Also in the Variorum Collected Studies Series

PETER LINEHAN
The Processes of Politics and the Rule of Law: Studies on the Iberian Kingdoms and Papal Rome in the Middle Ages

ANTHONY LUTTRELL
The Making of Christian Malta: From the early Middle Ages to 1530

BRIAN PATRICK McGUIRE
Friendship and Faith: Cistercian men, women, and their stories, 1100–1250

PETER LINEHAN
Past and Present in Medieval Spain

CONSTANT J. MEWS
Reason and Belief in the Age of Roscelin and Abelard

CONSTANT J. MEWS
Abelard and his Legacy

JAMIE C. KASSLER
Music, Science, Philosophy: Models in the universe of thought

H. COLIN SLIM
Painting Music in the Sixteenth Century: Essays in iconography

MADELINE H. CAVINESS
Art in the Medieval West and its Audience

SIDNEY H. GRIFFITH
The Beginnings of Christian Theology in Arabic: Muslim-Christian encounters in the early Islamic period

COLIN HEYWOOD
Writing Ottoman History: Documents and interpretations

DAVID R. KNECHTGES
Court Culture and Literature in Early China

SIMON FRANKLIN
Byzantium – Rus – Russia: Studies in the translation of Christian culture

VARIORUM COLLECTED STUDIES SERIES

Scholars and Courtiers: Intellectuals
and Society in the Medieval West

C. Stephen Jaeger

C. Stephen Jaeger

Scholars and Courtiers: Intellectuals and Society in the Medieval West

This edition copyright © 2002 by C. Stephen Jaeger.

Published in the Variorum Collected Studies Series by

Ashgate Publishing Limited
Gower House, Croft Road,
Aldershot, Hampshire GU11 3HR
Great Britain

Ashgate Publishing Company
131 Main Street,
Burlington, Vermont 05401–5600
USA

Ashgate website: http://www.ashgate.com

ISBN 0–86078–879–2

British Library Cataloguing-in-Publication Data
Jaeger, C. Stephen
  Scholars and Courtiers : Intellectuals and Society in the
  Medieval West. - (Variorum Collected Studies Series: CS753)
  1. Civilization, Medieval. 2. Humanism – Europe, Western –
  History – To 1500 3. Intellectuals – Europe, Western –
  History – To 1500 4. Europe – Intellectual Life
  I. Title
  940.1'46

US Library of Congress Cataloging-in-Publication Data
Scholars and Courtiers : Intellectuals and Society in the Medieval West/
  C. Stephen Jaeger.
      p.   cm. – (Variorum Collected Studies Series: CS753).
  Includes bibliographical references and index.
  1. Europe – Intellectual Life. 2. Europe – Court and Courtiers.
  3. Scholars – Europe. 4. Civilization, Medieval I. Jaeger, C. Stephen.
  II. Collected Studies: CS753.
  AZ183.E8 S36 2002
  305.5'52'094--dc21   2002074460

The paper used in this publication meets the minimum requirements of the
    American National Standard for Information Sciences – Permanence of
    Paper for Printed Library Materials, ANSI Z39.48–1984. ∞ ™

Printed by TJ International Ltd, Padstow, Cornwall

VARIORUM COLLECTED STUDIES SERIES CS753

CONTENTS

Introduction   vii

Acknowledgements   xi

SCHOLARS: THE LATIN CULTURE

I   Cathedral Schools and Humanist Learning, 950–1150   569–616
Deutsche Vierteljahsschrift 61. Stuttgart, 1987

II   Orpheus in the Eleventh Century   141–168
Mittellateinisches Jahrbuch 27. Stuttgart, 1992

III   Humanism and Ethics at the School of St. Victor in the early Twelfth Century   51–79
Mediaeval Studies 55. Toronto, 1993

IV   Peter Abelard's Silence at the Council of Sens   31–54
Res Publica Litterarum, 3. Kansas, 1980

V   The Prologue to the *Historia calamitatum* [of Peter Abelard] and the 'Authenticity Question'   1–15
Euphorion 74. 1980

COURTIERS AND COURTLY SOCIETY

VI   Patrons and the Beginnings of Courtly Romance   45–58
First published in The Medieval Opus: Imitation, Rewriting, and Transmission in the French Tradition, ed. Douglas Kelley. Amsterdam, 1996

VII   Courtliness and Social Change   287–309
First published in Cultures of Power: Lordship, Status, and Process in Twelfth-Century Europe, ed. Thomas N. Bisson. Philadelphia, 1995

VIII	L'amour des rois: structure sociale d'une forme de sensibilité aristocratique *Annales ESC 46. Paris, 1991*	547–571

THE UNITY OF SCHOOL AND COURT CULTURES

IX	Charismatic Body – Charismatic Text *Exemplaria, 9. North Carolina, 1997*	117–137
X	The Courtier Bishop in *Vitae* from the Tenth to the Twelfth Century *Speculum 58. Massachusetts, 1983*	291–325
XI	Beauty of Manners and Discipline (*Schoene Site, Zuht*): An Imperial Tradition of Courtliness in the German Romance *First published in Barocker Lustspiegel: Studien zur Literatur des Barock: Festschrift für Blake Lee Spahr, ed. Martin Bircher et al, Chloe: Beihefte zum Daphnis 3. Amsterdam, 1984*	27–45
XII	The Text as a Symbol of Decadence *First published in The Construction of Textual Authority in German Literature of the Medieval and Early Modern Periods eds James F. Poag and Claire Baldwin. North Carolina, 2001*	75–90
Index		1–7

```
This volume contains 12 + 312 pages
```

INTRODUCTION

Seven of the twelve studies included in this collection have morphed – generally shortened – into chapters in books since their first publication. Republishing them in their original versions in Ashgate's Variorum series serves a purpose that was brought home to me only in the last stages of reviewing them for republication. (Until then I was pleased simply that anyone might want to read them again.) While they had become a part of a focused thesis in the books in which they later appeared, they seemed to me, looking at them in this collected form, to add up to a whole greater than the sum of its parts and to form a monograph-like unity to the surprise of its author/editor. The 'argument' of this ensemble reaches farther than any of the individual books; what it amounts to is an argument for the vast subterranean influence of worldly clerical culture from the late tenth to the thirteenth century. Those learned clerics who created this culture divided their lives between two different social and intellectual realms: the cathedral communities and the secular courts. The essays show the diffusion between those realms of what I have called 'medieval humanism'.

If this book were to reignite the debate about what medieval humanism is, it will have served a good purpose. At the moment that term is defined and the phenomenon viewed very differently by two camps. The opposition might well be titled (for the sake of convenience – others preceded, and the 'opposition' never occurred directly), 'Knowles vs. Southern'. David Knowles sees medieval humanism as a literary culture whose style was based on classical models. R.W. Southern credits the existence of literary humanism but defined medieval humanism very differently. He sees it as founded on an ideal of the dignity of man, on the humanizing of God, on the cultivation of friendship human and divine, and on the idea of the rational intelligibility of the world. Knowles's medieval humanism begins in the early eleventh century and dies out in the first half of the twelfth; Southern's begins with Anselm of Bec and Canterbury and comes to its highpoint in the Scholasticism of the thirteenth century.

If 'humanism' applied to the Middle Ages is to be a concept with real content and not just an alluring term transferable *ad libitum* to unlike and opposed phenomena, then these two views need to be resolved.

It will be apparent from the first three studies in this collection that I am a Knowlesian. The humanism of the Middle Ages, in my view, goes back further than either Knowles or Southern believed. It arises with cathedral schools in the second half of the tenth century. It has (like its counterpart in both antiquity and the fifteenth century) a role to play in the active public life of courts secular and ecclesiastical. One of its most prominent features is the cultivation of a complicated Latin poetry based on classical models, especially Virgil, Horace and Martianus Capella. 'Orpheus in the Eleventh Century' (II) suggests a reason for the prominence of poetry in eleventh-century humanism. It served an idealized social mission of learned clerics, to educate, civilize, humanize the manners and 'tame the fury' of the secular nobility, particularly princes and kings. This mission is dramatically successful in shaping a code of social ideals that begins as an ethic structuring the behavior and manners of clerical court servants (*curiales*) and flows into the social code known as 'courtesy' or 'courtliness' (*curialitas*). The essays 'Cathedral Schools and Humanist Learning' (I) and 'The Courtier Bishop' (X) give a broader picture of the 'old learning' in its social and intellectual context.

The studies of clerical influence at worldly courts revise the earlier opinion that courtly ideals and courtly literature arose as ideas or values of the secular nobility. On the surface of it this idea is no more likely than that cowboys were the bearers and fashioners of the values projected onto them in Western movies. Courtliness, courtly love and the literature staging it were certainly fashioned by clerics trained in the 'old learning', who transmitted their social ideals to the secular nobles and – a stroke of genius of the age – fashioned the ideal Arthurian knight of romance as the embodiment of those values. In a perhaps greater stroke of genius, the same milieu shaped or helped shape an ideal of love in which bold combat and civil manners were made prerequisites of winning a woman's love.

An ennobling love, which raised the social and moral value of the lovers, had existed in Greek and Roman antiquity, and it appears at various royal courts in the earlier Middle Ages, but in the eleventh century this neo-classicistic cult of the high nobility filters through the various layers of aristocratic society, lay and clerical. It even spreads to some monastic communities, though generally is limited to individuals in the monastic life (Anselm of Bec, Aelred of Rievaulx), never establishing itself as a widely accepted social code of monks. Since the cult of passionate friendship emerges in one of its most extravagant and abundantly documented forms at the court of Charlemagne, reappears in Ottonian clerical culture, and is well-documented in cathedral communities of the early eleventh century, we can put aside R.W. Southern's idea that the cult of friendship originated with Anselm. It is a feature of aristocratic life in the earlier Middle Ages that has been severely understudied. I stress the classical, secular origins of the cult of friendship and its close ties to the moral code associated with courtly love in the essay 'L'amour des rois' (VIII). In the late eleventh century the cult of male friendship takes a direction that would have shocked and appalled Socrates or Cicero: not only did it allow women into the previously all-male social club of ennobling, virtue- and status-giving love, it made them into the administrators and teachers of that precious commodity. In the literature of courtly love at least (possibly also in the reality of high aristocratic love-practice as a public, social phenomenon) woman comes to take over a role assigned to paragons of male virtue in earlier ages, to philosophers and model gentlemen: to use the love of their devotees as an instrument of the enculturation of young men.

Two essays in the collection ('Charismatic Body – Charismatic Text' (IX) and 'The Text as a Symbol of Decadence' (XII)) try to frame the cultural changes from the eleventh to the twelfth century in terms different from what is implied in the almost universally accepted and highly misleading term, the 'Renaissance of the twelfth century'. An extremely turbulent conflict between an older culture and various new tendencies that merged with, combatted, and superseded it, are the overarching event of the age. This conflict rather than rebirth *ex nihilo* accounts for the great accomplishments of the twelfth century. Current notions of a renaissance, of the change from an oral to a written/literate culture, of the 'rise of Europe', of the 'discovery of the individual', or the unfolding of new cognitive stages, are all framed in the spell of a progressive view of history, and all of them ignore or discount the cultural importance of the worldly clerical culture that flourished from the tenth to the twelfth century. These two essays show the transition as a change from a 'charismatic' to an 'intellectual' culture. This point of view brings into sharp profile what is lost of the great richness in the older culture which died out in the course of the twelfth century, and it creates perspectives to judge the new trends of the period through the eyes of the old – from which perspective the new appears as anything but a 'renaissance'.

Finally, two of the essays concern Peter Abelard. 'Peter Abelard's Silence at the Council of Sens' (IV) studies Abelard's tendency to project himself and his own fate into characters from Christian history. This perspective allows us to reconstruct a whole set of biblical associations Abelard would have brought to bear to explain his failure to defend himself at the council of Sens in 1140, which led to his condemnation. Christ's and Susannah's silence before false judges were models he evoked and interpreted regularly in his sermons and elsewhere. They may well have helped him to fashion his 'strategy' of passive defense at Sens.

'The Prologue to the *Historia calamitatum*' (V) was written at a time when John Benton was arguing that the 'Historia' was a forgery, not a work of Peter Abelard. Benton himself recanted the argument shortly before my article appeared. The 'Historia' is demonstrably a work by Peter Abelard. Its prologue is just one of a large network of passages that link the work unquestionably to its author. The republishing of this article has some point at the present moment, partly because a conservative, rear-guard action still maintains the suspect character of some of the personal writings of Abelard and Heloise, partly also because a conflict is brewing at the moment over the ascription to the young Heloise and Abelard of a set of 113 love letters (the 'Epistolae duorum amantium'). 'The Prologue' offers some methodological guidelines for the use of stylistic criteria in authenticity disputes. It also cautions against the one-sided privileging of historical evidence and above stylistic arguments. A crediting of stylistic considerations might have saved John Benton and those who listened to him much wasted effort.

The work of R.I. Moore is presently laying the foundation for a new and richer understanding of the twelfth century's place in medieval culture. May the studies republished in this volume help in the construction work.

C. STEPHEN JAEGER

University of Illinois, Urbana, Illinois, USA.

ACKNOWLEDGEMENTS

Grateful acknowledgement is given to the following for permission to reproduce the articles in this volume: Freie Universität Berlin (II); Pontifical Institute of Mediaeval Studies (III); Salerno Editrice (IV); *Euphorion* (V); Rodopi (VI and XI); University of Pennsylvania Press (VII); Pegasus Press (IX); *Speculum* (X); The University of North Carolina Press (XII).

PUBLISHER'S NOTE

The articles in this volume, as in all others in the Collected Studies Series, have not been given a new, continuous pagination. In order to avoid confusion, and to facilitate their use where these same studies have been referred to elsewhere, the original pagination has been maintained wherever possible.

Each article has been given a Roman numeral in order of appearance, as listed in the Contents. This number is repeated on each page and quoted in the index entries.

I

Cathedral Schools and Humanist Learning, 950–1150

ABSTRACT

Der Humanismus des 12. Jahrhunderts formte sich in den Kathedralschulen des späten 10. und 11. Jahrhunderts. Aus einem an *ethica* und *moralitas* orientierten Kurrikulum ergab sich die Einheit der weltlichen Wissenschaften in Frankreich und Deutschland. Als dieser Humanismus durch die Frühscholastik verdrängt wurde, ging er in den Bereich der weltlichen Höfe über, um dort als höfische Erziehung hervorzutreten.

The curriculum of *litterae et mores* at cathedral schools of the late 10th and 11th centuries is essential in the formation of 12th century humanism. This curriculum, oriented to *ethica* and *moralitas*, accounts for the unity of secular learning in the period. When early Scholasticism displaced humanist learning at the schools, it passed into the realm of the courts and emerged as courtly education.

The humanist strain in twelfth century culture represented by figures like Bernard Silvester, John of Salisbury and Alan of Lille has its roots in the late tenth and eleventh centuries. Charles Homer Haskins knew very well that the more embracing renewal he called the "renaissance of the twelfth century" grew out of developments in the preceding age, and he called the eleventh century "that obscure period of origins which holds the secret of the new movement."[1] The factor that especially favors that obscurity and guards that secret is the apparent poverty of intellectual and artistic achievement in the centers of worldly learning, the cathedral schools. The privilege that modern historians of culture give to such sources is a hindrance to understanding the vitality of the eleventh century. It directs us where there is no path and blocks the way that is open to us.[2] If we privileged intellectual and artistic achievement in judging fourteenth and fifteenth century Italy, then we could scrap three-quarters of Burckhardt's *Civilization of the Renaissance in Italy*, put aside his idea that the

---

[1] C. H. Haskins, *The Renaissance of the Twelfth Century* (1927; rpt. 1972), p. 16.

[2] R. W. Southern made a fundamental point on the use of sources in his article, "The Place of England in the Twelfth Century Renaissance," *History*, 45 (1960), 201–16; rpt. in his *Medieval Humanism and other Essays* (1970), pp. 158–80: that it is necessary to look behind and beyond the most prominent documents to define that place. For Europe in the late tenth and eleventh centuries, it is necessary to look behind and beyond the lack of them.

state and statesmanship can themselves be regarded as works of art, and throw out his entire notion that political conditions, court life, and the development of ideals of the individual preceded the revival of learning, art and literature, and created the necessary presuppositions of that renewal.

If we compare the visible achievements of the century and a half between 950 and 1100 with its intellectual and cultural energy, the discrepancy is evident. Here are some indications that much was stirring in the period:

It produced a number of eminent men praised by contemporaries for their learning and teaching: Brun of Cologne, Gerbert of Aurillac, Fulbert of Chartres, Meinhard of Bamberg, Bernard of Chartres. And yet none of them wrote any works of note, apart from their letters.

The manuscript tradition of Plato's *Timaeus* virtually begins for the Middle Ages in the eleventh century.[3] For the period 850–900 one manuscript survives; for 900–950 two; for 950–1000 four. Then suddenly the first half of the eleventh century produces fifteen manuscripts, most of them from Germany; the second half fourteen, also largely from Germany. The preoccupation with Plato's work in that country was so intense that by the end of the century it provoked a polemic from Manegold of Lautenbach.[4] He attacks opinions and interpretations of German *philosophi*, some of which turn up a few decades later in works of Peter Abelard.[5] The thrust of the teaching which Manegold opposes is that the *Timaeus* is reconcilable with Christian doctrine. This is of course a favorite idea of the "School of Chartres." It provides the basis of Thierry of Chartres' Hexameron commentary.[6] And the more general problem of reconciling the ancient philosophers with Christian doctrine is the basic focus of Abelard's *Theologia Christiana*. In other words, some of the central problems that were to occupy the leading schools, or at least the leading representatives of secular philosophy in twelfth century France were intensely debated in eleventh century Germany. And that work which was to play such a major role in the philosophi-

---

[3] R. W. Southern, *Platonism, Scholastic Method, and the School of Chartres*, The Stenton Lecture 1978 (1979), p. 14. For the list of manuscripts see *Timaeus a Calcidio translatus commentarioque instructus*, ed. J. H. Waszink, Corpus Platonicum Medii Aevi: Plato Latinus, 4 (1975), pp. CVI–CXXXI. See also Margaret Gibson, "The Study of the 'Timaeus' in the Eleventh and Twelfth Centuries," *Pensamiento*, 25 (1969), 183–94.

[4] Manegold von Lautenbach, *Liber contra Wolfelmum*, ed. Wilfried Hartmann, MGH, Quellen zur Geistesgeschichte des Mittelalters, 8 (1972).

[5] This is one of the important findings in Wilfried Hartmann's study, "Manegold von Lautenbach und die Anfänge der Frühscholastik," *Deutsches Archiv für Erforschung des Mittelalters*, 26 (1970), 7–149, esp. p. 77 ff.

[6] N. M. Häring, "The Creation and the Creator of the World according to Thierry of Chartres and Clarenbaldus of Arras," *AHDLMA*, 22 (1955), 137–216. The text of Thierry's tract is also printed in Häring's edition *Commentaries on Boethius by Thierry of Chartres and his School*, Pontifical Institute of Mediaeval Studies: Studies and Texts, 20 (1971), 553–75. See the comments of Southern, *Platonism etc.* p. 25 ff.

cal commentary and poetry of France, Plato's *Timaeus*, first came to prominence in the eleventh century. We know of a Manegold, a German teaching in Paris around 1080, who was the teacher of William of Champeaux and Anselm of Laon, and is called *modernorum magister magistrorum*. This probably was that same Manegold of Lautenbach, himself a teacher of worldly philosophy and of the Platonic cosmology before he became an adversary.[7] And apart from the striking testimony of Manegold's polemic against Wolfhelm of Brauweiler, the writings against worldly learning by conservative monks like Peter Damian and Otloh of St. Emmeram show us a very lively academic scene, both in Italy and Germany.[8] Writings or not, there was plenty of activity.

The secular courts of Germany in the eleventh century also show us a lively scene, one that deserves to be called at least "prerenaissance."[9]

These are preliminary signs of renewal, symptoms of the coming outburst of brilliant cultural achievements in twelfth century France. The larger web of relationships in which the connections become evident has been hard to identify, partly because the rumblings occurred in Germany and the eruption they preceded occurred in France. The traditions of modern historical writing did not favor interpretations deriving the latter from the former. Drawing the lines of development in detail is not the object of this study. It aims at establishing the following points: 1) the humanism of the twelfth century has its roots in that of the eleventh; 2) there is a unity and continuity of secular learning in Germany and France in the period, which is disturbed and gradually supplanted by early scholasticism; 3) the needs of administration at secular and ecclesiastical courts determine a humanistic curriculum, oriented strongly to *ethica*. It has its institutional accommodation at cathedral schools. This symbiosis begins to break up in the second half of the eleventh century in Germany and in the middle decades

---

[7] For a thorough discussion and perhaps overly cautious weighing of the evidence for and against this identification, see Hartmann, "Manegold," p. 49ff.

[8] On Otloh's opposition to worldly learning, see Helga Schauwecker, *Otloh von St. Emmeram: Ein Beitrag zur Bildungs- und Frömmigkeitsgeschichte des 11. Jahrhunderts*, Diss. Würzburg (1962), pp. 165ff. On Peter Damian, J. A. Endres, *Petrus Damiani und die weltliche Wissenschaft*, Beiträge zur Geschichte der Philosophie im Mittelalter, 8,3 (1910); A. Cantin, *Les sciences séculières et la foi: Les deux voies de la science au jugement de S. Pierre Damien (1007–1072)* (1975). On this opposition in general, Martin Grabmann, *Die Geschichte der scholastischen Methode*, Vol. I (1909; rpt. 1957), pp. 215ff.; Pierre Riché, *Écoles et enseignement dans l'occident chrétien de la fin du Ve siècle au milieu du XIe siècle* (1979), pp. 335–344.

[9] On classical revival in the eleventh century see P. E. Schramm, *Kaiser, Rom und Renovatio: Studien zur Geschichte des römischen Erneuerungsgedankens vom Ende des karolingischen Reiches bis zum Investiturstreit*, 2nd ed. (1957); Reto R. Bezzola, *Les origines et la formation de la littérature courtoise en occident (500–1200)*: Vol. I: *La tradition impériale de la fin de l'antiquité au XIe siècle* (1944), pp. 239–282; C. Stephen Jaeger, *The Origins of Courtliness: Civilizing Trends and the Formation of Courtly Ideals, 939–1210* (1985), pp. 113ff.

of the twelfth in France. At this point humanist learning gradually passes into the realm of the secular courts and emerges as courtly education.

I. Cathedral Schools

The development of cathedral schools is our point of departure.[10] Episcopal schools existed since late antiquity, though they rose and fell in prominence with the coming and going of single masters. They stood in the shadow of monastic schools in Carolingian times, and indeed in the earlier period the nature of education there is hardly distinguishable from monastic education.[11] As institutions distinct from monastic schools, they appear not to have found a sustaining goal until the mid-tenth century. At that point they began to flourish. We hear praise of the Magdeburg school in mid-century, of the great crowds of students there, of the intense interest in secular studies aroused by the "second Cicero," Master Ohtricus, a teacher of such distinction and learning that he was later to debate with Gerbert of Aurillac in Ravenna before Otto II and his court.[12] By 952 Würzburg is flourishing under an Italian master, Stefan of Novara, called to the north by Otto the Great and Bishop Poppo of Würzburg.[13] By 953 the Cologne school comes into prominence under the episcopacy of Otto's brother, Brun of Cologne, a great educator and statesman, called by his biographer a reviver of the seven liberal arts.[14] This school will produce some of the most

---

[10] Paré, Tremblay and Brunet were quite right in making this the focal point of their study. *La renaissance du XIIe siècle: Les écoles et l'enseignement*, Publications de l'institut d'études médiévales d'Ottawa (1933). But their focus was so tightly on France and the seven liberal arts that many of the essential features of education at cathedral schools are not touched.

[11] See Josef Fleckenstein, *Die Bildungsreform Karls des Grossen als Verwirklichung der norma rectitudinis* (1953), p. 23; Rosamond McKitterick, *The Frankish Kingdom under the Carolingians, 751–987* (1983), p. 147f.

[12] On Magdeburg and Ohtricus, see *Vita S. Adalberti* III, MGH, SS 4, p. 582 (11.29–37); *Brunonis vita Adalb.* V, MGH, SS 4, p. 597 (1.14ff.); *Annales Magdeburgenses* a. 982, MGH, SS 16, p. 155 (1.40ff.). On Ohtricus and Gerbert, *Richeri Historiae* III, 55–65, MGH, SS rer. germ. in us. schol. (1839), pp. 136–43. For some discussion of the debate see Margaret T. Gibson, "The *artes* in the eleventh Century," in *Arts libéraux et philosophie au moyen âge*, Actes du quatrième congrès international de philosophie médiévale (1969), 121–126. On the Magdeburg school unter Ohtricus, F. A. Specht, *Geschichte des Unterrichtswesens in Deutschland von den ältesten Zeiten bis zur Mitte des dreizehnten Jahrhunderts* (1885), pp. 350–53.

[13] See Otloh of St. Emmeram, *Vita Wolfkangi* IV–V, MGH, SS 4, p. 528. On Stefan, L. F. Benedetto, "Stephanus grammaticus da Novara," *Studi Medievali*, 3 (1908–11), 499–508; Josef Fleckenstein, "Königshof und Bischofsschule unter Otto dem Grossen," *Archiv für Kulturgeschichte*, 38 (1956), p. 53 f.

[14] See Fleckenstein, "Königshof und Bischofsschule," passim. Otto Zimmermann, *Brun I., Erzbischof von Cöln und die in den Schulen seiner Zeit gepflegte Wissenschaft*, Diss. Leipzig, 1871.

illustrious intellectuals, statesmen, educators, and bishops of the next generation. By 954 we hear Hildesheim praised as a center of learning[15]; by 956 Trier.[16] In the last quarter of the century, under the guidance of the next generation of scholars – many of them students of Brun – Worms, Liège, Mainz, Speyer, Bamberg and Regensburg[17] come to life; in France Rheims under Gerbert[18], and some decades later Chartres under Gerbert's pupil, Bishop Fulbert (1006–28).[19] These schools are regularly referred to as "a second Athens," the better loved teachers as "noster Plato," "noster Socrates," "alter Cicero."[20] In a commemor-

---

[15] On Hildesheim, see Specht, pp. 343–50. G. von Detten, *Über die Dom- und Klosterschulen des Mittelalters, insbesondere über die Schulen von Hildesheim, Paderborn, Münster und Corvey* (1893). On the importance of Hildesheim for supplying the staff of Otto the Great, H. W. Klewitz, "Königtum, Hofkapelle und Domkapitel im 10. und 11. Jahrhundert," *Archiv für Urkundenforschung*, 16 (1938), p. 108ff. Also Herbert Zielinski, *Der Reichsepiskopat in spätottonischer und salischer Zeit (1002–1125)*, Teil I (1984), pp. 89–91, esp. 135–139.

[16] See Emil Lèsne, *Histoire de la propriété ecclésiastique en France*, Vol. V: *Les écoles de la fin du VIIIe siècle à la fin du XIIe* (1940), p. 368ff.

[17] On Regensburg see Specht, pp. 379–87; Bernard Bischoff, "Literarisches und künstlerisches Leben in St. Emmeram (Regensburg) während des frühen und hohen Mittelalters," in his *Mittelalterliche Studien: Ausgewählte Aufsätze zur Schriftkunde und Literaturgeschichte*, Vol. II (1967), 77–115, On Bamberg, Carl Erdmann, "Die Bamberger Domschule im Investiturstreit," *Zeitschrift für bayerische Landesgeschichte*, 9 (1936), 1–46; Zielinski, *Reichsepiskopat* (above, n. 15), pp. 84–86, 147; Johannes Fried, "Die Bamberger Domschule und die Rezeption von Frühscholastik und Rechtswissenschaft in ihrem Umkreis bis zum Ende der Stauferzeit," in *Schulen und Studium im sozialen Wandel des hohen und späten Mittelalters*, ed. Johannes Fried, Vorträge und Forschungen, 30 (1986), 163–201. On Liège, Charles Renardy, "Les écoles Liègoises du XIe et XIIe siècle," *Révue Belge de philologie et d'histoire*, 57 (1979), 309–328; Godefroid Kurth, *Notger de Liège et la civilisation au Xe siècle* (1905).

[18] See Lèsne, p. 271ff.; John R. Williams, "The Cathedral School of Rheims in the eleventh Century," *Speculum*, 19 (1954), 661–77; idem., "The Cathedral School of Rheims in the Time of Master Alberic, 1118–36," *Traditio*, 20 (1964), 93–114. On Gerbert, Oscar G. Darlington, "Gerbert the Teacher," *American Historical Review*, 52 (1946/47), 456–76; Uta Lindgren, *Gerbert von Aurillac und das Quadrivium: Untersuchungen zur Bildung im Zeitalter der Ottonen*, Sudhoffs Archiv, Beiheft, 18 (1976); Hélène Gasc, "Gerbert et la pédagogie des arts libéraux à la fin du dixième siècle," *Journal of Medieval History*, 12 (1986), 111–21.

[19] See Lèsne, p. 152ff. Also the introduction to Frederick Behrends edition, *The Letters and Poems of Fulbert of Chartres*, Oxford Medieval Texts (1976). And Loren C. McKinney, *Bishop Fulbert and Education at the school of Chartres*, Texts and Studies in the History of Mediaeval Education, 6 (1957); A. Clerval, *Les écoles de Chartres au moyenâge (du Ve au XVIe siècle)* (1895; rpt. 1965).

[20] Regensburg a "second Athens" (Specht, p. 382); Liège in the first half of the eleventh century "a second Athens... in literary studies it beggars Plato's academy, in the observance of religion it leaves Leo's Rome far behind" (Gozechinus or Goswin of Mainz, *Gozechini epistola ad Walcherum* VI, ed. R. B. C. Huygens, Corpus Christianorum, Continuatio Mediaevalis, 62 [1985], p. 15; earlier ed. PL 143, 889A). Hamburg-Bremen under Bp. Adalbert (d. 1072) "a second Rome" (Adam of Bremen, *Hamburgische Kirchengeschichte* XXIII, ed. B. Schmeidler, 3d. ed., MGH, SS rer. germ. in us. schol., 2 (1917; rpt. 1977), p. 167. Tournai under Master Udo (1087–92) a "second Athens" (Paré et al, *La*

574

ative poem from ca. 1012 Bamberg is praised as the "city of letters [or learning], [its citizens] no wit inferior to the Stoics, greater than the Athenians."[21]

In short, some 12 major cathedral schools emerged in the comparatively brief space of 60 years. Clearly some sort of sudden and dramatic growth was taking place in these centers in the second half of the tenth century, and equally clear is that the German schools preceded the French. The reasons for this renewal have been discussed by the historian Josef Fleckenstein in his article, "Königshof und Bischofsschule unter Otto dem Grossen" (above, n. 13). Fleckenstein understands this development as the work of Brun of Cologne in concert with his brother Otto the Great. These two form a purposeful conception of the role of cathedral schools, and this conception raises the fate of the schools above the vagaries of what professor happens to be where. That vagary may still determine the distinction of a particular school and its power to attract students at a given time, but not its educational goal. That remains more or less consistent until the rise of universities at the end of the twelfth and beginning of the thirteenth centuries. The first flourishing schools are in the episcopal centers favored by the emperor: Magdeburg, Würzburg, Cologne, Hildesheim and Mainz. Clearly imperial patronage was the impetus for their dramatic growth, as Fleckenstein argues.

The emperor had found a purpose for the episcopal school, one it had not had before. In the Carolingian revival, the schools had taken on the role of educating laymen and clerics to read the Bible and of preparing clergymen for their pastoral and liturgical duties. The goal was correction and reformation of the religious life according to the *norma rectitudinis*."[22] The new purpose was to educate statesmen and administrators. The goal was not knowledge for its own sake or knowledge for the glory and worship of God, but rather knowledge to be applied in the practical duties of running the empire. Brun of Cologne as imperial chancellor is known for transforming the royal chapel into a sort of

---

renaissance p. 23). Fulbert of Chartres, "noster Socrates" (Adelman of Liège to Berengar of Tours, ed. R. B. C. Huygens, "Textes latins du XIe au XIIIe siècle," *Studi Medievali*, 3rd ser., 8 (1967), p. 476; (earlier ed., PL 143, 1289A). Ohtricus of Magdeburg "Cicero unus" (MGH, SS 4, 597, l. 15).

[21] The poem is by Abbot Gerhard of Seeon. MGH, Poet. Lat., 5, p. 398 (ll. 33ff.): "Non minus ista Sepher Cariath [cf. Joshua 15, 15: *Sepher Cariath = civitas litterarum*] cluit arte scienter, / Inferior Stoicis nequaquam, maior Athenis."

[22] See Fleckenstein, *Bildungsreform* (above, n. 11), passim. Franz Brunhölzl, "Der Bildungsauftrag der Hofschule," in *Karl der Grosse: Lebenswerk und Nachleben*, ed. B. Bischoff, Vol. II: *Geistiges Leben*, p. 32: "Soweit das Bildungsprogramm die Schulen... betrifft, lässt es sich auf die kurze Formel bringen: Ziel des Unterrichts ist die Vermittlung der Fähigkeit, die Bibel zu lesen und zu verstehen; die artes liberales liefern die hierzu erforderlichen Grundfertigkeiten. Das wäre eine rein theologische, ja geistliche Zielsetzung."

academy of philosophy and school for imperial bishops.[23] The instruction that turned gifted young men into trained administrators and loyal supporters of the emperor originated at court, in the chapel. But it was so valuable that it spilled over the borders of that tiny, elite institution, and sought accommodation elsewhere. This gave cathedral schools their new role. The passage of Brun of Cologne from the imperial chapel to the see of Cologne is representative for the shift: he took this particular brand of instruction with him from the court to the cathedral. This, briefly summarized, is Fleckenstein's argument. Others before him noticed that individual schools took on the task of training men for administrative and state service,[24] but Fleckenstein's study is so important because he shows this role to be the impetus for the rise of cathedral schools generally in the mid-tenth century, and he shows the logical integration of these schools into the Ottonian "imperial church system." Cathedral school education becomes identical with preparation for service at court, be it secular or episcopal.[25] This is an insight of fundamental importance for our understanding of early medieval education and of the beginnings of the twelfth century renaissance.

II. Letters and Manners

The many studies of education in the earlier Middle Ages[26] have taught us a great deal about the curriculum. We have a good idea of the books read and the

---

[23] Cf. the description of his influence at court by his biographer, Ruotger, *Ruotgers Lebensbeschreibung des Erzbischofs Brun von Köln*, V–VIII, ed. Irene Ott, MGH, SS. rer. germ., N. S., 10 (1951), pp. 6–9.

[24] Klewitz, "Königtum, Hofkapelle und Domkapitel" (above, n. 16), and Erdmann, "Die Bamberger Domschule" (above, n. 18).

[25] Zielinski's recent book (above, n. 15) contains an important statistical and prosopographical study of the close interrelations of cathedral school, royal chapel and episcopate. It represents a strong confirmation of Fleckenstein's thesis: cathedral school education prepared men for service at the imperial court and in the episcopate.

[26] In addition to the major works by Specht, Clerval, Lèsne and Paré-Tremblay-Brunet already cited, the following more recent works deserve mention: Philippe Delhaye, "L'Organisation scolaire au XIIe siècle," *Traditio*, 5 (1947), 211–68; Luitpold Wallach, "Education and Culture in the Tenth Century," *Mediaevalia et Humanistica*, 9 (1955), 18–22; Hans Liebeschütz, "The Debate on Philosophical Learning During the Transition Period (900–1080)," in *The Cambridge History of Later Greek and Early Medieval Philosophy*, ed. A. H. Armstrong (1970), pp. 587–610; Margaret Gibson, "The Continuity of Learning circa 850–circa 1050," *Viator*, 6 (1975), 1–13; on Gerbert of Aurillac see the works cited in n. 19 above; Pierre Riché, *Education et culture dans l'occident barbare, VIe–VIIIe siècles*, 3rd ed. (1972); idem., *Les écoles et l'enseignement dans l'Occident chrétien* (above, n. 8); Cora Lutz, *Schoolmasters of the Tenth Century* (1977); Zielinski, *Der Reichsepiskopat* (above, n. 15), pp. 74–164; Rolf Köhn, "Schulbildung und Trivium im lateinischen Hochmittelalter und ihr möglicher praktischer Nutzen," in *Schulen und Studium* (above, n. 17), pp. 203–284. A number of essays relevant to our topic in *La scuola nell' occidente latino dell' alto medioevo*, Settimane di studio del centro Italiano di studi sull' alto

subjects taught. But it is not yet clear in what way the period 950–1100/1150 forms a unity, to what extent education at the cathedral schools in this period is distinguished from what came before, from what followed and from what was going on at the same time in monastic schools. The tendency to see all education against the monastic model and within the scheme of the seven liberal arts is a factor which particularly obscures the role of cathedral schools. But this obscurity is hard to dispel given the nature of the sources. Writings from the monasteries are many, and writings from the cathedrals are few. From the late tenth and early eleventh centuries we have some lists of *auctores*, some library catalogues,[27] schemes of studies and discussions of them. We have some descriptions of education in history and biography, some school poetry, and a handful of commentaries and tracts. Deriving our understanding of education at an eleventh century cathedral school from the authors read and the works written there is like writing history of the theater from lists of plays performed and from theoretical treatises by actors. If in a particular period the repertoire does not change much and there are no theoretical treatises (and there never are – actors do not write), then we might conclude that period was not original or productive. And if from the same period which we have just judged unoriginal and unproductive we have many rave reviews from critics, then we might say that given the lack of originality and productivity in the theater, such reviews must be taken as an indication of the low expectations and bad taste of the period. Of course, such an interpretation is based on a fundamental misunderstanding of what a theater is and what it does. This, I would suggest, is the predicament of historians of education for the eleventh century. There is a great deal of talk about flourishing schools and great teachers, but there are no works of philosophy, little poetry and few commentaries by masters. Therefore, the schools of Germany – and of course France, where the same holds true – must be judged to "show little vitality from within," as Haskins thought.[28]

But there is as strong a distortion in the sources as in the lack of them. To make a start in getting around it, I want to pursue the "scheme" or the framework of studies indicated in the formula *litterae et mores*, "letters" and – if I may translate it in this loose but convenient way – "manners."[29] The phrase is

---

medioevo, 19, 2 vols. (1972). The good survey by Robert Lerner, "Literacy and Learning," is easy to overlook because of the textbook nature of the publication it appeared in: *One Thousand Years: Western Europe in the Middle Ages*, ed. Richard De Molen (1974), pp. 165–223.

[27] See G. Glauche, "Die Rolle der Schulautoren im Unterricht von 800 bis 1100," in *La scuola*, vol. II (above, note 26), pp. 617–36.

[28] Haskins, *Renaissance of the Twelfth Century*, p. 16: "As we come into the eleventh century, German culture shows little vitality from within."

[29] Some observations on the formula in *Origins of courtliness*, pp. 213–19.

very common in descriptions of cathedral school education. It occurs in a variety of forms. As schoolmaster at Trier (ca. 957) Wolfgang, later Bishop of Regensburg, taught not only *liberales doctrinae* but also *morales disciplinae*.[30] Wazo as schoolmaster at Liège (1008–42) is said to have given instruction in the disciplines *tam morum quam litterarum*.[31] Bernward of Hildesheim was sent to school *litteris imbuendus, moribus etiam instituendus*.[32] The phrase occurs in variants like *sapientia et mores, ingenium et mores*. This is certainly not a topos without much content cribbed from ancient notions on the education of an orator. Examples outside of the standard topical section of a vita on the man's education show clearly the vitality of the formula. Some students of Würzburg wrote a poem in 1031 in answer to an attack on their school by the scholars of Worms. The poem praises the virtues of their school at length and calls it a flowing spring out of which one drinks the "doctrine of eloquence and of proper conduct of life" *(recte vivendi et dogma loquendi)*.[33] That is, their school teaches rhetoric or oratory (proper speaking) and ethics (proper living), clearly a variant of "letters and manners." In the context of an answer to an attack the phrase had to convey something of substance. Whether or not the school of Würzburg poured forth this two-fold doctrine as abundantly as its students claimed, such a doctrine had to exist; the students of Worms could not have been answered with an empty phrase.

A more telling example is from a letter of the Bamberg schoolmaster Meinhard written around 1060. This letter must be considered a major text in the history of education in the eleventh century. Meinhard answers a request from his bishop, Gunther of Bamberg, for a book on the Christian faith. He begins, "First you entangle me in all the busy cares of a headmaster, and now you are after me ... for another work, a task not just arduous but downright impossible." He goes on with this interesting complaint: "If the only task placed in my care were the instruction of young minds in the liberal arts – and many earlier writers argue for this single curriculum – then the rigors of the task and the reputation gained by it would be sufficient pay for me. Now however, those

---

[30] Otloh, *Vita Wolfkangi* VII, MGH, SS 4, 529, l. 3f.: "Juvenes... non solum liberalibus exercebat doctrinis, verum etiam moralibus informabat disciplinis."

[31] *Gesta ep. Leod.* XL, MGH, SS 7, 210: "In quarum [scolarum] studio tam morum quam litterarum vigilantissime exercuit disciplinam, eos qui pro his moribus essent, licet minus litteratos, longe his anteponens, quibus, ut in plerisque solet, scientia litterarum vanae gloriae peperisset stultitiam."

[32] *Vita Bernwardi* I, MGH, SS 4, 758 (ll. 16–17).

[33] *Die ältere Wormser Briefsammlung*, ed. Walther Bulst, MGH, Briefe der deutschen Kaiserzeit, 3 (1949), pp. 119-127, here p. 127 (ll. 264–65): "Istinc si discis, statim sensu resipiscis, / Recte vivendi potans et dogma loquendi."

who are placed at the head of schools are taxed in a dual function for the profit of the church: for they spend the first part of their fortunes in forming *mores* and squander the second part in teaching letters."[34] Here "letters and manners" cannot be an empty topos. Schoolmasters do not groan under the burden of meaningless formulae, certainly not when they explain to their bishops why they lack the time to write books. And bishops cannot be persuaded how hard their staff is working by the appeal to non-existent schemes of studies, any more than deans and provosts now can. Meinhard actually taught something called *mores*, and it took alot of his time, time he would rather have devoted to liberal studies. Particularly interesting is Meinhard's sense of the history of this double instruction within other schemes of studies. It is comparatively recent. Earlier masters got along without it. And while it is, unfortunately, not clear who or what is meant by the *studia veterum*, Meinhard knew Cicero and Quintilian well enough not to include them among the earlier writers who argued for a curriculum in the liberal arts alone. In any case it is the schoolmasters of the present ("Verum *nunc* qui prefecti scolarum habentur"), who are taxed doubly, not just in Bamberg but at schools generally. Telling also is that the instruction in letters and manners is given *pro ecclesiastico usu*, and that must mean in the midst of all this mercantile language, "to profit the church." Why the church? If *mores* meant proper comportment for young men and nothing more, then why not *pro scholarium usu?* I will offer some thoughts on this later.

Meinhard gives us a second telling bit of testimony to the reality of this formula. In another letter he commiserates with an unknown recipient on the death of the master of his school: now studies have died, the "light of letters" *(lumen litterarum)* is snuffed out, and "the moral discipline most excellently established and of long standing" is dead and buried. But Meinhard acknowledges with gratitude the arrival of a youth from this bereaved diocese, who has been sent to the Bamberg "workshop" for an education, so that those two marks of the school's former excellence, "letters and manners," may be revived

---

[34] *Briefsammlungen der Zeit Heinrichs IV.*, ed. Carl Erdmann and Norbert Fickermann, MGH, Briefe der deutschen Kaiserzeit, 5 (1950), pp. 238–39 (*Weitere Briefe Meinhards*, nr. 39): "Cum me negociosissimi magistratus cura implicueris, urgues tamen et instas... ut novam operam, non tam arduam et difficilem quam plane impossibilem suscipiam... Equidem si excubie nostre solis adolescentum ingeniis liberali erudicione excolendis assiderent, quod unicum curriculum pleraque veterum studia sibi vindicarunt, laboris mala fame nominisque momenta mihi pensarent. Verum nunc qui prefecti scolarum habentur, gemina pro ecclesiastico usu functione multantur: primas enim partes formandis moribus impendunt, secundas vero litterarum doctrine insumunt." Erdmann takes the letter to be the dedication to Meinhard's work *De fide*. See his *Studien zur Briefliteratur Deutschlands im elften Jahrhundert*, MGH, Schriften, 1 (1938), p. 23.

upon his return.³⁵ Again, an extraordinarily clear example of the real existence of "letters and manners" as a scheme of studies.

The choice of the Bamberg school as a "workshop" to prepare a master of "letters and manners" clearly made good sense. Bamberg gained a reputation for precisely this orientation of studies. We see this in a letter that the canons of Worms wrote ca. 1115 to their colleagues at Bamberg. They urge them to support their bishop elect, Burchard II, a former student of Bamberg ("vestris institutis fundatus a puericia"), "a son of Bamberg" "in litterarum scientia, in rerum agendarum pericia, in honestate morum, in gratia discretionum."³⁶ Whether this is flattery or a deserved reputation, it shows us a desirable curriculum for a school of future bishops: letters and manners, skill in governing or administering, and good judgment, presumably the kind a bishop/administrator, not an intellectual, requires.

In an earlier publication I have tried to show how the educational reforms that took place at Hildesheim in the middle of the eleventh century under Bishop Azelinus (1044–54) are understandable within this same framework of studies. A conservative chronicler complained about Azelinus importing the manners of the court *(curialitas)* into the comparatively rustic diocese, and this complaint has given that bishop the reputation of an epicurean corrupter of his church. But Azelinus also hired the gifted young cleric Benno, later the second bishop of Osnabrück by that name, as *magister scholarum*, luring him from the royal court with promises of great wealth. Benno implanted in the clergy a "zeal for the study of letters" and transformed Hildesheim into a center of learning second to none in the region. Hence we have a picture of the double role of Azelinus and Benno at Hildesheim, the bishop imposing courtly *mores* on the clergy, the schoolmaster instructing them in *litterae* (cf. *Origins of Courtliness*, p. 218f.).

I have given a number of references, not to smother the subject in documentation, but to establish as clearly and definitively as possible the overriding importance of a formula to which I can find no reference in scholarship on medieval education. The phrase "letters and manners" occurs so often not because it was the bearer of an inherited framework of studies, but because it was a formula by which the life of the schools was organized. Whatever is conveyed in the terms *mores, recte vivendi dogma*, and others we will encounter – *forma vivendi*,

---

³⁵ *Weitere Briefe Meinhards*, nr. 19, ed. Erdmann, p. 213: "Verum inter alia gravia et luctuosa hunc dolorem quasi capitalem deplorastis studium lumenque litterarum penitus apud vos occidisse nec minus disciplinam moralem egregie apud vos antiquitus institutam situ quodam et negligentia nunc dissolutam iam iamque obisse, immo sepultam esse. Quas ob res adolescentem vestrum officine nostre erudiendum informandumque tradidistis, ut duo pignora vestra, mores dico litterasque [sic], per eum vobis ... resuscitentur."

³⁶ Udalrici codex, nr. 172, *Bibliotheca rerum germanicarum*, ed. Philipp Jaffé, vol. V. *Monumenta Bambergensia*, p. 305.

disciplina vivendi, studium bene vivendi – students wanted it, and the schools had to provide it.

III. The Old Learning and Cultus Virtutum

I would suggest that the formula "letters and manners," with all it implies institutionally and pedagogically, indicates to us the essential unifying element in cathedral school education in the period 950–1100/1150. It was this dual instruction that aimed at shaping the statesman/educator, that is, attaining that goal which had given rise to cathedral schools in the mid-tenth century. Letters by themselves could of course be learned in monasteries. It is significant that in some of the best known descriptions of the education of monks from the period, only the term *litterae* occurs, not *mores*. Abbo of Fleury was sent to school *litteris imbuendus*; Otloh of St. Emmeram *pro litteris discendis*.[37] The study of *mores* was in part a preparation for secular administrative service, or for a secularized form of ecclesiastical service. Meinhard's statement that *mores* in the present day are added to *litterae* "pro ecclesiastico usu" makes sense only if we understand that instruction as combining the moral and ethical improvement of the individual with a preparation for service to the church. *Mores* could have been omitted from a monastic education, but it formed an important facet of instruction at the cathedral schools in our period. Letters had to be complemented by an ethical education,[38] which could become the main goal of instruction. Fulbert of Chartres wrote a letter to archbishop Ebalus of Rheims in 1023 recommending a student of his who wished to transfer to Rheims for the sake of the same study that had brought him to Chartres, namely, *causa discendae*

---

[37] On Abbo, *PL* 139, 389A; Otloh, *PL* 146, 38B. At Ramsey Abbo is said to have taught *litterarum scientia*, and in a long description of his teaching, no mention is made of *mores*. Cf. *PL* 139, 392B. The informative article by Peter Johanek, "Klosterstudien im 12. Jahrhundert," In *Schulen und Studium* (above, n. 17), pp. 35–68, shows that the monasteries took a considerable interest in the teachings of the schools. But his idea of a fundamental common purpose linking education at both kinds of institutions (e.g. p. 37) is misleading and ill-conceived. Neither the example of William of Champeaux continuing his teaching at St. Victor nor that of Wibald of Stablo's letter 167 to Manegold of Paderborn bear out the argument. The former fled from the threat of dialectic back to a teaching aimed at *venustas morum* (cf. Hildebert of Lavardin, Ep. 1, *PL* 171, 141A), that is, non-monastic. The latter gave advice appropriate to a worldly master, and apologized repeatedly for stepping out of his role as monk to do it.

[38] There is no doubt that the *mores* studied along with *litterae* is another name for the discipline called in the sources *ethica* and *moralitas*. Cf. Anselm of Laon, *PL* 162, 1590C: "Dicitur et auctor in Proverbiis ethicus, id est tractans de moribus." The identification of the two is standard in Conrad of Hirsau's *Accessus ad auctores*, ed. R. B. C. Huygens (1970), e.g. p. 21 (Cato): "Ethicae subponitur, quia ad morum utilitatem nititur"; p. 27 (Arator): "Ethicae subponitur, id est morali scientiae, quia tractat de moribus."

honestatis, to learn virtue or morality.[39] The acquisition of knowledge and the study of the seven liberal arts tended towards the higher goal of an ethical education, just as all studies in Carolingian times aimed at religious perfection. The subjects studied and authors read in secular learning may have changed little; but the underlying intent of education changed or broadened considerably. Now a great intermediate object swelled the area separating the arts from theology, and that intermediate object was called *mores, ethica*, or *moralitas*.[39a]

This explains in part the difficulty of assigning a place in earlier medieval education to the discipline called by these names. It is not an independent branch of study, even though in some schemes it may be assigned specifically to grammar or rhetoric.[40] Certainly, the association of ethics with grammar and rhetoric was a close one, hallowed since antiquity as the essence of an orator's education, cultivated and practiced in secular education in the Middle Ages.[41]

---

[39] Ep. 76, ed. Behrends, p. 136: "[Hubertus]... qui de patria sua causa discendae honestatis egressus..." Behrends misses the intent of the phrase, translating it, "for the sake of acquiring a sound education."

[39A] The strongly religious orientation of "letters and manners" in Carolingian education is evident in the following passage from the *Epistola de litteris colendis*, MGH, Leges 2, Capit. 1, nr. 29, p. 79: [Along with the "regularis vitae ordo" letters are to be studied]... qualiter, sicut regularis norma honestatem morum, ita quoque docendi et discendi instantia ordinet et ornet seriem verborum, ut, qui Deo placere appetunt recte vivendo, ei etiam placere non negligant recte loquendo." For a commentary, see Fleckenstein, *Bildungsreform*, p. 52. "Right living" is taken for granted; it is not an object of education. The learned skill is "right speaking." The end of both is "pleasing God." This is very far indeed from the *utilitas, elegantia* and *sublimitas* that Meinhard got from his studies, or from the *elegantia morum* and *dignitas vitae* that Onulf of Speyer set as the higher goal of rhetorical studies (below, n. 41).

[40] On the place of ethics in programs of studies, see the works of Philippe Delhaye, "La place de l'éthique parmi les classifications scientifiques au XIIe siècle," *Miscellanea moralia in honorem E. D. A. Janssen* (1948), 19–44; "L'Enseignement de la philosophie morale au XIIe siècle," *Mediaeval Studies*, 11 (1950), 77–99; "Grammatica et ethica au XIIe siècle," *RTAM*, 25 (1958), 59–110. It is evident from Delhaye's important works that the various subjects of the trivium could serve ethics. The latter should not be seen as a kind of pendant to the former; it was, or could be, the underlying motive. Some observations on the dependency in Köhn, "Schulbildung und Trivium" (above, n. 26), p. 224, 228.

[41] The short work by Onulf of Speyer *Colores rhetorici* (1071–76), ed. W. Wattenbach, Sitzber. der Preuss. Akad. der Wissenschaften (1894), pp. 361–86, gives us an especially good example of the subordination of rhetoric to ethics, or rather of the virtual disappearance of the discipline of rhetoric behind the ethical motive. Most of the prologue is lost. The work begins with the sentence fragment, most interesting for our purpose: "... arti rethoricae: morum elegantiam, compositionem habitus, vitae dignitatem amplectere" (p. 369). A conjecture in harmony with the rest of the work would see this as completing the thought, "The art of rhetoric is not confined to the framing of speeches, but includes the cultivation of elegant manners, composed bearing and dignity of conduct." The structure of the work is the outbidding of rhetorical definitions (from the *Rhetorica ad Herennium*) with moral precepts. E.g. *complexio* is an ornament of speech, but far better and more elegant is "amorem Dei... amorem proximi complectere" (III, 370). He wittily uses the

582

Gerbert of Aurillac gave a programmatic statement of the connection in saying that he refused to distinguish the art of speaking well from the art of living well.[42] This is the formula of humanist education for the eleventh and twelfth centuries as well as for Roman antiquity. But neither of those periods necessarily confined ethical education to the disciplines of grammar and rhetoric. Education generally had the purpose not just of conveying knowledge, but of forming the human being, of "attuning" his inner to his outer world, "composing" his manners according to inner virtues acquired through study and practice. Speech and gesture were the activities in which inner man and outer expression met most closely, but all the disciplines and arts could serve that purpose and ideally were pursued *causa discendae honestatis*. John of Salisbury strongly stated this dominant role of ethics. In the prologue to the first book of his *Metalogicon* he makes this trenchant claim: "Any pretext of philosophy that does not bear fruit in the cultivation of virtue *[cultus virtutis]* and the guidance of one's conduct is futile and false."[43] Elsewhere he lists and defines all the disciplines of liberal education and sums up: "Of all these branches of learning that which confers the grace of inner and outer beauty *[decoris gratia]* in the highest degree, is Ethics, the most excellent part of philosophy, without which the latter would not even deserve its name."[44] John here is the spokesman of what I will refer to from now on as "the old learning." It is a humanistic program of education based on the integration of knowledge and wisdom, or, to use the medieval emblem of that union, the marriage of Philology and Mercury. It dominated the cathedral schools in the eleventh century, and toward the end of the century it became locked in conflict with a new kind of learning, based on dialectic,

---

rhetorical figure under discussion to frame the moral precept. On Onulf see L. Wallach, "Onulf of Speyer: A Humanist of the Eleventh Century," *Medievalia et Humanistica*, 6 (1950), 35–56, and Carl Erdmann, "Onulf von Speyer und Amarcius," in his *Forschungen zur politischen Ideenwelt des Frühmittelalters*, ed. Fr. Baethgen (1951), pp. 124–34.

[42] *Die Briefsammlung Gerberts von Reims*, ed. Fritz Weigle, MGH, Briefe der deutschen Kaiserzeit, 2 (1966), p. 73 (Ep. 44): "Cumque ratio morum dicendique ratio a philosophia non separentur, cum studio bene vivendi semper coniuncxi studium bene dicendi..."

[43] *Ioannis Saresberiensis episcopi Carnotensis Metalogicon* I, Prol., ed. Clemens Webb (1929), p. 4: "Est enim quelibet professio philosophandi inutilis et falsa, que se ipsam in cultu virtutis et vitae exhibitione non aperit." English in text from *The Metalogicon of John of Salisbury: A Twelfth Century Defense of the Verbal and Logical Arts of the Trivium*, trans. Daniel McGarry (1962), p. 6.

[44] Translation taken, with some liberties, from McGarry, p. 67. *Metalogicon* I, 24, ed. Webb, p. 55: "Illa autem que ceteris philosophie partibus preminet, Ethicam dico, sine qua nec philosophi subsistit nomen, collati decoris gratia omnes alias antecedit." Cf. Abelard, *Dialogus inter Philosophum, Iudaeum et Christianum*, ed. Rudolf Thomas (1970), pp. 88–90 (ll. 1263–1314) (Ethics, based on the pursuit of the *summum bonum* is the highest discipline, the other liberal arts merely its handmaidens.)

disputation, and the systematizing of philosophical and theological problems: early scholastic philosophy, which from now on I will call "the new learning."[45]

One of the essential tasks of history of education for the tenth and eleventh centuries is to show how the *cultus virtutum* tended to penetrate into each of the seven liberal arts, to appropriate intellectual subjects for the purpose of ethical training. I pointed out Onulf of Speyer's appropriation of rhetoric for the study of *elegantia morum* and *dignitas vitae* (above, n. 41). The subject of cosmology and astronomy as an ethical discipline is a particularly rich and important one. I am preparing a study of it. Here I will just include a few observations.

The connection of ethics and cosmology is ancient and primitive in its origins. The Middle Ages had it most directly from Stoic philosophy, which made nature and the heavens into the pattern for man's moral development.[46] Cicero regarded the highest goal of moral conduct as "naturam sequi et eius quasi lege vivere" and formulated the pithy phrase, "natura optima vivendi dux."[47] John of Salisbury is fond of quoting it.[48] In the *Tusculan Disputations* Cicero traced the route by which public life leads distinguished men to philosophy, then to astronomy, thence to the search for the causes and origins of things, and ultimately to the good life. The Ciceronian joining of "natural science," ethics and public service had a vital meaning for the circles of statesmen/administrators in the eleventh century with whom we are concerned.[49] Boethius, in the *Consolatio philosophiae*, thanked Lady Philosophy for forming his *mores* in accordance with the celestial order and the movement of the planets.[50] If the

---

[45] The discussion of the period is getting a little crowded with "old-new" pairs, but given the transitional nature of the late eleventh-early twelfth century – the turn from subject matters taken over more or less uncritically from antiquity and from comparatively primitive, quasi-magical modes of thought – the terms are useful and accurate. "Old and new learning" are consistent with the framework formulated by Gillian Evans, *Old Arts and New Theology: The Beginnings of Theology as an Academic Discipline* (1980). On the transitional nature of the period see esp. the interesting studies by Charles Radding, *A World Made by Men: Cognition and Society, 400–1200* (1985); "Evolution of Medieval Mentalities: A Cognitive-Structural Approach," *American Historical Review*, 83 (1978), 577–97; and "Superstition to Science: Nature, Fortune and the Passing of the Medieval Ordeal," *American Historical Review*, 84 (1979), 945–69.

[46] See Maximilian Forschner, *Die stoische Ethik: über den Zusammenhang von Natur-, Sprach- und Moralphilosophie im altstoischen System* (1981).

[47] Cicero, *De legibus* I, 21, 56; *Laelius* V, 19.

[48] *Johannes Saresberiensis episcopi Carnotensis policratici sive de nugis curialium et vestigiis philosophorum libri VIII*, ed. Clemens Webb (1909), IV, 1 (Vol. I, 235, l. 13); VI, 21 (Vol II, 60, l. 1). See the study by Tilman Struve, "Vita civilis naturam imitetur: Der Gedanke der Nachahmung der Natur als Grundlage der organologischen Staatskonzeption Johannes von Salisbury," *Historisches Jahrbuch*, 101 (1981), 341–61.

[49] *Tusculan Disputations* V, 24–25, 68–72. Cf. the adaptation of this passage in the so-called *Regensburger rhetorischen Briefe*, ed. Norbert Fickermann, *Briefsammlungen der Zeit Heinrichs IV.* (see above, n. 34), p. 316 (Ep. 9).

[50] Boethius, *The Consolation of Philosophy* I, Prose 4, trans. & rev. H. F. Stewart, The Loeb Classical Library, 74 (1968), p. 142.

heavens are seen as a pattern for man's morals, then the study of astronomy is an object of ethics; it offers an approach to forming, or re-forming man's character.

This, I believe, is one of the main impulses for the study of Plato's *Timaeus* in the eleventh century. That stern critic of *Timaeus* studies, Manegold of Lautenbach, indicated this clearly when he conceded the value of Plato's work in "moral judgment aside from questions of faith," and that means the pursuit of the virtues appropriate to the "ecclesiastici rectores et gubernatores divine rei publice."[51] In other words, it is fine for civil and church administrators to study the *Timaeus* within a program of moral education, but let no one confuse it with theological truth. For medieval commentators the subject of Plato's work was "natural justice," the pattern of natural law implanted in the cosmic order at its inception, upon which men can draw to form their own characters: "Hence the subject matter of this book," writes William of Conches in the beginning of his *Timaeus* commentary, "is natural justice or the creation of the world: for he [Plato] treats the latter by way of investigating natural justice."[52] In his glosses on Boethius William also assigned both the *Timaeus* and *The Consolation of Philosophy* specifically to *ethica*.[53] This notion of the *Timaeus* legitimized as a work of ethics certainly helps explain the manuscript tradition of that work. The interest in the *Timaeus* in the eleventh century coincides with the advent of a program of ethical education at cathedral schools.

The more general Stoic connection of ethics with the study of nature also had far-reaching implications for our period. The author of the *Regensburger rhetorischen Briefe* sees *honestas* as a cosmic principle without which the entire *mundana fabrica* would collapse.[54] In Alan of Lille's *Anticlaudianus* the virtue of *Honestas* teaches the New Man to "love nature" and to embrace whatever nature has created.[55] Hugh of St. Victor gave the idea terse and sharp expression:

---

[51] *Liber contra Wolf.* XXII (above, n. 4), pp. 93–94.

[52] Guillaume de Conches, *Glosae super Platonem: Texte critique avec introduction, notes et tables* III, ed. E. Jeauneau, Textes philosophiques du moyen-âge, 13 (1965), p. 59: "Unde possumus dicere quod materia huius libri est naturalis iusticia vel creatio mundi: de ea enim propter naturalem iusticiam agit." On the origins of the idea of natural justice and its significance in the Middle Ages, see Gérard Verbeke, "Aux origines de la notion de 'loi naturelle'", in *La filosofia della natura nel medioevo: Atti del terzo congresso internazionale di filosofia medioevale* (1966), pp. 164–73.

[53] Cf. Delhaye, "L'Enseignement de la philosophie morale," p. 83, n. 13.

[54] *Reg. rhet. Briefe* nr. 15, p. 334.

[55] Alain de Lille, *Anticlaudianus: Texte critique avec une introduction et des tables* VII, 208ff., ed. R. Bossuat, Textes philosophiques du moyen-âge, 1 (1955), p. 163: "[honestas monet]... Ut vicium fugiat, Naturam diligat.../... amplectens quicquid Natura creavit."

... in the meaning of things lies natural justice, out of which the discipline of our own morals [*mores*] arises. By contemplating what God has made we realize what we ourselves ought to do. Every nature tells of God; every nature teaches man.[56]

The root impulse for the study of the creation and of nature in the eleventh and twelfth centuries lies in this idea. Any "science" based on this conception of the universe was necessarily a "humane" science, directed towards self-knowledge and moral perfection, towards good governance of the self and the state. The idea of macrocosm – microcosm, and with it the basic form of some of the most prominent works of twelfth century humanism, reveal this conception: William of Conche's *Philosophia mundi*, Bernard Silvester's *Cosmographia*, and Alan's *Anticlaudian*. In each case the point of departure is the cosmos and cosmic perfection, and following upon this, man and human perfection. This form came from the *Timaeus*, but the idea it proclaimed was no less vivid in the mind of these twelfth century humanists, no less vividly present in their works, than in Plato's. Eleventh and early twelfth century cosmology is in its basic impulse humane and ethical. The progress of science in the twelfth century towards Aristotelian empiricism, towards new Arabic astronomy, towards "natural science" in a sense approaching our understanding of the term, must be seen as a progress away from the pursuit of science in a humane, Stoic-Ciceronian sense.

IV. Teaching Virtue

How was virtue taught? Normally scholars point to the textbooks read in order to illustrate the contents of ethical instruction:[57] Cicero's *De officiis* and the adaptation of this work by Ambrose; the Distichs of Cato, Seneca, and medieval florilegia like the *Moralium dogma philosophorum* ascribed to William of Conches. But this does not help us distinguish the eleventh century clearly from the ninth or the thirteenth and brings us back to my comparison with theater history through lists of plays. Instruction in *mores* was vital enough to dominate studies for some two hundred years, and lists of textbooks reduce it to a collection of lifeless abstractions. What we miss and what is almost alto-

---

[56] *Hugonis de Sancto Victore Didascalicon De Studio Legendi: A Critical Text* VI, 5, ed. C. H. Buttimer, Catholic University of America Studies in Medieval and Renaissance Latin, 10 (1939), 123: "in illa [significatione rerum] enim naturalis iustitia est, ex qua disciplina morum nostrorum, id est, positiva iustitia nascitur. contemplando quid fecerit Deus, quid nobis faciendum sit agnoscimus. omnis natura Deum loquitur, omnis natura hominem docet..." English in text from *The Didascalicon of Hugh of St. Victor: A Medieval Guide to the Arts*, trans. Jerome Taylor, Records of Civilization: Sources & Studies, 64 (1961), p. 145.

[57] Cf. Delhaye, "L'Enseignement de la philosophie morale," p. 83.

gether unrecoverable is the life of the teacher himself.[58] This is the real textbook and exemplar of *mores*, and this form of instruction was conducted above all simply by *convictus*, a life shared by master and students, the imparting of the teacher's qualities to the student by force of example.[59] Meinhard of Bamberg wrote a letter to his former teacher in which he recalls nostalgically his student days: "That way of living *[convictus]* into which you received me in so profoundly humane a manner was more free and noble, more effective and practical *[ad utilitatem efficacius]*, more scrupulous in the cultivation of elegance *[ad elegantiam accuratius]*, more conducive to the highest a man can attain *[ad sublimitatem exquisitius]*, than any other whatsoever, even if my thickness of mind deprived me of its richer fruits."[60] The fruits of *convictus* are *utilitas, elegantia,* and *sublimitas*. There is no talk of the challenges of the mind, of analysis, of knowledge gained for its own sake, no talk of learning at all, but rather of the cultivation of a personal quality, called here "elegance,"[61] and of the practical benefits of a way of life shared with the master, and I take the practical side of this education to be indicated directly in *utilitas* and less directly, though still distinctly, in *sublimitas*, which may mean both the perfect life and the highest rank or office a man can attain.

Some testimony from Fulbert's school at Chartres bears out this picture of the master's role. Fulbert was known as a teacher of "both letters and manners,"[62]

---

[58] Also observed by Southern, *Platonism etc.* (above, n. 3,), p. 19: "In the schools it was the spoken world which was important: perhaps one should even say that it was the physical presence of the master..." And Behrends (*Letters of Fulbert*, p. XXVIII) observes sharply, "... it appears that what attracted [students] was Fulbert himself rather than the subjects which were studied."

[59] See the study by Caroline Bynum, *Docere verbo et exemplo: An Aspect of Twelfth-Century Spirituality*, Harvard Theological Studies, 31 (1979).

[60] *Hannoversche Briefsammlung*, nr. 65, *Briefsammlungen der Zeit Heinrichs IV.* (above, n. 34), p. 112–13: "Neque enim convictu vestro, quo apud vos humanissime acceptus sum, quicquam potest esse liberalius neque studio illo, tametsi mea ingenii malignitas me uberiorem eius fructum defraudavit, studio inquam illo nihil esse potest vel ad utilitatem efficacius vel ad elegantiam accuratius vel ad sublimitatem exquisitius." Erdmann conjectures that Meinhard's former teacher is Hermann of Rheims (*Studien*, p. 38f.), though the evidence for the identification is very slight.

[61] In general, beauty, elegance, grace – whatever the words in the context of *mores* may convey – were clearly important goals of study and learning. Recall John of Salisbury's words that *ethica*, more than any other discipline, confers *gratia decoris*, the grace of a beauty of both mind and manners (above, n. 44). Onulf of Speyer said that the study of rhetoric cultivates *morum elegantia* (above, n. 41). On "elegant" and "beautiful manners" as an ideal of worldly clergy, see *Origins of Courtliness*, pp. 128–52.

[62] The biographer of Abbot Angelran of St. Riquier says of his studies with Fulbert, "hic ei monitor, hic tam morum quam litterarum fuit institutor." *Vita Angel.* III, *PL* 141, 1406A. An interesting bit of testimony to Fulbert's dispensing of "letters and manner" is a letter of his former student and disciple, Hildegar. He writes to Fulbert with two requests: to correct a little work of his *(opusculum)* and to correct his vice of anger. Ep. 95, ed. Behrends, pp. 172–75. Hildegar regarded both his literary and his moral improvement, his letters and his manners, the province of his teacher.

and writings from his students make it clear that his instruction in *mores* was what they particularly valued. Adelman of Liège, later Bishop of Brixen, wrote a poem commemorating his former teacher and fellow students, *De viris illustribus sui temporis*. He praises Fulbert with the verses,

> Ah, with what dignity and diligence in questions of *mores*,
> With what gravity in subject
> matter, what sweetness in words
> He explained the mysteries of higher knowledge![63]

Here also: no praise of incisive intellect or of penetrating analysis, though presumably the reading of the Bible is the form of study in question. What roused this student's enthusiasm were the teacher's eloquence, gravity and dignity.[64] The eloquence and noble bearing of the master were what students wanted from Fulbert, undoubtedly at least as much as they wanted illumination of the "mysteries of higher knowledge." Adelman praises Fulbert's student, Hildegar, for having taken over and made his own the master's facial expression, tone of voice, and manners.[65] Fulbert's personal presence was a text from

---

[63] The critical edition of J. Havet is printed by Clerval in his *Les écoles de Chartres* (above, n. 19), 59–61, here p. 59:
> Eheu! quanta dignitate moralis industriae,
> Quanta rerum gravitate, verborum dulcedine,
> Explicabat altioris archana scientiae!

The lines intriguingly confuse Fulbert's style with the subject matter: Fulbert, and not the text, possesses *gravitas*; Fulbert's words, not those of the text, possess *dulcedo*. It is easy to read these as qualities of his text-interpreting (cf. R. W. Southern, *The making of the Middle Ages* [1953], p. 198). But *moralis industria* is not the level of interpretation called by nearly the same name, *moralitas*, as Southern reads it ("dignity of spiritual interpretation"). It is the striving to attain virtue, a discipline to which a text can lend itself. On Adelman see H. Silvestre, "Notice sur Adelman de Liège, évêque de Brescia (d. 1061)," *Révue d'histoire ecclésiastique*, 56 (1961), 855–71.

[64] Fulbert would seem to have a similar quality in mind when he refuses to send Hildegar, as schoolmaster at Poitiers, any teaching assistant who has not yet attained *gravitas morum* (ep. 92, ed. Behrends, p. 164).

[65] Adelman in Clerval, *Les écoles de Chartres*, p. 60: "Is magistrum referebat vultu, voce, moribus." Gozechin (Goswin) of Mainz praised his student Valcher for his seeming ability to transform himself wholly into his master: "... tu etiam totum magistrum in te videreris transfundere" (*Ep. ad walcherum* III, ed. Huygens, p. 12). See also Hugh of St. Victor, *De inst. nov.* VII, PL 176, 932D–933C. Ambrose in his adaptation of Cicero's *De officiis* had urged young men to attach themselves to wise and prudent teachers and imitate them to the benefit of their morals and their careers: "Ostendunt ... adolescentes eorum se imitatores esse, quibus adhaerent; et ea convalescit opinio, quod ab his vivendi acceperint similitudinem, cum quibus conversandi hauserint cupiditatem" (XX, 97, PL 16, 137B). The passage is worth quoting in this context not only because of the popularity and importance of Ambrose's work in this period, but also because it is quoted along with admonitions to students to imitate their teachers and to teachers to guide the morals of their students in Manegold of Lautenbach's *Liber ad Gebehardum* IX, MGH, Libelli de lite, I, 327–28. "Teacher imitation" remains an important formula of ethical pedagogy

588

which the students learned, his personal qualities a substitute for intellectual knowledge. Wibald of Stablo a century later was still speaking entirely within this conceptual framework when he urged a young master, Balderich of Trier,

> Let your mere presence be a course of studies for your students... Your position requires more than mere teaching. You must exercise strict severity, for you are, as you know, also one who supervises the correction of conduct. This teaching and this exercise is more subtle and in its fruits more important than any other.[66]

The physical presence of an educated man possessed a high pedagogic value; his composure and bearing, his conduct of life, could themselves constitute a form of discourse, intelligible and learnable. Willigis of Mainz is said to have "taught lovers of virtue how to live according to the norms of morality, not with his speech but with his actions, more with the language of his behavior than that of his words."[67] A comment of Gozechin, or Goswin of Mainz, gives us good reason to think that teaching merely by presence and personal authority was a recognized task at cathedral schools, opposed to the comparative busy work of presenting school learning. He distinguishes between some men who teach *auctoritate*, and others who teach *labore*. The former can stand the rigors of the job, "than which there is none more difficult," longer than the latter.[68]

If we can accept that the shaping of character through the person of the teacher, aided by written examples and by any of the seven liberal arts, was one of the central tasks of cathedral schools, the task indicated in the term *mores*, then we have come a long way toward understanding the nature and goal of

---

into the Renaissance. Cf. Castiglione, *The Book of the Courtier* I, 26, trans. Charles Singleton (1959), p. 42: "... whoever would be a good pupil must not only do things well, but must always make every effort to resemble and, if that is possible, to transform himself into his master."

[66] Ep. 91, in *Bibl. rer. Germ.*, ed. Philipp Jaffé, Vol. 1: *Monumenta Corbeiensia* (1864; rpt. 1964), p. 165: "Presentia tua tuis auditoribus disciplina sit... Plus habet locus tuus quam docendi officium; nam et censoriam exhibere debes severitatem, quoniam et corrigendis moribus prefectum te esse noveris. Quae disciplina et exercitatio omnibus est subtilior et in fructu cunctis propensior." Similarly his praise of Bernard of Clairvaux, Ep. 167, p. 286: "Quem si aspicias, doceris; si audias, instrueris; si sequare, perficeris."

[67] *Libellus de Willigisi consuetudinibus* IV, MGH, SS 15, 2, p. 745 (ll. 31–32): "Amatores virtutis, qualiter honesta moralitate deberent vivere, docuit in re, non ore, lingua magis morum quam lingua verborum." The thrust of this work (composed 1018/1039) is consistently Willigis' person as an ethical curriculum: he was "vitae honestissimae speculum" (p. 743, l. 35); "[from his life]... possunt exempla vivendi honestissima sumere qui student honestissime vivere..." (p. 744, l. 4f.); "... per assiduae lectionis honestaeque moralitatis [note the pair, letters and manners] exemplum honestissimum vitam non cessavit honestare multorum" (p. 744, l. 42f.). Cf. Caroline Bynum, *Docere exemplo et verbo*, p. 41: "... life almost becomes a form (a more effective form) of speech."

[68] *Ep. ad Walch.* XXVI, ed. Huygens, p. 30: "Cuius laboris tempus, quia nichil difficilius sub sole geritur vel quod magis operarii sui vires exhauriat, a sapientibus prefinitum est septuenne, nisi de cetero is qui preest auctoritate presideat, non labore."

education there and the role of *magister scholarum*, a position of incomparably greater stature than its modern counterpart, schoolmaster. It is a striking fact that the position of master is commonly a stepping stone on the way to the bishopric. A career followed by many of the most distinguished imperial bishops since Ottonian times led from student to schoolmaster to court chaplain to bishop, with perhaps stations in between as provost or chancellor.[69] Master of schools stood in a comparable relation to state service as today the law to government service. And the reason for this is, above all, that the schoolmaster had to embody those qualities he was to transmit to his students, and those qualities were ones that qualified a man for royal service, for administrative and diplomatic duties, for the episcopacy (see below). Hence a good schoolmaster was an obvious candidate for the royal chapel and the bishopric. The personal charisma of the great man, the diplomat, the statesman, the follower of the great Roman statesmen:[70] this was the aura that surrounded the successful teacher at the cathedral schools, and it was the main curriculum of *ethica*.

This notion of a pedagogy of personal charisma explains the exuberant praise of masters from the period. Students were swept away by the personal magnetism of the man suited for the service of the emperor and probably destined for it. And it mattered little what they taught, as long as they spoke well and exuded qualities like *gravitas, dignitas*, and *elegantia*. Recall that Abelard, a teacher in a completely different stamp from the masters of the old learning, was astonished that great crowds of students lavished devotion and respect on the venerable Anselm of Laon (whose school offered instruction in *litterae et mores*.[71]) Anselm spoke most beautifully, but his thought was obscure and he could not deal with the problems of philosophy he raised: "He had a remarkable command of words, but their meaning was worthless and devoid of all sense. The fire he kindled filled his house with smoke but not with light."[72] A description of the lecturing style of Berengar of Tours gives us an extraordinary glimpse of this aura of the great man. It was recorded by one of his enemies in the eucharist controversy, Guitmund of Aversa:

---

[69] Cf. Lèsne, *Les écoles*, p. 511f.

[70] One example of many that could be cited: Gerbert claims to be a faithful follower of Cicero "in otio et negotio." Ep. 158, ed. Weigle, p. 187. For other examples of Roman reminiscences in the conduct of this class of men, see *Origins of Courtliness*, p. 117ff.

[71] Helmold, *Chron. Slav.* LXV, MGH, SS 21, 47, 1.8ff.: [Vicelin went to Laon to study with Ralph, Anselm's brother, where] "... ad ea solum enisus est, que sobrio intellectui et moribus instruendis sufficerent."

[72] Abélard, *Historia calamitatum: Texte critique avec une introduction*, ed. J. Monfrin, Bibliothèque des textes philosophiques (1959), p. 68. English in text from *The Letters of Abelard and Heloise*, trans. B. Radice (1974), p. 62.

Whatever bespoke grandeur and distinction, he affected. This man, almost wholly ignorant, claimed to be a doctor of the arts, and persuaded people of it by virtue of his pompous posing, by elevating himself above others on a platform, by simulating the dignity of a teacher in his manner rather than by the substance of his teachings, by burying his head deep in his cowl, pretending to be in profound meditation, then finally, when the expectations of the listeners had been whetted by his long hesitation, giving forth in an extremely soft and plangent tone, which was effective in deceiving those who did not know better.[73]

Berengar is a figure very much on the border between the old learning and the new. His career took him between the cathedral schools and the courts of secular lords, his personal charisma won him many enthusiastic students, but his use of reason and analytic thought set him sharply apart from masters like Fulbert of Chartres and Meinhard of Bamberg. He had the style of the masters of the old learning, but he combined it with probing and exacting reason. We can put aside the criticism of this monk and student of Lanfranc that he was ignorant. These reproaches tell us more about the categories of judgment applicable to secular masters in the second half of the eleventh century than about the quality of Berengar's learning. Probably a great many teachers could substitute personal style, intellectually unrigorous moralizing, and grand self-presentation for scholarship, and students were more than willing to accept their education on those terms. Wibald of Stablo complains in the mid-twelfth century that students defend the sayings of their masters not because they are true, but because they love the men who pronounce them, and he sees one school set against another, not in the pursuit of truth through reason, but "in hate or love of individual teachers."[74] The teacher's main task, or one of them, was the cultivation of the self, of character, virtue, and eloquence in himself and his students; this is the essence of *cultus virtutum*, and knowledge, scholarship, rational analysis were somewhat beside the point, perhaps even dubious products of *curiositas* and the urge to novelties.

One may well think that then as now the cult of personal manners was a substitute for genius and a sign of the mediocrity of the age. Certainly to read what masters of the old learning did write cautions against thinking them alot of mute inglorious Miltons. Adalbold of Utrecht's commentary on Boethius' "O, qui perpetua," (early eleventh century) is wholly unoriginal. Arnulf of Speyer's *Colores rhetorici* is witty and amusing but one has the feeling that its author could have spun it out at great length with the intensity and incisiveness

---

[73] *PL* 149, 1428B.

[74] Ep. 167, ed. Jaffé, p. 277: "Discipuli magistrorum sentencias tuentur, non quia verae sunt, set quod auctores amant; scola adversus scolam debachatur, odio vel amore magistrorum." Cf. William of Conches' observation that students should love their teachers more than their parents: *Philosophia mundi* IV, 30, ed. G. Maurach (1980), p. 114f. (In the Migne ed., IV, 38, *PL* 172, 100A–B). And Abelard's, that students should not be duped by love of their teachers into believing that they make sense (below, n. 110).

of table talk, requiring no particular learning or intellectual rigor. Anselm of Besate's *Rhetorimachia* shows much eccentricity and little genius.[75] Can the explanation of personal greatness possibly cover all the sins of pedantry and self-congratulation this author commits? Henry III took Anselm into the royal chapel, supposedly as a reward for the *Rhetorimachia* (though we have only Anselm's word on it). Let us hope that the emperor did it because his judgment was numbed by the spell of Anselm's personality.

But a fair number of men in Anselm's position and with his ambitions were mute and glorious, whatever the quality of the unwritten works slumbering somewhere in their minds. The problem for us in the twentieth century is to get from the muteness to the glory. Silence means obscurity, and it is a pall over great men and mediocrities alike.

V. *The Civil Life as Productivity:* Disciplina Vivendi

The forum in which learning, intellect and brilliance were to be expressed was the active life, public service, not philosophical tracts. A cleric of Worms wrote a letter to his bishop, Azecho of Worms, around 1030, in which he sets forth an ideal of public administration as the fulfillment of philosophy:

Divine providence, in foreseeing the necessity of installing you as the governor of our republic, has placed you at the apex of pastoral care *in order that you may now translate into acts of public administration those things you have learned in your private studies.* The schoolmistress of all virtues [Philosophy] has taken up her abode in you, so that in all your undertakings you may follow in her footsteps.[76]

The letter was a job application, and the applicant was not only wheedling, but also putting forward his credentials by showing his mastery of Boethius and of the ideal of the learned administrator whose acts reveal the influence of philosophy. Public administration as a form of philosophy: it is a topic that would lead us back to Roman antiquity and into the heart of medieval humanism. Philosophy in the service of the *res publica* is a much cultivated educational and

---

[75] Anselm von Besate, *Rhetorimachia*, ed. Karl Manitius, MGH, Quellen zur Geistesgeschichte des Mittelalters, 2 (1958).

[76] *Ältere Wormser Briefsammlung*, nr. 52, p. 89: "Hinc divina providentia, cum te nostre rei publice regende necessarium previdisset, ad pastoralis cure apicem perduxit, ut quod inter secreta otia didiceras, in actum publice administrationis transferres. Magistra itaque Virtutum in te elegit sedem, ut in cunctis actibus tuis illius vestigia sequi videaris." Cf. Boethius, *De cons. phil.* I, 4,7: "Quod a te inter secreta otia didiceram, transferre in actu publicae administrationis optavi." Many texts on the combining of philosophy and public life in the *Regensburger rhetorischen Briefe*, e.g. nr. 1, p. 275 (quoting Cicero, *Tusc. Disp.*, V,2,5): "O vite dux philosophia, o virtutis indagatrix... tu inventrix legum, tu magistra morum et discipline fuisti." Also nr. 22, p. 348 f.

political ideal, one that required the alliance of schools with the apparatus of government.[77]

It is a major theme of the important letter collection, the *Regensburger rhetorischen Briefe*. The letters are only slightly fictionalized in the sense that the personae of the writers are loosely maintained. The basic situation is that a clerical administrator corresponds with friends asking them for advice and guidance in the trials and difficulties of public life. The source of advice, consolation, and statesmanly wisdom to which the writers regularly turn in addressing the problems raised is, generally stated, Philosophy, more specifically Cicero's, *Tusculan Disputations*. The latter is a work of major importance for the cathedral schools of the eleventh century. Meinhard of Bamberg had termed it the most important work of philosophy from Roman antiquity.[78] Its appeal lay in its combining of asceticism and rejection of the world with a stoically courageous affirmation of state service: persist, suffer through all the tribulations of the active life, and make the cult of virtues – identified with Philosophy – into your guide. That is the thrust of the *Tusculan Disputations*, and the author of the letters makes it into his theme. The appeal of this attitude to worldly clergy in the German empire in the second half of the eleventh century should be evident: torn between the parties in the investiture controversy, they could find in Cicero's work a rule of life, a philosophy that lent dignity to administrative service while at the same time casting serious doubt on it, that could idealize imperial statesmen while placing the emperor in the role of Nero, Herod, and Nebuchadnezzar (cf. nr. 9, p. 314), that reconciled *contemptus mundi* with *servitium rei publicae*. In one of the most remarkable of these letters, the author sets the trials of public life parallel with the sufferings of the martyrs and of Christ, and makes the courageous facing of those trials into an act of Christian *fortitudo*. Here is a passage that shows especially clearly the odd mingling of Christian and Roman heroism typical for this writer:

He himself [Christ] once fought for us. And should we now refuse to enter the field of battle for his sake? And would we, seeing his wounds, not suffer tribulations for his sake, having won salvation through the hate he faced? Spartan boys face tortures inflicted on them without crying out. Lacedaemonian youths in competitive fighting suffer blows and kicks and even bites, but would sooner suffer death itself than admit defeat. (nr. 9, p. 319)

I doubt that the sufferings of Christ have ever before or since been set parallel to the training of Spartan and Lacedaemonian boys. But it shows us a central concern of this author: to legitimize and sweeten a cleric's service to the state by appeal to ancient Greek and Roman ideals.

---

[77] On the combining of the intellectual and civil life in England see Southern, "England's Place" (above, n. 2), p. 174ff. Also Beryl Smalley, *The Becket Controversy and the Schools* (1973).

[78] *Briefe Meinhards*, nr. 1, ed. Erdmann, p. 193: "Unde hortor, ut Tusculanis tuis plurimus insideas, quibus Latina philosophia Cicerone parente nichil illustrius edidit."

But our point of departure was the combining of philosophy and the active life. The *Regensburger rhetorischen Briefe* find in the *Tusculan Disputations* a Roman model for this combination, one which must have had a deep resonance in the schools and courts of eleventh century Europe, at least among its statesman/intellectual class. Cicero observed in that work that philosophy was a fairly new discipline in the Rome of his time, and he recognized the superiority of the Greeks in the *writing* of it. But by way of explaining this to the advantage of his countrymen, he says that the early Romans did not write works of philosophy because they were so taken up with the great tasks of running the state, and they preferred to practice "that most bountiful of disciplines, the discipline of living well" *(bene vivendi disciplina)*. They pursued this more in their lives than in their writings: "Vita magis quam litteris persecuti sunt."[79] It is difficult to do justice in English to the phrase *disciplina vivendi*, and one takes recourse to spelling out its implications. It makes the conduct of public life into a form of philosophical discourse, a program of studies, a textbook. Wibald of Stablo was speaking within this trope when he urged Balderich of Trier to turn his mere presence into a discipline (above, n. 66). And the example of the Roman statesman who turns public life into a philosophical discipline gave allure to this substitute form of productivity: life itself could become a work of philosophy, a composition analogous to an oration or to a musical composition. This work of art, the composing of *mores*, was a major contribution of the eleventh century to "philosophy"[80] and to culture. It is the best answer to the question how that age could have been mute and glorious at the same time.

---

[79] *Tusc. Disp.* IV, 3, 5–6. Cf. *Regensburger rhetorischen Briefe*, nr. 1, p. 275; nr. 11, p. 329; nr. 12, p. 331f.; nr. 13, p. 333; nr. 16, p. 336; nr. 22, p. 348.

[80] Histories of philosophy almost without exception pass over the tenth and early eleventh centuries in silence, moving generally from Scotus Eriugena to Berengar of Tours. They would find their subject if they focused on the double orientation of philosophy in the period: not only intellectual but also ethical and civil. Isidor defined philosophy as "rerum humanarum divinarumque cognitio cum studio bene vivendi coniuncta" (*Etymologiae* II, 24, 1, ed. W. M. Lindsay [1911]). Alcuin echoes this, *De dialectica*, I, *PL* 101, 952A: "Philosophia est naturarum inquisitio, rerum humanarum divinarumque cognitio... Est quoque philosophia honestas vitae, studium bene vivendi, meditatio mortis, contemptus saeculi..." In the Worms letter collection Philosophy is the "magistra virtutum" (p. 89). She is depicted throughout the *Regensburger rhetorischen Briefe* as the "virtutis indagatrix" and "magistra morum." Cf. esp. nr. 1, p. 274ff. Eraclius of Liège (d. 971) was equal to the greatest philosophers, his biographer (mid-twelfth century) tells us, in part for his mastery of human and divine knowledge, but especially because his splendid manners "guilded his physical beauty" ("... presertim cum venustatem corporis mores etiam inaurarant splendidi" – MGH, SS 20, 562, l. 9f.). Hildebert of Lavardin consoled William of Champeaux that only on his retirement to St. Victor had he become a true philosopher, since "acquired knowledge" had only been a hindrance to cultivating *venustas morum*, presumably the true goal, at least the higher goal, of philosophy (*PL* 171, 141A). Wibald of Stablo encouraged an archdeacon of Liège to bring peace to his diocese, excusing himself from the negotiations because "Neque enim mores nostros ita

VI. The Statesman and other New Men

By its very nature, then, the end product of *cultus virtutum* is lost to recovery: it is the living administrator functioning at court, expressing philosophy through acts of governing. But we can recover some literary representations of this ideal type in portraits of bishops, in descriptions of an idealized education and of particular virtues within that education. The courtier and bishop embodied the ideals of a program of education in *mores* and *ethica*. *Cultus virtutum* was a preparation for those offices, and any study of qualifications for court service and the bishopric that concentrates on the conventional school subjects, letters and the liberal arts, is bound to end in uncertainty on the role of education in an ecclesiastical career. The school subjects provided the educational basis for a man's advancement only in conjunction with the study of virtue. Richard of St. Victor wrote a letter to Robert of Hereford congratulating him on his promotion from schoolmaster to bishop: "... all your students were filled with joyful hope [at the news of your promotion], and the entire school was heartened and roused to the love of letters and the cultivation of virtue [*cultus virtutum*] through the example of your efforts and your success."[81] Robert's promotion to the bishopric holds out hope to his and other students that the study of letters and *mores, cultus virtutum*, is rewarded by high office, and they redouble their efforts at those school subjects in the hope of repeating his success.

The content of that program of studies registers in the idealized portraits of men pursuing that education and those ambitions. Such portraits represent a humanistic view of man, an ideal of human dignity and greatness indebted – for its articulation – first and foremost to Roman antiquity, Cicero's *De oratore*, *Tusculan Disputations*, and *De officiis*, Quintilian's *Institutes of Oratory*. The formation of the courtier and bishop in the eleventh and twelfth centuries was the task of the old learning. But I stress that this type, the ideal educated bishop, the courtier bishop, was not in its origins a product of shaping ideas, but rather of political and social circumstances which favored the rediscovery and revival of those ideas. An office in the Ottonian imperial church system required a statesman/orator/administrator to fill it, and from that office and its require-

---

instituit et formavit illa vestra doctrix et domina, rerum divinarum et humanarum magistra et educatrix, philosophia..." (Ep. 331, ed. Jaffé, p. 462). Philosophy for Wibald, as for many of his contemporaries, is a force that forms men's character and guides them in the difficulties of public life.

[81] Ep. 1, *PL* 196, 1225A: "Magnam de promotione vestra concepit Ecclesia nostra laetitiam, et spe non modica hilarati sunt auditores vestri, tum universi scholares animati ad amorem litterarum, et cultum virtutum, vestri laboris et successus exemplo." On the connection between studies and promotion to the bishopric, see Zielinski, *Reichsepiskopat*, p. 110ff.

ments,⁸² an educational program, the cultivation of virtues in the old learning, took its major impetus in our period.

This program, as a survival from antiquity, had never completely died out in the earlier Middle Ages. The texts that transmitted it were a firm part of medieval education.⁸³ But it rose and fell in prominence, served a variety of educational goals, and maintained through all vicissitudes a fairly low profile until the end of the tenth century. Here suddenly it made itself felt distinctly – no longer just in tracts on education, like Alcuin's, but in the biographies of men who had received a statesman's education, imperial bishops.

I have talked elsewhere about this figure and the personal qualities requisite to his office, and I will not repeat here more than is necessary to lay the foundation for reading a few portraits. In the courtier bishop the German empire under the Ottos created a figure of great political and cultural significance. Important institutional changes took place through him and around him, the most immediate of which was the transformation of the court chapel and the cathedral schools into training grounds for future imperial bishops. This change laid the institutional groundwork for the career to which I referred earlier: from student to teacher to courtier to bishop.

The position had certain personal requirements, and one of them was charisma. There are many tales of the awe-inspiring presence of the great man from the episcopal milieu. William of Malmesbury tells of a bishop, the object of a murder attempt, who turns and faces his assailants, and the splendor of his presence is so dazzling to them that they drop their knives and flee. The story places us in the atmosphere of the saint's life, of the miraculous, but this bishop performs a humanist miracle; he is saved by his personal qualities, by the magical spell cast by his presence, not by divine intervention.⁸⁴ A bishop had to be tall, handsome and impressive in appearance: "statura procerus, vultu venerandus" are common terms of praise; *splendor* or *nitor personae* sums them up. Bishop Gunther of Bamberg (mid-eleventh century, Meinhard's bishop) was said to be so beautiful that on his crusade in Jerusalem crowds of locals

---

⁸² See my article, "The Courtier Bishop in Vitae from the Tenth to the Twelfth Century," *Speculum*, 58 (1983), 291–325.

⁸³ Alcuin speaks the language of the old learning clearly. His *Dialogus de rhetorica et virtutibus* (the connection of rhetoric and virtue already is indicative) is written for the person "qui ... civiles cupiat cognoscere mores" (*PL* 101, 919), and it ends with the master urging the pupil (Charlemagne), "Disce, precor, juvenis, motus, moresque venustos" (950). On the civil/ethical cast of ancient and early Christian education generally, see Joseph McCarthy, "Clement of Alexandria and the Foundation of Christian Educational Theory," *History of Education Society Bulletin*, 7 (1971), 11–18; idem., *Humanistic Emphases in the Educational Thought of Vincent of Beauvais*, Studien und Texte zur Geistesgeschichte des Mittelalters, 10 (1976), p. 58 ff.

⁸⁴ *De gestis pontificum Anglorum* I, 6, ed. N. E. Hamilton, Rolls Series, 52 (1870), p. 14.

596

gathered in front of a church he was in and prevented him from leaving, so eager were they to get a look at his fabled beauty.[85]

An important ideal of this figure is borne by the phrase, "the greater we are," or "the higher we are set above other men, the more we should bear ourselves as their inferiors." It is an ideal of aristocratic deference, not Christian self-denial. The phrase is borrowed from Cicero and quoted frequently.[86] Other qualities often praised are gentleness *(mansuetudo)*, affability and popularity, if I may put it that way – being all things to all men, making oneself loved of all men. Particularly important is a quality called "beauty of manners" and borne by a number of terms: *elegantia morum, venustas morum, gratia morum, pulchritudo morum*. We find out and out reference to this virtue as a qualification for royal service and the bishopric. Meinwerk of Paderborn is said to have been judged suited for service at the court of Otto III because of the elegance of his manners.[87] And Gerald of Wales complained that his Welsh nationality prevented him from receiving a bishopric from Henry II even though he had served the king loyally and had shown the requisite learning and "grace of manners," here evidently regarded as a prerequisite for advancement from the royal court.[88] This quality forms a bridge between the teachings of the schools and the entrance into the service of the king or bishop. "Beauty of manners" is an object of the study of *mores*, and at the same time a means of entry into the court and episcopacy.

The final quality I will mention here is one of overriding importance, though I know no name for it from the sources other than *decor*: a man must show the composition and harmony of his inner world by the grace, charm, poise, courtesy and urbanity of his outward bearing, by his gait, his table manners, his speech, the motions of his body and limbs. Outward elegance of bearing is taken as a manifestation of *compositio morum*.[89] It might be appropriate to

---

[85] Cf. "The Courtier Bishop," p. 298 ff.

[86] *De officiis* I, 26: "... quanto superiores simus, tanto nos geramus summissius." See *Origins of Courtliness*, p. 35 f.

[87] *Das Leben des Bischofs Meinwerk von Paderborn* V. F. Tenckhoff, MGH, SS rer. germ. in us. schol., 59 (1921), p. 7: "Meinwercus autem, regia stirpe genitus, regio obsequio morum elegantia idoneus adiudicatur evocatusque ad palatium regius capellanus efficitur."

[88] Gerald of Wales, *De principis instructione liber*, Praef. prima, ed. G. F. Warner, Rolls Series, 21, 8 (1891), p. LVIII: "Si quid enim gratiae morum gravitas, si quid litterae, si quid industria conferre potuit, totum id suspectum, totum infestum, totum exosum Gualliae nomen ademit." We recognize in this triad of frustrated qualities the pair "letters and manners."

[89] A history of this virtue from Cicero (who insists that outer *decorum* can never be present without inner *honestas*, nor *honestas* without *decorum*) to Shakespeare (whose Ophelia asks Hamlet, "Could beauty, my lord, have better commerce than with honesty?") would be a rewarding task. Here are a few references for our period. Ambrose echoes Cicero in maintaining that physical beauty is a decoration to inner virtue (*De officiis min., PL* 16, 48B). Poeta Saxo (888), *Annales* V, MGH, Poet. Lat. 4, 1, p. 60, ll.

Cathedral Schools and Humanist Learning

mention the resonance between this educational ideal and the Hellenic *kalos kai agathos*, as long as we insist that we are not dealing with a topos-like survival from an earlier culture where the ideal once was alive. It was alive in the eleventh century, and perhaps the best proof of its vitality is in a series of portraits to which we now turn.

Meinhard of Bamberg writes to a friend and former student, a cleric of high nobility, who is moving to Cologne, no doubt to take up a position at the episcopal court, and who will be exposed to the dangers and temptations of that city.[90] Meinhard warns him of a war to be waged there over his soul. Two courts will fight to gain his services, to make him a member of their retinue. The one is the noble court of virtues, the other the ignoble court of vices. The court of virtues summons him as its special favorite and places the entire business of the court in his hands because of the perfection of his manners *(specimen morum)* and the sharpness of his mind (again, letters and manners, or intellect and

---

211–220: "Interius radix operum latet exteriorum, / Mens moresque viri facta palam generant: / Qui solet esse domi constans prudensque decenter, / Perficit is crebro facta decora foris; / Intra se vitiis dominans rationeque pollens / Exteriora sibi nulla nocere sinit... / At cui mens torpet, mores neque corrigit in se, / Illum iure manet dedecus exterius." Bern of Reichenau, *Vita S. Udalrici, PL* 142, 1186B: "in corporis motu, gestu, incessu, foris ostendere [incipiebat], qualis habitus formaretur intus in mente." Decretum of Leo IX on the synod of Mainz (1049), *PL* 143, 623D: [Confirming Hugo as archbishop of Besançon, who deserves the splendid trappings of office] "... ut qui pollet meritorum laudabili dignitate, tam in virtutum scientia quam in morum honestate, polleat etiam ornamentorum pulchritudine in omni archiepiscopalis culminis plenitudine, semper meminerit in exteriore decore interiorem decorem procurare..." Here I find noteworthy, besides the idea of the bishop's robes and insignia as the outer signs of merit, the phrase *virtutum scientia*, the "science of virtues." Science must be taken to mean "skilled application [of virtues] learned through study." *Vita Adalardi* XXXIX (1055), *PL* 147, 1059: [though he wore vile clothes] "... non egebat aliqua corporis compositione, nihil enim sibi deerat pulchritudinis humanae, nihil etiam interioris animae." Conrad of Hirsau, *Dialogus de mundi contemptu vel amore,* ed. R. Bultot, Analecta Mediaevalia Namurcensia, 19 (1966), pp. 62–63: [in a discussion of the proper relation between *habitus* and *animus*] "... nihil vero prodesse cultum exteriorem virtutum gressus mentientem... Iunge utrumque, et habitum et animum, et summa voti perfectionis calculo constabit." Hugh of St. Victor, *PL* 176, 935B–D "... disciplina ... est membrorum omnium motus ordinatus et dispositio decens in omni habitu et actione... Disciplina est... frenum lasciviae, elationis iugum, vinculum iracundiae, quae domat intemperantiam, levitatem ligat et omnes inordinatos motus mentis atque illicitos appetitus suffocat. Sicut enim de inconstantia mentis nascitur inordinata motio corporis, ita quoque dum corpus per disciplinam stringitur, animus ad constantiam solidatur... Integritas vero virtutis est, quando per internam mentis custodiam ordinate reguntur membra corporis... Liganda ergo sunt foris per disciplinam membra corporis, ut intrinsecus solidetur status mentis." Thomasin von Zirclaere, *Der Wälsche Gast,* ed. Heinrich Rückert, Deutsche Nationalliteratur, 30 (1852), ll. 912 ff.: *"Der lîp wandelt sich nâch dem muot. / des lîbes gebaerde uns dicke bescheit, / hât ein man lieb ode leit."* Some sketchy comments on the subject in *Origins of Courtliness,* pp. 147–49.

[90] *Weitere Briefe Meinhards,* nr. 1, *Briefsammlungen,* ed. Erdmann, p. 192f. According to Erdmann, the receiver, called only G., is a future archbishop of Cologne on his way to be groomed for the office. See *Studien zur Briefliteratur,* p. 282.

manners as the prerequisite to court service). The other court calls to him with the allure of its "slippery, silky bodies," and tries to make him into a citizen of the second Babylon, Cologne. The allegory is a sort of psychomachia, as E. R. Curtius suggested (privately to Erdmann. See *Studien*, p. 282). But it is fabricated from the real situation of the competition between courts for a gifted courtier.[91] Meinhard now urges him to arm himself for this battle with the same virtues his father had possessed, whom he describes as

a man instructed in every kind of virtue, a man who enjoyed to an astonishing degree all the charm and grace of humanity, qualities visible far and wide not only in his dazzling blaze of manners *[flagrantia morum]* but also in the bright good humor which shone most graciously from his eyes.[92]

Presumably humanity, charm and grace, dazzling manners and gracious good humor are results of that instruction in the virtues which his father had received ("omni genere virtutis instructus"). The virtues are neo-classical, Ciceronian, and especially striking is Meinhard's use of *humanitas* in a context which shows that he understood the Ciceronian sense of the word very well.[93] It is a quality accompanied by charm and grace and one that is visible not only in his conduct and bearing, but in the joviality and charm of his facial expression. His inward qualities, a virtuous and humane disposition, shine forth outwardly like a blazing fire. We must remind ourselves that we are at a German cathedral of the eleventh century, not an Italian court of the sixteenth. It is also worth noting for our purpose that these virtues are placed exactly in the context of public life: they are what the cleric and future bishop requires to assert himself and survive in the conflicts of court life, and it is just at this point in his letter that Meinhard recommends to the young man Cicero's *Tusculan Disputations*, "than which Latin philosophy has produced nothing more illustrious." This teacher of *mores* knew perfectly well that that philosophy was vital to a man entering court service.

The description is not isolated. From the eleventh century on we find great men said to embody virtues like these: beauty of soul, composition of manners,

---

[91] On the competition for "sought after men" *(viri expetibiles) Origins of Courtliness*, p. 52.

[92] *Weitere Briefe Meinhards*, nr. 1, p. 193: "Est enim vir ille omni genere virtutis instructus, omni lepore humanitatis mirifice conditus, que in eo non solum flagrantia morum latissime redolet, sed ex ipsa oculorum hilaritate gratiosissime renidet. Atque sic in te animi ornamenta redundent, ut illa ocularis gratia relucet."

[93] Other occurrences of *humanitas*: *Briefe Meinhards*, nr. 74, p. 122; nr. 75, p. 123; nr. 80, p. 130; *Weitere Briefe Meinhards*, nr. 14, p. 206; nr. 21, p. 216; nr. 24, p. 222. Erdmann has a few comments on Meinhard's classicism, *Studien*, p. 61, pp. 104–5. On *humanitas* in the Middle Ages, see Rolf Sprandel, *Ivo von Chartres und seine Stellung in der Kirchengeschichte* (1962), pp. 9–31. And especially Peter von Moos, *Hildebert von Lavardin 1056–1133: Humanitas an der Schwelle des höfischen Zeitalters*, Pariser historische Studien, 3 (1965).

inner qualities that express themselves outwardly in the good humored appearance, the graceful gait and elegant bearing of the courtier/statesman. Otto of Bamberg (d. 1139) is praised by one of his biographers for manifesting his elegant breeding and his inner harmony in each and every act of the outer man, in his table manners, his speech, gestures and dress.[94] By the twelfth century the ideal appears to have permeated the milieu of the worldly clergy in Germany, France and England. One of the most impressive statements of it comes from Bernard of Clairvaux, certainly not the typical spokesman for external elegance, but here one of the most eloquent. He explains the line from Psalm 92, "The lord desireth your beauty," which he takes to mean beauty of soul *(decor animae)*:

> What then is beauty of the soul? Is it perhaps that quality we call ethical goodness *[honestum]*?... But to understand this quality we must observe a man's outward bearing... The beauty of actions is visible testimony to the state of the conscience... But when the luminosity of this beauty fills the inner depths of the heart, it overflows and surges outward. Then the body, the very image of the mind, catches up this light glowing and bursting forth like the rays of the sun. All its senses and all its members are suffused with it, until its glow is seen in every act, in speech, in appearance, in the way of walking and laughing ... When the motions, the gestures and the habits of the body and the senses show forth their gravity, purity, modesty... then beauty of the soul becomes outwardly visible.[95]

Bernard's description has much in common with Meinhard's. Both are using a basically Ciceronian ethical vocabulary; both employ the image of the powerful light breaking forth from within to express the relation of inner virtue to outward grace. We see the sign of the monastic writer in Bernard's indication that "beautiful" bearing manifests, not the quality Meinhard had called *lepor humanitatis*, but rather a pure conscience. But we are still in a conceptual environment where behavior – speech, gesture, dress, gait – is estheticised and regarded as a visible manifestation of inward beauty and harmony.[96]

Alan of Lille's *Anticlaudian* is a poetic *summa* of the old learning. At the

---

[94] See *Origins of Courtliness*, p. 128 ff.

[95] *Super Cant.* Sermo 85. 10–11, *Sancti Bernardi Opera*, vol. II, ed. J. Leclerq, C. H. Talbot, H. M. Rochais (1958), p. 314: "In quo ergo animae decor? An forte in eo quod honestum dicitur?... De honesto autem exterior interrogetur conversatio... Siquidem claritas eius testimonium conscientiae... Cum autem decoris huius claritas abundantius intima cordis repleverit, prodeat foras necesse est... Porro effulgentem et veluti quibusdam suis radiis erumpentem mentis simulacrum corpus excipit, et diffundit per membra et sensus, quatenus omnis inde reluceat actio, sermo, aspectus, incessus, risus... Horum et aliorum profecto artuum sensuumque motus, gestus et usus, cum appareverit serius, purus, modestus... pulchritudo animae palam erit..."

[96] Consistently *gestus, habitus, gressus* or *incessus, motus corporis, locutio* or *sermo, cibus* and *potus* are seen as the measurement of inner virtue. These and their relation to virtue are the subject of the last chapters of Hugh of St. Victor's *De institutione novitiorum*.

same time it is the highpoint of twelfth century humanism and in many ways exemplifies the renaissance spirit of the period. Much of the work, but particularly Alan's portrait of the New Man, must be read against the background of *cultus virtutum*. Late in the poem the New Man is equipped by a parade of allegorical virtues for his battle with the vices.[97] First comes Bounteousness *(copia)*, then Favor and Fame, then Youth and Laughter. Chastity makes him rival the patriarch Joseph. Modesty follows. She "composes" the whole man according to the law of *moderamen*, the golden mean ("Totum componit hominem"). She moderates his action, measures his speech and his silence, weighs his gestures, judges his bearing and restrains his senses. She sets the tilt of his head in a middle position, not too far up towards the heavens to show scorn of the world of men, nor too far down to sink into the material. Constancy comes next; she arranges his gestures and his gait, his hairdo and the style of his dress. Next comes Reason, who gives him good sense for making judgments in practical affairs, prevents him from taking any course of action hastily, teaches him to prepare all undertakings carefully, to make few promises and give many gifts wisely. *Honestas* then gives him love of his fellow men while still preserving the integrity of his inner life.

A series of recent studies has shown that the court and the civil duties of the court administrator are the context in which this description is to be located.[98] Michael Wilks calls the *Anticlaudian* "a species of court poetry," and locates it, approximately, in the genre of education of princes. This seems to me accurate for one important aspect of the work, though I doubt that Alan intended a specific reference to Philip Augustus and a prediction of his victory over the Plantagenets, as Wilks and Linda Marshall argue.[99] The virtues of Alan's New Man are a summing up of the moral instruction of the old learning. As a preparation for court life, it applied to courtiers no less than to kings. It is a preparation through civil virtues for battle against civil vices. The gifts of Reason associate the passage especially clearly with *ethica* and *practica* and its products, the perfect statesman or courtier. Reason's gifts have to do with governing and administering, not with analysis, thought, argumentation. *Ratio* here is a virtue of the active life; it is that principle by which, according to the traditions of the cathedral schools, both the cosmos ("O, qui perpetua mundum *ratione* gubernas...") and the composed human being were governed. It is also the virtue by which the man of well composed *mores* governed the state. The

---

[97] *Anticlaudianus*, VII, ll.77ff., ed. Bossuat, p. 159.

[98] Linda Marshall, "The Identity of the 'New Man' in the 'Anticlaudianus' of Alan of Lille," *Viator*, 10 (1979), 77–94; Michael Wilks, "Alan of Lille and the New Man," *Studies in Church History*, 14 (1977), 137–57. Also of interest for our topic is P. G. Walsh, "Alan of Lille as a Renaissance Figure," *Studies in Church History*, 14 (1977), 117–35.

[99] John W. Baldwin is also sceptical about this connection: *The Government of Philip Augustus: Foundations of Royal Power in the Middle Ages* (1986), p. 571.

concept experienced a fundamental transformation from the civil to the intellectual realm at the hands of the early scholastics.[100] *Ratio,* in the passage just discussed, comes into effect in administrative, not intellectual, activity. None of the virtues of this parade are abstract inner qualities, cloistered or scholastic virtues. All of their gifts aim at external perfection. What *constancia* gives is not loyalty, not faith to oaths and vows, not steadfastness, but an elegant gait, measured gestures, correct clothes and hairdo. The virtues do not bestow the inner qualities they govern: rather they *are themselves* those inner qualities, and what they bestow are the external signs of their presence. The logic at work is that of virtues made visible, beauty or harmony of soul shining forth from every action, down to dress, personal grooming and table manners.

My purpose here and throughout this section in juxtaposing texts from the eleventh and twelfth centuries, from Germany and France, was of course to suggest lines of development, perhaps even lines of dependency. The virtues of Bernard's *decor animae* and of Alan's New Man are anticipated in the values embodied by German courtier bishops. The perfect, elegant, humane gentleman/courtier, who receives his armor from civil virtues, does battle with civil vices, and shows outwardly the beauty within, occurs in Meinhard's letter from the mid-eleventh century. What these common features suggest is that the fates of the old learning and twelfth century humanism were linked, that the one was the bearer and transmitter of the other, and the institutional basis of this humanism was the cathedral school in its relation to court service. The common features of these portraits also teach us to regard the humanism of the eleventh and twelfth centuries as a more or less homogeneous phenomenon. Meinhard and Alanus produced such similar portraits of idealized future statesmen because they taught programs of *ethica* that were not essentially different in either content or purpose.

VII. Old Learning Vs. New

Gradually in the second half of the eleventh century and precipitously in the first half of the twelfth, the masters of the old learning became threatened by a new kind of teacher offering a new kind of studies: the disputatious philosopher-scholar-teacher in the stamp of Peter Abelard. Both Italy and the north apparently bred this type, because in reports from the monastic as well as the cathedral communities we see the schools teeming with cavillers whose breasts swell with pride in their knowledge, and who even contradict and show up their own teachers. We start this section by pursuing some early examples of teacher

---

[100] Cf. Grabmann, *Geschichte der scholastischen Methode,* I, 272–336.

insulting. In observing clashes between masters and bright, irreverent students we locate a fundamental characteristic of the old learning and a fundamental weakness.

The saintly Wolfgang of Regensburg, as a student at Würzburg in the midtenth century, had commented so astutely on Martianus Capella that his erudition became an affront to his teacher, Stefan of Novara, that Italian master called to the north by Otto the Great.[101] Stung to anger and threatened by the loss of his students, Stefan undertook to stifle Wolfgang's further progress. But the inner flame of divine erudition only burned the more brightly for the attempt to snuff it out, "as a fire flares when fanned by blasts of wind." Still, the future saint might have saved himself alot of trouble by not giving offense at all, especially to this sensitive foreigner. Clearly some etiquette was violated here when Wolfgang complied with the request of his fellow students for a commentary on Martianus superior to that of their master. The incident brings us close to the circumstances in which the young Abelard outdid Anselm of Laon in explaining Biblical texts.

Abelard's intellectual arrogance is foreshadowed also in the insult dealt to the clergy of Limoges by a Lombard grammarian, Benedict of Chiusa, who visited Limoges in 1028 and disputed the claim that the local patron, St. Martial, was an apostle. Our source, Ademar of Chabannes, tells the story by way of holding this pompous windbag up to ridicule. He quotes a long speech which he attributes to Benedict. In it the latter boasts of his knowledge of grammar, claims that all of Aquitaine and most of France are ignorant of this art, that after nine years of study his own wisdom is so perfect no one under the sun can match him.[102] The monks of St. Denis a century later would undoubtedly have liked to place such discrediting speeches in the mouth of Peter Abelard, whom, out of the arrogance of his learning, they took to be diminishing the authority of their patron.[103] It may be that Benedict and Abelard were entirely right in disputing the beliefs of the local monks. The validity of the claims against those beliefs, the historical truths at stake, did not matter; reasoning and proof, when pitted against venerable authority, textual or personal, were pernicious instruments of pride that invited discrediting and were seen as deserving it.

But gradually in the course of the later eleventh century, knowledge, reasoning, success in disputation and in proof, become ends in themselves. Grave and

---

[101] Otloh of St. Emmeram, *Vita Wolfkangi* IV–V, MGH, SS 4, p. 528. In view of the fact that Stefan's countryman Gunzo had his grammar corrected by the monks of St. Gall, one wonders whether Italian masters were fair game in the North. They certainly were sensitive to contradiction.

[102] *Epistola de S. Martiali*, PL 141, 107 ff. See H. E. J. Cowdrey, "Anselm of Besate and some North-Italian Masters of the Eleventh Century," *Journal of Ecclesiastical History*, 23 (1972), p. 119.

[103] Cf. *Historia calamitatum*, p. 90, ll. 963 ff.

dignified orations are no longer the object of intellectual effort, but definitions and systematizing, frameworks of argumentation, and harmonizing of inconsistencies.

The contest between old and new learning is as much a part of twelfth century intellectual life as is the clash between the new learning and monastic orthodoxy, though the latter has commanded much more interest from historians. In many ways the old learning and monasticism were allies in opposition to the new. They had, it is true, a traditional antagonistic relationship in the eleventh century (polemics of monks against worldly professors), but at the same time an easy reciprocal relationship (many professors converted). The rise of the new learning brought their common interests and characteristics into clear focus. Representatives of both ganged up on Berengar of Tours and Peter Abelard. The intellectual world of the monasteries had much in common with that of the schools. Philosophical Realism was fundamental to both. The eucharist controversy showed this in the late eleventh century; the dispute on universals in the early twelfth. Also common to both was authority as the basis of argumentation and of instruction. The basic intellectual reorientation of the period has long been regarded, quite rightly, I believe, as the clash between reason and authority. But some understanding of the old learning helps us to see the nature of authority in a clearer light. It does not only reside in texts and traditions. It is also a human quality, one of considerable importance both as an instrument and a goal of pedagogy.

A letter of Adelman of Liège to Berengar of Tours allows us to see this form of authority at work in the eucharist controversy. The letter is a trenchant rejection of Berengar's position on the divine presence in the sacrament, but it is written in a tone of loving correction from one former student of Fulbert to another. The body of the letter is a dossier of arguments against reasoning, novelties, and heresy. Of interest to us is its introduction. Adelman evokes at length the figure of Fulbert of Chartres, their former master, and in doing so he recreates vividly and emotionally the atmosphere of the old learning:

I have called you my fellow suckling and foster brother in memory of that sweetest and most pleasant of times we spent together, you a mere youth, I somewhat older, at the Academy of Chartres under our venerable Socrates. We have more cause to glory in the common life of studies [convictus] shared with him than had Plato, who gave thanks to nature for bringing him forth as a man rather than as an animal in the days when Socrates was teaching.[104]

---

[104] R. B. C. Huygens ed., "Textes latins du XIe au XIIIe siècle," *Studi Medievali*, 3rd ser., 8 (1967), 476–89, here p. 476, ll. 3–8: "Conlactaneum te meum vocavi propter dulcissimum illud contubernium, quod tecum adulescentulo, ipse ego maiusculus, in achademia Carnotensi sub nostro illo venerabili Socrate iocundissime duxi, cuius de convictu gloriari nobis dignius licet quam gloriabatur Plato, gratias agens naturae eo, quod in diebus Socratis sui hominem se et non pecudem peperisset."

Berengar and Adelman have experienced ("experti sumus") the more saintly life and sound doctrine of Fulbert, and now can hope to benefit from his prayers in heaven, since the regard and Christlike charity in which he held them, as in a maternal womb, still live on; indeed his death has only intensified them. Fulbert watches them from heaven and calls to them with his vows and silent prayers to follow him,

> entreating us through all those intimate evening colloquies he used to hold with us in the little garden next to the chapel in the city... and beseeching us, by the tears which broke forth and interrupted his lecture whenever the force of divine ardor overflowed within him, to hasten thither with all diligence, treading in a straight path the royal road, adhering with utmost observance to the footsteps of the holy fathers, lest we should be detoured, turning aside into some new and false path and succumbing to the snares of scandal...[105]

In other words, Adelman conjures him by the person of their former teacher; if Berengar holds the memory of Fulbert dear, he will not deviate from the path of the fathers. These are arguments from authority: the personal authority of the great man. He tries to dissuade Berengar from "false," at least deviant opinions, by the force and authority of Fulbert's personality, by pulling him back into the orbit of the master's charisma. The nostalgia of the scene he paints – Fulbert weeping during evening colloquies, overcome by the force of divinity breaking forth in his lecture – derives straight from the rhetoric and ideals of the old learning. We see how true the statement by Wibald of Stablo rings, that students defend what their teachers say because they love the men, not the truth in their pronouncements. "I conjure you by the tears of our teacher..." This is the poetry and the mood music of the old learning, unthinkable in a scholastic disputation,[106] powerful in an atmosphere where love of teacher substitutes for thought, where the teacher's person constitutes a kind of orthodoxy. For Adelman there was more truth in Fulbert's tears than in Berengar's logic.

This gives us the common strand in the examples cited earlier of authority defied: the old learning responds to conflict and intellectual challenge by asserting and defending the authority of the masters. An ideal of demonstrable truth

---

[105] P. 476–77, ll. 14–21: "... invitat ad se votis et tacitis precibus, obtestans per secreta illa et vespertina colloquia, quae nobiscum in hortulo iuxta capellam de Civitate illa ... sepius habebat, et obsecrans per lacrimas, quas, interdum in medio sermone prorumpens, exundante sancti ardoris impetu emanabat, ut illuc omni studio properemus, viam regiam directim gradientes, sanctorum patrum vestigiis observantissime inherentes, ut nullum prorsus [in] diverticulum, nullam in novam et fallacem semitam desiliamus, ne forte in laqueos et scandala incidamus..."

[106] Werner of Basel's debate poem from the mid eleventh century, "Synodus," *AHDLMA*, 8 (1933), 397 ff., is a disputation carried on in this climate. The Old Testament embodied debates with the New; Sophia is judge. The atmosphere is marked by harmonious intellectual exchange, loving cooperation towards a common goal. Sophia's judgment: "... vos non certastis, amici, sed bene cantastis... / Nec clamavistis."

approachable through arguments represented a powerful threat to men whose instruction was based on eloquence and personality. And this points up the fundamentally irrational nature of an education based on the formation of character. It relies on the personal moral authority of the teacher, and reasoning – certainly critical, independent thought – can become an offense against him, can diminish his authority. The old learning made the masters into an image of God, and the student's goal was to fashion himself in that image.[107] Disputation and reasoning are fundamentally at odds with this goal. Awe and reverence are appropriate to it.

The cult of personality in the old learning was the form of irrationality that Peter Abelard was up against long before he faced that of the Cistercians. In his early conflicts with masters of the old learning, as in so many incidents, Abelard's life is exemplary for the tendencies of the time. An entire system of education was caught in a conflict between a traditional kind of teaching that tended toward the acquisition of human qualities and a new kind that tended toward rational inquiry. This conflict forced the separation of letters and learning from manners.[108] The clash between Abelard and Anselm of Laon is a good illustration. It is as if whatever forces of history shaped the general conflict had designed Abelard and Anselm to embody it: they brewed the intellect and character of Anselm with an overbalance in favor of *mores* and eloquence (the products of the old learning). Then, like chemists performing an experiment, exactly reversed the proportions in brewing Abelard. Anselm and the type he represented may have lacked penetration and analytical sharpness, but they

---

[107] Hugh of St. Victor uses this conceit in urging students of the *schola virtutum* and *recte vivendi scientia* to imitate the examples of good men. *De inst. nov.* VI, *PL* 176, 932D: "In ipsis [good men] siquidem similitudinis Dei forma expressa est, et idcirco cum eis per imitationem imprimimur, ad ejusdem similitudinis imaginem nos quoque figuramur."

[108] The letter of Goswin of Mainz (Gozechinus) to his former student Walcherus (above, n. 20) is an important document on the conflict of old and new learning in Germany. He contrasts the school of Liège where he once taught ("ad omne quod civile sit et moribus conducat informat et instruit" VI, p. 14) with the schools of the present day (ca. 1065) which suffer from rejecting *mores* and *disciplina* (XXVII, p. 31). Young students, who ought to be taught beneath the rod, flee instruction on the "gravity of moral discipline" and are blown about like light chaff in the wind of every doctrine: they follow vain and pestiferous novelties and questions (XXVII, p. 31). Certain pseudo-masters wander about giving new readings of texts, seducing students to flee discipline and seek the levity of novelties (XXVIII, p. 32). Since the whole church is being poisoned by this lust for novelty and the abandoning of discipline, few can be found who will work for the true institutes of a good life (XXXII, p. 34). Many fine teachers, men of outstanding repute and high authority – Hermann of Rheims, Drogo of Paris, Huzmann of Speyer, Meinhard of Bamberg – have abandoned teaching for theology (XXXIII, p. 35). The golden age of the schools, when the gravity of discipline ruled and all studies were for the utility of the republic and of *honestas*, when the beauty of virtues and the liberal arts flourished, is now past (XXXIV, p. 36f.). The passage is full of sentiments we encounter a few decades later in France. It is not only an old, disillusioned teacher's empty *laudatio temporis acti*.

were masters of the discipline of living well. Abelard may have known a great deal and possessed a keenly analytical mind, but he was a failure at the discipline of life.[109]

Abelard's opposition to authority was two-fold: he called it into question in its written form in his *Sic et non*, and he challenged it in its living personification by opposing, contradicting and outdoing his own masters. Besides the clashes with Anselm and William of Champeaux, we have his written testimony to this opposition in his poem to his son, Astralabe. He prefaces the work with cautionings against some of the underlying principles of the old learning: "Care not who speaks, but what the value of his words are. Things well said give an author his reputation. Neither put your faith in the words of a master out of love for him, nor let a learned man hold you in his influence by his love alone." The pointedness of these precepts is quite evident against the background presented above, but Abelard accommodated the modern reader in locating the sentiments within the actual flux of trends in the schools, because he immediately restated them in the formulations he had used against Anselm of Laon in the *Historia calamitatum*: "We are nourished not by the leaves of trees, but by their fruits. The meaning is to be preferred to the mere words. The rhetoric of ornate words may capture minds effectively, but true learning prefers plain speech. A wealth of words conceals a poverty of understanding."[110]

"Plain speech and ideas which bear up to criticism": the formula, combined with a willingness to contradict, to assert the truth of one's own opinion over the teacher's, was fateful for the masters of the old learning. The combination of reason and impudence answered their riddle, dissolved the magic spell of their authority. They were as vulnerable as their aura of venerability: tarnish it

---

[109] Abelard came to the ethics of the old learning by betraying them. He is arguing against himself in his poem to his son Astralabe when he says, "No man becomes wise by mere sharpness of mind; character and a good life make a man wise. Wisdom professes itself in actions, not in words, and the gift [of such actions] is conferred only on good men" (*Petri Abaelardi carmen ad Astralabium filium*, B. Hauréau ed., *Notices et extraits des manuscrits de la bibliothèque nationale*, 34 (1895), p. 158: "Ingenii sapiens fit nullus acumine magni, / Hunc potius mores et bona vita creant. / Factis, non verbis, sapientia se profitetur; / Solis concessa est gratia tanta bonis"). Also p. 180: "Pluris sit morum tibi quam doctrina librorum..." He was keenly aware of the ancient distinction between the wise man, who lived well, and the philosopher, who knew a great deal (cf. Heloise's purported advice to him, *Hist. cal.*, pp. 78–9), and distinguished between the philosopher, who sees the hidden causes of things, and the practical man, who foresees the results of his acts (*Ad Astral.*, p. 159).

[110] *Ad Astral.*, p. 157: "Non a quo, sed quid dicatur, sit tibi curae; / Auctori nomen dant bene dicta suo. / Ne tibi dilecti jures in verba magistri, / Nec te detineat doctor amore suo. / Fructu, non foliis pomorum quisque cibatur, / Et sensus verbis anteferendus erit. / Ornatis animos captat persuasio verbis, / Doctrinae magis est debita planities. / Copia verborum est ubi non est copia sensus." It is a constant theme in Abelard's works: "Do not regard the person of the teacher but the weight of his ideas; do not respect the ornament of his words, but their sense."

and they fell; contradict them convincingly and they faced early retirement. They had only faith, charisma and tradition to fall back on, not a systematically worked out philosophical position. Stefan of Novara sensed that a systematic commentary on Martianus Capella, one that satisfied the intellectual curiosity of his students, was a serious threat to his authority as a teacher. William of Champeaux shows such fears to be well-founded: his teaching career was seriously deflected[111] because he lost to Abelard in their exchanges on the nature of universals. The very foundation of the old learning, personal authority, was at the same time its Achilles heel.

Anselm and William were not the only masters in the old tradition to suffer rough treatment. John of Salisbury tells of his own teachers, William of Conches and Richard the Bishop, who were forced to give up teaching "when popular opinion veered away from the truth" and they were "overwhelmed by the rush of the ignorant mob."[112]

John's *Metalogicon* is the most important monument to the conflict of old and new learning. The general intention of that work is to defend humanist learning against purely scholastic and to urge an integration of the two. John sees studies and all civilized life threatened by the tendency of contemporary scholars and teachers to cultivate specialized subjects, to privilege dialectic, to separate learning from ethics and thus end the fruitful relationship between philosophy and state or church administration. In a passage that is a touchstone for these concerns, he complains about the tendency to see dialectic as separable from other disciplines and from the active life. To exercise dialectic without broad learning and a practical context for it is senseless and harmful, like a pigmy trying to wield the sword of Hercules. Learning must find its fulfillment in domestic life or at court or in the church, not remain merely a "school" discipline. And he sounds a theme central to the old learning when he asks, "What moral philosopher does not fairly bubble over with laws of ethics so long as these remain merely verbal? But it is a far different matter to exemplify

---

[111] He retired from Notre Dame to found the new community of St. Victor and its famous school. But though he remained active as a teacher, he had burned his fingers on dialectic and was denied participating in the more vital life of the Paris schools. For a good summary of the founding and history of the school of St. Victor see Stephen C. Ferruolo, *The Origins of the University: The Schools of Paris and their Critics, 1100–1215* (1985), pp. 27–44.

[112] *Metalogicon* I, 24, ed. Webb, p. 57f. Trans. McGarry, p. 71. On this passage and the "retirement" of William and Richard, see R. L. Poole, *Illustrations of the History of Medieval Thought and Learning*, 2nd ed. (1920), pp. 310–14. John says that William of Conches took over the teaching method of Bernard of Chartres. This statement and John's mention of a shift in popular opinion make William's position fairly clear: a master of the old learning has his position undermined by a new fashion.

these in his own life."¹¹³ John's description of the teaching of Bernard of Chartres (*Metalogicon* I, 24) is a classic portrayal of the old learning. Bernard, like his predecessor, Fulbert, fit the old model in the teaching of eloquence and ethics together, in his use of the classics, in his holding of evening colloquies, in the adulation accorded him by his students, and in not producing a single written work.¹¹⁴

John of Salisbury's attempt to reconcile the old and the new had no hope of succeeding. It was a conservative, humanistic, rear-guard action. The days of friendly and emotional colloquies and symposia in cloister gardens between a magisterial teacher and a handful of socially and intellectually elite disciples were past.

VIII. *The Schools and the Courts*

In the course of the twelfth century the old learning dwindled, collapsed, was forced out of the schools. John of Salisbury was shocked that twenty years after he had studied in Paris the learning there was merely "scholastic," seemed to consist of abstract school exercises. Cathedrals and the new schools of Paris may have remained training grounds for administrators,¹¹⁵ but they were no longer schools of virtue. The *cultus virtutum* still had life in it, as we see in a work like the *Anticlaudianus*. But now it had to seek accommodation elsewhere, and it found it in the institution that had originally accounted for its rise in the tenth century, the prince's court. Courts secular and ecclesiastical had after all been the hidden context of the old learning for the centuries of its prominence. Cathedral schools had handled the overflow from the court chapel and had aimed at preparing men precisely for service in the chapel and what came to be called the chancellery.

The fading of the old learning at cathedral schools coincides with the rise of an education which we must now call "courtly," and no longer merely "for the court."¹¹⁶ There is an old controversy on the question, whether actual schools

---

[113] *Metalogicon* II, 9, ed. Webb, p. 77: "Quis ethicus morum regulis, dum in lingua versantur, non habundat? Sed plane longe difficilius est ut exprimantur in vita." Trans. McGarry, p. 94.

[114] A possible exception, his *Timaeus* commentary. See Paul Edward Dutton, "The Uncovering of the *Glosae super Platonem* of Bernard of Chartres," *Medieval Studies*, 46 (1984), 192–221. But the comparative anonymity and the difficulty of the ascription tends to confirm the rule.

[115] See John W. Baldwin, "Masters at Paris from 1179 to 1215: A Social Perspective," in *Renaissance and Renewal in the Twelfth Century*, ed. R. L. Benson and G. Constable (1982), pp. 138–164.

[116] The contemporary terms are *aulica* or *curialis nutritura*. See *Origins of Courtliness*, p. 215f.

existed at worldly courts.[117] The question to my mind is a misleading one, because as soon as we determine that in the post-Carolingian period schools at court no longer existed *as institutions*, we are also tempted to conclude that teachers and instruction had little role at court. The Carolingians needed court schools. They had not discovered, as their successors did, that cathedral schools could function as a more secular alternative to the monasteries. But we would shoot over the mark if we turned this around and said, the Ottonian and Salian kings did not require palace schools, because the cathedral schools had taken over their function. More accurate would be: from Carolingian times on there is no useful distinction to be made between the court school and the life of the court itself. Hincmar formulated for Louis the German the ideal of the court as a school of letters and manners:

> The king's court is indeed called a school, that is a course of studies, not because it consists solely of schoolmen, men bred on learning and well trained in the conventional way, but rather a school in its own right, which we can take to mean a place of discipline, that is correction, since it corrects men's behavior, their bearing, their speech and actions, and in general holds them to the norms of a good life.[118]

Hincmar considered the court a school of *mores*, to which might have been added formal instruction in letters. This does not change in Ottonian times. The statements of Ruotger that Brun of Cologne as chancellor at Otto the Great's court rescued the seven liberal arts from their decline, attracted philosophers and intellectual "refugees," held philosophical disputations, improved the Latin of the court members, and served personally as an exemplar of wisdom, piety, and justice (*Vita Brun.* V, ed. Ott, p. 6f.) cannot be emptied of their content merely because no traces of an institutionalized court school can be found. Ruotger's words make perfect sense when we understand the nature and goal of the old learning and distance ourselves from a conception of education limited to notions of classroom and textbook, learned lecturing and writing. Ruotger speaks unmistakably the language of the old learning: letters are combined with manners, the person of the teacher is a large part of the curriculum, philosophy, learning, and public life are inseparable. The masters of the old learning were courtiers in their capacity as teacher, and teachers in their capacity as courtier.

---

[117] See Lèsne, *Les écoles*, p. 39ff.; Fleckenstein, "Königshof und Bischofsschule" (above, n. 13), p. 40f.; idem, *Die Bildungsreform Karls des Grossen* (above, n. 11), p. 24ff.; Brunhölzl, "Der Bildungsauftrag der Hofschule" (above, n. 22), p. 28f.; Rosamond McKitterick, "The Palace School of Charles the Bald," in *Charles the Bald: Court and Kingdom*, ed. M. Gibson and J. Nelson, BAR International Series, 101 (1981), 385–400.

[118] *Epist. syn. Karisiac.* XII, MGH, Leges 2, Capit. 2, p. 436, ll. 2–6: "Et ideo domus regis scola dicitur, id est disciplina; quia non tantum scolastici, id est disciplinati et bene correcti, sunt, sicut alii, sed potius, ipsa scola, quae interpretatur disciplina, id est correctio, dicitur quae alios habitu, incessu, verbo et actu atque totius bonitatis continentia corrigat." For other references to the Carolingian "court school" see Lèsne, p. 39ff.

What need for institutionalized schools at court; the court itself was a school, where the pedagogy of personal charisma was at work more immediately and effectively than at more formally constituted schools. Every educated man at court was, ideally, philosophy embodied and translating itself into acts of public administration. What changed around 950 and in the following years is that this sort of education became more strongly oriented to classical models of the statesman and orator and was transferred out of the courts and into the cathedral schools, where hitherto secular and sacred letters had formed the curriculum. After ca. 1150 letters joined to manners returned to the courts and left the schools to "scholastic" endeavors.

The career of William of Conches is exemplary for this development. He began teaching either in Paris or Chartres or both around 1120 or 1125.[119] His student John of Salisbury tells us that he taught in the manner of Bernard of Chartres and that he had to withdraw from the schools because his students left him for other disciplines and for teachers who promised greater success with shorter studies.[120] It is a fate like the one that Stefan of Novara feared and William of Champeaux suffered. William of Conches left the schools and consoled himself with a position as tutor to the young Plantagenet prince and future king Henry II of England. He had written his work *Philosophia mundi* under the influence of the *Timaeus* for use in the schools; he now rewrote it in dialogue form for the education of the prince and gave it the title *Dragmaticon*. It was probably William who composed the work *Moralium dogma philosophorum*, which has stood in the center of the discussion of a "ritterliches Tugendsystem." The intended audience of this work is uncertain. It is dedicated to a "vir optimus atque liberalis Henricus," who may be Henry II.[121] The work is located, like William himself and like the old learning itself, between schools

---

[119] On William of Conche's career, see Jeauneau, *Glosae super Platonem* (above, n. 52), p. 9ff.; Max Manitius, *Geschichte der lateinischen Literatur des Mittelalters*, vol. III, Handbuch der Altertumswissenschaft, 9, 2, 3 (1931; rpt. 1973), p. 215ff. Bradford Wilson in his edition, Guillaume de Conches, *Glosae in Iuvenalem*, Textes philosophiques du moyen âge, 18 (1980), p. 75ff.

[120] "... impetu multitudinis imperite victi, cesserunt." *Metalogicon* I, 24, ed. Webb, p. 58. Throughout his *Philosophia mundi* William's defensive posture is apparent; he was threatened with the loss of his students. Cf. his attack on teachers who fawn on students and on students who pass judgment of their masters (*Phil. mundi* IV,Prol., ed. Maurach, p. 88). Also his statement that he cares not for the multitude, but only for the probity and love of truth of the few (II, Prol., p. 41). John's notice about William's and Richard's "retirement" makes a comment by William appear especially poignant: he says that the true teacher teaches out of love of learning, not an urge for popularity, "nec, si deficiat multitudo sociorum, deficiet [alt. desinet]..." (IV, 30, p. 114). Undoubtedly trends at the schools, new professors offering dialectic and short periods of study, cost William his students, not the attack of William of St. Thierry, as Wilson (above, n. 119, p. 76) suggests.

[121] The editor of the *Moralium dogma*, John Holmberg, takes this to be Henry II (*Das Moralium dogma philosophorum des Guillaume de Conches: Lateinisch, Altfranzösisch, Mittelniederfränkisch* [1929], p. 6f.) Manitius disagrees (*Gesch. lat. Lit.*, vol. III, p. 219).

and secular courts. But the example of William is especially significant, because his activity for worldly courts followed upon his "retirement" from teaching at schools. The new developments in the schools of France and the drift towards dialectic forced this humanist schoolmaster to transfer his pedagogy, oriented to the Platonic view of man and the world and to ancient Roman ethics, to a secular court, one which by no coincidence was to be closely associated with the rise of courtly literature.

Brun of Cologne was exemplary for the shift of court education from the chapel to the cathedral schools in the tenth century, William of Conches for its return to the courts in the twelfth.[122]

Two examples of the old learning in the setting of the court will show us some of the ties between *cultus virtutum* and courtly education.

Thomas Becket took up a position at the court of Theobald, Archbishop of Canterbury after returning from his studies in Paris. Here he worked together with many men distinguished for their learning, William Fitzstephen tells us, and while Thomas was not their equal in letters, he surpassed them all in, as Fitzstephen puts it, the far superior endeavor of *mores*. He applied himself to *moralitas* and *prudentia*, and distinguished himself in this study: "litteris adhuc inferior, moribus conspectior et acceptior..."[123] Fitzstephen describes his character and appearance as follows:

He was of a placid and beautiful countenance, noble in stature, his nose long and straight, his body vigorous and adept; he was skilled in eloquence, subtle in mind, great in soul, and because he tread the path of virtue in a higher sense, he showed himself amiable to all men... generous and witty [or sophisticated or courtly: *facetus*]... (ch. 7, p. 17)

Upon his promotion to chancellor of England, he maintained a household that rivalled that of the king for pomp and magnificence. He loved and excelled in courtly games, especially chess, also the hunt with dogs and falcons. He gave splendid banquets where richly clothed guests ate from gold plates and drank from gold goblets. In the next chapter the biographer tells us that Becket, rich, popular, famous, and burdened with the business of state, takes over the duties of court tutor. The king places his own son and heir, Henry, in his hands, and many princes of the land entrust their sons to his care. He prepares them for knighting.[124]

---

[122] Another instructive example is William of Champeaux. Forced from Paris, he founded the school at St. Victor, where a later master, Hugh, was to write important educational tracts presenting the ethical views of old learning. But this path was a dead end. The future of a classically oriented ethics was at the courts, not in the church.

[123] *Materials for the History of Thomas Becket, Archbishop of Canterbury*, ed. J. C. Robertson, Rolls Series, 67, 3 (1877), p. 16 (William Fitzstephen, *Vita S. Thomae* V).

[124] XII, p. 22: "Cancellario et regni Angliae et regnorum vicinorum magnates liberos suos servituros mittebant, quos ipse honesta nutritura et doctrina instituit, et cingulo donatos militiae ad patres... remittebat... Rex ipse, dominus suus, filium suum... ei nutriendum commendavit..."

This biography shows us a man who becomes a master of *mores* and *moralitas* in the schools of London, Paris and Canterbury then turning into an educator in *mores* at court. The moral instruction of the schools transfers comfortably to the courts; the *moralitas* of the educated cleric prepares its possessor as an educator of princes or knights. Here we see also the successful courtier/administrator as educator. Even in the highest state office next to the king, burdened with work, Becket becomes tutor to the children of nobles. Of course we must not imagine him holding classes in grammar, dialectic and the classics.[125] Letters were not his strong point; *mores* were. His "students" served him ("servituros mittebant"), watched him in action, probably received an occasional tip in comportment, possibly learned Latin names for strategies of political/social behavior, which they learned to regard as the functioning of "virtue." The busy chancellor had little time to instruct *verbo* but instruction *exemplo*, through the *lingua morum*, was what counted. Becket presided over this "court school" by his authority, leaving the *labor* to others. In his role at court he was the perfect embodiment of what the old learning aimed at.

Nothing in the text states outright that the *moralitas* Becket pursued as a young clerk at Canterbury had anything in common with the education he gave to aspiring knights as chancellor of the king and court tutor, that *moralitas* and *curialitas* had approximately the same content by this time.[126] But our second example makes the connection clear.

Gottfried von Strassburg's romance *Tristan and Isold* is the highpoint of literary humanism in medieval Germany. The author includes a scene that is a mirror of courtly education. After Tristan, disguised as a minstrel at the Irish court, is nursed back to health from a poisoned wound, he takes over the task of educating princess Isold from her previous tutor, a learned courtly cleric. This scene deserves a prominent place in the history of medieval education. The princess, already instructed in foreign languages, music and composition, learns various kinds of diciplines from him, but she devotes most of her attention to the one called *moraliteit*:

> *under aller dirre lere*
> *gab er ir eine unmüezekeit,*
> *die heizen wir moraliteit.*
> *diu kunst diu leret schoene site.*[127]

---

[125] It is not out of the question that such instruction took place at the court, however. William Fitzstephen tells us that Becket as chancellor had fifty-two clerics in his service, most of whom were attached to his household staff. *Vita Thomae* XVIII, p. 29.

[126] However Matthew Paris (mid-thirteenth century) tells that the king sent his son to Becket "to be instructed in manners and courtly ways." *Historia Anglorum (Historia minor)*, ed. F. Madden, Rolls Series, 44, 1 (1866), p. 316: "rex filium suum... beato Thomae cancellario commisit alendum, et moribus et curialitatibus informandum."

[127] Gottfried von Strassburg, *Tristan und Isold*, ed. F. Ranke, 11th ed. (1967), ll. 8002–5.

All women, he continues, should occupy themselves with this "sweet discipline" from youth on. It teaches them to please God and the world, and without it they will attain neither wealth nor honor. The results of this instruction for Isold:

> hie von so wart si wol gesite,
> schone unde reine gemuot,
> ir gebaerde süeze unde guot. (8024–26)

In the six months of her instruction she improved her "learning and comportment" *(lere unde gebare)* to such an extent that the fame of her talents spread throughout the land. When guests come to court she entertains them with her arts: she sings, writes and reads. Then follows a dazzling description of the "double" beauty of her singing: she not only performs a masterpiece, she herself is one; the audible beauty of her song is matched by her "unheard" song, the visible beauty of her person. The passage is one of the most sublime statements of the human presence as a work of art from the Middle Ages and beyond. There follows a final summary of the results of this education: Tristan's instruction gave her "sweetness of mind" *(suoze gemuot)*, lent charm to her manner and her bearing. She mastered all kinds of courtly games and pastimes, could compose letters[128] and songs (cf. 8132ff.).

It is immediately evident against the background of our previous discussion that Gottfried speaks the language of the *cultus virtutum*. Many of his terms and his turns of thought translate easily into that vocabulary: *moraliteit* is the art that teaches *schoene site*; "moralitas est ars quae morum elegantiam docet."[129] *Lere unde gebare*, which Gottfried also varies as *rede unde gebare*, comes close to *litterae et mores*. Isold learns many arts, but the one to which she devotes most attention is *moraliteit*. Like John of Salisbury Gottfried sets *moralitas* as the highest goal of learning. The princess receives from this discipline beauty of mind or temperament *(schone gemuot, süeze gemuot*; cf. *decor animae, compositio morum* or *mentis)*, and both references to this "well-tempered" quality are followed by the statement that her manners and her comportment, her gestures and bearing were pleasing and charming. The implica-

---

[128] In the three translations I consulted (Hatto, von Ertzdorff, Krohn) Gottfried's phrase *brieve und schanzune* (8139) is rendered as some variation of "words and songs," though neither Gottfried's usage nor any other Middle High German citation in the standard lexica justifies translating *brieve* with "song text." Gottfried's meaning is clear when we read this scene as a "mirror of courtly education": she composed letters and songs. Translating *brieve* as lyrics was the translators' means of preserving the sanctity of her artistry which would appear diminished to modern sensibilities by combining her role of siren with that of secretary. But that is what Gottfried intended: to juxtapose administrative tasks and courtly pastimes, *otium* and *negotium*.

[129] See my article, "Beauty of Manners and Discipline *(schöne site, zuht)*: An Imperial Tradition of Courtliness in the German Romance," in *Barocker Lust-Spiegel: Festschrift für Blake Lee Spahr* (1984), 27–46.

tion is that her pleasant gestures are a result of her spiritual beauty; elegant bearing expresses inner harmony.[130]

But what we observed first as an ethical ideal taught to aspiring worldly clerics at cathedral schools recurs here as an education in courtliness aimed at princesses and other noble ladies. Far from representing a contradiction, however, this simply shows us in a clear light what had been a feature of the old learning since its emergence in the eleventh century: that it is a preparation for court life and court service, both worldly and ecclesiastical. Here that education has shed all its religious trappings and shows the educational goal – refinement of mind and manners – as a means to wealth, honor, and reputation at court, as a prerequisite to administrative skills (reading and writing letters) and court entertainments (games, music, composing). The only remaining trace of a religious orientation of *moralitas* is the observation that it is pleasing to God and the world. But in Gottfried's romance the emphasis is decidedly on "world".

In the second half of the twelfth century a single master at the schools could still produce a grand *summa* of the old learning, the *Anticlaudianus*. But from the mid-century on the cult of virtues registers largely in works from the courtly milieu: tracts on the education of princes, nobles and noble children like Gerald of Wales' *De principis instructione* and Thomasin von Zirclaere's *Der welsche Gast*. Vincent of Beauvais' *De eruditione filiorum nobilium* is a particularly rich summation of this learning and the virtues it sought to cultivate. Vincent still preserves the basic formula of that education: "... litterarum erudicioni morum eciam instructio copulanda es..."[131] and his ethical vocabulary and concepts, though richer, still draw from the old learning and the authorities who formulated it.[132]

The renaissance of the fifteenth century experiences the rebirth of an education based on the ethical formation of man according to classical models. In reading the humanist tracts on education that W. H. Woodward has edited and translated, we encounter vocabulary and concepts familiar to us from the humanism of the eleventh and twelfth centuries: *moralitas* and *ethica* are the most important disciplines; they are "learned" by imitation of classical models

---

[130] Gottfried shows his familiarity with the notion of *decor* in a number of passages. Cf. *Origins of Courtliness*, p. 148f.

[131] Vincent of Beauvais, *De eruditione filiorum nobilium* XXIII, ed. A. Steiner, Mediaeval Academy of America Publication, 32 (1938), p. 78. Also LXIII, p. 176: "... congruum est, ut litteris imbuantur et moribus instruantur..."

[132] Cf. his discussion of the "two-fold discipline" of *moralis composicio*. It has an inner and an outer aspect, the inner consisting in the cultivation of virtue, the outer "in decenti composicione membrorum," involving "membrorum omnium motus ordinatus et dispositio decens in omni habitu et actione." His best source is Hugh of St. Victor, whose *De institutione novitiorum* he quotes at great length. *De eruditione* XXXI, p. 117ff. On Vincent as an informant on courtly ideals, see Rosemary Combridge, "Ladies, Queens and Decorum," *Reading Medieval Studies*, 1 (1975), 71–83.

and of the teacher; Philosophy is identified with the pursuit of virtue, and "school" subjects are subordinated to that pursuit.[133] Humanist education gradually moved from the courts back to the universities. In Tudor England the abolition of Catholicism rendered the dominant curriculum of canon law unimportant at the English universities and created a great space in which humanist courtier administrators could restructure university education on humanist principles.[134] When Sir Humphrey Gilbert designed an academy for courtier/ statesmen for the Elizabethan government, he provided for a Reader of Moral Philosophy (he is to receive 100 pounds yearly salary; the reader in natural philosophy receives only 40), who "... shall teach civill policy and warres. By directing the Lectures to thendes afforesaid, men shall be taught more witt and policy than Schole learninges can deliver... the greatest Schole clarks are not always the wisest men."[135] And the formula "letters and manners" once again looms large. Castiglione writes in the *Libro del Cortegiano*: "good masters teach children not only letters, but also good and seemly manners in eating, drinking, speaking and walking, with appropriate gestures."[136]

Conclusion

There is much to be said on the growth and spread of humanist learning. Here I have only been able to characterize it. I hope to have indicated where in the previous centuries the roots of twelfth century humanism lie. The immediate social and intellectual context of the works we traditionally associate with that direction in twelfth century culture – Bernard Silvester's *Cosmographia* and *Aeneid* commentary, John of Salisbury's *Metalogicon* and *Policraticus*, Alan's *Anticlaudian* – is the *cultus virtutum* of the cathedral schools and its application in administrative service. The old learning flowed into and extensively informed these writings, and an acquaintance with its content and goals teaches us to regard those works as the last flowering of a movement, based on the alliance of

---

[133] W. H. Woodward, *Vittorino de Feltre and Other Humanist Educators*, Classics in Education, 18 (1897; rpt. 1963), p. 221: "It is a marked characteristic of Humanism to limit Philosophy, as a serious study, to Ethics, to the entire exclusion of Metaphysic." See also his *Studies in Education during the Age of the Renaissance 1400–1600* (1924).

[134] See Joan Simon, *Education and Society in Tudor England* (1966), and J. H. Hexter, "The Education of the Aristocracy in the Renaissance," in his *Reappraisals in History* (1962), pp. 45–70. On Humanist influence and the role of ethics in the founding of University of Vienna, see Jan-Dirk Müller, *Gedechtnus: Literatur und Hofgesellschaft um Maximilian I.*, Forschungen zur Geschichte der älteren deutschen Literatur, 2 (1982), p. 43 ff.

[135] Sir Humphrey Gilbert, *Queene Elizabeths Achademy*, ed. F. J. Furnivall, EETS, Extra Ser., 8 (1849), p. 3.

[136] Cf. Baldesar Castiglione, *The Book of the Courtier* IV, 12, trans. Charles Singleton, (1959), p. 297.

school and court, learning and government, that preceded them by some two hundred years. The most impressive *written* testimony to humanism surfaced well after the establishment of humanist learning in the courts and cathedrals, the administrative centers of Europe. But the same is true of humanism in ancient Rome and in fifteenth century Italy: its ideals were formulated in the active civil life first, then in written testimony.

The continuity of secular learning in the period 950–1150 is not to be sought in texts and artifacts, but in personalities and the cultivation of personal qualities. Our notions of humanism and humanistic education remain one-sided and lifeless as long as we insist on separating the learning of the period from the lives of its educated statesmen. That is a difficult fact for the historian of literature and culture to deal with. We interpret texts and comment on artifacts, and when we look at the eleventh and twelfth centuries we can still read the works of Abelard and John of Salisbury, and we can still see the sculpture and architecture of the early Gothic. But the ideal of the statesman and the education that formed him are no longer visible. The ideal was as perishable as the men who embodied it, and it died with them, like a dance or a stage performance. And now we can only catch glimpses of its shaping ideals of humanity, deference and elegant comportment in the writings of the schools and courts, and we can find them, sublimated, in the figure of the chivalric knight of courtly romance.

II

Orpheus in the Eleventh Century

The learned poetry of the eleventh century wards off broad interest by its obscure diction and its display classicism that brings down on it the characterization of 'school poetry' and 'rhetorical exercises' with the sober opprobrium those terms convey. In addition, its powerful neighbor, the twelfth century, pulls much that preceded into its orbit. There is a tendency to read Marbod, Baudri and Hildebert looking forward, not backward, as precursors, not as fulfillers.

The 'school poetry' had a greater role in learning and society than current perceptions credit[1]: «Warum dichtete man? Man lernte es auf der Schule.» The tone in the master's voice here excluded contradiction and convicted the sensible question, «Why learn poetry?», in advance of impertinence.

We can get some impression of the distance that separates the learned eleventh century poet from the 'Vagant' of the twelfth in a satirical portrait of the perfect worldly cleric by Peter Damian[2]:

Hodie ... in Romana urbe frater advivit, ortus de summis proceribus Galliarum ... Cui nescio an aliquid utilitatis desit, tot siquidem exteriorum bonorum floribus enitescit: nobilis ut imperator; pulcher aspectu quodammodo; sicut Tullius loquitur; ut Virgilius poetatur; tuba vehemens in Ecclesia; perspicax et acutus est in lege divina; scholastice disputans, quasi descripta libri verba percurrit; vulgariter loquens, Romanae urbanitatis regulam non offendit.

The satirist's point is that these are vain and empty attainments, but his lucid picture places the values and ambitions of worldly clerics in sharp focus. The only quality that gives pause is poetry: *ut Virgilius poetatur*. Poetry a «useful» quality[3], parallel to

---

[1] E. R. CURTIUS, Europäische Literatur und lateinisches Mittelalter (Bern 1954) 462 (Exkurs 7: «Die Existenzform des mittelalterlichen Dichters»).

[2] Petrus Damianus, De sancta simplicitate 7, ed. Paolo BREZZI, trad. Bruno NARDI, S. Pier Damiani, De divina omnipotentia e altri opusculi (Edizione nazionale dei classici del Pensiero Italiano 5), Firenze 1943, 163–201, here 188.

[3] The word is used in the sense of *utilitas ecclesiae* or *rei publicae*, that is, personal qualities beneficially engaged in the business and administration of church and state. Both contexts are addressed in Peter Damian's portrait of a certain Ugo of Parma, see De sancta simplicitate 6, ed. BREZZI (note 2) 184 and 186: ... *quot utilitatum dotes habuerit, non enumero*, so ambitious in the arts he had an astrolabe fashioned of pure silver. He aspired to the position of bishop, and so «had himself appointed to the chapel of Emperor Conrad» (*dum aspiraret ad episcopale fastigium, Conradi imperatoris se constituit capellanum*). The classical definition is Cicero, De inventione II 168–169. Cf. the adaptation in Bernard of Utrecht, Comm. Theodul., in: Accessus ad auctores. Bernard d'Utrecht. Conrad d'Hirsau, Dialogus super auctores, ed. R. B. C. HUYGENS (Leiden 1970) 68, 245–249.

high nobility, physical beauty, forensic eloquence, political influence and legal training?

The apparent anomaly can perhaps be dissolved by regarding Virgil's skill as another expression of the verbal eloquence the passage stresses. This study argues, against such a reading and its premises, that the writer had a concept of poetry that regarded it as an attainment valuable in public life, parallel, possibly, to noble birth and definitely to legal skill, a talent closely allied with one of the major missions of educated clergy in western Europe in the period – not merely advanced rhetoric. The learned poet of the eleventh century is more likely to be found in furs and silks in high church positions than wandering homeless and hopeful of patronage for the evening's bread[4].

The eleventh century cathedral schools were the nurturing ground of a concept of poetry useful to church and state. The extraordinary status of poetry in the period is evident in the poem 'De mensa philosophie' from the Cambridge Songs. It sets a rich table of philosophical food and drink, but serves only poetry[5]:

> *Ad mensam philosophie   sitientes currite*
> *et saporis tripertiti   septem rivos bibite,*
> *uno fonte procedentes   non eodem tramite,*
> *Hinc fluit gramma prima,*
> *hinc poetica ydra,*
> *lanx hinc satiricorum,*
> *plausus hinc comicorum,*
> *letificat convivia*
> *Mantuana fistula.*

This is not a niggardly 'let them eat poetry!'; it is the best dish the host has to offer. The age had a loose hold on the quadrivium, but it had a sense that in poetry Virgil was not always its equal[6]. There is good testimony to the fervid devotion to poetry

---

[4] Rudolf SCHIEFFER's case for identifying the Archpoet with a schoolmaster of Cologne gains persuasiveness from this point of view, even though the stature of poetry was changing radically since the beginning of the twelfth century: Bleibt der Archipoeta anonym?, in: MIÖG 98 (1990) 59–79. The evidence is not yet fully persuasive for this identification. Johannes FRIED accepts the general line of SCHIEFFER's argument, but proposes identification with another cleric of Cologne: Der Archipoeta, ein Kölner Scholaster?, in: Ex Ipsis Rerum Documentis. Beiträge zur Mediävistik, Fs. für Harald Zimmermann, ed. Klaus HERBERS et al. (Sigmaringen 1991) 85–90.

[5] Carmina Cantabrigiensia 37, ed. Walther BULST (Heidelberg 1950) 65. *Mantuana fistula* = Virgil's pastoral poetry.

[6] The sense of outbidding antiquity is evident in much of the school poetry. It imposed an obligation on the poet which had disastrous effects on his Latin style. Cf. the dedicatory letter of Anselm of Besate, Rhetorimachia, ed. Karl MANITIUS, Gunzo, Epistola ad Augienses und Anselm von Besate, Rhetorimachia (MGH Quellen zur Geistesgeschichte des MA.s 2), Weimar 1958, 97–100. Anselm associates the deeds of Henry with Augustus Caesar and himself with Virgil, whose task was to praise the deeds of Augustus. Since Henry's are more famous than Caesar's, it follows – though it is not stated outright – that poetic talents beyond Virgil's are called for, and Anselm is his man – that is stated outright. Anselm was offered a position in Henry III's chapel, presumably as a response to his 'Rhetorima-

in school[7]. A poem written by a student of Würzburg in 1031 as a polemic against the school of Worms also testifies to the stature of poetry in that flourishing but poorly documented school at that early period[8]. The master is praised as *Princeps primatum, qui pandunt abdita vatum* (v. 21); he is «refulgent with the light of many poets» (v. 24: *poetarum fulget decus omnigenarum*), a striking formulation that implies a mystification of the self built on poetic knowledge – he 'beams' poetry, as he might exude humanity, grace and charm; the master teaches composition above all other subjects (v. 26): *Preter scripture studium nihil est sibi cure*[9]; he qualifies his students for office, and himself and them for heaven, through learning and virtue (cf. vv. 75–82).

Still towards the end of the period (ca. 1125), when studies and poetry in France had gone new ways, a learned German, Ulrich of Bamberg, could make the skilled composition of verse and prose into the measure of learning (vv. 31–39)[10]:

---

chia'; see Carl ERDMANN, Anselm der Peripatetiker, Kaplan Heinrichs III, in: (id.) Forschungen zur politischen Ideenwelt des Frühmittelalters (Berlin 1951) 119–124. – Cf. two recent studies of Anselm's style: Beth S. BENNETT, The Significance of the 'Rhetorimachia' of Anselm de Besate to the History of Rhetoric, in: Rhetorica 5 (1987) 231–250; (eadem), The Rhetoric of Martianus Capella and Anselm de Besate in the Tradition of Menippean Satire, in: Philosophy and Rhetoric 24 (1991) 128–142.

[7] Guibert of Nogent claimed that in his youth he had «immersed my soul beyond all measure in poetry so I considered scripture ridiculous vanity». He read Ovid and the bucolics, and composed love poetry himself; see Peter STOTZ, Dichten als Schulfach: Aspekte mittelalterlicher Schuldichtung, in: Mlat. Jb. 16 (1981) 1–16, esp. 9–13.

[8] The poem is edited as supplement to Die ältere Wormser Briefsammlung, ed. Walther BULST (MGH Die Briefe der dt. Kaiserzeit III), Weimar 1949, 119–127 (cited here), and in: Die Tegernseer Briefsammlung, Carm. XLIII, ed. Karl STRECKER (MGH Epistolae selectae 3), Berlin 1925, 125–134. For commentary on the poem and historical circumstances, see Georg SCHEPSS, Zu Froumunds Briefcodex und zu Ruodlieb, in: ZfdPh 15 (1883) 419–433; J. KEMPF, Zur Kulturgeschichte Frankens während der sächsischen und salischen Kaiser. Mit einem Excurs: Über einen Schulstreit zwischen Würzburg und Worms im 11. Jahrhundert (Programm d. kgl. Neuen Gymnasiums Würzburg 1914/15), Würzburg 1915; E. HAEFNER, Die Wormser Briefsammlung des 11. Jahrhunderts (Erlanger Abhandlungen zur mittleren und neueren Geschichte 22), Erlangen 1935; Max MANITIUS, Geschichte der lat. Literatur des Mittelalters, II (München 1923) 522–523, takes Froumund of Tegernsee to be the poet, the bishop of Würzburg, not the schoolmaster, Pernolf, to be the figure defended, but neither identification is tenable.

[9] The meaning is clearly the study of composition, not of Scripture. Cf. vv. 160–161, where *scriptura* refers to the Worms poem to which the Würzburger is responding: *quod cor non celat, quoniam scriptura revelat / Versibus oblatis mendacibus inmodulatis*; also Ältere Wormser Briefsammlung, Ep. 19, ed. BULST (note 8) 36, 10: *De scriptura* (= the outer shell, the written form) *non erit curandum, cum magis ad sententie nucleum ... sit respiciendum*; and some verses in the Tegernsee letter collection, ed STRECKER (note 8) 122 (Carm. XLI): *Me bene scribentem faciat, precor omnipotentem. / ... / Artem scripture sectandi sit tibi cure.*

[10] See Franz BITTNER, Eine Bamberger ars dictaminis, in: Bericht des Historischen Vereins Bamberg 100 (1964) 145–171, here 156; *componere* (v. 33) here refers to poetry as well as prose. Cf. vv. 58–59: *Nam versus dulces scribendo pectora mulces, / Mulces egregie scribens metri sine lege*. On Ulrich's so-called 'Ars dictandi' and its two introductory poems, see I. S. ROBINSON, The 'colores rhetorici' in the Investiture Contest, in: Traditio 32 (1976) 209–238, here 213.

> ... Fateor me iudice nemo,
> Si concedis idem, carissime, doctus ad unguem
> Nec perfectus erit, qui nil componere novit
> Auditu dignum; quod maius dic rogo signum
> Aut argumentum, quod certius est documentum
> Divitis ingenii, frater dulcissime, quam si
> Dictator mentes et grate mulceat aures?
> Hic est aut nusquam quod quaerimus, hic erit inquam
> Fructus longorum, ni fallor ego, studiorum.

I

The period made Orpheus into the representative of its lofty conception of poetry[11]. A close reading of three poems, two from the last two decades of the century, one probably from mid-century, opens this conception to view[12].

---

[11] Specifically on the Orpheus figure in the Middle Ages, see Peter DRONKE, The Return of Eurydice, in: Classica et Mediaevalia 23 (1962) 198–215; Klaus HEITMANN, Orpheus im Mittelalter, in: Archiv für Kulturgeschichte 45 (1963) 253–294; J. B. FRIEDMAN, Orpheus in the Middle Ages, Cambridge, Mass. 1970. For general discussions including the Orpheus figure, cf. Peter GODMAN, Poets and Emperors: Frankish Politics and Carolingian Poetry (Oxford 1987) passim; Winthrop WETHERBEE, Platonism and Poetry in the Twelfth Century (Princeton 1972) 78–79, 96–103 (exclusively on William of Conches); Hennig BRINKMANN, Mittelalterliche Hermeneutik (Tübingen 1980) 205–206 (he reads the 11th-century sources as *integumenta* referring to Christ).
A few references to update BRINKMANNS extensive bibliography of studies of Orpheus from antiquity to the present: Max WEGNER, Orpheus. Ursprung und Nachfolge, in: Boreas 9 (1988) 177–225; E. SCHWARTZ, Aspects of Orpheus in Classical Literature and Mythology, Diss. Harvard Univ. 1984; Orpheus: The Metamorphosis of a Myth, ed. J. WARDEN, Toronto 1982; W. S. ANDERSON, The Artist's Limits in Ovid: Orpheus, Pygmalion and Daedalus, in: Syllecta Classica 1 (1989) 1–11; Detlef C. KOCHAN, Literarische Spuren einer Symbolfigur, Orpheus zum Beispiel, in: Literarische Symbolfiguren von Prometheus bis Svejk. Beiträge zu Tradition und Wandel, ed. Werner WUNDERLICH (Facetten dt. Literatur 1), Bern & Stuttgart 1989, 37–63; P. PRIGENT, Orphée dans l'iconographie Chrétienne, in: Revue d'histoire et de philosophie religieuses 64 (1984) 205–221; I. R. JOHNSON, Walton's sapient Orpheus, in: The Medieval Boethius, ed A. J. MINNIS (Cambridge 1987) 139–168; C. Munro PYLE, Le thème d'Orphée dans les œuvres latines d'Ange Politien, in: Bulletin de l'Association Guillaume Budé 1980, 408–419; Arnfried EDLER, 'Die Macht der Töne'. Über die Bedeutung eines antiken Mythos im 19. Jahrhundert, in: Musik in Antike und Neuzeit, ed. M. von ALBRECHT/W. SCHUBERT (Quellen und Studien zur Musikgeschichte von der Antike bis in die Gegenwart 1), Frankfurt 1987, 51–65. On the two endings of the story (following DRONKE, Return of Eurydice), see M. Owen LEE, Orpheus and Eurydice: Myth, Legend and Folklore, in: Classica et Mediaevalia 26 (1965) 402–412; D. SANSONE, Orpheus and Eurydice in the Fifth Century, in: Classica et Mediaevalia 36 (1985) 53–64.

[12] The main poems treated here are: 'De nuptiis,' 'Quid suum virtutis' and 'Liège song' nr. 3 by Gautier; as to the editions see note 13, 21 and 33. The best commentaries on these poems develop a powerful consensus that they are to be read as «school poetry» and «rhetorical exercises»; cf. DRONKE (note 11) 210: ('Quid suum', Liège song, and Godefroy of Rheims' Orpheus version are) «more in the nature of literary exercises»; HEITMANN (note 11) 260, giving a broader boundary to the same perspective: «Man muß diese Stücke,

We start with a text that is broadly conceived and useful for placing Orpheus and the poetry he stands for in the context of learning. It is an adaptation of Martianus Capella by a poet either in or acquainted with the Rheims circle towards the end of the century. He knew the works of Godfrey of Rheims and Marbod of Rennes. His poem is confusingly titled in the two manuscripts that have preserved it 'De nuptiis Mercurii et Philologie'[13]. This verse adaptation of Martianus deserves a detailed study. No reading I know takes seriously its joining of a survey of the liberal arts with the Orpheus figure. Boutemy himself tends to discount the first part and regard the poem as «a version of the Orpheus legend». A more searching reading would reveal the poem as a summary of learning at cathedral schools of the eleventh century. Like Alan of Lille's 'Anticlaudian', though on less grand a scale, it is an allegory of the ideal education[14].

As in Martianus Capella, the work begins with the marriage of Mercury and Philology. The wedding feast is presided over by *sapientia*. Apollo calls upon the nine muses, who «cling closely to study» (v. 82 *studio cohibente*) in order to «magnify the arts». Then each of the muses sings the praises of one of the arts. After the celebration of the arts, the «ethereal chorus of philosophy» sings a song praising *sapientia*. Next Orpheus appears with his wife Eurydice. No reason is given for his entrance. He simply is «there» (v. 242): *Ecce novus vates vatumque ferens novitates*. He calls for silence and begins to sing. The song he sings is of no particular importance, though it goes on at some length (vv. 242–366). It is a series of 'hymns' to gods and heroes, essentially the brief retelling of myths. Eurydice follows and sings of some of the paramours of Jove, and is awarded the laurel wreath, gems and gold for her song[15]. When she ends the feast is over (v. 402). Now follows a lament on death and

---

wenngleich für die besten von ihnen der Mythos gewiß mehr als ein bloßer Vorwand für die Erprobung dichterischer Geschicklichkeit war, doch ihrer Genesis entsprechend vor allem unter formal-rhetorischem Gesichtspunkt lesen»; FRIEDMAN (note 11) 164: «exercise poems», «rhetorical elaborations on the myth»; 165: «of minor interest poetically, but they are very important as evidence for the portrait of Orpheus as a romance hero»; 166 ('Quid suum'): «more interested, one feels, in the rhetorical possibilities of the myth than in the myth itself.» This judgment seems to me to warn off readers from taking them seriously.

[13] See A. BOUTEMY, Une version médiévale inconnue de la légende d'Orphée, in: Hommages à Joseph Bidez et à Franz Cumont (Collection Latomus 2), Bruxelles 1949, 43–70.

[14] BOUTEMY's title 'Une version ... de la légende d'Orphée' tends to conceal the broad sweep of the poem. Only in that light is it intelligible that the poem has been omitted in the useful study by Gabriel NUCHELMANS, Philologia et son mariage avec Mercure jusqu'à la fin du XIIe siècle, in: Latomus 16 (1957) 84–107. I have not found any reference to it in the literature on education in the 11th and 12th centuries. One of the major documents on 11th century learning is currently masked as «a version of the Orpheus legend».

[15] I know of no other version from any period in which Eurydice herself performs as a singer. The extravagant reward seems to aim at legitimizing praise of women. Cf. vv. 398–400:
    Leta cohors superum laudesque probans mulierum
    Euridicis totis referunt preconia votis,
    Utque decet lauro, gemmis redimitur et auro.
Can anyone explain this untypical bit of feminist advocacy? Possibly because some sources make her into a daughter of Apollo? Cf. Mythographus Vaticanus I 75, 1–2, ed. Peter KULCSAR (CChr 91 C), Turnholt 1987, 33: *Orpheus Oeagri et Caliope muse filius, ut quidam*

the inevitability of the decrees of fate. The logic of its inclusion, not evident at once, is that we are now, with no transition, into the story of Orpheus and Eurydice. She is bitten by the serpent, he descends to recover her, softens the flinty hearts of the infernal beings, and, following the Ovidian 'unhappy ending', loses redeemed Eurydice by looking back.

What does it mean that a poem celebrating the union of eloquence and wisdom through the muses and the liberal arts ends in the story of Orpheus and Eurydice? Essentially, the message is that education is fulfilled in poetry and music[16]. Martianus Capella's work also ended with music. The ninth and final book of his 'De nuptiis' is devoted to Harmony. Banished from earth, she joins the wedding party to celebrate the union in song. Orpheus is also present, along with Amphion and Arion. His song and his failed rescue are mentioned, but with no particular profile. He is one of several emblems of Harmony's working. Martianus Capella's work ends with a long-winded rehearsal of the laws of harmonics and metrics. The overall conception of the two works is comparable: a survey of studies ends in the art which fulfills them. But the eleventh century poet thoroughly changed his source to highlight Orpheus and his role.

The underworld scene is the key to the poem's guiding conceptions. Orpheus meets the harshest, cruelest and most inflexible beings God and nature have created, and his song softens their hearts and turns them into advocates of compassion. The fates are overcome in short order and beg the king, Dis, to relent and spare Eurydice (v. 571): *Flectuntur Parce, que dicunt: «Rex pie, parce!»* The furies, described as *ferva, trux, torva*, reproach Dis for his harshness (v. 574): *Sevitiam Ditis reprobant cum murmure litis*. The tortured in hell forget their sufferings (v. 575). Sensual nostalgia is the dominant tone struck in Orpheus' plea to Dis: «Hymen» has driven him to invade the land of hell (v. 534); Orpheus is «a youth bound by the reins of love»

---

putant, *Appolinis filiam habuit uxorem Euridicen*. This still doesn't explain *laudes probans mulierum*. The article on Eurydice in PAULY/WISSOWA, RE VI 1, 1322–1327, does not mention a singing Eurydice or a daughter of Apollo.

[16] There are a few details that confirm the poet was working within a structure where poetry fulfills the arts. The «ethereal chorus of philosophy» sings, in praise of *sapientia* (vv. 227–229):

> At hominum sensus, duce te, sapiendo remensus
> Appetit internas herebi penetrare cavernas,
> Discutiens utique secreta polique solisque.

This marks the catabasis as symbolic of the continuing quest for understanding; to «penetrate the caverns of the underworld» means to investigate the secrets of the heavens. BOUTEMY (note 13) 52 points to the lines as foreshadowing the descent of Orpheus, but he regards the Orpheus story as tacked on, not the fulfillment of learning. Likewise the striking parallel between the role of rhetoric as presented by Calliope (vv. 136–159) and the judicial pleading for Eurydice in the underworld (vv. 593–616) is discussed below.

Baudri of Bourgueil assigned the same preeminent role to music. The headbord of the allegorical bed in Countess Adela of Blois' bedchamber is inscribed with a representation of Philosophy and the liberal arts, see Carm. 134, ed. K.-H. HILBERT (Heidelberg 1979) 149–187. Music is located at the right hand (v. 975), or at the feet (v. 1002) of Philosophy herself, because she is the force that keeps the other sisters in harmony with each other (vv. 1001ff.).

(v. 535); his dead bride had «hardly even in her girlish mind tasted the union with a man, still knew not how to love or be loved» (vv. 538–539); Eurydice, roused from the dark regions by her lover's voice, «desires to embrace him» (v. 559). The romantic pathos seizes the residents of hell and awakens love and compassion in all of them. A chorus of the furies and the damned together plead with Pluto for Orpheus (v. 586): «Love presses them all with its urgings, from all sides the clamor for forgiveness rings out» (*Omnibus instat amor, venie sonat undique clamor*). The lord of the underworld is at first irritated and hardens his heart (v. 588: *Pluto cor indurat neque vati parcere curat*). But this love-inspired plea for mercy from a unanimous chorus softens and renders him «modest and placid» (v. 617: *Rex prius infestus placida iam mente modestus*) and «lightens the fatal law» (v. 618). But Orpheus violates his condition. Eurydice is lost forever, and the poet is left with only the consolation of his song, which retains its power to mitigate sorrow and anger (vv. 642–643):

> *Mitigat arte lyre fera dampna doloris et ire,*
> *Quaque fuit victus lugens redit arte revictus.*

The essential moment in the scene is the conversion of the underworld, the remarkable metamorphosis from cold, dead rage and vengeful fury to warmth, compassion, and love. This is the power of Orphic music. Love-inspired music soothes and conquers the fury and anger of the harshest and cruelest. Poetry softens fate and prevails over the gods and the laws of nature.

A central thought of the poet emerges in the meeting of Orpheus and Dis. It is modeled on a courtroom scene: Orpheus is pleading a case, the chorus of the furies and damned speak in his support, Dis is a king sitting in judgment and enforcing or relaxing laws[17]. This conceit of the poet's makes poetry and judicial rhetoric into allies in legal dealings, and reiterates a remarkable passage earlier in the poem, the presentation of rhetoric by the muse Calliope (vv. 138–145)[18]:

---

[17] The judicial nature of the proceedings is quite evident. The chorus gives the «king» advice on the treatment of the accused and convicted in general (v. 594): *Parcere prostratis decus est et honor pietatis*. They invoke points of law (vv. 598–599): *ne modo maiora pereant concede minora, / Ne vicio regis titubet sententia legis*. They appeal to «the law» itself (v. 599 *sententia legis*; v. 604 *lex tua*). The issue glides from death vs. life over into innocence vs. guilt (vv. 607–608): *Innocuos dure non sit tibi perdere cure / Sitque satis diram pretendere sontibus iram*. Eurydice's plight is a *casus* (v. 610) and a *causa* (v. 611). They demand that condemnation be based on proof (v. 609): *Non bene dampnatur qui non meruisse probatur*. – A near-contemporary text describing (satirically) legal procedures and drawing on the same vocabulary: Gozechini epistola ad Walcherum, XXXV 800ff., ed. R. B. C. HUYGENS (CChr Cont.Med. 62), Turnholt 1985, 37–38.

[18] BOUTEMY (note 13) 50:
> *Ars docet hoc, leges tenet in moderamine reges,*
> *Milicie gentem Mavorcia tela gerentem*
> *Doctrina vigili studioque reformat herili,*
> *Hoc iuvenum mores struit, instituit seniores,*
> *Perpete mensura cohibens civilia iura.*
> *Quatuuor ornatur virtutibus et decoratur.*
> *Omnia discrete moderatur, cuncta quiete*
> *Temperat ...*

«This art teaches the following: it holds kings to moderation in exercising the law, it reforms [or reeducates] the knighthood, who bear the weapons of Mars, with the doctrine of vigilance and study of lordly ways; it instructs youths in manners and guides the mature; it constantly holds the civil laws close to the rule of moderation ... It moderates everything wisely and gently tempers all things ...»

The softening, taming effect of Orpheus' song is answered in this passage by the moderating, tempering effect of rhetoric. In both, a king is «held to moderation in exercising the laws». Judicial pleading and poetry meet in the function of urging clemency by softening the emotions of the judge or king. This correspondence shows us again that the first and second parts of the poem are knit in a unified conception. It also shows us the remarkable symbolic staging that is the highpoint of the underworld scene: poetry/music joins forces with judicial rhetoric to soothe, and this makes allies of Orpheus and the residents of hell.

Orphic poetry has a civilizing mission like that of rhetoric as the educator of warriors and temperer of royal judgment. It inspires mercy and «brings low impious rage» (v. 600: *Carminibus vatis occidit furor impietatis*). It replaces cruelty and vengefulness with love. The conception of poetry as softening and civilizing force has a long history, and the story of Orpheus and Eurydice was frequently its vehicle[19]. But the eleventh century gave a profile to this role that was not received from classical or earlier medieval sources[20]. Orpheus and Eurydice becomes a defining myth for the mission of the educated man.

---

[19] On Orpheus' song as a civilizing force, see HEITMANN (note 11) 267–269, and in the Renaissance, John WARDEN, Orpheus and Ficino, in: Orpheus: The Metamorphosis of a Myth (note 11) 89–91, with some parallels to the eleventh century figure; cf. also 90: Orphic song in its civilizing capacity is «a social and political program».

[20] Ovid has no interest in this aspect of the myth (see Met. X 1–63, XI 1–66); nor does Virgil, Georg. IV 453ff.; Quintilian, Inst. I 10, 9, makes of Orpheus a musician, philosopher and poet in one, who by the power of his song *rudes quoque atque agrestes animos admiratione mulceret*; Horace presents him as the primal civilizer (Ars poet. 391–393):
> Silvestris homines sacer interpresque deorum
> caedibus et victu foedo deterruit Orpheus,
> dictus ob hoc lenire tigris rabidosque leones.

Boethius mentions the softening effect of song with the casualness of a received motif (Cons. III m. 12), though he was to treat the civilizing aspect of music at length in his 'De inst. musica.' For classical authors Orphic song is a producer of *mirabilia*, not a force aimed at a widely accepted social mission. The more detailed description of his civilizing power in Eusebius, see FRIEDMAN (note 11) 56–57, suggests that it is a product of Christian modelling of the ancient myth.

Still, this aspect virtually disappears from Merovingian and Carolingian sources. On Orpheus and the conception of poetry in Venantius Fortunatus, see Peter GODMAN (note 11) 1–37 («Orpheus among the Barbarians»). Venantius does not develop the civilizing force of Orphic song. *Dulcedo* of poetry is the central idea. Where he exploits the obvious parallel of Orpheus in the underworld to his own mission among the barbarians, it dissolves in irony; far from taming and civilizing them, he himself is turned into a barbarian (GODMAN 1). But see Cassiodorus, Variae II 40, 17 (MGH Auct. ant. XII 72): *facturus aliquid Orphei, cum dulci sono gentilium fera corda domuerit*. Orpheus in Carolingian poetry has a pale, representative role as emblem of poetic excellence. Cf. Theodulf, Carm. 27, 24–25 (MGH Poetae I 491):

The poem 'Quid suum virtutis'[21] places the story of Orpheus between an opening section castigating contemporary vices and the decline of virtue (vv. 1–498) and a closing section offering lessons in virtue (vv. 1025–1190). The poem is a showpiece of the 'manneristic' style of eleventh century poetry. The placement of the Orpheus story again is significant. It is introduced to illustrate the virtues that the present age has lost. Those are study and hard work that develop «art» (vv. 499–504):

> Arti materne iunctum sudando laborem
> Manibus extorsit Orpheus Euridicen.
> Non hic frenaret fluvios, non saxa moveret,
> Vellet si blande se dare desidie,
> Sed studio dictante sagax dum temperat odas
> Muse demulcens omnia blandiciis.

> Rideat Orpheum Tityrus aurisonum.
> Orpheus in silvis putridas tu pasce capellas,
> Tityrus aulenses delicias sequitur.

Versus de eversione monasterii Glonnensis 1–2 (MGH Poetae II 147; cf. also II 642, 10ff.):

> Dulces modos et carmina praebe, lyra Treicia,
> commota quis cacumina planxere yperborea.
> Montes simulque flumina illa putent nunc Orphea,
> respondeantque carmina silvae canant melliflua.

Sedulius Scotus, Carm. 49, 9–10 (MGH Poetae III 211): *Scriptor sum (fateor), sum Musicus alter et Orpheus / Sum bos triturans* ...; Carm. 68, 9–10 (Poetae III 222): *Armonicen videas melicas depromere voces, / Quam vix Orpheus Trax similare potest.*
The learned tradition preserves the poet's civilizing role more than the poetic. Edgar DE BRUYNE, Études d'Esthétique médiévale, I (Bruges 1946/1975) 211–212, cites a Carolingian commentary on Horace, 'Ars Poetica': *Cum in scripturis non invenitur Orpheus deterruisse silvestres homines, sed potius lenire tigres, posset videri fictum esse ... Cujus sit figura ostendit [poeta de Amphione]: dictus est saxa i.e. saxea corda et dura movere dulcedine cantus ... Nam fuit intentio primorum dare praecepta de moribus, ut silvestria et saxea corda redderent mollia, ut Amphion.* Paschasius Radbertus, De vita S. Adalhardi 84 (MIGNE PL 120, 1550A-C), gives a full paraphrase of the Orpheus story (as received from Boethius) to illustrate the futility of mourning a lost spouse. The varied and disparate character of this tradition testifies to the eleventh century's more unified conception of Orphic song.

[21] 'Quid suum virtutis'. Eine Lehrdichtung des 11. Jahrhunderts, ed. A. PARAVICINI (Editiones Heidelbergenses 21), Heidelberg 1980. Variously attributed to Thierry of St. Trond and Hildebert of Lavardin. The most recent editor suggests an anonymous poet writing under the pseudonym of Mamucius (possibly also Kalphurnius) and a date prior to 1043–1046 (based convincingly on an allusion to the poem in 'Ecbasis captivi', cf. PARAVICINI 8–9). Its origin remains uncertain. Manuscript distribution suggests it was most popular in southern Germany, but also in Belgium and northern France, see PARAVICINI (14) who conjectures (10) that it may have been written for the instruction of a prince by a member of a court chapel. It is a significant testimony to the unity of French and German school culture in the mid-eleventh century that this poem has proved so hard to locate. For B. HAURÉAU, Les mélanges poétiques d'Hildebert de Lavardin (Paris 1882) 41, it was the «most interesting and admirable work of Hildebert». And E. R. CURTIUS, Die Musen im Mittelalter, in: ZRPh 59 (1939) 129–188, here 183–185, found in it «die echte, wahre, widerspruchsfreie Auffassung Hildeberts von der Aufgabe der Poesie, von der Antike, vom Musendienst». A poem written in mid-century, before Hildebert's birth, possibly in Germany, can be taken by two of his most learned students as the very core of his work.

Orpheus is the representative of uncorrupted «study» leading to virtue, that is, the embodiment of the instruction the poet offers. The text does not locate this kind of study directly at schools, but the values are those of the cathedral schools[22].

The effects of Orpheus' music before the descent to the underworld are described in terms familiar from the 'De nuptiis'. It «soothes with its sweetness»[23]. His muse is «sweet»[24]. It delights and brings happiness[25]. It can create a variety of moods according to the temper of the mode, the «gravity of the spondee» calms anger and brings peace to the soul[26], though harsher tones stir rage and belligerence (vv. 795–796). But the dominant mode of music is conciliating, soothing, harmony. The learned author integrates these effects into Boethian ideas of cosmic and human music (vv. 749–764)[27]:

> Huius Musa viri mundum dulcedine tali
> Dum permulcebat, esse palam dederat,
> Vis armonie quia rerum temperet esse
> Unanimi nodo dissona concilians, ...
> Et que maioris eadem moderando minoris
> Naturam mundi lex copulat numeri ...
> Hec anime corpus, hec federat ima supernis,
> Hec mores ornat, membra dolore levat.

He goes on to derive the inner constitution of man from the effect of music (vv. 799–802):

---

[22] Stress on 'natural talent brought to fruition through learning' since Brun of Cologne: See Ruotger, Vita Brunonis 1, in: Lebensbeschreibungen einiger Bischöfe des 10.–12. Jahrhunderts, ed. and transl. Hatto KALLFELZ (Ausgewählte Quellen zur dt. Geschichte des MA.s 22), Darmstadt ²1986, 3; Sigebert of Gembloux, Vita Deoderici ep. Mettensis, ed. G. H. PERTZ (MGH SS IV), Hannover 1841, 464. 48–465. 16 (also quoting Horace, Carm. IV 4, 33: *Doctrina vim promovet insitam*); Marbod of Rennes, Vita Licinii 1 (MIGNE PL 171, 1495B): *bonis omnibus animae et corporis a natura ditatus, felicitatem suam virtutis studio cumulavit.*

[23] Quid suum virtutis 675–676 (note 21): *Quem non invitat, que non precordia mulcet / Musica?*; 749–750: ... *dulcedine tali / ... permulcebat*; 781–782: ... *ira resedit, / ... pax et adest animi*; 953–956: *Exhilarant umbre frontem presente Megera, / Dum lira permulcet, pena dolore caret. / Ad nectar cantus hilarescit ovans Rhadamantus, / Ridet permulsus carmine trux Eacus.*

[24] Quid suum virtutis 677 (note 21): ... *pisces muti vocis dulcedine capti*; 692: *Dulcis eum Muse sola fames tenuit*; 721: *Sic Musa dulci dulcis fuit Orpheus orbi*; 749–750: *Huius Musa viri mundum dulcedine tali / Dum permulcebat*; 809–810: ... *Musa tui, sacer Orpheu, / Tanti dulcoris extiterat superis.*

[25] Quid suum virtutis 723–724 (note 21): *Tot res et tante letantur eo modulante, / Has et que vegetat musica letificat*; 829–830: *Leta ... / Stix, qua nil umquam tristius esse potest*; 943–944: *Numquam leta prius, Charon, tua ... senectus / ... gaudet*; 991–992: ... *Parce / ... hilares.*

[26] Quid suum virtutis 780–782 (note 21): *Mox, ut spondei succinuit gravitas, / ... ira resedit, / ... pax et adest animi.*

[27] Cf. Boethius, De institutione musica libri quinque I 2, ed. G. FRIEDLEIN (Leipzig 1867 / Frankfurt a. M. 1966) 187–189, and a recent English translation with commentary and bibliography: Fundamentals of Music: Anicius Manlius Severinus Boethius, trans., introd. & comment. Calvin M. BOWER, New Haven/London 1989.

II

Orpheus in the Eleventh Century 151

> *Et cum nunc mulcet, nunc asperat et modo pacat*
> *Affectum mentis musica temperies,*
> *Certo certius est hominis subsistere totum*
> *Apte coniungi temperie numeri.*

Man's harmonious constitution renders him susceptible to the tempering and 'educating' influence of music, since the 'ornament of manners' registers the body's harmonious coherence with the soul, for which song and number are responsible.

The descent and journey through hell are powerfully described, and the representation is based on a conception as distinct and as fundamental to our topic as the corresponding scene of 'De nuptiis'. Everywhere are scenes of sadness, suffering, cruelty and inhumanity. Orpheus passes through these dead realms singing. His music casts a magic spell, transforming rage and vengefulness into love and gentleness. The «sweetness» of his music softens hell, «destroys the Stygian law», and brings streams of tears to the eyes of the Eumenides (vv. 809–812):

> *Nec mirum dictu, quod musa tui, sacer Orpheu,*
> *Tanti dulcoris extiterat superis:*
> *Tartara flexisti, legem Stigis annichilasti,*
> *Te modulante madent Eumenides lacrimis.*

The stones themselves weep (v. 817). The poet's ebullient imagination produced a scene unique in the Orpheus myth: the music of Orpheus sets the monsters of hell dancing (vv. 921–922):

> *Quelibet in portu Stigio stabulantia monstra*
> *Alternis gradibus membra movent fidibus.*

They do not dance well (*incompositas ... choreas*), but then they are not used to music (vv. 931–932). The ferryman Charon, who has never experienced a happy day in his life grows joyful in his bitter old age, and works his pole with renewed pleasure in the task (vv. 943–944):

> *Numquam leta prius, Charon, tua cruda senectus*
> *indulgens conto gaudet in obsequio.*

The raging waves themselves grow glad (v. 945). Hairy Cerberus now fawns on the poet with wags of his tail and nods of his triple-throated maw; he turns sociable and becomes the companion of the Hydra (vv. 951–952). The gloomy aspect of the shades grows cheerful (v. 953), and at the dulcet sounds of the lyre and the «nectar of the voice», pain loses its sting, Rhadamanthus grows cheerful and festive, while cruel (*trux*) Eacus, deeply moved, breaks into smiles (vv. 954–956). The «king» of the underworld (v. 961 *rex Tartareus*) himself sits, as though on a throne (v. 965: *In cuius medio maiestas fulta tyranni*), in the middle of a black fire which overwhelms the vision[28] and leaps as a sulphurous whirlwind into the heights. Attended by Agony, Lamentation and Horror (the editor stresses the personification by capitalizing

---

[28] Quid suum virtutis 963 (note 21): *Excedens visum niger estuat ignis in altum* – or «leaps out of sight»? The urge to overwhelm is so prominent in the rest of the passage, the more powerful reading seems preferable.

the names), he feeds the guilty into his consuming fire. At the sound of Orpheus' music the tyrant is astonished to feel how his teeth-gnashing fury is calmed, and he is transformed from his former self into a gentle creature (vv. 989–990):

> *Miratur flecti frendens furor ipsius Orci*
> *Mansuescendo stupens se periisse sibi.*

This remarkable scene shows us the cumulative and outbidding impulse not merely producing poetic flotsam, but engaged in the crucial moment of the poem. The guiding idea is the transformation of this entire society from savage inhumanity to courteous sociability through the agency of music. One monster after another turns into a mild-mannered courtier, until the entire underworld is a festive[29] grand ballroom with the guests greeting each other affably, walking arm in arm, dancing, smiling, making charming and blandishing comments and gestures. If the model for hell in 'De nuptiis' was the king's court dispensing law, in 'Quid suum virtutis' it is the king's court as social center. The disparity, comical to the modern reader, is high seriousness for the eleventh century poet.

Finally, in an anticlimactic single line, Orpheus' wish is granted (v. 996): *Odis empta viro redditur Euridice*. Orpheus leads her out, but in this case, as opposed to the 'De nuptiis', love works against him. It forces him to look back. And so he whom no effort or exertion could conquer, is thwarted by love (v. 1008)[30]. Euridyce vanishes, and Orpheus is eager to return and work his marvelous effect again, taking courage from the power of his lyre, but is dissuaded by his revulsion at the thought of petitioning evil[31]. But the divine power of song has already enabled him

---

[29] Cf. Quid suum virtutis 955 (note 21): *ovans Rhadamantus*; *ovans* is the festive mood for the triumphal entry: *ovans urbem ingrederetur* (Liv. V 31); *ovans triumphavit* (Vell. II 96, 3). Glosses from LEWIS/SHORT, Latin Dictionary (New York 1879) 1285.
[30] The motif is from Boethius, Cons. III m. 12, 47–48.
[31] Quid suum virtutis 1013–1018 (note 21):
> *Muse confisus rursum fidicen generosus*
> *Squalores imi mox repetens baratri*
> *Conciliante lira molliret saxea corda,*
> *Placaret Parcas, flecteret Eumenides,*
> *Deflens pulsaret, pulsando preces iteraret,*
> *Sollers effectum nec negat ingenium.*

Orpheus' urge to return and engage hell again is present in Ovid, Met. X 72, but is thwarted by the ferryman. The eleventh century poet makes the power of poetry into the motivating force, frustrated by the poet's revulsion at the thought of hell's evil. The lines leave some room for seeing here a second descent and successful rescue of Eurydice, cf. DRONKE (note 11) 199, an outcome that would be more consistent with the poet's faith in powerful song and genius. It would also eliminate the awkward artifice of an Orpheus ready and willing to return but repelled by the thought of dealing with such monsters, «even bearing gifts». But the subjunctives (*molliret, placaret* etc.) followed by (1019–1020): *Sed fugit exosus Stigios .../Indignans supplex nequitie fieri*, seem clear, and the upbeat conclusion (1022–1023: *Fortiter extorsit a Stige, quod voluit. / Sic ars naturam vicit ...*) probably looks backwards past the poet's failure through love to the initial success through song. Read this way, the conclusion states: «What powerful song accomplished, ungovernable love undid.»

to win a great victory over Styx, and this shows how «art, with the mediation of fervent study, conquered nature, proving that all things yield to Lady Virtue»[32].

Our next text is a short poem (60 lines) from the so-called 'Liège Songs'[33]. It dates from the end of the century and was written by a certain 'Gautier', who had ties to Marbod, Baudri of Bourgeuil, and probably was himself active at Rheims[34]. The element of study and education that played such a prominent part in both the other poems is absent. The entire poem is given over to the effects of Orpheus' song on the residents of the underworld. The ideas and the conception – transformation from cruelty to mercy and kindness – differ little from what we have observed so far. It is important for the following analysis to have the vocabulary of this transformation before us, and I will limit the discussion of this poem to pointing out the terms of what I will call from now on 'Orphic discourse'.

Here also, Orpheus' music is imagined as penetrating all of hell and working its magic on all its denizens (vv. 1–3)[35]: *Carmine leniti tenet Orpheus antra Cocyti /.../ Carmine placavit quod quisque mali toleravit.* Where there was fury, at the sound of the song there is deep peace and quiet (c. 4): *Fit, quod erat rabies, carmine summa quies.* Those bound in chains forget their pain and anger at the love that the lyre spreads (vv. 7–8): *Immemores penę, quos constrinxere catenę, / Inmemores irae fecit amore lirae.* This Orpheus also changes the laws of hell (v. 13): *Arte lireque sonis mutavit iura Plutonis.* As he proceeds, the «dark faces and loathsome figures» he passes «transform their grim countenances and greet him cordially» (v. 41): *Intuitus mutant torvos blandeque salutant.* Facing the gods of the underworld, Orpheus «takes away their raging fury and alleviates the fierceness of their hearts» (v. 56): *Sic rabiem demit, sic fera corda premit.* The god of the underworld is overcome, and his «imperial command» returns Eurydice to the poet.

The eleventh century poets show an interest in representing the underworld that is unprecedented in the Orpheus tradition. They were far less interested in the fate of Eurydice than in the civilizing of hell. The conversion of Dis and his realm to kindness is the basic manifestation of Orphic poetry functioning.

---

[32] Quid suum virtutis 1021–1024 (note 21):
    Numine sic artis fidens industria mentis
    Fortiter extorsit a Stige, quod voluit.
    Sic ars naturam vicit studio mediante
    Virtuti domine cedere cuncta probans.

[33] Carmina Leodiensia, ed. Walther BULST (SB Heidelberg 1975, 1), Heidelberg 1975, 1–47, here 11–12 (carm. III).

[34] See Maurice DELBOUILLE, Un mystérieux ami de Marbode: le 'redoutable poète' Gautier, in: Le Moyen Âge 57 (1951) 205–240.

[35] The seven-fold repetition of *carmine* and *carmina* in the first eight lines suggests that the poet knew Godfrey of Rheims' poem to Enguerrand of Soissons, in which an anaphora with *carmine* is sustained over five lines, and likewise the power of poetry is the theme. See André BOUTEMY, Trois Œuvres inédites de Godefroid de Reims, in: RMAL 3 (1947) 342 (vv. 99–103).

We can conclude from the three poems surveyed that 'Orphic' poetry has two major characteristics: it is the fulfillment of learning – liberal and ethical – and it transforms the cruel and vengeful into gentle, loving, compassionate beings. That it «conquers nature» and is an instrument in the pursuit of virtue, as the 'Quid suum virtutis' depicts it, is for the eleventh century part and parcel of cathedral school learning based in large part on *cultus virtutum*[36], hence is consistent with poetry's role in education.

We know from sources outside the Orpheus poems that these two aspects of poetry (it fulfills education, it soothes hard hearts and creates compassion) were accepted views of its role in studies and life[37]. In this light the lines on poetry by Ulrich of Bamberg quoted earlier have programmatic character (vv. 32–37, see note 10 above):

> *Si concedis idem, carissime, doctus ad unguem*
> *Nec perfectus erit, qui nil componere novit*
> *Auditu dignum; quod maius dic rogo signum*
> *Aut argumentum, quod certius est documentum*
> *Divitis ingenii, frater dulcissime, quam si*
> *Dictator mentes et grate mulceat aures?*

It is a pithy statement of the conclusion just stated: poetry that can «soothe», «charm», or «delight» (*mulcere*), attests to thorough learning (*doctus ad unguem*)

---

[36] See C. Stephen JAEGER, Cathedral Schools and Humanist Learning, 950–1150, in: DVjs 61 (1987) 569–616. The formula «overcoming nature» expresses one of the central educational ideals of the eleventh century cathedral schools. Here a few references, the interpretation of which must be reserved for a more detailed study: Quid suum virtutis 1022–1023 (note 21): *Sic ars naturam vicit studio mediante / Virtuti domine cedere cuncta probans*; Sigebert of Gembloux, Passio Thebeorum I 260–261, ed. E. DÜMMLER (note 55) 55: *Quando potens virtus naturam vincere gestit, / Hic opus est ultra naturę tendere iura*; and III 598–601 (112): *Naturę columen per nostrum excrevit acumen, / Venis naturę studii dum plurimus usus / Montis acutibiles tanquam de marmore cotes / Elicuit plures excudit et extudit artes*; Hildebert, Carm. min. 36, 33–34, ed. A. B. SCOTT (Leipzig 1969) 24: *non potuit Natura deos hoc ore creare, / quo miranda deum signa creavit homo*. Perhaps related, Marbod of Rennes, De molesta recreatione 5, ed. W. BULST, Liebesbriefgedichte Marbods, in: Liber Floridus. Mittellateinische Studien, Paul Lehmann ... gewidmet, ed. B. BISCHOFF (St. Ottilien 1950) 296: *Cuius dulce melos transcendit acumine celos*. I believe the formula, «Orpheus conquered the gods», in the Liège song nr. 3 (note 33) reiterates in mythological circumscription the same idea (v. 10): *Orpheus ante deos, carmine vicit eos.*

[37] Cf. Tegernseer Briefsammlung (Froumund), carm. XXXII 9–10, ed. STRECKER (note 8) 81: *Nunc facito versus, omnis, qui scribere nosti, / Ut modo pellatur mentibus ira suis*. Hildebert still cultivated a poetry aimed at calming, soothing and consoling. Cf. Peter VON MOOS, Hildebert von Lavardin, 1056–1133. Humanitas an der Schwelle des höfischen Zeitalters (Pariser Historische Studien 3), Stuttgart 1965, 26–27: «[H.] ... sieht den höchsten Sinn der Dichtung in der Vermittlung menschlicher Gunst, im Freundesdienst ... Dichtung soll 'erleichtern', die Sorgen vergessen lassen, das Dasein angenehmer machen ... [Der Dichter] hilft den anderen, beschwichtigt, bringt Ruhe und Ordnung in bedrängte und erregte Herzen.»

II

Orpheus in the Eleventh Century 155

and virtue (*perfectus*)[38]. Ulrich elaborates on the effects of poetry a few lines later. His unnamed friend is known as a man of strong and kind genius (vv. 56–62):

> ... *quis te subtilem nesciat esse?*
> *Ingenii venam tibi quis neget esse benignam?*
> *Nam versus dulces scribendo pectora mulces,*
> *Mulces egregie scribens metri sine lege.*
> *Moribus haec ornas, cum sit tibi prona voluntas*
> *Semper ad omne bonum ...*

The structure of thought is essentially the same as in the previous passage: genius (*subtilis*) and virtue (*benignus, prona ad bonum*) are shown forth in poems and prose compositions that «charm and delight». Skilled poetry and virtue are again closely joined in the phrase: *moribus haec ornas*. The statement is close to the basic idea of both 'De nuptiis' and 'Quid suum virtutis'. Ulrich is defining poetry as «Orphic» without any reference to Orpheus.

II

Orphic poetry[39] is not an aesthetic idea separable from social circumstances and moral obligations. The concept as the eleventh century schools developed it analyses situations of conflict. That is, those who observed and described conflict themselves called on the Orpheus myth for their formulations.

The poem glorifying the Würzburg school cited earlier (see p. 143 above) is a response to some students of Worms, who in the autumn of 1030 wrote a poem criticizing the school at Würzburg and its master, and extolling their own[40]. It may well

---

[38] The *vir perfectus* is the fulfillment of moral training. Cf. Martin of Braga, Formula vitae honestae VI 1ff., ed. Claude BARLOWE (New Haven 1950) 247; and the work of Hildebert dependent on it, Liber de quatuor virtutibus vitae honestae (MIGNE PL 171, 1055–1056C): *Quarum* [namely the four virtues] *se formis si mens humana coaptet, / Perfectum faciet integra vita virum*; (1063B): *His ... formis virtutes commemoratas / Perfectum constat reddere posse virum*. See the lengthy description of the education of S. Lambert of Utrecht in the Vita S. Lamberti 5 (MIGNE PL 132, 645); also Petrus Alfonsi, Disciplina clericalis, prol., ed. A. HILKA/W. SÖDERHJELM (Sammlung mlat. Texte 1), Heidelberg 1911, 1; Peter of Blois, Ep. 126 (MIGNE PL 207, 377AB).

[39] From now on I will not put this term in quotation marks, but assume the conception as defined.

[40] Editions, see above, note 8. The Würzburg school flourished in Ottonian times under Stefan of Novara, summoned from Italy to the north by Otto the Great and Poppo of Würzburg. Witness the biography of Wolfgang of Regensburg, who challenged the master on interpreting Martianus Capella and caused a flap: see Otloh of S. Emmeram, Vita S. Wolfkangi 4–5, ed. G. WAITZ (MGH SS IV, Hannover 1841, 528. In the 1030's a «widely famed» master Pernolf is attested; Bishop Heribert of Eichstätt called on him to test the qualifications of a school master whose learning he doubted. Apart from the poem in question and a few letters spun off from it in the Worms letter collection, total obscurity. That is the condition of the eleventh century German schools, and a brilliant light like this polemical poem and the responding letters shows that documentation depends on chance, and

have begun as an exercise in composition[41], but it took the form of a taunt and quickly turned serious. Several other letters in the Worms collection illuminate the aftermath, and they leave no doubt that the poem was at the center of a storm that had unpleasant results (for the Worms perpetrators, it seems), and not merely a literary squabble with no social implications[42].

The passages that interest us juxtapose the peace of the Würzburg school with the hell of contentiousness at Worms. The poet depicts Würzburg as an Elysian realm of studies, an academy of poetry and virtue, its students and master a harmonious community, knit together as if «by a single vow» (v. 46). They lead a «dolce vita» of peacefulness and friendship (vv. 108–109):

> *An nos mellitam nescis hic ducere vitam,*
> *Undique pacatos et de nullis superatos?*

The students are «happy» about their teacher (v. 49 *de principe letus*); with «subtle care he keeps watch over his flock» (v. 42: *Cura subtili proprio vigilabit ovili*) and makes moderate use of the rod (v. 25); he does not despise the less gifted in favor of the talented students (v. 44); when the sons of nobles win his love, submission to his tutelage does them no dishonor (vv. 57–58); his word brings the «joys of life» (v. 52); the poet wishes him «who is replete with virtue», serenity and prosperity, «may he remain safe from all harm», and may he rejoice, «having shed all sad things», secure on all sides, and may he enjoy the far-famed joys of true peace (vv. 64–67):

> *Virtutum plenus sit prosperitate serenus,*
> *Nil eventurum cui quod maneat nociturum,*
> *Tristibus exutus letetur et undique tutus,*
> *Gaudia veracis sibi sint celeberrima pacis.*

The Worms poet has stormed into this citadel of love as a raging enemy of peace. He is a «sower of wrath and destroyer of friendships» (v. 105: *sator irarum et destructor amicitiarum*), filled with «frenzied rage, mad with the love of Mars» (vv. 141–142: *bacharis.../... /Martis amore furendo*); he has fomented between them the «discord of dire wrath» (v. 130 *ire ... discordia dirę*). His «message of contention» (v. 107 *nuncia litis*) disturbs the «sweet life of Würzburg» and the peace that rules on all sides (vv. 105–109).

The peace-breaker's penchant to anger, rage and combat is consistent with the studies at his school, the poet claims. At Worms they worship «spiritual monsters»

---

behind the lack of it is a vital school life. On the Würzburg school, apart from the literature in note 8 above, see R. BLANK, Weltdarstellung und Weltbild in Würzburg und Bamberg vom 8. bis zum Ende des 12. Jahrhunderts (Bamberg 1968) 47–75; Herbert ZIELINSKI, Der Reichsepiskopat in spätottonischer und salischer Zeit (1002–1125), I (Stuttgart 1984) 86–87.

[41] Cf. the comment of the perpetrators at Worms, Ältere Wormser Briefsammlung, Ep. 15, ed. BULST (note 8) 32: ... *litem, quam cum Herbipolensibus exercitii causa habuimus.*

[42] Cf. Ältere Wormser Briefsammlung, Epp. 15, 25, 26, 42, ed. BULST (note 8) 31–32, 46–49, 77–79.

Orpheus in the Eleventh Century 157

(v. 206); they lack all art and put their faith in the quarrels of Mars (v. 207); they call back to life the gods of the underworld (v. 213 *Inferni divos ... redivivos*) and prefer their worship to the society of the living under the «law of instruction» (vv. 211ff. *ius documenti*); they worship the «black demons», who, while they lived, are engaged in «constant contentions» (vv. 224ff.); they will never prevail in the present combat, «even though the prince of the underworld himself should leave hell to render them aid» (vv. 269–270)[43]:

> *Nos non devinces, licet Inferni tibi princeps*
> *Infernum linquat, sic auxiliando propinquat.*

We are suddenly in the underworld scene of the Orpheus myth, though there has been no signal of it nor any reference to that story. The «sower of wrath» has chosen to revive the gods of hell, those whom the law of Pluto has condemned to the dragon's jaw, but there is no resonating lyre to soften his (Pluto's) anger. No pleading can rescue those who enter his kingdom (vv. 213–216):

> *Inferni divos cur optabis redivivos?*
> *Quos lex Plutonis damnavit fauce draconis,*
> *Non resonante lira cuius mulcebitur ira,*
> *Quicquid hic acceptat, nullius iam prece reddat.*

The Worms poet, in other words, is caught in the hell of contention he has created, and has no soothing lyre and no redeeming Orpheus[44] to soften the rage of the beasts he consorts with. Wrathful contentiousness is stylized as a descent to the underworld; hell is the place of anger, fury and war. The poet could evoke the story without telling it; the circumstances themselves called for an Orpheus[45].

If there is an Orpheus in the poem, it is the Würzburg poet. His foe is in the position of Eurydice, caught in hell and locked into the law of Pluto. It takes an Orpheus with his *lyra concilians* to redeem him. The poet implies but does not state this interpretation. The roles he has cast himself and his adversary in suggest that that model guided his conception: he is the peace-maker and reconciler. Having railed against the war-like posture of Worms, he makes an extravagant offer of peace: «Now let the discord and cruel anger between us fade. Let us shun war and become joined as twins in our love. A bond like that of David and Jonathan will join us. No cruelty

---

[43] The reproach translates into an attack on the excessive study of the classics at Worms. A student of Mainz, writing to his colleagues at Worms in the following year to refuse the requested support in their continuing conflict with Würzburg, makes an ironic reference to this reproach in his salutation, see Ältere Wormser Briefsammlung, Ep. 26, ed. BULST (note 8) 48: *Eximie iuventuti Wormatiensium, insudanti studiis et artibus Atheniensium, R. Mogontinus non Grecus, sed vix effectus Latinus, amicitiam indivulsam, fidem inconcussam.* The letter is filled with sarcasm and 'Schadenfreude' at the straits of the Worms students.
[44] This may well reiterate the contempt the Würzburger feels for his foe as a poet. Cf. vv. 143–148.
[45] The early date of the poem can put to rest any reservation about the advent of the Orpheus figure in the capacity as restorer of peace and love. The indirectness of the treatment suggests this interpretation of the myth is well known.

will disturb us now or ever more. Those caught up in unending quarrels will marvel to see such a friendship between us» (vv. 130–135):

> *Inter nos ire fugiat discordia dirę,*
> *Expertes belli nos simus amore gemelli,*
> *Fedus Davidis mecum Ionathęque subibis,*
> *Nil nosmet sevum conturbet nunc et in evum.*
> *Multum mirantur nam, talia cum speculantur,*
> *Sunt qui cum rixis nobis in pignore fixis*[46].

This posture of unquestioning forgiveness of wrongs, overlooking of insults, restoration of peace and friendship with no sense of vengefulness was an admired one. The poet is showing his *mansuetudo*[47]. That is the reconciling oil he pours forth to sooth this dispute. His own poem is the bringer of it. The final lines represent the poet as the redeemer of his wrathful colleague at Worms, sowing seeds of peace in the divine field by his song and praying for aid from God, «by whose gifts I master the melody of reason»[48].

This poem shows us actual social circumstances that commended the figure of Orpheus as a representative of peace and conciliation. Peace, friendship, love in cathedral schools was a sacred law. To violate it is serious[49].

The Würzburg poem is not the only case in which a breach of claustral tranquillity conjured Orpheus as the reconciler. Two letters from the Hannover collection show us the same logic at work. The first is written (between 1054 and 1079) by a group of students residing at the Hildesheim cathedral school, evidently as guests (*hospites*), not members of the chapter. They are starving. In their salutation, they

---

[46] The last line is confusing. See STRECKER's and BULST's puzzlement in their editions (note 8) 130 resp. 123. But the sense if fairly clear: many who cannot end their disputes will marvel at the model of conciliatory restraint and loving friendship these two provide, having been transformed from bitter enemies to a David and Jonathan.
[47] See C. Stephen JAEGER, Origins of Courtliness: Civilizing Trends and the Formation of Courtly Ideals, 939–1210 (Philadelphia 1985) 36–42, 149–150, 198–199.
[48] Cf. vv. 273–279 (BULST 127):
> *Istic prescriptum metrico modulamine dictum,*
> *Cum precor eius opem necnon venerabile nomen,*
> *De cuius donis modulo fungor rationis, / ... /*
> *Nobis ductores verbi dum posco satores*
> *Agrum divinum plantantes semine primum.*
[49] The later letters addressing the conflict at Würzburg suggest some legal action was taken, at least threatened, against the perpetrators, cf. Ältere Wormser Briefsammlung, Ep. 25, ed. BULST (note 8) 46–47.
Another case is that of Wazo of Liège. He protested the tyrannical rule of Provost John at Liège ca. 1021–1025 by quitting his post as schoolmaster and writing a strong letter. But the future bishop was the loser in the conflict. John made representations to Bishop Durandus, calling Wazo a contumacious hot-head (*iracundus, obstinatio iracundiae*) and attributing Wazo's protest to his contentiousness (*studio litigii*). John's position carried the day, even though he was accused of inciting local wine-merchants to set the dormitory on fire in order to kill Wazo. See Anselm of Liège, Gesta episcoporum Leodiensium 41, ed. R. KÖPKE (MGH SS VII), Hannover 1846, 211–215.

sign themselves «famished men whose flesh barely clings to their bones» and wish Bishop Hezilo «the satiety of celestial grace, full of the bread of life»[50]. They play changes on their hunger, describing the physical effects in detail. They compare themselves to the tortured in hell, except that their own tortures are worse (Ep. 27, p. 62):

> ... videmur nobis Tantalo apud inferos antepositas regales epulas tangere non auso miseriores, Ixionę rote volubili astricto calamitosiores, Sisipho saxum iam iamque relapsurum volvente magis damnati, Titione, cuius renascens iecur insaciabilis vultur rodit, gravius puniti et omnino adhuc in corpore pęnis infernalibus traditi.

They beg the bishop to release them from «the jaws of hell»[51]. Having set up the bishop for the role either of Pluto or Orpheus, they end discreetly by casting themselves as Orpheus pleading for Bishop Hezilo before God. Just as the lyre of Orpheus liberated 'Erudicen' from hellish creatures who know no forgiveness, they pray that «the cithara of their devotion» will win from God whatever Hezilo wishes (Ep. 27, p. 63):

> Si Erudicen ab inferis ignoscere nescientibus Orphei liberaverat lira, quęlibet optanda benedictissime tuę animę apud Dominum impetrabit nostrę devotionis cythara.

A letter from Walo, abbot of St. Arnulf in Metz, to Archbishop Manasses of Rheims, written in 1074, is not so discreet[52]. The unhappy abbot heaps vituperation on the Archbishop, who has wronged him. The substance of his complaints is not relevant, just the phrasing and concepts. He grieves for the errors of Manasses, as is appropriate to anyone moved by the «affection of true love». He has grieved far more for the «ragings» of his injurer than for the injuries done himself. He shudders to recall the misery he has suffered under the «barbarous rule» (barbaro dominio). He declines to enumerate the threats and the curses he has received from Manasses. Had he been anything but a simple fool, he would not have come to so «ungentle, so cruel, so violent, so monstrous a beast» (ad te tam inmitem tam trucem tam violentam tam inmanem bestiam). Manasses has had the nerve to suggest that Walo, being a peaceful, humble and quiet man (pacificum, humilem et quietum), and constantly given to reading, is not comfortable with the «French manners» of Manasses. Only a monster barren of all virtue, Walo says, could imagine a life tempered by peace,

---

[50] Briefsammlungen der Zeit Heinrichs IV., Ep. 27, ed. Carl ERDMANN/Norbert FICKERMANN (MGH Die Briefe der deutschen Kaiserzeit V), Weimar 1950, 61–63, here 61: Domno patri et episcoporum dignissimo H. famelici et vix hęrentes ossibus Hiltinisheimensium scholarum hospites uberem cęlestis gratię sacietatem, plenam panis vivi, qui est Christi, refectionem. The editors identify vix hęrentes ossibus as an echo of Virgil, Ecl. III 102.

[51] Briefsammlungen der Zeit Heinrichs IV., Ep. 27 (note 50) 63: ... eripe ex ipsis leti faucibus. Letum can be read as «death», but in the context of the Orpheus story, it must mean death personified.

[52] Briefsammlungen der Zeit Heinrichs IV., Ep. 108 (note 50) 182–185. On Walo's conflict with Manasses, see M. MANITIUS (note 8) II 724–725, also John R. WILLIAMS, Manasses I of Rheims and Gregory VII, in: American Historical Review 54 (1949) 804–824, here 809–810.

modesty and sobriety to be lower in virtue than one given to harsh and bold combat. The rehearsal of the archbishop's perverse ideas continues: peace weakens the spirits of powerful men, while combat strengthens the weak and idle. But, Walo replies, Cicero has shown the superiority of the toga to weapons.

The opposition of peaceful, gentle Walo to fierce and barbarous Manasses gives the structure that invokes Orpheus. Walo says he has tried to mitigate the fury of Manasses by citing scripture and «celestial words» (Ep. 108, p. 183):

> O quotiens adhibui tibi medicamina scripturarum! quotiens cęlestibus verbis quasi quibusdam carminibus tuum temptavi mitigare furorem! quotiens non Treicia sed Davitica cythara conatus sum illud vel expellere vel sedare dęmonium, quo vexaris!

The rejection of the «Thracian cithara» only confirms the appropriateness of Orpheus in the circumstances. It is a gesture, like the 'rejection of the muses' in invocations[53], that christianizes a domain legitimately occupied by the classical tradition, and in so doing concedes a strong sense of obligation to what it rejects. The reference to the harp of David illustrates through its isolation how accepted the jurisdiction of Orpheus in the correction of *furor* and *saevitia* was. David curing Saul would have had a higher degree of legitimacy, but the Old Testament singer is seldom invoked as a soother of royal anger, though his poetry is often compared to that of Orpheus[54].

Sigebert of Gembloux gives us a second example of Christian superseding Orphic opposition to violence and rage in his 'Passio Thebeorum' (ca. 1070)[55]. He represents Emperor Maximian as the raging king: (I 613) *nec civilis multum, nec amicus amicis*; (I 617–618) *Est trux ira animos ... / Nunquam corde reses, ceu mansuescens leo deses*; (I 621) *ferox et naturaliter atrox*; (I 627) *barbaricus sensus*[56]. He orders the (Christian) Theban legion to slaughter the foe (a rebel gallic tribe and Christians) mercilessly (II 36–37, p. 72): *nec vos miseratio flectat. / Non sit qui parcat, nullus sit qui miserescat*. In a speech full of fine ironies (II 25–159, pp. 71–75), the emperor's speaker warns the (converted) legion against the dangers of Christianity: their God is taking over, snatching the trident from Neptune, etc. Soon he will command the underworld – rightly so, since Dis, harder than stone, is deaf to the pleas and blind

---

[53] See CURTIUS (note 21) 129–188.
[54] On the frequent comparison of David and Orpheus see FRIEDMAN (note 11) 148–155; DRONKE (note 11) 206–208; PRIGENT (note 11) 205–221; E. IRWIN, The Songs of Orpheus and the new Songs of Christ, in: Orpheus: The Metamorphosis of a Myth (note 11) 51–62 (a dense and informative study); Fabrizio VISCONTI, Un fenomeno di continuità iconografica: Orfeo citaredo, Davide salmista, Cristo pastore, Adamo e gli animali, in: Augustinianum 28 (1988) 429–436. Walo is the only monk quoted so far. It may be that in monastic communities the Old Testament figure was the preferred calmer of rage. Also noteworthy for its omission in favor of Orpheus in hell: Christ harrowing hell. Cf. DRONKE (note 11) 208.
[55] Sigebert von Gembloux, Passio Sanctae Luciae Virginis und Passio Sanctorum Thebeorum, ed. Ernst DÜMMLER (Abh. Berlin 1893, 1), Berlin 1893, 1–125.
[56] Sigebert, Passio Theb., ed. DÜMMLER (note 55) 65–66; cf. Passio Theb. III 204–297 ('*De furore Cęsaris*') 101–103.

Orpheus in the Eleventh Century 161

to the tears of the wretched. Dis could not even be softened by the tearful songs of Orpheus and refused to grant the life of Eurydice (II 67–70, pp. 72–73):

> 'Pluto duritia vincens adamantina saxa,
> Non potuit flecti lacrimosis cantibus Orphei,
> Quis tygres, rupes, silvas flectebat et amnes,
> Ut daret Euridicis vitam pretium modulanti'.

But «this new fellow Jesus» (II 64, p. 72 *hic novus Iesus*) hears the pleas of all and has compassion with all, even to the point of returning the dead to life.

This is the only version known to me in which Eurydice is not saved even once and the song of Orpheus fails to soften Dis/Pluto. Sigebert obviously required an inflexible king and a thwarted Orpheus in order to create a space for a Christ whose redeeming mission overcame the ineffectual pagan means of arousing mercy. This shows how casually variable and governed by authorial intention the fate of Eurydice is. The purpose of the individual author can override tradition and 'Stoffzwang'.

This section looked at the Orpheus story as a structuring myth for conflict in actual social-political circumstances. Sigebert's 'Passio Thebeorum' helps establish the point even though it is an imaginative narrative poem. The same narrative metaphor was at the disposal of any learned cleric who described conflict situations. It gave a powerful analogue to the learned man of peace softening the rage of rulers, no matter what the ultimate success.

III

The soothing and civilizing role of verse was more than a conceit of school poetry. Orphic discourse formulated important duties of secular clergy: restraining and soothing the anger of princes and rulers, making peace, effecting reconciliations, teaching civilized manners to knights, nobles, kings, and, when the occasion warranted, to archbishops. «Mitigating the fury of kings» is mentioned as a matter of praise in Carolingian sources[57], though it is not common and Orpheus is not associated with it. Gerbert of Aurillac formulated the task programmatically. He strikes the Ciceronian posture that the art of speaking well must be inseparable from the art of living well. The necessity for combining good speaking and good living is the 'mitigating' task of the statesman[58]:

> ... nobis in re publica occupatis utraque necessaria. Nam et apposite dicere ad persuadendum et *animos furentium suavi oratione ab impetu retinere* summa utilitas.

---

[57] Cf. Walahfrid Strabo, In Natalem S. Mammetis Hymnus, ed. E. DÜMMLER (MGH Poetae II 296):

> 5. Mitis domans immitia,   6. Adiutus armis spiritus
>   illisque promens mystica,   *vicit furores principum,*
>   Vivebat inter bestias,   saevi draconis conterens
>   quo cive gaudent angeli.   sacris caput conatibus.

[58] Die Briefsammlung Gerberts von Reims, Ep. 44, ed. Fritz WEIGLE (MGH Briefe der dt. Kaiserzeit II), Weimar 1966, 73. Emphasis mine.

The discourse of fury and anger mollified was present in the tenth century, and the man whose charisma had peace-making force was an admired ideal. Ruotger says that Brun of Cologne was born to be a peacemaker, just at the time when his father had «tamed the savageness of the barbarians» (*perdomita barbarorum sevicia*)[59], «turned back the danger of internal strife», and proceeded to rebuild a peaceful kingdom. Brun always cultivated peace, «as if it were the nourishing force and crown of all other virtues». He believed that tranquillity was the atmosphere that strengthens virtue, while strife weakens it[60].

The first abbot of Gembloux, Erluin (d. 987), was described by his contemporary the monk Richarius, in verses transmitted by Sigebert of Gembloux, as the embodiment of the peacemaking task[61]:

> Quam patiens et quam dulcis quantumque benignus
> Iugiter extiterit, quis memorare queat?
> Nam placidus degens lenibat corda furentum
> In mores pacis de feritate vocans.
> Alloquia blandus, mira gravitate modestus,
> Non asper, non trux, non violentus erat ...

---

[59] This becomes the formula for describing victories over foreign invaders or rebellious states. Cf. the dedicatory poem believed written by Brun for Otto the Great, ed. K. STRECKER (MGH Poetae V 2), Berlin 1939, 377–378 (vv. 23–26):
> Caecaque secula barbaries
> Seva premebat et error iners.
> At tua dextra ubi sceptra tenet,
> Publica res sibi tuta placet.

Cf. also Anselm of Besate, Rhetorimachia, Ep. to Henry III, ed. K. MANITIUS (note 6) 98: [it is matter of praise for him that] *gentes feras et atrocissimas domuisti animos crudos nefarios ab humanitate derelictos.*

[60] Ruotger, Vita Brunonis 2 (note 22) 182–184. Cf. also Vita Brunonis 25 (216), Brun's *pietas* renders battle-hardened men war-shy and timid: ... *quos nulla umquam acies, nulla inflexit asperitas, hos huius viri pietas inbelles et timidos faciebat.* The mere sound of his name put an end to wars, ushered in peace and established the study of the arts: ... *nominis quoque eius fama, quousque pervenit, bella sedaret, pacem formaret, studium in omnibus bonis artibus firmaret.* Chs. 18 and 19 (202–206) show Brun attempting to pacify and reconcile Otto the Great's rebellious son Liudolf. It is oratory (204: *vir bonus, dicendi peritus*) at its Ottonian best, working to mitigate the fury (Liudolf is possessed by an «Erinye») of princes with the suasions of eloquence – the ideal function of the statesman as Gerbert had formulated it (above, p. 161).

[61] Sigebert, Gesta abbatum Gemblacensium 3, ed. G. H. PERTZ (MGH SS VIII), Hannover 1848, 524. 32–42. On the text see WATTENBACH/HOLTZMANN, Deutschlands Geschichtsquellen im Mittelalter: Deutsche Kaiserzeit I (Tübingen 1948) 149 and note 220. Cf. the commemorative lines by Eugenius Vulgarius (southern Italy, ca. 911), ed. Paul MAYVAERT, A Metrical Calendar by Eugenius Vulgarius, in: AB 84 (1966) 349–377, here 364 (vv. 104 bis 108):

> ... Iohannes
> Inferior nulli veterum probitate priorum,
> Cuius in octonis mundus suffragia clamat
> Quatinus indomitas ęvi demulceat iras
> Ingentesque animi curarum mitiget ęstus.

> *Quem mestum vidit, quem tristem quemque dolentem,*
> *Affectu patris subveniebat ei;*
> *Affatu dulci merentia pectora mulcens.*

It is not likely that this early portrait drew even indirectly on the image of Orpheus doing with his song what the abbot did with his speech and his mere presence. But the language dramatically shows the affinities between a clerical ideal and the Orpheus myth. More likely this language of the peace-bringing personality was pre-formed in clerical-monastic circles close to the Cluny reform[62], and then appropriated in the cathedral schools with their stress on poetry and classical learning, to describe the music of Orpheus.

Fulbert of Chartres seems to have radiated the effect of soothing tinged with friendship and love implied in *mulcere*. He received a letter from his disciple Hildegar asking that the master correct his student's vice of anger, since he «emits the sweetest fragrance of mature holiness» through his virtues[63]. We see Fulbert at work in this capacity in his letter to King Robert the Pious restraining his anger against Bishop Odolricus of Orléans[64]. In Fulbert this clerical obligation connects with engagement in the peace movement. His poem in praise of peace shows how close the conception of a new civilization based on law, moderation and restraint was to goals of the peace movement[65]. It would be surprising if that movement did not call on the image of the soothing, calm-restoring man of peace mollifying the raging of barbarians, but in fact this language is nowhere in evidence in the legislation of peace and truce, though sermons and orations could draw on it[66].

---

[62] Odo of Cluny praises Gerald of Aurillac for exercising this influence in Aurillac in his Vita Geraldi IV 8 (MIGNE PL 133, 700D): *Incolae autem regionis illius mores valde ferinos habere solebant, sed aliquantulum exemplo vel reverentia sancti hominis esse mitiores videntur.* Passage cited by Thomas BISSON, The Organized Peace in Southern France and Catalonia, ca. 1140–ca. 1233, in: American Historical Review 82 (1977) 290–307, here 292.

[63] The Letters and Poems of Fulbert of Chartres, Ep. 95, ed. & trans. Frederick BEHRENDS (Oxford 1976) 172: ... *te propter mores tuos matura sanctitate suavissime redolentes erga tibi subditos eo animo esse intelligo, ut bonos sinceri amoris gratia conplectaris.*

[64] Fulbert, Ep. 94, ed. BEHRENDS (note 63) 170–171. – Peter Damian is going about the same duty in his tract: De frenanda ira et simultatibus exstirpandis (MIGNE PL 145, 649–660). Cf. also the example of Thierry of St. Hubert and Manasses of Rheims (note 67 below).

[65] Fulbert, Carm. 149, ed. BEHRENDS (note 63) 262–263:
> *Ad normam redigit qui subdita secla pravitati,*
> *Potens novandi sicut et creandi,/.../*
> *Iam proceres legum racionibus ante desueti*
> *Quae recta discunt strenue capessunt.*

[66] This observation is based on a reading of the sources in Ludwig HUBERTI, Studien zur Rechtsgeschichte der Gottesfrieden und Landfrieden, Ansbach 1892, and on the documents in MGH, LL IV, Const. 1, ed. L. WEILAND (Hannover 1893) 596–617. That the contemporary commentary on legislation and its ends could draw on Orphic discourse is evident in a speech of Archbishop Guido of Vienne in the Council of Langres (1116): Concilium Lingonense (Recueil des Historiens de la France XIV), Paris ²1877, 223, and MANSI, Concil. Collect. Suppl. 2 (1748) 159. Guido's speech to open the council lamented the depradations on the church. The effect of his speech, delivered in *mellita oratione*: '*His et huiuscemodi declamatis a viro facundissimo coepere audientium mitescere pectora et in pacis modestiae-*

Archbishop Manasses I of Rheims with his rough warrior ways seems to have brought out this quality in the gentler clergy around him. The biographer of Abbot Thierry of St. Hubert (Ardennes), writing ca. 1090, describes Thierry's soothing effect on Manasses[67]:

«... by nature and by [acquired] manners he was more fierce than appropriate, but he [Abbot Thierry] behaved to him in so laudable a way that he made him his friend ... And so he put aside his harsh ways to a great extent at his admonitions ... and though to many men he was frequently ungentle and truculent, to this man alone ... he was always gentle and placid.»

This complex of concerns comes together in Bern of Reichenau's letters to Henry III praising him as peace-maker[68]. In a letter written before 1044 he explained to the king the significance of his royal title[69]:

Veterum satis declarat auctoritas, quod hi, qui nunc reges dicuntur, olim ob crudelem morum ferocitatem tyranni vocabantur, sed crescente sacrae religionis studio reges appellati sunt a recte regendo, dum bestiales motus comprimunt et per discretionis vim se rationales ostendunt.

This is a result of clerical instruction of kings since it occurs «as the zeal of religion grows» (*crescente sacrae religionis studio*)[70]. It is a significant connection. It indicates the clergy's sense of being engaged in a mission of civilizing the laity that registers in many sources in the eleventh and twelfth centuries[71]. Bern's letters in praise of

---

que velle concurrere sacramenta' (cited by HUBERTI 430). Also the speech of this same Guido (now Pope Calixtus II) at the council of Rheims (1119), after hearing much bickering and contention from a host of complainants: The Ecclesiastical History of Orderic Vitalis XII 21, ed. & trans. Marjorie CHIBNALL, VI (Oxford 1978) 262; cited also by HUBERTI 431–432.

[67] Vita Theoderici abbatis Andaginensis 20, ed. W. WATTENBACH (MGH SS XII), Hannover 1856, 49. 9–14: ... *natura et moribus plus quam oporteret ferus, propter laudabilem conversationem eius sibi amicum eum fecerat ... . Multum ergo feritatis ab eo admonitus deposuit ... et cum pluribus esset frequenter immitis et truculentus, huic uni ... semper fuit mitis et placidus*. The biographer wrongly takes Manasses' predecessor Gervasius to be the object of this pacifying activity. On the error, see J. R. WILLIAMS (note 52) 806, note 7. – Walo, abbot of St. Arnulf in Metz (see p. 159–160 above), in accepting the abbacy of St. Remi, let his good judgment be overruled by the prospect of «tempering the truculence» of Manasses (cf. MIGNE PL 150, 879–880, here 879D) and sought to transform his «canine manners», «savageness of mind» and «bestiality of manners» into «most gentle charity and charitable gentleness», see Briefsammlungen der Zeit Heinrichs IV., Ep. 108 (note 50) 183.

[68] Franz-Josef SCHMALE, Die Briefe des Abtes Bern von Reichenau (Veröffentlichungen der Kommission für geschichtliche Landeskunde in Baden-Württemberg, Reihe A: Quellen 6), Stuttgart 1961, 55–64. For a commentary see Karl SCHNITH, Recht und Friede. Zum Königsgedanken im Umkreis Heinrichs III., in: Historisches Jahrbuch 81 (1962) 22–57.

[69] Bern, Ep. 26, ed. SCHMALE (note 68) 55–56, here 55.

[70] SCHMALE cites Isidore, Etym. IX 3, 19–20, as Bern's source for this etymology, but it is evident from Isidor's passage that the idea of a transition from barbarity to reason inspired by «sacred religion» is Bern's addition.

[71] See JAEGER, Origins of Courtliness (note 47) 211–235. I now believe that the peace movement was a vital precursor of medieval courtliness, as has been argued by G. DUBY, Hommes et structures au moyen âge (Le savoir historique 1), Paris 1973, 227–240 (ch. «Les laics et la paix de Dieu»).

Henry III as peace-maker show the language of the peace movement and that of instruction in *mores* intersecting[72].

The obligation to soothe and calm the ruler registers in 'Ruodlieb' and here again is significantly connected with goals of the peace movement, possibly with the amnesties of Henry III[73]. The *rex maior* thanks his «kind and gentle» courtier, Ruodlieb, for dispelling his anger (V 405–407)[74]:

> ... «absit, ut is de me tribuletur ⟨ut hostis,⟩
> A quo sum numquam minimam commotus in ⟨iram,⟩
> Quin irascentem me mitem reddit ut ag ⟨num⟩ ...».

«Soothing the anger» of the king was no minor bit of personal royal psychological counseling, but rather a fundamental way of doing business, accomplishing personal and political goals. This was suggested in Gerbert's comment that the ability to

---

[72] In a later letter, Ep. 27, ed. SCHMALE (note 68) 56–64, Bern praises the king for uniting in his own heart mercy and truth, justice and peace (an echo of Psalm 84, 11). These unions have created a kingdom so peaceful and harmonious as the world has never seen (p. 57). He compares Henry with King David, who was *mitis, humilis, mansuetus* (p. 59, cf. p. 60 the form of address: *omnium regum ... mitissime*). Henry is the imitator of David cutting the piece from Saul's mantle and refusing to raise his sword against his enemy (p. 59): *cum non solum inimicos diligitis, verum etiam omnes in regno vestro sub uno karitatis et pacis vinculo constringitis*. The concord of his kingdom invites comparison with the period of Christ's birth, Bern continues. Henry takes no vengeance against those who have wronged him, and with «marvelous charity» he favors, aids and restores them. Bern 'loves' the king for these qualities (p. 60): «There is nothing in this life more cheerful, more dear, more loveable, since good cheer reigns in the kingdom while peace and concord persist.» The monk of Reichenau never mentions the peace-maker Orpheus, but the peace-maker David and the prince of peace he prefigures play that role. Again, we see that the structure of Orphic discourse is present before that figure entered it, an appropriation that had already taken place at Würzburg.

[73] See Karl HAUCK, Heinrich III. und der Ruodlieb, in: PBB 70 (1948) 372–419.

[74] Ruodlieb. Faksimile-Ausgabe des Codex Latinus Monacensis 19486 der Bayerischen Staatsbibliothek München und der Fragmente von St. Florian, II 1: Kritischer Text, ed. Benedikt VOLLMANN (Wiesbaden 1985) 103. Ruodlieb's personal qualities are tailored to this effect. He is *mitis* and *benignus* (V 400), «ready to serve and in all things well mannered, envious of none, and dear to all», the king's «most beloved» and «dearest of all the retinue» (V 419–422):

> ... promptus eras et in omni morigerebas;
> Hinc habeo grates tibi, dilectissime, grandes.
> Invidus es nulli sed plebi karus es omni
> ... karissime cunctigenorum,

(v. 421 *invidus* seems to be preferable to VOLLMANN's conjecture *gravis*). The atmosphere of the king's court is determined by *amor* and *clementia*; see Helena M. GAMER, Studien zum Ruodlieb, in: ZfdA 88 (1957/58) 249–266. Even the tamed wild animals that the court teems with become representatives of the civilizing power of these virtues. Likewise the king's generous and merciful treatment of his conquered adversary illustrates the nobility of not seeking revenge, but reconciling enemies through friendship and love and invites comparison with Henry III (see notes 72 and 73 above). These values were represented as institutionalized at the school of Würzburg in the poem from 1031 discussed above.

soothe is *nobis in re publica occupatis ... necessaria* and *summa utilitas* see p. 161 above). There is good testimony to Orphic discourse functioning in royal business[75]. In this context it may be that the king's 'anger' at its palest is little more than a circumscription for his refusing requests. The language of royal favor or disfavor is a language of the emotions: the king's favor is 'love', his disapproval, 'hate' or 'anger'[76].

The task of soothing, pacifying and instructing princes and moving the lay nobility away from barbarity to *mores compositi* registered in tracts on the obligation to shun anger and cultivate clemency. An early example is Wipo's 'Tetralogus'[77]. The last two of the four admonishers of the king in this «tetralogue» are the Law and Grace. *Gratia* urges the softening and moderating of the precepts that *Lex* had urged on him (vv. 225–229):

> *Et post iudicium veniae mulcedo sequatur / ...*
> *Lex odium regi generat feriendo nocentes;*
> *Ut sit carus item rex idem, Gratia suadet.*

In showing mercy, Henry imitates Jove himself, who punishes crimes by forgiveness (vv. 243–244: *... parcendo crimina punit!*). Wipo cites a consecration formula for the girding on of the king's sword[78], built on the antithesis of the king's killing weapon to his preserving mercy (vv. 249–255):

---

[75] «Placating the king», «soothing his anger» as business: The siege of Troja lifted when Henry II's rage and anger are softened by the children of the city; see Rodulfus Glaber, The Five Books of the Histories III 4, ed. Neithard BULST (Oxford 1989) 100–102. – Peace-making = «placating his anger»: Anselm of Liège, Gesta episcoporum Leodiensium 34 (MGH SS VII 208): Bishop Wolbodo has displeased Henry II. He sets out with money to «placate» the king, but on the way considers that *frustra terrenum principem placari* if he angers God – and he gives all the money away. Wazo of Liège restrains the French king (Henry I, in 1046) from attacking Aix merely by writing an eloquent letter (says his idealizing biographer Anselm, Gesta 61, 226. 14): *Qua sententia viri Dei audita, tyrannica rabies confestim est sedata*. On another occasion Wazo defies a prohibition of Henry III and is solemnly summoned to court to account for it. He is fined 300 pounds of silver, and this mundane act of compensation is described as «softening the indignation of that powerful mind» (Gesta 66, 229. 36: *potentis animi indignatio non aliter visa est posse leniri*), and «placating the emperor» (229. 39: *imperator postea placatus*). – The language of royal business and affairs of state regularly draws on the concept: The Admont collection (mid-twelfth century) has an interesting series of letters; see Die Admonter Briefsammlung nebst ergänzenden Briefen, Epp. 55–62, ed. G. HÖDL/P. CLASSEN (MGH Briefe der dt. Kaiserzeit VI), München 1983, 107–116: Frederick I summons Archbishop Eberhard I of Salzburg (Ep. 55), who refuses (Ep. 56), thus arousing the king's anger (Epp. 57, 58, 59). Through intermediaries the king's anger is placated (Epp. 60 and 61), and the Archbishop agrees to appear before the king (Ep. 62).

[76] See C. Stephen JAEGER, L'amour des rois: structure social d'une forme de sensibilité aristocratique, in: Annales ESC 46 (1991) 547–571.

[77] Die Werke Wipos, ed. Harry BRESSLAU (MGH SS rer. Germ.), Hannover/Leipzig 1915, 75–86.

[78] Evidently Wipo's invention. The admonition to compassion does not occur in any preserved royal ordination. Cf. BRESSLAU (note 77) 83–84, note 6.

> *Dum rex iratus fueris, miserando quiesce.*
> *Dura foventur aquis, durescunt lenia flammis,*
> *Alternatque vices moderatae ius rationis.*
> *Hinc adamas durus solvetur sanguine molli / ...*
> *Et natura iubet mutari tristia blandis.*

This section of the poem is a verse tract on tempering justice with mercy. The eleventh and twelfth centuries produced a fair number of preceptive writings on the subject[79].

IV

We can conclude that the Orpheus figure was an emblem for a certain obligation of clergy in their dealings with lords clerical and secular and that this obligation had wide social and political resonance. But is it anything more than an emblem? Did poetry itself actually function in this capacity? The testimony to learned men using music and poetry in this capacity is scarce, at least I have not found it in abundance[80]. Wipo's 'Tetralogus' and 'Quid suum virtutis' might qualify as 'orphic' poems in the sense we have given the word. Fulcoius of Beauvais wrote poetry advocating the cause of Manasses I of Rheims in his conflict with Rome. Fulcoius has much in common with that ideal cleric whose portrait was quoted at the beginning of this article: both were French nobility, lived in Rome, were skilled in law, rhetoric and poetry[81]. Peter Damian died too early to have had Fulcoius in mind, but he certainly would have recognized in him a representative of the species. Fulcoius wrote several verse epistles to Alexander II (Ep. 7) and Gregory VII (Ep. 2) seeking reconciliation. When Manasses was excommunicated by Hugh of Die, Fulcoius wrote a

---

[79] For instance Peter Damian's tract on suppressing anger: De frenanda ira et simultatibus exstirpandis (note 64); Hildebert's letter to Countess Adela of Blois (Ep. I 3; MIGNE PL 171, 144–145), a little treatise on clemency, drawing on Seneca and using the language of Orphic discourse; also Bernard of Clairvaux, Sermo super cant. 12, ed. J. LECLERQ/ C. H. TALBOT/H. M. ROCHAIS, Sancti Bernardi Opera I (Rome 1957) 60–67; and Peter of Blois' fictional dialogue against royal anger between Henry II and the abbot of Bonneval (MIGNE PL 207, 975–988).

[80] Adam of Bremen, Hamburgische Kirchengeschichte III 39, ed. B. SCHMEIDLER (MGH SS rer. Germ.), Hannover/Leipzig 1917, 183, says that Archbishop Adalbert (d. 1072), though not partial to *fidicines*, called on them to «relieve his anxieties»: *Raro fidicines admittebat, quos tamen propter alleviandas anxietatum curas aliquando censuit esse necessarios*. But this is probably standard medical practice with little evocation of the Orpheus figure.

[81] Cf. one of the epitaphs on Fulcoius cited by Marvin L. COLKER (ed.), Fulcoii Belvacensis Epistulae, in: Traditio 10 (1954) 191–273, here 192:
> *Legem, consilium, rationem, carmina, linguam*
> *Sparsa quis hospitio colligit huic simili?*
> *Quis queat actorem titulare? Quis anser olorem*
> *Hunc pro tot titulis carminibusque suis?*

On Fulcoius, see also WILLIAMS (note 52) 808 and 813–814; André BOUTEMY/Fernand VERCAUTEREN, Fulcoie de Beauvais et l'intérêt pour l'archéologie antique au XIe et au XIIe siècle, in: Latomus 1 (1937) 173–186; M. MANITIUS (note 8) III 836–840, and G. BERNT, Fulcoius von Beauvais, in: LexMA IV (1989) 1019.

conciliatory letter in verse commending the many good qualities of his patron, arguing against the «hatreds» which beset Manasses, and urging him to exercise mercy before justice and lift the excommunication (Ep. 3). Fulcoius is at work with his poetry mollifying the anger of Manasses' foes. It is not improbable on this model to imagine gifted and learned men serving the interests of their lords through poetry.

This sets forth the broader social context which drew the Orpheus figure into its orbit and made of the ancient singer the prototypical softener of royal anger. We know that learned clerics felt an obligation to perform this function, and that poetic composition was part and parcel of their education. A man showed his own *mores compositi* by mitigating the anger of lords, bishops, brothers, and if he ornamented his *mores* with poetry (or vice versa in Ulrich of Bamberg's formulation), then he gave testimony to excellent moral training and powerful genius. Peter Damian's portrait of the futile perfection of a worldly cleric virtually reiterates the educational ideals of the poem 'De nuptiis'. The combination of judicial rhetoric, knowledge of the law and poetic composition, was the best the cathedral schools had to offer.

This conception of the role of poetry virtually died out at the schools after the end of the eleventh century. The Orpheus myth was dissolved into religious or psychological allegories[82], and Orpheus' civilizing mission was absorbed into the broader role of Orpheus/Christ or Orpheus/Reason. It hangs on as reminiscences[83]. A passage in the fourth homily on the Virgin Mary of Bishop Amadeus of Lausanne (mid-twelfth century) adapts an earlier view of Orpheus to describe creation, conversion and moral training[84]:

> ... *suavitate mirificae cantilenae suscitavit [deus] de lapidibus filios Abrahae, et ligna silvarum, id est corda gentilium ad fidem commovit. Feras quoque, id est feros motus et incultam barbariem moraliter composuit, et homines ab hominibus eductos in numerum deorum instituit.*

Orpheus is not mentioned, but it is clear where the ideas came from.

The fate of Orpheus in the twelfth century schools does not show that the ancient singer has at last reemerged and come into his own. It shows the concept losing the firm contours it had had in the previous century. In the eleventh century the Orpheus figure bore a vital educational ideal with broad social and political significance, and maintained this role in competition with Christ and King David.

---

[82] See HEITMANN, WETHERBEE, BRINKMANN (note 11).

[83] Bernard Silvester's treatment in his commentary on Virgil's 'Aeneid' is instructive. He develops the myth in the interpretation that became shared by the 'School of Chartres': Orpheus is Reason, which combines wisdom and eloquence, Eurydice is natural desire etc. The only trace that remains of the eleventh century Orpheus is Bernard's comment on his lyre, cf. The Commentary on the First Six Books of the Aeneid of Vergil commonly attributed to Bernardus Silvestris VI 119, ed. J. & R. JONES (LINCOLN, N. B./LONDON 1977) 54: *Lenimen huius ad aliquod honestum opus pigros excitat, instabiles ad constantiam vocat, truculentos mitigat.* There is a clear reminiscence of the eleventh century Orpheus in John of Salisbury, Policraticus V 10, ed. C. J. WEBB, I (Oxford 1909) 326, 20–27.

[84] Amédée de Lausanne, Huit homélies mariales IV 17–22, ed. G. BAVAUD (Sources Chrétiennes 72), Paris 1960, 110–112.

III

HUMANISM AND ETHICS AT THE SCHOOL OF ST. VICTOR IN THE EARLY TWELFTH CENTURY

The humanism of the twelfth century shares with that of the fifteenth a program of learning that combines the arts of language with the discipline of conduct.[1] The term that conveys this program in the eleventh and twelfth centuries is "letters and manners" (*litterae et mores*). It is so widespread in descriptions of curriculum and teaching as to suggest comparison with the formula of contemporary liberal education in America, "arts and sciences," and I have found it to be one of the best lexical guides to studying the learning of the cathedral schools.[2]

"Letters" are easier to study and have dominated in modern scholarship.[3] *Mores, ethica, moralitas* are hard to study. *Mores* constituted a curriculum oriented more to the person of the teacher than to text books. It is the discipline of behavior, manners, something inherently ephemeral, whose formulation is closer to literature than to discursive philosophy, and whose

---

[1] Leonardo Bruni defined the *studia humanitatis* in terms of this combination. See his letter to Niccolò Strozzi: "Let your study be twofold, first in the skill of letters ... and second in the knowledge of those things which pertain to life and *mores*. These two are therefore called the humanities, because they perfect and adorn a human being" ("Studium vero tibi sit duplex, alterum in litterarum peritia ... alterum in cognitione earum rerum quae pertinent ad vitam et mores, quae propterea humanitatis studia nuncupantur, quod hominem perficiant atque exornent," ed. Eugenio Garin, *La disputa delle arti nel quattrocento* [Florence, 1947], 7). On the study of *mores* in the Renaissance, see Paul Oskar Kristeller, "The Moral Thought of Renaissance Humanism," in his *Renaissance Thought* II: *Papers on Humanism and the Arts* (New York, 1965), 20-68; see also William Harrison Woodward, *Studies in Education During the Age of the Renaissance, 1400-1600* (Cambridge, 1924), 100 (referring to Rudolf Agricola's letter now called *De formando studio*): "'Mores,' conduct and principle, are placed above knowledge. They are the end to which all else leads up. But the place of Letters in relation to conduct is all-important, for character is moulded and strengthened by the study ... of great examples. ..." The best work on ethical training in the twelfth century is a series of studies by Philippe Delhaye, "L'enseignement de la philosophie morale au xiie siècle," *Mediaeval Studies* 11 (1949): 77-99; "'Grammatica' et 'ethica' au xiie siècle," *Recherches de Théologie ancienne et médiévale* [*RTAM*] 25 (1958): 59-110.

[2] See my article, "Cathedral Schools and Humanist Learning, 950-1150," *Deutsche Vierteljahrsschrift für Literaturwissenschaft und Geistesgeschichte* 61 (1987): 569-616.

[3] See the study by Rolf Köhn, "Schulbildung und Trivium im lateinischen Hochmittelalter und ihr möglicher praktischer Nutzen," in *Schulen und Studium im sozialen Wandel des hohen und späten Mittelalters*, ed. Johannes Fried, Vorträge und Forschungen 30 (Sigmaringen, 1986), 203-84.

historical recovery poses problems comparable to the reconstruction of a stage performance from only the scenario and a few notes on the rehearsals. Ethical education at cathedral schools was regarded as more important than its partner, letters.[4] But important or not, it produced no primary texts.

The same is not true of the houses of canons regular that burgeoned since the end of the eleventh century.[5] These communities based the instruction of novices on spiritual formation according to several documents that went under the name "Rule of St. Augustine,"[6] according to Carolingian customs formulated in the *Regula canonicorum* of Aix from 816, and according to customs formulated by individual communities for their own use, often leaning on the previously mentioned documents and the Rule of St. Benedict. The command of St. Augustine that each canon should make himself an example for all others to imitate translated into formal arrangements and an ethos of life in which virtually the entire house could regard itself as a school.[7] The duty of teaching through example was for canons regular what pastoral duties were for secular clergy. It also distinguished them from monastic communities, in which teaching and learning had a very different status and could not be regarded as an entirely legitimate activity of monks.[8]

---

[4] John of Salisbury claimed in the *Metalogicon* that any philosophy that did not bear fruit in *cultus virtutis* and the guidance of conduct was "futile and false" (*Ioannis Saresberiensis episcopi Carnotensis Metalogicon*, prologue, ed. Clemens C. I. Webb (Oxford, 1929), 4. Cf. also ibid. 1.24, p. 55 (ethics, which confers *decoris gratia*, the most excellent of the branches of learning).

[5] See the fundamental works by Charles Dereine, *Les chanoines réguliers au diocèse de Liège avant Saint Norbert*, Mémoires, Académie royale de Belgique, 2d ser., vol. 47 (Brussels, 1952); "Chanoines," in *Dictionnaire d'histoire et de géographie ecclésiastiques*, vol. 12 (Paris, 1953), 353–405; "Vie commune, règle de saint Augustin et chanoines réguliers au xie siècle," *Revue d'histoire ecclésiastique* [*RHE*] 41 (1946): 365–406; "Les origines de Prémontré," *RHE* 42 (1947): 352–78; see also J. C. Dickinson, *The Origins of the Austin Canons and Their Introduction into England* (London, 1950); Caroline Walker Bynum, *Docere verbo et exemplo: An Aspect of Twelfth-Century Spirituality*, Harvard Theological Studies 31 (Missoula, Montana, 1979); eadem, "The Spirituality of Regular Canons in the Twelfth Century: A New Approach," *Medievalia et Humanistica*, n.s., 4 (1973): 3–24; Jean Châtillon, "La crise de l'église aux xie et xiie siècles et les origines des grandes fédérations canoniales," *Revue d'histoire de la spiritualité* 53 (1977): 3-45; M.-D. Chenu, "Monks, Canons, and Laymen in Search of the Apostolic Life," in his *Nature, Man, and Society in the Twelfth Century: Essays of New Theological Perspectives in the Latin West*, trans. Jerome Taylor and Lester K. Little (Chicago, 1968), 202–38; Ludo Milis, "Ermites et chanoines réguliers au xiie siècle," *Cahiers de civilisation médiévale* 22 (1979): 39–80.

[6] On the so-called Rule of St. Augustine, see Luc Verheijen, *La Règle de saint Augustin*, 2 vols. (Paris, 1967).

[7] Bynum's *Docere verbo et exemplo* is the standard study of this phenomenon and the works that express it.

[8] See for instance Bynum, *Docere verbo et exemplo*, 4–5, 18–21; Philippe Delhaye, "L'organisation scolaire au xiie siècle," *Traditio* 5 (1947): 225–34.

These communities produced two kinds of documents that are the best evidence for education in *mores* from the twelfth century: the *consuetudines* of the house,[9] which ordinarily include detailed instructions for the reception, initiation, and instruction of novices; and tracts that reflect on the nature and goals of the training of novices.[10] The earliest of these is Hugh of St. Victor's *De institutione novitiorum* written probably in the early 1120s.[11]

The community of canons regular at St. Victor of Paris in the first half of the twelfth century has left the best documentation on ethical training from the period. The combination of its richly detailed customary, the *Liber ordinis Sancti Victoris*,[12] and Hugh's *De institutione* gives us a uniquely clear picture of this instruction from the heyday of medieval humanism in France. Reading these works along with other tracts and letters from St. Victor gives us a picture of the life and teaching in that community united by a common core of ethical thought and a common ethical motive.[13]

---

[9] On customaries, see Dereine, "Chanoines," 386-91; idem, "Coutumiers et ordinaires de chanoines réguliers," *Scriptorium* 5 (1951): 107-13; idem, "Les coutumiers de Saint-Quentin de Beauvais et de Springiersbach," *RHE* 43 (1948): 411-42; idem, "Saint-Ruf et ses coutumes aux xie et xiie siècles," *Revue bénédictine* 59 (1949): 161-82; Josef Siegwart, *Die Consuetudines des Augustiner-Chorherrenstiftes Marbach im Elsass (12. Jahrhundert)*, Spicilegium Friburgense 10 (Freiburg, 1965), 4-14.

[10] Bynum, *Docere verbo et exemplo*, is the best guide to sources.

[11] On the date of the work, see Damien Van den Eynde, *Essai sur la succession et la date des écrits de Hugues de Saint-Victor*, Spicilegium Pontificii Athenaei Antoniani 13 (Rome, 1960), 113-15. Van den Eynde places it just after the *Didascalicon*, that is, prior to 1125. But Roger Baron is sceptical about a specific dating: *Études sur Hugues de Saint-Victor* (Paris, 1963), 69-89, esp. 71.

[12] *Liber ordinis Sancti Victoris Parisiensis*, ed. L. Jocqué and L. Milis, CCCM 61 (Turnhout, 1984). See Fourier Bonnard, *Histoire de l'Abbaye royale et de l'ordre des chanoines réguliers de St.-Victor de Paris*, 2 vols. (Paris, 1904-7), 1:47-48; Jean Châtillon, *Théologie, spiritualité et métaphysique dans l'œuvre oratoire d'Achard de Saint-Victor*, Études de philosophie médiévale 58 (Paris, 1969), 63-66. Jocqué is preparing a historical study of the *Liber*.

[13] On the school of St. Victor, see Bonnard, *Histoire* 1:85-140; Beryl Smalley, *The Study of the Bible in the Middle Ages*, 3d ed. (Oxford, 1983), 83-195; Jean Châtillon, "De Guillaume de Champeaux à Thomas Gallus: Chronique d'histoire littéraire et doctrinale de l'école de Saint-Victor," *Revue du moyen âge latin* 8 (1952): 139-62 and 247-72; idem, "Les écoles de Chartres et de Saint-Victor," in *La scuola nell'occidente latino dell'alto medioevo*, vol. 2, Settimane di studio del Centro Italiano di studi sull'alto medioevo 19 (Spoleto, 1972), 795-839; idem, *Théologie, spiritualité et métaphysique*, 53-85; M.-D. Chenu, "Civilisation urbaine et théologie: L'école de Saint-Victor au xiie siècle," *Annales* 29 (1974): 1253-63; Jean-Pierre Willesme, "Saint-Victor au temps d'Abélard," *Abélard en son temps: Actes du colloque international organisé a l'occasion du 9e centenaire de la naissance de Pierre Abélard* (Paris, 1981), 95-105; Stephen C. Ferruolo, *The Origins of the University: The Schools of Paris and their Critics, 1100-1215* (Stanford, 1985), 27-44. Earlier works by E. Michaud, *Guillaume de Champeaux et les écoles de Paris au xiie siècle* (Paris, 1867), and by Martin Grabmann, *Die Geschichte der scholastischen Methode*, vol. 2 (Freiburg, 1911; rpt. 1957), 229-323, are still valuable.

It also helps fill out an important aspect of the humanism of Hugh of St. Victor, easily overlooked, since it stands in the shadow of his major work on liberal studies, the *Didascalicon*.[14]

HUGH ON *MORES*: *DE INSTITUTIONE NOVITIORUM*

The *De institutione* is one of Hugh of St. Victor's most popular works (172 manuscripts have survived, as compared to 125 for the *Didascalicon*) and it is one of his oddest. As a tract of spiritual instruction, it lacks the gravity, coherence, and systematic conception of other representatives of the genre (like Hrabanus Maurus's *De institutione clericorum* and Philip of Harvengt's work of the same title). Regarded alongside comparable works, it appears downright eccentric. It reads like a first draft. The organizing principle is a quotation from Psalm 118: "Bonitatem et disciplinam et scientiam doce me."[15] But the work is exclusively about *disciplina*. Hugh treats *scientia* briefly, essentially as a category of ethical learning,[16] and covers *bonitas* with almost jocular brevity in the final line of the work: "We have said these few things to you, brothers, concerning learning and discipline. As for goodness, pray that God give it to you" ("Haec vobis, fratres, de scientia et disciplina interim nos diximus: Bonitatem vero orate ut vobis det Deus," 952B). From beginning to end the work is about how to behave and how to learn good behavior.[17] Typical of the work's priorities is that the chapter on gesturing takes up six full columns in the *Patrologia* edition (938A–943D), while the chapter on sacred Scriptures takes up nineteen lines, barely half a column (933D–934A).

Its religious intent deserves a more critical analysis than it has received. It is not easy to understand as preparation for the apostolic life. Although this is not the place to treat the question in detail, an example or two

---

[14] Roger Baron, in his *Science et sagesse chez Hugues de Saint-Victor* (Paris, 1957), defines Hugh's humanism in terms of thought, not behavior. See p. 95: "L'humanisme de Hugues et essentiellement un humanisme de pensée. Il est à la recherche de la vérité."

[15] PL 176:925C.

[16] See PL 176:927A: "[scientia] quae ad institutionem recte et honeste vivendi pertinet. . . ."

[17] Cf. Baron, *Science et sagesse*, p. xxix n. 48: "On pourrait se demander si le contenu de cet ouvrage (qui traite surtout du comportement extérieur) est en accord avec ce que nous savons de Hugues." Baron excuses the work referring to Hugh's comment that everything is worth learning. But the suggestion that it is an inferior work, qualifying for Hugh's authorship by a generous extension of boundaries, does it an injustice. It is in a sense the heart of Hugh's and of Victorine thinking. Jean-Claude Schmitt in his recent book, *La raison des gestes dans l'occident médiéval* (Paris, 1990), also reads the work as aimed basically at externals, and is the first to place it in the context: the decorum of gesturing. He also suggests the proximity of Hugh's lessons to humanism (193–94) and to courtly manners (197). He also points out the importance of the "aesthetic dimension" to Hugh's instruction (178).

HUMANISM AND ETHICS AT THE SCHOOL OF ST. VICTOR

can characterize the problem. The purpose of the work, stated in the prologue, is to show the way to God through the "discipline of virtue" to men to whom "all earthly glory and beauty is as a heap of dung" (". . . omnem gloriam atque decorem quasi stercora reputatis," 926C). But this purpose is almost wholly absorbed in matters of external conduct. The fervent conjuring of *contemptus mundi* and the apostolic life in the prologue gives way to lessons on walking, talking, gesturing, and eating.

In its second half the work takes on a tone that Hugh himself describes as satirical. In a number of passages he shows a quality I have not found in any other work of his, a sense of humor. Here he describes ill-disciplined gesturing:

> Some men are incapable of listening without jaws agape, and as if meaning entered the mind via the mouth they open it wide to take in the words of the speaker. And others (far worse!), when they do something or listen to someone, stick out their tongue like a thirsty dog and revolve it around their mouth like a millstone, twisting their lips from the effort. Others stick out their finger while speaking, raise their eyebrows, and roll their eyes; or they stand rooted to the spot in profound meditation and an outward pretense of some inner magnificence.[18]

It goes on in this vein until Hugh interrupts to remind himself that he is teaching, not writing satire, and that modesty and restraint are called for.[19] But the satire persists and the *modestia* he conjures is put aside to make way for it.[20]

---

[18] "Sunt enim quidam qui nisi buccis patentibus auscultare nesciunt, et quasi per os sensus ad cor influere debeat, palatum ad verba loquentis aperiunt. Alii (quod adhuc pejus est!) in agendo vel audiendo quasi canes sitientes linguam protendunt, et ad singulas actiones velut molam labia torquendo circumducunt. Alii loquentes digitum extendunt, supercilia erigunt, et oculos in orbem rotantes, aut profunda quadam consideratione defigentes, cujusdam intrinsecus magnificentiae conatus ostendunt" (PL 176:941C-D).

[19] Chap. 12 (after quoting Horace): "Sed ne forte satiram potius quam doctrinam edere videamur . . . modestiae hic quoque oblivisci non debemus" (PL 176:942C).

[20] An especially rich passage is in chap. 19, on table manners: "Caution is required in the choice of food, lest one request things excessively lavish and refined, or rare and unusual. Nor should one desire things prepared in an excessively sumptuous or refined way. . . . But there are some men whose gorges are afflicted with a quite laughable infirmity, in that they cannot swallow anything that is not rich and delicate. And if on occasion sparse and ordinary food is offered them, they pass it by, offering frivolous excuses, as for instance, that it will cause them indigestion or asthma or headaches. Others disdain culinary delicacies and luxuries with great constancy, but at the same time despise altogether the common cuisine in a way equally intolerable. They demand new and unusual kinds of food, so that often for the sake of one man's stomach, a throng of servants must run through all the nearby villages to return at length with some rare roots plucked from distant desert mountains, or with a few little fishies fished through enormous effort from the deep, or with strawberries plucked out of season from the thirsting bramble bushes, all this to quell the petulance of one man's appetite" ("Observatio in eo quid sumat, id est ut neque nimis pretiosa et

The work's stated intention is at odds with its tone and contents. In its preoccupation with external decorum, it omits the major themes of the Benedictine and Augustinian traditions.[21]

RECTE VIVENDI SCIENTIA — DISCIPLINA VIVENDI

I will argue that the themes and concerns of the *De institutione* are dictated by classical models. Its dissonances are the unresolved contradictions between two ethical traditions which Hugh was combining. The relation of ancient Roman ethics to Christian ethics was a problem that faced twelfth-century society generally. Abelard with his keen eye for intellectual irresolution attempted a serious reconciliation of the two in his "Dialogue between a Christian, a Philosopher, and a Jew,"[22] subordinating the classical to the Christian tradition and deriving all virtues from Christian *caritas*.

Whatever the discursive success of such resolutions in early and high Scholasticism, the classical tradition continued to loom, its subtlety, humanity, and eloquence evident to Christian writers whose ethical traditions stressed renunciation of the world, not the reasoned guidance of life in the world.[23] Roger Bacon was to concede outright the superiority of the ancients:

delicata expetat, nec nimis rara et insolita requirat, nec nimis laute et accurate praeparata concupiscat. ... Sunt namque quidam quorum fauces satis ridicula infirmitate aegrotant, quae nisi pinguia et delicata deglutire non possunt. Et si quando eis parci aut frugales cibi oblati fuerint, statim aut indigestionem stomachi aut pectoris siccitatem, aut obripilationem capitis, aut si qua sunt talia, ad frivolas excusationes praetendunt. Alii delicias et luxum ciborum magna constantia aspernantur, sed ab eis iterum non minori aut tolerabiliori petulantia communium cibariorum usus omnino despicitur. Nova quaedam et insolita ciborum genera exquirunt, ita ut saepe propter unius ventrem hominis per omnes circum pagos turba famulorum discurrat, et vix tandem vel ignotas de desertis procul montibus radices evellendo vel pauculos de imis gurgitibus profunda scrutatione pisciculos trahendo, sive intempestiva de arentibus rubetis arbuta colligendo, unius appetitus petulantiam compescere queat," PL 176:950A-B).

[21] The work does not treat fasting, penance, self-denial, and mortification of the flesh. *Obedientia*, the dominant virtue in the Benedictine Rule, occurs three times in the entire work (PL 176:931A and 933A), two of the occurrences in a single sentence, subordinated to the topic of following examples (933A). Chastity, which looms large in both the rules of Benedict and Augustine, is not mentioned. *Caritas* does not occur in the work. This omission gains profile against a passage from Hugh's work *De scripturis et scriptoribus sacris:* the philosophers of the gentiles wrote books on ethics, he says, but they sever the members from the body of goodness, which has no life apart from charity (PL 175:9-10).

[22] Peter Abelard, *Dialogus inter Philosophum, Iudaeum et Christianum*, ed. Rudolf Thomas (Stuttgart-Bad Cannstatt, 1970). On Abelard's ethical thought, see D. E. Luscombe, *Peter Abelard's "Ethics": An Edition with Introduction, English Translation and Notes* (Oxford, 1971), introduction; also Ermenegildo Bertola, "La dottrina morale di Pietro Abelardo," *RTAM* 55 (1988): 53-71.

[23] Bernard of Clairvaux's *De consideratione* is a serious effort at a Christian ethic for the active life free of influence from classical ethics.

The beauty of the moral sentences is a delight. . . . We should receive them all the more avidly, since we Christians who philosophize are able to attain neither their depth of insight into wisdom nor their degree of elegance in persuasion.[24]

Hugh of St. Victor, while maintaining the superiority of Christian to ancient Roman ethics, owes much more to the latter in his *De institutione*. It would be appropriate to turn Hugh's criticism of pagan ethics (n. 21 above) against his own work: he deals with a few members from the body of virtue and pays no attention to their source, *caritas*.

DISCIPLINA

"Discipline" is the central ethical/pedagogical conception of the *De institutione novitiorum*. It occurs in a variety of formulations: *disciplina virtutis, morum disciplina* describe the training of novices; the abbey is the *schola disciplinae; custodia disciplinae* is the maintenance of acquired virtue through vigilant self-examination; the human face is the *speculum disciplinae;* the end point of ethical learning is the *forma disciplinae; disciplina vivendi* is another term for ethics. It designates both the content and the process of ethical training ("Sunt . . . loca . . . pro disciplina et instructione morum," 946A; ". . . in illis locis ubi de disciplina agendum est . . . ," 946B).

Throughout Hugh's works "discipline" is the process of learning virtue, the central activity of ethical education. The word has no other general area of application,[25] except in the *Didascalicon* where it occurs in the

---

[24] ". . . delectat sententiarum moralium pulcritudo. . . . Et tanto avidius recipiendae sunt, quanto nos philosophantes Christiani nescimus de tanta morum sapientia percogitare, nec tam eleganter persuadere" (Roger Bacon, *Opus Majus* 7.3.15, ed. John H. Bridges, 3 vols. [Oxford, 1900; rpt. Frankfurt, 1964], 2:322).

[25] Even in *Didascalicon* the major area of reference of *disciplina* is ethical. Cf. *Hugonis de Sancto Victore Didascalicon De Studio Legendi: A Critical Text*, ed. Charles Henry Buttimer, The Catholic University of America Studies in Medieval and Renaissance Latin 10 (Washington, D.C., 1939), praef., pp. 2–3: ". . . legentibus vitae suae disciplinam praescribit . . ."; 3.12, p. 61: ". . . cavendum ei qui quaerit scientiam, ut non negligat disciplinam"; 1.11, p. 22: [*practica*] "quae morum disciplinam instituit"; 3.6, p. 57: [the three things necessary to study: *natura, exercitium, disciplina*] "disciplina, ut laudabiliter vivens mores cum scientia componat"; same passage in *De modo dicendi et meditandi*, PL 176:877B–C. Cf. also *Epitome Dindimi in philosophiam* 2.19, *Hugonis de Sancto Victore Opera propaedeutica*, ed. Roger Baron, University of Notre Dame Publications in Mediaeval Studies 20 (Notre Dame, 1966), 195: "Ethica . . . ordinem modumque uirtutum ac morum disciplinam, que ad probitatem et religionem spectant, instituit"; ibid. 2.22, p. 196: "Ethica moralis interpretatur, ex re nomen sumens, quia morum disciplinam instituit"; *Expositio in Hierarchiam Coelestem S. Dionysii* 1.1: [*ethica*] "modum vivendi rectum, et disciplinae formam secundum virtutum instituta disponit" (PL 175:927B); *De arca Noe morali* 2.6: [mere knowledge is not useful in itself,

III

conventional sense of *disciplina* = *ars*, and *disciplinae* = "the disciplines."[26] The singularity of Hugh's usage is apparent in the definition he gives in *De institutione* (and in the fact that he gives a definition at all, which suggests that the term is not part of a shared conceptual vocabulary):

> Discipline is good and proper behavior; to attain it one must not only avoid evil but also strive to appear above reproach in all things that one does well. Discipline is also the governed movement of all members of the body and a seemly disposition in every state and action.[27]

This definition expressly limits its meaning to an etiquette of conduct, bearing, control, and governance of the body. It also insists that good is constituted not just in the performance of good and omission of evil acts but also in the *appearance* of goodness, its outward semblance. Goodness should be visible in the governed movement of the body.

We need to supply a context in which the uniqueness of this definition becomes evident. Hugh is speaking an ethical language that he does not share with monastic tradition or with the traditions of canons regular, where *disciplina* as a process of ethical training ordinarily meant the teaching and learning of the rule, or simply the rule itself,[28] and had nothing like the

unless one strives to imitate the virtues he admires in others and to make them his own] "per exercitium disciplinae et formam recte vivendi" (PL 176:640A). Jerome Taylor, *The "Didascalicon" of Hugh of St. Victor: A Medieval Guide to the Arts* (New York, 1961), 213 n. 49, refers to Cicero, Quintilian, Augustine, and Boethius as sources for the idea, but qualifies it: "Note, however, that in the words which follow Hugh gives his own definition to each term, altering particularly the sense of *disciplina* from 'art' to moral excellence." See also Ferruolo, *Origins*, 37–38, on the unconventional narrowing of *disciplina:* ". . . Hugh defines discipline not as academic training but as moral excellence. This definition seems intended to suggest the clear advantage of studying at St. Victor, where the rules of learning were inseparable from the rules of the canonical life."

[26] *Didascalicon* 1.11, ed. Buttimer, p. 20: "logicae peritia disciplinae"; 1.11, p. 22: "disciplinae exordium" (= the invention of the arts); 2.1, p. 23: "artes et disciplinae"; 2.1, p. 24: "disciplina . . . quae in speculatione consistit et per solam explicatur ratiocinationem"; 2.6, p. 30: "astronomicae disciplinae peritia."

[27] "Disciplina est conversatio bona et honesta, cui parum est mala non facere, sed studet etiam in iis quae bene agit per cuncta irreprehensibilis apparere. Item disciplina est membrorum omnium motus ordinatus, et dispositio decens in omni habitu et actione" (chap. 10, PL 176:935A–B).

[28] Common formulations in rules and constitutions are *regularis disciplina, canonica disciplina, monachica disciplina, disciplina ecclesiastica, disciplina claustralis,* and *disciplina ordinis*. Fairly standard is Sigebert of Gembloux's description of the education of his teacher, Abbot Olbert: "in disciplina monachica regulariter nutritus" (*Gesta abbatum Gemblacensium* 26, MGH SS 8 [Hannover, 1848], 536, line 4). Cf. also Ulrich of Cluny, *Consuetudines antiquiores Cluniacenses* 2.4: "quia sermo est de instituendis novitiis . . . per ordinem dicatur de ea disciplina [= the rule] qua jugiter ille tenetur qui nobiscum voluerit conversari" (PL 149:704D–705A). These examples and the monastic usage generally are consistent with patristic usage. Cf. Walter Dürig, "'Disciplina': Eine Studie zum Bedeutungsumfang des Wortes in der Sprache der Liturgie und der Väter," *Sacris Erudiri* 4 (1952): 245–79; also

profile it has in the *De institutione novitiorum*. We can contrast it with an instructive passage from the *Constitutiones* of Springiersbach on the reception and "discipline" of novices. It distinguishes between two kinds of lay converts: the one fit by youth and mental aptitude to study letters and become clerics; the other somewhat older and duller of mind. The latter should imitate the canonical life and be governed under a rule by means of a discipline appropriate to them:

> alii prouectiores et natura hebetiores in eo, quo sunt statu, imitantur uitam canonicam et sub quadam regula positi reguntur per congruam sibi disciplinam.[29]

In a "tracking" system of teaching novices, the older and duller of mind are assigned "merely" to discipline under "some rule." The suggestion that "discipline" is the slow track was not thinkable at St. Victor, where, on the contrary, ethical discipline was a major attraction to recruits, even to those who had completed a program of liberal studies elsewhere, as was the case with Godfrey of St. Victor (see pp. 73–74 below).

Disciplina morum, disciplina vivendi, and other terms for ethical training from the *De institutione*[30] form part of the tradition of moral training inherited from classical antiquity and taught in worldly courts at least since Carolingian times and at courts and cathedral schools since Ottonian times.[31] This is the tradition that asserts itself strongly and with the appearance of anomaly in Hugh's *De institutione,* and it is taken over by other canonical and monastic communities in the course of the twelfth century.[32] A good

---

M.-D. Chenu, "Disciplina," *Revue des sciences philosophiques et théologiques* 25 (1936): 686–92. I have found nothing to compare with Hugh's definition, *disciplina = ordinatus motus corporis.*

[29] *Consuetudines canonicorum regularium Springirsbacenses-Rodenses* 40, ed. Stefan Weinfurter, CCCM 48 (Turnhout, 1978), 124 (par. 233).

[30] *Disciplina virtutis* (PL 176:925B); *scientia vere discretionis* (926A); *scientia ... ad institutionem recte et honeste vivendi* (927A); *recte vivendi scientia* (927A); *schola virtutum* (931B); *schola disciplinae* (933D); *peritia bene agendi* (932C). A useful comparison with the last formulation: a letter from the canons of Worms to their colleagues at Bamberg ca. 1115 asking for support of their newly elected bishop, who had studied in Bamberg and acquired *litterarum scientia, rerum agendarum pericia, honestas morum, gratia discretionum* (Udalrici codex, ep. 172, *Monumenta Bambergensia,* vol. 5 of *Bibliotheca rerum germanicarum,* ed. Ph. Jaffé [Berlin, 1869], 305).

[31] See Jaeger, "Cathedral Schools and Humanist Learning."

[32] Cf. Adam of Perseigne, *Lettres: Texte latin, introduction, traduction et notes,* ed. Jean Bouvet, Sources Chrétiennes 66, Textes monastiques d'occident 4 (Paris, 1960), Ep. 5.59, p. 124: "Bonitatem, inquit, et disciplinam et scientiam doce me [Ps 118:66]. ... Maturum quippe reddit hominem disciplina quae est membrorum omnium motus ordinatus et compositio decens in omni habitu et actione." The Pseudo-Vincent of Beauvais compendium, *Speculum morale* 1.3.42, vol. 3 of *Speculum maius* (Douai, 1624; rpt. 1964), 307–8, quotes Hugh's definition of discipline in full.

indication of its affinities with court/courtly education is that the *De institutione* is appropriated in the thirteenth century by courtesy books and "mirrors of princes."³³

Disciplina vivendi and *bene vivendi disciplina* are originally Ciceronian formulations. In the *Tusculan Disputations* Cicero explains the late blooming interest of his countrymen in philosophy by representing their civic activities as a surrogate philosophy, or rather a genuine one, a discipline of life. They preferred to practice "that most bountiful of disciplines, the discipline of living well" (*bene vivendi disciplina*). They pursued this more in their lives than in their writings: "Vita magis quam litteris persecuti sunt."³⁴ The phrase does not occur in Seneca or Quintilian. Isidore varied it to define philosophy as "rerum humanarum divinarumque cognitio cum studio bene vivendi coniuncta."³⁵ And from the early Middle Ages on the two were joined as the constituents of philosophy. Alcuin echoes Isidore:

> Philosophia est naturarum inquisitio, rerum humanarum divinarumque cognitio. . . . Est quoque philosophia honestas vitae, studium bene vivendi, meditatio mortis, contemptus saeculi. . . .³⁶

Hincmar of Rheims in his letter of instruction to Louis the German represents *disciplina* as the cultivation of *mores:*

> The king's court is indeed called a school, that is, a course of studies, because it not only consists of schoolmen, men bred on learning and well trained in the conventional way, but is rather a school in its own right, which we can take to mean a place of discipline, that is correction, since it corrects men's behavior, their bearing, their speech and actions, and in general holds them to the norms of a good life.³⁷

---

³³ Vincent of Beauvais borrows wholesale from *De institutione* in his *De eruditione filiorum nobilium*, ed. Arpad Steiner, The Mediaeval Academy of America Publication No. 32 (Cambridge, Mass., 1938). His chap. 31 borrows extensively from *De institutione*, taking over the definition of *disciplina* word for word, and Hugh's work is quoted and adapted in many other passages. Aegidius Romanus adapts Hugh's *De institutione* in his influential *De regimine principum*, e.g., 2.2.13: "Gestus autem dicuntur quilibet motus membrorum ex quibus iudicari possunt motus animae. . . . Disciplina autem, quae est danda in gestibus, est, ut quodlibet membrum ordinetur ad opus sibi debitum. Homo enim non audit per os, sed per aurem" (*D. Aegidii Romani . . . De regimine principum libri III* [Rome, 1556; rpt. Frankfurt, 1968], 192r–v). My thanks to David Fowler for pointing out this passage to me.

³⁴ Cicero, *Tusculan Disputations* 4.5–6. Cf. ibid. 4.17; *De officiis* 2.15.

³⁵ Isidore, *Etymologiae* 2.24.1, ed. W. M. Lindsay (Oxford, 1911), vol. 1 (unpaged).

³⁶ Alcuin, *De dialectica* 1, PL 101:952A. Also Hrabanus Maurus, *De universo* 15.1, PL 111:413B.

³⁷ "Et ideo domus regis scola dicitur, id est disciplina; quia non tantum scolastici, id est disciplinati et bene correcti, sunt, sicut alii, sed potius ipsa scola, quae interpretatur disciplina, id est correctio, dicitur, quae alios habitu, incessu, verbo et actu atque totius

This brings us close to the context in which Hugh places discipline. Both texts identify it with the teaching and correction of *habitus, incessus, verbum et actus.*

The author of the collection of letters from the late eleventh century known as the *Regensburg Rhetorical Letters* speaks a distinctly Ciceronian ethical language. He picks up the idea of life as an exercise in discipline as opposed to writing and reading, adapting the passage from *Tusculan Disputations* quoted above:

> . . . eos audire delectat, qui vivendi viam magis disciplina quam literis persecuntur. . . .[38]

Later in the work the burdened statesman who is one of the fictive authors finds consolation in the philosophy of those men who regard their discipline as a law of living, not a means of learned ostentation.[39]

WALKING AND GESTURING: *INCESSUS, MOTUS CORPORIS*

The ethical vocabulary of *De institutione* deserves a detailed study. Its leading terms and concepts are discretion or judgment (*discretio*), moderation and the golden mean (*mensuram et modum tenere; rationis moderamen*), the examined life (*custodia; assidua inspectio operum et morum suorum; facta sua circumspicere*), imitation of the examples of good men, renewal and reformation of the self (*ad novae vitae similitudinem reformari; se reformare in melius*), and gentleness and modesty of mind which display themselves in speech, disposition, gestures, and carriage of the body. It is important to stress the role of outward display as the guarantor of inner harmony and well-governed virtues in the school of St. Victor. This is by far the dominant concern of Hugh's teaching: gesture and carriage (*usus corporis, gestus, motus corporis*). It is the feature on which the present study concentrates.

Hugh's definition of discipline as "membrorum omnium motus ordinatus, et dispositio decens in omni habitu et actione" (chap. 10, 935B) shows the cooperation of Christian and classical traditions and takes us into an essential element of ethical training in both the religious and the secular life. The

bonitatis continentia corrigat" (*Epistola synodi Carisiacensis* 12, MGH *Leges* 2, *Capit.* 2 [Hannover, 1893], 436, lines 2–6).

[38] *Die Regensburger rhetorischen Briefe*, Ep. 16, in *Briefsammlungen der Zeit Heinrichs IV.*, ed. C. Erdmann and N. Fickermann, MGH *Briefe der deutschen Kaiserzeit* 5 (Weimar, 1950), 336. Cf. ibid., Ep. 1, p. 274, lines 15–16: [a cleric in the service of the emperor returns to "philosophy"] "quia ad recte vivendi viam studio et disciplina veniendum est."

[39] Ep. 22, p. 348, lines 24–25: ". . . qui disciplinam suam non ostentationem scientiae, sed legem vitae putent." Cf. Cicero, *Tusculan Disputations* 2.11.

III

idea that elevates these external questions of etiquette and decorum to a major object of ethical discipline is the congruence of external carriage and inner state. The composition of the inner world is the job of *ethica*, and for Hugh of St. Victor, the job begins with the body:

> Just as inconstancy of mind brings forth irregular motions of the body, so also the mind is strengthened and made constant when the body is restrained through the process of discipline. And little by little, the mind is composed inwardly to calm, when through the custody of discipline its irregular motions are not allowed free play outwardly. The perfection of virtue is when the members of the body are governed and ordered through the inner custody of the mind.[40]

This means that virtue is acquired by physical training and restraint. For a teacher with this presupposition, *usus corporis*[41] becomes identical to *cultus virtutis*.

Hugh's lengthy chapter on gesturing takes his morality of carriage to its logical conclusion: the body can be read for the virtues of the mind. He infers from various styles of gesture and carriage the attendant virtue or vice:

> There are six kinds of reprehensible gesture and movement, namely, an effeminate glide, a swagger, a listless shuffle, a hasty stride, a wanton strut, and a turbulent dash. The effeminate step indicates lasciviousness; the swagger, slovenliness; the shuffle, laziness; the stride, inconstancy; the strut, pride; the dash, wrathfulness.[42]

The principle of governance is applied to the control of the body, since "the body is a kind of republic" ("Est enim quasi quaedam respublica corpus humanum," 943A), each member of which has its own duty; vice is when one usurps the duty of another. The ordinate functioning of all together produces *concordia universitatis*. His elaborations on this topic also are puzzling and alien: "the eyes should see, the ears hear, nostrils smell ... ,

---

[40] "Sicut enim de inconstantia mentis nascitur inordinata motio corporis, ita quoque dum corpus per disciplinam stringitur, animus ad constantiam solidatur. Et paulatim intrinsecus mens ad quietem componitur, cum per disciplinae custodiam mali motus ejus foras fluere non sinuntur. Integritas ergo virtutis est, quando per internam mentis custodiam ordinate reguntur membra corporis" (chap. 10, PL 176:935B–C).

[41] Hugh gives three contexts for "propriety in every act" ("quid deceat ... in omni actu ... ," PL 176:927A): worship and the liturgy, "human obligations" ("humana officia"), and the governance of the body ("quae ad usum corporis pertinent," 927B). The focus of *De institutione* is exclusively on the latter two.

[42] "... hic sex modis reprehensibilis invenitur, scilicet si est aut mollis, aut dissolutus, aut tardus, aut citatus, aut procax, aut turbidus. Mollis significat lasciviam, dissolutus negligentiam, tardus pigritiam, citatus inconstantiam, procax superbiam, turbidus iracundiam" (chap. 12, PL 176:938A–B).

the hands manipulate, the feet walk . . ." (". . . oculi videant, aures audiant, nares olfaciant, os loquatur, manus operentur, pedes ambulent . . . ," 943B). Moderation is the virtue that holds contrary vices, to which the body is prone, in check and produces a particular grace:

> . . . a man's gestures ought to be graceful without effeminacy, nonchalant without swagger, grave without listlessness. . . . The turbulent dash tempers the effeminate gesture, and the effeminate tempers the turbulent . . . because the median line between opposing vices is virtue.[43]

Of the various surprises the work affords the reader—primed to read a work of spiritual instruction for men to whom all worldliness is bitter as absinth—this strict identification of *cultus corporis* and *cultus virtutis* is perhaps the most striking.

The final two-thirds of the tract are concerned with rules for walking, gesturing, dressing, speaking or remaining silent, eating, and drinking.[44] The sense of a random and unorganized sequence of chapters in the first third now ends, and the work is organized around the subject of proper manners in external things.

It is clear from the Victorine customary that novices indeed received rigorous training in the points of etiquette stressed by Hugh.[45] The customary also makes the importance of this training obvious. Its prescripts indicate a life in which virtually every moment in the daily round of rising, performing the liturgy, eating, dressing, and going to bed is governed by rules

---

[43] ". . . gestus hominis in omni actu esse debet gratiosus sine mollitie, quietus sine dissolutione, gravis sine tarditate. . . . Mollem gestum temperat turbidus, et turbidum mollis . . . quia inter vitia contraria medius limes virtus est" (chap. 12, PL 176:943C–D). On the presence of this Aristotelian definition of virtue in the earlier Middle Ages, see C. J. Nederman, "Aristotelian Ethics before the *Nichomachean Ethics:* Alternate Sources of Aristotle's Concept of Virtue in the Twelfth Century," *Parergon*, n.s., 7 (1989): 55–75.

[44] The chapter headings after chap. 10, "Quid sit disciplina, et quantum valeat," take the form "De disciplina servanda in habitu" (chap. 11), ". . . in gestu" (chap. 12), ". . . in locutione" (chap. 13), and after chapters on "quid, cui, ubi, quando, quomodo loquendum," chap. 18 continues with "De disciplina servanda in mensa . . . et primo in habitu et gestu"; chap. 19: "De triplici observatione disciplinae in cibo, et primo quid comedendum"; chap. 20: "Secundo, quantum comedendum"; chap. 21: "Tertio, quomodo comedendum." After a final cautioning to eat not too fast or slowly, the work breaks off abruptly with the advice to pray to God for goodness, Hugh having taught them *scientia* and *disciplina*.

[45] *Liber ordinis*, chap. 22, CCCM 61:106–7, lines 229–42: "In scola diligenter instruendus est de inclinationibus, de *incessu et statu, et omni gestu suo*, et quomodo uestimenta sua in omni actione circa se coaptare debeat, et *membra sua ordinate componere*, oculos demissos habere, submisse et non festinanter loqui. . . . Postremo de omnibus actionibus suis et uerbis. . . . perfecte eum instruat. . . ." Rendered perfect, the novice will be able to hold to "bonum modum et competentem mensuram in omnibus uerbis et actionibus. . . ." Much of the wording is so close to *De institutione* it is clear that Hugh was writing with the *Liber*, at least with the discipline of living it commended, in mind.

of etiquette, proper carriage, considerateness, and good manners—rules that presuppose a rigorous discipline in the areas of behavior presented in the *De institutione*. The *Liber ordinis Sancti Victoris* is exceptional among customaries for its detailed prescriptions and for its insistence on courtesy and humanity in the ordering of the daily life.

The concern with proper gestures, walking, and talking is shared by other houses of canons regular.[46] But its roots in Christian traditions are shallow; prior to the eleventh century they show a minor and peripheral interest in the subjects Hugh deals with. The biblical texts he cites as exempla of proper dress, gait, gesture, and table manners are often pressed into service from contexts that do not fit the concerns of his work well.[47] The Benedictine Rule says nothing about *incessus* and *gestus*, and its prescriptions for dressing and eating are very different from those in Hugh's *De institutione* and the *Liber ordinis Sancti Victoris*.[48] The passing references in the Rule of St. Augustine, the Rule of Chrodegang, and the *Regula canonicorum* of Aix simply do not prepare us for the serious and methodical preoccupation with the subject in Hugh's *De institutione*.

Gesture and carriage as serious pedagogic concerns come from the classical tradition of an orator's education. They are an important part of oratory,

---

[46] Rule of St. Augustine, *Praeceptum* 4.2–3 "Quando proceditis, simul ambulate; cum ueneritis quo itis, simul state. In incessu, in statu, in omnibus motibus uestris nihil fiat quod cuiusquam offendat aspectum . . ." (ed. Verheijen 1:423). Cf. *Regula canonicorum* of Aix (816), chap. 123: ". . . intus forisque non solum habitu et actu, sed etiam ipso incessu inreprehensibiles existant . . ." (ed. A. Werminghoff, *Concilia Aevi Karolini I*, MGH *Leges* 3, vol. 2, pt. 1 [Hannover and Leipzig, 1906; rpt. 1979], 403, lines 20–21); ibid., chap. 131: [enter the church] ". . . non pompatice aut inhoneste vel inconposite, sed cum reverentia . . ." (p. 408, lines 4–5); *Regula clericorum* ("Petrus de Honestis") 1.2: ". . . gravitatem non solum in loquendo vel operando, sed et in eundo vel stando teneant; decorem morum, sanctitatem, honestatem non solum actionum, sed et locutionum habeant" (PL 163:709C); *Consuet. Marbac.*, chap. 3: [the novice given to the charge of a brother] ". . . qui doceat eum regulam, usum et disciplinam monasterii, primum qualiter ambulare, supplicare, stare, sedere debeat, et in omnibus motibus suis signum habere humilitatis . . ." (ed. Siegwart, p. 104, par. 5); *Expositio in Regulam S. Augustini* (Pseudo-Hugh of St. Victor): "Tunc enim religiose vivimus . . . si membra et sensus nostros studeamus restringere, ut non possint lasciviae et levitati deservire . . . ut sit . . . in incessu gravitas, status cum reverentia, motus cum maturitate, habitus cum religione . . ." (PL 176:898C); *Consuet. Springiersbach*, chap. 40: ". . . admonendi sunt [nouitii], ut sint prouidi et circumspecti in incessu, statu, habitu, in omnibus motibus nihil fiat, quod cuiusquam offendat aspectum . . ." (CCCM 48:126, par. 236).

[47] For a biblical attack on *inordinati motus corporis* (PL 176:938B) he cites Proverbs 6:12–13: ". . . vir inutilis graditur ore perverso, annuit oculis terit pede digito loquitur." Against the *mollis* and *procax* gesture (938D) he cites Isaiah 47:1–3: "descende sede in pulverem virgo filia Babylon, sede in terra. . . . tolle molam et mole farinam, denuda turpitudinem tuam discoperi umerum, revela. . . . revelabitur ignominia tua. . . ."

[48] *Benedicti Regula*, ed. Rudolph Hanslik, CSEL 75 (Vienna, 1960), chaps. 6, 7, 39, 40, 55.

since they add the force of personal authority to forceful speech, and when the latter is lacking, they can make up for faults of voice and thought. For Cicero the motion of the body is itself a kind of eloquence: "Est enim actio quasi sermo corporis."[49] Apart from the *De inventione* his writings on oratory were not available to Hugh, but bits of them came to the Middle Ages through other routes, for instance Ambrose, who calls gestures "a kind of voice of the mind."[50]

Cicero includes motions of the body in his discussion of temperance and *decorum* in *De officiis*. When the body and the spirit are in harmony with nature, he says, then the motions (emotions) of each find approbation (1.100). After a long discussion of control of the passions (*motus animi*), he commends *constantia* in all acts, and this brings him to the *motus corporis:*

> ... the propriety to which I refer shows itself also in every deed, in every word, even in every movement and attitude of the body. And in outward, visible propriety there are three elements—beauty, order, and embellishment appropriate to the act it accompanies.[51]

To achieve beauty, order, and appropriate embellishment, we need to follow nature in our motions:

> ... in standing or walking, in sitting or reclining, in our expression, our eyes, or the movements of our hands, let us preserve this decorum. We must avoid especially the two extremes: our conduct and speech should not be effeminate and affected on the one hand, nor coarse and boorish on the other.[52]

The beauty of conduct is of two kinds, he continues. The one called "loveliness" (*venustas*) is feminine, the other (*dignitas*) manly. Let a man therefore avoid any *ornatus* of dress that is not dignified, and the same applies to gesture and motion. The principle to follow is the golden mean (*mediocritas;* cf. 1.130–31). This means that we should walk and gesture neither too slowly nor too fast, since this puts us out of breath, distorts the face, and is a strong indication that inner constancy is lacking:

---

[49] Cicero, *De oratore* 3.222. Cf. *Orator* 55: "Est enim actio quasi corporis quaedam eloquentia. ..."

[50] "Vox quaedam est animi" (Ambrose, *De officiis ministrorum* 1.18.71, PL 16:44C [2d ed., 49A]).

[51] "... decorum illud in omnibus factis, dictis, in corporis denique motu et statu cernitur idque positum est in tribus rebus, formositate, ordine, ornatu ad actionem apto ..." (Cicero, *De officiis* 1.126; translation adapted from Cicero, *De officiis*, trans. Walter Miller, Loeb Classical Library [Cambridge, Mass. and London, 1975], 129).

[52] "... status incessus, sessio accubitio, vultus oculi manuum motus teneat illud decorum. Quibus in rebus duo maxime sunt fugienda, ne quid effeminatum aut molle et ne quid durum aut rusticum sit." (Cicero, *De officiis* 1.128–129; cf. trans. Miller, p. 131).

III

Cavendum autem est, ne aut tarditatibus utamur in ingressu mollioribus . . . aut in festinationibus suscipiamus nimias celeritates, quae cum fiunt, anhelitus moventur, vultus mutantur, ora torquentur; ex quibus magna significatio fit non adesse constantiam (1.131).

In these passages fitting gait and gesture into a philosophy of "natural" behavior, Cicero represents beauty of gesture as a response to and symptom of an inner harmony. Elsewhere he uses the image of the harmonically composed soul playing inaudible music, a kind of visible melody, on the instrument of the body (*Tusc. Disp.* 1.19–20). Grace, beauty, and dignity are the result when inner constancy finds its expression in natural external gestures.

Ambrose picked up some of these ideas and made proper walking and gesturing into an important duty of the Christian statesman. Composed gesture and movements are signs of *verecundia*, reluctance to give offense:

Est etiam in ipso motu, gestu, incessu tenenda verecundia. Habitus enim mentis in corporis statu cernitur. . . . Itaque vox quaedam est animi, corporis motus.[53]

He demands a kind of gesture and movement which bespeak authority, gravity, and tranquillity.[54]

Though it is possible to find occasional praise of good carriage among Carolingian clerics,[55] it clearly is not a prominent topic in that period.

An ideal of elegant bearing based on classical models came to prominence with a new program of education at European cathedral schools in the mid-tenth century. It formed part of the curriculum of *mores*. A portrait from the second half of the eleventh century, striking for the purity of its Ciceronian pedigree, can serve to illustrate some of its ideal virtues. The Bamberg schoolmaster Meinhard wrote to a former student heading off to Cologne, possibly to be groomed for the archbishopric. He admonishes him to imitate the virtues of his father, whom he describes as

---

[53] Ambrose, *De officiis ministrorum* 1.18.71, PL 16:44C–D (2d ed., 48D–49A). Ambrose tells two anecdotes to illustrate the importance of decorous movement: He rejected a friend for membership in the clergy—though his stringent performance of duties commended him—because his gestures were in very poor taste (". . . gestus eius plurimum dedeceret"); another, already a cleric, he ordered never to walk in front of him, because his gait offended his eyes, like a slap in the face (44D–45A [2d ed., 49A]). Both men met bad ends, which Ambrose believes he could have predicted from their way of walking.

[54] Ibid. 1.18.75, PL 16:45B (2d ed., 49C): "Est etiam gressus probabilis, in quo sit species auctoritatis, gravitatisque pondus, tranquillitatis vestigium."

[55] Eigil, *Vita sancti Sturmi*, MGH SS 2 (Hannover, 1829), 366, line 33: "gressu composito." Alcuin urges Charlemagne, "Disce, precor, juvenis, motus moresque venustos. Laudetur toto ut nomen in orbe tuum" (*De rhetorica et virtutibus*, PL 101:949–50). But this classical ideal combining "rhetoric and the virtues" appears to have been restricted to court and civil education.

... a man instructed in every kind of virtue, a man who enjoyed to an astonishing degree all the charm and grace of humanity, qualities visible far and wide not only in his dazzling blaze of manners but also in the bright good humor which shone most graciously from his eyes.[56]

It is also visible in a portrait from the middle of the twelfth century of Bishop Otto of Bamberg, praised by his biographer for his

... special gift of singular fastidiousness ... of elegant and urbane discipline. Never under any circumstances, in eating, drinking, in word, gesture, or dress, would he tolerate anything indecorous ... but rather in every act of the outer man he manifested the harmony within him, conspicuous as he was for his goodness, discipline, and farsighted wisdom.[57]

The ensemble of qualities is called by the name, *elegantia morum, venustas morum, gratia morum, pulchritudo morum*.[58] It makes outward grace and fine bearing into the measure of inner virtue.

This ethic found a prescriptive formulation in the *Moralium dogma philosophorum*, a kind of *summa* of Ciceronian ethics.[59] The authorship of William of Conches has been generally accepted, though not proven.[60]

---

[56] "Est enim vir ille omni genere virtutis instructus, omni lepore humanitatis mirifice conditus, quae in eo non solum flagrantia morum latissime redolet, sed ex ipsa oculorum hilaritate gratiosissime renidet. Atque sic in te animi ornamenta redundent, ut illa ocularis gratia relucet" (*Weitere Briefe Meinhards von Bamberg*, in Erdmann, *Briefsammlungen*, 193, no. 1). Erdmann cannot date the letter exactly; he places it between 1057 and 1088 (see also *Studien zur Briefliteratur Deutschlands im elften Jahrhundert*, MGH *Schriften* 1 [Leipzig, 1938], 282).

[57] "... quandam ... cuiusdam singularis mundicie atque, ut ita dixerim, elegantis et urbane discipline prerogativam habebat, ita ut nichil unquam indecens aut ineptum inhonestumve quid in cibo aut potu, sermone, gestu vel habitu admitteret. Sed in omni officio exterioris hominis, quenam esset composicio interioris, ostendebat, bonitate, disciplina et prudencie cautela conspicuus" (*Herbordi Dialogus de vita S. Ottonis* 2.16, ed. J. Wikarjak and K. Liman, *Monumenta Poloniae Historica*, n.s., vol. 7, fasc. 3 [Warsaw, 1974], 90). The last line raises the question whether the influence of Hugh's *De institutione* shows in this biography written ca. 1155. The resonance of Herbord's *bonitas, disciplina et prudencia* with Hugh's *bonitas, disciplina et scientia* is worth noting. On the diffusion of the *De institutione*, see Rudolf Goy, *Die Überlieferung der Werke Hugos von St. Viktor: Ein Beitrag zur Kommunikationsgeschichte des Mittelalters* (Stuttgart, 1976), esp. 340–67, 496–500. Bavaria was an interested recipient of the work (ibid., 367). But of course the echoes do not require the explanation of direct influence, just a shared ethical language and a curriculum in *mores* at both French and German schools.

[58] See my study, *The Origins of Courtliness: Civilizing Trends and the Formation of Courtly Ideals, 939–1210* (Philadelphia, 1985), 32–34 and 128–52.

[59] *Das Moralium Dogma Philosophorum des Guillaume de Conches: Lateinisch, Altfranzösisch und Mittelniederfränkisch*, ed. John Holmberg (Uppsala, 1929), 77: "intentio ... est summatim docere ethicam Tullianam et Tullium et Senecam imitari."

[60] See Ph. Delhaye, "Une adaption du *De officiis* au xiie siècle: Le *Moralium dogma philosophorum*," *RTAM* 16 (1949): 227–58; 17 (1950): 5–28. See also Holmberg's introduction.

The work dates from the first half of the twelfth century. The only guide to a more specific dating is the uncertain identification of the "Henricus" of the prologue with the young Henry of Anjou, future Henry II of England. Lacking positive evidence of date and authorship, the work cannot be fit into the dossier of connections between William of Conches and Hugh of St. Victor.[61] But the ethical language and concepts shared by Hugh and this Ciceronian-Senecan compendium make the comparison valuable.

The following passages illustrate the proximity of thought and language:

> 1) *Moral. dog. phil.*, p. 42: Modestia est cultum et motum et omnem nostram occupationem ultra defectum et citra excessum sistere. De hac dicit poeta: "Est modus in rebus, sunt certi denique fines. . . ."
>
> *De institutione*, 943B: Secunda est custodia disciplinae in gestu, ut unumquodque membrum id quod facit, eo modo atque mensura faciat quo faciendum est, id est nec plus nec minus. . . .
>
> 2) *Moral. dog. phil.*, p. 42: Malus enim ornatus exterior male composite mentis nuntius est.
>
> *De institutione*, 935B: . . . de inconstantia mentis nascitur inordinata motio corporis. . . .
>
> 3) *Moral. dog. phil.*, p. 42: In corporeo [motu] cauendum est ne in tardationibus adeo molli gressu utamur, ut . . . in festinationibus non suscipiamus nimias celeritates. Que cum fiant, anelitus mouentur, uultus mutantur, ora torquentur; ex quibus magna significatio fit non adesse constanciam. . . . Curandum igitur est ut ratio presit, appetitus obtemperet. Si enim non pareant appetitus rationi . . . non modo animi perturbantur sed etiam corpora.
>
> *De institutione*, 938A–C: Gestus . . . reprehensibilis invenitur . . . si est aut mollis, aut dissolutus, aut tardus, aut citatus. . . . cum mens interius a custodia sui solvitur, membra foris ad omnem actum inordinate commoventur. . . . in omnibus quae agit nullo rationis moderamine gubernatur.

These passages do not argue direct influence, but they certainly indicate shared ethical concepts. The debt to Cicero is obvious in the case of the *Moralium dogma philosophorum;* it is not obvious but palpable in the case of Hugh's work. Hugh is using different words for the same ideas.[62] The comparison makes evident the veiled Ciceronianism fundamental to his work.

---

[61] Taylor's notes to the *Didascalicon*, which constitute an important study of Hugh's intellectual obligations, suggest strong connections between him and William of Conches (see Taylor, *The "Didascalicon" of Hugh of St. Victor*, esp. intro., 6–7, and 160–61 nn. 15, 16).

[62] One example leads the reader to wonder whether Hugh read the work. The *Moral. dog. phil.* treats *providentia* and *circumspectio* one after the other (ed. Holmberg, 9–10). Hugh's chap. 9 urges, ". . . homo . . . sit circumspectus et providus" (PL 176:934B); these virtues foresee *futurum eventum* and *rerum exitus* in *Moral. dog. phil.* (p. 9); in *De institutione* it is the *finis actionis* and *finis operis* (934B–C). The *Moral. dog. phil.* commends caution:

The adaptation of Ciceronian ideas in the *De institutione* still leaves us with the puzzle, why Hugh, in outlining a program of spiritual renewal, placed so little stress on ideals of the apostolic life and so much on a few facets of an ethic inherited ultimately from antiquity and immediately from cathedral schools.

A School for Gentlemen

St. Victor was an urban community, or comparatively urban. It attracted many noble clerics of high learning.[63] It enjoyed royal patronage;[64] a visit from the king was as much to be reckoned with as a visit from the local bishop, and the *Liber ordinis* makes provisions for receiving him.[65] Its connections at the highest levels of church and state administration were excellent.[66] Its school was open to outsiders until approximately the death of Hugh of St. Victor in 1141,[67] and its traditions of ethical training persisted at least until the death of Richard of St. Victor in 1173. As Jean Châtillon suggests, the more communities of canons tend to the monastic life, the more their schools tend to disappear,[68] and accordingly, St. Victor prior to Hugh's death was a non-monastic community, open to the exciting atmosphere of ideas in the other schools of Paris, though conservative in regard to method, intellectual orientation, and ethical training. Dialectic and disputation never found a home there.

Other fashions in aristocratic society at the turn of the century did, however, come to St. Victor; at least they made their way to the door. *De institutione* is directed to nobles. It enjoins on them an aristocratic ethic—its canonical elements notwithstanding—and it warns them against vices typical

---

"Cautio est discernere a uirtutibus uitia uirtutum speciem preferentia"; it helps the cautious avoid deception of *occultiores insidie* (p. 10, lines 18 ff.). Cf. *De institutione:* [through *circumspectio*] "... plane vitium esse dignoscitur, in quo prius sibi animus falso de virtute blandiebatur" (934C), and it helps him avoid future deception if he has succumbed to *insidia inimici* (934D).

[63] Robert of Torigny, *De immutatione ordinis monachorum*, chap. 5: "Sub cujus [i.e., Gilduin's] regimine multi clerici nobiles saecularibus et divinis litteris instructi, ad illum locum habitaturi convenerunt" (PL 202:1313A).

[64] Bonnard, *Histoire*, vol. 1, chaps. 1–3.

[65] *Liber ordinis Sancti Victoris*, chap. 33, CCCM 61:162, lines 168–69: "Si rex uel episcopus uel abbas in capitulum adducitur, fratres assurgentes omnes ei inclinent...."

[66] Dickinson, *Austin Canons*, 86: "Favoured by the highest officials of Church and State, esteemed all over the Western world, the haven of scholars and nursery of bishops, St. Victor's displayed perhaps more than any other house the potential of the regular canonical life."

[67] Smalley, *Study of the Bible*, 83–84; Ferruolo, *Origins*, 30.

[68] Châtillon, "Les écoles de Chartres et de St. Victor," 812.

of the aristocracy, or vices imputed by other writers to the nobles. The passage quoted earlier warning against excessively dainty dishes is a good example (n. 20 above). It presupposes men with delicate palates, sensitive nervous systems, and finicky stomachs (they complain about asthma and indigestion when they are offered coarse food). It also presupposes that they have numbers of servants at their disposal to send for the rare fish and berries that alone will satisfy their tastes.[69] Of course, there may not have been a single novice or member of the community who really indulged in this vice after his entry into the religious life. To have its impact the satire does not require the actual abuse, but it does require the unfulfilled inclination. The barb would be blunted and the humor diluted if none of them kept servants or if they were men to whom rude and impoverished lives, or even ascetic lives of renunciation, were an accepted norm.

The prescriptions on dress and gesture reject fashions of the secular world which other clerics in many places in Europe were attacking throughout the twelfth century. Hugh says that clothes should not be "nimis ... subtilia vel mollia," nor in any way "distorted according to worldly vanity" ("secundum saeculi vanitatem detorta," 936A). He numbers among the vanities clothes that flow too fully and those pulled so tight as to reveal every curve of the body. This he calls shameless turpitude and vain ostentation; such fashions make women, or rather prostitutes, of men, who seem to change their sex along with their clothes (936C–D). Men should show modesty and humility in their clothing. But there are certain hard and rebellious souls, he continues, who can only be reined in with a jagged bit (938A). Then follows the chapter on gesturing already discussed.

The language that Hugh speaks here is widely shared and easy to locate. These vanities and worldly ways are part of a broad wave of fashion that swept the European aristocracy from the middle of the eleventh century on.[70] Worldly fashions may have been as extravagant before that time, but the church reform produced a reaction against them that brought them into sharp profile. From the mid-eleventh century, wherever men touched by the spirit of the reform come into contact with worldly men, complaints like Hugh's surface. The *De institutione* responds in no small part to an

---

[69] The *Liber* in fact forbids guests of whatever rank to bring their own cooks and have special dishes prepared by their own cooks, as Bonnard points out (*Histoire* 1:68): "Just as all guests receive our care, so all must eat our fare" ("... sicut de nostro procurantur, ita etiam et nostras apparationes sustineant, oportet," chap. 17, CCCM 61:69, lines 247–48).

[70] See H. Platelle, "Le problème du scandale: Les nouvelles modes masculines aux xie et xiie siècles," *Revue belge de philologie et d'histoire* 53 (1975): 1071–96; see also Jaeger, *Origins of Courtliness*, 176–94.

infestation of bad manners that became a shared object of attack among clerics who regarded their duty in life as teaching and correcting the laity. And it should not be surprising if this project commended itself to a master responsible for formulating the education of novices at an abbey near Paris attractive to noblemen, a community whose rigorously structured life was conceived as a curriculum and whose "teaching" was exercised in the very act of living that life.

SCHOLA VIRTUTUM: THE BEGINNINGS OF ST. VICTOR AND *VENUSTAS MORUM* AS A CURRICULUM

The threat of a spreading corruption of *mores* was answered not only by polemics but also by a moral discipline aimed at the nobility that made moderated external elegance into the sign of inner virtue. Clerics at worldly courts were the main transmitters of this ethic to the laity, but some houses of canons regular had a role to play in this civilizing process.

The constitutions of Marbach are the earliest rule showing a strong influx of the vocabulary of courtesy.[71] It is tempting to pursue this lead and a possible connection with the urbane humanity of St. Victor, since the author of the earliest sections of this rule, Manegold of Lautenbach, is possibly the same as that Manegold, *modernorum magister magistrorum*, who was the teacher of William of Champeaux. But both this connection and the dating of the Marbach *Constitutiones* are too uncertain. Manegold's contributions to the rule date from around 1103; other sections were added between 1122 and 1136.[72]

---

[71] See the passage from the Marbach constitutions cited in n. 85 below; also chap. 149 (on the prior): "Sit sermo aedificans, vita imitabilis. Sit caritate eminens, mansuetus, humanus, hilaris, severus, largus, cunctis affabilis atque amabilis . . ." (ed. Siegwart, p. 254). On the Latin vocabulary of courtesy, see Jaeger, *Origins of Courtliness*, 127–75.

[72] See Josef Siegwart in the introduction to the *Consuet. Marbac.*, 30–31. On Manegold, see Wilfried Hartmann, "Manegold von Lautenbach und die Anfänge der Frühscholastik," *Deutsches Archiv für Erforschung des Mittelalters* 26 (1970): 47–149. A student from Bamberg who studied at St. Victor in its early years is an important witness to William's teaching. His testimony also bears on the influence of Manegold. He wrote a letter to his prior in Germany (asking for money) and praised William, who "gave up all his possessions to live in some miserable little church to serve only God. There he showed himself kind and devoted to all who came to him, and he received them gratis . . . in the manner of Master Manegold of blessed memory" (". . . omnibus quae possidebat dimissis, in praeterito pascha ad quandam pauperrimam ecclesiolam, soli Deo serviturus, se contulit; ibique postea omnibus undique ad eum venientibus gratis . . . more magistri Manegaldi beatae memoriae, devotum ac benignum se praebuit," Udalrici codex, ep. 160, ed. Jaffé, p. 286). He was in a good position to observe William's cordiality and liberality and to judge them as the continuing influence of Manegold. Of course that does not help us figure out whether this was the same as that Manegold of Lautenbach, author of the core of the Marbach customs.

III

In 1108 William of Champeaux left the schools of Paris to set up a new community at an abandoned hermitage dedicated to St. Victor just outside of the city gates of Paris. He had suffered a defeat or a series of defeats in debate with Peter Abelard that put his authority as a teacher of dialectic in question, or if he managed to maintain his following as a teacher, at least it had the result of souring him on the new atmosphere of contentiousness that dominated the schools.[73] He continued to teach in the new community of St. Victor, and this, according to Abelard, irritated many people and cast doubt on the sincerity of his conversion.[74] What did he teach there?[75] Probably not dialectic and the theory of universals. True, Abelard claims to have dealt him his final defeat on this question at St. Victor, but he went there to study rhetoric with William (*Historia calamitatum*, p. 65, line 81), and Abelard was probably not one to let himself be diverted from what he wanted to talk about by what his teacher wanted to teach.

After his retirement to St. Victor, William received a letter from Hildebert of Lavardin that helps us deal with this question. He urged him to continue his teaching and mapped out in illuminating comments the area of curriculum open to him. The letter begins,

> My soul rejoices and exults in your conduct and conversion, giving thanks for these acts of grace to Him from whose gift you have at long last decided to begin philosophy. For what you have done until now did not savor of philosophy. You merely gathered knowledge from philosophers; you did not bring forth in yourself beauty of conduct. But now you begin to draw out

---

[73] The tendency of scholars to advocate William of Champeaux by denying Abelard's account of a resounding defeat has persisted since Bonnard (*Histoire* 1:4–5). See also Dickinson, *Austin Canons*, 85; and Châtillon, *Théologie, spiritualité et métaphysique*, 55. Since Abelard is the only one to report it, this might have some ability to persuade, but the demise of a humanistic or old-fashioned master at the hands of a brash young Turk was too common a phenomenon in the period (cf. the testimony of Goswin of Mainz on the "retirements" of Hermann of Rheims, Drogo of Paris, Huzmann of Speyer, and Meinhard of Bamberg; also the testimony of John of Salisbury on William of Conches and Richard the Bishop) to be just a product of Abelard's ego, however much he may have favored himself in the account.

[74] Abelard, *Historia calamitatum: Texte critique avec une introduction*, ed. J. Monfrin (Paris, 1959), p. 65, lines 78 ff.

[75] The letter cited in n. 72 above is perhaps some help on the question. The student admires William's eloquence; his words were so sweet he seemed more like an angel than a man. The student seeks *bonum sapientie* and *scientia cum caritate*. These *doctrina et studium* erase vices, inculcate virtue, and arm the mind against the attacks of this life (ed. Jaffé, pp. 286–87). Since he is asking for money, the pious stance is suspect, but the array of subjects—eloquence and virtue—is plausible within a framework of studies known at other schools.

from it [i.e., beauty of manners] the pattern of good behavior like honey from the comb.[76]

The philosophy abandoned is an ungenuine one, mere acquired knowledge; the philosophy embraced is pressed out of the very self, like honey from the comb: beauty of manners. This change occurs because William has subjected himself to a new rule of the religious life, which makes him into a true philosopher. Against the advice of those who urge William to give up teaching Hildebert says, "Virtue is to administer the material of virtue, even to one who will not put it to good use" ("Virtus est, etiam male usuro, virtutis ministrare materiam," 142B).

The point is clear: he now has a new curriculum to administer, *virtus* and *morum venustas*. Its content (*bene agendi formula*) is the honey that flows out of the comb of beauty of manners. The letter is not an admonition to continue the teachings of the schools but rather an admonition to administer the rule of a new life. And the new philosophy he is enjoined to teach is behavior. Hence Hildebert's rejoicing both at his conversion and his conduct (*conversio et conversatio*).

This testimony to the "philosophy" of *conversatio* at St. Victor is not isolated. One of the few and extremely valuable witnesses to the teaching of Hugh of St. Victor from his student, Lawrence of Westminster, is of help to us. Lawrence tells us what drew him to Hugh as master:

> With all possible dispatch I chose that excellent and unique doctor, and I embraced his teaching with supreme diligence, since the moral excellence of his life decorates his learning, and the saintliness of this teacher illuminates his polished doctrine with beauty of manners.[77]

Godfrey of St. Victor entered the community around 1155 or 1160, after completing ten years of study in liberal arts and sacred letters, and he explained its attractions in his quasi-biographical poem, *Fons philosophiae*. The life of canons regular drew him because it is a "faultless" norm learned

---

[76] "De conversatione et conversione tua laetatur et exsultat anima mea, illum prosequens actione gratiarum, cujus muneris est, quod nunc tandem philosophari decreveris. Nondum enim redolebas philosophum, cum ex acquisita philosophorum scientia, morum tibi minime depromeres venustatem. Nunc autem sicut e favo mellis dulcedinem, sic ex ea bene agendi formulam expressisti" (PL 171:141A). On the letter, see Châtillon, *Théologie, spiritualité et métaphysique*, 56–57.

[77] ". . . illum eundem, quam cicius potui, precipuum ac singularem doctorem delegi, eius doctrinam cum summa diligencia amplexatus sum, veluti cuius scienciam vite honestas decorat et doctrinam morum venustate conditam sanctitas docentis illuminat" (Bernhard Bischoff, "Aus der Schule Hugos von St. Viktor," in *Aus der Geisteswelt des Mittelalters: Studien und Texte Martin Grabmann . . . gewidmet*, ed. Albert Lang et al., Beiträge zur Geschichte der Philosophie und Theologie des Mittelalters, Supplement 3.1 [Münster i. W., 1935], 246–50; edition of letter and cited passage on p. 250).

III

from the "great examples" of the "fathers." They are men "instructed in the salutary ways of the sacred rule, equal in manner of living, dressing, eating, and gesturing" (*vita, votis, habitu, victu, gestu pares*). The "master's elegance, the assessors' probity, the ministers' skill" drew him. The "mere appearance of things" (*ipsa rerum facies*) compels him to sit at the master's feet. After his entrance, he studied *ethica* and theology. Ethics removed all childish emotions (*pueriles motus*) from his mind and at the same time bathed his outward bearing (*habitus*) and his body, transforming him in "miraculous newness."[78] He learned to govern his tongue. Finally his mind was strengthened and his vagrant body restrained to a fixed measure (*figitur ut meta*).[79]

It is evident from our earlier discussion that Godfrey is describing a program of instruction common to the *Liber ordinis Sancti Victoris* and Hugh's *De institutione*. The training of novices aims at strengthening the mind for virtue through external culture. The outer appearance of the individual, like that of the institution (*facies rerum foris*), expresses the inner renewal. It is not at all farfetched to assume that William of Champeaux was one of the major architects of this program.

CARITAS ET HUMANITAS: COURTESY AT ST. VICTOR

These texts bring us close to the "new" teaching of William of Champeaux, his "true philosophy," in which the training of novices in *ethica* was an attraction that ranked next to the study of theology. A final look at the *Liber ordinis Sancti Victoris* shows us another aspect of the *forma vivendi* developed there.

The *Liber* was written around 1116 by Gilduin, William's disciple and first abbot of St. Victor, probably with help from other members of the community.[80] It has a distinctive character compared with other works of its genre. Its recent editor, Ludo Milis, characterizes the Victorines, as they

---

[78] "Newness," "renewal," and becoming a "new man" are topoi of entry into a religious community and of the reform of the church in general. See Giles Constable, "Renewal and Reform in Religious Life: Concepts and Realities," in *Renaissance and Renewal in the Twelfth Century*, ed. Robert C. Benson and Giles Constable (Cambridge, Mass., 1982), 37–67.

[79] Godfrey of St. Victor, *Fons philosophiae*, ed. Pierre Michaud-Quantin, Analecta Mediaevalia Namurcensia 8 (Namur, 1956), lines 741–84. Interesting insights into ethical training also in lines 401–4. The Victorine masters identify the "path of morality" with "beautiful manners" (*pulcri mores*). These distinguish the individual and help govern the family and the state. This is the threefold division of *practica* presented in *Didascalicon* 3.1: "practica dividitur in solitariam, privatam, publicam" (ed. Buttimer, 48). *Fons phil.*, lines 413–16, places among the masters of *practica* (meaning ethics) some whom probity has made kings of the church, dukes (i.e., leaders) of souls, and even secular princes of lands who govern many peoples. Clearly *practica* aims at administration and governing.

[80] For literature on the *Liber ordinis Sancti Victoris*, see n. 12 above.

represent themselves in the *Liber ordinis,* as "plus originaux dans la formation de leur genre de vie, plus courtois (même au sens littéral du mot) et plus urbains" (*Liber,* avant propos, p. vi). I have only a few notes to add to this comment. The qualities Milis describes are evident in every chapter of the *Liber.* One example will suffice here: the reception and treatment of guests.

The gate keeper (*portarius*) is the first to welcome arrivals. He must be

> a man of proven character, affable and kind-hearted, instructed in the discipline of manners and speech, who can serve as an example to all and embody the reputation of the entire house.[81]

Someone who troubles arriving guests with questions and delays is not suited, particularly if his rejoinders are abrasive or wounding. If he turns people away for any reason, he must beg their pardon humbly and explain himself, "lest they be hurt by his repulse" ("... ne aliquatenus de repulsa sua perturbentur ...," chap. 15, p. 55). Guests arriving for the first time must be met *cum magna benignitate et humanitate.* If they arrive on horseback, the porter should approach the one he takes to be the superior, and with a smiling face (*hilari vultu*) he should receive his reins and stirrup and say, "May our lords be welcome" ("'Bene ueniant domni nostri,'" p. 56). The authors of courtly romances were to depict welcoming scenes with manners, gestures, and emotions close to the *Liber.* Here is the way the knight Calogrenanz describes his reception at an unknown castle in Chrétien de Troyes's *Yvain:*

> "I saw the master of the castle. I had no sooner saluted him than he came forward to hold my stirrup and invited me to dismount. ... Then he told me more than a hundred times at once that blessed was the road by which I had come thither."[82]

The courtesy and humanity of the early Victorines as represented in the *Liber* is evident in many passages.[83] But the reception of guests by the porter

---

[81] "... probatus moribus, affabilis et benignus, qui, morum atque uerborum disciplina instructus, cunctis quasi exemplum et titulus tocius domus proponatur" (chap. 15, CCCM 61:55).

[82] *Le chevalier au lion (Yvain),* ed. Mario Roques, Les classiques français du moyen âge 89 (Paris, 1960), lines 198-206. Cited here from Chrétien de Troyes, *Arthurian Romances,* trans. W. W. Comfort (London and New York, 1975), 182.

[83] Beyond the gentleness, modesty, considerateness, humanity, and charity typical of Benedictine monasticism and canonical communities, St. Victor appears to have cultivated amicability particularly. See *Liber,* chap. 17: [if someone should meet the guests of a brother] "laetam faciem demonstret"; [if the porter is not there] "benigne eos alloquatur" (CCCM 61:68); chap. 18: [someone who sees a brother wearing superfluous clothes] "amicabiliter et caritatiue ammonebit fratrem suum" (p. 75). See also the comments of Odo of St. Victor cited below, p. 77.

is the outstanding example. There is a strong strain of courtesy and humanity in the Benedictine Rule and the traditions it founded. It also calls for a humane and compassionate reception of guests.[84] The virtues of *caritas* and *humanitas* are active in both the Benedictine Rule and the *Liber*, but the mood is different.[85] The injunctions in the *Liber ordinis* not to offend the feelings of guests, to receive them *hilari vultu*, and to represent in their bearing inner virtues are best described with the terms Milis uses, "courtly and urbane." The Victorine prescripts provide a little mirror of courtly ritual.[86]

The moment of reception, the mood of good humor and humane kindness, is especially important for reasons other than external etiquette: "from their first impressions of the outside they form an estimate of the things concealed within":

> ... primo occursu cum magna benignitate et humanitate recipiendi sunt ... ut ex his, quae extrinsecus vident, eorum, quae intrinsecus latent, existimationem colligant ... (1.19–22, p. 56).

---

[84] Cf. *Reg. Ben.*, chap. 53: every guest is to be received as if he were Christ. The prior or the brothers welcome him *cum omni officio caritatis*. But the tone and the actions are quite different from the St. Victor ritual: the welcomers and the newcomer pray together; the bearing proper to the welcomer is humility, shown by bowing the head or lying prone before the guest.

[85] A look at other customaries gives the Victorine ritual sharper profile. The Rule of St. Augustine gives no precepts for receiving guests. A recension of the Rule of Chrodegang of Metz calls for a porter who is "probabilis vitae, sobrius, patiens, et sapiens," a man who knows how to receive and render a response, who does his job "summa obedientia et humilitate"; he should not be drawn into any nonsense by outsiders but should receive guests "cum charitate" and close the door well (*Regula canonicorum*, chap. 12, ed. L. d'Achéry; printed in PL 89:1064). The *Decreta* of Lanfranc are dry and practical: the brother who receives guests should have various kinds of equipment ready—beds, towels, etc. (*The Monastic Constitutions of Lanfranc*, ed. David Knowles [New York, 1951], 87). The Premonstratensian custom is positively dour: when a guest knocks, the porter opens, asks humbly who it is and what he wants (*Institutiones patrum Praemonstratensium* 2.15, ed. E. Martène, *De antiquis ecclesiae ritibus*, 4 vols. [Antwerp, 1736–38; rpt. Hildesheim, 1967], 3:913). The *Regula clericorum* ("Petrus de Honestis") is more concerned with the porter's character, but is not very interested in the reception of guests (PL 163:747–48). The customs of Springiersbach and Arrouaise give no rules for receiving guests. The comparison shows us again that Victorine custom is close to the customs of Marbach, which stipulate, [the brother who serves guests] "debet esse dulcis, benignus, humanus et discretus. . . . Super omnia vero debet apparere affectus animi, voluntas bona et larga, vultus hilaris et clarus, affabilitas pulchra et honesta . . ." (chap. 127, ed. Siegwart, p. 231).

[86] The precepts for receiving guests bear comparison with Andreas Capellanus's advice to women for the courtly reception of their lovers. *Andreas Capellanus on Love*, ed. and trans. P. G. Walsh (London, 1982), 160, section 410: ". . . hilari scilicet facie et urbanitatis quemlibet receptu suscipiant . . ."; 162, section 414: "hilari vultu in suo quemlibet adventu suscipere et suavia sibi responsa praestare" [= *opus curialitatis*]; ibid., section 417: "ad vos venientes hilari receptione suscipitis et curialitatis verba secum adinvicem confertis. . . ."

III

This comment strikes a rich chord. It recalls Hugh's ideal of behavior in the *De institutione*, echoed in Godfrey of St. Victor's first impression of the community ("Ipsa rerum facie cogor assidere," *Fons phil.*, line 761). It suggests a conceptual unity underlying the life of St. Victor, Hugh's ethical thought, and his theology. Just as the exterior behavior of the disciplined man gives testimony to the composition of his mind, so also the behavior of the "outer man," the porter, symbolizes the interior ideals, *benignitas, humanitas, caritas*. It might be stretching the point a bit to apply to the porter of St. Victor's Hugh's definition of a sacrament,

> Disc.: Quare dicitur sacramentum sacrae rei signum?
> Mag.: Quia per id quod foris visibile cernitur, aliud interius invisibile significatur,[87]

but not much. The congruence of inner and outer was an idea so widely shared in the school of St. Victor that it forms something like a unifying moral/intellectual concept.[88]

These observations suggest that Hugh's moral philosophy and at least a part of his theology are the life at St. Victor turned into philosophy. But this is just what Hildebert of Lavardin had enjoined on William of Champeaux: he was to make a philosophy out of *conversatio* and *venustas morum*. The strain in the thought, teaching, and behavior of Hugh of St. Victor just noted suggests that Hildebert's letter has programmatic character.

The courtesy of St. Victor must have been some of the honey pressed from *venustas morum*. It was no doubt part of moral training. But it served the interests of the house as well. It made it attractive to converts. Just as the monastic communities put the cult of friendship to practical use in recruitment,[89] St. Victor beckoned to those outside with the attractions of its courteous and affable society. Odo of St. Victor wrote a letter to a brother living outside the community, recalling to him the cordiality of their society, their *dulce consortium* and *dulce colloquium*, and commending his brothers as

> ad societatem amabiles, ad imitandum utiles. Sunt, inquam, amabiles ad societatem, tum pro vitae sanctitate, tum pro morum suavitate.[90]

---

[87] *De sacramentis legis naturalis et scriptae*, PL 176:34B. Cf. *De sacramentis* 1.9.2, PL 176:317C. Here the comparison between sacrament and significatum, the human body and soul, and scriptural letter and meaning, suggests a common symbolic structure uniting theology (sacraments), ethics (body-soul), and textual studies (Scripture).

[88] Cf. Richard of St. Victor, *Explicatio in Cantica Canticorum*: ". . . disciplina loquendi . . . foris pulchram animam demonstrat. . . . Ubi vero composita fuerint verba . . . testimonium dant constantiae mentis" (PL 196:462A). See also Odo of St. Victor, Ep. 4, PL 196:1408B–C.

[89] Jean Leclerq, *Monks and Love in Twelfth-Century France: Psycho-Historical Essays* (Oxford, 1979), 8–23.

[90] Odo of St. Victor, Ep. 2, PL 196:1403C. For some discussion of his letters, see Bynum, *Docere verbo et exemplo*, 44–45, 81–82.

The teaching of *mores* at St. Victor had another use. It was seen as a means of promotion in the church. *Elegantia morum, venustas morum*, the result of a discipline in *ethica*, were not only private virtues; they were also qualifications for church office; they were among the constituents of *idoneitas*.[91] It is not easy to say whether the study of letters or the study of manners was the more practical in regard to advancement. Thomas Becket had not been an expert in letters, but he worked hard on *mores* and excelled in that study.[92] Wazo of Liège favored the students who distinguished themselves in *mores* over those who merely excelled in letters.[93] A letter from Richard of St. Victor to Robert of Melun congratulating him on his promotion to Bishop of Hereford gives us an interesting insight into Victorine attitudes on the subject. Robert had taught briefly at St. Victor before his election. Richard writes congratulating him:

> ... all your students were filled with joyful hope [at the news of your promotion], and the entire school was heartened and roused to the love of letters and the cultivation of virtue through the example of your efforts and your success.[94]

Joined to the love of letters, *cultus virtutis* was not entirely disinterested personal ethical formation—not a kind of aesthetic-spiritual self-perfecting—but also a study that shaped men for the service of church and state.[95]

Conclusion

The humanism of St. Victor is fed by the diffusion of an ethic that spread from the cathedral schools in the course of the eleventh century. It picks

---

[91] See Jaeger, *Origins of Courtliness*, 32–34.

[92] William Fitzstephen, *Vita Thomae*, chap. 5: "Thomas minus litteratus erat; sed longe quidem altior est ratio morum quam litterarum, et ipse studuit moralitati et prudentiae intendere, ut inter eos, litteris adhuc inferior, moribus conspectior et acceptior appareret" (ed. James Craigie Robertson, *Materials for the History of Thomas Becket*, Rolls Series 67.3 [London, 1877], 16).

[93] Anselm, *Gesta episcoporum Leodiensium*, chap. 40, MGH SS 7 (Hannover, 1846), 210–11: "In quarum [= scolarum] studio tam morum quam litterarum vigilantissime exercuit disciplinam, eos qui pro his moribus essent, licet minus litteratos, longe his anteponens, quibus, ut in plerisque solet, scientia litterarum vanae gloriae peperisset stultitiam."

[94] "... spe non modica hilarati sunt auditores vestri, tum universi scholares animati ad amorem litterarum, et cultum virtutum, vestri laboris et successus exemplo" (PL 196:1225A). Perhaps somewhat revealing on the connection between the life of canons regular and promotion in the church is Abelard's accusation that William of Champeaux converted "ut quo religiosior crederetur ad majoris prelationis gradum promoveretur ..." (*Historia calamitatum*, ed. Monfrin, p. 65, lines 74–75). The suggestion that the canonical life had this effect must have weight whether or not that was William's intention.

[95] See the discussion in Jaeger, "Cathedral Schools," 594–601.

up ideals of "beautiful manners" and the congruence of inner world and outer appearance that found a good, perhaps an ideal context in the lives and customs of canons regular with their stress on humanity, charity, and irreproachable appearance in external things. The Ciceronian-Ambrosian ethic of beautiful conduct "sat" perfectly in this context. A worldly ethic stressing fine manners and courtesy tended to overrefinement and ostentation in secular and episcopal courts. The founders and early teachers at the School of St. Victor superimposed an ethic of refined bearing onto the ideals of the apostolic life, equality of manners and renunciation of possessions. This created a quasi-monastic courtesy, an ascetic Ciceronianism, with a degree of legitimacy that the old imperial program of cathedral school education with its more worldly Ciceronianism could never again attain in the wake of the investiture controversy. It occupies a middle position between the worldly ethic of the secular courts and the asceticism of the new monastic movements.

But apart from its social and historical context, Victorine humanism had its own content. Acquisition of virtue through training of the body, self-presentation made into a work of art, carriage and bearing as a symbolic code that conveys through outward elegance inner beauty and harmony: these are what the training of novices at St. Victor promised, and they must have represented powerful incentives to conversion. They spoke above all to worldly men of high nobility. If men wanted sainthood and escape from the self, they went to monastic communities. St. Victor offered "letters," beautiful manners, theological illumination, the "good"—that is the ordained and regulated—life, a life that left open the possibility of advancement in the church.

The first two constituted its particular form of humanism. The two major works that convey that humanism are Hugh's *Didascalicon* (letters) and his *De institutione novitiorum* (*mores*). The history of humanistic education in the Middle Ages changes its aspect altogether, depending on which side of that formula we look at. "Letters" have commanded most scholarly attention. The Victorine writings are invaluable because they also offer such good testimony to the teaching of *mores* and even indicate what form "beautiful manners" took when embodied in a trained and disciplined brother.

Impressive as the *Didascalicon* is in its breadth and coherence, the eccentric and unevenly composed *De institutione* formulated the *studium vivendi*, at least as attractive and important in the schooling at St. Victor as the *studium legendi*.

IV

Peter Abelard's Silence at the Council of Sens

Peter Abelard's failure, or refusal, to defend himself at the council of Sens in 1140 [1] has provoked sharply contradictory explanations. For some years these have lived side by side without confrontation, and this long peace between irreconcilable opposites suggests that the topic has been exhausted. The evidence which bears on it is well known, and to my knowledge there are no new documents in sight. [2] The purpose of this study is to analyse Abelard's treatment of the trials of Christ and Susanna in his Sermons 11, 12 and 29. My argument, briefly stated, is that Abelard's failure to respond to his accusers at his «trial» [3] was an example of «eloquent silence»: [4] he was acting on an ideal of silent and passive suffering of injustice, which crystallized around the figures of Christ and Susanna, but which fit into a broader complex of ideas and convictions in his thought. He formed these ideas after his castration and public humiliation in 1118. They are detectable in his conduct at his trial in 1121 at Soissons as described in the *Historia calamitatum*, [5] and were expressed elsewhere in the *Historia*, in the *Problemata Heloissae*, in his hymns and other writings for the Paraclete. A reading of the relevant texts makes it apparent that his failure to defend himself was an assertion of conviction and that his sermons on Christ and Susanna constitute a forecast of this behavior.

The sequence of events leading up to the council began in 1139. [6] In that year William of St. Thierry collected excerpts from Abelard's works and sent them to Bernard of Clairvaux and Geoffrey of Chartres, the papal legate for France and a former supporter of Abelard. In the accompanying letter William called on them to read and test the orthodoxy of Abelard's works. [7] Some time in 1140 Bernard responded by writing his *Tractatus contra quaedam capitula errorum Abaelardi*. [8] Bernard sent the tract to Pope Innocent, and it soon began circulating in Paris. In addition to the *Tractatus*, Bernard wrote a series of letters to Rome in which he attacked Abelard in the most virulent terms. [9] For the time being his complaints to Rome accomplished nothing. Abelard had strong support there. Bernard turned to local authorities, first Henry, Archbishop of Sens, then Stephen, Bishop of Paris. In both cases he was not successful in bringing action. [10] The news of all this reached Abelard, many of whose students were employed in the church administration. Now Abelard seized the offensive. He pressed Archbishop Henry of Sens and Bishop Stephen of Paris until they set a date for a confrontation. [11] Bernard was taken aback when informed of the bishops' action. He had wanted the condemnation of Abelard's patent heresies, not intricate discussions of the faith; now he was to face Abelard and bandy about its secrets with this «vir bellator,» a seasoned warrior in disputation. [12] At this point, Abelard wrote a letter announcing the planned confrontation and inviting his supporters to Sens.[13] This was a bold move. Bernard had not yet agreed to the confrontation;[14] in fact he was still reluctant to meet Abelard face to face. But Abelard's letter made Bernard's further resistance impossible. His withdrawal or refusal to participate would be put down to cowardice. The letter forced Bernard into the open and effectively put an end to a campaign waged against Abelard behind his back. Abelard's aggressiveness in precipitating the meeting has generally been interpreted as the stirring of his old arrogant self-confidence.[15] I seriously question this. He was entering a desperate final encounter in which he had little or no hope of vindicating himself. He had suffered (or believed he had suffered) injustice at the hands of an ecclesiastical court at Soissons nineteen years before. The memory of the machinations of his enemies at that trial, trumped up charges, biased judges, had not left him. Some ten to fifteen years after Soissons he still wrote in the *Historia* that he never heard of an assembly of churchmen without imagining that they had convened in order to condemn him as a heretic.[16] He knew that in provoking Bernard he was not dealing with relatively minor characters like Alberic of Reims or Lotulf of Novara, his chief antagonists at Soissons. Bernard was one of the most powerful men in the church, and Abelard profoundly mistrusted him, as the letter to his *socii* indicates.[17] Having abandoned at Soissons any illusions he may have had about the impartiality of judges, he cannot have entered the proceedings at Sens with visions of vindication dancing in his head.[18]

Abelard would have been very naive not to anticipate treachery and machinations. In fact a group of clergymen met on the evening preceding the trial, at the invitation of Bernard, to discuss the proceedings on the following day. The list of accusations was agreed upon, and Bernard got them to consent to what in effect was a verdict in advance.[19] And so on the next day it was possible for Bernard to offer Abelard the chance to defend himself, and he could rest somewhat assured that his maneuver would guarantee him some buffer from the awesome flow of words that — as he supposed — his enemy commanded.

The only eyewitness reports of Abelard's behavior at the council were written by his opponents, with the exception of the somewhat scatterbrained account of Abelard's student Berengar of Poitiers.[20] Bernard began the proceedings against Abelard by reading the nineteen *capitula,*[21] the list of allegedly heretical propositions attributed to Abelard. According to Bernard's own account, when he was only part way through the reading, Abelard interrupted him, announced his intention of appealing to Rome, and left.[22] The presiding bishops, on the other hand, report that when Bernard finished the reading of the *capitula*

> Master Peter Abelard appeared to be at a loss what to do; and in order to make a way of escape refused to reply, although he had a free hearing given to him, a safe place, and impartial judges; but appealing to you in person, most holy father, he left the assembly with all his supporters.[23]

Geoffrey of Auxerre, a former student of Abelard, later Bernard's secretary and biographer,[24] was present at the council and gave the following account:

> He [Abelard], unwilling to pull himself together and unable to resist the wisdom and spirit which spoke, appealed, to gain time, to the Apostolic See. But afterwards

> he was admonished by that excellent advocate of the catholic faith that he might reply freely and safely in the knowledge that nothing would be done to harm his person, and that he would be heard and indulged in all patience. This too he refused altogether. For he confessed afterwards to his followers that in that moment, as they say, his memory had been thrown into confusion, his reason had clouded over, and his inner sense fled him. 25

The latter two accounts, the first written shortly after the council, the second some fifteen years later, agree that Abelard failed to react after Bernard read the *capitula*. Hence we can probably discount Bernard's statement that Abelard interrupted him and walked out. Also, both the bishops and Geoffrey indicate that there was a period of silence after Bernard's reading, during which all waited for Abelard to reply. But he remained silent («respondere noluit»). Although Bernard urged him repeatedly to answer, he still refused to speak («et postea... monitus... hoc quoque omnimodis recusavit»). Geoffrey may well be magnifying Bernard's generosity here, listing the various inducements he used to encourage Abelard to answer, since the bishops' report seems to indicate that Abelard left immediately after announcing his appeal. Still, there is a lacuna in the proceedings here, which Geoffrey and the bishops interpret as faltering and uncertainty («visus diffidere»; «nec volens resipiscere, nec valens resistere...»; «memoria ejus turbata fuerit, ratio caligaverit»). Bernard's account at least makes sense of this apparently senseless pause by omitting it altogether. Abelard's repeated refusal to speak is, on the surface of the matter, difficult to understand as a rational act. I hope that the following discussion will clarify it.

The various attempts to explain Abelard's failure to defend himself derive for the most part from one or the other of two general ideas: either he was prevented by some physical or mental failure from speaking; or, upset by the machinations preceding the council, he refused to participate and left to take his case to Rome. The former explanation is the one put forward by the bishops and Geoffrey of Auxerre, and the claim that Abelard's mind and nerve failed him at a crucial moment becomes the common explanation by partisans of St. Bernard. 26 As impartial an historian as R. L. Poole echoes this view:

> Abelard's fortunes turned upon the alternations of his inner mood. He believed his actions to be under the mechanical control of his mind; yet he was really the creature of impulse. At the critical moment that lofty self-confidence of which he boasted would suddenly desert him and change by a swift transition into the extreme of despondency, of incapacity for action. 27

Though there is much to credit in Poole's assessment of Abelard's character, still it pictures him as the bold egotistical warrior in disputation, buoyed up, even shortly before his second trial, by a «lofty self-confidence,» from which his faltering at Sens was a momentary lapse. More likely is that by 1140 self-confidence came over Abelard only in rare moments, dispelling the «despondency and incapacity for action» which by then were the normal state of his emotions and will. Though his intellect was still vital, his ego was considerably eroded. 28

It has also been suggested that Abelard's health in large part accounts for his failure to speak. 29 According to the theory of Dr. Jeannin, Abelard was suffering from Hodgkin's disease and was stricken by a serious flare-up during the council. This made it impossible for him to defend himself. His physical condition must have been wretched to be sure, [30] but this interesting idea is still not convincing. He left the council claiming that he intended to appeal in person to Rome; on this the sources agree. But a sick man in the very moment of an extreme attack does not seize on the idea of long trips to make good what his infirmity has confounded. If illness prevented the one, it would have shut out all thought of the other. It is possible to appeal to Rome without walking there. [30a]

The other line of thought on this problem relies on historical evidence and is the more favorable to Abelard. The first methodical statement of it comes from S. M. Deutsch, who argued that Abelard's behavior resulted from his realization that the sentence against him had been agreed upon on the day before the council; all hope of victory was denied him in advance, and the chance to reply to the charges, which was undoubtedly offered to him, was only a sham. Therefore he refused to cooperate with the proceedings. [31] Deutsch's theory has undergone corrections and variations, but in its main points it is still accepted. [32] It offers a neat package into which the facts fit, and it is completely rational. It allows us to hold on to the traditional picture of Abelard as a vigorous, brash intellectual rebel, a picture that we are, perhaps understandably, reluctant to abandon. But there are some troublesome objections to it. It cannot account for Abelard's silence and his slowness in leaving the hall. It pictures Abelard changing his tactics suddenly when confronted with the injustice of the proceedings. [33] But this ignores the fact that he had gone through a similar experience once before in 1121 and had brooded on his defeat for at least ten years (the *terminus post quem* of the *Historia* being 1131) and probably longer. In the 1130s he had been in mortal fear that a council of ecclesiastics would be called in order to condemn him, and he profoundly mistrusted Bernard. It is quite unlikely that a rational man in this position would not have prepared himself well in advance for machinations. At Soissons after all he had been denied all right to speak. [34] By comparison Bernard's maneuver seems a minor miscarriage. At Sens he was in fact given the chance to speak. And even in the unlikely event that he was overcome by sudden indignation by this predictable maneuver, much could have been salvaged if he had spoken out. He could at least have denied those opinions wrongly ascribed to him, and he could have toppled the most ill-conceived of the arguments against him, as Robert of Melun did for him in a bold and powerful polemic a few years after the council. [35] He could have shown in person a little of the vehemence and urge for self-justification that he showed in the *Apologia* «*universis*», written either immediately before or after the council. [36] By speaking out he could at least have made the guilty verdict embarrassing to the bishops. Also, a man suddenly stung by the injustice of the proceedings would surely have cried to high heaven against the prearranged verdict. The accusation of illegal goings-on would have fully legitimized his appeal. But Abelard does not make it. Probably he was not suddenly stung, but rather was passively accepting a situation which he had long since anticipated. The picture of an Abelard indulging in sanguine visions of objective debate on his own terms and of councils of ecclesiastics hearing his justifications with impartial and unprejudiced minds, then suddenly disappointed when he finds it is not so, ought to receive more scepticism than it has.

Undoubtedly the theory of Deutsch, with elaborations by Klibansky, Borst, Murray and others, gives accurately the historical background to the unfair condemnation. But as an explanation of Abelard's behavior it is incomplete. [37] If his silence was nothing more than a reaction to the prearranged verdict, then it was not very good strategy, to put it mildly. Through remaining silent, he caused the momentary confusion of his opponents and offered them a slight affront which must have been much more welcome to them than energetic compliance with their expectations. Abelard lost much by refusing to defend himself. He left his accusers more powerful. They could claim that he had not replied so that he could avoid refutation and so prolong his iniquity. [38] A more serious result was that his failure to speak opened him to the reproach that his appeal to Rome was unjustified, that he had been accorded a fair trial, but had not taken advantage of it, and his appeal was therefore superfluous. This argument, which the bishops did not omit in their letter to Pope Innocent, [39] must have carried weight at Rome, and so his silence possibly hastened his final condemnation. Finally, through his silence he disappointed the friends and students he had invited to the council and made any further defense of him difficult.

The paradox is that Abelard himself requested the council, invited his friends, preparing them for a grand encounter, and then did not do anything. The swift change from aggressiveness to passivity invites us to conclude either irrational behavior or a change in tactics. I will argue that there is no contradiction and no change in tactics, but that Abelard called for the assembly in order to create for himself a forum at which he could remain silent.

The evidence for this is in his sermons. [40] While Abelard was abbot of the dissolute monastery of St. Gildas, [41] he wrote a series of thirty-four sermons for a variety of occasions and audiences, and he assembled them for use at the Paraclete. [42] In Sermons 11 *(De rebus gestis in diebus passionis)* and 12 *(De cruce)* he relates and discusses the trial of Christ, and he devotes a good deal of commentary to Christ's determined, aggressively passive silence before his judges, a subject which did not provoke much commentary in twelfth-century writings on the passion. [43] The four Gospels agree that Christ refused to answer his judges at some point in his trial. According to Matthew and Mark, he is silent when confronted with false evidence. [44] In Luke he refuses to reply to the many questions Herod puts to him; [45] and according to John, he remained silent when Pilate questioned him. [46] Abelard comments on Christ's silence in Sermon 11, but there are problems with the text. The second half of it is corrupt; there are jumps in thought; it is disorganized; occasionally one has the impression of reading a first draft; [47] and, exasperatingly, the sermon breaks off at the point where the high priest is questioning Jesus, who has just refused to make any reply to false testimony brought against him. Fortunately, Abelard commented earlier in the sermon, out of context, on Christ's refusal to answer. He is explaining the fear that Jesus suffered on Mt. Olivet, and he refers to his subsequent silence before his judges as another example of strength rising out of fear:

> How steadfastly he met his passion and persisted through it any judge who notes carefully the enormity of his fear, the incomparable fortitude in him [...[48]] Other things aside, who will not marvel at what we hear from him when interrogated by Pilate, he would make no response: [49] «You will not speak to me? Do you not know

> that I have the power to set you free?» [John 19.10]. Also when he was sent to Herod by Pilate, since he fell within his jurisdiction as a Galilean, so that thus he might be able to free him easily, he did not deign to respond to him, though questioned with many words...[50]

Abelard clearly wants to stress the fact that Christ could have been set free had he only spoken. The quotation from John is abbreviated. In the Bible it reads, «I have the power *to crucify you* and to set you free» (John 19.10). Abelard omits the threat and cites only the promise, and thus stresses that Christ's silence represents determined acceptance of his fate: the victim is in control of events and will not be deprived of his martyrdom. Also, in Luke there is no indication that Pilate sent Christ to Herod, «ut sic per eum facile liberari posset,» as Abelard says.

The above passage was the presentation of Christ's silence *ad litteram*. The explanation follows:

> The fact that the indeed seems to grow weary and perturbed from terror — as if to say in his despair «What is there to say?» — all these are not signs of cowardice or lack of confidence, but rather of the deepest fear at the testing of the frailty he had taken upon himself.[51]

Later, at the end of the sermon, an unambiguously positive construction is placed on Christ's silence before the high priest, as reported in Matthew. In this case it was disdain: he refused to answer, thinking the testimony so manifestly false as not to merit response.[52]

In Sermon 12, Abelard again discusses the trial scene and presents Christ's silence in a more consistent way. He was brought before Pilate bound and standing:

> With how much constancy he persisted there is clearly shown when, interrogated by Pilate, he makes no response. Marvelling at his confidence and at what seems his contempt, Pilate says: «Do you not know that I have the power to crucify you and to release you?»[53]

He then retells the scene before Herod nearly as in Sermon 11, and finally comments: «A principibus itaque interrogatus, qui ad eum liberandum plurimum poterant, responsione sua dignos eos non censuit...» (PL 178:482A).

In Abelard's presentation, then, Christ's silence was motivated by contempt for the judges and for proceedings which are manifestly unjust; his bearing showed a confidence and perseverance that caused even his opponent to marvel. It was an act of passive defiance, all the more admirable in that some action on his part, a plea for pardon, could have set him free. I stress again that these commentaries are in Abelard's sermons by the choice of the author, not by the press of convention. As indicated above (note 43), one is hard put to find more than a mention of Christ's refusals to answer his interrogators in contemporary writings on the passion. Ruberg's extensive collection of texts (Beredtes Schweigen, pp. 119 ff.), ranging from patristic times to the seventeenth century, tends to support this. Other sources mention the silence and gloss it in various ways, but it is clear that Abelard, by comparison with other writers, was preoccupied with the subject. In Sermons 11 and 12 we find three treatments of Christ's silence. The longest of these passages is not even in the context of the trial; he brought in the silence as an illustration of something which on the surface is quite unrelated. If the text of Sermon 11 were complete, we would surely have yet another commentary on Christ's silence. The context in Sermon 12 is worth considering also. It is a sermon on the cross; its theme is the suffering of Christ. He mentions only two moments in the trial: the mocking of Christ, which is relevant to the theme, and Christ's silence, which is not particularly relevant. This is clear from the clumsy transitions with which the subject is introduced in the sermon: «Ubi, inter caetera...» (PL 178:481C); «responsione sua dignos eos non censuit; qui tamen, ut supra meminimus...» «482A). The phrases «inter caetera» and «tamen, ut supra meminimus...» are the devices of an embarrassed writer forcing a subject into his text where it does not belong. Clearly Christ's aggressively passive behavior interested Abelard particularly.

Besides these direct comments on Christ's silence, there is much on the periphery of Abelard's treatment of the trial that resonates with his own actions at Sens, or at least casts a particular light on them. I will briefly summarize the entrance into Jerusalem as Abelard presents it in Sermon 11. He comes, surrounded by followers, and enters the temple. Seeing the impious conditions there, he leaves and returns to Bethany determined to return the next day to exact vengeance («vindicta,» PL 178:459B; cf. Mark 11. 11). He defers his wrath, so says Abelard, to show that we must know in advance about errors and evils which we wish to correct, and Jesus deferred punishment lest anyone think his confidence came from the crowds surrounding him; he would act without crowds (459B). He leaves Jerusalem, not the Jerusalem called «visio pacis» but a Jerusalem made the asylum for tyrants, since the leaders of the city already conspired against him and denied him a place to stay. He ordered his disciples to return, bring a donkey to him, and it was done, though he was well aware of the conspiracy against him («cum tamen in se conspirationem factam non ignoraret,» 459D). Concerning which (i.e. the conspiracy) he said to the disciples whom he sent, «Ite in castellum quod contra vos est» (Matth. 21.2). Go, he says (I am paraphrasing Abelard), confidently into this place, though it can hardly be called a place of men living together in justice, but rather a fortress of tyrannical entrenchment, a place indeed opposed to you. «And if any man say ought unto you, ye shall say, The Lord hath need of them» (Matth. 21.3). «O marvellous power of confidence!» Abelard comments, «as if the Lord issued commands to them whom he knew to be vigorously conspiring for his death» (459D).

Here Abelard has focused on Christ's state of mind in facing the conspiracy against him. There is no mention of his miracles, preaching or healing. But there is much talk of the facing of treacherous enemies, revenge, the aggressiveness with which Christ faces men conspiring against him. Two motifs stand out particularly in this passage and in what follows. The first is Christ's foreknowledge of the conspiracy against him. It was mentioned several times in the passage just surveyed, and it is pointed out energetically a few columns later in Abelard's commentary on Matth. 26. 3-5 («Then the high priests came together, and the leaders of the people took counsel to seize Jesus by guile and kill him. But they said, not on the holiday...») Abelard's commentary: «*not on the holiday,* that is lest the crowds which received him in exultation ... should be stirred up against them and should snatch him away. O blind and evil men! You seek to take him by guile, as though he were ignorant of your machination...»[53a] Again, before Christ's arrest, when he goes forward to meet the soldiers: «And so Jesus went ahead to meet all things which were to come upon him. While men prepare to do violence to God, quickly the Lord goes to meet his passion, not dragged along behind, as he himself said, "No man taketh it (i.e. my life) from me, but I lay it down of myself, knowing all things,"[54] that is, not being ignorant of their machinations...»[54a] Christ asks the soldiers whom they are seeking, «tanquam ignorans eorum nequissimam inquisitionem...» (PL 178:471B).

The second prominent motif is the presence of crowds of followers who received and accompanied Christ. It recurs with real insistence. When Jesus descends from Mt. Olivet: «Bene autem descendens de monte Dominus a turbis glorificatur...» (PL 178:456B). He entered Jerusalem «cum multo exsultantium turbarum comitatu» (458B); «cum magno comitatu turbarum laudes acclamantium templum ingressus...» (458D). He was reluctant to destroy the temple, «quasi praedictarum turbarum confisus ope» (459B). Abelard's Sermon 7 *(In ramis palmarum)* opens with the scene of the crowds receiving Christ: «Hodierna solemnitas et tanquam imperialis pompae jucunditas, qua Dei filius regio more a turbis est susceptus...» (430C). Here also the crowds are mentioned repeatedly: «a turbis hodie recognitus est et susceptus» (431A); «susceptus est hodie a turbis» (435B). Of course Christ was received by crowds on Palm Sunday, but still the frequency of these references does seem unusual.[55] In Sermon 7 he gives an explication of the crowds. Christ wished to be received by crowds, he explains, as a token of greater honor, and he threw out the moneychangers and sellers from the temple, overturned the tables of the vendors and healed the blind and lame who came to him, «so that thereby he could arouse the envy of perverse men against him all the more, so that they could hasten to complete what they had long since wanted, and he himself would supply the means of implementing what they sought.»[56] And he sums up: «But so that those who already negotiated for the death of the Lord would be spurred on by even greater envy and so that they would be more enraged against God, seeing him honored thus, he permitted on this day more honor to be shown him than ever had been shown to any king.»[57]

The exaltation of Christ by the crowds on Palm Sunday is variously explained in medieval exegesis. It represents either a prefiguring of Christ's impending glory,[58] or, as Abelard explains it here, a goad to the envy of his enemies.[59] While the latter idea is not original with Abelard, still the affinities between his own reaction to Bernard's attacks and his explanation of Christ's behavior are striking. Abelard vigorously demanded a confrontation in a meeting of ecclesiastics («crebro nos pulsare coepit, nec... voluit desistere,» above, note 11), an event which he feared and knew to be the worst possible forum of vindication for himself. The meeting would clearly be dominated by a man whom he knew to be circulating charges against him behind his back and who had tried repeatedly to bring action against Abelard without involving himself. When the day was set, Abelard wrote the letter inviting friends and associates. Bernard heard about Abelard's letter. It both intimidated him and it goaded him into action: «Exiit sermo ad omnes, et non potuit me latere,» Bernard wrote afterwards to Pope Innocent:

«At first I held back ... At length, yielding to the advice of my friends — though much against my will and with tears — *who saw how all were getting ready, as if for a great spectacle* and feared that our absence would result in a scandal among the people and horns for our enemy, ... I hastened to the appointed place on the appointed day.» [59a] In other words, Abelard's premature announcement of a confrontation to which his opponent had not yet agreed was the single decisive factor in overcoming Bernard's reluctance; he was forced into confronting Abelard by Abelard. Thus Abelard provided his enemy with the means of carrying out his campaign against him, and this is how he had described Christ's motives for his aggressive surrender: «ut quod jamdudum voluerant, perficere maturarent, et ab eo daretur facultas, in quibus praecesserat voluntas» (PL 178: 435D). Both Christ and Abelard goaded their enemies into action, then remained silent at their trials.

Also, there is the role of the «turbae.» He came to Sens with crowds of supporters and was no doubt met by many more. [60] For Abelard the very word «turba» must have been laden with associations flattering to his ego, since his ability to attract crowds had been part of his triumph as a teacher. [61] And it was, among other things, the throngs of students he attracted that made him appear dangerous to Bernard and William of St. Thierry. [62]

Finally, the crowds and the honors shown to Christ were intended, says Abelard, to inflame the envy of his enemies. But it was envy, «invidia,» which Abelard had regarded as the main motivation of his own enemies ever since his persecution on intellectual grounds had begun. [63].

The passages discussed above should also make us very sceptical of the idea that the scheming of his opponents at Sens took him by surprise. He obviously admired Christ's foreknowledge of machinations and the aggressive surrender it provoked. It made him the master of his own demise, the stager and manipulator in a tragedy of which he was the main character. It is quite likely that the psychological mechanism which compels a man to press for an end to protracted sufferings, albeit a tragic one, was also at work in Abelard's pressing for the council and inviting his friends. [64]

In short, there are many affinities between Abelard's presentation of Christ's arrest and trial and his own posture before and during his trial at Sens. It remains to be shown that these are anything more than chance correspondences. After all, his sermons were written some ten to fifteen years before Sens. Nonetheless, there is much that argues that the depictions of Christ's trial represent a foreshadowing of his behavior at Sens. First, we should recall that the sermons were written around the same time as the *Historia calamitatum*. This work had recalled vividly to him the shame of his condemnation at Soissons, and the fear he had felt of being called before a council of clergymen and condemned as a heretic was still with him (see above, note 16). Where a trial scene occurs in the sermons it is hard to imagine that Abelard would have staved off his own fear of trials, machinations, false witnesses, prejudiced inquisitors, and written wholly unengaged commentaries on scenes which had such vivid meaning for him. If a man is in mortal fear of being dragged before a council and condemned, he is going to put some thought into the question of what to do when that eventuality comes about, and faced with so powerful an example as Christ's silence, it is very probable that he will allow his own «strategy» to pattern itself on this model. Second, in Abelard's description of his trial at Soissons the author occasionally casts himself in the role of Christ. Jacques Monfrin pointed this out and indicated that the subject is worth investigation.[65] Third, the image of Christ at his trial was in Abelard's mind around the time of his own. The *Apologia* «*universis*» borrows phrases from the speech of Christ before the high priest as recorded in John 18:

Abelard's *Apologia*:	Christ before the high priest: [66]
Multa in scholis multis locutus sum nec unquam aquas furtivas vel panem absconditum habuit mea doctrina. Palam locutus sum ... et quaecumque scripsi, libenter omnibus exposui, ut eos judices, non discipulos haberem [PL 178: 105].	Ego palam locutus sum mundo. Ego semper docui in synagoga et in templo quo omnes iudaei conveniunt, et in occulto locutus sum nihil. Quid me interrogas? Interroga eos qui audierunt quid locutus sum ipsis. Ecce hi sciunt quae dixerim ego [John 18. 20-21].

This passage was written either immediately before or immediately after his trial at Sens. In it he lifts phrases directly from the speech of Christ refusing to cooperate with one of his interrogators and reproduces in paraphrase the train of thought of Christ.[67] The further events of Christ's trial must also have occurred to him and served him as a model for his action, as Christ's words served him as a model for part of his written statement. This is the only evidence from the time of the council that Abelard went into the proceedings with some sense of identification with Christ at his trial.[68]

But obviously he did not orchestrate his own demise as an elaborate imitation of Christ's. Abelard appealed to Rome,[69] and Christ did not. And besides appealing he wrote three *Apologiae* around the time of the council.[70] This shows an un-Christlike eagerness, not only to justify, but also to save himself by having the verdict overturned. The most we can say is that Abelard had a conception, formed around the figure of Christ, of silence as proper behavior for a man falsely condemned.

That Abelard did regard silence as proper behavior in such circumstances we find confirmed in his treatment of the figure of Susanna in his Sermon 29. Susanna, whose story was an appendage to the prophetic book of Daniel, was not a particularly important figure for the Middle Ages.[71] Though she interested Abelard for a variety of reasons,[72] his sermon focuses on the themes of a rigged trial, an unjust accusation, false witnesses and judges, and a miraculous acquittal after the condemnation.

She is led to the judgment, Abelard says, «with her parents, her children and all her acquaintances» (PL 178:558D). This is in the text of Daniel, but still the detail might have aroused in Abelard's mind an echo of those «turbae» which received Christ in Jerusalem. He repeats it several times: «Flebant non solum sui, sed omnes, qui noverant eam» (559A); «Anxius maritus, anxii tam parentes quam filii, et omnes qui noverant eam ... » (559A); «Circumstantes suos, virum, parentes, filios, cognatos... et omnes qui noverant eam ... cernebat» (560C). Abelard describes her bearing after the condemnation at some length:

> ... when the people believed the false testimony of the old men, and condemned her to death, she called out in a loud voice, and said: «Eternal God, who knows hidden things, who knew all things before they were created, you know that they have given false testimony against me, and behold, I shall die, though I have done nothing.» The verdict having been assigned her earlier [in judicio prius constituta] when the men had testified in accusation of her, now she is said, not to speak, but to weep, and to look up to heaven, so that first her patience may be shown, which also the prophet had predicted of Christ with these words: «He is led as a lamb to the slaughter, and as a sheep before its shearers is silent, so he openeth not his mouth» (Isaiah 53. 7). [72a]

Abelard's interpretation of her loud outcry to God as silence rests on the standard interpretation by Jerome,[73] and of course the analogy to Christ's silence encourages this interpretation, the Isaiah quotation connecting the two. Abelard continues and describes the decisive moments:

> She silently awaited there the sentence of her condemnation, and silent before men, she spoke in weeping to God alone. But now having received the condemnation, she protested her innocence —in order to excuse herself, not in order to free herself— she resolved to save her reputation rather than her life ... [73a]

There are two steps in her «defense»: first, passive, determined silence («Exspectabat ibi tacita damnationis suae sententiam»); then, having received the judgment, a loud protest to God, inaudible to the crowds around her. Her «appeal» to God, Abelard stresses, aims only at protecting her reputation. He pointed this out twice in the above passage. Shortly thereafter he repeats it with insistence:

> Was it that she turned to prayer so that she would be freed from a punishment she had not merited by her own fault? By no means was that her intention... Nor was she so concerned with death as with throwing off the infamy ... [73b]

But God, he continues, judges men by what is in their conscience, not by what is on their tongues. Hence he freed her, not only from the infamy, but also from death, since the truth had been put forth in such certainty in her silent and inward confession (cf. 562A). Such a silent confession, spurning the use of words and the judgment of men, he says, is the most reliable vehicle of truth:

> Indeed the most certain testimony of innocence or of guilt is the final confession of the condemned, especially when they despair that what they say before men will do them any good, and are the more eager for truth to be served, the more anxious they are to hasten to the divine judgment. [74]

In these passages from Sermon 29, it seems to me, is indicated very intimately the train of thought that was translated into action (or inaction, more accurately) at Sens. He would refuse to make any response to trumped-up charges and a prearranged verdict (like Susanna, he faces his accusers «prius in judicio constitutus»); and having learned of the verdict earlier, he is in the position of those who «despair that what they say before men will do them any good»; hence he maintains a meek but resolute silence to show the judges that he has no intention of crediting the proceedings; finally he appeals to Rome, not to save his skin, but to save his reputation («ad excusationem sui, non liberationem ... famae potius quam vitae decrevit consulere»). All this apparatus of explication, worked out in such detail in his sermons on Christ and Susanna, he would have undoubtedly brought to bear on his own behavior, had he given us a written report of it. His spokesmen at Rome he would surely have cast in the role of Daniel, as he had done with Thierry at Soissons (see above, note 72). But of course reality did not arrange itself according to Biblical precedent. Abelard did not make it to Rome, and his spokesmen did not have a chance to intervene, as Daniel intervened for Susanna.

Besides the affinities between his treatment of Susanna and his own behavior at Sens, and besides his own preoccupation with his good name [75] (a preoccupation which lagged far behind the loss of it), two further considerations argue for this reconstruction. First, Abelard at Sens did not say anything about the prearranged verdict. But if it had been his intention to have the verdict overturned, then he would have done so. His silence on this crucial point of the legality of the proceedings is so contrary to his self-interest that it must be explained either as an irrational failure to act or as a silent «final confession of the condemned.» Second, I reveals in the *Apologia* «*universis*» that his attitude towards the condemnation at Sens and his appeal was indeed close to that which he had imputed to Susanna in his Sermon 29. He calls upon God as the witness to his innocence («Deum testem et judicem in animam meam invoco...,» PL 178:105). His knowledge of his innocence assures him of his ultimate acquittal («pietatem vestram exoro ne innocentiam meam, *quam a culpa veritas liberat,* nemo respergendo delinquat,» 107; emphasis mine.) And the writes the *Apologia* for two reasons only: to protect his reputation, and lest his silence be taken as a sign of his guilt. [76] Thus the question of guilt or innocence is settled only between himself and God, and the writing of *apologiae* can only serve the purpose of defending the reputation. [77] This *Apologia* puts forward quietly the suggestion that the judges who have judged him (will judge him) have no right to do so. He has always taught openly, he says, and considered his students his judges, and the brief work ends with the injunction, «judge not that ye be not judged: condemn not that ye be not condemned» (107). The comparison of this statement of innocence with his Sermon 29, and his earlier identification with Susanna during his trial at Soissons (see above, note 72) place beyond all reasonable doubt the idea that his actions at Sens were in part modelled on Susanna.

The appeal to Rome appears incongruous, indeed hypocritical, if we wish to see Abelard entering Sens with visions of the replaying of Christ's trial in his mind. But the example of Susanna shows us how to understand the connection: his explanation of Christ's and Susanna's trials and his silence at Sens, all are expressions of a consistent pattern of thought on proper behavior in the face of unjust condemnation, and the example of Susanna is particularly important, because it showed the possibility of higher vindication beyond the judgment of false judges.

But the fact remains, Abelard appealed to Rome at a time when his reputation and his career were at stake. And St. Bernard's assurances that his person was in no danger [78] suggest Abelard's uneasiness on that point. He knew both that a successful appeal could turn aside all these dangers, and that he could rely on powerful support in the curia, support that Bernard himself feared: Guido di Castello, for instance, and the sub-deacon Hyacinth (later cardinal, then Pope Celestine III), [79] a former student who was present at the trial at Sens and at the meeting of officials on the previous day, and who spoke out strongly for Abelard, even to the point, it appears, of threatening Bernard (see Bernard, Ep. 189, PL 182:357A; Ep. 338, PL 182:543D). And so Abelard's appeal can be seen as a calculated political act. Therefore we must distinguish between the purity of motivation behind his refusal to defend himself on the one hand and behind his appeal on the other. Biblical parallels provide a satisfactory explanation for Abelard's silence, which is unintelligible as a political act. To explain the appeal as an ideal act or an assertion of conviction is more strained. Susanna merely stood there and was the passive beneficiary of divine intervention; Abelard trudged off for Paris, and after some three or four weeks of waiting, for Rome. But the problem is not that we are attempting to judge Abelard's actions by a false comparison — the precedent of Susanna is obviously the correct comparison, a parallel which Abelard himself would invoke — but rather that there is a discrepancy between thought and deed in his appeal to Rome. But this is not a concern of the present study. I have tried to demonstrate that there is in Abelard's writings a whole complex of ideas on the proper behavior of an innocent man unjustly condemned. He considered himself at Sens to be in circumstances to which those ideas applied. Both in the general outline of his behavior there and in particular details of his «defense» he bore himself as those ideas dictated.

Abelard's interpretation of Susanna's behavior and the connection of her silence with that of Christ may well have come to him via a sermon of Augustine urging silence as the proper defense of the just man.[80] But the examples of Christ and Susanna before their judges and Augustine's commendation of silence went largely unheeded by Christians unjustly accused, as far as I have been able to determine. The trial of Thomas More offers some interesting parallels, since he also maintained an obstinate silence before his interrogators. But More's motivations were wholly different from those of Christ or Abelard.[81] There is no tradition of silent insistence on condemnation or martyrdom. In Christian hagiography voluble protestations of the martyr's faith become the rule. In fact in some saints' legends the pagan judges complain of the loquacity of the defendant.[82] St. Paul, the aggressive wrangler at court, and St. Stephen, whose speech before his persecutors takes up fifty-one verses in the Acts of the Apostles,[83] became models for the hagiographer.

There is one final piece of shoring that needs to be put into place before my argument is complete. The argument depends in large part on the idea that Abelard abstracted patterns of behavior from biblical examples. Now if he never tended to identify with Christ, saints, Old Testament figures and church fathers, then the probability that he did so at Sens would be very slim. But the opposite is the case. He regularly projected his problems, circumstances, thoughts, into biblical characters; this is a well known and much studied feature of his thought and writings.[84] Christ and St. Jerome were the figures with whom he identified most strongly.[85] In his *Planctus,* his own circumstances often account for his choice and treatment of the subject matter, a fact turned up in several incisive analyses of his poems devoted to Samson and Jephtha's daughter.[86] The figure of

Mary Magdalene in Abelard's writings will be of interest to anyone who studies this aspect of his thought. She occurs frequently in his writings for the Paraclete. [87] She is clearly a figure whom Abelard wished to hold up to Heloise as an admonishing example, inviting her to identify with this sexual sinner who had turned to Christ. Furthermore, Abelard has furnished us with a direct statement of his subjective relationship to Scripture. In the letter establishing a rule for the Paraclete, he urges the nuns to read and study Scripture, which is, he says, «a mirror of the soul ... in which anyone who gains life by reading and benefit by understanding will recognize the beauty or deformity of his own behavior. [88] This gives us further assurance that in sensing affinities between his life and his reading of the Bible, we are rediscovering relationships that Abelard perceived before us. [89]

Finally, Abelard's reading of the trials of Christ and Susanna and his own behavior at Sens are consistent with a tendency towards inwardness, introspection, self-denial and the idealizing of passivity which becomes pronounced in the years after his castration. Passivity and a certain inept meekness characterize his «defense» at Soissons. From his own report on the proceedings, it appears that he neither actively defended himself nor demanded the right to do so. He never mentions outright defiance or outrage on his part at what he claims to have been an unfair action against him. If he had defied his judges he surely would have reported it himself. At least he was not reticent in reporting his attacks on William of Champeaux and Anselm of Laon, men of much greater status than his accusers at Soissons. Abelard defends himself on intellectual grounds, not personal. He is invincible in disputes on the nature of the Trinity, [90] but is prostrate in the face of machinations and outright injustice. There is a good deal of truth about Abelard's character in the nasty comment of Otto of Freising about Bretons in general (made with Abelard in mind): Brittany is «a land of clerics who possess minds that are acute and keen in the study of the arts, but who are near-idiots when it comes to other matters.» [91] Geoffrey of Chartres, Abelard tells us, offered him advice on dealing with his enemies at Soissons. This dubious advice is that he should become meek in the same proportion as his enemies become violent and open in their persecutions. The manifest envy behind their actions will harm them more than Abelard *(Hist. cal.,* p. 87). This is a concise statement of Abelard's «strategy» at Soissons: the more severe and openly unjust the attacks, the more passive the reaction. Probably Abelard put this advice into Geoffrey's mouth (as he put the speech of Daniel into Thierry's), the advice so clearly suits Abelard's own temperament at this point. We hear much about his tears and anguish in his account of Soissons and its aftermath *(Hist. cal.,* p. 89, lines 905 f., 917 f.), but nothing of his anger. Having inspired powerful outrage in others, possibly he was incapable of rousing it in himself. [92]

Abelard ends his autobiography commending a martyrlike patience to those suffering wrongs:

> ... the more undeserved the wrongs that befall us, the more cheerfully we should bear them ... *[Hist. cal.,* p. 108].
>
> This is what that wisest of wise men meant when in his *Proverbs* [12.21] he said: «Whatever befalls the just man will not trouble him.» In this he clearly shows that those who are angered by some tribulation, though they know that God ordained it,

leave the path of justice, submit to their own rather than God's will, and in their secret thoughts rebel against the meaning of the words, «Thy will be done,» placing their own desires before God's *[Hist. cal.,* p. 109].

He gives a detailed exposition of this stance — passivity as ideal behavior in the face of wrongs [93] — in *Problemata Heloissae* 14 (commenting on Lam. 3.27 ff.):

And lest he should exult in his virtues, he is to be humbled by persecutions, so that his virtue, having been tested, may be crowned through that patience which makes the poor in spirit truly meek. Therefore he will turn the other cheek to the man who strikes him, and he is heaped with abuse, for when he is injured with words or with deeds, he is refreshed by them and delights in them as in a feast [PL 178:699A-B].

This is an extreme statement of a position which Abelard repeatedly gave expression to, in word and in deed, in the years between his castration and his death. [94]

My conclusion is that Abelard's actions at Sens were consistent with a broad complex of ideas on patience and passivity in the face of injustice in his writings. His reading of Scripture, his ethical thought and his own bent towards idealizing passivity funnelled into his silence at his trial in 1140. This furnishes a much more credible explanation for his failure to defend himself than the idea of some physical or mental failing. My explanation is for the most part consistent with Deutsch's rendering of the historical facts, and it helps fill out some of the lacunae in Deutsch's theory.

In the light of these findings, it is clear that the Abelard who faced Bernard at Sens was not the arrogant, brash dialectician, whose self-confidence derived from unbounded faith in his own intellect. It was Abelard the monk, ascetic and martyr, a man bent on ending years of uncertainty, whose self-confidence came from the sure knowledge of his impending condemnation. But there is also a militant aspect to his capitulation, or passivity, at Sens. Though his silence hastened his condemnation, it also expressed a proud refusal to cooperate with the unjust proceedings. It asserted Abelard's conviction that he is obligated to satisfy only the conscience and that words would be wasted on men who have determined their judgment in advance. It is a public insistence on the privacy of moral determinations.

NOTES

1. On the date of the council (June 2, 1140), see Giles Constable, *The Letters of Peter the Venerable,* 1 (Cambridge, Mass., 1967), 318-319.

2. According to a note of Jean Leclercq («Notes Abélardiennes,» *Bulletin de philosophie médiévale* 8/9 [1966/67], p. 62), P. Zerbi is preparing an extensive historical study of the council.

3. I shall refer throughout to the proceedings at Sens as a «trial» for the sake of convenience. It was a hearing at a church council which was called at Abelard's own initiative. On the nature of the proceedings and their historical development, see Jürgen Miethke, «Theologenprozesse in der ersten Phase ihrer institutionellen Ausbildung: Die Verfahren gegen Peter Abaelard und Gilbert von Poitiers,» *Viator* 6 (1975), 87-116.

4. The tradition of «eloquent silence» from antiquity to the 17th century has recently been studied by Uwe Ruberg, *Beredtes Schweigen in lehrhafter und erzählender deutscher Literatur des Mittelalters,* Münstersche Mittelalter-Schriften 32 (Munich, 1978).

5. Citations are from the edition by J. Monfrin, *Historia calamitatum: Texte critique avec une introduction* (Paris, 1962). The authenticity of the *Historia* and of the personal letters ascribed to Abelard and Heloise has long been suspect. There is a recent summary of the controversy by Peter von Moos, *Mittelalterforschung und Ideologiekritik: Der Gelehrtenstreit um Heloise*, Kritische Information 15 (Munich, 1974). Since von Moos' book appeared, two studies by John Benton have appeared seriously questioning the authenticity of the *Historia*, personal letters, and parts of the letters of instruction: «Fraud, Fiction and Borrowing in the Correspondence of Abelard and Heloise,» *Pierre Abélard — Pierre le Vénérable: Les Courants philosophiques, littéraires et artistiques en occident au milieu du XIIe siècle*, Colloques internationaux du CNRS 546 (Paris, 1975) — henceforth cited as *Colloque* — pp. 437-512; also J. Benton and F. P. Ercoli, «The Style of the *Historia calamitatum*: A Preliminary Test of the Authenticity of the Correspondence Attributed to Abelard and Heloise,» *Viator* 6 (1975), 59-86. Benton's ideas have found some support (see H. Silvestre, «Réflexions sur la thèse de J. F. Benton relative au dossier Abélard-Héloïse,» *Recherches de théologie ancienne et médiévale* 44 [1977], 211-216), but mainly opposition. See Peter Dronke, *Abelard and Heloise in Medieval Testimonies*, University of Glasgow, W. P. Ker Memorial Lecture 26 (Glasgow, 1976); C. Stephen Jaeger, «The Prologue to the *Historia calamitatum* and the "Authenticity Question",» *Euphorion* 74 (1980), 1-15. Some recent works which are not mainly concerned with the authenticity dispute but which bring forward evidence linking Abelard to the *Historia* and personal letters are Mary McLaughlin, «The Correspondence of Abelard and Heloise and Abelard's Other Writings for the Paraclete» (unpublished paper read at the 1974 meeting of American Historical Association); eadem, «Peter Abelard and the Dignity of Women: 12th Century "Feminism" in Theory and Practice,» *Colloque*, pp. 287-333; Peter von Moos, «Lucan und Abaelard,» *Hommages à André Boutemy*, ed. Guy Cambier, Collection Latomus 145 (Brussels, 1976), 413-443. The strongest opposition to Benton's ideas has come from Chrysogonus Waddell in unpublished research refuting some of the central arguments in Benton's studies. As a result of Waddell's studies, Benton recently (at the Internationale Studientage — Petrus Abaelardus, in Trier, 16-20 April 1979) considerably modified his earlier position, conceding the authenticity of the greater part of the *Historia*. We may safely treat it as an authentic work of Abelard in this study. Mary McLaughlin is now preparing a detailed critical review of the authenticity dispute, to appear in *Speculum*.

6. For detailed studies of the events, see Arno Borst, «Abälard und Bernhard,» *Historische Zeitschrift* 186 (1958), 497-526; and R. Klibansky, «Peter Abailard and Bernard of Clairvaux: A Letter by Abailard,» *Medieval and Renaissance Studies* 5 (1961), 1-27. See also Miethke, «Theologenprozesse» (cited above, note 3).

7. The 13 *capitula* and William's accompanying letter are printed among Bernard's letters, PL 182:531-533 (Ep. 326). See Klibansky, «Peter Abailard,» p. 11f. For a discussion of William's *capitula* and the other polemical writings against Abelard preceding the council, see D. E. Luscombe, *The School of Peter Abelard* (Cambridge, Eng., 1969), pp. 116-142.

8. Bernard's Ep. 8, PL 182:1053-1072. Contrary to earlier opinions, this tract was written before the council of Sens, since Abelard refers to it in his letter to his *socii* (ed. Klibansky, cited in n. 6, above), written shortly before the council. But there were successive redactions: see Jean Leclercq, «Les Formes successives de la lettre-traité de Saint Bernard contre Abélard,» *Révue Bénédictine* 78 (1968), 87-105.

9. Epistolae 188, 192, 193, 330, 331, 332.

10. Cf. Borst, «Abälard und Bernhard,» pp. 512-513.

11. [Magister Petrus] ... crebro nos pulsare coepit, nec ante voluit desistere, quoad ad dominum Clarae-Vallensem abbatem super hoc scribentes, assignato die ... Senonis ante nostram submonuimus venire praesentiam ...» (from the report of the bishops to Pope Innocent II written after the council, among Bernard's letters, Ep. 337, PL 182:541B).

12. He described these hesitations in his letter to Pope Innocent II written after the council: Ep. 189, PL 182:354-357.

13. Published by Klibansky (cited above, note 6) and by Jean Leclercq, *Analecta sacri ordinis Cisterciensis* 9 (1953), 104-105.

14. Abelard writes to his *socii:* «Nondum vero audivimus, quale ipse responsum dederit litteris illis» (ed. Klibansky, p. 7).

15. Cf. Leif Grane, *Peter Abelard: Philosophy and Christianity in the Middle Ages,* trans. F. and C. Crowley (New York, 1970), p. 136: «He took this decision [viz. to defend himself at Sens] on the basis of a supreme confidence in his intellectual superiority.» Also J. G. Sikes, *Peter Abailard* (Cambridge, Eng., 1932; repr., New York, 1965), pp. 227-228.

16. *Hist. cal.,* p. 97: «Deus ipse mihi testis est, quotiens aliquem ecclesiasticarum personarum conventum adunari noveram, hoc in dampnationem meam agi credebam. Stupefactus ilico quasi supervenientis ictum fulguris, expectabam ut quasi hereticus aut prophanus in conciliis traherer aut sinagogis.»

17. Abelard calls him «Ille quippe occultus iam dudum inimicus, qui se huc usque amicum, immo amicissimum simulavit...» (ed. Klibansky, p. 6), and says that Bernard had spoken against him at Sens and Paris «de profundo nequitiae suae...» (p. 7). In his article «Abälard und Bernhard,» pp. 504-505, Borst has argued that relations between Bernard and Abelard were good prior to 1139. Hence he denies that Abelard's Letter 10, justifying the form of the Lord's prayer he ordained at the Paraclete, is a polemic against Bernard, who objected to the wording of the prayer. The idea has found strong support: Chrysogonus Waddell, «Peter Abelard's *Letter 10* and Cistercian Liturgical Reform,» *Studies in Medieval Cistercian History* 2, ed. John Sommerfeldt, Cistercian Studies Series 24 (Kalamazoo, Mich., 1976), 75-86; E. F. Little, «Relations between St. Bernard and Abelard prior to 1139» (Paper read at the Cistercian Studies Conference, University of Dallas, Texas, 1972). Jürgen Miethke has argued convincingly against the idea: «Abaelards Stellung zur Kirchenreform,» *Francia* 1 (1972), pp. 187 ff.

18. True, he had called for a council two decades earlier at which he could confront his former teacher Roscellinus because, as Abelard alleged, «multas in me contumelias et minas evomuerit» (PL 178:356D, Ep. 14), and this is a clear parallel to his challenge to Bernard at Sens. But the challenge to Roscellinus came before Abelard's defeat at Soissons, and this changed his attitude towards councils. Also, Roscellinus as a condemned heretic and Bernard on the way to sainthood were opponents of quite unequal stature.

19. As the letter of the bishops openly concedes: «... sententias pravi dogmatis ipsius... non solum falsas, sed et haereticas esse evidentissime comprobatas, *pridie* ante factam ad vos appellationem *damnavimus*» (Ep. 337, PL 182:542B; emphasis mine.)

20. Printed among Abelard's works: *Berengarii Scholastici Apologeticus contra Bernardum et al.* PL 178:1857-1870. On Berengar, see Luscombe, «Berengar, Defender of Peter Abelard,» *Recherches de théologie ancienne et médiévale* 33 (1966), 319-37, and *School of Peter Abelard,* pp. 29-49.

21. Cf. Bernard, Ep. 189; PL 182:356B: «... producta sunt quaedam capitula de libris ejus excerpta...» These are the 19 *capitula,* of uncertain authorship, of which Jean Leclercq has published a recent edition: «Les Formes successives de la lettre-traité,» (cited above, note 8), pp. 103-104. See also J. Rivière, «Les "Capitula" d'Abélard condamnés au concile de Sens,» *Recherches de théologie ancienne et médiévale* 5 (1933), 5-22; L. Grill, «Die neunzehn "Capitula" Bernhards von Clairvaux gegen Abälard,» *Historisches Jahrbuch* 80 (1961), 230-239. For discussions of recent literature on them, see Jean Leclercq, «Notes abélardiennes,» *Bulletin de philosophie médiévale* 13 (1971), pp. 68 ff. and E. F. Little, «The Source of the *Capitula* of Sens of 1140,» *Studies in Medieval Cistercian History* 2 (full citation above, note 17), pp. 87-91.

22. Ep. 189, PL 182:356B: «Quae [capitula] cum coepissent legi, nolens audire exivit...»

23. «visus diffidere magister Petrus Abaelardus, et subterfugere, respondere noluit; sed quamvis libera sibi daretur audientia, tutumque locum et aequos habere judices, ad tamen, sanctissime Pater, appellans praesentiam vestram cum suis a conventu discessit.» (Ep. 337, PL 182:542B; here lightly emended.)

24. On Geoffrey, see W. W. Williams, *Studies in St. Bernard of Clairvaux* (London, 1927), p. 9 ff. Also, Jean Leclercq, *Recueil d'études sur St. Bernard et ses écrits,* 1 (Rome, 1962), pp. 27-46.

25. «At ille, nec volens resipiscere, nec valens resistere sapientiae et spiritui qui loquebatur, ut tempus redimeret, Sedem apostolicam appellavit. Sed et postea ab egregio

illo catholicae fidei advocato monitus, ut vel jam sciens in personam suam nihil agendum, responderet tam libere, quam secure, audiendus tantum et ferendus in omni patientia, non sententia aliqua feriendus; hoc quoque omnimodis recusavit. Nam et confessus est postea suis, ut aiunt, quod ea hora, maxima quidem ex parte memoria ejus turbata fuerit, ratio caligaverit, et interior fugerit sensus.» *(Vita prima* 3.5, PL 185:311C.) With no hesitation we can ignore Geoffrey's claim that Abelard's students had learned from their master of this mental failure and reported it to him.

26. The most radical statement of this view comes from Henri Daniel-Rops, *Bernard of Clairvaux* (New York, 1964), p. 85: «Surprised by [Bernard's] attack, disconcerted, overwhelmed at the start under a deluge of citations drawn from the Scriptures ... Abelard felt the ground swept from beneath his feet and he staggered before the assault.» But, of course, since Bernard's tract had been circulating in Paris, probably for weeks before the council, Abelard had had ample time to prepare himself for the «deluge.»

27. R. L. Poole, *Illustrations from the History of Medieval Thought and Learning* (London, 1920), p. 144.

28. For a sensitive and eloquent treatment of the gradual dissolution of identity Abelard suffered in the years after his castration, see Mary McLaughlin, «Abelard as Autobiographer: The Motive and Meaning of his "Story of Calamities",» *Speculum* 42 (1967), 463-488.

29. J. Jeannin, «La Dernière Maladie d'Abélard: Une Aliée imprévue de St. Bernard,» *Mélanges St. Bernard* (Dijon, 1953), 109-115.

30. In 1140 Abelard was 61 years old. He had broken a bone in his neck in a fall from a horse while abbot at St. Gildas and had probably never fully recovered. Possibly he already suffered from the skin disease which Peter the Venerable mentioned in his letter to Heloise after Abelard's death (Letter 115, ed. Constable, 1:307: «... Scabie et quibusdam corporis incommoditatibus gravabatur...»). And surely his castration had effects far beyond the period in which it occurred. Cf. McLaughlin, «Abelard as Autobiographer,» p. 467: «His castration could hardly have failed to intensify, if it did not produce, the instability often exhibited in the emotions and actions of his later life.»

30a. On the permissive laws of appeal and the abuses of this right in the early 12th century, see Stanley Chodorow, «Dishonest Litigation in the Church Courts, 1140-98,» *Law, Church, and Society: Essays in Honor of Stephan Kuttner,* ed. Kenneth Pennington and Robert Sommerville, The Middle Ages Series (Philadelphia, 1977), pp. 187-206.

31. S. M. Deutsch, *Die Synode von Sens 1141 und die Verurtheilung Abälards* (Berlin, 1880).

32. For recent treatments, see Borst, «Abälard und Bernhard,» and Klibansky, «Peter Abailard»; also A. V. Murray, *Abelard and St. Bernard* (Manchester, 1967), p. 41, and D. W. Robertson, *Abelard and Heloise* (New York, 1972), p. 142.

33. Cf. Borst, «Abälard und Bernhard,» p. 517: «Er musste sich hintergangen fühlen... er hatte ein Schieds-gericht gewollt und wurde nun vor ein Gericht gestellt. Das war gegen die Verabredung; Abälard brauchte sich an seine Zusage nicht mehr gebunden zu fühlen... Abälard würde sich zu verteidigen haben und sein System nicht frei entwickeln können.» And Klibansky, «Peter Abailard,» pp. 24-25: «Up to the last moment Abailard thought of the dispute in terms of a personal contest, an ἀγών, in a spirit entirely foreign to Bernard.»

34. *Hist. cal.,* p. 87: «... sine ullo discussionis examine meipsum compulerunt propria manu librum memoratum in ignem proicere...» Otto of Freising, *Gesta Friderici* 1.47, MGH SS 20:377: «... libros quos ediderat, propria manu ab episcopis igni dare coactus est, nulla sibi respondendi facultate ... concessa.»

35. See Raymond M. Martin, «Pro Petro Abaelardo: Un plaidoyer de Robert de Melun contre S. Bernard,» *Révue des sciences philosophiques et théologiques* 12 (1923), 308-333.

36. This brief *Apologia seu fidei confessio* «universis» is printed in PL 178:105-107. On the date see Borst, «Abälard und Bernhard,» pp. 514-515. He argues convincingly that it was written shortly before the council.

37. Deutsch is the harshest questioner of his own theory. He gives some strong arguments against it and concedes that it gives only the external explanation of events *(Synode von Sens,* pp. 32-33.)

38. Archbishop Samson of Reims, along with others in Bernard's camp, writes after the council to Innocent: «... ut suam prolongaret iniquitatem, Sedem apostolicam appellavit» (Among Bernard's letters, Ep. 191, PL 182:357D).

39. Ep. 337, PL 182:542B: «... licet appellatio ista minus canonica videretur...» Also Bernard, Ep. 189, PL 182: 356B: «... exivit, appellans ab electis judicibus, quod non putamus licere...»

40. PL 178:379-611. A new edition is being prepared by Louk Engels. It will appear in the *Continuatio Mediaevalis* of *Corpus Christianorum*.

41. On this period of Abelard's life, see Sikes, *Peter Abailard*, pp. 22-25; McLaughlin, «Abelard as Autobiographer,» pp. 476-477; Miethke, «Abaelards Stellung zur Kirchenreform,» p. 170 ff. According to *Hist. cal.*, pp. 98-101, he suffered constant persecutions there, but there is surprisingly little evidence to confirm Abelard's statement that «there is no longer anyone who does not know» about his sufferings *(Hist. cal.*, p. 99). Another witness to Abelard's problems there is Bernard, who writes of Abelard's return from St. Gildas: «Siluerat jam per multos dies: sed quando siluit in Britannia, concepit dolorem, et nunc in Francia concepit iniquitatem» (Ep. 331, PL 182:536D).

42. See P. D. Van den Eynde, «Le recueil des sermons de Pierre Abélard,» *Antonianum* 37 (1962), 17-54.

43. Rupert of Deutz comments at length on Christ's trial and explains his silence as follows: «"... et dicit Pilatus ad Iesum: Unde es tu? Iesus autem responsum non dedit ei." Nimis importuno tempore hoc interrogabat, quia tempus maxime tacendi erat, et ipse audire indignus erat, quia non credere volebat. Praeterea quia iam eundem agnum Dei male totonderat, id est flagellaverat, ideo coram illo iuste obmutescebat et non aperiebat os suum» *(Ruperti Tiutensis Commentaria in Evangelium Sancti Johannis* 13, ed. R. Haacke, Corpus Christianorum, Continuatio mediaevalis 9 [Turnholt, 1969], p. 735). The *Enarrationes in Matthaeum* ascribed to Anselm of Laon gives the following commentaries: «Jesus autem non respondebat, sciens, ut Deus, quaecunque respondisset torquendum in calumniam.» (PL 162:1478A-B); citing St. Hilary: «... Huic enim nihil respondere voluit, ne crimen diluens dimitteretur, et ita crucis utilitas differretur.» (1482A-B). On this explanation see Ruberg, *Beredtes Schweigen*, pp. 128-129. St. Bernard in his sermons on the passion mentions the trial only in reference to the mocking of Christ. Though he twice quotes Isaiah 53.7 («Sicut ovis ad occisionem ducetur etc.») he connects the quotation only with Christ's patience, not with his silence before his judges: «... "non aperuit os suum," non adversus Patrem murmurans a quo missus fuerat...» *(S. Bernardi Opera* 5, ed. J. Leclercq and H. M. Rochais [Rome, 1968], p. 57.) Ordericus Vitalis *(Hist. eccl.* 1.1.13) makes a cursory mention of his silence: «... Et cum accusaretur, ut Matthaeus ait, a principibus sacerdotum et senioribus populi nihil respondit, quod ex mansuetudine fecit.» (PL 188: 56C-D). Peter Comestor treats it in a dependent clause: «Cumque non respondisset Jesus, exsurgens Caiphas dixit ad Jesum: Adjuro te etc.» *(Hist. scholast. in Evang.* 160, PL 198:1624). In general his silence is interpreted as a sign of patience and humility. Cf. Alanus de Insulis, Sermon 2, PL 210:225A: «Contra has iniurias patientissimus fuit, quia nec verbum respondit, unde: Tanquam ovis ad occisionem ductus est.» And John of Ford, Sermon 30.5: «Humilitatem et taciturnitatem in tanta accusatorum improbitate miratus est [Pilatus] vehementer, teste evangelista» (ed. E. Mikkers and H. Costello, Corpus Christianorum, Continuatio mediaevalis 17 [Turnholt, 1970], p. 247). Petrus Riga does not mention Christ's silence at all in his treatment of the passion. Cf. *Aurora. Petri Rigae Biblia versificata* 2, ed. P. E. Beichner, University of Notre Dame Publications in Mediaeval Studies 19 (Notre Dame, 1965), pp. 523-524. Ruberg's collection of sources on Christ's silence tends to confirm my statement that the silence did not inspire much commentary. The citations in *Beredtes Schweigen*, pp. 119-138, are brief explanations, glosses, often only a brief mention of the silence without comment.

44. Matt. 26.62-63: «et surgens princeps sacerdotum ait illi, nihil respondes ad ea quae isti adversum te testificantur? Iesus autem tacebat.» Mark 14.60-61: «et exsurgens summus sacerdos in medium interrogavit Iesum dicens, non respondes quicquam ad ea quae tibi obiciuntur ab his? ille autem tacebat et nihil respondit.» Mark 15.4-5: «Pilatus autem rursum interrogavit eum dicens, non respondes quicquam? vide in quantis te accusant. Iesus autem amplius nihil respondit, ita ut miraretur Pilatus.»

45. Luke 23.9: «interrogabat autem illum multis sermonibus, at ipse nihil respondebat.»
46. John 19.9-10: «et ingressus est praetorium iterum, et dicit ad Iesum, unde es tu? Iesus autem responsum non dedit ei. Dicit ergo ei Pilatus, mihi non loqueris? Nescis quia potestatem habeo crucifigere te et potestatem habeo dimittere te?»
47. He indicated to Heloise in the introductory letter to the sermons that they were composed in haste: «...nonnulla...opuscula sermonum...scribere praeter consuetudinem nostram maturavi» (PL 178:379).
48. The sentence is incoherent and incomplete. What is there seems like notes rather than a corrupted text. The intriguing subject, «quisquis judex» is left hanging.
49. The logic of the sentence escapes me. Who hears from whom? It prepares us to marvel at what Christ said, then reports the words of Pilate.
50. «Quam constanter autem Dominus passioni occurreret et in passione persisteret, quisquis diligenter attendit judex secundum magnitudinem timoris, incomparabilem in eo fortitudinem...enim omittam caetera, quis non illud miretur, quod a Pilato interrogatus cum respondere nollet, ab eo audierit: "Mihi non loqueris? Nescis quia potestatem habeo dimittere te..." Qui etiam ab ipso ad Herodem missus, tanquam ad ejus potestatem pertinens, cum esset Galilaeus, ut sic per eum facile liberari posset, nil ei respondere dignatus est, cum multis interrogaretur sermonibus...» (469C-D).
51. «Quod ergo pavendo taedere, vel perturbari adeo videtur, ut quasi desperans diceret: Et quid dicam? signa sunt omnia non ignaviae vel diffidentiae, sed timoris maximi ad infirmitatis probationem assumptae...» (469D). On Abelard's ideas on the moral value of fear, see. A. Teetaert, «Doctrine d'Abaelard au sujet de la valeur morale de la crainte des peines,» *Estudis Franciscans* 36 (1925), 108-125.
52. Cf. PL 178:479A. On this motivation for the silence, see Ruberg, *Beredtes Schweigen*, pp. 129-130.
53. «Quanta autem constantia illic persisteret, patenter ostenditur, ubi interrogatus a Pilato, responsum ei non reddebat. De qua ejus confidentia, et quasi de suo contemptu Pilatus admirans: "Nescis," inquit, "quia potestatem habeo crucifigere te et potestatem habeo dimittere te?"» (481D).
53[a]. «...hoc est ne turbae, quae illum cum exsultatione susceperant...in eos commoverentur, et ipsum eriperent. O caeci et pessimi! dolo eum vultis tenere, tanquam ignarum machinationis vestrae...» (462A).
54. The attitude of proud and aggressive surrender expressed in the Biblical quotation (John 10.18) evidently impressed Abelard. Cf. Sermon 7, PL 178:435D; Sermon 9, 445C; *Comment. Epist. ad Rom.* 3 in *Petri Abaelardi Opera Theologica*, 1, ed. E. Buytaert, Corpus Christianorum, Continuatio Mediaevalis 11 (Turnholt, 1969), p. 179; *Expos. Symboli Apost.*, PL 178:672A.
54[a]. «Jesus itaque omnia quae ventura erant super eum praecessit. Dum homines Deo vim facere parant, sponte Dominus, non intractus, occurrit passioni, sicut ipse dixerat: "Nemo tollit a me animam meam, sed ego pono eam. Sciens," inquit, "omnia": hoc est non ignoras eorum machinamenta...» (471A).
55. See also Sermon 7, PL 178:433B, 436A; Sermon 8, 436C (twice); Sermon 10, 452C; Sermon 15, 496A (twice), 496B, 497C, 497D, 498A.
56. «...eo amplius invidiam perversorum contra se commovit, ut quod jamdudum voluerant, perficere maturarent, et ab eo daretur facultas, in quibus praecesserat voluntas» (435D).
57. «Ut autem majori incitarentur invidia, qui de morte Domini jam tractabant, et Deo magis indignarentur, quo amplius eum honorari viderent, tantum sibi honoris hodie permisit exhiberi, quantum nulli regum legimus exhibitum» (436A).
58. Cf. Rupert of Deutz, *Comment. in Joan.* 10, ed. Haacke, pp. 575-576; Ivo of Chartres, Sermon 16, *In ramis palmarum*, PL 162:587B; Abelard, Sermon 15, PL 178:497C-D.
59. See the *Glossa ordinaria* on Matt. 21.10: «Quod ideo factum est [viz. Christ being called king] ut amplius illorum adversum se excitaret invidiam, quia iam tempus passionis instabat» *(Biblia sacra cum glossa ordinaria* 5 [Antwerp, 1617], p. 345). The same gloss occurs for Luke 19.37 (ibid., p. 942).

59a. «Dissimulavi primum... Cedens tamen (licet vix, ita ut flerem) consilio amicorum, qui videntes quomodo se quasi ad spectaculum omnes pararent, timebant ne de nostra absentia et scandalum populo, et cornua crescerent adversario...occurri ad locum et diem...» (Ep. 189, PL 182:355D-356A; emphasis mine).

60. Bernard, Ep. 189, PL 182:355D: «vocavit multos, congregavit complices;» letter of Samson of Reims et al. Bernard, Ep. 191, PL 182:358A: «homo ille multitudinem trahit post se, et populum qui sibi credat, habet...»; Bernard, Ep. 337, PL 182:542A: «adfuit magister Petrus cum fautoribus suis»; ibid., 542B: «cum suis...discessit.»

61. Heloise says of his early fame, «Quis etenim regum aut philosophorum tuam famam exaequare poterat? Quae te regio aut civitas seu villa videre non aestuabat? Quis te rogo in publicum procedentem conspicere non festinabat...» (Ep. 2 [using the numbering of the Migne edition], ed. J. T. Muckle, «The Personal Letters between Abelard and Heloise,» *Mediaeval Studies* 15 [1953], 71). At the Paraclete, Roscellinus says in a letter to Abelard full of ugly abuse, he gathered around him «from all parts a throng of barbarians» («undique congregata barbarorum multitudine»; Ep. 15, PL 178:370C). During this period Abelard attracted such a crowd of followers that he himself can imagine his enemies saying of him what the Pharisees said of Christ: «Ecce mundus totus post eum abiit» *(Hist. cal.,* p. 94; cf. John 12.19). Otto of Freising said of him, probably referring to the period after 1136 when Abelard was once more teaching in Paris: «maximamque post se sociorum multitudinem traheret...» *(Gesta Frid.* 1.48, MGH SS 20:337). One of Abelard's epitaphs calls him «turbae lucerna scholaris» (PL 178:105A).

62. Bernard, Ep. 332, PL 182:537C: «Accedit non solus, sicut Moyses, ad caliginem in qua erat Deus, sed cum turba multa et discipulis suis.» Ep. 189, PL 182:355A: «Volant libri ... Urbibus et castellis ingeruntur pro luce tenebrae ... Transierunt de gente in gentem, et de regno ad populum alterum.» William's letter to Bernard and Geoffrey of Chartres (among Bernard's letters, Ep. 326, PL 182:531B): «libri ejus transeunt maria, transiliunt Alpes... per provincias et regna deferuntur, celebriter praedicantur...»

63. See Klibansky, «Peter Abailard,» p. 22 ff.

64. Klibansky, after comparing Abelard's comments on the trial at Soissons with his behavior at Sens, suggested that this mechanism was at work («Peter Abailard,» p. 24). We learn from his treatment of the passion in his sermons that he certainly understood the urge to hasten a tragic end. Cf. also his praise of Jephtha's daughter in Ep. 7 (Ep. 6, ed. Muckle): «Dimissa per duos menses a patre libera, his completis redit ad patrem occidenda. Sponte morti se ingerit et *eam magis provocat quam veretur*» (ed. J. T. Muckle, «The Letter of Heloise on Religious Life and Abelard's First Reply,» *Mediaeval Studies* 17 [1955], 270). And his Hymn 98, *In festis martyrum, in 2. nocturno:* «Sed ut poena / protendatur, / Poenae finis, / mors differtur, / Optant mori / Diu torti / Martyres...» *(Peter Abelard's Hymnarius Paraclitensis,* 2, ed. Joseph Szövérffy, Medieval Classics: Texts and Studies 3 [Albany, N. Y., 1975], pp. 204-205).

65. J. Monfrin, «Le Problème de l'authenticité de la correspondance d'Abélard et d'Héloïse,» *Colloque,* p. 420: «Il est frappant de voir comment le récit de son arrivée à Soissons, avant le concile, utilise — vocabulaire, citations explicites et implicites — le récit évangelique des préparatifs de la Passion.»

66. Abelard had quoted the entire speech of Christ in his sermon on the passion (Sermon 11, PL 178:478B) and cites the speech, abbreviated, in Sermon 12, 481C.

67: One of the clearest departures from the words of Christ («nec unquam aquas furtivas vel panem absconditum habuit mea doctrina»; cf. Proverbs 9.17) is possibly a reply to a charge of Bernard: «Aquas furtivas et panes absconditos domesticis suis apponit in libris...» (Ep. 332, PL 182:537C).

68. But he was clearly in a mood to conjure up important precedents for his own tribulations. Cf. letter to his *socii*, ed. Klibansky, p. 6: «Probabile satis est ad gloriam Vincentii Martyris quod descriptis eius gestis titulo invidit inimicus. Tale aliquid mihi nunc accidit...» Berengar of Poitiers paints the proceedings against Abelard as a parody of the trial of Christ, but without making any connection between the refusal of both to defend themselves: see PL 178:1860A-B.

69. Abelard had considered appealing to Rome for satisfaction after his castration, possibly even after his attackers had been brutally punished (by castration, blinding and

confiscation of their goods). But he decided against it, in part dissuaded by Fulk of Deuil in a letter of consolation he wrote to Abelard (Ep. 16, PL 178:371-376). The passage discouraging Abelard from appealing to Rome is not printed in the Patrologia. See P. D. Van den Eynde, «Détails biographiques sur Pierre Abélard,» *Antonianum* 38 (1963), p. 219, who prints the deleted passage and suggests that its anti-papal sentiments account for its omission.

70. Besides the *Apologia* «*universis*» there is the *Apologia contra Bernardum* «*Ne iuxta Boethianum*,» of which only a fragment has survived: *Petri Abaelardi Opera theologica*, 1:359-36. The editor, Buytaert, dates this apology — contrary to earlier opinion — before the council, probably in the winter 1139-1140 (ibid., pp. 352 ff.). And the *fidei confessio ad Heloisam*, PL 178, 375-78.

71. In 12th century treatments of Susanna, I find none which has any ties to Abelard's. In general the seduction is of much more interest than the trial. Cf. Hildebert of Lavardin, *Versus de Sancta Susanna*, PL 171:1287-1292; Petrus Riga, *Aurora* 1, ed. Beichner, pp. 360-367. Bernard includes her in a sermon on the Annunciation, but is not the least interested in the trial, her silence, or her acquittal: *In Annuntiatione dominica, Sermo 3, De Maria et adultera et Susanna* in his *Opera* 5:37-39.

72. He had held her up to the nuns of the Paraclete as an example in his letter encouraging the study of the Biblical languages (Ep. 9, PL 178:325-336). At Soissons one of the two men who spoke up for Abelard, a certain Thierry («Terricus quidam, scolaris magister»; *Hist. cal.*, p. 88; Thierry of Chartres?) upbraided the judges upon Abelard's condemnation by quoting the words of Daniel upbraiding the Israelites for accepting the judgment against Susanna: «Sic fatui, filii Israel non judicantes, neque quod verum est cognoscentes, condempnastis filium Israel. Revertimini ad judicium, et de ipso judice judicate, qui talem judicem quasi ad instructionem fidei et correctionem erroris instituistis; qui cum judicare deberet, ore se proprio condemnavit, divina hodie misericordia innocentem patenter, sicut olim Susannam a falsis accusatoribus, liberante» *(Hist. cal.,* p. 88; cf. Daniel 13.48-49). Undoubtedly Abelard himself wrote this speech and placed it in the mouth of Thierry. But even in the unlikely event that «a certain Thierry» actually spoke these or similar words, the speech is a powerful indication that Abelard before his judges felt an identification with Susanna before hers.

72[a]. «cum falso testimonio senum populus credidisset, et eam ad mortem condemnassent, exclamavit voce magna, et dixit: "Deus aeterne, qui absconditorum es cognitor, qui nosti omnia antequam fiant, tu scis quoniam contra me falsum tulerint testimonium, et ecce morior, cum nihil horum fecerim." In judicio prius constituta, cum illi in accusationem ejus testificarentur, non loqui, sed flere, et in coelum suspicere narratur, ut ejus patientia primum probaretur quam et in Christo propheta praedixerat his verbis: "Tanquam ovis ad occisionem ducetur, et quasi agnus coram tondente se obmutescet, et non aperiet os suum." Exspectabat ibi tacita damnationis suae sententiam, et tacens hominibus, soli Deo fletu loquebatur» (PL 178:561B-C).

73. *Comment. in Dan.* (included in *Glossa ordinaria*): «*"Exclamavit autem Susanna voce magna"* etc. Cordis affectus, et mentis pura confessio, et bonum conscientiae, vocem ejus fecit clariorem, unde erat magna exclamatio ejus Deo, quae ab hominibus non audiebatur» (PL 25:582A); cf. Augustine, *Enarratio in Psalmum 137*, PL 37:1775.

73[a]. «Exspectabat ibi tacita damnationis suae sententiam, et tacens hominibus, soli Deo fletu loquebatur. Nunc vero damnationis accepta sententia, ad excusationem sui, non liberationem, suam innocentiam protestata, famae potius quam vitae decrevit consulere...» (PL 178:561C).

73[b]. «Nunquid orando adjecit ut liberaretur a poena quam non meruerat ex culpa? nequaquam id rogare decreverat... nec tam de morte quam de infamia propulsanda curabat...» (PL 178:561D-562A).

74. «Certissimum quippe vel innocentiae vel culpae testimonium est extrema confessio damnatorum, maxime cum quidquid jam dicatur apud homines, sibi profuturum desperent, et tanto amplius de servanda veritate sunt solliciti, quanto se magis ad divinum judicium propinquare trepidant» (PL 178:561C).

75. Cf. *Hist. cal.*, pp. 80, 89, 102; also «Le Poème adressé par Abélard à son fils Astralabe,» ed. B. Hauréau, *Notices et extraits de quelques manuscrits latins de la Bi-

bliothèque Nationale 34,2 (Paris, 1893), 158: «Detrimentum tuae caveas super omnia famae.» The authenticity of the poem has been questioned, but not, to my knowledge, on substantive grounds; see F. J. E. Raby, *A History of Secular Latin Poetry in the Middle Ages*, 2, 2nd ed. (Oxford, 1957), 2-7. A new edition of the *Carmen ad Astralabium* is being prepared by Mrs. J. Rubingh-Boscher. On the theme of reputation in Abelard, see Georg Misch, *Geschichte der Autobiographie* 3,2 (Frankfurt, 1959), p. 549.

76. «Cum enim dicat Beatus Augustinus: "Crudelis est, qui famam suam negligit," ac, juxta Tullium, "Taciturnitas imitatur confessionem," quae scripta sunt contra me capitulis aequum duxi respondere...» (PL 178:105). The same quotations are repeated in the *Apologia* «Ne iuxta Boethianum» in Abelard's *Opera Theologica*, 1:361.

77. That is, his justification has nothing to do with the question of his guilt or innocence, but only with external matters, like reputation. The judgment of innocence or guilt is dispensed «*in foro interno.*» Clearly his spurning of his judges at Sens is an act consistent with his ethical thought. For recent works on Abelard's ethics, see the introduction to *Peter Abelard's Ethics*, ed. D. E. Luscombe (Oxford, 1971), and Luscombe's article «The Ethics of Abelard: Some Further Considerations,» *Peter Abelard: Proceedings of the International Conference, Louvain, May 10-12, 1971*, ed. E. Buytaert (The Hague, 1974), pp. 65-84. Also M. de Gandillac, «Intention et loi dans l'éthique d'Abélard,» *Colloque*, pp. 585-610.

78. Ep. 337, PL 182:542B, and *Vita Prima*, PL 185:311C.

79. On Guido see Luscombe, *School of Peter Abelard*, pp. 20 ff.; on Hyacinth, ibid., pp. 22 ff.

80. *Sermones supposititii*, Serm. 152, PL 39:2040-41: «Accusationem ergo suam Dominus tacendo non firmat, sed despicit non repellendo. Bene enim tacet, qui defensione non indiget. Ambiat defendi, qui metuit superari. Festinet loqui, qui timet vinci.. Melior est igitur causa quae non defenditur, et probatur: plenior justitia, quae non verbis astruitur, sed veritate fulcitur. Taceat lingua necesse est, ubi ipsa veritas sibi adest... Scivit enim Salvator, ... quomodo tacendo vinceret, quomodo non respondendo superaret... Sed quid de Deo Christo loquar? Susanna mulier inimicos suos tacuit et vicit...» Cf. Ambrose, *Expos. Evang. secundum Lucam* 10.97, PL 15:1828B. The passage found its way into the *Glossa ordinaria* (5:975-976), but I have not found it in sermons or commentaries from the 12th century. On dating the parts of the *Glossa*, see Beryl Smalley, *The Study of the Bible in the Middle Ages* (Notre Dame, 1970), p. 62 ff.

81. See E. E. Reynolds, *The Trial of St. Thomas More* (New York, 1964), p. 120 ff.

82. See *Four Martyrdoms from the Pierpont Morgan Coptic Codices*, ed. E. A. Reymond and J. W. Barnes (Oxford, 1973), p. 146, n. 11. The editors point to various versions of the story of St. Coluthus, who in an early account refused to answer the questions of his judge. The more romanticised the story becomes, the more «prolix, sententious and insolent» the saint becomes (ibid., p. 13). My thanks to Prof. Richard Kieckhefer for this valuable reference.

83. Abelard treats the death of St. Stephen in his Sermon 32. When interrogated before the council, Stephen showed great constancy and fortitude in his answers, says Abelard, but this expressed itself «non tam verbis, quam ipsa sua praesentia» (PL 178: 575D). It is perhaps noteworthy that Abelard ignores Stephen's lengthy speech (Acts 7.2-53) and praises his mere presence in the face of false charges.

84. Wolfram von den Steinen, «Abaelard als Lyriker und der Subjektivismus,» in *Menschen im Mittelalter: Gesammelte Forschungen, Betrachtungen, Bilder*, ed. Peter von Moos (Bern, 1967), p. 226: «[es ist] das Kennzeichnende und, wenn man so will, bahnbrechende an Abaelards Gedichten, dass er die Bibel selber auf persönliche Weise liest und sich subjektiv in ihre Gestalten hineindenkt.» Other works that study this aspect of Abelard's writings are cited in the next two notes. Recently Thomas Renna has prudently warned against excessively «subjectivizing» interpretations of Abelard's works: «St. Bernard and Abelard as Hagiographers» (to appear in *Citeaux*). Of course the study of Abelard's subjectivism requires caution, but it is an element of his work that should not be ignored.

85. Donald K. Frank, «Abelard as Imitator of Christ,» *Viator* 1 (1970), 107-113; Mary McLaughlin, «Abelard and the Dignity of Women,» p. 303. On his obsession with suffering and his identification with Christ's passion, see von den Steinen, *Der Kosmos des*

Mittelalters (Bern, 1959), p. 300 ff. On Abelard and Jerome, Mary McLaughlin, «The Correspondence of Abelard and Heloise» (cited above, note 4) and Thomas J. Renna, «Abelard vs. Bernard: An Event in Monastic History,» *Cîteaux* 27 (1976), 196. On Abelard's sense of personal identification with figures from antiquity, see Gabriella D'Anna, «Abelardo e Cicerone,» *Studi Medievali* 10 (1969), 333; Peter von Moos, «Lucan und Abaelard,» (cited above, note 4), pp. 438-439. David Knowles points to Abelard's sense of reliving the lives of great men of the past as one of the distinguishing characteristics of medieval humanism: «The Humanism of the 12th Century,» in *The Historian and Character and Other Essays* (Cambridge, 1963), pp. 29-30.

86. On the *Planctus Israel super Samson (Analecta Hymnica Medii Aevi*, 48, ed. Guido M. Dreves [Leipzig, 1905], pp. 228-229) see Peter Dronke, *Poetic Individuality in the Middle Ages* (Oxford, 1970), pp. 114-149. On the *Planctus de filia Iephtae (Anal. Hymn.* 48: 225-228), see von den Steinen, «Die Planctus Abaelards: Jephthas Tochter,» *Mittellateinisches Jahrbuch* 4 (1907), 122-144; Misch, *Geschichte der Autobiographie,* 3,2: 688; McLaughlin, «Abelard and the Dignity of Women,» pp. 213 f.

87. Ep. 7 passim; Sermon 11, PL 178:455; *Prob. Hel.* 5, PL 178:683; Hymns 59, 124, 127, 128, 129, (ed. Szövérffy, pp. 129, 254-257, 262-269). (See Joseph Szövérffy, «Peccatrix quondam femina: A survey of the Mary Magdalen Hymns,» *Traditio* 19 [1963], 79-146). These are only a few of the more prominent passages. She is ubiquitous in the works for the Paraclete. She was on the calendar for the Paraclete, and one of the first priories of the convent, Trainel, was dedicated to her. On her importance in the Middle Ages, see V. Saxer, *Le Culte de Marie Madeleine en Occident*, Cahiers d'archéologie et d'histoire 3 (Paris, 1959); Wiltrud aus der Fünten, *Maria Magdalena in der Lyrik des Mittelalters*, Wirkendes Wort, Schriftenreihe 3 (Düsseldorf, 1966).

88. Ed. T. P. McLaughlin, «Abelard's Rule for Religious Women,» *Mediaeval Studies* 18 (1956), 285: «Speculum animae scripturam sacram constat esse in quam quilibet legendo vivens intelligendo proficiens, morum suorum pulchritudinem cognoscit vel deformitatem deprehendit...» It must have been a common feature of Abelard's teaching on the Bible. Heloise wrote to him in the introduction to the *Problemata* (PL 178:678B): «Quibus [viz. to us at the Paraclete] *saepius* intantum Scripturae sacrae doctrinam commendasti, ut eam animae speculum dicens...» (emphasis mine).

89. On Abelard's «subjectivism» see von den Steinen, «Abaelard als Lyriker und der Subjektivismus»; Jean Leclercq, «Modern Psychology and the Interpretation of Medieval Texts,» *Speculum* 48 (1973), 481-485; G. Verbeke, «Peter Abelard and the Concept of Subjectivity,» *Peter Abelard: Louvain Conference*, pp. 1-11.

90. See his description of his debate with Alberic of Reims before the council of Soissons: *Hist. cal.*, pp. 84-85.

91. Gesta Frid. 1.47, MGH SS 20:376.

92. Cf. *Carmen ad Astralab.*, p. 186: «indignare tibi cum te tua culpa flagellat, / Non illi aut dat verbera justa tibi.»

93. Cf. *Carmen ad Astralab.*, p. 181: «Quidquid contigerit justo non provocat iram; / Disponente Deo scit bene cuncta geri. / ... / Justus pressura se consolatur in omni, / Quod meditatur et hanc disposuisse Deum.»

94. One of Abelard's clearest formulations of the ideal of inwardness and passivity in the face of persecution is in his hymn to the martyrs (Hymn 97, ed. Szövérffy, p. 200-201): «In cunctis periculis / Persistit immobilis. / ... / Pugnat totus / mundus extra, / Salvat unus / Deus intra, / Ferro, flammis / Caecus hostis / Saeviens, / Nescit, intus / Quae sit virtus / Protegens. / Crebros ictus / Dat assultus / Vehemens, / Sed est intus / Dei virtus / Praevalens.» On passivity as a monastic ideal peculiar to Abelard, see Renna, «Abelard vs. Bernard,» pp. 193-196.

V

The Prologue to the *Historia calamitatum* and the "Authenticity Question"*

The author of the *Historia calamitatum*, who either was or claimed to be Peter Abelard, opened his work with a few lines of introduction explaining its purpose and setting forth its contents. It reads as follows:[1]

> Sepe humanos affectus aut provocant aut mittigant amplius exempla quam verba. Unde post nonnullam sermonis ad presentem habiti consolationem, de ipsis calamitatum mearum experimentis consolatoriam ad absentem scribere decrevi, ut in comparatione mearum tuas aut nullas aut modicas temptationes recognoscas et tolerabilius feras.

This unadorned bit of prose would not merit much attention in Abelard studies,[2] except for the fact that recently the ascription to Abelard has been questioned with meticulous argumentation based on the supposition of extensive historical contradictions within the *Historia*.[3] In this context the prologue to the work looms large.

---

* Postscript: The present uncertainty about the authenticity of Abelard's autobiography rests on the works of John Benton cited in note 3 below. At a recent conference in Trier (Internationale Studientage – Petrus Abaelardus, 16–18 April, 1979), Benton, in response above all to criticism from Fr. Chrysogonus Waddell, retracted some central points in his own studies and conceded the authenticity of the greater part of the *Historia*. And so the present study, written almost a year earlier, is in the position of running at doors that were opened during its approach. Its appearance may still serve the purpose of warding off future doubts about the authenticity of the *Historia*, providing a commentary on its prologue, and offering some guide lines and bibliographical references for others engaged in authenticity disputes.

[1] Citations from *Historia Calamitatum: Texte critique avec une introduction*. Ed. J. Monfrin. Paris 1959, here p. 63 (= *Bibliothèque des Textes Philosophiques*).
[2] For a convenient survey of the "authenticity question" up to 1972, see Peter von Moos, *Mittelalterforschung und Ideologiekritik: Der Gelehrtenstreit um Heloise*. Munich 1974. (= *Kritische Information*, Nr. 15). Unfortunately von Moos' book appeared just at the front of a wave of interest in the authenticity of the *Historia* and personal letters. Besides the studies by Benton and Ercoli (below, n. 3), J. Monfrin, *Le problème de l'authenticité de la correspondance d'Abélard et d'Héloise*. In: *Pierre Abélard / Pierre le Vénérable: Les courants philosophiques, littéraires et artistiques en occident au milieu du XIIe siècle, Abbaye de Cluny, 1972*. Paris 1975, pp. 409-424 (= *Colloques internationaux du CNRS*, nr. 546; henceforth cited as *Pierre Abélard / Pierre le Vénérable*); Mary McLaughlin, *The Correspondence of Abelard and Heloise and Abelard's other Writings for the Paraclete*. (Paper delivered at the 1974 meeting of the American Historical Association in a section devoted to the authenticity controversy); Peter Dronke, *Abelard and Heloise in Medieval Testimonies*. Glasgow 1976 (= *W. P. Ker Memorial Lecture*, Nr. 26).
[3] J. F. Benton, *Fraud, Fiction and Borrowing in the Correspondence of Abelard and Heloise*. In: *Pierre Abélard / Pierre le Vénérable*, pp. 469-506. Benton's arguments have met with some opposition. See the comments following his article (ibid., pp. 507-511). Also those of Dronke, *Medieval Testimonies*, p. 1lff. The stiffest opposition comes from Fr. Chrysogonus Waddell in still unpublished research refuting some of Benton's central points. Support has been scattered and faint. See Hubert Silvestre, *Reflexions sur la thèse de J. F. Benton relative au dossier Abélard-Héloise*. In Recherches de théologie ancienne et médiévale 44 (1977), pp. 211–216. Also J. Szöverffy, *Peter Abelard's Hymnarius Paraclitensis: An annotated Edition with Introduction*. Albany, New York and Brookline, Mass. 1975, vol. 1, p.

V

2

If Peter Abelard wrote it, then he also wrote a letter of consolation narrating his calamities, *consolatoriam de ipsis calamitatum mearum experimentis,* which, considering the undisputed unity of style, structure, intent and thought of that work[4], and the many features which link it to Abelard,[5] could only be the *Historia calamitatum.* Whoever wrote the preface wrote all, or nearly all, the body of the text.

The opening sentence of the *Historia* comprises a formulation, with a few individual traits, of a commonplace idea: *plus movent exempla quam verba.* The idea has

---

15. (= *Medieval Classics: Texts and Studies,* vol. 2); D. W. Robertson, Review of von Moos, *Mittelalterforschung.* In: Cahiers de civilisation médiévale 21 (1978), p. 197. More recently Benton and F. P. Ercoli have published the results of a word count study broadly comparing the frequency of occurrence of common words and constructions in the *Historia,* genuine works of Abelard, works of other 12th century writers and of Gregory the Great: *The Style of the "Historia calamitatum": A Preliminary Test of the Authenticity of the Correspondence Attributed to Abelard and Heloise.*
In: Viator 6 (1975), pp. 59–86. They find that certain words and constructions occur much more frequently in the *Historia* than in the other works sampled. Benton and Ercoli are cautious and modest in evaluating their findings. They suggest only that these findings make a broader study advisable. They follow the methodology of F. Mosteller and D. Wallace in their statistical study of the Federalist Papers. This study was successful in confirming conventional wisdom about the ascription of certain papers to certain authors. Mosteller – Wallace, and following them Benton – Ercoli, select common "function words" for sampling – connectives, particles, adverbs – words and constructions which are not "context sensitive." The question of methodology in this area is a tower of Babel. A reading of the studies collected by D. Erdman and E. Fogel, *Evidence for Authorship: Essays on Problems in Attribution.* Ithaca, New York 1966, will bear out my metaphor. The endless squabbles about approach presented there will commend the broadest eclecticism in the study of attribution. There is a school of thought opposed to the sampling methods of Mosteller-Wallace, Benton-Ercoli. It began with G. U. Yule's classic work, *The Statistical Study of Literary Vocabulary.* Cambridge, England 1944. Yule finds nouns and adjectives the most reliable markers of an author's identity. This preference is born out in the impressive and valuable study by M. P. Brown, *The Authentic Writings of Ignatius: A Study of Linguistic Criteria.* Durham, North Carolina 1963. More recently G. Herdan in the second edition of his awesome work *The Advanced Theory of Language as Choice and Chance.* New York 1966 (= *Kommunikation und Kybernetik in Einzeldarstellungen,* vol. 4), vigorously attacks the reliance on "function words" as markers of style. See his chapter, "The Fallacy of Determining Style by Differences in Frequency of a few Grammar (,Function') Words," ibid., p. 171, pp. 172ff. Herdan stresses that wide variations in the use of common words indicate nothing about authorship, since they can represent conscious choice on the part of the same author. If so, then Benton and Ercoli's results must be regarded as inconclusive. If the large scale computer analysis of the *Historia* recommended by Benton and Ercoli is nonetheless undertaken, it could certainly profit from the debate on the authenticity of Paul's letter to the Ephesians, conveniently summarized by G. B. Caird, *Paul's Letters from Prison.* Oxford 1976, p. 11ff.

[4] Cf. Benton, *Fraud Fiction and Borrowing,* p. 497: "The stylistic and thematic unity of the *Historia calamitatum* suggests to me that later additions cannot make up more than a small fraction of the whole letter." And loc.cit.: "... it is hard to believe that most of it was not written by one author." The literary unity of the *Historia* has been one of the most studied aspects of that work in recent years. E. g. R. W. Southern, *The Letters of Abelard and Heloise.* In: *Medieval Humanism and Other Studies.* Oxford 1970, pp. 86-104; D. W. Robertson, *Abelard and Heloise.* New York 1972, esp. pp. 99ff.; P. von Moos, *Palatini quaestio quasi peregrini.* In: Mittellateinisches Jahrbuch 9 (1974), pp. 124-158. Against this approach and its presuppositions, see Dronke, *Medieval Testimonies,* p. 11 et passim.

[5] Von Moos could write in 1974: „Der radikale Zweifel an der Authentizität der gesamten *Historia calamitatum* dürfte seit der kommentierten Mitteilung der *Epistola Petri Abaelardi contra Bernhardum* durch R. Klibansky endgültig begraben sein, da sich darin bei aller Berücksichtigung topischer Elemente doch erstaunliche sprachliche und inhaltliche Parallelen zur Autobiographie finden lassen..." (*Mittelalterforschung,* p. 87). Recent studies that connect the *Historia* in thought, temperament and intellectual obligation with Abelard are M. McLaughlin, *Abelard as Autobiographer: The Motive and Meaning of his "Story of Calamities".* In: Speculum 42 (1967), pp. 463-488; McLaughlin, *Peter Abelard and the Dignity of Women: Twelfth Century "Feminism" in Theory and Practice.* In: *Pierre Abélard / Pierre le Vénérable,* pp. 287-333; D. K. Frank, *Abelard as Imitator of Christ.* In: Viator 1 (1970), pp. 107-113; P. von Moos, *Lucan und Abelard.* In: *Hommages à André Boutémy.* Ed. G. Cambier. Brussels 1976, pp. 413-443 (= *Collections Latomus,* vgl. 145).

direct counterparts in antiquity.[6] It is fairly common among patristic writers,[7] but Gregory the Great brought it into prominence[8]. Of the frequent instances of the motif in Gregory,[9] two have particular affinities with the opening of the *Historia*. He writes in the *Moralia in Job*, Bk. 25:

> ... quia ne divina praecepta nos terreant, antiquorum patrum nos exempla confortant, et ex eorum comparatione facere nos posse praesumimus, quod ex nostra imbecillitate formidamus. (PL 77, 329B-C)

and in the prologue to Bk. 1 of the *Dialogi*:

> ... sunt nonnulli, quos ad amorem patriae coelestis plus exempla quam praedicamenta succendunt. Fit vero plerumque audientis animo duplex adjutorium in exemplis patrum, quia si ad amorem venturae vitae ex praecedentium comparatione accenditur, etiam si se esse aliquid existimat, dum meliora de aliis cognoverit, humiliatur. (PL 77, 153A)

In both cases statements are opposed to examples to the favor of the latter; the writer then commends comparison of examples to the lives of the readers for whom they are intended. This mirrors very closely the structure of the opening of the *Historia*.

In the 12th century the motif occurs often enough and in prominent enough works to indicate that it is not the private property of an individual author in that age.[10] Nonetheless, the thought on which it is based and the particular phrasing in which it is couched in the *Historia* have a place in Abelard's writings. The beginning of his Commentary on the Epistle to the Romans shows some clear similarities. Scripture, it begins, like a rhetorical oration, intends either to instruct or to move the listener:[11]

---

[6] See the citations in H. Kornhardt, *Exemplum: Eine bedeutungsgeschichtliche Studie*. Göttingen 1936, p. 3ff., 59ff. The idea of Seneca that "in admonishing anyone we begin with precepts and end with examples" (*Ad Marciam de consolatione*, 2, 1) has an interesting affinity with the opening of the *Historia*, but had next to no resonance in the Middle Ages. See the commentary of P. von Moos, *Consolatio: Studien zur mittellateinischen Trostliteratur über den Tod und zum Problem der christlichen Trauer*. Munich 1971, vol. 3, p. 287 (= *Münstersche Mittelalterschriften*, vol. 3).
[7] Cf. Ambrose, *PL* 16, 207B; *PL* 17, 236C, 254C. Jerome, *PL* 26, 618 B.
[8] On the "exemplum" tradition in the Middle Ages and Gregory's influence on it, see J.-Th. Welter, *L'Exemplum dans la littérature religieuse et didactique du moyen âge*. Paris & Toulouse 1927, p. 14f. (= *Bibliothèque d'Histoire Ecclésiastique de France*).
[9] Cf. *PL* 76, 326C, 328A, 318C (three times), 329B, 329C, 330A. This is a small sampling. In the *Moralia* alone the motif occurs 26 times. For these citations I am most indebted to Professor Gerhard Ladner, who, along with two student assistants at UCLA, has prepared a computerized text of the *Moralia*, from which I have drawn this information. In preparing this text, Ladner had the help of Dr. David Packard, whose equipment was used in providing the information given above. The genesis of this project and Packard's role in it are described in Ladner's article, *Gregory the Great and Gregory VII*. In: Viator 4 (1973), pp. 1-31.
[10] Cf. Bernard of Clairvaux, *Sermo 59 in Cant. Sancti Bernardi Opera*. Ed. Leclerq, Talbot, Rochais. Rome 1958, vol. 2, p. 137; Giraldus Cambrensis, *Gemma Ecclesiastica*. Ed. J. F. Dimrock. London 1877, vol 2, p. 6 (= *Rolls Series*, vol 7). For a discussion of the motif in prologues to historical works, see G. Simon, *Untersuchungen zur Topik der Widmungsbriefe mittelalterlicher Geschichtsschreiber*. In: Archiv für Diplomatik 5/6 (1959/60), pp. 103-105. The commendation of *exempla* at the beginning of a saint's life is also common (cf. St. Bernard, *Vita Malachiae, Opera*, vol. 3, p. 307). On the interesting subject of hagiographic aspects of the *Historia calamitatum*, see Th. Renna, *St. Bernard and Abelard as Hagiographers* (to appear in the journal Cîteaux).
[11] *Petri Abaelardi Opera Theologica*. Ed. E. M. Buytaert. Brepols 1969, vol. 1, p. 41 (= *Corpus Christianorum Continuatio Mediaevalis*, vol 11). The opening of this commentary is adapted from Augustine, *De Genesi ad litteram* (cf. *PL* 34, 245). But the threefold division into precepts, admonitions and examples, is Abelard's work.

> *In Veteri nempe Testamento lex, quae in quinque libris Moysi continetur, praecepta Domini primum docet. Deinde prophetiae vel historiae cum ceteris scripturis, ad ea quae iam praecepta erant, opere complenda adhortantur et affectus hominum ad obediendum praeceptis commovent.*

When the prophets and patriarchs, he continues, saw that precepts alone did not suffice to procure the obedience of the people, they resorted first to admonitions and warnings, then to examples: *Exempla quoque ex historiis necessarium erat adiungi ...* The subject of *commovent* is *historiae*, or *exempla ex historiis* (as the subject of *adhortantur* is *prophetiae*). Hence the thought can be paraphrased, *exempla affectus hominum commovent plus quam praecepta*. This very nearly repeats the opening sentence of the *Historia*. In both texts the unillustrated verbal utterance takes second position to examples; both texts speak of "stirring human emotions" (*Hist.*: *humanos affectus*; *Comm. Rom.: affectus hominum*).[12]

The opposition of examples to words has a place in Abelard's thought. Words are the first step in moral instruction; examples are its fulfillment:

> *At vero Dominum decebat hoc suae orationis exemplo nos maxime ad patientiae virtutem et ad summae dilectionis exhibitionem exhortari, ut quod ipse docuerat verbis... proprio exemplo nobis exhiberet in opere.*[13]

The opposition of words to examples as a turn of phrase is also quite common in Abelard's works.[14] This opposition is consonant with a more general idea in Abelard: the rejection of frail words in favor of some higher means of conveying truth. Language, he maintains, is a man-made tool, invented as an emergency measure to stave off sheer chaos and arbitrariness in the communication of thought;[15] there are more reliable means of generating understanding. A spectrum of ideas in Abelard's works breaks from this single thought: *res* as opposed to *verba*;[16] *intellectus* or *sen-*

---

[12] I believe this wording is characteristic of Abelard. Cf. *Comm. Rom.*, p. 280: *Ipsa quidem verba, quae proferimus, affectum nostrum et devotionem intellectu suo in Deum excitant et commovent...* Hymn 111, (Ed. Szöverffy, vol. 2, p. 231): *Et humana/Moves corda/Signis et prodigiis*. There is a clear resonance in *Historia*, p. 100: *Quippe quo feminarum sexus est infirmior, tanto earum inopia miserabilior facile humanos commovet affectus...* As for *Exempla provocant*, cf. Abelard's Hymn 119, (Ed. Szöverffy, vol. 2, p. 241): *Verbis nos instruunt,/ exemplis provocant...* Cf. Ep. 3 (old numbering), *The Personal Letters between Abelard and Heloise*. Ed J. T. Muckle. In: Mediaeval Studies 15 (1953), p. 76: *... ut exemplo maxime superiorum ad orationis instantiam inferiores provocarentur*
[13] *Peter Abelard's Ethics*. Ed. & Trans. D. E. Luscombe. Oxford 1971, p. 60 (= *Oxford Medieval Texts*). Also Ep. 9, *PL* 178, 325B, ibid., 333B; Sermo 13, *PL* 178, 488B; Sermon 17, *PL* 178, 504C; Sermon 33, *PL* 178, 594A.
[14] His Ep. 9 begins and ends with it (*PL* 178, 325B, 336A). Also *PL* 178, 239A, 396B, 488B; *Ethics*, p. 106; ibid., p. 120; Ep. 8, Ed. T. P. McLaughlin, *Abelard's Rule for Religious Women*. In: Mediaeval Studies 18 (1956), p. 284. Cf. *Historia*, p. 108; Ep. 2 (Ed. Muckle), p. 73. Though the phrase *tam exempla quam verba* is commonplace, this list (by no means complete) is somewhat telling. By comparison, the opposition of words to examples occurs only once in St. Bernard's 86 Sermons on the Song of Songs and the *De consideratione* (citation in note 10, above).
[15] Cf. Ep. 8 (Ed. McLaughlin), p. 245; *Theologia Christiana*. Ed. Buytaert. vol. 2, p. 198, p. 230, p. 237, p. 245 (= *Corpus Christianorum Cont. Med.*, vol. 12); *Theologia "Scholarium" (Intro. ad Theologiam)*, *PL* 178, 1063D-64A; *Expos. in Hex.*, *PL* 178, 781; Sermon 1, *PL* 178, 386B. On the subject see Arno Borst, *Der Turmbau von Babel*. Stuttgart 1959, vol. 2, pt. 2, p. 632.
[16] The most impressive formulation of the opposition of *res – verba* as an idea (not merely a turn of phrase) is in the *Theologia Christiana*, p. 198; also ibid., p. 230, p. 266, p. 268; *Apologia "ne iuxta Boethianum"*, *Opera Theol.* Ed. Buytaert, vol. 1, p. 359; *Comm. Rom.*, p. 78, p. 188, pp. 243-244, p. 301; *Probl. Hel.*, *PL* 178, 709A; *Sic et Non*, *PL* 178, 1343B; Sermon 30, *PL* 178, 568D; Sermon 33, *PL* 178, 604B. Also, in works of questioned authenticity: *Historia*, p. 67, line 148, line 153; ibid., p.

sus-verba;[17] *facta* or *opera-verba.*[18] The motif already discussed, *exempla – verba,* has its place here as well.

Peter Abelard, then, might well have written the opening sentence of the *Historia.* But this is the most we can conclude from these observations. The fact that the conventional motif seems to share its particular wording only with other uses of it in Abelard's works is at best worth noting. There may be abundant instances of the phrase *exempla provocant* or *commovent humanos affectus* in other Latin works which I have overlooked.[19] The fact that there are some noteworthy parallels to the opening of the *Historia* in Gregory the Great likewise points vaguely towards Abelard. Considering his close ties to Gregory, both in style and thought,[20] it would not be at all surprising if he had adapted a phrase or a train of thought he found in the *Moralia* or the *Dialogi.* But that does not distinguish him sharply from many other writers.

It is possible to speak with more assurance about the second part of the prologue.[21] He writes the letter of consolation to his friend, ...*ut in comparatione mearum tuas aut nullas aut modicas temptationes recognoscas et tolerabilius feras.* The author

71, p. 99, p. 106; Ep. 2 (Ed. Muckle), p. 68, p. 69; Ep. 3, p. 74, p. 75; Ep. 5, p. 88. For discussions of "things and words" in the 12th century, see M.-D. Chenu, *Théologie symbolique et exégèse scolastique aux XIIe et XIIIe siècles.* In: *Mélanges Joseph de Ghellinck.* Gembloux 1951, esp. p. 520; also the important article by F. Ohly, *Vom geistigen Sinn des Wortes im Mittelalter.* In: Zeitschrift für deutsches Altertum 89 (1959), pp. 1-24; and on this topic in quite a different context, with a useful bibliography, H. Steger, *Philologia Musica: Sprachzeichen, Bild und Sache im literarisch-musikalischen Leben des Mittelalters: Lire, Harfe, Rotte und Fidel.* Munich 1971, p. 62ff. (= *Münstersche Mittelalter-Schriften,* vol. 2).

[17] On this motif as a feature of Abelard's style, see L. Engels, *Abélard écrivain.* In: *Peter Abelard: Proceedings of the International Conference, Louvain, May 10-12, 1971.* Ed. E. Buytaert. The Hague 1974, p. 19ff. On the place of the idea in Abelard's thought, L.-M. De Rijk, *La signification de la proposition (dictum propositionis) chez Abélard.* In: *Pierre Abélard / Pierre le Vénérable,* pp. 547-555, and J. Jolivet, *Arts du langage et théologie chez Abélard.* Paris 1969, p. 71ff. In addition to the citations given by Engels, I would point out the following: *Theol. Christ.,* p. 270; Sermon 19, *PL* 178, 514A; *Intro. ad. Theol., PL* 178, 1052D; *Expos. Symb. Apost., PL* 178, 619B; *Petrus Abaelardus Dialectica.* Ed. L. De Rijk. Assen ²1970, p. 92. And in works of questioned authenticity: *Historia,* p. 68, p. 83, p. 84, p. 85; Ep. 8 (Ed. McLaughlin), p. 286; *Le poème adressé par Abélard à son fils Astralabe.* Ed. B. Hauréau. Paris 1893, p. 157 (= *Notices et extraits de quelques manuscrits latins de la Bibliothèque Nationale,* vol. 34, nr. 2).

[18] *Theol. Christ.,* p. 161; *Comm. Rom.,* p. 78; Ep. 12, *PL* 178, 346B; Ep. 13, *PL* 178, 356B; Sermon 27, *PL* 178, 550C; Sermon 29, *PL* 178, 562D; *Carmen ad Astralabium,* p. 166, p. 171, p. 177, p. 180, p. 182.

[19] Though I doubt it. H. Walther lists only one occurrence of it: *Proverbia Sententiaeque Latinitatis Medii Aevi.* Göttingen 1963, vol. 1, p. 1067: *Exemplo melius quam verbo quisque docetur.* The only close parallel I have found is in Thomas Aquinas, *Summa Theologiae,* Part II, i. Quaest. 34, Art. 1: *In operationibus enim et passionibus humanis, in quibus experientia plurimum valet, magis movent exempla quam verba.*

[20] On Abelard and Gregory, see Engels, *Abélard écrivain,* p. 29f., p. 36f. On Gregory and Abelard's monastic thought, J. Leclerq, *'Ad ipsam sophiam Christum': Le témoignage monastique d'Abélard.* In: Révue d'ascetique et de mystique 46 (1970), p. 163. On the stylistic dependency of the *Historia* on Gregory, see Muckle, *The Personal Letters,* pp. 52-54, esp. p. 52: "... they [i. e. the *Historia* and personal letters] resemble the style of St. Gregory's *Moralia* so closely as to make one suspect it was derived from that work."

[21] Its beginning, the motif "presence – absence", is not important for my purpose, but see the discussion by Peter von Moos, *'Palatini quaestio',* (above, note 4), p. 126f. On the concept of the letter as a continuation of a conversation in absence of one partner, *sermo absentium,* see G. Constable, *Letters and Letter Collections.* Turnholt 1976, p. 13f. p. 19 (= *Typologie des Sources du Moyen Âge occidental,* vol. 17).

restates this purpose in the same formulation near the end of the work: ...*ut, sicut in exordio praefatus sum epistolae, oppressionem tuam in comparatione mearum aut nullam aut modicam esse judices...* (p. 107). The phrase recurs, almost word for word, in Abelard's Sermon 12, though here Christ offers the consoling example of the greater sufferer to the martyrs, the lesser sufferers:

> *Conferant martyres quae passi sunt, et videant in comparatione Dominicae passionis nulla esse vel parva quae passi sunt. (Pl* 178, 483A)

Similar phrasings are to be found here and there in Abelard's works. For instance, he writes in the *Apologia* "*Universis*": ...*cum pauca scripserim, parva, vel, ad comparationem aliorum, nulla...* (*PL* 178, 105). The phrase *aut nulla aut parva* is common enough in Abelard,[22] but also elsewhere. Hence a formulation in the preface to the *Historia* corresponds very closely to a formulation in Abelard's Sermon 12, a work whose authorship cannot be contested. This correspondence must be carefully analysed.

First it should be noted that the prologue to the *Historia* is an integral part of that work and could not have been added later onto the body of the work.[23] Not only does the work begin and end with a variant of the phrase, *ut in comparatione mearum tuas aut nullas aut modicas temptationes recognoscas*,[24] but the perspective it suggests is one element that lends a structural unity to the work as a whole. Abelard's calamities intensify progressively in the course of the *Historia*. Occasionally he looks back, compares his past with his present sufferings, and finds the former "either nothing or only slight." After his defeat at Soissons, he compares his suffering with the pain caused by his castration:

> *Conferebam cum his que in corpore passus olim fueram quanta nunc sustinerem; et omnium hominum me estimabam miserrimum. Parvam illam ducebam proditionem in comparatione hujus injurie...* (p. 89)

At St. Gildas he compares the barenness of his life with the fruits of his earlier teaching (p. 99). The comparison brings him nearly to the point of despair, and he no longer considers his previous torments as anything at all (...*priores molestias quasi jam nullas reputans...* --p. 100). Hence the second sentence of the *Historia* states a narrative perspective from which the author regarded Abelard's calamities in the body of the work: comparison of sufferings. Heloise, or the author of the first letter ascribed to her, perceived this structure and reiterated it in summing up the *Historia*: (You fulfilled what you promised your friend in the beginning of your letter) ...*ut in*

---

[22] *PL* 178, 489C, 559A, 603A; *Hymn. Paraclit. Praef.* (Ed. Szöverffy), vol. 2, p. 10.

[23] As for instance Aegidius of Paris in the early 13th century added a prologue to the *Aurora* of Petrus Riga, with the justification, *Vulnificabat eum defectio magna libellum / Cui neque que decuit ianua prima fuit* (*Petri Rigae Biblia Versificata*. Notre Dame, Indiana 1965, vol. 1, p. 12 [= *University of Notre Dame Publications in Mediaeval Studies*, vol 19].) Works written without a prologue apparently aroused the impression of incompletenesss, hence invited tampering. Robert of Melun wrote to his friend Gilbert Foliot urging him to add a prologue to his commentary on the Song of Songs, and Gilbert agrees to do so, *ut sic operis completio digna foret* (*PL* 202, 1148A).

[24] On the construction *ut* plus subjunctive in the *Historia* and personal letters, see Muckle, *The Personal Letters*, p. 53f.; Benton and Ercoli, *The Style of the "Historia"*, p. 72, p. 79ff.

comparatione tuarum suas molestias nullas vel parvas reputaret (Ep. 2, ed. Muckle, p. 68). This consistent perspective confirms the assumption that was my point of departure: the ascription of all or most of the *Historia* hangs on the ascription of its prologue.

The purpose of the *Historia*, according to its preface, is to console: "Abelard" wants to console an absent friend (whose identity is a mystery) suffering temptations and grief by telling him the story of his own tribulations, so that by comparison, those of the friend will appear trivial. The treatments of this statement of purpose by Georg Misch, R. W. Southern and Peter von Moos connect the *Historia* with the traditions of consolatory rhetoric.[25] But with the exception of Misch, these scholars place the statement of purpose in the prologue only very obliquely within that tradition. For my purposes it is important to determine to what extent this opening is conventional, since if the formulation in question is purely conventional, then the occurrence of the same phrase in Abelard's Sermon 12 can be accounted for as a chance of common literary obligation, and we cannot conclude that Abelard wrote both passages. However, the statement of purpose in the preface to the *Historia* is undoubtedly not a conventional turn of phrase, at home among the topoi of consolatory rhetoric. Peter von Moos in his monumental work, *Consolatio*, mentions this preface in his discussion of the category which he calls "Paradigmentrost", consolation through examples. He describes this category as follows: "Der Gedanke an die 'anderen', die Gleiches erleiden, soll den Trauernden aus seiner Isoliertheit erlösen..." (*Consolatio*, vol. 3, p. 115). The conventional formulation of this type of consolation in the Middle Ages derived from Seneca, *Ad Polybium de consolatione* I, 4:

> *Maximum ergo solacium est cogitare id sibi accidisse quod omnes ante se passi sunt omnesque passuri; et ideo mihi videtur rerum natura, quod gravissimum fecerat, commune fecisse, ut crudelitatem fati consolaretur aequalitas.* (Cited in *Consolatio*, vol. 3, p. 110)

The opening of the *Historia* is obliquely related to this figure, since it promises consolation through examples. But the turn of thought, "Take comfort. My sufferings are far worse than yours. By comparison yours are trivial," would be decidedly out of place in consolatory rhetoric. It would be an unfeeling consolor who tried to convince the bereaved that his sorrow amounted to nothing! and there is a certain cold egotism in regaling a mourner with tales of one's own tribulations.[26] "Paradigmentrost" tries to persuade the mourner that his troubles, though great, have been faced and overcome by others; it is radically egalitarian (cf. *aequalitas* in the passage from Seneca), and the preface to the *Historia* is certainly not. Von Moos is entirely right

---

[25] G. Misch, *Geschichte der Autobiographie*. Frankfurt 1959, vol. 3, pt. 1, p. 550: „Hier kommt eine antike philosophische Tradition zum Vorschein..."; Southern, *The Letters of Abelard and Heloise*, p. 89-90: "It was necessary to say something like this [in consolatory epistles]: 'your misfortunes, however great, have all happened to other and better men.'"

[26] And in fact the reaction of Heloise to this "consolation" suggests that it accomplished the opposite of its intended effect. Cf. Ep. 2 (Ed. Muckle), p. 68: *Tanto dolores meos amplius renovarunt*, [i. e. the story of Abelard's suffering] *quanto diligentius singula expresserunt et eo magis auxerunt, quo in te adhuc pericula crescere retulisti ut omnes pariter de vita tua desperare cogamur...* Ep. 4, p. 77: ... *quibus consolationis remedium afferre debuisti, desolationem auxisti, et quas mitigare debueras excitasti lacrymas.*

in mentioning the prologue to the *Historia* in connection with "Paradigmentrost", though for obvious reasons he was not interested, in *Consolatio*, in Abelard's highly individualistic variation of the figure.[26a]

The notion that consolation or edification comes from the comparison of greater with lesser examples is traceable directly to the thought and teaching of Peter Abelard. An idea that recurs frequently in his work is that the saints and Biblical figures provide examples against which the reader can measure himself. In his Sermon 29, he holds up the figure of Susanna as a model,

> ... ut in comparatione, si quae sacri propositi feminae minus quam noverint habeant, de suo defectu erubescant. *(PL* 178, 555D)

In Sermon 26, the purity of the Virgin is compared with that of the faithful:

> Etsi enim multi amici Dei dicantur... comparatione tamen Dominicae Matris... nulla est fidelium anima immunis a macula. *(PL* 178, 543B)

In the *Problemata Heloissae*, he says that Paul commended first the example of the saints, then that of Christ to the Ephesians, *...ut ejus comparatione humiliores ac ferventiores in ejus dilectione teneamur* (XXIX, *PL* 178, 714B). In Sermon 33, he says that Job was shown examples of just and continent men leading the solitary life, so that by comparison with his wedded life he would be restrained from pride (*...ut eorum scilicet comparatione se compescat ab elatione* -- *PL* 178, 582C). In excusing the sinner-Pope Marcellinus, in Sermon 27, he points to the examples of yet worse sins committed by the apostles:

> Quod si post Petrum, Paulum quoque summum coapostolum ejus Marcellino conferamus, levissimam Marcellini culpam in hac transgressione censebimus. *(PL* 178, 548B-C)

These various examples of the fruits of comparison (gotten only from a scanning of the works for the Paraclete -- there are more instances[27]) are typical of Abelard's use of figures from Scripture in teaching the nuns of the Paraclete. In the letter of direction for the Paraclete, he admonishes them to read Scripture, since it is a "mirror of the soul" in which the reader can see reflected the beauty or ugliness of her own soul.[28] And it is just this process in which he invites them to take part, when for instance he commends the figure of Susanna to them so that by comparison with her virtues, they will be ashamed of their own faults (555D). There is consolation for the saints in the comparison of their own sufferings with those of Christ (483A), and in

---

[26a] The rhetorical *locus* of this prologue is, as Peter von Moos kindly pointed out to me, *exemplum impar, ex maiore ad minus ductum.* See. H. Lausberg, *Handbuch der literarischen Rhetorik: Eine Grundlegung der Literaturwissenschaft.* Munich 1960, vol. 1, pp. 230–231, parag. 420b.

[27] Cf. Ep. 7, *The Letter of Heloise on Religious Life and Abelard's First Reply.* Ed. J. T. Muckle. In: Mediaeval Studies 17 (1955), p. 271, p. 272. Abelard's fondness for the construction *in comparatione* plus genitive in the context of self evaluation shows again the influence of Gregory the Great. Cf. *Moralia, PL* 75, 990C; *PL* 76, 21A, 81B, 121D, 156D, to mention only a few instances.

[28] Ep. 8, (Ed. McLaughlin), p. 285: *Speculum animae scripturam sacram constat esse, in quam quilibet legendo vivens, intelligendo proficiens, morum suorum pulchritudinem cognoscit vel deformitatem deprehendit, ut illam videlicet augere, hanc studeat removere.* Heloise restates the principle in her prefatory letter to the *Problemata, PL* 178, 678B: *Quibus* [viz. to us at the Paraclete] *saepius intantum Scripturae sacrae doctrinam commendasti, ut eam animae speculum dicens, quo decor eius vel deformitas cognoscatur* ... Clearly comparison of self to Biblical examples was an important part of Abelard's teaching on the Scriptures. He has impressed it on them *saepius.*

The Prologue to the Historia calamitatum

the same way there is consolation for Abelard's unnamed friend in comparing his own calamities with those of Abelard. Hence the second sentence of the prologue to the *Historia* not only employs phrasing which Abelard also used, but the process of comparison it urges is closely tied to Abelard's thought.

It is difficult to account for such correspondences by any other explanation than that the passages under discussion all come from Abelard. But we should seek another explanation anyway. The kind of textual evidence just presented would normally count as proof of Abelard's authorship, at least of the passage in question,[28a] but the implications of John Benton's studies --however one evaluates the historical evidence he brings forward -- force us to be sceptical of any simple evaluation of conventional philological evidence for authenticity. In order to account for the historical discrepancies he finds in the *Historia* and for various inconsistencies and contradictions in the letters of direction, Benton proposes the hypothesis,

> "that sometime in the 13th century a forger, or a pair of forgers, motivated by a desire to modify the institutions of the Paraclete, compiled and reworked the eight letters we can read today in ms. T, making use of both authentic writings of Abelard ... and a twelfth century 'autobiographical' letter which was itself a work of imaginative fiction, produced perhaps by some skilled student of the *ars dictaminis*." (*Fraud, Fiction and Borrowing*, p. 472).

The presence of authentic Abelardian material in these letters might be accounted for by the idea that "a forger both covered his tracks and lightened the load of the amount he had to create by filling as much as a half of his book with extracts from the writings of Abelard" (p. 491). The many traces of Abelard's thought and style in the *Historia*, then, may be the result of imitation by that skilled student of the *ars dictaminis*, either lending authenticity to his false ascription or paying homage to an admired master. With such a suspicion about the composition of the *Historia* in the air, stylistic arguments for authenticity, like the ones I have presented, must be tested with caution and scepticism.

The following bit of evidence linking the *Historia* to Abelard illustrates the problems of evaluating stylistic evidence, and can help us formulate some criteria for evidence useful in determining the authenticity of an individual passage. In the *Historia* we are told that Abelard's students gathered around him and mourned after his castration, and the author exclaims,

> ...*quanta stuperet ammiratione, quanta se affligeret lamentatione, quanto me clamore vexarent, quanto planctu perturbarent, difficile, immo impossibile est exprimi.* (p. 80)

Abelard used this syntactic frame in his Sermon 29 to describe the anguish of the relatives of Susanna as they watch her being led off to her trial:

> ...*quanto pudore confusi, quantis lacrymis perfusi ejus innocentiam deplorarent, quis commemorare vel cogitare non plorando queat? (PL* 178, 559A)

[28a] A good example of the use of traditional inner-textual material to determine authenticity is Van den Eynde's treatment of Abelard's sermons: *Le recueil des sermons de Pierre Abélard*. In: Antonianum 37 (1962), pp. 17-54. Brown's study of the Ignatian corpus of letters (above, note 3) is important for testing and validating stylistic criteria in authenticity disputes. See also Yale, *The Statistical Study of Literary Vocabulary* (above, note 3), pp. 221-280, where he tests the ascriptions of the *De imitatione Christi* to Thomas à Kempis and Jean Gerson with an eye to working out valid stylistic criteria for determining authenticity.

Stylistically these passages are nearly identical. Besides the anaphora, *quanto... quanto*, there are in both cases rhyming verbs following the conjunction: *ammiratione... lamentatione... vexarent... perturbarent* in the one, *confusi... perfusi* in the other.[29] The main clause in both cases, besides meaning practically the same thing, makes use of an intensifying repetition: *difficile, immo impossibile*; *commemorare vel cogitare*. Both are loosely metrical.[30] Also striking is the similarity in context. In a moment of tragic crisis, many friends gather in public around the tragic figure and weep and lament:

> Sermon 29: *Deducitur illa ... ad judicium cum parentibus et filiis, et universis cognatis suis.* (558D) ... *Flebant non solum sui, sed omnes qui noverant eam*[31] ... *In medium matrona sancta trahitur...* (559A)
> Historia: *Mane autem facto, tota ad me civitas congregata ... intolerabilibus me lamentis et ejulatibus cruciabant...* (p. 80)

Abelard admired and perhaps felt some sense of identification with the figure of Susanna, one that is expressed in works of unquestioned authenticity,[32] and in the *Historia*.[33] It may be that these affinities encouraged him to cast the "lament for Abelard" in the same syntactic frame as the "lament for Susanna" (or vice-versa, depending on which was written first[34]). But on the other hand, the near identity of these passages can be neatly accounted for by the fraud-fiction hypothesis. The "lament for Abelard" could be the work of a clever student, perhaps a student of Abelard, someone who knew his works well. Possibly Pseudo-Abelard worked with a copy of the master's sermons in hand, read the scene of Susanna's arrest, connected this scene with the lamenting for Abelard's castration (in which he may even have taken part[35]) and conceived a similar scene to include in his fictive biography. He then lifted the syntax from that passage[36] and used comparable rhyme and metre. Such

---

[29] Cf. Engels, *Abélard écrivain*, p. 33: "... il est hors de doute que, chez Abélard, celle-ci [viz. rhyme] n'est pas seulement un résultat fortuit, mais, très souvent, un effet voulu..."

[30] On Abelard and the *cursus*, see K. Polheim, *Die lateinische Reimprosa*. Berlin 1925, p. 418; Engels, *Abélard écrivain*, p. 33, note 95: "Abélard me semble pratiquer sur une assez grande échelle la théorie du 'cursus'". But also Benton and Ercoli, *The Style of the "Historia"*, p. 75, note 44.

[31] Cf. Daniel, 13, 33.

[32] In Ep. 9, he commends the figure of Susanna to the nuns of the Paraclete as an example of a learned woman living in "the world" who because of her learning was able to "condemn the priests and judges who had condemned her" (*PL* 178, 332D), and he devotes an entire sermon to her (Sermon 29, *PL* 178, 555-564).

[33] When Abelard is condemned at Soissons, a certain Thierry, *scolaris magister*, perhaps Thierry of Chartres, upbraids the judges in the words of young Daniel berating the judges of Susanna. Cf. *Historia*, p. 88.

[34] The *terminus post quem* of the *Historia* is 1131, since the author mentions the papal privilege for the founding of the Paraclete issued in that year. Van den Eynde dates the sermons some time after 1129/1130 (*Le recueil des sermons*, p. 20), but before 1135/36 (ibid., p. 54). See also Van den Eynde, *Chronologie des écrits d'Abélard à Héloise*. In: Antonianum 37 (1962), pp. 337-349.

[35] There may be some confirmation of the statement in the *Historia* that not only many of Abelard's students, but "the entire city" mourned for him after his castration, in the letter of Fulk of Deuil, written shortly after that event. Cf. *PL* 178, 374C-D (among Abelard's letters, Ep. 16): *Plangit ergo hoc tuum vulnus et damnum ... liberalium canonicorum ac nobilium clericorum multitudo. Plangunt cives, civitatis hoc dedecus reputantes... Quid singularum feminarum referam planctum... Tantus ergo omnium luctus exstitit, ut melius mihi videaris te debere velle periisse quam servasse quod periit*.

[36] And in fact liked the formulation well enough to use it throughout the *Historia*. Cf. p. 74 (lines 379-383): *O quantus in hoc cognoscendo dolor avunculi! quantus in separatione amantium dolor ipsorum!*

a process of imitation is not improbable. Stylistic reliance on an admired master was part and parcel of the study of composition in the 12th century; John of Salisbury indicated this in his description of the teaching methods of Bernard of Chartres.[37] This could apply to the imitation of a contemporary or near-contemporary model, as well as to a classical or patristic one. The superb new edition of the *Architrenius* of Johannes de Hauvilla by Paul Schmidt[38] allows us to observe the process of imitation in some detail. It becomes clear in Schmidt's extraordinarily detailed citings of quotations and echoes of other writers in the *Architrenius* that a poet imitated rare wording, polished phrasing, striking syntactic formulations. John of Hauville, needless to say, was an eclectic imitator. Though he borrowed heavily from Alain of Lille, he did not of course consistently imitate the style and thought of a single author. The author of the *Historia*, by contrast, did consistently reproduce the style and thought of Peter Abelard, and if this work was a forgery, then it stands alone in the Middle Ages.[39] Pseudo-Abelard, if he existed, was a writer whose stylistic virtuosity is equal to, or rather far superior to, that of Abelard, since Abelard gained a reputation for *suavitas eloquii* (*PL* 178, 372B, Ep. 16) by producing naturally and, as it were, unreflectingly his own style, whereas Pseudo-Abelard re-produced in a long and impressive work the style and thought of another man by calling on special talents which permitted him to do so! Be that as it may, in dealing with individual passages, evidence like that of the two just discussed must be put aside in determining whether one passage is ge-

---

quanta sum erubescentia confusus! quanta contritione super afflictione puelle sum afflictus! quantos meroris ipsa de verecundia mea sustinuit estus! Loc. cit., lines 400-402: ...*quanto estuaret dolore, quanto afficeretur pudore, nemo nisi experiendo cognosceret.* Ibid., p. 89: *Quanto autem dolore estuarem, quanta erubescentia confunderer, quanta desperatione perturbarer, sentire tunc potui, proferre non possum.*

[37] *Metalogicon*, I, 24.
[38] Johannes de Hauvilla, *Architrenius*, Ed. P. G. Schmidt. Munich 1974.
[39] On literary forgeries in the Middle Ages, see H. Fuhrmann, *Einfluss und Verbreitung der pseudoisidorischen Fälschungen von ihrem Auftauchen bis in die nuere Zeit*. Stuttgart 1972, vol. 1, p. 73 ff. (= *MGH*, Schriften, vol. 24). The work by Wolfgang Speyer, *Die literarische Fälschung im heidnischen und christlichen Altertum: Ein Versuch ihrer Deutung*. Munich 1971 (= *Handbuch der Altertumswissenschaft*, vol. 1, pt. 2) treats only antiquity and early Christianity. An interesting case in vernacular literature is the imitation-forgery of Wolfram von Eschenbach by Albrecht von Scharfenberg in his work which has come to be called *Der jüngere Titurel*. There is a fine recent study of the literary dependence of Albrecht on his model by Linda Parshall, *The Art of Narration in Wolfram's Parzival and Albrecht's Jüngerer Titurel*. Dissertation, London. The study will appear in the Cambridge series of German monographs, *Anglica-Germanica*. Parshall shows that Albrecht, for all his borrowings and imitation, comes nowhere near successfully concealing his stylistic identity, much to his own disadvantage. This points up a principle of both literary forgeries and imitations in the Middle Ages: the style and temperament of the forger-imitator are never submerged in those of his model. According to M. P. Brown (above, note 3), not even Pseudo-Ignatius, certainly a more clever imitator than Nicholas of Clairvaux, and in the judgment of Brown a more educated man and more accomplished stylist than his model Ignatius, took pains to conceal his idiosyncrasies. Cf. *The Authentic Writings of Ignatius*, p. 46, p. 52, p. 95. The so called „Trierer Stilübungen" offer a good example of this principle from the 12th century. See the study by Norbert Höing, *Die ‚Trier Stilübungen': Ein Denkmal der Frühzeit Kaiser Friedrich Barbarossas, I. Teil.* In: Archiv für Diplomatik 1 (1955), pp. 257–359. They consist of three letters composed by a single author and ascribed by him to Frederick Barbarossa, Archbishop Hillin of Trier, and Pope Hadrian IV. While the enterprising author characterized each purported writer by varying ideas and attitudes, the style of the three shows no variation whatsoever. Höing can confirm the judgment of Jaffé, „. . . dass die drei Schreiben überhaupt die gleiche Ausdrucksweise haben und dieselbe Sprache sprechen" (Part I., p. 289).

nuine or not, since the very features which argue for authenticity also lend probability to the fiction-imitation hypothesis. We can conclude beyond all reasonable doubt that one passage was modeled on the other, but not that the same author wrote both. The "lament for Susanna" is impressive and conspicuous, both for its drama and for its rhetorical coloration, and an imitator would have been drawn to just such a passage.

The only kind of stylistic features useful for determining the authenticity of an individual passage in a work suspected of being a literary imitation are phrasings and syntactic formulations which are unique and inconspicuous, combine two or more unimportant and unrelated phrases and occur infrequently, preferably only once, in genuine works.[40] The recurrence of such a formulation in the *Historia* would place the authenticity of the passage in which it occurs beyond all reasonable doubt. The phrase in Sermon 12, *videant in comparatione dominicae passionis nulla esse vel parva quae passi sunt,* would seem to fit these criteria. The combination of the inconspicuous *in comparatione* plus the genitive[41] with the homely *nulla vel parva* is wholly idiosyncratic. A forger might have hit on one of these features (particularly *in comparatione* plus the genitive, since it is somewhat prominent in other works), but that he could have combined them just as Abelard combined them in Sermon 12 is out of the question.[42] Nor is it likely that he would have hit on that passage to imitate: neither the context in Sermon 12[43] nor the wording commended it as a model.

If the correspondences in question are the result of imitation, then the motive was not aesthetic. Hence we must seek another explanation, one that can account for Pseudo-Abelard's interest in the dross of literary expression rather than the gold. One possibility is that a clever forger reproduced even insignificant details of phrasing and syntax in order to lend an air of authenticity to his work. The idea of imitating an author's style in order to support a false ascription was not wholly unknown. Wolfgang Speyer can point to several examples in antiquity, and to one in early Christian writings, namely Pseudo-Ignatius.[44] In the high Middle Ages one can point to the case of Nicholas of Clairvaux, the personal secretary of St. Bernard. Nicholas, a man of some learning and a skilled stylist, allegedly took advantage of Bernard's trust to forge letters in the abbot's name, using his seal without Bernard's knowl-

---

[40] Hence common words and phrases in Abelard, like *tanto-quanto, detrimentum famae, vehementer, res ipsa clamat, fragilior sexus* — the kind of evidence on which the stylistic study of the *Historia* has relied since Schmeidler — are quite useless, even as clues, where there is a suspicion of literary imitation. The study of the authenticity of this work would profit from dropping these traditional means altogether. The first task of anyone who suspects its authenticity is to show what vocabulary (particularly nouns and adjectives) Pseudo-Abelard employs but does not share in common with Abelard. However, the irreplaceable basis of an authenticity study must be a thorough knowledge of Abelard as a writer and of the institutional history of the 12th century. In this I heartily agree with von Moos, *Mittelalterforschung,* p. 90, parag. 41.1.

[41] I have not found a single occurrence of *in comparatione* plus genitive in Bernard's 86 sermons on the Song of Songs, and only one occurence in his *De consideratione*.

[42] The combination never occurs in Gregory's *Moralia*.

[43] Unless of course we assume that the author of the *Historia* connected Abelard with Christ. But who is more likely to have made this connection than Abelard! Cf. Frank, *Abelard as Imitator of Christ* (above, note 5).

[44] *Die literarische Fälschung,* p. 82. But there were of course other instances. Cf. Constable, *Letters and Letter Collections,* p. 50.

The Prologue to the Historia calamitatum

edge. Bernard dismissed him from his service and wrote a vitriolic letter to Pope Eugenius denouncing his former friend (Ep. 298, *PL* 182, 500-501).[45] Bernard's charge is that Nicholas wrote false letters using the abbot's seal, but — if the charge was true at all, — it may be that he also "authenticated" the letters by imitating Bernard's style. He did so in authorized letters. In 1146 Bernard had him write to the English nobility encouraging them to take up the cross in the 2nd crusade. This task called for hortatory skill, and Nicholas relied more on that of Bernard than on his own. He modelled his letter on Bernard's Epist. 363 (*PL* 182, 564ff.) written with the same purpose shortly before to the clergy and people of Eastern France. Here then is a case in which "a skilled student of the *ars dictaminis*" with alleged inclinations to forgery imitated a near-contemporary model, and we can assume that there would have been little difference between the "honest" and dishonest imitation of Bernard's style. How then did Nicholas operate? He opens with some turgid Biblical phrasing borrowed directly from Bernard:

Nicholas:

Commota est et contremuit terra, quia Rex coeli perdidit terram suam, terram ubi steterunt pedes ejus. (Inter Bern. Ep. 468, *PL* 182, 671B)

Bernard:

Commota est siquidem et contremuit terra, quia coepit Deus coeli perdere terram suam. (*PL* 182, 565A)

Some further correspondences:
Vides et dissimulat ille magnus providentiae oculus, ut videat si est intelligens aut requirens Deum, si sit qui doleat vicem ejus... (*PL* 182, 671C)

Respicit [Deus] filios hominum, si forte sit qui intelligat, et requirat, et doleat vicem ejus. (566A)

Et quia terra vestra fecunda est virorum fortium, et militari juventute referta, decet vos inter primos, et cum primis ad tam sanctum opus accedere, et armatos ascendere ad serviendum Deo viventi. Eia igitur, fortissimi milites, accingimini; et qui non gladium habet, emat eum. (*PL* 182, 672B)

Quia ergo facunda est virorum fortium terra vestra, et robusta noscitur juventute referta, sicut laus est vestra in universo mundo, et virtutis vestrae fama replevit universum orbem; accingimini et vos viriliter, et felicia arma accipit Christiani nominis zelo. (566C)

These borrowings fall under the heading of literary imitation. Nicholas copies stirring and memorable phrasing. He lifts passages which serve the same purpose in his letter as they served in its model. Nicholas did not pick up insignificant phrasing from his model. He regarded the opening as critical, and so he set the earth shaking in the first sentence; Bernard had opened with protestations of humility.

---

[45] For a summary of Nicholas' career and his problems with Bernard, see G. Constable, *The Letters of Peter the Venerable*. Cambridge, Mass. 1967, vol. 2, pp. 316-330.

No firm conclusions can be drawn from comparing these borrowings with the opening of the *Historia*. We cannot say that by analogy to Nicholas of Clairvaux Pseudo-Abelard ought also to have wished to put some more prominent phrasing of his model at the beginning of his work. Each literary forgery is a work of individual genius; no conventions and rules apply which would make the *modus operandi* of forgers predictable. The comparison does however force us again to ask the question: if the opening of the *Historia* rests on imitation of Abelard, then what was the forger's motive? Nicholas was clearly aware that the opening of his work was a critical point: it puts forth dramatically the famed eloquence of Bernard. But the author of the *Historia* at this point produced the phrase, ... *humanos affectus aut provocant aut mittigant amplius exempla quam verba*, part commonplace, part Abelard; and he recalled or hit on the phrase in Sermon 12: *videant comparatione dominicae passionis nulla esse vel parva quae passi sunt*, which is inconspicuous and unique in genuine works. We can only conclude that if the prologue to the *Historia* was composed in imitation of Abelard, then this imitation was wholly unmotivated and disinterested. It does not lend grace, elegance or force to the work; it does not assure the contemporary reader of Abelard's authorship.

Furthermore we can say with certainty that no sensibility existed in the high Middle Ages to which a process of subtle and detailed imitation would have responded. It does not require the reproduction of minute details of genuine phrasing in order to convince even learned readers in the 12th century of the authenticity of a forged work. The critical attitude to forgeries was strictly limited,[46] and even where some sense of the philological integrity of a text is evinced, it is restricted to striking features of style and the most crude sort of anachronisms.[47] And here we are speaking of official documents, texts where there is a powerful practical incentive for determining authenticity. To imagine a literary forger reproducing unmemorable details of phrasing as part of his plan to defraud is to confuse modern philological sensibilities with medieval ones. When James McPherson set out to write the poems of a bard named Ossian in the 18th century, he reckoned with sceptics of the stamp of Dr. Johnson, and this anticipation of sharp critical abilities, combined with the personal genius of the forger, brought forth a forgery brilliantly reproducing an alien style. If the "forger" of the *Historia calamitatum* tried to lend authenticity to his handiwork by modelling part of his prologue on an insignificant clause in Abelard's Sermon 12, then he was covering tracks that no one in his day would have dreamed of looking for, and he was performing a feat that none of his contemporaries could have appreciated, except of course Abelard.

If we are to avoid making the weaker argument the stronger, then we must put aside the idea that the prologue to the *Historia* is based on skillful imitation of Peter

---

[46] Cf. Fuhrmann, *Die Pseudo-Isidorischen Fälschungen*, vol. 1, pp. 112-136.
[47] See H. Bresslau, *Handbuch der Urkundenkritik für Deutschland und Italien*. Leipzig ²1912, vol. 1, pp. 15-19; Fuhrmann, *Pseudo-Isidor*, vol. 1, pp. 123-127.

Abelard.⁴⁸ The correspondences in question are much more satisfactorily accounted for by supposing that Peter Abelard wrote that prologue. Mary McLaughlin has shown that there is a unity of thought, motive and style underlying Abelard's writings for the Paraclete.⁴⁹ The echoes of Abelard's style in the opening to the *Historia* are undoubtedly part of that unity. My conclusion is that this preface constitutes a statement, the authenticity of which is beyond all reasonable doubt, that Abelard wrote a letter of consolation narrating his own calamities in order to comfort an absent friend and to convince him of the comparative triviality of his sufferings. That letter is of course the *Historia calamitatum*.

---

⁴⁸ It might be objected that the possibility of imitation, likely or not, gains strength because of the evidence of historical inaccuracy in the text of the *Historia*; we must account for anachronisms and contradictions somehow. I for one am not convinced that the historical evidence against its authenticity is best accounted for by a hypothesis of forgery and fiction. The means of corrupting a genuine text are many and well known: scribal error, wilful tampering, large scale additions. But the means of producing a fictional autobiography which bears many traces -- both obvious and subtle -- of the style, temperament and thought of the man to whom it is ascribed, are extremely limited; very few litterati in the Middle Ages would have commanded or would even have dreamed of mustering such means.

⁴⁹ In: *Peter Abelard and the Dignity of Women* (above, note 5).

VI

Patrons and the Beginnings of Courtly Romance

The purpose of this study is to question the influence of patronage on the origins of romance. "Origins of romance" is used here not in the sense of literary history — history of narrative forms, history of style and motifs — but rather in the sense of the social forces that encouraged the creation of a new narrative form. What moved Wace, Benoît de Sainte-Maure, Chrétien de Troyes, Heinrich von Veldeke and Hartmann von Aue, to form a conception of human destiny, of chivalric manners, of the knight's relation to society and to women, so starkly different from that of the heroic epic and chanson de geste?

There are big issues at stake in trying to identify the forces that nourished this new form. The question of patronage has received a lot of attention in recent years. To some extent it has defined the issues. It is one of those questions that comes trailing implications. Assume patronage made romance, and the following chain of arguments falls into place: rich secular nobles wanted courtly narrative and hired poets to produce it; the poets either were rewarded in advance or after composing their work — at least they wrote for the lord with the hope of reward; since they ate — or hoped to eat — his bread, they also sang his song; accordingly the works of courtly narrative poets reflect the values of the nobles who commissioned them or who were their potential patrons; like court poets generally, they flattered the patron, if not directly, then in their means of representation; the lord in fact hired them with the unspoken but obvious assumption that their entertainment would also flatter him, at least tell him things he wants to hear; finally, the relation of poet to patron is the key to understanding how the material requirements of poetry were provided.¹

These are strong assumptions. They stake out important positions on the nature, purpose and origins of courtly narrative. If courtly narrative poets wrote in the hire of feudal nobles, then chivalry, courtliness, and courtly love were not creations *of the poet*, not their intellectual property, but those of their patrons and of their class — the poets were not the spontaneous creators of a new vision of the sublime chivalric life, but hired image makers.

These assumptions do not hold up to a critical view. The historical evidence — for the beginnings of romance — is against them.

To bring my thesis to a formula: patrons did not make courtly romance; courtly romance made patrons.

It is easy to argue the first of these claims, especially with the help of Joachim Bumke's book on patronage.² It is one of the best works on the social history of courtly literature yet written. Its point of departure is the dependency of medieval literature on patronage: "Mittelalterliche Kunst ist Auftragskunst und muß so verstanden werden" (*Mäzene*, p. 9). Bumke can show this persuasively for Germany from the second third of the thirteenth century and beyond. But the role of patronage in the twelfth century is unclear. Next to nothing is known about the patronage of worldly vernacular narrative in the period of its beginnings. We know nothing about the patronage of Wace's *Brut*, of the romances of antiquity, of Chrétien's first romances, *Erec*, *Cligés*, and *Yvain*. Likewise in Germany, with few exceptions, there is only conjecture on the patronage of twelfth- and early thirteenth-century narrative, courtly and pre-courtly, as is evident from some of the conclusions on individual twelfth-century German works in Bumke's book: On Lamprecht's *Alexander*: "Unfortunately the text gives no sort of indication where, when and in whose service the Cleric Lamprecht composed" (p. 75). On the *Kaiserchronik*: "As in Lamprecht's *Alexander*, so also in the first German rhymed chronicle, no patron is

---

¹ For instance Erich Köhler, "Literatursoziologische Perspektiven," in *Le roman jusqu'à la fin du XIII* siècle*, GRLMA 4/1 (Heidelberg: Winter, 1978), p. 84: "Die Rezeption antiker epischer Stoffe ... steht im Zeichen geschichtlicher Legitimation dynastischer Machtansprüche. ... primär interessegeleitet ... im Dienste eines gesellschaftlich-politischen Primats..." Joachim Bumke, *Mäzene im Mittelalter: Die Gönner und Auftraggeber der höfischen Literatur in Deutschland 1150-1300* (Munich: Beck, 1979), p. 9f. For an original view of the relationship of poetry to patronage, see Raymond Cormier, "Medieval Courtly Literature, Royal Patronage, and World Harmony, I," *Aevum* 64 (1990), 269-77.

² Joachim Bumke, *Mäzene im Mittelalter* [note 1 above].

mentioned" (p. 78). On *König Rother*: "Perhaps the bad state of manuscript transmission of *König Rother* accounts for the fact that we do not know who the patron of this work was" (p. 91). And so it goes through the list of early German narrative poetry, on into the high courtly period. We know nothing about the patronage of Hartmann's and Gottfried's narratives; Wolfram names no patron of his first romance and only finished narrative, *Parzival*. We have certainty only about Konrad's *Rolandslied*, Herbort's *Liet von Troye* and Albrecht von Halberstadt's Ovid translation. Veldeke's *Eneit* is a special case to which we return later. The evidence for the first romances shows clearly that twelfth- and early thirteenth-century narrative poets almost never name patrons, and praise is as rare as names.

I would like to propose a guideline for determining the importance of patronage and the role of patrons. This guideline seems to me simple and common sensical. It is: If no patron is mentioned, then none exists; and if a poet writes a narrative work in the hope of attracting a patron, he says so. It makes no sense to think that patronage produced courtly romance when patrons are so seldom mentioned. For a poet to have a patron and not say so is to deprive his employer of immortality, and that is an important reward patrons get for their pay, apart from some education, a few nights' entertainment, and a pile of parchment. Nor does it make sense to imagine that there is a patron behind the work, even when he or she is not named. There are cases where the name itself is not decisive: a patron is referred to but not named (Marie de France, Ulrich von Zatzikhoven, Albrecht von Scharfenburg). This suggests that other considerations were more important than recognizing and honoring the person for whom the work is written. In any case, my "guideline" is not a litmus test, but a point of departure for analysing more complex relationships.

As an approach to the origins of romance and the interrelationships of the poet and his noble audience, there is a more useful question: What was the social class of the poets, and what was the relation of this class to the courtly audience? We can find some clear answers to these questions, at least in the general outline. By and large *clerics* wrote romance, as, by and large, laymen and laywomen composed lyric. With few exceptions, romance, and twelfth-century narrative generally, are the work of clerical poets. The list of cleric-romanciers includes Geoffrey of Monmouth, Wace, the authors of the *Roman d'Eneas* and *Roman de Thèbes*, Benoît de Sainte-Maure, author of the *Roman de Troie*, Herbort von Fritzlar, Albrecht von Halberstadt, and Ulrich von Zatzikhoven. There is good reason to think that Chrétien de Troyes, Heinrich von Veldeke, the Nibelungen poet, and Gottfried von Straßburg were clerics, and no reason at all to think they were knights or laymen. Marie de France is of course a special case: a woman with an education, and that means, with the learning of a worldly cleric. The knights or laymen who wrote courtly narrative prior to the year 1200 in France, England, and Germany are quickly named: Robert de Boron, Renaut de Beaujeu (or de Bâgé), and Hartmann von Aue. Courtly romance in its early phase, clearly, was the province of clerics.

So, what was their interest in this new narrative form? What did they want to accomplish with it? What effect was it supposed to have on the courtly audience? These questions also are answerable, though more complex. In this paper I can just point to a couple of indicators of the relationship between the courtly world and the class of men in which the romance originated.

We know that clerics attached to a court or those who just appeared at a court to help a lord or bishop conduct his business, or for any reason, stood fairly high in the social hierarchy of the court. We know this for instance from witness lists and table arrangements, in which a rigid sense of precedence is observed. At the court of King John of England all laymen beneath the rank of earl will always be seated beneath any cleric, and will always appear after him on a witness list. Clerics always take precedence over anyone described as a knight. Such indications must be taken seriously in a society in which men killed each other over the right to hold the king's stirrup or pour his wine. Clerical status by itself gave social standing, unquestionably above knights. The unfree knights at courts seem generally to have been kicked around and sworn at. It is a sign of particular courtesy in a lord that he treats his knights well.[3] But education and church affiliation generally assured a cleric immunity from bad treatment at court. In the debate poem "Phyllis and Flora" on the relative merits of knight and cleric as lovers, Flora, the cleric's advocate, says:

> By custom all things favor the cleric,
> And he bears the sign of the empire in his crown.
> He commands knights, and he dispenses gifts.
> After all, he who commands is greater than he who serves [i.e. the knight].[4]

---

[3] Cf. the praise of Geoffrey the Fair of Anjou by Jean de Marmoutier, *Chroniques des comtes d'Anjou et des seigneurs d'Amboise*, ed. Louis Halphen and René Poupardin, CTSEEH 48 (Paris: Picard, 1914), p. 177.

[4] *Carmina Burana*, ed. Alfons Hilka and Otto Schumann, 2 vols. (Heidelberg: Winter, 1930-70), Poem 92, stanza 38: "Universa clerico constat esse prona, / et signum imperii portat in corona. / imperat militibus et largitur dona: / famulante maior est imperans persona."

Phyllis does not contradict her on this, and with good reason. Clerics at or near courts in a sense commanded, at least dictated to, all of court society on certain matters. There were two good reasons for clerics to go near worldly courts. There were plenty of bad reasons, and these are regularly imputed to court clerics by their critics. But the good reasons were: to educate people of the court and to correct their worldly ways: *eruditio* and *correctio*. The most venal and ambitious cleric, asked to justify following the court, will claim he is there for this pious reason. And the best of the clerics were there, in part at least, for that reason. They were meant to be patterns of conduct, exemplary figures, to the laity, to instruct them by precept and by example.[5]

Let us take some instances of clerics assuming this teaching posture vis à vis the patron of their work. First, a bit of evidence from twelfth-century Germany, the encyclopedic work called *Lucidarius*. In Bumke's opinion its prologue is one of the most valuable pieces of evidence on early patronage (*Mäzene*, p. 137). The authors of the *Lucidarius* were the chaplains of Henry the Lion. A prologue written by the original author makes no reference to the work's patron. He gives the work two different names: *Lucidarius* and *Aurea gemma*. A later prologue, added after the death of Duke Henry but still no doubt from the circle of his court clerics,[6] tells that the work was written at "the request and command" of the Duke. The author of the later prologue records two disagreements between the work's patron and its commissioned writers:

> God Himself gave the idea and meaning of this work to the duke who arranged for its composition. He charged his chaplains to find the words in written books and asked them to write it down without rhymes, for it was his wish that they should write nothing but the truth as in the Latin sources. They did this willingly for Duke Henry at his command and request... Had it been up to the master, he would have written the work in rhymes. It was the duke's wish that the book be

---

[5] On this justification of the cleric's court service, see my *Origins of Courtliness: Civilizing Trends and the Formation of Courtly Ideals, 939-1210* (Philadelphia: University of Pennsylvania Press, 1985), pp. 213-27.

[6] See the study by Georg Steer, "Der deutsche *Lucidarius* — ein Auftragswerk Heinrichs des Löwen?" *Deutsche Vierteljahrsschrift* 64 (1990), 1-25. Steer's relegating of the A-prologue to an unreliable later addition to the "genuine" B-prologue was rejected by Joachim Bumke, "Heinrich der Löwe und der *Lucidarius*-Prolog," *Deutsche Vierteljahrsschrift* 69 (1995), 603-633. See also Steer's answer, "Der A-Prolog des deutschen *Lucidarius* — das Werk eines mitteldeutschen Bearbeiters des 13. Jahrhunderts: Eine Replik," *Deutsche Vierteljahrsschrift* 69 (1995), 634-665.

called *Aurea gemma*. But it seemed preferable to the master to call it *Lucidarius*, because it is an illuminator.[7]

This recovers moments in a dialogue between the patron and his commissioned writers: they debate points of composition, exchange opinions, and resolve their differences. It is clear that the authority relations are flexible. One difference was resolved in the duke's favor (no verse), the other in the master's (the title). The dispute registers in the original prologue (B), written while the duke was alive and interested. It begins by naming the book as the master wished (line 1) and later on (line 9) also mentions the title the duke wanted, but omits any reference to the discussion that accounts for the double naming. The later prologue (A) gives us the clue to reading the double title: the master had his way; the second title is token recognition of the duke's wishes. The duke was pliant and acceded on one point to the plans of his learned chaplain, and the A-prologue writer thought it worth recording — not praise or flattery of the duke, but his success in contradicting him. This is the way educated clerics ideally spoke to their lords, secular or ecclesiastical, and this is the way, ideally, the masters listened to them.

The point is not that the patron has authority; that is a given of political and economic relations; what we learn is that the poet/master/chaplain had an authority that could override that of the patron. While different circumstances may have applied to a learned work gleaned and translated from the Latin tradition than to vernacular romance and history, we can also confirm the same situation for more popular genres. A recent study of Wace's *Roman de Rou* and its relations to the Plantagenet court argues that Wace refused to distort historical truth to flatter his patrons: "One would naturally expect... that a writer of vernacular history dependent upon a royal patron would slant his narrative to suit the political interests of the ruling house... However, Wace was neither a propagandist nor a panegyrist; his loyalties lay more with his conception of the

---

[7] *Der deutsche "Lucidarius": Band 1: Kritischer Text nach den Handschriften*, ed. Dagmar Gottschall and Georg Steer (Tübingen: Niemeyer, 1994), pp. 102*-103* (both prologues are given also in Steer, "Der deutsche *Lucidarius*" [n. 7 above], pp. 5-9) A-prologue, lines 10-31: "Got selbe hat den sin gegebin / deme herzogen, der ez schribin liez. / Sine capellane er hiez / die rede suchen an den schriften / und bat, daz sie ez tichten / an rimen wolden, wan si ensolden / nicht schriben wan die warheit, / als ez zu latine steit. / Daz taten sie willecliche / dem herzogen heinriche, / der es in gebot und bat. /.../ Ez enwere an dem meister nicht bliben, / er hette ez gerimet, ab er solde. / Der herzoge wolde, / daz man ez hieze da / Aurea gemma. / Do duchte ez den meister bezzer sus, / daz ez hieze lucidarius, / wan ez ein irluchter ist."

actual nature of past events than with his patron's personal or political ego."[8]

John of Salisbury's *Policraticus* is also instructive for the relations of writer to patron. The *Policraticus* (1159) is a work for and about the court by a court cleric, though not a fictional narrative. John wrote it for Thomas Becket while Becket was Chancellor of the English court under Henry II. Becket was famous for his courtly ways, his interest in riding and hunting, even in knightly combat. He wore splendid clothes, gave fabulous banquets, led the life of an elegant bon vivant, hunted, played chess, and occasionally courted women in the manner of lovers.[9] John of Salisbury dedicated the work to Becket, made him its patron, and praised him abundantly. Well and good. The *Policraticus* is a patronized work in the broader sense in which that expression is used: a work which designates a patron, is dedicated to him and sent to him in hope of reward. And John, a clerk of the Archbishop of Canterbury, did indeed dream of reward. He foresaw that Becket was to become next Archbishop of Canterbury, and he said so in the long introductory poem, the *Entheticus*. In other words, he wrote the work for the man he thought would be his future boss, the man on whose good will his hopes and ambitions rested.

So, how does he represent the life of the court, of which his patron was so fond? In three words, he mistrusted, despised and condemned it — and represented it accordingly.[10] He criticizes the courtier's love of hunting, of feasting, of fine clothes. And to make a long story short, the *Policraticus* is a trenchant attack on that very life for which Thomas Becket, its patron, had made himself a reputation.[11] John's prologue is a masterpiece of subtlety. He explicitly names the culprit against whom the work is directed. It is: none other

---

[8] Jean Blacker-Knight, "Wace's Craft and his Audience: Historical Truth, Bias, and Patronage in the *Roman du Rou*," *Kentucky Romance Quarterly* 31 (1984), 355-62, here p. 357.

[9] On Becket as courtier see C. Stephen Jaeger, *The Envy of Angels: Cathedral Schools and Social Ideals in Medieval Europe 950-1200* (Philadelphia: University of Pennsylvania Press, 1994), pp. 297-310.

[10] On John's court criticism, see Claus Uhlig, *Hofkritik im England des Mittelalters und der Renaissance: Studien zu einem Gemeinplatz der europäischen Moralistik* (Berlin, New York: De Gruyter, 1973), pp. 27-54.

[11] It is true that the work develops positions on clerical immunity and the limits of royal power close to those of archbishop Thomas Becket (see Anne Duggan, "John of Salisbury and Thomas Becket," in *The World of John of Salisbury*, ed. Michael Wilks [Oxford: Blackwell, 1984], p. 430), but since Thomas was still the king's loyal chancellor at the time, it only underscores the point: the author of the *Policraticus* does not assume comfortable positions vis à vis his patron.

than he himself, John of Salisbury. *He* embodies all the frivolities of courtiers. Of course, he adds, others may sense that the shoe fits them. If they do, then they should wear it. John's intention shines through that filter clearly. Becket is to be confronted with his own vices and to receive lessons in living virtuously while at court.

This is a case where a writer hoping for patronage endears himself by criticising his patron, and his criticism takes the form of teaching, compared to that of Seneca and Jerome for their pupils.[12]

Orderic Vitalis gives an example closer to narrative literature in his *Historia ecclesiastica*. He tells of a cleric living at the court of Hugh of Avranches, a court renowned for its splendor and worldliness. This chaplain, Gerold of Avranches, was a man of piety and learning. He made a collection of tales of combat of famous knights from bygone days, including tales of Biblical warriors, Charlemagne, and William of Orange. His purpose is to convert the men of the court to a better life: *ad emendationem vitae*, and to combat their "carnal impetuosity" by examples of heroic virtue from the past.[13] This cleric, then, used tales of knighthood as an instrument of correction. He fabricated from historical examples of the warrior life a pattern of moral excellence for the courtiers to follow. He may have idealized activities native to the warrior class, but he did so to criticize his contemporaries, not to flatter them. It is arguable that this is also the intention out of which courtly romance generally was written.

We encounter this pedagogic tone of voice in many Latin writings from the worldly clerical milieu: the learned master speaks to persons in his charge, as to his pupils, or as to men caught in error and in need of guidance. He is responsible for their spiritual edification and for warding off their sins before they commit them; he helps them to suppress their anger and cruelty, govern their sexuality and dampen their grief over death, encourages them to substitute compassion and forgiveness for revenge, and in general strives to bring them to norms of self-control, discipline, temperance. It is surprising to us, who have certain expectations of the way subordinates speak to masters, to read letters like those of the Bamberg schoolmaster Meinhard to Bishop Gunther (died 1065) chiding him for sleeping late, for staying away from Bamberg too long, and —

---

[12] See John of Salisbury, *Policraticus*, ed. C. C. I. Webb, 2 vols. (Oxford: Clarendon Press, 1909) Book I, Prologue.

[13] *The Ecclesiastical History of Orderic Vitalis*, ed. and trans. Marjorie Chibnall (Oxford: Oxford University Press, 1969-80), vol. 3, p. 216 (*Hist. eccl.* 6.2). See the analysis in *Origins of Courtliness* (n. 6 above), p. 231f.

a famous reproach in literary history — for being more interested in the tales of Attila and Dietrich of Bern than in the word of God.[14] But this is the tone typical in letters of clerics — no matter where in the church hierarchy — to bishops, kings, dukes, counts, to any men exposed to the dangers and temptations of public life. It did not matter in what degree of dependence or independence these clerics stood to noblemen, rulers, pontiffs, or what hopes of favor they cherished. Whatever respect they show for worldly authority, the tone of the letters is condescending and admonitory, teaching and preaching.[15]

It goes without saying: this was an idealized stance. The cleric speaks to the prince as his wise counselor and instructor, as Aristotle spoke to Alexander the Great, as Joseph spoke to Pharaoh. It also goes without saying that there must have been many flatterers among clerics, who assented to everything their lords wanted. Thomasin von Zirclaere, in his polemic against worldly courts, says that clerics do not need an education to thrive at court. All they need is a single phrase: "Yes, mylord."[16] But even for the educated spineless sycophant, the sanctioned pose was the teacher and corrector of vices, and if they did not at least strike it, they were betraying their order, acting inordinately.

This relationship of clerics to noblemen secular or ecclesiastical marks out a model of the relationship of clerical narrative poet to noble court audience. The poets spoke to their potential readers/listeners, not as supplicants, not as hired scribes, and not as prince-pleasers, but as teachers, as men responsible for the moral and social improvement of the laity.[17]

---

[14] Meinhard's letters are available in the collection *Briefsammlungen der Zeit Heinrichs IV.*, ed. Carl Erdmann, MGH: Briefe der deutschen Kaiserzeit 5 (Weimar: Böhlau, 1950). On the letter reproaching Bishop Gunther for excessive interest in worldly tales, see Erdmann, "'Fabulae curiales': Neues zum Spielmannsgesang und zum Ezzoliede," *Zeitschrift für deutsches Altertum* 73 (1936), 87-98.

[15] I would just mention the letters of Berengar of Tours to King Philip I of France; of Philip of Harvengt to Philip of Flanders and Henry the Liberal of Champagne; of Peter of Blois to Henry II of England.

[16] *Der Wälsche Gast des Thomasin von Zirclaria*, ed. Heinrich Rückert (Berlin: De Gruyter, 1965), v. 6401-02.

[17] In stark contrast to Georg Steer's claim that the apparent independence of the "master" of the *Lucidarius* presupposes a "phenomenon of the emancipation of self-conscious mastery" that did not develop until the thirteenth century (Steer, "Der deutsche *Lucidarius*," [n. 7 above], p. 17). Also against Steer's view on this point, Bumke, "Der *Lucidarius*-Prolog," (n. 7 above), p. 614 and n. 73. The sense of self-conscious mastery faded rather than emerged in the course of the thirteenth century.

Virtually every work of pre-courtly or early courtly narrative presents itself as teaching and transmitting wisdom, not magnifying its patron. Some examples:

— The author of the *Kaiserchronik* mentions no patron, but tells his listeners that they will learn important lessons from his work, lessons that can increase their wisdom; it is a true book about the ancient popes and kings, not the kind of lying fable many poets sing.[18]

— Chrétien begins *Erec et Enide*, his first Arthurian romance, with a proverb and the admonition to study always, and strive to speak and teach what is right. He is rescuing the Erec story, he says, from those paid singers who regularly mangle it in the presence of kings and counts. He mentions no patron.[19]

— Marie de France begins her *Lais* by indicating that she considers herself duty bound to proclaim truth by the exercise of her poetic talent, because this brings forth great fruit. She indicates that there is a hidden meaning in her writing which she has placed there in the manner of the ancient philosophers, "so that those who came after might study with greater diligence to find the thought within their words." She writes them down in order that the great deeds of men of an earlier age will not be forgotten, She also dedicates them to a king whom she does not name.[20]

And so on through the early period of romance: that whole series of romancers who are silent about their patrons regularly name as the impulses behind their works didactic and historical ones. We sense in the background another impulse: the competition between poets who write and teach by doing it, and those who sing and earn money by doing it. Occasionally we hear hopes of rewards and sense the profit motive, but in approximately one of ten cases.

I do not know of any good reason to doubt these statements of purpose of the early romancers. If we accept them at face value, then a whole train of evidence (not assumptions) about the social and cultural impulses behind courtly narrative falls into place. Clerics taught and corrected the ways of laymen. They put forward ideal models of behavior for imitation, and that means they were free to create ideals of behavior. They used letters, histories, "Fürstenspiegel,"

---

[18] *Die Kaiserchronik eines Regensburger Geistlichen*, ed. Edward Schröder, MGH: Texte des Mittelalters 1/1 (1895; rpt. Berlin: Weidmann, 1964), lines 6-14.

[19] *Erec et Enide*, ed. Mario Roques, CFMA 80 (Paris: Champion, 1952), v. 1-22.

[20] *Les Lais*, ed. Jeanne Lods, CFMA 87 (Paris: Champion, 1959), Prologue. On the uncertainty of the unnamed "noble reis," see Lods's introduction, p. vi. Also, Rita Lejeune, "Le Rôle littéraire d'Aliénor d'Aquitaine," *Cultura Neolatina* 14 (1954), pp. 35, 39.

their own behavior, to do it. And some especially clever clerics invented a new form: courtly romance. This form should be seen as part of that greater body of literature aimed at educating and instructing princes, rulers, lords and knights, all of which served and functioned within the great wave of educating in progress from the eleventh century on: the civilizing of the feudal nobility. The romance satisfied the craving of lay society for fabulous tales of miraculous adventures, and it incorporated those tales into classical ethical-esthetic ideals of elegant, controlled behavior. The educating and civilizing impulse smuggled itself in via the love of the fantastic among all levels of lay society. In some of the major romances, the primary underlying motive of the narrative — ethical education — coincides with the theme: the education of the knight or lady or both.

Seeing the beginnings of romance from this perspective gets us around a difficult problem in both the popular and scholarly understanding of courtly society, a problem that the patronage question again and again entangles us in. The problem is this: we look at the romances and see elegant, courtly, humane gentleman-warriors, pardoning their vanquished enemies and treating ladies and inferiors with sublime regard, thinking and feeling with greatness and refinement of soul. Then we look in contemporary history and we hear horror stories of violence and brutality, of iron sensibilities and dark-hearted inhumanity, of a world lit only by fire.[21] We compare these historical "realities" with the portraits of noble and humane knights in the literature which the same feudal nobility is supposed to have commissioned, and only one conclusion is possible: courtly romance is a form of lying. Or we ask the motive of the idealizing veil masking brutality, and find in romance an instrument of ideology: a means of maintaining and legitimizing the power of a ruling elite.[22]

There is a more compelling historical model explaining the rise of courtly romance: in the eleventh and twelfth centuries, the violence of the times produced a reaction, a trend toward civilizing that began in a class of worldly clerics brought up to restraint and moderation, to courteous, humane, delicate, compassionate ways. It became a task of this class to oppose the violence of lay

---

[21] The title of William Manchester's work of popular scholarship is devoted to the brutality and barbarity of the period, *A World Lit only by Fire: The Medieval Mind and the Renaissance: Portrait of an Age* (Boston: Little, Brown, 1992). See also Bumke, *Höfische Kultur* (Munich: Deutscher Taschenbuchverlag, 1986), pp. 9-13, 558-82, and Arno Borst, "Das Rittertum im Hochmittelalter: Ideal und Wirklichkeit," *Saeculum* 10 (1959), 213-31.

[22] See n. 1 above.

society. They did it in a variety of ways. But their most effective instrument was the romance. The courtly knight of romance is, as Bumke has shown, an educational ideal,[23] and the works that convey that ideal were meant to oppose knightly violence, not to gloss it over. Popular fiction played an important part in creating new social ideals,[24] and the lay nobility snatched them up as eagerly as any fashion.

So much for the first part of my thesis, "patrons did not make courtly romance." The second part of the formula was: "courtly romance made patrons." The evidence on this is fairly clear also. The Norman poet Wace finished his verse adaptation of Geoffrey of Monmouth, the *Roman de Brut*, in 1155.[25] Since he does not mention a patron we can assume he did not have one, that is, following the guideline proposed earlier. A later adapter, Layamon, says that Wace gave his book to Queen Eleanor. That statement tells us very little. It is an apocryphal comment, rather like the statement of the *Klage* poet that Bishop Pilgrim of Passau commissioned a Latin *Nibelungenlied*. Why should Wace have deprived his patroness, or would-be-patroness, of the slice of immortality he had to bestow by not mentioning her in the poem? In spite of that consideration, Eleanor is mentioned regularly in respectable scholarship as the patroness of the *Brut*.[26]

What we do know as a fact is that a few years after the *Brut*, King Henry II, husband of Eleanor, asked Wace to write a history of the dukes of

---

[23] Joachim Bumke, *Studien zum Ritterbegriff im 12. und 13. Jahrhundert*, 2nd ed., Beihefte zum Euphorion 1 (Heidelberg: Winter, 1976), pp. 147-48.

[24] See C. Stephen Jaeger, "Courtliness and Social Change," in *Cultures of Power: Lordship, Status, and Process in Twelfth-Century Europe*, ed. Thomas N. Bisson (Philadelphia: University of Pennsylvania Press, 1995), pp. 287-309.

[25] On the patronage of Wace and his relation to the Angevin court, see Jean Blacker-Knight, "Wace's Craft and his Audience" (n. 9 above); Jean-Guy Gouttebroze, "Henri II Plantagenet: Patron des historiographes anglo-normands de langue d'oïl," *La littérature angevine médiévale Cesbron: Actes du colloque du samedi 22 mars 1980/Université d'Angers Centre de recherche de littérature et de linguistique de l'Anjou et des Bocages* (Maine et Loire: Herault, 1981), pp. 91-105; Diana B. Tyson, "Patronage of French Vernacular History Writers in the Twelfth and Thirteenth Centuries," *Romania* 100 (1979), 180-222; Bumke, *Mäzene im Mittelalter*, p. 13f. and notes 3-5 (extensive bibliography prior to 1979).

[26] M. D. Legge, "La littérature anglo-normande au temps d'Aliénor d'Aquitaine," *Cahiers de civilisation médiévale* 29 (1986), 113-14; Rita Lejeune, "Rôle littéraire d'Aliénor d'Aquitaine et de sa famille," *Cultura neolatina* 14 (1954), 25-27; and Diana B. Tyson, "Patronage," pp. 193-95.

VI

Patrons and Courtly Romance

Normandy, which became the *Roman de Rou*. Wace tells us so in an introduction to that work. The patronized work mentions a patron. He praises Henry and Eleanor, especially their generosity, and expresses his hopes of receiving a reward. Later in the work he mentions that Henry gave him a prebend as canon of Bayeux, — which he did, — around 1169. Here patronage and gifts followed literary success.

The same is true of Benoît de Sainte- Maure. His *Roman de Troie* is without dedication, and nothing is known of a patron. But in the wake of its success, he was hired by Henry II to write a chronicle of the Norman dukes, a job probably taken out of the hands of Wace.[27]

Chrétien wrote his two first romances, *Erec et Enide* and *Cligés*, and probably *Yvain*, before he received a commission: Marie de Champagne gave him the story of Lancelot, both *matière* and *sens*, and he produced most of the work — with what degree of willingness it is not clear from his possibly ironic dedication.

In Germany, Heinrich von Veldeke mentions Landgraf Hermann von Thüringen in the epilogue to his *Eneit*.[28] But the landgrave encouraged and patronized Veldeke's work only when it was nearly finished. Nine years earlier he had entrusted his work to the Countess of Clèves only to have it stolen by a lady of her court. We know nothing of a commission to begin the writing; we know only of a patron who came late.[29]

In all these cases, the work, finished and successful, made the patron; in none of these cases did a patron make the work.

We should stop giving credit to patrons and patronage in the early history of romance, as somehow the originators of that form and the vision of life it conveys. The lay nobles do not deserve it. They did not pay for the early romances; they did not help the authors. In part it was the bad behavior of their class and of their knights that provoked the romance-writer's antithetical vision of a civilized knighthood. And they waited to bestow their patronage — with the faint-heartedness typical in those who have to judge talent — until the poets had proven themselves. Samuel Johnson's description of a patron applies well to medieval Maecenases: "Is not a patron ... one who looks with unconcern on a

---

[27] On Benoît, see Bumke, *Mäzene*, p. 14 and notes 4-5.

[28] See Bumke, *Mäzene*, pp. 113-118.

[29] Veldeke does praise Countess Margaret of Clèves for her generosity in the epilogue, but probably as the wife of Landgrave Hermann, not as the earlier patroness of his work. Bumke doubts that she commissioned it and states the plain fact that "Der erste Auftraggeber der 'Eneit' bleibt unbekannt" (*Mäzene*, p. 116).

man struggling for life in the water, and, when he has reached the ground, encumbers him with help?"[30]

---

[30] Letter to Lord Chesterfield, in James Boswell, *The Life of Samuel Johnson* (London, New York: Macmillan, 1900), vol. 1, p. 186.

VII

Courtliness and Social Change

> ich schilt die âventiure niht, / swie uns ze liegen geschiht / von der
> âventiure rât, / wan si bezeichenunge hât / der zuht unde der wârheit.
>
> (What the romances tell us may be a pack of lies, but I do not criticize
> them, for they contain symbols of courtesy and truth)
> —Thomasin von Zirclaere, *Der welsche Gast*, 1121–25

This study suggests ways of assessing the part played by courtly literature and courtly ideals in the social changes of the twelfth century. It is not easy to assess the role of literature and ideas in any climate of social crisis and change.[1] For twelfth-century court society, where imaginative literature forms a large part of the documentation, the problems are great, and that makes methodology a fundamental concern. Courtly literature is fantastic and artificial;[2] the society in which it arose was rough, rude, and violent.[3] The society produced social codes that seem to mediate between literature and reality, or at least to occupy an intermediary position,[4] but there is no

---

1. Gabrielle Spiegel, "History, Historicism, and the Social Logic of the Text in the Middle Ages," *Speculum* 65 (1990), 59–86; and Spiegel, "Social Change and Literary Language: The Textualization of the Past in Thirteenth-Century Old French Historiography," *Journal of Medieval and Renaissance Studies* 17 (1987), 129–48. See the extensive survey of research by Otto H. Baumhauer, "Kulturwandel: Zur Entwicklung des Paradigmas von der Kultur als Kommunikationssystem: Forschungsbericht," *Deutsche Vierteljahrsschrift* 56 (1982), Sonderheft, 1–167.
2. See Erich Auerbach's reading, in *Mimesis: The Representation of Reality in Western Literature*, tr. Willard R. Trask (New York, 1957), pp. 107–24 ("The Knight Sets Forth").
3. See Joachim Bumke, *Höfische Kultur: Literatur und Gesellschaft im hohen Mittelalter*, 2 vols. (Munich, 1986), 1: esp. 9–14, 430–32; tr. Thomas Dunlap, *Courtly Culture: Literature and Society in the High Middle Ages*, (Berkeley, CA, 1991); Arno Borst, "Das Rittertum im Hochmittelalter: Ideal und Wirklichkeit," *Saeculum* 10 (1959), 213–31, rpt. in *Das Rittertum im Mittelalter*, ed. Arno Borst, Wege der Forschung 349 (Darmstadt, 1976), pp. 212–46; Georges Duby, "Youth in Aristocratic Society," in his *The Chivalrous Society*, tr. Cynthia Postan (London, 1977), pp. 112–22.
4. For instance, on chivalric honor, see Jean Flori, *L'idéologie du glaive: préhistoire de la chevalerie* (Geneva, 1983); Flori, *L'essor de la chevalerie, XIe–XIIe siècles* (Geneva, 1986). On courtly manners, see C. Stephen Jaeger, *The Origins of Courtliness: Civilizing Trends and the Formation of Courtly Ideals, 939–1210* (Philadelphia: University of Pennsylvania Press, 1985); and courtly love, Bumke, *Höfische Kultur* pp. 503–82, and Rüdiger Schnell in a series of works,

From *Cultures of Power* edited by Thomas N. Bison. Copyright © 1995 by University of Pennsylvania Press. Reprinted with permission.

agreement on the ability of such codes to set standards of social behavior.[5] And yet one of the hard and accepted facts of the history of chivalry is that the ideal of the chivalric courtly knight in literature created a social ideal;[6] shortly after the emergence of courtly literature, "knighthood" has risen from humble beginnings as mounted soldiers to a noble order comprising the entire nobility.[7] And dukes, counts and kings are proud to have themselves and their ancestors represented in family chronicles as modest, debonair gentlemen, who overlook insult and abuse and never seek revenge.[8]

Society changed; it sought the trappings of chivalric romance;[9] it staged festivals that were themselves the stuff of romance.[10] But did warriors become "verhöflicht," and if they did, what part did courtly literature have in their reformation?[11] There is a large gap that separates the sublime idealism of romance from the realities of court society. What, if anything, does that gap say about the engagedness of courtly literature in the process of civilizing the knighthood?

Romantic and Victorian scholarship tended to make courtly literature into documentation of social realities.[12] For the past few decades the major

---

most recently, "Die 'höfische Liebe' als 'höfischer Diskurs' über die Liebe," in *Curialitas: Studien zu Grundfragen der höfisch-ritterlichen Kultur* ed. Josef Fleckenstein (Göttingen 1990), pp. 231–301. Also his *Causa amoris: Liebeskonzeption und Liebesdarstellung in der mittelalterlichen Literatur* (Bern-Francke, 1985).

5. See Bumke, *Höfische Kultur,* pp. 439ff. The non-existence of "courtly love" as a social practice is virtually an accepted tenet of current literature. Cf. Schnell in *Curialitas,* p. 300, referring to the current scholarly consensus: "der höfische Frauendienst war keine gesellschaftliche Realität; die 'höfische Liebe' existierte lediglich als 'a mode of thought' bzw. nur in der Literatur."

6. The result of Joachim Bumke's *Studien zum Ritterbegriff im 12. und 13. Jahrhundert,* 2nd ed. (Heidelberg, 1977).

7. Bumke, *Studien* esp. pp. 130ff.; also Bumke, *Höfische Kultur* (with extensive bibliography); Georges Duby, "The Origins of Knighthood," in *The Chivalrous Society* (note 3 above), pp. 158–70; Maurice Keen, *Chivalry* (New Haven, CT, 1984); Flori, *L'idéologie* and *L'essor* (note 4 above).

8. Jaeger, *Origins,* pp. 195–210.

9. See Bumke, *Höfische Kultur,* pp. 137–275 ("Sachkultur und Gesellschaftsstil").

10. See Bumke, *Höfische Kultur,* pp. 276–318; also the studies in *Höfische Repräsentation: Das Zeremoniell und die Zeichen,* ed. Hedda Ragotzky and Horst Wenzel (Tübingen, 1990); *Das Fest,* ed. Walter Haug and Rainer Warning (Munich, 1989); *Feste und Feiern im Mittelalter,* ed. Detlef Altenburg, Jörg Jarnut, and Hans-Hugo Steinhoff (Sigmaringen, 1991). The study by John Baldwin, "Jean Renart et le tournoi de Saint-Trond: Une conjonction de l'histoire et de la littérature," *Annales ESC* 45 (1990), 565–88, is valuable for showing the literary representation of court practice.

11. "Verhöflichung der Krieger" is Norbert Elias's term: *Über den Prozess der Zivilisation: Soziogenetische und Psychogenetische Untersuchungen,* 2d ed., 2 vols. (Bern, 1969), 2: 351–69. See Sabine Krüger, "'Verhöflichter Krieger' und miles illitteratus," in *Curialitas,* pp. 326–49.

12. For instance, Alwyn Schultz, *Das höfische Leben zur Zeit der Minnesinger,* 2 vols., 2d ed. (1889; rpt. Osnabrück, 1965); Hans Naumann continues this tradition and represents the

work in the area has reacted against that trend. It was an important corrective to the nineteenth-century view of the middle ages. But it has its limits. It tends to relegate courtly literature and the social values it conveys to the realm of "the ideal" and privileges non-fictional documents as spokesmen of "reality." This view has prominent adherents: Johan Huizinga,[13] Erich Auerbach, and Erich Köhler. Joachim Bumke recently published a study of major importance that draws in part on this paradigm for its conceptual framework.[14] E. R. Curtius deserves mention in this connection for tending to isolate literature in a realm by itself. Curtius helped us look on literature as a composite of received forms, isolated in literary traditions—as texts generated by earlier texts—and discouraged us from looking on it as texts charged with ideas and social issues alive and influential in the period which produced them.[15]

The opposition of the ideal and the real accommodates post-

moral values of courtly literature as actual social values in *Deutsche Kultur im Zeitalter des Rittertums* (Potsdam, 1938). See Bumke, who comes to terms with this entire trend in *Höfische Kultur* pp. 14–17. It is easy to do an injustice to much of the earlier literature in a kind of wholesale dismissal of its premises. Still instructive for the moral force of courtly literature, without succumbing to the fallacies Bumke warns against, is Kenelm Digby's *The Broad Stone of Honor or, The True Sense and Practice of Chivalry*, 4 vols. (London 1877). See the fascinating survey by Mark Girouard, *The Return to Camelot: Chivalry and the English Gentleman* (New Haven, CT, 1985).

13. Huizinga represents the strengths and weaknesses of the Ideal vs. Real paradigm. His judgment of chivalry as a historiographical idea: "The confused image of contemporaneous history being much too complicated for their comprehension, they simplified it, as it were, by the fiction of chivalry as a moving force.... A very fantastic and rather shallow point of view, no doubt. How much vaster is ours.... Still, this vision of a world ruled by chivalry, however superficial and mistaken it might be, was the best they had.... It served them as a formula to understand, in their poor way, the appalling complexity of the world's way" (*The Waning of the Middle Ages: A Study of the Forms of Life, Thought, and Art in France and the Netherlands in the XIVth and XVth Centuries*, tr. F. Hopman [London, 1924], p. 68). The voice of the patriarch chastising his silly, ungovernable subjects sounds wherever Huizinga talks of chivalry. Its ideals are symptomatic of "the spirit of a primitive age, susceptible of gross delusions and little accessible to the correction of experience" (p. 129). They are comforting lies: "In order to forget the painful imperfection of reality, the nobles turn to the continual illusion of a high and heroic life. They wear the mask of Lancelot and Tristram. It is an amazing self-deception. The crying falsehood of it can only be borne by treating it with some amount of raillery" (p. 80).

14. Bumke, *Höfische Kultur*, esp. pp. 9–14, 430–50; also Auerbach, *Mimesis*; Erich Köhler, *Ideal und Wirklichkeit in der höfischen Epik* (Tübingen Niermeyer, 1970); Johanna Maria van Winter, *Rittertum: Ideal und Wirklichkeit* (Munich, 1969); Klaus Schreiner, "Hof (*curia*) und höfische Lebensführung (*vita curialis*) als Herausforderung an die christliche Theologie und Frömmigkeit," in *Höfische Literatur, Hofgesellschaft, Höfische Lebensformen um 1200: Kolloquium am Zentrum für Interdisziplinäre Forschung der Universität Bielefeld*, ed. Gert Kaiser und Jan-Dirk Müller (Düsseldorf, 1986), pp. 67–138.

15. Ernst R. Curtius, *European Literature and the Latin Middle Ages*, tr. Willard R. Trask (New York, 1963). See Peter Godman, "The Ideas of Ernst Robert Curtius and the Genesis of *European Literature and the Latin Middle Ages*," Epilogue to *ELLMA* (rpt. Princeton, NJ, 1990), with extensive bibliography on recent studies of Curtius.

VII

structuralist thinking without being beholden to it. It creates a category into which literature can be banished to a detached aesthetic existence with no ties to the other category, "the real." That is the direction in which post-structuralist theory tends to push literature.[16] Chivalry and courtly love, the norms governing behavior in courtly literature, are placed in a kind of limbo, and to ask about them as social realities is to repeat the mistake of Don Quixote.

In the present state of the question, a central methodological problem is how to judge the historical value of texts that bear on knighthood in the twelfth century when a large body of documentation gives sharply conflicting views.[17] The following reflections deal with the process by which determinants of social behavior are established through a conflict of ideas and interests.

Sociologists and cultural anthropologists have wrestled with the inherent impossibility of documenting the "realities" of social behavior reliably, and have tended to focus discussion on the "patterns of and models for behavior, received and transmitted by symbols,"[18] or on "the conceptual structures individuals use to construe experience."[19] The "cultural patterns" that organize experience and the "conceptual structures" that explain

---

16. See the methodological reflections of Gabrielle Spiegel, "History, Historicism, and the Social Logic," who summarizes a large body of theoretical literature and suggests possibilities for historical criticism in a post-structuralist theoretical climate. On the problem of non-referentiality and post-structuralist conceptions of the text, Rodolphe Gasché, *The Tain of the Mirror: Derrida and the Philosophy of Reflection* (Cambridge, 1986), esp. pp. 109–76, rescuing Derrida from an over-simplified view that sees him as abolishing referentiality ("There is nothing outside of the text"—Gasché, *The Tain,* pp. 278–93). Whatever its precise views on referentiality, post-structuralism moves away from questions like literature's role in social change and towards the questions raised by problematized discourse and hermeneutic. A general criticism of post-structuralism, Manfred Frank, *Was ist Neostrukturalismus?* (Frankfurt, 1984); trans. *What Is Neostructuralism?,* tr. Sabine Walke and Richard Gray (Minneapolis, 1989).

17. A problem analyzed evenhandedly by Yuri Bessmertny in his study "The Peasant as Seen by the Knight (Based on French Data of the 11th–13th Centuries)," in Bessmertny, *Social and Political Structures of the Middle Ages* (Moscow, 1990), pp. 45–61. Cf. p. 49: "The gap [between the ideal and the real] did not preclude the ideal from performing its ideological functions, nor did it preclude the ideal from making an impact on social realities."

18. A. L. Kroeber and Clyde Kluckhohn, "Culture: A Critical Review of Concepts and Definitions," *Harvard University Peabody Museum of American Archeology and Ethnology Papers* 47 (1952), 189. For more recent literature see the survey of research by Baumhauer, "Kulturwandel."

19. Clifford Geertz, "The Politics of Meaning," in Geertz, *The Interpretation of Cultures: Selected Essays* (New York, 1973), p. 313.

VII

Courtliness and Social Change 291

it are the object of ethnology, and not some comprehensive inventory of the actual observable forms of behavior. Cultural anthropology aims at formulating "the norms for and standards of behavior . . . the ideologies that legitimize certain select patterns of behavior or give them a rational explanation."[20] The discussion of courtly literature and courtly society would profit by moving to this more abstract level, at which symbolic models compete for dominance in a conflict of ideas aimed at establishing norms, instructing, informing, explaining, and representing behavior.

A letter of Peter of Blois will get us into the issues.[21] Letter 94 is addressed to a certain Archdeacon John. It criticizes the behavior of his two nephews, who are knights, and develops a general criticism of knighthood. He makes the following accusations. Knights slander and malign clerics; their speech is scurrilous; their behavior is inordinate; they esteem most him whose speech is filthiest and whose curses are foulest, who fears God and the church least; they claim the license to rob and slander; hardly girded with the sword, they turn to plundering the church, persecuting the poor and suffering mercilessly; they let their exorbitant lusts and desires run wild; they are slothful and drunken; corrupted by *otium,* they neglect the practice of arms; they go to battle as if to a banquet, their pack animals laden with wine, cheese, sausage, and roasting forks instead of weapons; they carry gilt and jewel-encrusted shields, which of course they are concerned to protect from sword blows; they have scenes of combat painted on their saddles and shields, "so that they may take pleasure in a kind of fantasy vision of battles [*quadam imaginaria visione*], which in reality they would not have the courage so much as to look upon, let alone take part in."[22]

Listing the accusations in this bald way strips the letter of its rhetorical structure and of the social values which move it. Now we should try to restore the syntax of thought and of argument in which these criticisms are imbedded.

The occasion for writing is the slandering of clerics. Knights have an obligation to defer to clerics, which they are neglecting shockingly. The

20. Kroeber and Kluckholn, "Culture," 189.
21. *PL,* 207, 293–97. Bumke called attention to the letter. He quotes it at length opposing its realism to the idealism of the courtly knight of romance (*Höfische Kultur,* 2: 430ff.). Some brief comments on the letter in Flori, *L'essor,* pp. 332–33. Informative on Peter of Blois's letters, though not for our context, Ethel Cardwell Higonnet, "Spiritual Ideas in the Letters of Peter of Blois," *Speculum* l 50 (1975), 218–44. Also R. W. Southern, "Peter of Blois: A Twelfth Century Humanist?" in Southern, *Medieval Humanism and Other Studies* (Oxford, 1984), pp. 105–32.
22. *PL,* 207: 296A: "Bella tamen et conflictus equestres depingi faciunt in sellis et clypeis, ut se quadam imaginaria visione delectent in pugnis, quas actualiter ingredi, aut videre non audent."

tensions between knights and clerics are a reality of social life in the period. The many testimonies to them[23] include the debate poems on the question of the comparative virtues of knights and clerics as lovers. Peter of Blois is speaking in the interests of his own social group. He has not fabricated the social tensions in which the letter originates, nor is he standing back from a disengaged distance.

The language of his accusations is conventional and easily recognized. The concerns of the peace movement since the late tenth century register in some of the complaints: the knights' obligation to protect clerics, the church, the poor, widows, and the suffering; the attack on the ungovernable and contentious character of knights and lay nobles.[24] But alongside this discourse is another: an attack on sloth, corruption, debauchery, drunkenness, and the resultant slackening of the warrior spirit. This is the language of polemics against the corruption of knights through life at the court, polemics that surfaced in the mid-eleventh century and continued into the thirteenth.[25] In Peter of Blois's letter both directions of the polemics are represented: the knights are violent outdoors; they are slothful, debauched, and corrupt at court.

Along with Peter of Blois's polemical language there is a language of chivalric ideals. He posits an "order" of knighthood, high in dignity and excellence, and a code governing its behavior.[26] Each of the knightly abuses is presented as a betrayal of the knightly code. In the conceptual syntax of his argument, ideal and abuse are set in a relationship of mutual interdependency. The knights' maligning of clerics comes from the conviction of "the eminence of knighthood"[27]; they ignore the "code of knights" in abusing clerics and in not tempering their scurrilous speech with "a kind of maidenly modesty"[28]; their corruption is all the worse because as youths they learned from their uncle "modesty and good conduct" (*modestia et hones-*

23. See Josef Fleckenstein, "Miles und clericus am Königs– und Fürstenhof: Bemerkungen zu den Voraussetzungen, zur Entstehung und zur Trägerschaft der höfisch-ritterlichen Kultur," in *Curialitas*, pp. 302–25.
24. See, among many other works, Hans-Werner Goetz, "Kirchenschutz, Rechtswahrung und Reform: Zu den Zielen und zum Wesen der frühen Gottesfriedensbewegung in Frankreich," *Francia* 11 (1983), 193–239.
25. See Henri Platelle, "Le problème du scandale: les nouvelles modes masculines aux XIe et XIIe siècles," *Revue Belge de Philologie et d'Histoire* 53 (1975), 1071–96; Jaeger, *Origins of Courtliness*, pp. 176–94.
26. On the gradual development of a knightly code of honor in the eleventh and twelfth centuries, see Flori, *L'essor*, pp. 265–67.
27. 293C: ". . . vitae militaris eminentiam jactitantes clericorum sortem multiplici detractione depravant."
28. 293D–294A: ". . . si essent milites, aut quae militum professio esset, cognoscerent, deferrent clericis; et se a scurrilitate verborum quadam puellari modestia temperarent."

VII

Courtliness and Social Change 293

tas)²⁹; they receive their swords from the altar, only to turn them against the church³⁰; they dishonor both the reputation and the ethics of knighthood³¹; they have received the "solemn honors" or "solemn distinction" of knighthood (= were knighted).³²

This pattern shows us the dominant structure of the letter, the perversion of an ideal order: "their honor is dishonor; their modesty is immodesty; their weapons are sausages." Of course the agenda of this polarized discourse requires it to position knights squarely at the negative pole. But that pole plays its part as the negation of an ideal, not as an unopposed perspective onto the real world of knights. Knighthood true to its "order" is "eminent" and "excellent." It behaves with "girlish modesty," it follows the law of *honestas*. "Ordinate" knights protect widows and orphans and fight boldly for a good cause. Membership is acquired through solemn, sanctifying rituals.³³

An important element of this idealizing is the projection into the Roman past of the ideal of knighthood. It has its exemplary embodiment in Aeneas, Scipio Africanus, Trajan, Pompey, and Caesar³⁴. The military discipline, boldness, and self-sacrifice of the ancient Roman heroes are conjured to show how far the nephews of Archdeacon John have declined.

The letter gives us abundant material to convict medieval knights of bad habits. But it also sets tensions in place between an ideal and a corrupted knighthood. So, shall we credit the abuses, or the ideal, with a higher degree of "reality"?

Peter of Blois's writing gives us a second perspective on his character as polemicist. It is a help in judging the value of his polemics as testimony to real conditions. He wrote a letter against the clerics of Henry II's court which became a classic work of court criticism. His accusations were as vehement and extreme as those against the knights, but in this case he received an answer. The chaplains wrote a reply, unfortunately lost, which brought their accuser up short. He then wrote a chastened apology (Let-

---

29. 294A: ". . . illi a pueritiae cunabulis solam in vobis modestiam noverint, solam a vobis didicerint honestatem."
30. 294B: ". . . et hodie tirones enses suos recipiunt de altari, ut profiteantur se filios Ecclesiae . . . Porro res in contrarium versa est . . ."
31. 294C: ". . . vitam . . . degenerem in immunditiis transigentes nomen et officium militiae dehonestant."
32. 297A: ". . . nepos vester S. . . . solemnes militiae titulos acquisivit"
33. For a balanced view of ideals set against abuses, see Flori, *L'essor*, pp. 271–84. It is clear from Flori's discussion of critics of knighthood (particularly Orderic Vitalis) that blame sits in the larger context of praise.
34. *PL* 207: 295 A–C.

ter 150) with fervent praise of court clerics, their good offices, and their "laudable and glorious service." He commends them for virtues which are the reverse of the vices his first letter attacked.[35]

So much for the polemicist as spokesman for "reality." If he was deflating what Huizinga called "an amazing illusion" or tearing off the "mask of Lancelot or Tristram,"[36] then he certainly could not be relied on to stick to his guns. As soon as he was challenged he retreated. His swift retraction shows that he was back-pedaling on his own exaggerations. The principle of gross, barely defensible exaggeration probably applied to his attack on knighthood as well, as it does to much of medieval polemics especially in and after the investiture controversy.[37]

Peter's two letters show us what social pressures were exerted on courtiers and knights, not what an entire class "was really"—something we can never learn. A social class is not like a chemical element with a single discernible internal code which governs its behavior. The two letters mark off a field of social forces within which the court clerics and the knights live and work, and the two extremes are the parameters within which—in the reality of late twelfth century knighthood—an unlimited variety of individual behavior could take place. The polemicist pressures them towards compliance with the values of a code. In the case of the clerics of Henry II's court, we see the courtier's code emerge as a real functioning ethic, because the polemicist backs into it and away from his criticism (though of course the courtiers' vigorous defense says nothing about the degree of compliance, only that a code exists to which they can appeal against charges of abuse). Peter of Blois's polemic against knights likewise confirms ex negativo the existence of chivalric ideals as social values.

Reading polemics against knighthood along with the idealizing litera-

---

35. Epist. 14, *PL* 207: 42–51. On court criticism, see Bumke, *Höfische Kultur*, pp. 583–94. On Peter's Epist. 14, Claus Uhlig, *Hofkritik im England des Mittelalters und der Renaissance: Studien zu einem Gemeinplatz der europäischen Moralistik* (Berlin and New York, 1973), pp. 99–105; Rolf Köhn " 'Militia curialis': Die Kritik am geistlichen Hofdienst bei Peter von Blois und in der lateinischen Literatur des 9.–12. Jahrhunderts," in *Miscellanea Mediaevalia 12: Soziale Ordnungen im Selbstverständnis des Mittelalters*, ed. A. Zimmermann (Berlin and New York, 1979), pp. 227–257. For letter 150, *PL* 207: 439–42.
36. Note 13 above.
37. An illustrative exchange is the letter of Abbot William of Hirsau accusing the Saxon clergy of simony and corruption (ca. 1082–1085) and the answer from the accused. The former is a model of extreme polemics, the latter a model of measured, reserved correction of the abbot's hyperbole. *Briefsammlungen der Zeit Heinrichs IV.*, ed. Carl Erdmann and Norbert Fickermann, *MGH*, Briefe der deutschen Kaiserzeit 5 (Weimar, 1950), pp. 41–46 (Hildesheimer Briefe, Epist. 18 & 19).

ture would seem to leave us either with the category ideal-real, or stymied in indeterminism. I want to suggest a way around this difficulty.

The two sides of Peter of Blois's polemics work together. Medieval social criticism in general operates within a two-pronged discourse: one prong skewers the objects of attack on their gross abuses, the other fixes them into codes and norms. The first finds or invents inflated wrongs, the second fashions sublime ideals.[38] In the polemics of Peter of Blois the dichotomy of good knight-bad knight, restraint and violence, is a unified discourse aimed at urging civilized behavior on the warrior class.

A hindrance to integrating both aspects of the discourse in reading medieval polemics is a mode of interpreting that I will call the mimetic fallacy. This is the assumption that a text like Peter of Blois's letter 94 operates in the mode of empirical, mimetic observations, that it wants to reproduce reality. It is a fallacy because it accepts the illusion of objectivity as a fact of the text's discursive mode. Certainly any medieval writing that brings disapproval to bear on a social group or practice is speaking a polemical language of extreme distortion. The statement, "knights are slothful brutes" has the historical value of the statement, "police are violent racists." Both comments conceal an agenda of social change beneath the appearance of an objective observation. They say silently, "disapprove of brutality." They mask the imperative or optative mode in the indicative.

This mask only exercises deception and creates a misread modality once the issues it faces die, fade, or disappear. No one living in a crisis of competing social values would fail to recognize the engagedness of statements that take positions on the issues at stake. "Police brutality" will certainly now find a lot of agreement, but also a lot of opposition. But a hundred years from now a historian will face that statement with a methodological problem. Once the issues die, the statements remain, and the appearance of objective observation establishes itself as the "true" mode of the statements. The undertow of their agenda for change no longer exercises its pull. That is precisely the condition in which Peter of Blois's polemics or Wolfram's *Parzival* confront the modern historian. The issues on which they took a strong position are no longer present in the mind of

---

38. This helps us deal with the difficult case of Guibert of Nogent, regarded as at once the most scurrilous and the most "objective" and "critical" historian of the Middle Ages. See the survey of views on Guibert in John Benton, *Self and Society in Medieval France: The Memoirs of Abbot Guibert of Nogent* (New York, 1970), pp. 7–11.

the reader, and the texts take on the appearance of "art" or some kind of objective imitation of reality.

Readings of panegyric literature are especially susceptible to the mimetic fallacy. We can imagine a poem in praise of a king, describing him as chaste, generous, wise, and clement. In the spell of mimesis, we think him admirable. Then we read other sources, and these persuade us that in reality he was lascivious, stingy, foolish, and vengeful. Still in the spell of mimesis, we now see the poem as lying flattery because we are measuring its "genuineness" by its loyal rendering of reality. Since it appears to have betrayed that principle, we brand it a lie. The panegyrist's extravagant praise may well be intended to oppose the vices of a notoriously vicious king by fulsome praise of what he lacked. He was prodding and stinging the king by false praise, pushing him to change, and if the rest of the court heard it, so much greater the power of its irony to push him toward reform.[39] But that motive and that immediate effect are lost to the view of the modern reader, since the agenda of reform has vanished, and a mimetic thrust the text never contained is the only one we credit. The exemplary thrust of panegyric in general—that is, not only in ironic praise—removes it from the mimetic mode, and tries to impose its idealizing on reader and subject alike. A modern reader's urge to find the man "as he really was" behind panegyric is ordinarily naïve, not because it is lying flattery, but because it aims at recreating the subject and others in the image of its ideals. It does not represent anything objectively.

Another anti-mimetic element in representation is policy, its documentation, legitimation, and monumentalizing. Any portrait of a ruler aims at more than representing the man "as he was," an aspect necessarily subordinated to the monumentalizing intent. If an art historian writing centuries later read the portrait for its physiognomic information, he would be in the spell of the mimetic fallacy.

The same process by which the illusion of mimesis replaces the reality of advocacy is at work in Peter of Blois's letters. With his polemics he wanted to change reality; he did not care particularly about describing it in some sense we would call "objective." Advocacy is the modality of texts engaged in an economy of competing social issues exercising power and exerting pressure through the written or spoken word. That is why the dis-

---

39. An example of this didactic impulse in ironic praise is a letter from a student of the Mainz cathedral school to the students of the school at Worms (1033), *Die ältere Wormser Briefsammlung,* ed. Walther Bulst, *MGH,* Briefe der deutschen Kaiserzeit 3 (Weimar, 1949; rpt. 1981), pp. 47–48.

course of polemics is polarized. Its negative pole is insult and ridicule: the abuses opposed have to cry out to heaven, and if they do not, the polemicist will invent them. His voice is shrill to muster disapproval.[40]

Its positive pole does the opposite. It speaks a language of ideals that allure and promise social rewards (esteem, prestige, honor), and that have the exemplary force of a charismatic human being, the power to draw others into its orbit. One pole works through extravagant glorifying, the other through extravagant vilifying. The knighthood placed between these two poles is meant to be repelled by the negative and attracted by the positive, and extreme exaggeration at both ends turns up the pressure.

Peter of Blois's response to the alleged violence and sloth of knights was a push to turn them into members of that *ordo militiae*, modest as maidens, serving the needy, the clergy, and the *res publica*, hard, wise, and disciplined as that elite order of ancient knights. This aligns them with many clerics engaged in an important contest of social ideals from the second half of the eleventh century on, among them the authors of courtly romance, who opposed the violence of the lay nobles with ideals of restraint, moderation, and courtesy. We will look at examples of this conflict first in social history, then in literature.

In late 1073 or early 1074 Abbot Walo of St. Arnulf (Metz) wrote two letters to his Archbishop, Manasses I of Rheims (1070–1080), explaining his resignation from the abbacy of St. Remi of Rheims after a brief, unhappy period as abbot.[41] These letters and the other documents that touch on the clash of Walo and Manasses are a lucid illustration of the issues. The abbacy of St. Remi had been vacant since 1071, and this caused concern in Rome.[42] By the end of 1073 Manasses had appointed Walo, who resigned the position within a short time of accepting it. In the letters the freed abbot wrote to Manasses, he heaps vituperation on the archbishop. The latter appears in the letters as an abusive monster who has insulted, threatened, and cursed Walo. "I must have been a fool," he complains, "to

---

40. See Laura Kendrick's paper on Marcabru in this volume. It is instructive to read the ugly polemics against Henry IV in Bruno of Merseburg, *Brunos Buch vom Sachsenkrieg*, ed. Hans-Eberhard Lohmann, *MGH*, Deutsches Mittelalter: Kritische Studientexte des Reichsinstituts für ältere deutsche Geschichtskunde 2 (Leipzig, 1937), cc. 5–15, pp. 16–22, along with the critical commentary by Karl Hampe, *Herrschergestalten des deutschen Mittelalters*, 6th ed. (Heidelberg, 1955; rpt. Darmstadt, 1978), pp. 134–46.

41. On Manasses I, see John R. Williams, "Archbishop Manasses I of Rheims and Pope Gregory VII," *AHR* 54 (1949), 804–24. Also Max Manitius, *Geschichte der lateinischen Literatur des Mittelalters*, 3 vols. (Munich, 1923; rpt. 1976), 2: 724ff.

42. See William, "Manasses I," p. 808–9. Manasses received a letter from Gregory VII urging him to fill the vacancy post haste and to mind his manners, *Das Register Gregors VII.*, ed. Erich Caspar, 2 vols. (Berlin, 1920–23), 2: 1 Epistle 13 (June 30, 1073).

come to a beast so ungentle, so fierce, so violent, so horrendous!"[43] Part of Walo's inducement to accept the position in the first place was the opportunity to convert a man so fierce and truculent from his harsh ways.[44] And indeed he claims in one letter to Manasses that he repeatedly tried to "mitigate his raging" by citing holy scripture, singing it to him, as it were, to drive out the demon in his soul, like another David before Saul.[45] But Manasses holds to his warrior-like ways. It becomes evident that he is not clinging to inborn and habitual savagery, but to an ideal of behavior. He is wrathful and violent as a privilege of his class, and he has the nerve, moreover—says Walo—to suggest that the abbot, being a peaceful, humble, and quiet man, constantly given to reading, is not comfortable with the "manners of the French" and of Manasses.[46] This perversion of values sets off a tirade:

> O monster whom no single virtue redeems from vice! Is it not true that you regard a life tempered by peace, modesty, and sobriety as lower in virtue than one given to harsh and bold combat in wars, since [as you claim] peace is wont to weaken strong minds, while battle strengthens the weak and idle? That distinguished orator has argued justly, ingeniously, and persuasively that weapons take second place to the toga, since those who can live continently

---

43. Walo's letter, *Briefsammlungen der Zeit Heinrichs IV*, p. 184 "nisi enim ego follis fuissem, ad te tam inmitem tam trucem tam violentam tam inmanem bestiam non venissem."; also in *PL*, 150: 879–80, together with other letters of Walo. Also on Manasses's rude ways, *Vita Theoderici Abb. Andaginensis*, c. 20 *MGH SS* 12: 49 (ca. 1090): "in disciplina liberalium artium apprime eruditus, vir saeculi dignitatem nobiliter natus, ad omnia sagax et strenuus, episcopatu quidem dignus, sed natura et moribus plus quam oporteret ferus . . ." Abbot Theoderich's influence on Manasses: "Multum ergo feritatis ab eo admonitus deposuit . . . et cum pluribus esset frequenter immitis et truculentus, huic uni pro gloria et admiratione virtutum eius semper fuit mitis et placidus." The biographer identifies this archbishop wrongly as Gervasius, Manasses's predecessor. On the error, see Williams, "Manasses I," p. 806, note 7.

44. *PL* 150: 879–80, referring to "illius ferae pessimae monstrique horribilis saevitia," he believed the promises of Manasses and accepted, "non levis meriti minimaeve remunerationis arbitrans fore, si per me posset illius truculentia temperari." Hanover collect. Epist. 108, *Briefsammlung*, p. 183: [he desired the archbishop's release from "canine manners"] "ut, si fieri posset, mentis sevitia morumque bestialitate deposita tu quoque mecum de suavissima caritate et carissima suavitate gauderes." See also note 43 above, Abbot Theoderich's influence on Manasses.

45. *Briefsammlung*, Epist 109, p. 183: "O quotiens adhibui tibi medicamina scripturarum! quotiens celestibus verbis quasi quibusdam carminibus tuum temptavi mitigare furorem! Quotiens non Treicia sed Davitica cythara conatus sum illud vel expellere vel sedare demonium, quo vexaris!"

46. Epist 109, p. 183: "Asserebas enim in illis litteris tuis me hominem esse pacificum, humilem et quietum, lectioni semper intentum, ac per hoc non me Francigenarum tuisque moribus convenire."

in peace are rarer than those who can suffer the toils and dangers of warfare patiently.⁴⁷

This passage has the flavor of a continued debate between the two men, and it is not improbable to imagine this kind of debate crystallizing around Walo's efforts to tame the wildness of Manasses.

But the clash is also a debate between two classes defending their social mores at a critical moment in the history of those mores, when they were in a serious struggle for dominance the one over the other. Manasses is the spokesman of archaic warrior ways (a posture known in high clergy, though all the more flagrant and inordinate for that reason in the eyes of the pacifiers), Walo the advocate of peace. The abbot places the archbishop's values in the context of warfare and armed combat. His complaint is that the archbishop has brought warrior ways to bear also on domestic and ecclesiastic affairs. This debate is in the air in the eleventh and twelfth centuries.

Walo's letters show us Manasses spitted on the two-pronged discourse of ideal and abuse. The other documents that bear on Manasses's period of office show the champion of warrior ways losing to the party of peace and restraint. He was excommunicated and never restored to his office.⁴⁸

It was not a foregone conclusion that the Christian-courtly agenda of civilizing would win the day against militant nobles generally. An archbishop was more vulnerable than a count or baron. The move to civilize the warrior class operated in a larger field of forces, where it was opposed by assertions of the right to violence and warlike ways as the "customs of our ancient ancestors." For many nobles, lay and cleric alike, "maidenly mod-

---

47. P. 485:

O monstrum nulla virtute redemptum a vitiis, putasne inferioris esse virtutis in pace temperanter, modeste et sobrie conversari quam in bello acriter et fortiter preliari, cum pax soleat fortes etiam animos enervare, pugna vero inbelles et desides roborare? Unde non immerito ille insignis orator arma toge cedere persuadet subtiliter, nimirum considerans pauciores esse, qui possint in pace vivere continenter, quam qui pati bellorum labores et pericula patienter.

The "insignis orator" is Cicero. Cf. *De officiis* 1, 22, 77 (ref. from Erdmann ed., p. 185, n. 2).

48. There were other things at stake, but fierceness versus charity, friendship, and "suavitas" recurs in virtually all the documentation (cf. notes 42–47 above). Also Guibert de Nogent, *Autobiographie*, 1.11 ed. Edmond René Labande (Paris, 1981), pp. 62–64. Whatever the issues of policy at stake, the discourse of peace vs. violence structured the rhetoric.

VII

esty" meant womanish cowardice, a sense of shame was an excuse not to fight, and politeness was a form of lying. Warrior ways were their traditions, and restraint meant effeminization and sapping the strength of their manly customs.

The resistance to courtesy is badly recorded.[49] It probably expressed itself ordinarily in acts of violence. But the conflict of violence and restraint also played itself out on the field of literary representations—in fact far more abundantly and dramatically than in non-literary ones.[50] The literary medium of this opposition to restraint, mercy, and moderation was the heroic epic and chanson de geste, though it registers in numerous clerical complaints about the slackening of the warrior spirit. Both kind of sources appeal to "the customs of our ancient ancestors," though the ancestors are not Julius Caesar and Trajan but Dietrich of Bern, Roland, and Raoul de Cambrai. An arch-conservative like Saxo Grammaticus, resisting precisely the civilizing trends of courtly society and lumping together civility and corruption, could even advocate a fierce warrior ethic of revenge.[51] The poet of the *Nibelungenlied*, if he did not represent revenge as glorious, did show it as heroic and awe-inspiring as opposed to the prissy niceties of courtliness. This conservative trend sought to restore an archaic ideal of warrior honor that was in a crisis, and it could do so often by pitting it directly against courtly-Christian values. In the chanson de geste *Raoul de Cambrai*, Bernier tricks his enemy into stepping naked into a fountain, then refuses to kill the helpless man. This chivalric act of restraint makes him an object of scorn for the rest of his life.[52] Siegfried defers to King Gunther in *Nibelungenlied* just before getting speared in the back, and the poet comments: "That was the reward for his courtesies."[53]

The literary advocate of restraint was the courtly romance. This new

---

49. A brief comment by Hugh of Flavigny gives us a rare look at the ideology of noble fierceness. He says that Richard of Saint-Vanne's efforts to institute the *treuga Dei* in France met with resistance from "certain perverse and indomitable spirits," who regarded "peace by divine revelation" as a "violation of ancestral institutions through the adoption of new and unheard of ideas" (*Chronicon*, 2.30 [*anno* 1041], ed. G. H. Pertz, *MGH SS* 8: 403). The passage shows how resistance to the issues reverses the positive and negative poles: peace is "unheard-of novelty"; unobstructed warfare is "ancient custom." See the commentary of Hartmut Hoffmann, *Gottesfriede und Treuga Dei* (Stuttgart: Hiersemann, 1964), pp. 87–88.

50. See Jaeger, *Origins of Courtliness*, pp. 176–94.

51. *Origins of Courtliness*, pp. 185–90.

52. Cited in Sidney Painter, *French Chivalry: Chivalric Ideas and Practices in Medieval France* (Ithaca, NY, 1967), p. 33.

53. *Das Nibelungenlied*, ed. Karl Bartsch and Helmut de Boor, 12th ed. (Leipzig, 1949), Stanza 980, 1: "Do engalt er sîner zühte."

narrative form from the mid-twelfth century appropriates clerical norms of courtesy and uses them to represent the behavior and speech, the combat and lovemaking, of knights. Its hero combines warfare and courtly-Christian restraint. The romance creates a model in which ideals of courtly restraint are integrated into an exalted lay aristocratic style of life. In some romances both poles of the discourse we observed in Peter of Blois's letter are present.

The Parzival romance of Wolfram von Eschenbach is the best example. Written within a decade of Peter of Blois's letter, it dramatizes the poles of ideal and abuse by showing a knight's progress away from the bad and toward the good. Its hero starts out as a blunt rustic with a good heart, and ends as Grail king, highly honored in both the Arthurian and the quasi-religious Grail court. He spans this broad ethical gap by a progress away from unfeeling egotism. He is held responsible for the death of his mother and the disgrace of a young woman whom he all but rapes; in his blind eagerness to become a knight he attacks and kills another man and strips the armor off his corpse; his victim turns out to be his own uncle; he is responsible for prolonging the sufferings of the old Grail king and his community. Lack of compassion is generally seen as the fundamental flaw that permits the commission of this string of atrocities.[54] Ill-digested lessons from three teachers of uneven quality harm him as much as they help. In the end, suffering, loyalty to his wife, and insistence on the value and dignity of his identity bring him to the virtues of a true knight, husband, and Grail king: gentleness, modesty, loyalty, compassion, and a sense of shame.

This progress covers the same span as the polemics of Peter of Blois. Parzival's misdeeds and the moral flaws from which they derive are comparable to those of Archdeacon John's nephews. In part Parzival's educators Gurnemanz and Trevrizent speak the same ethical language as Peter of Blois.[55] Peter of Blois and Wolfram were clearly addressing some of the same social issues. They share a program of social change, and employ both prongs of a polemical discourse, the negative more strongly emphasized in the one, the positive in the other. The common issue is the move of the warrior class from violence to restraint, from irresponsibility to social en-

---

54. See the summary of the problem in Joachim Bumke, *Wolfram von Eschenbach*, 6th ed. (Stuttgart, 1991), pp. 128ff. (with recent literature).
55. *Wolfram von Eschenbach*, ed. Albert Leitzmann, 6th ed. (Berlin, 1926), 170, 25: "iuch sol erbarmen nôtec her: / gein des kumber sît ze wer / mit milte und mit güete. / vlîzet iuch diemüete"; 171, 13: "gebet rehter mâze ir orden"; 171, 25: "lât die erberme bî der vrevel sîn."

VII

gagement, a move that the clergy had advocated in varying contexts and ideologies since the tenth century.[56]

Wolfram von Eschenbach and Saxo Grammaticus were evidently engaged in the same conflict of social ideas, and they took up positions near opposite ends of the spectrum. Their works testify to that conflict and its acuteness, no less than do the letters of Walo of St. Arnulf and Peter of Blois.

Works that engage in the project of shaping and changing social and political consciousness do so by entering into the competition of ideas clustered around issues. Competition that occurs when the norms, values, mores, and laws of a society are in flux or crisis generates friction among contending groups, and this friction places a heavy charge on language and concepts that address the issues at stake. The competition of ideas for dominance gradually focuses power and shapes consensus. The stakes are always high in conflicts for the shaping of social consciousness. If they were not, there would be no friction and no competition of ideas.

But in fact every generation experiences the convulsiveness of such competitions. A systematic ordering of society through widely accepted mores and values is troubled when new values emerge and challenge the old. Then a once systematic ordering of forces turns chaotic. Ideas, sentiments, and convictions—old, new, and intermediate—are tumbled about in this chaos. The combatants carry them like shields and hurl them like weapons. The ideas, sentiments, and convictions are generated by a spectrum of interests that break from the issues at stake. While social practices dominate society unchallenged, they create vested interests, and a challenge to them produces conservative resistance and an ideology that supports it. Along the line formed by the two outer parameters, challenge and resistance to it, a variety of intermediate positions and their defending ideologies form, and all of these vie for consensus and victory. The analysis of such an unstable system is complex and could be aided by a kind of "chaos theory" of social change. The analysis of historical conflicts is especially fraught with the danger of over-simplifying, since the unstable system has normally come to equilibrium when anyone besides journalists begins

---

56. For recent literature on the peace movement, see note 24 above; also *The Peace of God: Social Violence and Religious Response in France around the Year 1000*, ed. Thomas Head and Richard Landes (Ithaca, NY, 1992).

to analyse it. By the time the historian gets to it its issues and positions have rigidified, amalgamated, or disappeared altogether. Some ideas which fought bravely succumb and fade; others which stood on the sidelines and watched emerge strong, and the historian is confronted with the appearance of a unified system, because all possible outcomes of a once complex and chaotic melee ossify into a single constellation; an unstable and complex mix of issues comes to equilibrium. The point is not to describe the ossified constellation but rather, so to speak, to restore it to chaos in order to see once again the issues in their various interactions.

In the case of the present issue—violence vs. restraint—a dynamic is at work that stands above particular social circumstances, and could be formulated abstractly as a general theory of social change and used to analyse a variety of similar historical and social trends.[57]

The ideas engaged in conflicts of social ideology are borne by any available medium: fiction, lyric, polemics, epistle, broadsheet, legislation. The primary medium is the human beings who are engaged in the conflict. The clash of Walo and Manasses shows the embodiment of ideas that later will confront each other in the writings of Saxo Grammaticus and Wolfram von Eschenbach. This means for the historian that narrowing the body of documentation on a social issue is bad methodology. Considerations of genre inject one-sidedness into selection of texts, and while studies like "the investiture controversy in late eleventh century lyric" are valuable as building blocks and contributions to the narrower discipline, the greater picture of social and institutional change must be drawn from the broadest possible base of documentation.

The same applies to the transition from warrior society to courtly society. Ideas in conflict do not select a particular medium as their bearer, though they may favor one over another. A saint's life may bear on the point of friction as much as church legislation, panegyric as much as slander. The spectrum of competing attitudes unfolds in a variety of statements, acts, legislations, and written documents. The issues generate what we might call their own culture, and a broadly comparative reading of that culture is the basis of good methodology.

An essential characteristic of the conflict of social ideologies is that opposite generates opposite. Offensive attitudes, acts, or statements call

---

57. Norbert Elias, *Prozess der Zivilisation*, formulated this dynamic for European lay aristocratic society. But the context in that case was the life of the court, and his theory cannot account for the role of spiritual sanctions and popular opinion in the first phase of resistance to warrior ways.

forth opposing attitudes; these provoke and strengthen opposition, which claims as sanctioned behavior what appears to be abuse. Rape, mistreatment of women, and anti-feminism call forth a cult of the revered woman and an ethical obligation to respect and speak well of ladies.[58] Facing this opposition, anti-feminism articulates itself all the more vehemently and self-righteously, looking to any writings for ammunition, but finding it especially in scripture and antiquity. Andreas Capellanus's *De amore* is a self-enclosed friction zone, where the tendencies to idealize and to vilify women face each other in an oddly static confrontation.[59] It both instructs in courtly love mores and opposes them by a fierce anti-feminism. Feuds, private wars, and despoiling of church goods call forth opposition in the peace movement with its rich culture. The recalcitrant nobility responds by appeal to ancestral customs.

In these two cases it would be justified to say that if women were not being raped and mistreated, there would be no cult of woman in courtly literature, and if there were no private wars and church ransacking, there would be no ideal Christian knight. The abuse gives offense, causes suffering, and calls forth the corrective, or at least creates a discursive net to throw over the offenders. The corrective exercises whatever force on the abuse it can muster, using extreme idealizing models, extreme slander, and maligning. Those who are slandered, maligned, and provoked are sensitized to the issue and respond, perhaps capitulate, perhaps retaliate. Then the opposition culture arises. It is highly unlikely that the courtly love lyric arose as a response to a widely-shared adulation of woman, but it is quite likely that it responded to their wretched treatment.

Now let us consider three propositions about conflicting social ideologies.

First. the conflict of ideologies can only exist when norms are in crisis and flux. If the prevailing norms are strong, they may still generate opposition, but opposing ideas have no strength. They are suppressed, voted

---

58. In reading through the documents on the peace movement for this and another study, it became evident that the protection of women emerges gradually as a social concern. Early documents include women among the threats to peace, later ones among the threatened. It is a rewarding research topic. Cf. the study by Werner Rösener, "Die höfische Frau im Hochmittelalter," in *Curialitas*, pp. 171–230 (with rich bibliography).

59. The two dominant voices recently on the reading of this dissonant work, Rüdiger Schnell, *Andreas Capellanus: Zur Rezeption des römischen und kanonischen Rechts in De Amore* (Munich, 1982); and Alfred Karnein, *De amore in volkssprachlicher Literatur: Untersuchungen zur Andreas Capellanus-Rezeption in Mittelalter und Renaissance* (Heidelberg, 1985).

down, or shouted down as soon as they surface. The norms dominate either in public opinion or in the mechanisms of enforcement or both. There were democratic sentiments in Iraq before the Gulf War, but there was no effective voice advocating them; there was opposition to anti-semitism in Nazi Germany, but it was silent.

Second. no statements addressing the issues in competition can be made that do not engage in the conflict. Where social values are being re-forged and asserting themselves against conservative opposition, everything touching on the conflict is polemical, and the intentions of the author cannot change that.[60] Talking about peace or clemency when these values are asserting themselves against an ethic of revenge is asking for conflict, no matter in what mode or tone of expression the talk is couched. If the vital interests of a social group depend on or are perceived as depending on enforcement through revenge, then the advocate of peace is asking for a fight. The American scientist (a white man) who claimed experimental results arguing the genetic inferiority of blacks experienced the working of this principle. His "research" addressed a fiercely fought social issue, and his appeal to alleged scientific objectivity, far from pacifying the contestants, gave offense and inflamed the issues. His position was comparable to that of a man who enters a battle zone armed with a rifle and wearing the uniform of one side. He can claim neutrality, but he will be shot at anyway.

This proposition also applies in whatever medium or genre the issues in conflict are propagated. It is a principle well known to any office of censorship serving a tyrannical government. A children's fairy tale suffused with ideology can be as inflammatory as a propaganda leaflet and far more effective indoctrination. Imaginative literature can have a much more powerful effect on the imagination than polemical prose.

Third. ideas engaged in competition for dominance in a society have the power to influence behavior. This includes the ideas on the offensive and those on the defensive. This proposition is axiomatic because such competitions aim at establishing dominant social values, and social values determine behavior. Any group of Americans can at present be polarized, troubled, outraged, or sensitized by a charge of anti-feminism or racism.

---

60. A vital point for weighing the engagedness of courtly romance in social change. It suggests that the idiom of courtliness was engaged in the competition of ideas no matter which author speaks it. The frivolous voice of courtly entertainment narrative is a provocation to the opposing front no less than the high ethical tone of Wolfram's *Parzival*. Authorial intention plays no role.

VII

These charges throw a discursive net over anyone they are directed at, a net that holds them captive in a certain field of conflict. The reaction would be strong whether or not the charge is true. The same result would not be achieved by calling any group of contemporary Americans a pack of Cathars, Anabaptists, or Unitarians. These are curiosities with no power to offend, fossils from dead friction zones, though all were once issues over which blood was spilled and reputations ruined. An accusation of racism now exerts power and influence over the person it is directed at, true or not. It makes that person a combatant in a social issue. It puts him either on the offensive or the defensive. It sets off an internal alarm system which makes him guard his words and those of other people against traces of racism. That is, it creates sensibility, and that means it has successfully influenced behavior in favor of its agenda.

Was courtly romance a factor in the spread of courtly values? Was the outward enthusiasm with which this genre was accepted by lay society answered by an internal realignment of ethical values? The framework developed in this article says yes. Both Peter of Blois's Letter 94 and Wolfram's *Parzival* addressed social issues engaged in an important contest. The literary work broke through the aesthetic encapsulation within which literary historians have tended to view courtly literature. If the three propositions developed above are valid, then *Parzival* was probably more effectively engaged than Peter of Blois's polemical letter.

But in order not to subject historical analysis to the power of the syllogism, I close with two questions that offer the criterion of falsification or verification of a thesis that courtly literature favored the social acceptance of courtly values.

First. did courtly romance compel identification with its hero and his values? The hero of narrative embodies the crisis playing itself out in the society or social group generally. He or she dramatizes the contradiction at the root of the crisis. He repeats in the phylogeny of his personal development the ontogeny of social change and its stages: normal conditions, anomaly, polarization, and so on. He is charged with the whole field of forces pressing for and against social change. Through identification and immersion, the reader/listener can live in the friction zone, and feel the advantages of the author's agenda and the disadvantages of the opposite. The narrative exemplum charged with authority is one of the most important didactic instruments, certainly in the Middle Ages,[61] perhaps in human society generally. Hence there is no reason to rule out the effectiveness of the courtly-chivalric knight as "Bildungsgedanke."[62] But this is not an argument, only a methodological suggestion.

There is a passage of Peter of Blois's Letter 94 that bears directly on the problem, and it is worthwhile interpreting it in the context of the first question. He says that the corrupted knights want battle scenes painted on their saddles and shields "so that they may take pleasure in a kind of fantasy vision of battles, which in reality they would not have the courage even to look upon, let alone take part in."[63] Here a contemporary observer points to a predilection of knights themselves for the "ideal" in preference to a "reality" they would rather not face. Hartmann von Aue expressed a similar attitude at the beginning of his adaptation of Chretien's *Yvain*. He says that in King Arthur's day men loved bold deeds and actions. But while men of the present day are no longer bold, they have the stories of those men of action. If he, Hartmann, had to choose, he would prefer the present life with the pleasures of these stories to the past with its story-less life of action.[64] In both cases avoidance of action finds compensation in the artifice of chivalric representation.

Did the courtly romance have the effect of alienating its readers from a life of action? Did it pamper the sloth of a slackened warrior class, hand them over to a decadent aesthetic existence, and render them yet more useless for the active life? Extravagant fantasy does seem to work a kind of enchantment. It did on Don Quixote. Samuel Johnson was "immoderately fond of reading romances of chivalry" throughout his life, and he attributed "to these extravagant fictions that unsettled turn of mind that prevented his ever fixing in any profession."[65]

But this should not encourage us to imagine a warrior class stunned

61. See the exhaustive study by Peter von Moos, *Geschichte als Topik: Das rhetorische Exemplum von der Antike zur Neuzeit und die historiae im 'Policraticus' Johanns von Salisbury* (Hildesheim, Zürich, New York, 1988), passim, esp. pp. 13–21.

62. Bumke, *Studien zum Ritterbegriff*, p. 147: "Das adlige Rittertum, von dem die höfische Dichtung erzählt . . . ist ein Erziehungs– und Bildungsgedanke von weitreichender Bedeutung und ein Phänomen der Geistesgeschichte viel mehr als der Sozialgeschichte." On the Arthurian literature and the model of Arthur as an instrument of education of nobles, see Peter Johanek, "König Artus und die Plantagenets: Über den Zusammenhang von Historiographie und höfischer Epik in mittelalterlicher Propaganda," *Frühmittelalterliche Studien* 21 (1987), esp. pp. 358–60.

63. See note 22 above.

64. Hartmann von Aue, *Iwein*, 7th ed., ed. G. F. Benecke, K. Lachmann, and L. Wolff (Berlin, 1968), vv. 54–58: "ichn wolde dô niht sîn gewesen, / daz ich nû niht enwaere, / dâ uns noch mit ir maere / sô rehte wol wesen sol: / dâ tâten in diu werc vil wol."

65. *Boswell's Life of Johnson*, ed. G. B. Hill and L. F. Powell, 3 vols. (Oxford, 1934), 1: 49.

VII

to inaction by the recitation of romances or by "imaginary visions" of a Camelot world and of chivalric combat. That charge is part of Peter of Blois's polemics, and like medieval polemicists generally, he represents the extreme as the norm. Far more likely is an interpretation that sees in this passage testimony to the power of chivalric representation to compel identification. There is much more evidence for that argument, the Arthurian imitations of Ulrich von Lichtenstein being among the earliest and best known.[66] The Arthurian–chivalric cast of courtly representation in many courts of the late Middle Ages and Renaissance represents the dramatic success of courtly enculturation through romances. The madness of Don Quixote and the instability of Samuel Johnson—the possibility that derangement lurks at the dark fringes of courtly enculturation—does not deny the romance's power over behavior, but rather confirms it.

The second question: did courtesy and courtly love become factors in the economy of honor and prestige at court? Did behavior like Gawain's raise a man's standing and did behavior like Kei's lower it? Did it do a woman honor and raise her reputation to receive homage from a knight in the form of a love declaration? Parzival behaved like a boor, and the result was disgrace and exclusion. Did boorishness actually spell exclusion from aristocratic society?[67] The answer tells us whether the lay nobles internalized the ethical values of the courtly knight or merely appropriated from romance the trappings of court festivals and rituals. If courtesy became integrated into the economy of honor at court, then it was not only a real social force, but an indispensable instrument of worldly esteem, and that is the prime moving force of aristocratic society. Those who sought to live in court society without it might well find reason to regret their neglect of the lessons of chivalric romance.

But that is a conjecture that further research would have to test. My purpose here has been to provide a framework within which courtly ideals can be studied as real forces shaping behavior, not just a fanciful overlay

---

66. David Tinsley, "Die Kunst der Selbstdarstellung in Ulrich von Lichtensteins 'Frauendienst,'" *Germanisch-Romanische Monatsschrift* 40 (1990), 129–40; Jan-Dirk Müller, "Lachen–Spiel–Fiktion: Zum Verhältnis von literarischem Diskurs und historischer Realität im Frauendienst Ulrichs von Lichtenstein," *Deutsche Vierteljahrsschrift* 58 (1984), 38–73; Ursula Peters, *Frauendienst: Untersuchungen zu Ulrich von Lichtenstein und zum Wirklichkeitsgehalt der Minnedichtung* (Göppingen, 1971).

67. These values were thoroughly integrated into the society of Theresa of Avila. She complained about religious houses turned into "courts and schools of good breeding." Her fears of giving offence to people "who think these observances essential to their honor" competed with her religious observances. Santa Teresa de Jesús, *Libro de la Vida* (chapter 37), ed. Otger Steggink (Madrid, 1986), p. 506.

of disengaged discourse beneath which reality could go its dreary way. I believe that the answers to these questions, based on historical data, will reveal the close connections between the ideals of courtly romance and the realities of contemporary social life. The unreality of courtly narrative, its enchantments, wizards, dragons, noble combats, and sublime love affairs are not masks over society's imperfections. If they mask anything, it is an agenda of social change.

VIII

L'AMOUR DES ROIS :
STRUCTURE SOCIALE D'UNE FORME
DE SENSIBILITÉ ARISTOCRATIQUE

En 1187 la campagne militaire de Henri II en France s'enlisa lorsque son fils Richard Cœur de Lion, à qui il avait confié le commandement du quart de l'armée anglaise, s'éprit du roi ennemi, le jeune Philippe Auguste. Le chroniqueur Roger de Howden décrit cette relation en ces termes :

> (le roi de France)... l'honorait tant depuis si longtemps qu'ils mangeaient chaque jour à la même table et dans le même plat, et le soir le lit ne les séparait pas. Et le roi de France l'aimait comme son âme ; et ils s'aimaient tant l'un l'autre que le roi d'Angleterre était profondément étonné par l'amour véhément qui existait entre eux[1].

Le texte ne semble pas équivoque : deux hommes s'aiment et partagent la même couche. Leur affection ne cherche pas d'excuse : ils la manifestent ouvertement. Mais ce texte comporte quelques éléments qui invitent à ne pas le lire comme un constat d'amour homosexuel. Premièrement l'attitude des deux observateurs, le roi et le chroniqueur, mérite d'être relevée :

> Henri II était profondément étonné par l'amour véhément qui existait entre eux et se demandait ce qu'il pouvait signifier. De façon à prendre des précautions pour l'avenir, il reporta ses projets de retour en Angleterre jusqu'à ce qu'il pût déterminer quelles intrigues cet amour soudain laissait présager.

Il s'agit là de la réaction d'un général trahi et non de celle d'un père outragé. La stratégie militaire est le seul souci de Henri II. Cette affaire entre deux hommes menace ses projets guerriers et non l'honneur de sa famille. La seule mesure qu'il prend consiste à modifier ses projets de voyage. Le chroniqueur lui-même, par son silence sur la question essentielle, confirme que les hésitations politiques du souverain étaient la réaction appropriée[2].

VIII

Il semble possible de voir une forme de désapprobation déguisée dans l'étonnement du roi que Roger de Howden souligne. Mais c'est essentiellement un effet de l'intérêt que nous-mêmes portons à ce point. Le texte ne suggère rien de cela. L'étonnement emprunte sa coloration morale à son contexte qui ne met en évidence qu'une relation exaltante. Cela apparaît clairement dans les termes employés par le chroniqueur. L'amour du monarque français « honorait » Richard : « *in tantum honoravit... quod...* ». Plus loin il rapporte avec émerveillement que lorsque les deux princes se retrouvèrent quelques années plus tard en Terre sainte ils reprirent leur amour ancien. « Il semblait que l'affection d'amour mutuel entre eux était si puissante qu'elle ne pourrait être brisée, ni que jamais ils ne pourraient trahir leur amour »[3].

Le ton est celui de l'étonnement devant une relation sublime qui dépasse toute suggestion de scandale et dont la valeur se mesure à l'aune d'une fidélité durable, en des termes qui conviendraient à des amants romantiques. L'expression « il l'aimait comme son âme » *(« dilexit eum rex... quasi animam suam »)* tend aussi à exalter cette relation mais fait vibrer une corde quelque peu différente. Il s'agit d'une expression assez courante pour qualifier une amitié intense, mais ici elle est aussi probablement une réminiscence voulue de l'amour de Jonathan et de David que la Vulgate décrit dans les mêmes termes : « *dilexit eum Ionathan quasi animam suam* » (Samuel I, 18 : 1) : « *diligebat enim eum quasi animam suam* » (18 : 3) ; « *sicut animam enim suam ita diligebat eum* » (20 : 17). La constellation, Henri-Richard-Philippe Auguste, reprend de manière frappante celle de l'Ancien Testament, Saül-Jonathan-David. Dans chaque cas les deux princes conspirent pour désarmer la colère d'un roi dirigée contre l'un d'entre eux ; l'amitié qui les unit dépasse les liens du sang entre père et fils. Il n'est pas improbable que Roger de Howden ait eu recours à l'Ancien Testament pour « romancer », c'est-à-dire magnifier, ce qui est par ailleurs (par exemple pour Gervase de Canterbury) une trêve mondaine[4].

Pour de nombreuses raisons, certaines présentes dans le texte, d'autres non, nous pouvons écarter toute suggestion dans ce passage à une relation homosexuelle entre le roi de France et le duc d'Aquitaine, futur roi d'Angleterre. L'une de ces raisons est la grande franchise du récit. Si ces gestes et ces actes avaient eu le moindre pouvoir de condamnation, le chroniqueur, qui n'hésite pas à critiquer la famille royale, l'aurait indiqué ou nous aurait prévenu contre une telle pensée. L'accusation d'homosexualité était une charge sérieuse[5]. Le geste timide consistant à fournir aux lecteurs la preuve de l'accusation sans assumer soi-même l'accusation ne correspond pas à son *modus scribendi*.

Il n'est guère probable qu'il s'agisse là d'un exemple de cette tolérance à l'égard de l'homosexualité caractéristique, selon John Boswell, de la culture chrétienne avant le XIIIe siècle[6]. Cette attitude tolérante, en particulier dans la sphère du pouvoir de deux grands royaumes, aurait pu se manifester sous la forme d'un comportement scandaleux auquel on se serait discrètement livré et non par l'affirmation franche d'une passion entre rois. Le ton du texte est empreint d'admiration et ne suggère pas un écart de conduite princier.

L'examen d'autres descriptions de relations entre des rois et leurs favoris nous persuadera rapidement que l'amour de Richard et de Philippe Auguste n'est pas une relation individuelle et « privée » et que nous avons affaire à un discours qui a non seulement un caractère d'approbation mais aussi une fonction ennoblissante.

VIII

L'AMOUR DES ROIS

L'amour et la passion (ainsi que l'amitié, *amicitia,* sentiment proche mais plus modéré) constituaient un mode d'expression de la faveur royale. La cour carolingienne parlait une langue particulièrement extravagante [7]. Alcuin écrit à Charlemagne pour le réconforter au cours d'une maladie :

> Mon très adoré seigneur, mon très doux maître, le plus désiré de tous les hommes, mon David, votre Flaccus est attristé par votre infirmité. Je souhaite et prie Dieu de tout mon cœur que vous vous rétablissiez rapidement, de façon que notre joie trouve en vous son accomplissement... [8].

Après le rétablissement de l'empereur il écrit :

> La douceur de votre amour sacré calme et soulage fortement l'ardeur de mon cœur à chaque heure, chaque minute ; et la beauté de votre visage, vers lequel je tourne constamment mes pensées amoureuses, emplit tous les canaux de ma mémoire de désir et d'une joie immense, et dans mon cœur la beauté de votre bonté et de votre apparence m'enrichit comme le feraient les trésors les plus grands [9].

Quel que soit le type de relation évoqué dans ces lettres d'amour, il ne s'agit pas d'homosexualité. A l'époque où le vieux sage, à 65 ans environ, écrivait ces lignes enflammées à l'empereur, ils édictaient ensemble l'*admonitio generalis* qui, entre autres choses, condamnait la « sodomie » dans le royaume et établissait des châtiments sévères. Alcuin écrivit aussi une lettre en son nom propre à un ancien étudiant vivant en Angleterre et dont on disait qu'il avait eu des relations homosexuelles. Sa condamnation est sans équivoque. Il le met en garde contre une pratique qui représente une menace à la fois pour sa position sociale et pour son salut [10]. Cela doit signifier que les lettres et les poèmes passionnés d'Alcuin à ses amis hommes ne pouvaient suggérer ou proposer une relation de caractère illicite ou viser à renforcer une telle relation déjà existante. Si telle avait été son intention, il aurait poursuivi ces rapports sous une forme autre que celle qu'il avait choisie, c'est-à-dire une lettre faisant partie de sa correspondance officielle.

La langue de l'amitié virile passionnée était l'idiome principal permettant de décrire la faveur royale sous Othon III et ses successeurs. Othon « aimait beaucoup » Burchard de Worms [11]. Il appréciait tant son clerc Tammo qu'ils portaient les mêmes vêtements et mangeaient dans le même plat à la même table, leurs mains se joignant lorsqu'elles se rencontraient au-dessus de la nourriture [12]. Son conseiller et courtisan, l'évêque Adalbert de Prague, devint son « très doux compagnon de chambre », et il restait à ses côtés jour et nuit parce qu'« il l'aimait » [13]. Meinwerk de Paderborn exprima à l'empereur Henri II « la flamme de son amour intime » [14]. Une atmosphère d'amour, d'amitié, d'affabilité, tel était l'idéal courtois des rois othoniens et saliens [15]. Cependant cela ne se réduisait pas seulement à l'Empire. Le roi David d'Écosse « aimait avec passion » son intendant, le jeune Ailred de Rievaulx, et « l'embrassait avec amour » [16].

Le langage de l'amour conservera ce rôle jusqu'à la Renaissance et même après. Shakespeare lui-même l'utilise encore. Lear ne dit-il pas à Kent « Tu me sers et je t'aimerai » (I, IV, 89) [17] ?

VIII

Le langage de l'amitié passionnée dans certains monastères à la fin du XIe siècle et au XIIe siècle est fort proche de cela. Je reviendrai plus loin sur les liens existant entre l'amour des rois et celui des moines ; on peut noter que l'un des caractères qu'ils partagent est l'innocence apparente du langage érotique dont une lettre d'Anselme de Bec accueillant deux novices au sein de la communauté nous donne un bon exemple :

> Mes yeux sont impatients de voir vos visages, bien aimés ; mes bras se tendent pour vos enlacements. Mes lèvres désirent vos baisers ; tout ce qui me reste de vie désire votre compagnie afin que la joie de mon âme soit complète dans les temps à venir... Vous êtes venus, vous m'avez embrasé ; vous avez fondu mon âme et l'avez amalgamée à la vôtre ; cette âme qui est nôtre peut dorénavant être déchirée, elle ne pourra jamais être séparée [18].

Seraient-ce là les paroles d'un homme animé d'une violente passion du corps et de l'âme ? D'une passion pour deux hommes à la fois ? Rien ne pourrait être plus éloigné de la vérité. Anselme n'avait encore vu aucun des deux hommes à l'époque où il écrivait ces lignes. C'était pour lui une manière d'accueillir avec chaleur deux nouveaux venus, et non de les recevoir dans un antre d'érotisme viril illicite. Les études et les commentaires consacrés à Anselme confirment cette analyse (voir *supra*, n. 18).

Un tel état de choses ne peut que laisser le lecteur moderne perplexe : un chroniqueur médiéval pouvait fort bien dire qu'un roi aimait un courtisan avec passion, qu'il l'enlaçait avec l'ardeur de l'amour le plus intime, l'embrassait avec désir, qu'il dormait à son côté et partageait les mêmes vêtements ; un clerc ou un abbé pouvait écrire qu'il désirait embrasser son ami, se perdre dans ses bras et unir son âme à la sienne, qu'il léchait sa poitrine et baignait son sein de ses larmes sans qu'aucune de ces formulations ne suggérât quelque attachement de type homosexuel.

Le lecteur moderne est victime devant ces textes d'une forme d'illusion d'optique d'ordre moral. Si nous les examinons à la lumière de notre propre discours sur la sexualité, ils expriment une chose mais ne la signifient pas pour autant. Notre paradigme ne nous donne pas les outils nécessaires pour décoder le sens de ces textes. Il est donc nécessaire de rechercher quelle était l'optique des écrivains de l'époque. Dans cet essai je m'efforcerai de reconstruire et d'analyser cette sensibilité perdue, le discours qui la véhiculait et le contexte social qui lui était propre. J'étudierai le rôle social de l'amour et de l'amitié en tant que forme d'auto-représentation aristocratique.

L'*Histoire de la vie privée* répond en partie au projet de Lucien Febvre d'écrire une « histoire des sensibilités » qui reconstituerait « la vie affective d'autrefois »[19]. Elle met en évidence une limite importante : en général les poètes et les historiens du Moyen Age étaient indifférents à ce que nous nommons aujourd'hui la vie privée. Nous pourrions déduire de l'introduction de Duby au volume II qu'un tel concept n'existait pas, que la vie était entièrement publique et que les actes qui avaient pour cadre la sphère privée étaient tout simplement des actes publics sans spectateurs. La vie privée, avant d'exister en soi, n'était donc que l'absence de vie publique. L'étymologie conforte cette interprétation : *privatus* signifie « privé de », « dépourvu de ».

VIII

L'AMOUR DES ROIS

Le silence des sources médiévales sur la sexualité est particulièrement remarquable. L'aristocratie et l'intelligentsia dont l'intérêt pour l'amour était proche de l'obsession abordaient ce sujet dans des écrits d'éthique ou de fiction. La séduction et ses difficultés en étaient le thème et non la sexualité considérée ici comme domaine privé, à l'écart, protégé par des droits et des privilèges. La sexualité, aussi importante qu'elle ait pu être, ne généra pas de discours qui lui fût propre. Ainsi Peter Brown a pu comparer l'intérêt de saint Augustin pour ce sujet à celui que nous portons « aux bruits de la plomberie dans l'appartement du voisin ».

L'Europe victorienne et post-victorienne donna naissance à un discours sur la sexualité. L'atmosphère superficiellement répressive du XIXe siècle eut pour effet curieux d'accroître l'intérêt pour les comportements sexuels, intérêt qui se manifeste aujourd'hui par une véritable débauche discursive. Foucault dans son *Histoire de la sexualité* analyse la volubilité moderne et l'oppose au silence relatif qui caractérise les époques antérieures[20]. Il soutient que la répression superficielle et l'atmosphère lourde de tabous sont les signes extérieurs d'une relation symbiotique entre le pouvoir et le discours sur la sexualité. Les interdits créent un besoin de parler de la chose érotique, de confesser des désirs cachés et des activités secrètes, et cela rétablit le contrôle de l'État — qui a perdu son droit ancien de disposer comme bon lui semblait de la vie — sur le corps des individus.

Foucault soutient que, dans leur désir de faire apparaître la sexualité au grand jour, les puissances répressives de l'ère victorienne coopérèrent avec les forces du libertinage et de la perversion ; le père confesseur désirait — dans le cadre d'un discours sur le sexe — essentiellement la même chose que le marquis de Sade. La réaction contre la mentalité victorienne prude et répressive créa une nouvelle obligation intellectuelle : celle de libérer la vie sexuelle de ses fers. La psychologie freudienne apparaît comme le point culminant de cette entreprise.

Ces divers développements éclairent les difficultés que l'on rencontre dans l'analyse de l'enchevêtrement des signaux et de la traîtrise des perceptions que les textes cités plus haut nous présentent. Nous ne disposons pas de termes susceptibles de nous aider à comprendre les relations évoquées : « homo-érotisme », homosexualité ou même amitié virile sont des expressions qui suggèrent quelque relation de type physique. Même lorsque l'érotisme n'est pas affirmé (dans le cas de l'amitié virile), les termes opèrent encore dans un champ de forces dans lequel la sexualité demeure le fondement référentiel non perceptible.

Ce champ de forces est ce que je nommerai le paradigme freudien. On ne peut séparer de ce paradigme un discours où le niveau littéral d'un texte et le niveau des apparences dans les relations humaines sont des voiles cachant les véritables forces agissantes. Il fait de l'inconscient le terrain d'interprétation et la source de vérité ; il situe l'explication réelle des motifs, des actions et de la culture elle-même dans la libido dont l'exploration devient une obligation et une tâche intellectuelle majeures. Les pulsions refoulées et cachées de la libido se voient conférées une force de persuasion sans appel. Elles deviennent le fondement final d'une argumentation qui n'admet pas de réfutation et là où des signes et des signaux sont à l'œuvre à la surface d'un texte et mettent en évidence une allusion sexuelle cachée, ce fondement apparaît encore plus justifié.

VIII

La meilleure preuve peut-être que nos textes ne fonctionnent pas selon ce paradigme est qu'ils ne contiennent pas de signaux subtils, d'allusions à des motifs sexuels sous-jacents, de « lapsus » ou d'ambiguïtés. Ils sont parfaitement directs et francs. Une lecture pré-critique de ces écrits suggère l'image d'une homosexualité tolérée et sans retenue parmi le clergé et la noblesse laïque. Mais cela pose un problème au lecteur freudien dont l'herméneutique se nourrit de déjouer nos tendances au refoulement. Ces textes fonctionnent comme s'ils n'avaient rien à cacher. Toute lecture de type psychologique que l'on pourrait en faire doit expliquer pourquoi ils échappent à l'emprise du paradigme freudien, pourquoi leurs auteurs n'ont nullement cherché à sublimer ou à réorienter l'objet de leurs propos. Loin de dissimuler ce qui était pour tous un comportement honteux et condamnable ils l'ont proclamé hautement.

L'amour du roi s'exerce au sein d'une structure d'émotions non privée. Son discours nous est étranger et il nous faut un vocabulaire conceptuel qui puisse rendre compte d'un amour public et supra-personnel[21]. Je désignerai son acte fondamental par l'expression « geste social ». Il y a « geste social » lorsqu'un modèle de sentiment exaltant se manifeste publiquement. Le fait pour un individu de se comporter selon une émotion idéalisée — l'amour, la compassion et le courage par exemple — revient à affirmer qu'il accepte les valeurs éthiques de la société. C'est une source de prestige, un moyen de prouver sa valeur, d'élever son statut social que pratiquent aussi ceux qui sont incapables d'éprouver cette émotion exaltante ou ceux qui lui sont indifférents.

Le geste social trouve son fondement dans une émotion expérimentée. Ils renvoient l'un à l'autre comme le signe renvoie au signifié. L'acte public est « lu » pour sa congruence avec l'émotion vécue et le geste social ne peut être authentifié que si cette adéquation existe. Prenons un exemple ; le discours d'un général avant une bataille doit donner à voir dans chacun de ses aspects — l'articulation, la gestuelle, l'intonation de la voix et l'expression du visage — les émotions dont il est censé être l'émanation : l'engagement pour une cause, l'amour du pays, l'acceptation de la mort. Si le général ne se transforme pas, en cet instant critique, en une œuvre d'art à la gloire du courage et du patriotisme, la cause à laquelle il cherche à rallier ses troupes perd de sa légitimité. La ferveur affirmée doit être perçue comme émanant d'une ferveur vécue, et si elle en découle effectivement cela n'en sera que mieux. Les prouesses guerrières tout comme les rodomontades vaines doivent avoir pour fondement affectif le courage ; sans cela elles ne sont qu'une forme de mensonge.

La congruence de l'émotion vécue et du geste social n'est pas moins importante dans les déclarations d'amour. L'amour en tant que geste public inverse la relation entre l'acte signifiant et l'expérience signifiée qui existe dans la vie privée où l'on peut ignorer le geste mal fait. Cependant pour les actes publics l'importance des gestes extérieurs en tant que garants de l'implication, de l'engagement ou de la ferveur, est bien plus grande et le fait de savoir que les intentions sont bonnes n'est jamais une excuse pour de mauvaises représentations. Les actes publics développent leur typologie et leur style propres et ceux-ci se diffusent à travers la hiérarchie politique et sociale donnant d'abord naissance à une mode puis à une coutume sociale.

Le déploiement de modèles idéalisés de sentiments dans la vie sociale et politique fait du geste social un événement « textuel » toujours conçu pour être lu,

VIII

L'AMOUR DES ROIS

interprété et évalué pour permettre les ajustements de rang et de statut de ceux qui le pratiquent et de ceux à qui il est destiné. Cela impose aussi la nécessité prosaïque d'établir une distinction entre la sincérité et l'affectation. Dotés d'un rôle social, d'une structure d'interaction leur permettant d'être mis à l'épreuve et d'un discours leur servant de véhicule, les actes de courage, de compassion ou d'amour, deviennent un *locus* pour les comportements les plus élevés comme pour l'hypocrisie la plus vile. Ils composent un décor théâtral d'émotions encore en usage dans la vie politique contemporaine. Au cours de la campagne présidentielle de 1988, Michael Dukakis fut accusé de manquer de compassion, critique qui fut à l'origine de l'une des crises qui devaient finalement entraîner son échec. Cette crise fut suffisamment sérieuse pour l'obliger à paraître à la télévision et montrer qu'il était capable d'éprouver des émotions. Il exprima sa compassion pour les gens qui souffraient et, s'adressant au public, il dit : « Je vous aime ». Que Dukakis ait ou non ressenti ce sentiment, que cette déclaration ait correspondu à une émotion vécue ou non, il s'agissait de se conformer à une norme de comportement exaltant idéal, c'est-à-dire à un geste social.

Le geste social sépare les émotions qu'il évoque du champ de forces de l'interprétation freudienne. Il découle de la politique et de l'intentionnalité et, comme tout autre texte, il est le produit du calcul et de la planification. Il n'a pas cette qualité propre à l'exécution irréfléchie des impulsions qui sont les fruits spontanés de la libido. Depuis la fin du régime monarchique, la vocation publique de l'émotion a perdu en importance, mais elle conserve sa puissance politique quelle que soit sa discrétion. Dans la déclaration d'amour de Dukakis ce qui était à l'œuvre ce n'était pas un sentiment d'affection personnelle pour les Américains, mais bien quelque chose d'extrêmement important pour le gouvernement et qui retirait toute pertinence à la question « Nous aime-t-il vraiment ? » ou en révélait la naïveté. Cette question confond émotion publique et émotion privée et l'on retrouve cette même confusion si l'on s'interroge sur les préférences sexuelles des monarques du Moyen Age passionnément amoureux de leurs « mignons ».

A son niveau le plus primitif l'amour des rois est une structure d'émotions qui est inscrite dans la règle charismatique ou qui en est l'émanation [22]. L'aura du corps du roi dessine un cercle magique. Le fait de pénétrer dans ce cercle, comme celui de se retrouver en présence d'un dieu et de participer soudain de la divinité, a un effet d'enchantement. La légitimation de la règle par la déification du roi n'est pas simplement un moyen de préservation du pouvoir. C'est une réponse au charisme royal, une interprétation de ce charisme. La représentation que le roi donne de lui-même vise à renforcer chez le sujet le sentiment d'être le témoin d'un être supérieur jouissant de liens privilégiés avec le monde surnaturel.

La présence du roi a des effets particuliers. Elle tend à annihiler la volonté et à effacer l'individualité ; elle crée, à partir d'un grand nombre d'individus, quelque chose de comparable à un être unique. Elle a des effets proches de ce que Nietszche nomme le Dionysiaque. Il faut les lire tous les deux comme des phénomènes de psychologie des foules. La présence du roi induit même au sein d'une assistance privée des réactions du type de celles des rassemblements de foule.

L'un de ces effets curieux est l'intensification des sentiments. L'amour et la

VIII

dévotion, l'hommage et la crainte respectueuse sont suffisamment forts pour que la vie du sujet perde toute signification et que celui-ci soit prêt à la sacrifier avec joie pour préserver l'existence et le pouvoir du roi. Les pleurs et les comportements hystériques sont des réactions normales de la foule en présence du souverain. L'amour, la soumission volontaire et le désir du sujet de se modeler à l'image et à la ressemblance du monarque sont des réactions individuelles communes [23].

Une forme d'amour qui trouve son fondement dans l'aura du souverain et non dans quelque impulsion libidineuse est l'un des effets du charisme. Ses manifestations premières sont la crainte et le respect devant l'objet aimé, mais ces sentiments génèrent le désir. Une observation particulière dans la biographie de Gérald d'Aurillac (mort en 909) montre fort clairement cet objet politique du désir. Gérald régnait sur ses vassaux dans un climat d'amour mutuel (ainsi que l'écrit son biographe fort idéalisateur, Odon de Cluny mort en 942) [24]. La séduction qu'il exerçait sur ses sujets était nettement d'ordre physique. Sa beauté (qui n'était pas de type à susciter luxure ou fierté, nous assure Odon) émanait de tout son corps mais son cou « était si rayonnant *(candidulum)* et d'une forme si parfaite que vous pensiez n'avoir jamais vu quoi que ce fût de si beau » (650 C : I, 12). Les personnes qui lui étaient proches avaient « coutume de lui baiser le cou avec grande joie » et elles le faisaient sans aucun sentiment d'avilissement (651 A : I, 12). L'amour pour Gérald suscite le désir de baiser la partie la plus belle de son corps mais ce baiser n'exprime que respect et hommage, quel que soit le désir d'ordre sexuel que ce geste peut évoquer. *Ingens veneratio,* une « vénération énorme » (661 B : I, 32) lie Gérald à ses vassaux et amis et cela stimule un désir dont la motivation ultime est politique.

La faveur du prince ou un avancement étaient le motif caché de ce désir et cela quelle qu'ait pu être la sincérité de l'affection existant entre le souverain et son courtisan ou vassal. L'introduction de la dynamique de la passion dans la sphère politique avait pour effet de l'intégrer à la dynamique du pouvoir. L'arrière-pensée du monarque était d'asseoir son autorité. Sa cour devient une famille, les courtisans lui sont attachés en tant que *familiaritas, amicitia* et *caritas.* Le système de récompenses et de châtiments passe par un discours des émotions : amour et haine tiennent lieu de faveur ou de disgrâce ; l'air sombre du monarque ou son déplaisir non seulement indique son état d'esprit particulier mais aussi le climat politique. La personne du roi et l'État, ses sentiments et sa politique, ne font plus qu'une seule et même chose.

Il est facile de réduire l'amour du roi à un jeu du pouvoir et de l'intérêt personnel véhiculé par un discours déplacé de son objet réel. Mais cela privilégie un élément d'un mode de sentiments et d'expressions extrêmement riche. Il est aussi tentant de le réduire à la rhétorique, de dire que « l'amour politique » était langage ou geste et rien de plus. On peut voir dans le spectacle des vassaux baisant le cou de Gérald une obligation féodale ritualisée, comparable au geste de baiser la main du pape ou d'un évêque. Mais la description qu'en donne Odon montre qu'il s'agit d'autre chose, d'un comportement lié à la personne du comte. L'admiration et le désir sont à l'origine de ce baiser. Ce texte nous rapproche d'une époque où l'amour politique était un amour vécu et non un geste social vide. Même si cette scène n'est qu'une invention d'Odon elle suggère que les rituels du baiser en général puisent leurs racines dans l'émotion [25]. Elle est

L'AMOUR DES ROIS

comparable au respect somatique primitif pour le roi qui en faisait un symbole de fertilité et qui donna naissance à une coutume comme celle du « droit de cuissage »[26]. Le *Jus primae noctis* et l'amour du roi ont connu des développements historiques similaires. Avec le temps le droit de dépucelage du roi ne fut plus considéré comme une bénédiction de type divin ou une promesse de fertilité, mais comme une abomination. De même le désir supra-personnel qui prenait le souverain pour objet s'estompa progressivement au cours du Moyen Age. Quelle qu'ait été la force de l'amour pour le roi, à la Renaissance le désir non romancé dont il aurait pu être l'objet aurait été perçu comme une chose curieuse et primitive.

L'amour en tant que relation dominante dans la vie publique unissant le souverain et la cour, le souverain et le vassal, est un sujet qui mériterait qu'on lui consacrât un livre entier. Nous examinerons ici un autre aspect de l'amour du roi en tant qu'émotion vécue.

Avant le XIIe siècle la société aristocratique ne connaissait qu'une forme d'amitié, l'amitié entre hommes. Cette amitié est chose banale dans les sociétés de guerriers où les circonstances de la guerre et de la vie militaire créaient entre les hommes des liens forts qui n'avaient aucun rapport avec le désir[27]. Elle donna naissance à une tradition sociale et à un corpus d'écrits éthiques et philosophiques dans les sociétés hellénique, hellénistique et romaine, dont le développement se poursuivit au Moyen Age et à la Renaissance. L'amour platonique en est une forme première[28]. L'amitié devient le terrain d'expérimentation de la morale grecque avec ses idéaux de maîtrise et de contrôle de soi[29]. L'essence de l'amitié dans la tradition gréco-romaine est l'amour de la vertu qui existe chez un autre homme, un amour dont le premier mobile est l'acquisition de la vertu et l'élévation de l'honneur chez chacun des partenaires. L'amitié devient le véhicule de la perfection éthique. Le désir libidineux peut être présent mais les freins et les limites qui lui sont imposés sont les pierres de touche de la force morale. La maîtrise et la discipline du désir sont les objets premiers de cette amitié.

Cette forme d'amitié était exaltante, elle était le signe d'une noblesse intérieure, de l'*areté*[30]. Dans le *Banquet* de Platon, Phèdre présente l'amour entre hommes comme une force morale qui les incite à la bravoure, les pousse aux actions d'éclat ou à défendre leur pays[31]. Perfection dans la vertu et réalisation d'actions d'éclat, tels sont les objectifs éthiques de l'amitié virile. Il est intéressant de noter que ce sont aussi les objectifs de ce que l'on nomme l'amour courtois au Moyen Age.

L'affirmation d'Aristote selon laquelle les termes « ami » et « homme de bien » sont identiques devint le thème du traité de Cicéron, *De amicitia*[32], qui devait servir de manuel sur l'amitié à l'aristocratie européenne jusqu'au XVIIe siècle. Pour Cicéron l'amitié n'est possible qu'entre les hommes les meilleurs ; l'amitié intime est une prérogative de l'aristocratie :

> Il est si peu vrai que l'on cultive l'amitié par besoin de secours que ce sont précisément les hommes matériellement bien pourvus et possédant la meilleure des sauvegardes, la vertu, n'ayant par suite besoin de personne, qui sont les plus généreux et les plus bienfaisants[33].

VIII

La mise en parallèle de la fortune, du pouvoir et de la vertu, était en quelque sorte le programme politique et social de l'aristocratie européenne et probablement de l'aristocratie en général. Il s'agit d'une auto-consécration et dans le même temps d'un impératif moral : l'aristocratie se définit comme détentrice de la vertu, il lui faut donc se montrer vertueuse. La capacité à se créer des amitiés et à les conserver était un signe de supériorité morale et de classe. Cette équivalence eut une grande influence sur la constitution des idéaux sociaux de l'aristocratie occidentale. L'identification de « l'amitié » et de « l'alliance » puise probablement ses racines dans une expérience humaine commune mais l'aristocratie européenne développa une espèce de culte de l'amitié qui conférait une stature plus importante aux individus et aux alliances [34] et permettait au pouvoir de se masquer discrètement derrière un voile de bonté, d'affabilité, de sincérité.

Dans l'amour platonicien la possession physique était la dernière étape, la plus basse et la moins importante. Mais à partir de l'époque hellénistique elle devint progressivement taboue et fut bannie du culte de l'amitié et de ses pratiques [35]. Elle n'a aucune place dans le *De amicitia* de Cicéron ni dans les traditions romaines et médiévales ayant trait à l'amitié. L'abstinence totale et ses relations visant seulement au perfectionnement de l'âme étaient des marques d'*askesis*, de *disciplina* et de maîtrise de soi. Les relations sexuelles ne pouvaient que souiller et ruiner l'amitié. Le désir libidineux au sens étroit du terme était certainement souvent présent dans l'amitié virile mais, pour l'éthique post-hellénique, il ne pouvait être considéré que comme un danger à éviter [36].

L'expérience de l'amitié finit par se structurer et se déployer en tant que geste social et politique. Cet idéal, ce mode de sentiment ennoblissant, devint un signe de distinction. C'était un bien trop précieux pour demeurer caché dans le cadre des relations privées entre individus, et personne ne songeait d'ailleurs à le maintenir dans ce contexte. L'amitié raffinée et vertueuse devint la monnaie du royaume ; elle avait cours dans l'économie du statut aristocratique et permettait d'acquérir estime et reconnaissance.

L'amour comme geste social jouait un rôle de soutien pour l'une des constantes de la société aristocratique, à savoir le besoin d'affirmer ou de prouver sa supériorité [37]. Le terme *aristoi*, qui signifie « les meilleurs », implique en fait cette obligation. Pour que le gouvernement fût exercé par les meilleurs — c'est-à-dire par l'aristocratie — ceux-ci devaient structurer la société de façon à manifester leur position et à la préserver par l'exclusion et diverses formes de coercition. Ils devaient aussi mettre en évidence et illustrer leur position au sommet de la hiérarchie qu'ils avaient édifiée. Le décor de cette mise en scène est bien connu : raffinement des costumes et de l'apparence, manières distinguées et style de vie grandiose, architecture impressionnante.

Mais la nécessité de la représentation de soi s'affirmait aussi dans le champ des sensibilités et de la morale. La noblesse du sang devait se justifier par la noblesse de l'esprit et de l'âme. Les raffinements extérieurs et la beauté physique n'étaient rien s'ils n'étaient pas les signes visibles d'une valeur intérieure. Le Beau était l'enveloppe du Bien. L'idéal du *kalos kai agathos* faisait de la vertu, *areté*, la force intérieure que les raffinements extérieurs révélaient. Cet idéal contraignait l'aristocratie à adopter certains types de comportement : générosité, condescendance, bonté, affabilité. L'élitisme de la vie affective englobait tous ces comportements et trouvaient son expression dans des actes sublimes d'empathie. Cela est vrai de l'aristocratie grecque et romaine. Nous retrouvons cet élitisme dans les idéaux courtois que la littérature chevaleresque attribuait à la classe des chevaliers du Haut Moyen Age. La langue chevaleresque et les sentiments courtois firent cause commune à la Renaissance. Le culte du raffinement demeure vivace jusqu'au XVIIIe siècle et au-delà, atteignant peut-être son apothéose avec *La princesse de Clèves* de Madame de Lafayette.

Dans toutes ses mises en scène historiques l'aristocratie faisait appel au sentiment comme à l'un des fondements de sa supériorité : les individus les meilleurs avaient les sentiments les plus raffinés et les plus élevés. C'est dans ce cadre que le culte de l'amitié fonctionnait comme geste social. L'amour dépouillé de connotations érotiques ennoblissait[38]. Après avoir dépassé le premier stade, celui de la pédérastie hellénique, qui avait contribué à sa promotion dans la hiérarchie des mœurs, il se transforma en une amitié sublimée et une passion de caractère non libidineux qui trouva son expression la plus élevée dans les communautés monastiques du Haut Moyen Age. L'amitié témoignait de la vertu, au même titre que la beauté physique et les manières nobles ; c'était le signe d'un raffinement aristocratique ou d'une spiritualité chrétienne. Alcuin pouvait déclarer son amour pour Charlemagne et pour Arn de Salzbourg de manière aussi directe précisément parce que plus le ton de l'expression était passionné, plus la relation était innocente. Loin de le stigmatiser comme sodomite, l'amour du roi en faisait un homme de la vertu la plus élevée. Roger de Howden pouvait dépeindre l'amour de Richard et de Philippe Auguste de manière aussi franche pour la même raison.

Quelques communautés monastiques des XIe et XIIe siècles intégrèrent les pratiques aristocratiques de l'amitié passionnée à la vie religieuse et les transformèrent en une forme de spiritualité chrétienne plus intense et plus élevée[39]. Cette revendication d'une origine religieuse fut imposée car elle ne correspondait à aucune tradition de la spiritualité monastique. Le concept d'amitié spécifiquement chrétienne, d'origine monastique, n'a pas de réalité propre[40]. Afin d'exister en tant que telle, l'amitié « monastique » devait s'imposer contre l'idéal chrétien de type ascétique des pères du désert qui jugeaient suspectes toutes les relations humaines[41]. Elle devait donc résister aux traditions monastiques et, dans le même temps, elle se voyait sans cesse assimilée aux traditions séculières. Les écrits majeurs de l'époque prennent Cicéron pour référence ; ils élèvent « l'amitié spirituelle » sur les fondations mêmes de l'amitié séculière, et leur opposition à Cicéron n'est que la reconnaissance déguisée de la dette immense qu'ils ont à son égard[42].

Dans les monastères l'amitié était une ramification du culte de l'amitié aristocratique. Nombre de documents mettent en évidence son caractère public. Un exemple frappant nous est donné par une lettre de saint Anselme, abbé du Bec, adressée à son ami Maurice[43]. Il écrit que leur correspondance est nécessaire, non pour réaffirmer leur amitié qui repose sur des bases inébranlables, ni pour échanger quelques propos, ce qu'ils font régulièrement par l'intermédiaire de messagers, mais plutôt pour donner un témoignage public et visible de leur affection. Ils écrivent « de crainte que quiconque, en quelque circonstance, ne pense que leur amour tiédit ». Cet amour doit « être vu » dans sa ferveur véritable et la lettre en fait quelque chose de manifeste.

VIII

> Le fait même que je ne puisse t'avoir près de moi, bien que je te désire et que tu me désires, loin de l'atténuer, accroît mon amour pour toi. Je sais combien tu es digne d'amour quand je vois des hommes plus grands et meilleurs que moi être épris de toi au point de ne pas souffrir ton absence. Cela me pousse à me demander si je dois me réjouir ou m'affliger : me réjouir que tu sois digne de tant d'amour ou m'affliger de ne pouvoir jouir de la présence d'une personne aussi aimable.

Tout comme l'amour d'Anselme est stimulé lorsqu'il voit son ami aimé d'hommes meilleurs et plus grands que lui, sa déclaration accroît l'amour que d'autres hommes éprouvent pour lui. Cette lettre était sans aucun doute connue des membres de la communauté; dans le cas contraire sa déclaration d'intention n'aurait aucun sens. Elle laisse de côté les aspects personnels de l'amitié et se tourne vers la société pour trouver une confirmation et peut-être une stimulation du sentiment amoureux. Elle crée une espèce d'émulation entre ceux qui aiment Maurice. Elle « donne une contenance » à Maurice, l'honore, l'élève dans la communauté. Sur cet arrière-plan d'amour centrifuge, tourné vers le public, la puissance de la réputation à inspirer l'amour (que l'on retrouve exprimée dans le lieu commun « je t'aimais avant même de t'avoir vu ») acquiert une certaine crédibilité.

On affirme souvent que le culte de l'amitié dans les monastères du Moyen Age représente la sexualité sublimée, chez les hommes privés de tout érotisme. Il s'agit là encore d'un argument sans appel qui nous ramène aux mécanismes de l'inconscient et échappe dans ce contexte à toute réfutation. Mais sa valeur explicative dépend d'un acte de foi dans une théorie particulière de la psyché. L'exemple de la lettre d'Anselme à Maurice montre clairement que l'amitié monastique ne peut s'expliquer ainsi. La sexualité « sublimée » ne trouve pas son expression dans des déclarations d'amour, extravagantes pour des hommes, portées délibérément à la connaissance du public. La sublimation impose que l'interdit passe par le canal du licite ou en adopte les formes. Ainsi des moines, pour sublimer leur sexualité, se livraient aux travaux agricoles avec plus de fougue, enluminaient nombre de manuscrits ou rédigeaient des commentaires passionnés du Cantique des Cantiques.

L'amitié monastique n'étaient pas mue par l'énergie de la sexualité sublimée ou la révolte contre l'ascétisme chrétien, mais par ce type particulier de discipline et de contrôle de soi inhérent à la pratique de l'amitié aristocratique depuis l'Antiquité. C'était le champ d'expérimentation (ainsi que la vitrine) de la vertu. Parler d'amour monastique (ou d'amour du roi) n'a pas de sens si la dimension sexuelle a fait l'objet d'une sublimation. Le sexuel est présent comme un danger vaincu, à la manière de ces singes (symboles de luxure) que l'on représentait enchaînés auprès de gentes dames sur les tapisseries ou les manuscrits enluminés. L'amour devait avoir la luxure pour adversaire. L'âme est le lieu d'une opposition entre forces égales, la psychomachie, qui constitue le modèle psychique dans le cadre duquel cet amour opérait, et non pas d'une coopération entre forces répressives et forces refoulées comme dans un modèle freudien. La franchise du discours sur l'amour fait de la luxure un antagoniste visible et non un complice caché.

La continuité d'un culte aristocratique de l'amour et de l'amitié nous apparaît clairement dans l'amour courtois du Moyen Age et de la Renaissance et dans la galanterie aux xviie et xviiie siècles. Dans cette analyse je mets l'accent sur le parallèle existant entre l'amour du roi et ces deux formes plus tardives et mieux connues [44].

Une étude de ces trois sentiments dans le cadre d'une phénoménologie commune contribuerait grandement à préciser la nature et le contexte social de l'amour courtois, questions épineuses de l'histoire sociale et littéraire du Moyen Age [45]. Leur caractéristique commune est de partager la même fonction sociale. Dans les trois cas l'amour, sous son aspect public, confère du prestige à ceux qui le pratiquent [46] ; il accroît leur valeur sur le marché humain de la cour [47].

Si nous considérons l'amour courtois comme proche de la *philia* et de l'*amicitia,* le changement essentiel dans les mœurs amoureuses au xiie siècle nous apparaîtra être l'entrée des femmes comme acteurs majeurs dans une pièce qui avait été jusque-là exclusivement réservée aux hommes. Au lieu de s'interroger sur la fonction sociale du culte des femmes tel qu'il est représenté dans la littérature courtoise, les chercheurs se sont demandé quelles étaient ses conventions littéraires formelles, de quelles autres conventions littéraires celles-ci découlaient et quel était le « système » d'amour qu'elles impliquaient. Cela devait enfermer la question dans l'impasse où elle se trouve actuellement [48].

C'est une erreur d'imaginer que l'amour représenté dans la littérature de l'aristocratie avant la Renaissance (et, dans certains cas, après) ne se rapporte qu'à des affaires d'ordre privé. Certaines difficultés de compréhension de l'amour entre hommes et de l'amour courtois des hommes pour les femmes à partir du Haut Moyen Age seraient aplanies si nous considérions que ces modes de sentiments sont tout d'abord publics et investis d'une fonction sociale importante et si nous les envisagions, dans un second temps seulement, sous leur aspect individuel et privé. Les recherches sur l'amour courtois ont aussi cherché à définir ce que sont les relations amoureuses « réelles » vécues, auxquelles la littérature courtoise se réfère et elles se sont trouvées confrontées au même problème d'ordre conceptuel et méthodologique que nous avions lorsque nous nous posions la question « Michael Dukakis aime-t-il vraiment les Américains ? » Il a même paru possible de dénier toute existence réelle à la pratique de l'amour courtois, démarche comparable à celle qui consisterait à nier que l'amour est un facteur de la politique moderne parce que nous manquons d'éléments prouvant que les hommes politiques aiment vraiment le public.

Un document remarquable nous permet d'analyser le rôle des femmes dans l'amour des rois et dans l'ennoblissement des relations amoureuses en général. Il s'agit d'une « lettre d'amour » adressée par une gente dame, Constance, sœur du duc Conan de Bretagne, au roi de France Louis VII en 1160. Cette lettre était incluse dans la correspondance officielle du roi dans la collection de son chancelier, Hugues de Champfleury. Il est donc peu probable que les contemporains aient pu juger cette proposition d'amour, d'échange de présents et de rencontre, comme choquante ou inconsidérée. Lisons-la.

> A Louis, vénérable et excellent roi de Gaule, Constance, fille d'Alain, comte de Bretagne, [adresse] ses salutations et [offre] le lien de son amitié. Je désire faire connaître à Votre Dignité que j'ai longtemps gardé mémoire de vous et que je n'ai jamais accepté les nombreux présents que, par amour,

VIII

nombre d'hommes m'offraient. Mais s'il plaisait à votre libéralité de m'envoyer à moi qui t'aime au-delà de ce que je peux exprimer, quelque signe d'amour, un anneau ou autre chose, je le tiendrais à plus haut prix que le monde tout entier. Je vous remercie d'avoir reçu avec tant d'honneur mon messager. Et si il y a quelque chose en nos provinces qu'il vous plairait d'avoir, un faucon, un chien, ou un cheval, je vous prie de ne pas en différer la commande auprès de moi par le porteur de la présente lettre. Soyez sûr que si la fortune refusait de me sourire de toutes ses lèvres, je préférerais être unie à l'un de tes sujets, même humble, plutôt que de devenir reine d'Ecosse. Et je vais le prouver par le fait, car dès que mon frère le comte C. sera revenu d'Angleterre, j'irai à Saint-Denis pour prier, et pour pouvoir jouir de votre présence. Portez-vous bien, afin que je me porte bien [49].

Sous l'apparence d'une déclaration enflammée, nous avons là une proposition d'alliance politique. Conan avait besoin pour conserver son titre de duc d'un soutien dans ses luttes contre une opposition locale [50]. Au nombre de ses alliés, il comptait son suzerain, Henri II d'Angleterre, qui l'avait confirmé dans son titre de duc de Bretagne en 1158 et le roi d'Écosse dont il épousa la fille en 1160. Le roi de France devait apparaître comme un apport de valeur dans ce réseau d'alliances. Les allusions à l'Angleterre et à l'Écosse présentes dans cette lettre font discrètement référence à ces liens. Le rappel de la présence de son frère en Angleterre a la valeur d'une menace subtile et vise à exercer une pression politique sur le roi de France avant une rencontre éventuelle à Saint-Denis. La mention de l'éventualité pour Constance de devenir reine d'Écosse si la « fortune » lui était défavorable va dans le même sens. C'était la vérité. Malcolm IV d'Écosse était un parti possible mais peut-être cette union avait-elle perdu de sa signification en termes d'intérêts dynastiques depuis que Conan avait contracté une alliance avec Malcolm en épousant sa sœur. Cependant l'éventualité du mariage de Constance avec le roi d'Écosse demeurait une réalité et ne pouvait apparaître comme une simple métaphore (ce qu'elle peut nous sembler être aujourd'hui) aux yeux de Louis VII, menacé par un pacte qui aurait uni la grande et la petite Bretagne (la Normandie, l'Anjou et l'Aquitaine étant déjà sous contrôle anglais).

La date de la lettre, 1160, suggère une explication possible des circonstances immédiates de sa rédaction. Cette année-là Louis, qui eut trois femmes, se trouvait temporairement sans épouse [51]. Sa deuxième femme, Constance de Castille, était morte en couches et quelque cinq semaines plus tard il épousait Adèle de Champagne, future mère de Philippe Auguste. Si la lettre fut écrite au cours de ce bref veuvage, la maison de Bretagne saisissait là ce qui lui semblait être une occasion propice. Le roi qui gardait la tête froide résista à ces flatteries politiques et au léger parfum érotique qui pouvait en émaner [52]. Toujours est-il qu'il n'épousa pas Constance.

Plus que l'arrière-plan politique ce qui nous intéresse ici c'est le premier plan, le style d'auto-représentation aristocratique mis en œuvre. L'amour passionné est la langue dont se parent les objectifs politiques et qui leur permet de s'affirmer, c'est une fiction structurante qui permet à la stratégie du pouvoir de se représenter. La lettre de Constance est-elle un exemple d'« amour courtois »? Je pense qu'il s'agit bien d'une illustration à peine déformée de cet amour en tant que pratique sociale. Peters et Köhn ont mis en évidence certains

VIII

L'AMOUR DES ROIS

éléments que cette lettre partage avec la poésie et le roman courtois (« Liebeswerben », p. 188 ss) : l'échange de présents *(munera amoris causa),* le faucon et la bague comme gage d'amour, le messager portant une lettre et l'invitation à se rencontrer. Cette lettre montre clairement l'aspect pragmatique du langage de l'amour courtois, aspect rarement visible dans la littérature d'imagination. Ce qui manque ici c'est le sentiment de révérence de l'homme pour la femme que les formes normales de la poésie et du roman courtois nous font espérer. Mais elle fournit quelques indications sur la position plus élevée de la femme dans les relations amoureuses. Il est vrai qu'ici la femme a l'initiative. L'allusion à ses prétendants malheureux en fait une femme désirable qui peut maîtriser et repousser les avances des hommes et cela contribue à évoquer la figure de la *domna* hautaine.

Cependant le fondement ultime de cette lettre n'est pas la littérature mais bien la pratique sociale, l'amour du roi. Depuis l'époque carolingienne au moins, les courtisans déclaraient leur amour pour le roi, exprimaient leurs désirs et cherchaient à plaire. Ce qui est nouveau ici ce sont le langage et le sexe des protagonistes et non la coutume ; pour la première fois dans les documents historiques une femme doit se donner le rôle de séductrice d'un roi, la passion amoureuse est proposée comme type de relations et la tâche importante consistant à négocier une alliance politique passe par le canal d'une déclaration d'amour écrite. Cela aurait été impossible un siècle plus tôt, ce type de tractation étant traditionnellement mené par les parents ou des membres puissants de la famille.

Le rôle de la femme et le moyen employé, une lettre d'amour, sont choses impensables sans l'influence des mœurs courtoises. La passion amoureuse féminine a connu une revalorisation radicale ; le duc de Bretagne et sa famille avaient jugé bonne la stratégie consistant à entamer une importante démarche diplomatique par une lettre d'amour, écrite de surcroît par une femme. C'est là un signe manifeste de la promotion de la femme dans la société courtoise. C'était évidemment un honneur pour le roi de France de recevoir une proposition d'alliance politique sous la forme d'une lettre d'amour rédigée par une femme, en partie parce qu'il s'agissait d'une femme de qualité, exigeante et courtisée, et en partie aussi parce que cela reléguait à l'arrière-plan les réalités sévères et banales les remplaçant par une élégante fiction courtoise. Le langage de l'amour s'imposait ici car il honorait et exaltait même les personnes qui en faisaient usage pour conduire leurs affaires. Il en fut ainsi pour Richard Cœur de Lion lorsqu'il conclut une trêve avec Philippe Auguste comme pour Constance de Bretagne lorsqu'elle rechercha une alliance avec Louis VII.

Nous nous sommes efforcés jusqu'à présent de restituer une sensibilité, son discours et son développement dans la société aristocratique européenne. Ce discours soulève une question importante qu'il est nécessaire d'examiner à présent. Il tend à se situer aux marges de l'illicite tout en revendiquant comme ses caractères propres la vertu, l'exaltation et même la chasteté. Il est en équilibre entre le sublime et l'immoral. On peut se demander pourquoi l'élitisme des sentiments recherchait le langage de la passion et des amours interdites, tantôt homosexuelles, tantôt adultères, pour exprimer sa supériorité morale. Il aurait pu, après tout, avoir recours au langage bien plus modéré de l'amitié. Pourquoi aucun de ces écrivains ne craignit que ces déclarations publiques d'amour, de

VIII

désir et d'envie, ne fussent déformées, mal interprétées ou retournées contre elles-mêmes ?

Le langage de l'illicite loin de servir à exprimer une condamnation servait de système de défense et protégeait ceux qui en faisaient usage des soupçons qu'une lecture littérale ne pouvait manquer de suggérer. L'homme ou la femme qui use du langage de l'érotique montre innocemment que l'illicite est certes proche mais évité ou ignoré. Il est maîtrisé, contrôlé, maintenu à sa place. Les déclarations publiques d'amour impliquent le message suivant : « Des gens tels que nous sont au-dessus des désirs bas, inaccessibles à leurs dangers. L'obscène et l'interdit n'ont d'emprise que sur les âmes faibles. Notre passion est amour de la vertu ». Les textes que nous venons d'examiner affirment une supériorité sur la passion et l'érotique en montrant publiquement et ouvertement une passion fougueuse maîtrisée. Ce mode de sentiment se définit lui-même et fonde sa supériorité en faisant abstraction des dangers qu'il a, dans un premier temps, évoqués puis soumis à sa loi. Cette attitude implique un héroïsme moral et une maîtrise de l'économie de la vertu et de la passion dans l'âme [53].

Mais ce discours ne pouvait préserver sa position souveraine que parce qu'il comportait aussi un mécanisme qui réduisait la critique au silence, une stratégie rhétorique qui écartait tout reproche et invitait le lecteur ou l'observateur à ignorer, comme le locuteur lui-même, tout soupçon d'illicite. Il présentait des modèles et des structures de relations sublimes, des archétypes platoniques à l'œuvre au niveau social, et il invitait la cour, le royaume et le lecteur à les partager. Il montre des rois, des comtes, des courtisans et de gentes dames, dominant la nature et se comportant comme le font les dieux, avec une autorité supérieure à celle du commun des mortels. Si le lecteur ou le spectateur accepte cette affirmation d'un raffinement élevé dans les relations exprimées, il montre qu'il est capable d'éprouver de tels sentiments ; s'il se montre critique, il nie cela et s'exclut de l'élite du sentiment. Cette stratégie partage les individus en deux catégories, les cœurs nobles et les êtres vulgaires.

Ce discours protège aussi ses locuteurs en lançant un défi. Les affirmations de supériorité mises en avant dans le langage de l'illicite invitent l'auditeur à commettre une espèce de crime de lèse-majesté. Comme dans le cas de tout défi, l'accepter et s'élever contre les termes qu'il pose revient à provoquer une réplique et à déclencher le mécanisme de sanctions qui en est le garant. « Démasquer » l'amour du roi revient pour un membre de la cour à s'exposer aux risques d'une exclusion ou, dans les cas extrêmes, à ceux d'un duel, d'un emprisonnement ou d'une condamnation à mort. Soutenus par ces menaces les actes et les affirmations exprimés dans ce discours trouvent en eux-mêmes leur propre légitimité, leur validation et leur sauvegarde. Cela explique pourquoi leur puissance d'exaltation excède leur puissance de condamnation.

La littérature et l'historiographie des cours européennes fourmillent d'exemples. L'histoire de la création de l'Ordre de la Jarretière, la distinction la plus élevée que le roi d'Angleterre puisse conférer, illustre ce mode discursif particulièrement bien. Il est difficile aujourd'hui de faire la part de l'anecdote, des faits réels et de la légende, dans cette histoire qui trouve ses origines dans une scène publique embarrassante mais assumée avec courage, retournement curieux de la tendance consistant à magnifier les sources pour en faire des mythes.

VIII

L'AMOUR DES ROIS

La légende rapporte que le roi Edouard III (1312-1377) dansait soit avec la reine, soit avec sa maîtresse (un autre récit affirme qu'il s'agissait de Joan, comtesse de Kent et de Salisbury), lorsqu'une jarretière bleue glissa de la jambe de la dame et tomba. Certains courtisans se moquèrent mais le roi ramassa la jarretière, la mit à son mollet en prédisant que bientôt ils révéreraient l'objet dont ils riaient à présent et il lança l'avertissement qui devait devenir la devise de l'Ordre et qui pourrait bien être celle du type de discours que nous examinons ici : « Honi soit qui mal y pense ». En portant ainsi une jarretière le roi s'abaisse et laisse croire à quelque relation intime avec sa propriétaire. Mais ce même geste l'élève : il s'agit d'un acte sublime de galanterie. Le roi écarte toute critique en multipliant les causes d'embarras et en les prenant à son compte, et cela inscrit son comportement dans la structure d'un acte chevaleresque ennoblissant. Le privé et l'intime révélés perdent leur pouvoir de scandale parce que le geste du monarque les transpose comme par magie dans la sphère de l'invulnérabilité qui lui est réservée, où le vulgaire, l'obscène et l'illicite ne sont qu'illusions et où tout est noble et digne de vénération ; du même coup, il les sauve.

Il s'agit aussi d'un défi. Il place les courtisans témoins entre deux champs de perception : ils peuvent y voir le signe d'une liaison entre le roi (marié) et sa maîtresse. Mais ils peuvent décider que ces analyses sordides sont incompatibles avec la dignité des courtisans et des rois et qu'une explication plus noble s'impose : il s'agit d'un acte de chevalerie, de courtoisie sur le mode héroïque, à la manière d'un Lancelot s'abaissant pour protéger sa maîtresse. D'une part nous avons une attitude vulgaire et insultante, d'autre part un geste exaltant. Selon le cas, l'embarras et le déshonneur inhérents à la situation retombent sur les courtisans (ainsi, ne l'oublions pas, que la colère du monarque) ou ceux-ci se trouvent promus membres d'une élite chevaleresque. Renforcé par ces motivations le sublime réduit le vil au silence.

Les seules sources primaires contemporaines d'Edouard sont l'Ordre lui-même, son symbole et sa devise. L'anecdote de la jarretière perdue n'a pratiquement aucune base dans l'historiographie [54]. La tendance de la recherche historique consiste depuis quelque temps à n'accorder aucun crédit à la légende et à expliquer la jarretière et la devise à la lumière des ambitions politiques d'Edouard concernant la France [55]. Ce rapprochement est tout aussi sujet à caution que l'histoire de la jarretière fièrement arborée et la thèse que Barber et Vale défendent me semble tout aussi fragile. L'invasion de la France par l'Angleterre devait être perçue et présentée comme une entreprise héroïque, en particulier face aux invectives de l'ennemi, or une jarretière de femme arborée par un homme est une marque de déshonneur.

Barber soutient que les jarretières étaient, dans les années 1350, une parure d'homme et que la jarretière de l'Ordre était probablement la ceinture que l'on recevait au cours de la cérémonie d'élévation au titre de chevalier (*Edward,* p. 87) et non un signe de déshonneur. Certaines analogies avec le roman en moyen anglais *Sir Gawain and the Green Knight* apportent un éclairage intéressant, bien que je n'aie trouvé aucune référence à ce texte dans les écrits récents sur l'Ordre de la Jarretière. Les études consacrées à *Sir Gawain* font en général état de certains liens entre le roman et l'Ordre [56]. Sir Gawain reçoit d'une dame une ceinture ou « girdel » comme talisman et gage de leur amour secret. Le fait de l'accepter le protège et le déshonore à la fois. Lorsque Sir Gawain se repro-

VIII

chera sa lâcheté et sa trahison devant la cour, le roi Arthur déclarera que tous les chevaliers et toutes les dames devront dorénavant arborer un ruban vert.

Ici aussi la parure intime est un signe érotique qui déshonore celui qui la reçoit mais elle devient distinction honorifique lorsque le roi en fait un symbole d'appartenance à la cour.

L'auteur de *Sir Gawain* vivait à l'époque de la fondation de l'Ordre. Il est difficile de dater précisément cette œuvre que l'on juge généralement avoir été rédigée au cours du dernier quart du XIVe siècle. Le seul manuscrit que l'on connaisse remonte aux alentours de l'an 1400. Il s'achève par les mots « hony soyt qui mal pence » ajoutés peut-être un peu plus tard d'une écriture différente de celle du scribe. Cette mention, quel qu'en soit l'auteur, nous apporte une interprétation de la devise de l'Ordre à moins d'un siècle de sa création. Le scribe, le lecteur ou le propriétaire du manuscrit, établit un lien entre les événements contés dans le roman et l'Ordre de la Jarretière. Il utilise la devise pour conjurer le déshonneur symbolisé par un sous-vêtement de femme. Il est peu probable qu'il ait fait cela si les traditions de l'Ordre avaient rattaché la devise aux guerres d'Edouard III en France. La jarretière devait être perçue comme un signe de disgrâce, au même titre que la ceinture verte.

On trouve la première version complète de la fondation de l'Ordre dans l'*Historia Anglica* (1534) de Polydore Vergil[57]. Il s'agit d'un texte précieux pour nous parce que ce récit des événements est aussi une méta-narration définissant le discours qui nous concerne. Polydore Vergil considérait la jarretière de l'Ordre comme un sous-vêtement féminin[58] et pour lui les origines de l'Ordre, telles qu'il les rapporte, étaient « triviales et sordides » (*parva sordidaque*, p. 374). Mais il reprochait aux historiens anglais d'avoir passé sous silence la « véritable » histoire, par crainte de manquer de respect à l'égard de la monarchie et parce qu'ils n'avaient pas compris comment le déshonneur pouvait devenir marque d'honneur, en particulier lorsqu'il trouvait ses origines dans l'amour.

> La véritable origine de l'Ordre de la Jarretière ne devrait donc pas être cachée, même s'il est né de l'amour, car il n'est rien de plus noble que cela comme le dit Ovide : « la noblesse se cache sous l'amour ».

Non seulement Polydore Vergil rapporte les événements mais il explique au lecteur comment les interpréter. Italien vivant en Angleterre il traite les historiens anglais comme Edouard III avait traité les rieurs de la cour : il retourne le sentiment de déshonneur contre eux et montre comment le sublime peut être tiré des griffes du vulgaire.

L'historicité des événements n'importe guère pour l'analyse d'un discours et du code social qu'il véhicule. En revanche la légende, parfaitement constituée — du moins complètement révélée — quelque deux siècles plus tard, importe davantage. Son émergence graduelle montre comment un code social « corrige » les événements et les met en concordance avec ses lois. La version remaniée véhicule les lois discursives en vigueur bien mieux que ne le ferait le rapport direct de quelque observateur qui n'auraient pas eu pour tâche de commémorer ce code.

La logique qui unit la jarretière et la devise supposait un acte de déshonneur sur lequel asseoir les fondations de l'ordre, et si les sources historiques ne le fournissaient pas il était impératif de l'inventer. La devise n'a aucun sens si elle

L'AMOUR DES ROIS

ne concourt pas à dévier l'opprobre qui s'attache à un acte déshonorant. Un événement embarrassant tel que la révélation publique d'une liaison cachée, ou tout simplement celle du vêtement intime d'une gente dame ou de la reine, donne son sens à la logique inhérente de la jarretière et de la devise et fournit un modèle dans lequel le combat opposant le vil au sublime s'achève par la victoire de ce dernier.

Cet événement crée un ordre qui est bien plus général qu'un simple club de « gentlemen » anglais. Il représente une communauté qui partage un discours d'élite, qui nourrit toutes les visions idéalisatrices nécessaires et condamne leur dévoilement. Le symbole du contrat discursif qui unit ses membres est la jarretière ainsi arborée. Ils vénèrent un signe de déshonneur immunisé contre sa valeur symbolique première dès lors que le roi l'assume dans la sphère publique. Ainsi les membres de l'Ordre affirment qu'ils sont au-dessus du déshonneur et de ses causes.

Cette structure discursive unissait toute la société aristocratique occidentale, au moins à partir du début du Moyen Age. Le roi devait être considéré par la cour comme moralement irréprochable : il fallait donc étoffer certaines perceptions de sa majesté. Parfois ses qualités personnelles donnaient à celles-ci quelque consistance ; le plus souvent il s'agissait d'illusions ou de fictions ennoblissantes. Cependant ce n'étaient pas de simples mensonges ; elle étaient en partie le résultat de l'enchantement qui émanait de sa présence. A ce contact tout ce qui était vil semblait acquérir de la noblesse. Il suffisait au roi de traverser ses terres et cet enchantement émanait de sa personne comme la chaleur de l'astre solaire. Sous l'effet de son charisme ses sujets percevaient la réalité comme une vision de rêve néoplatonique et chevaleresque. Si tel n'était pas le cas et qu'ils l'avouaient ils risquaient rien moins que le déclassement social : menace terrible.

★

La compréhension de cette force de sensibilité et de sa structure sociale permet de dégager divers niveaux d'interprétation, qui n'étaient pas visibles à première lecture dans le texte concernant l'amour de Richard Cœur de Lion et de Philippe Auguste. L'un de ces niveaux est l'affirmation d'une amitié exaltante entre les deux princes qui s'exprime dans la langue et avec les gestes de la passion amoureuse et jette un voile élégant sur les réalités politiques en jeu. Un autre renvoie à la négation implicite de toute accusation d'attachement de caractère homosexuel entre les deux princes. En déclarant haut et fort qu'ils s'aiment et qu'ils dorment ensemble, Roger de Howden affirme la pureté de leur amitié. Ce paradoxe apparent devrait être à présent résolu. Il se peut que les soupçons concernant l'homosexualité de Richard aient fait d'une telle affirmation quelque chose d'important. Les historiens modernes ont constitué un dossier sur cette question [59], mais le texte de Roger de Howden échappe à leurs travaux. Loin de soutenir l'accusation il constitue un défi pour quiconque la formule.

VIII

NOTES

1. ROGER OF HOWDEN, *Gesta Regis Henrici Secundi*, dans *The Chronicle of the Reigns of Henri II and Richard I*, William STUBBS éd., Rolls Series (RS) 49 : 2, Londres, 1867, p. 7.

2. GERVASE DE CANTERBURY décrit les mêmes événements sans jamais suggérer qu'une passion amoureuse ait pu troubler la campagne militaire. *The Historical Works of Gervase of Canterbury*, W. STUBBS éd., RS 73 : 1, Londres, 1879, pp. 370-371.

3. ROGER OF HOWDEN, *op. cit.*, p. 126.

4. Sur les relations entre Jonathan et David comme modèles d'amitié au Moyen Age, voir Brian P. McGUIRE, *Friendship and Community: The Monastic Experience 350-1250*, Cistercian Studies Series 95, Kalamazoo, Mich., 1988, p. XVII ss. Sur le roman médiéval, Louise H. REISS, « Tristan and Isolt and the Medieval Ideal of Friendship », *Romance Quarterly*, 33, 1986, pp. 131-137.

5. Voir Vern L. BULLOUGH, « The Sin against Nature and Homosexuality », dans *Sexual Practices and the Medieval Church*, V. BULLOUGH et J. BRUNDAGE éds, Buffalo, N. Y., 1982, pp. 55-71. James BRUNDAGE, *Law, Sex and Christian Society in Medieval Europe*, Chicago, 1987, pp. 534-535 (fin du Moyen Age).

6. John BOSWELL, *Christianity, Social Tolerance and Homosexuality: Gay People in Western Europe from the Beginning of the Christian Era to the Fourteenth Century*, Chicago, 1980.

7. Voir BOSWELL, pp. 188-191, ainsi que Heinrich FICHTENAU, *The Carolingian Empire*, trad. Peter Munz, Oxford, 1957, pp. 93-94.

8. *Epist.*, 118, *MGH Epistolae* IV : *Epist. Karolini Aevi* 2 : 173, ligne 21 ss.

9. *Epist.*, 121, *ibid.*, p. 176, ligne 3 ss. Les lettres et les poèmes adressés par Alcuin à son ami l'archevêque Arn de Salzbourg sont encore plus enflammés. Voici deux exemples : *MGH Poetae* 1 : 236, N° 11 :
L'amour a percé mon cœur de sa flamme.
Et l'amour brûle toujours d'une ardeur nouvelle.
Ni terre ni mer, ni collines, bois ou monts
Ne peuvent obstruer ou fermer le chemin à celui,
Père aimant, qui lèche son sein
Et baigne, bien aimé, votre poitrine de ses larmes.
Et *Epist.*, 19, p. 36, ligne 2 ss : « Je me rappelle avec force et dans un doux souvenir votre amour et votre amitié, très saint père, et j'attends avec impatience le moment heureux où je pourrai vous enserrer amoureusement entre les doigts de mes désirs. O pouvoir être transporté comme Habacuc : comme je m'abandonnerais à vos embrassades paternelles avec des mains empressées, comme je presserais mes lèvres sur vos yeux, vos oreilles et votre bouche, mais aussi sur chaque doigt de vos mains et de vos pieds, et pas seulement une fois mais de façon répétée ».

10. *Admonitio generalis, MGH, Leges* II. *Capitularia regum Francorum* 1 : 57, n° 22, article 49 (qui prescrivait « des châtiments sévères et stricts » pour ceux qui « pèchent contre nature avec des animaux ou des hommes »). Lettre à son ancien élève, *Epist.*, 249, *op. cit.*, pp. 451-452. Selon moi BOSWELL (pp. 178 et 191) sous-estime la force de ces deux documents.

11. *MGH,* SS 4 : 833, ligne 23.

12. PETRUS DAMIANI, *Vita Romualdi*, ch. 25, *PL* 145 : 975C.

13. *Vita Adalberti,* ch. 23, *MGH,* SS 4 : 591. « Très cher compagnon de chambre » : *dulcissimus cubicularius*. Sur le jeu de mots, voir McGUIRE, *Friendship* (note 4 ci-dessus), p. 154. Après avoir dit qu'ils étaient des compagnons de chaque instant, échangeant baisers et embrassades, le biographe exclut toute critique possible en expliquant qu'il ne s'agissait pas de vanité de la part d'Adalbert. Ainsi l'accusation qui doit être écartée est celle d'ambition mondaine. La relation intime n'entraînait pas d'accusation d'homosexualité.

14. *Vita Meinwerci,* ch. 10, F. TENCKHOFF éd., *MGH,* script. rer. germ. in us. scholarum 59, Hanovre, 1983, p. 17.

L'AMOUR DES ROIS

15. Voir mon *Origins of Courtliness: Civilizing Trends and the Formation of Courtly Ideals, 939-1210,* Philadelphie, 1985, p. 170 ss.

16. *The Life of Ailred of Rievaulx by Walter Daniel,* ch. 2, M. POWICKE éd., Oxford, 1950; réed. 1978, p. 2.

17. Un tiers environ des références au terme « love » dans l'index lexical de l'œuvre de Shakespeare ont pour signification « faveur » ou « alliance ». Le commencement du *Roi Lear* thématise les deux formes d'amour, publique et privée ; Lear demande à ses trois filles de déclarer l'importance de leur amour pour lui ; il récompense deux d'entre elles en leur donnant une part proportionnelle du pouvoir et châtie la troisième qui refuse de faire le geste demandé en la reniant. Les sens cachés ne devaient pas échapper au public de l'époque. Lear et Cordelia sont tous deux victimes d'une perception étroite et tragique de l'amour causée par une séparation stricte des conceptions publique et privée. Lear agit comme si l'amour ne comportait pas d'élément personnel, Cordelia comme s'il n'avait pas de dimension politique.

18. *Epist.,* 120, *Sancti Anselmi Cantuariensis Archiepiscopi Opera Omnia,* F. S. SCHMITT éd., Edimbourg, 1946, 3 : 258-259. Cité et analysé dans R. W. SOUTHERN, *Saint Anselm and his Biographer: A Study of Monastic Life and Thought 1059-c. 1130,* Cambridge, 1963, p. 72 ss. Sur Anselme voir aussi Adele M. FISKE, *Friends and Friendship in the Monastic Tradition,* Cidoc Cuaderno 51, Cuernavaca, Mexico, 1970, section 15, pp. 1-32 ; BOSWELL, pp. 218-220 ; B. P. MCGUIRE, « Love, Friendship and Sex in the Eleventh Century: The Experience of Anselm », *Studia Theologica,* 28, 1974, pp. 111-152 ; et son *Friendship and Community,* pp. 210-221.

19. Lucien FEBVRE, « La sensibilité et l'histoire : comment reconstituer la vie affective d'autrefois ? » *Annales,* 1941, pp. 5-20.

20. Michel FOUCAULT, *Histoire de la sexualité,* vol. 1, Paris, 1976.

21. Pour une analyse fine du problème de l'honneur comme force intérieure et démonstration publique, voir Julian PITT-RIVERS, « Honour and Social Status », dans *Honour and Shame: The Values of Mediterranean Society,* J. G. PERISTIANY éd., Chicago, 1966, pp. 19-77, en particulier p. 21 ss. Pour une théorie générale de l'amour reposant sur la distinction entre privé et public, voir Niklas LUHMANN, *Liebe als Passion: Zur Codierung von Intimität,* Francfort, 1982. La conception de LUHMANN inverse la relation du public au privé telle qu'elle est présentée ici. Selon lui la sémantique de l'amour, son système de communication au niveau du privé et du personnel, est une habitude acquise, une réponse à un codage qui se fait au cours de l'évolution des systèmes culturels et sociaux au niveau du public.

22. Sur le charisme royal et le pouvoir charismatique voir les études désormais classiques de Max WEBER, *Max Weber on Charisma and Institution Building: Selected Papers,* S. N. EISENSTADT éd., Chicago, 1968 ; Marc BLOCH, *Les rois thaumaturges: étude sur le caractère surnaturel attribué à la puissance royale en France et en Angleterre,* nouv. éd., Paris, 1983 ; Ernst KANTOROWICZ, *Les deux corps du roi: essai sur la théologie politique au Moyen Age,* Paris, 1989 ; Norbert ELIAS, *La société de cour,* Paris, 1974 ; Clifford GEERTZ, « Centers, Kings and Charisma : Reflections on the Symbols of Power », dans son *Local Knowledge: Further Essays in Interpretative Anthropology,* New York, 1983, pp. 121-146 (éd. frse, *Savoir local, savoir global,* Paris, 1986).

23. Cf. les vers de Richard FANSHAME sur Charles Ier, « To his Highness... in the West... 1646 », dans *Shorter Poems and Translations,* W. BAWCUTT éd., Liverpool, 1964, p. 71 : « ... le peuple fixe les yeux sur / Le Roi, n'admire, n'aime, n'honore que lui. / En lui, comme en un miroir, leurs manières contemplent / Et forment, et copient ce qu'ils le voient faire / Ce que le canon meurtrier ne peut imposer, / Ni les escadrons d'acier empanachés, ni les chevaux étincelants, / L'Amour le peut... » cité et analysé dans R. Malcolm SMUTS, *Court Culture and the Origins of a Royalist Tradition in Early Stuart England,* Philadelphie, 1987, p. 245. Si ces vers ne font pas intentionnellement écho à l'hommage que Lady Percy rend à Hotspur mort (*Henry IV,* II, III, 21 ss) la comparaison révèle un sentiment partagé de la force métaphorique du charisme humain dans l'Angleterre des Tudors et des Stuarts. Cf. Thomas ELYOT, *The Book of the Governor,* II, II.

24. *Vita Geraldi,* I, 30, *PL,* 133 : 660A : « ... il était aimé de tous parce qu'il les aimait tous ». *Ibid.,* I, 25, 657B : « ... les citoyens et les clercs de ses terres... l'aimaient avec l'affection due à un père ».

25. Cf. Nicholas PERELLA, *The Kiss Sacred and Profane: An Interpretative History of Kiss Symbolism and related Religio-Erotic Themes,* Berkeley, 1969.

26. Voir Carl SCHMIDT, *Jus primae noctis: Eine geschichtliche Untersuchung,* Fribourg, 1881.

27. Les circonstances du *comitatus* dans la société germanique par exemple. Sur l'époque carolingienne voir R. SCHNEIDER, *Brüdergemeine und Schwurfreudschaft: Der Auflösungsprozess des Karlingerreiches im Spiegel der caritas-Terminologie in den Verträgen der Karlingischen Teilkönige des 9. Jahrhunderts, Historiche Studien,* 388, Lübeck-Hambourg, 1964; W. FRITZE, « Die Fränkische Schwurfreundschaft der Merowingerzeit : Ihr Wesen und ihre politische Funktion », *Zeitschrift für Rechtsgeschichte,* Germ. Abt. 71, 1954, pp. 74-125.

28. A. W. PRICE, *Love and Friendship in Plato and Aristotle,* Oxford, 1989 ; Jean-Claude FRAISSE, *Philia: la notion d'amitié dans la philosophie antique. Essai sur un problème perdu et retrouvé,* Paris, 1984.

29. Michel FOUCAULT, *Histoire de la sexualité,* vol. 2 : *L'usage des plaisirs,* Paris, 1984.

30. Werner JAEGER, *Paideia : The Ideals of Greek Culture,* vol. 1 : *Archaic Greece, the Mind of Athen* (trad. Gilbert Highet), New York, 1965, p. 194 ss.

31. *Symposium* 178.

32. ARISTOTE, *Ethique à Nicomaque,* IX, I, 1155a. Cf. CICERON, *De amicitia,* XIV, 50 et XXI, 79.

33. *De amicitia,* XIV, 52 ; CICÉRON, *De la vieillesse, De l'amitié, Des devoirs,* trad. par Ch. APPUHN, Paris, Garnier-Flammarion, 1967, p. 82.

34. Voir R. A. BRUNT, « "Amicitia" in the Late Roman Republic », *Proceedings of the Cambridge Philological Society,* n. s. 11 (o. s. 191), 1965, pp. 1-20.

35. Ce développement est le sujet même de l'ouvrage de M. FOUCAULT, *Histoire de la sexualité,* vol. 3 : *Le souci de soi,* Paris, 1984.

36. Cf. l'analyse que fait BOSWELL de Saint Augustin et d'Ailred de Rievaulx dans *Christianity,* pp. 134-135 et 222 ss. Boswell n'aborde pas les problèmes que pose à son interprétation la répugnance que les deux hommes ressentaient pour leurs penchants charnels. Ce sont des questions difficiles à résoudre en termes de tolérance ou même d'indifférence à l'égard de l'homosexualité mais faciles en termes de tension entre amitié avilissante et amitié exaltante.

37. Cf. Jonathan POWIS, *Aristocracy,* Oxford, 1984, en particulier p. 6 ss ; ELIAS, *La société de cour, op. cit.*

38. Voir Kevin SHARPE, *Criticism and Compliment: The Politics of Literature in the England of Charles Ier*, Cambridge, 1987, p. 23 ss, sur le culte de l'amour platonique à la cour en Italie et en Angleterre.

39. McGUIRE dresse une vaste bibliographie sur le sujet dans *Friendship and Community.* Signalons pour leur intérêt particulier, Paul CONNER, *Friendships between Consecrated Men and Women and the Growth of Charity,* thèse, Rome, 1972; Adèle M. FISK, *Friends and Friendship* (n. 17 ci-dessus) ; Jean LECLERCQ, « L'amitié dans les lettres au Moyen Age », *Revue du Moyen Age latin* 1, 1945, pp. 391-410, ID., *Monks and Love in Twelfth Century France,* Oxford, 1979.

40. McGUIRE, dans *Friendship and Community,* analyse les sources majeures de l'amitié monastique sans chercher à localiser ses origines en tant que pratique sociale. Mais il est clair d'après son étude qu'il s'agit d'un emprunt à la société séculière. Il n'existait pas de tradition d'amitié monastique avant la fin du XIe siècle et cette tradition s'enracine dans le *De amicitia* de CICERON.

41. Cf. McGUIRE, p. 3 ss et *passim.* P. 17 « ... comme très souvent dans la littérature monastique, les amis appartiennent au monde et il faut les abandonner lorsqu'on devient moine ».

42. Les deux traités majeurs sur l'amitié de type spirituel, le *De spirituali amicitia* d'AILRED et le *De amicitia Christiana* de PIERRE DE BLOIS sont des réponses au *De amicitia* de CICERON. Dans le roman aussi l'amitié chrétienne se définit comme transcendance de l'amitié mondaine et non comme quelque chose d'indépendant des traditions séculières. Voir en particulier Hartmut FREYTAG, « Höfische Freundschaft und geistliche *amicitia* im Prosa-Lancelot », *Wolfram-Studien,* 9, 1986, pp. 195-212. Ainsi que Xenja von ERTZDORFF, « Höfische Freundschaft », *Der Deutschunterricht,* 14, 1962, pp. 35-51.

43. *Epist.,* 69, SCHMITT éd., 3 : 189. Cf. McGUIRE, *Friendship,* p. 217 ss.

VIII

L'AMOUR DES ROIS

44. P. S. ALLEN et H. M. JONES suggèrent un parallèle entre le culte de l'amitié virile à la cour des Carolingiens et l'amour courtois au XIIe siècle, *The Romanesque Lyric Chapel Hill*, 1928, p. 148 : « Les Francs accordaient autant de valeur que Socrate aux liens entre amis... à une amitié suffisamment intense pour mériter le nom d'amour... c'est un analogue très proche de la dévotion chevaleresque à l'égard des femmes ». Cette observation conserve sa justesse tant que nous considérons cet amour comme une pratique sociale supra-personnelle.

45. On pourrait à partir de trois prémisses concevoir une approche nouvelle de l'amour courtois : il se fonde sur l'expérience publique et non privée ; en Occident ses antécédents doivent être recherchés dans l'amour et l'amitié entre hommes et non entre hommes et femmes ; ses idéaux ne sont pas une forme de tromperie, une structure rhétorique ironique se réfutant elle-même, ou une fiction masquant une « réalité » totalement antagoniste, mais un système opérationnel de règles et de valeurs qui, d'une part régit le comportement et d'autre part sert les intérêts de ceux qui le respectent et le défendent. La méthodologie de cette approche trouve ses bases chez ELIAS, *La société de cour* (prémisse 3) et FOUCAULT, *Histoire de la sexualité* (prémisses 1 et 2). Foucault n'a pas écrit une histoire des pratiques sexuelles mais une histoire des interdits qui leur étaient imposés, de la discipline morale à laquelle le désir est soumis et de l'empire de la maîtrise de soi sur le besoin de plaisir. L'originalité de son ouvrage réside dans la résistance qu'il oppose à un consensus universitaire puissant et à un consensus populaire plus puissant encore qui ne reconnaît aucun sens à un amour dont l'objet ultime ne serait pas la satisfaction du plaisir et il se défie de toute autre motivation.
Le thème des interdits sexuels et de l'abstinence est dans l'air du temps. Cf. Peter R. L. BROWN, *The Body and Society: Men, Women and Sexual Renunciation in Early Christianity,* New York, 1988. Bernd THUM, *Aufbruch und Verweigerung: Literatur und Geschichte am Oberrhein im hohen Mittelalter: Aspekte eines geschichtlichen Kulturraums,* Waldkirch, 1980. L'article de Carolyn BYNUM « The Body of Christ in the Later Middle Ages : A Reply to Leo Steinberg », *Renaissance Quaterly,* 39, 1986, pp. 399-439, illustre bien la nécessité de corriger les interprétations de caractère non historique inspirées par une réflexion critique centrée sur le sexuel. Notre étude a pour origine une polémique fondée sur des prises de position semblables à celles qui opposent Steinberg et Bynum : « Mark and Tristan : The Love of Medieval Kings and their Courts », dans *In höhem prise: A Festschrift in Honor of Ernst S. Dick,* Winder MCCONNELL éd., Göppingen, Göppinger Arbeiten zur Germanistik, 480, 1989, pp. 183-197.

46. Le motif développé chez Andreas CAPELLANUS et dans la poésie de l'amour courtois, « l'amour élève la valeur de soi à la fois intérieurement et par rapport au monde », témoigne de cette fonction. Stephen KAPLOWITT dans son étude consacrée à ce motif littéraire, *The Ennobling Power of Love in the Medieval German Lyric,* Chapel Hill, NC, 1986, soutient, en contradiction avec le vaste corpus de documents présentés, que la prépondérance de la poésie amoureuse n'ayant pas de rapport avec le thème en démontre l'insignifiance. Mais la poésie n'a pas besoin de se référer constamment à sa fonction sociale propre pour en avoir une. Castiglione est un bon informateur pour la Renaissance italienne. Il distingue deux sortes de relations amoureuses, l'une motivée par la passion, l'autre par le prestige et le statut que l'on confère et que l'on reçoit (le courtisan use de paroles et de manières raffinées pour gagner la faveur des femmes) « ... non seulement lorsqu'il est mû par la passion, mais souvent aussi pour honorer la dame avec laquelle il s'entretient, car il pense que lui montrer qu'il l'aime prouve qu'elle est digne de cet amour et que sa beauté et ses mérites sont tels qu'ils obligent tous les hommes à la servir ». *The Book of the Courtier,* II, 53, trad. Charles Singleton, New York, 1959.

47. Norbert ELIAS, *La société de cour, op. cit.*

48. Cf. Joachim BUMKE, *Höfische Kultur,* Munich, 1986, p. 504, résume les résultats de toute une tradition de recherches universitaires : « Nous avons moins de certitudes aujourd'hui sur ce qu'est l'amour courtois qu'il y a une centaine d'années ». Pour un état des recherches universitaires voir Roger BOASSE, *The Origin and Meaning of Courtly Love: A Critical Study of European Scholarship,* Manchester-Totowa, N. J., 1977 ; Ursula LIEBERTZ-GRUN, *Zur Soziologie des « amour courtois »: Umrisse der Forschung,* Heidelberg, Beihefte zur Zeitschrift Euphorion 10, 1977. Plus récemment, avec une bibliographie et un état des recherches, Rüdiger SCHNELL, *Causa Amoris: Liebeskonzeption und Liebesdarstellung in der mittelalterlichen Literatur,* Berne-Munich, 1985 ; Ursula PETERS, « Höfische Liebe : Ein Forschungsproblem der Mentalitätsgeschichte », dans *Liebe in der deutschen Literatur des Mittelalters,* Jeffrey ASHCFOFT éd. et alii, Tübingen, 1987, pp. 1-13.

49. *Recueil des historiens des Gaules et de la France,* Léopold DELISLE éd., Paris, 1878, 16, p. 23.

50. La lettre et ses circonstances historiques sont discutées dans Ursula PETERS, « Höfische Liebe », pp. 11-13. Voir en particulier l'article récent de PETERS et de Rolf KÖHN, « Höfisches Liebeswerben oder politisches Heiratsangebot ? : Zum Brief der Konstanze von Bretagne an Ludwig VII von Frankreich », *Beiträge zur Geschichte der deutschen Sprache und Literatur,* 111, 1989, pp. 179-195. Peters et Köhn considèrent que cette lettre a été envoyée à l'insu du duc, de manière clandestine, parce que sa rédactrice ressentait un désir personnel pour le roi. Cela me semble improbable. Elle dit qu'elle se rendra à Saint-Denis lorsque son frère sera revenu d'Angleterre, détail superflu si elle n'établit aucun lien entre ses voyages et ceux de son frère, et s'il lui importe peu que le roi connaisse les activités de celui-ci. Si la lettre était aussi politique, en fait aussi subversive que Peters et Köhn le soutiennent, l'allusion à son frère et à ses liens avec l'Angleterre irait à l'encontre de son but prétendûment amoureux. Mais ces références ont dû paraître à Constance, ou plus probablement à sa famille, aller dans le sens de l'affaire en cours.

51. Pour une analyse des mariages de Louis VII, voir Georges DUBY, *Le chevalier, la femme et le prêtre. Le mariage dans la France médiévale,* Paris, 1981, p. 201 ss.

52. La phrase « j'irai à Saint-Denis pour prier et user/jouir de votre présence » est moins anodine en latin : «... *itura sum ad Sanctum-Dionysium orationum causa, et ut vestra praesentia uti valeam».* L'expression « user de votre présence » a des connotations érotiques et, juxtaposée à *« orationum causa »,* elle prend un tour presque frivole.

53. Les jeunes hommes et les jeunes femmes « d'extraction noble » qui se retirent à la campagne dans le *Décaméron* de BOCCACE adoptent une attitude qui était largement admirée : « Malgré de joyeux récits, de nature, peut-être, à éveiller les désirs de la chair, malgré nos airs de musique et nos chansons — tous motifs qui pourraient incliner à moins de pudeur les âmes chancelantes —, je n'ai observé ni chez vous ni chez nous le moindre geste, la moindre parole, le moindre fait qui méritât le blâme. Une honnêteté qui ne se dément pas, une concorde soutenue, une intimité fraternelle de tous les instants, tel est le tableau que j'ai eu, voilà ce que j'ai cru comprendre. Rien assurément n'est moins cher pour votre honneur et le mien ». (BOCCACE *Le Décaméron,* trad. Jean Bourciez, Paris, Classiques Garnier, 1988, Dixième Journée, p. 713). Le rôle de Sir Gawain dans le roman arthurien était de maintenir ce fragile équilibre. Ses aventures le montrent au bord de la catastrophe dans ses relations amoureuses et c'est son habileté dans les situations périlleuses qui le sauve. Wolfram von ESCHENBACH a défini ce rôle de façon paradigmatique « er ist doch âne schande/liget er in minnen bande » (« il est sans déshonneur/bien qu'enchaîné par les liens de l'amour »). (Wolfram von ESCHENBACH, *Parzival,* Albert LEITZMANN éd., Tübingen, 1963, 2, p. 154, 532, 24 f.).

54. Un commentaire indirect de Mondonus Belvaleti dans son essai sur l'Ordre (1463), texte antérieur à Polydore Vergil, constitue un document d'un grand intérêt. BELVALETI écrit : « De nombreuses personnes affirment que cet ordre a pour origine le sexe féminin » (*Tractatus ordinis serenissimi domini regis Anglie vulgariter dicti la Gerretiere,* Cologne, 1631, p. 7. Cité dans George F. BELTZ, *Memorials of the Most Noble Order of the Garter,* Londres, 1841 ; réed., New York, 1973, p. XLII, n. 2). La discrétion de l'auteur est si manifeste qu'elle constitue une preuve en elle-même. Elle semblerait confirmer la remarque de Polydore Vergil selon laquelle les historiens de la Jarretière ont gardé le silence sur ses origines par crainte d'aborder des questions si sensibles qu'elles relèvent de l'ordre du crime de lèse-majesté.

55. Beltz fut le premier à suggérer cela, mais il prit soin de montrer qu'il ne s'agissait que d'une conjecture (*Memorials,* p. XLVII). Cf. Juliet VALE, *Edward III and Chivalry : Chivalric Society and its Context 1270-1350,* Woodbridge, 1982, p. 76 ss ; Richard BARBER, *Edward, Prince of Wales and Aquitaine : A Biography of the Black Prince,* Londres, 1978, p. 80 ss ; Maurice KEEN, *Chivalry,* New York-Londres, 1984, p. 194. Le rejet de la thèse de Margaret GALWAY soutenant qu'une liaison entre Edouard et Jeanne de Kent serait à l'origine de l'Ordre est unanime (« Joan of Kent and the Order of the Garter », *University of Birmingham Historical Journal,* 1, 1947, pp. 13-50 encore que James L. GILLESPIE, « Ladies of the Fraternity of Saint George and of the Society of the Garter », *Albion,* 17, 1985, p. 260 ss, ait récemment renouvelé l'hypothèse selon laquelle le témoignage contemporain de Jean le Bel pourrait impliquer un lien entre Jeanne et la création de l'Ordre. Pour une discussion approfondie et nuancée voir D'Arcy BOULTON, *The Knights of the Crown: The Monarchical Orders of Knighthood in Later Medieval Europe, 1325-1530,* Woodbridge, Suffolk, 1987, en particulier pp. 152-161.

56. Ce rapprochement fut mis en évidence par Israel GOLLANCZ, *Pearl: An English Poem of the Fourteenth Century,* Londres, 1891, p. XLI ss. Voir aussi Oscar KARGILL et Margaret SCHLAUCH, « The *Pearl* and its Jeweler », PMLA, 43, 1928, pp. 118-123, et une série d'études de Henri L. SAVAGE, résumées dans *The Gawain-Poet: Studies in his Personality and Background,* Chapel Hill, NC, 1956 ; La position adoptée par Barber et Vale n'est pas compatible avec l'existence possible d'un lien entre *Sir Gawain* et l'Ordre. Comme ce lien est généralement admis, il faut à Barber et à Vale soit s'en accommoder soit modifier leur position. BOULTON établit un rapprochement entre la ceinture du roman et l'Ordre de la Jarretière, *Knights of the Crown,* p. 158 mais ne signale pas la récurrence de la devise et du déshonneur symbolisé par la ceinture verte, ce qui impliquerait de reconnaître à la jarretière de l'Ordre la même signification.

57. *Polydori Vergilii Urbinatis Anglicae Historiae Libri XXVI,* Bâle, 1534. Vergil était plus un détracteur qu'un créateur de mythes. Il se méfiait de la légende et se considérait comme un sceptique lucide, irrespectueux du silence pieux des premiers historiens, lorsqu'il révélait au grand jour l'histoire des origines de l'Ordre. Voir l'étude de Denis HAY, *Polydore Vergil: Renaissance Historian and Man of Letters,* Oxford, 1952, p. 109 ss.

58. *Anglica Historia,* p. 373, « ... *garter lingua Anglica, id ligaculum significet, quo mulieres tibiarum tegmenta sibi ligant* ».

59. Sur les thèses pour ou contre l'homosexualité de Richard, voir BOSWELL, *Christianity,* p. 231 ss ; James BRUNDAGE, *Richard Lion Heart,* New York, 1974, p. 88 ss, p. 287 ss.

IX

Charismatic Body — Charismatic Text

Hildebert of Lavardin visited Rome in the last years of the eleventh century. Probably on his return to the north in 1100 he wrote an elegiac praise of the city's ancient ruins, *Par tibi Roma nihil*. At the poem's core is an admiration for the art of the ancient Romans so exuberant that it clouds the bishop's Christian loyalties. In one of the most impressive passages of medieval poetry, Hildebert admires the crumbling statues of the ancient gods; he imagines the gods themselves in their full glory appearing bodily before their statues and comparing the original—i.e., themselves—with the copy:

> cura hominum potuit tantam componere Romam,
> quantam non potuit solvere cura deum.[1]
> hic superum formas superi mirantur et ipsi,
> et cupiunt fictis vultibus esse pares.
> non potuit Natura deos hoc ore creare,
> quo miranda deum signa creavit homo.
> vultus adest his numinibus,[2] potiusque coluntur
> artificum studio quam deitate sua.[3]

---

[1] *Cura hominum ... cura deum* is a play on words that cannot be reproduced in English. Implied in the latter is the "worship" of the gods, i.e., a benighted pagan faith. In other words, human art was above religious matters. The worship of false gods could not destroy the human art created to honor them.

[2] See the exchange on this line between Otto Zwierlein, "Par tibi Roma, nihil," *Mittellateinisches Jahrbuch* 11 (1976): 92–94, and Peter von Moos, "Par tibi, Roma, nihil: Eine Antwort," *Mittellateinisches Jahrbuch* 14 (1979): 119–26. My translation follows von Moos's reading.

[3] Hildebertus, *Carmina minora* 36.29–36, ed. A. Brian Scott (Leipzig: Teubner,

IX

118   *Charismatic Body—Charismatic Text*

> The art of men once made a Rome so great
> That the art of the gods could not destroy it.
> Divinities themselves look awe-struck on divinities sculpted,
> And wish themselves the equals of those sembled forms.
> Nature could not make gods as fair of face
> As man created the wondrous images of gods.
> Carved likenesses improve these deities;
> They merit worship more for the sculptor's art than their own divinity.[4]

He invests the gods with aesthetic judgment and constructs a contest of beauty and skill between sublime art and sublime beings. That Nature creates gods—and not vice versa—is a bold idea.[5] Also bold is the outcome: Nature loses the contest to the human artist. The statues—crumbling though they are—are superior to the living gods, as their artist is superior to the "sculptor" of the gods, Nature. The Roman sculptor's art does not just imitate and represent the gods; it corrects their maker. It shows Nature possibilities beyond her own imagination. As if the Platonic process of imprinting ideas on matter were turned upside down, the copy teaches its archetype what beauty is.

It is enough to make iconoclasts of the gods. Here is the very reason gods forbid graven images: the images and not that which they represent become the object of worship ("potiusque coluntur / artificum studio quam deitate sua"). They suffer an envious disquiet at this usurpation of charisma, since they wish themselves, in momentary forgetfulness of their stature and dignity, the equals of their fictions. They gawk at their magnificent copies, which ignore their models and gaze past them in Olympian indifference. If we could also see the bested gods collect their wits and overcome their surprise, we could imagine them challenging the artist: "How dare you depict us more beautiful than we

---

1969), 22–24. For commentaries, see Wolfram von den Steinen, "Humanismus um 1100," in his *Menschen im Mittelalter: Gesammelte Forschungen, Betrachtungen, Bilder,* ed. Peter von Moos (Berne and Munich: Francke, 1967), 196–214, especially 201–3, and also Peter von Moos, *Hildebert von Lavardin, 1056–1133: Humanitas an der Schwelle des höfischen Zeitalters,* Pariser Historische Studien 3 (Stuttgart: Hiersemann, 1965), 240–45, 251–58.

[4] All translations are my own, except as noted.

[5] For instance, in two grand allegorical poems of creation, Bernard Silvestris's *Cosmographia* and Alan of Lille's *Anticlaudianus,* the secondary spirits and minor gods precede nature, at least are not created by her. Nature's work is man.

are!" To which the Roman sculptor would reply, "Learn through me to be more god-like."

This passage from Hildebert's poem is a myth of representation, comparable to the stories of Narcissus or Pygmalion. In all three the created or reflected image produces a kind of enchantment in the maker or model. But in the two ancient myths, the source of astonishment is the interchangeability of life and art. Narcissus sees an image of himself indistinguishable from the living being it reflects; Pygmalion makes a statue so close to life that his desire is enough to overcome the narrow distance between art and life. Both are myths of mimetic representation. Against this, the hyper-mimesis of the medieval "myth" posits the victory of representation over nature. It is about overcoming and going beyond mimesis. Hildebert's "myth" presupposes an art that we can call "charismatic," because it competes with the charismatic beings par excellence, the gods, and surpasses them. It is not enough within this mode of representation for art just to be like "life," merely to imitate nature. It wants to be grander and more beautiful than nature, as the statues are more beautiful than the gods they are modelled on.

* * *

Hildebert's "myth" of representation has a general aesthetic aspect, which this essay touches on, but does not take as its focus. My subject is the interaction of personal and textual[6] charisma as a historical dynamic at work in the transition from the eleventh to the twelfth century. Hildebert's Rome poem dramatizes aesthetic change as cultural change. The superseded gods—this is the argument—stand for the passing age, the charismatic statues for the coming one; the gods stand for a declining mode of representation, the statues for an ascending one. The date "circa 1100" is a significant perch from which the poem looks in two directions in time and intellectual history and reflects on the cultural transformation in progress.

The period is in many ways the watershed between the ancient and the modern world. Its transitional nature has been the focus of critical attention recently. Charles Radding has used Piaget's model of the growth of consciousness to understand a whole variety of phenomena, such as the abolition of the ordeal, in the twelfth century.[7] The current

---

[6] Here and throughout I use "text" to mean any form of representation. This is a convenience, not a deconstructionist extension of textuality to any form of experience.

[7] Charles M. Radding, *A World Made by Men: Cognition and Society, 400–1200* (Chapel Hill: University of North Carolina Press, 1985).

discussion of the transition in media has made use of the categories of oral culture and literate culture.[8] I want to propose a reading of the passage from Hildebert's Rome poem based on the fundamental opposition of bodies and texts, a relationship that is central for culture generally, not only for medieval culture. Hildebert's lines offer a paradigmatic metaphor for a transitional moment in the relations of bodies and texts.

Paul Zumthor has urged the rediscovery of the voice in literary texts.[9] Courtly literature, he suggests, contains a voice that has fallen silent and implies a performance that preceded textualizing, a performance that becomes sublimated in the text. But voice and performance are aspects of a greater act of sublimation on which art in a certain phase rests. At a level hardly accessible to critical excavation and altogether blocked by post-structuralist aesthetics, the foundation of the charismatic text is the charismatic body.

The goal of this essay is to locate Hildebert's image along the trajectory of the body-text dynamic in its development in the eleventh and twelfth centuries.

The shift from bodies to texts in that age[10] is close to the transformation of consciousness that Walter Benjamin observed in "The Work of Art in the Age of Mechanical Reproduction."[11] Benjamin compares the work of art in two phases. Prior to mechanical reproducibility, it is characterized by "authenticity" and "aura." The mode of reception—even of wholly secularized art—is "the cult." But given mechanical reproduction, it experiences "the decay" and the "withering of its aura."

---

[8] See, for instance, Brian Stock, *The Implications of Literacy: Written Language and Models of Interpretation in the Eleventh and Twelfth Centuries* (Princeton: Princeton University Press, 1983). Also of interest is Ivan Illich, *In the Vineyard of the Text: A Commentary to Hugh's Didascalicon* (Chicago: University of Chicago Press, 1993).

[9] See, for instance, Zumthor, *Oral Poetry: An Introduction*, trans. Kathryn Murphy-Judy (Minneapolis: University of Minnesota Press, 1990); "Körper und Performanz," *Materialitaet der Kommunikation*, ed. Hans-Ulrich Gumbrecht et al. (Frankfurt am Main: Suhrkamp, 1988), 703–13; "The Text and the Voice," *NLH* 16 (1984/85): 67–92.

[10] These ideas are developed in more detail in my book, *The Envy of Angels: Cathedral Schools and European Social Ideals, 950–1200* (Philadelphia: University of Pennsylvania Press, 1994), introduction.

[11] Walter Benjamin, "The Work of Art in the Age of Mechanical Reproduction," *Illuminations*, tr. Harry Zohn, ed. Hannah Arendt (New York: Schocken, 1969), 217–51.

The reproducible work of art can only emerge and gain legitimacy at the cost of "a tremendous shattering of tradition," which undermines the authority and authenticity of art.

Benjamin's scheme links aesthetic change to historical change, and its terms apply well to the transition underway in the twelfth century. This transition plays out a contest between two stages of culture which is not restricted to a particular historical setting, but recurs at various points in Western history: in fifth- and fourth-century Athens, in Rome from the Republic to the Empire,[12] in the European Middle Ages from the eleventh to the twelfth centuries, and again from the late Middle Ages to the Renaissance. We can call the two stages "charismatic" and "intellectual." Their relationships are basically agonal, but also dynamic and productive.

Charismatic cultures are familiar to us almost exclusively as heroic, warrior cultures, tribal societies with a powerful sense of clan identity and aristocratic honor, and an authoritarian hierarchic structure, at the top of which is a charismatic leader.[13] But the warrior aspect of charismatic culture is one of many. "Heroism" is a modality which takes in other aspects of life: intellectual, sexual, romantic, poetic and artistic. In a charismatic culture, the scholar, intellectual and artist—and not just the warrior—operate in a heroic mode. This is not to turn poets, monks and schoolmasters into titans. "Heroic" means action—and not reflection; presence—and not representation; the glorifying of the lived moment, the *kairos*, and of the elegant human response to it—not art. The glorifying of representation is the realm of intellectual, textualizing culture, a restorative phase when real and present charisma is passing out of existence, and artists and poets are struggling to rescue and preserve it in texts, pictures and statues, as the disciples of Socrates and Christ tried to hold firm the physical and spiritual presence of the dead master. Prior to the stage where representation becomes a cult, there is a mode of art, poetry, learning, whose effect is tied to the charisma of personal presence, not to the allure of the artifact. We fetishize texts and artifacts, and we are so suspicious of personal charisma that it takes

---

[12] A good contemporary formulation of the opposition of charismatic to intellectual is Cicero's scheme of the development of Roman philosophy in *Tusculan Disputations* 4.2.3.

[13] See *Max Weber on Charisma and Institution Building: Selected Papers*, ed. S. N. Eisenstadt (Chicago: University of Chicago Press, 1968), and Clifford Geertz, "Centers, Kings and Charisma," in his *Local Knowledge: Further Essays in Interpretive Anthropology* (New York: Basic Books, 1983), 121–46.

careful excavation to recover the mentality of an age that derived its values from the charismatic presence.

The irreplaceable center of charismatic culture is the human body, and the memorializing text or artifact is a fairly indifferent item. The body and the physical presence are the mediators of cultural values; they have pedagogic, "curricular" force. The controlled body with all its attributes—grace, charm, sensuality, beauty, authority—is the work of art of a charismatic culture.

The school life of the eleventh century is particularly rich in examples.[14] The person and physical presence of the teacher played a role in the culture of the eleventh century cathedral schools that is hard to overestimate. A poem from the school of Würzburg in the early century uses an oddly mystical formula to praise the master for his teaching of poetry: "He beams with the light of many poets."[15] This reverses the normal relationship of teacher to curriculum. The Würzburg master does not illuminate the texts that he reads and explains; *the texts illuminate him*. This poem has a clear conception of a sacral professorship; the master teaches by divine right.[16] The living presence of the teacher is the curriculum.[17] The personal aura is the locus of pedagogy, and the language of the body is its medium.[18] The charismatic teacher ushers the student into the charged field of his personality and transforms him, demiurge-like, into a little copy of himself. Hugh of St. Victor used the image of a seal and wax to describe this relationship: the

---

[14] See Guy Beaujouan, "The Transformation of the Quadrivium," in *Renaissance and Renewal in the Twelfth Century*, ed. Robert Benson and Giles Constable (Cambridge, Mass.: Harvard University Press, 1982), 463–87; Horst Wenzel, *Hören und Sehen, Schrift und Bild: Kultur und Gedächtnis im Mittelalter* (Munich: Beck, 1995).

[15] "Ipse poetarum fulget decus omnigenarum," *Die ältere Wormser Briefsammlung*, ed. Walther Bulst, MGH, Briefe der deutschen Kaiserzeit 3 (Weimar: Böhlau, 1949), 119–27, line 24.

[16] For instance lines 28–30 (ibid.):

> Vim talem mentis dono tenet omnipotentis.
> Doctrine rivus fluit eius pectore vivus,
> Eternum numen sermonum dat sibi flumen.
>
> He retains his power of mind by the gift of the Almighty.
> The living stream of learning flows from his breast.
> The eternal divinity gives him his flow of speech.

[17] See Jaeger, *The Envy of Angels*, 76–83; Wenzel, *Hören und Sehen*, 25–37.

[18] Willigis of Mainz is said to have instructed "lovers of virtue" more by the "language of his conduct" (*lingua morum*) than by his speech. MGH, SS 15.2, 745, lines 31–32.

naster impresses the stamp of his character on the soft wax of the tudent.[19] The school of St. Victor offered a curriculum in "manners"—
)ne of the attractions of that school—in which the learning of virtue
)egan in the disciplining of the body to ideals of elegant gait and gesures, posture and speech.[20]

This is the central conception of an education oriented to the body: t identifies control of the body with control of self; the controlled, dis-:iplined self is defined as a work of art, described with the vocabulary)f aesthetics, conceived as parallel to well-made statues.[21] The cultivaion of external presence is identical with the cultivation of virtue. 3ernard of Clairvaux is a good witness to this cult of the person. His lescription of a beautiful young woman of high nobility, whom he :alls only "the virgin Sophia," mixes the vocabulary of sculpture with he language of moral pedagogy to articulate the ideal of virtue made /isible in the well-governed body:

> O quam compositum reddit omnem puellaris corporis statum, nedum et mentis habitum, disciplina? Cervicem submittit, ponit supercilia, componit vultum, ligat oculos, cachinnos cohibet, moderatur linguam, gulam frenat, iram sedet, format incessum. Istiusmodi circumdata varietate virginitatis, cui gloriae merito non praefertur? Angelicae? Angelus habet virginitatem, sed non carnem, sane felicior quam fortior in hac parte. Optimus et optabilis valde ornatus iste, qui et angelis possit esse invidiosus.

> Oh, how well-composed does discipline render every posture not only of the virginal body, but even more so of the mind! It sets the angle of the head, orders the eyebrows, composes the facial expression, masters the set of the eyes, suppresses laughter, moderates speech, reins in appetite, controls anger, and shapes the way of walking. What splendor can compare with this? The splendor of

---

[19] Hugh of St. Victor, *De institutione novitiorum* 7, PL 176: 932D–33A.

[20] See Jean-Claude Schmitt, *La raison des gestes dans l'occident médiéval* (Paris: Gallimard, 1990); Jaeger, *Envy of Angels*, 244–68.

[21] Hugh of St. Victor makes the equation explicit:

> We long to be perfectly carved and sculpted in the image of good men, and when excellent and sublime qualities ... stand out in them, which arouse astonishment and admiration in men's minds, then they shine forth in them like the beauty in exquisite statues, and we strive to recreate these qualities in ourselves.

De institutione novitiorum 8, PL 176: 933B–C.

angels? An angel has virginity, but no body. He has happiness, certainly, but not strength. Best and most desirable is that distinction which angels themselves might envy.[22]

This is not primarily praise of virginity, something which any angel can have. Sophia has something they can never have: a body. That is what the angels envy, and not her virtue. She possesses in her body the theater and staging ground of self-control, and her staging of virtue gives her a heroism (strength) which the angels in their wan eternal "happiness" can never attain. Virtue disembodied cannot exercise the demiurgic function of shaping others in its image and likeness.[23] The angels envious of the charismatic body (the living virgin Sophia) are like the gods envious of charismatic art (their statues in Hildebert's Rome poem); the parallel shows how the image of astonished supernatural beings works as a device to highlight the age's ethical/aesthetic values.

These are some reflections on a charismatic culture. It is oriented to the body to the extent that the physical presence becomes the medium for aesthetic and educational ideals. In eleventh-century secular culture, the body was the work of art of the inner world, its text, statue, and poem; it was meant to be read, interpreted, imitated.

Whatever area of twelfth-century culture we compare with its counterpart in the eleventh, we see a move in orientation from "real presence" to symbolic. This is most evident in the area from which I have borrowed the terms: the Eucharist controversy.[24] The belief in the real

---

[22] Bernard of Clairvaux, epistula 113, *Sancti Bernardi Opera*, ed. Jean Leclercq et al. (Rome: Editiones Cistercienses, 1957), 7: 290.

[23] Bernard of Clairvaux himself evidently beamed charismatic force. Hildebert of Lavardin addressed him in the salutation of a letter as "the one in the church with the ability to educate others to virtue, in word as in example" ("... didicimus, te in Eccclesia eum esse, qui ad eruditionem virtutis et exemplo sufficias et verbo"; Hildebert, epistula 18, PL 171: 294C). Wibald of Stablo gave a dithyrambic praise of Bernard: "The mere sight of him educates you; the mere sound of his voice refines you; merely following him perfects you" ("Quem si aspicias, doceris; si audias, instrueris; si sequare, perficeris"; *Wibaldi epistolae*, epistula 167, Bibliotheca rerum Germanicarum, vol. 1: Monumenta Corbeiensia, ed. Philippe Jaffé [Berlin, 1864; rpt. Aalen, Scientia 1964], 286).

[24] See Radding, *A World Made by Men*, 165–72; J. de Montclos, *Lanfranc et Bérengar: La controverse eucharistique du XIe siècle* (Louvain: Spicilegium Sacrum Lovaniense,

presence of Christ's body and blood in the sacrament yields to the conception of bread and wine as *symbols* of body and blood. The shift registers also in the dispute about universals: the move from realism to nominalism abolishes universal archetypes, or places them in a realm inaccessible to human reason, and it changes language from God-given, thing-like signifiers into a man-made symbolic code. In secular rule, the change from itinerant kingship (real presence of the king) to administrative kingship (the king "represented" through documents, contracts, bailiffs, and so on) is part of the same transformation of consciousness.[25] Procedures for electing bishops and abbots change from a system based on charismatic selection (virtue, personal authority, miracle) to one based on bureaucratic selection (canonical procedure formulated in texts and documents).[26]

We can add to these various oppositions the opposing pair, body and text, and the shift from a charismatic to an intellectual culture. The direction of change in each case is towards textualizing. From the eleventh to the thirteenth century, charisma passes, as in a massive transfusion, from the body and the real presence to the text and the symbolic presence.

The twelfth century learned to transpose body into text—without knowing initially that it was setting into motion a process that could not be reversed. A visible symptom of this process is the gradual fading

---

1971); R. W. Southern, "Lanfranc and Berengar," in *Studies in Medieval History Presented to Frederick Maurice Powicke*, ed. R. W. Hunt et al. (Oxford: Oxford University Press, 1948), 27–48; a number of recent studies in *Auctoritas und Ratio: Studien zu Berengar von Tours*, ed. Peter Ganz, Wolfenbütteler Mittelalter-Studien 2 (Wiesbaden: Harrasowitz, 1990).

[25] Warren C. Hollister and John Baldwin, "The Rise of Administrative Kingship: Henry I and Philip Augustus," *AHR* 83 (1978): 867–905. Recent work has revised the conventional progressive, evolutionary view of the period: R. I. Moore, *The Formation of a Persecuting Society: Power and Deviance in Western Europe, 950–1250* (Oxford: Blackwell, 1987), and Ute-Renate Blumenthal, *The Investiture Controversy: Church and Monarchy from the Ninth to the Twelfth Century* (Philadelphia: University of Pennsylvania Press, 1991).

[26] See Hayden F. White, "The Gregorian Ideal and Saint Bernard of Clairvaux," *Journal of the History of Ideas* 21 (1960): 321–48, and John Sommerfeldt, "Charismatic and Gregorian Leadership in the Thought of Bernard of Clairvaux," *Bernard of Clairvaux: Studies Presented to Dom Jean Leclercq* (Washington, D.C.: Cistercian Publications, 1973). 73–90. See also Blumenthal, *The Investiture Controversy*.

from the scene of the dominant genres of the eleventh century, the biography and the personal letter, both of which presuppose real presence, and the emergence of a welter of new forms of artistic expression which do not. By the second half of the twelfth century a new form of narrative is popular among the aristocracy, the courtly romance. In charming and flowing narratives, knights are shaped, educated, formed into models of chivalrous conduct, and tested at the hands of charismatic damsels, whose mere presence infuses virtue.[27] The new narrative creates a new fashion of imitating romances among the nobles, expressed in pageantry and ceremony, in fashions of clothing and naming. At the same time a new mode of representing the human body in sculpture is on the rise. It creates supple, clinging garments, gives to the curve and posture of the body a grace and elegance not seen in representation since classical antiquity and to the facial expression a life-like realism and a supernatural serenity and beauty; it reproduces remarkably the very features and virtues that Bernard of Clairvaux admired in the body of the virgin Sophia.

Credit for these trends in literature and art is often given either to a "renaissance" spirit or to the "discovery" of new styles. Both explanations are formed in the spell of a progressive conception of cultural change; they presuppose that nothing, or nothing significant, went before to which the artistic modes respond. The model of charismatic body-charismatic text, however, suggests a different explanation: the emergence of charismatic literature and art occurred in a historical moment in which a rising intellectual culture came to terms with a fading charismatic culture. The heroism of the passing age entered a textual contract with the scribes, clerics, storytellers, sculptors and stonemasons of the scholastic age. Charisma of the body, which had previously defined itself as sculpture-like and imagined gods and angels envying it, now was re-incorporated in courtly literature and Gothic sculpture.

The sublimated presence of body in the art and literature of the twelfth century results from a nostalgic relation to the passing age. Its literature and sculpture are attempts to capture and restore the fading charisma of a "heroic" culture of personal presence. Hildebert's image of the gods shame-faced and embarrassed at seeing their charisma

---

[27] On the parallel of schoolmaster and courtly damsel as administrators of virtue, see Georges Duby, *Love and Marriage in the Middle Ages*, trans. Jane Dunnett (Chicago: University of Chicago Press, 1994), 33.

usurped by statues is a metaphor for this development. What Walter Benjamin referred to as "a tremendous shattering of tradition" is at work, and it occurs in the form of a transference of "aura and authenticity" from human beings to art.

The general aesthetic at work here is a big subject, but it might be worthwhile to articulate briefly the term "textual contract" and the contest between body and text of which this is the resolution.

Bodies need texts. The living human presence has vitality, emotion, sexuality, authority, charisma and fate. But these qualities weaken, play themselves out, fade and die. Of course "it" (if I may generalize the agent of this wish and locate it in the body itself) wants to maintain these desirable but perishable qualities. For this purpose the body seeks textualizing, and it goes to the artist to get it, not awed by art's grandeur—a comparatively modern and unheroic sensibility—but as a down-at-heels prince goes to a money-lender.

This dynamic works smoothly, because the interests of the text coincide with those of the body: texts also need bodies. They have their own form of incompleteness. They have no substance. They are nothing in themselves but words and sounds, weaving and patching, ink and paper, stone and canvas. They are not alive, but also not exactly dead. They are worthless unless they can persuade humans that they are sublime, immortal, permanent. That is the agony of texts: their condition of life is illusion, imitation, artifice. They need the qualities of body, which can never arise naturally from within the work of art. The unique and exclusive originating place of voice, authority, sensuality, is the body. Even if the artist produced, by great rhetorical skill, the semblance of a heroic human being and the whole drama of the heroic existence, it remains a form of cheating. The work of art is a beggar with pretensions to glory. Its existence is based on a long-term lease. It is nothing without life, a state it always longs for,[28] but can never attain.

The textual contract arises from this mutual insufficiency of bodies and texts. Because each has what the other lacks, they enter an agreement. The body says to the text: "Give me permanence, and I may

---

[28] Therefore the persistence of myths and folktales of the statue's awakening to life, e.g., Pygmalion, Shakespeare's *Winter's Tale, Pinocchio, One Touch of Venus.*

have something you want." The text answers the body: "If you give me life and life-likeness, I will make you immortal."

This is the birth of the charismatic work of art from the charismatic presence. The desiccated word- and sign-magic of the text is pumped full of the charisma of the body, and takes on the appearance of life.

The working of the textual contract in Western art is evident by contrast to charismatic cultures which refused to enter such an arrangement:[29] the stiff, hieroglyphic character of Egyptian art; the hieratic, symbolic codes of native American art; the runic-hieroglyphic character of Scandinavian art of the Viking age. The art of heroic cultures shows in its sparseness a refusal to inject life into images, an aristocratic unwillingness to profane the mysteries of the precious flesh by showing them forth, vulgarly publicizing them in substitute signs and symbols. Texts may be important for such cultures, but they, and not the charismatic body, are the beggars and petitioners.[30] This posture has a counterpart in the reluctance of many cultures to make images, or to speak the true name, of their gods. The modern Westerner stands in awe in front of a portrait by Holbein. But viewed by someone outside of a culture bound by the textual contract, life-like, idealizing portraiture may seem out and out dishonorable. A native American chieftain or warrior might well wonder what kind of a man its subject could have been to allow a workman to entrap his charisma in canvas and pigment—the better the art, the greater the subject's act of self-betrayal. The modern Westerner, having no concept of the rejection of representation, imagines that the charismatic culture is aesthetically less advanced than his own, since its art is so unlifelike. And the end-point of this ignorance is the idea that the abstractness and chasteness of non-representational heroic art must, after all, be somehow lifelike and

---

[29] It is also evident in its unravelling in the twentieth century: the loss of representation in art, the "withering of aura" in literature, the return of charismatic forms (cinema, rock concerts, performance art), and in the academic discussions of literature's/language's inability to convey reality. The grand panorama of these developments is formulated by Michel Foucault in his *The Order of Things: An Archaeology of the Human Sciences* (New York: Vintage, 1973).

[30] The tattooing worn in Oceanic societies is an instance, observed and wonderfully described in Melville's *Moby Dick*, ch. 109. The harpooner, Queequeg (a wandering chieftain), has his body covered with tatooings representing "a complete theory of the heavens and earth and a mystical treatise on the art of attaining truth." The mysteries are of course "destined to molder away with the living parchment whereon they were inscribed," but it does not matter. The irreplaceably valuable, sanctified flesh of the chieftain is a far more worthy medium for knowledge than dead animal skin or paper.

mimetic in the eyes of the cultures that produced it. Charismatic cultures never have a cult of the artist. They barely distinguish the poet from the historian or the magician, because art's purpose is either memorializing or incantatory.

Not all cultures enter a textual contract, because the cost of it is high. This cost registers in the development of art compared with the "progress" of culture in the European Middle Ages. Some paradigm texts can mark the stages of this development. They show charismatic presence giving way to representation. The first is a description of Bernard of Clairvaux by his biographer Geoffrey of Clairvaux:

> Through numerous signs and miracles God raised his loyal servant, the abbot, to glory. But the first and greatest miracle was the man himself. Serene of face, modest in his bearing, cautious in speech, pious in action.... In his body there was a certain visible grace and charm [or gift, talent—*gratia*], which was spiritual and not physical. His face beamed with light, in his eyes there shone an angelic purity. His inner beauty was so full that it broke forth in visible external signs.[31]

Charisma of person is intact in this passage and unchallenged by representation. The element of symbolic representation rests in the "signs and miracles" the man performs. They are the text narrating the story of his inner virtue via the medium of his body. But the biographer warns the reader away from overvaluing either physical (*gratia spiritualis, non carnalis*) or performed charisma. He insists on the priority of body over mediating code: the great miracle is the man himself, not any medium of expression or representation, miracles included. That inner core of the human being is what creates his perfection, according to Geoffrey, and it is marvelously infused into his body and inadequately expressed in acts. The biographer sees Bernard, in his body and his person, as the thing itself, proto-spirit and proto-truth, prior to encoding and narrating.

The structure of thought here implies a contest between charisma of person and representation. It is the agonal relationship of body and text which also is implicit in Hildebert's poem. The same biographer regu-

---

[31] Geoffrey of Clairvaux, *Vita prima* 3.1, PL 185: 303C.

larly drew on this logic to praise Bernard. At one point he regrets the inadequacy of his attempts to explain what Bernard was, and refers the reader to Bernard's own writings:

> We have treated in a few words the sacred manner of living of our father, but it emerges much more clearly from his own writings, and in his letters you will recognize the man. His own image is as easy to read out of them as if you saw him in a mirror.[32]

Bernard's writings have this effect not because he represented himself in them, but because his person, voice, and presence have passed naturally over into them, as into a second body, and his writings exist in that state of primary dependence on real presence, not in that restorative mode the biographer himself writes in. Bernard's writings are his second self. Geoffrey shows Bernard musing over his own mission of sanctity in terms that suggest a half-serious, half-playful reflection on the interactions of body and text. Bernard ruminates:

> facta sunt aliquando signa per sanctos homines et perfectos, facta sunt et per fictos. Ego mihi nec perfectionis conscius sum, nec fictionis.
>
> Signs are sometimes made through holy and perfect men and sometimes through fictitious men. I for my part am neither aware of my perfection nor my fiction.[33]

A remarkable formulation. It amounts to saying, "as far as I know, I am not literature," and that disclaimer may owe more to the rhetoric of humility than to his conviction of his non-fictional character. Moving towards "holiness and perfection" he was living in the condition of textuality while in the flesh.

The second text shows physical and textual charisma in balance. It is from Gottfried von Strassburg's *Tristan*, the description of Princess

---

[32] Ibid., 3.8, PL 185: 320. An example of a similar logic with priority given to presence over text, in Herbert of Bosham's biography of Thomas Becket:

> Let us now open the pages of our exemplar [i.e., Becket himself] and continue to read in it. For acts of virtue are certainly read more fruitfully in men themselves than books, just as deeds speak more effectively than words.

Vita Thomae 3.13, *Materials for the History of Thomas Becket, Archbishop of Canterbury*, ed. James Craigie Robertson, Rolls Series 67.3 (London: Longman, 1877), 208.

[33] *Vita prima* 3.7, PL 185: 314D-15A. The word play *perfectos . . . per fictos*, repeats the glide from living men to textual men.

Isolde playing the harp and singing before the court of Dublin. This virtuoso description speaks the language of the agonal relationship between charismatic body and charismatic text. Her playing was a double performance, the poet says. Isolde sang two songs at once, one public and the other private, one audible and the other visible. The public song was the one that all heard, the music of her voice and instrument. The private song was the singer herself, her presence:

> so was der tougenliche sanc
> ir wunderlichiu schoene,
> diu mit ir muotgedoene
> verholne unde tougen
> durch diu venster der ougen
> in vil manec edele herze sleich
> und daz zouber dar in streich,
> daz die gedanke zehant
> vienc unde vahende bant....

her secret song was her wondrous beauty whose spiritual melody stole hidden and unseen through the windows of the eyes into many noble hearts and smoothed on the magic which took thoughts prisoner suddenly....[34]

There is no competition between person and text. Song and singer appear as equivalent conveyors of beauty and inspirers of desire. Body and text are both divided and united by the stark parataxis of the thought: here audible, here visible music; here performed, here embodied melody. The song is represented as something in itself, perhaps separable, at least imaginable separated from the body which produces it. But at the same time the poet makes it into a quality of Isolde's body, that quality which stirs the erotic imagination, sets it vibrating and creates desire: the body's beauty and the harmonic interaction of physical form and gesture, of motion and line. Her physical presence is inaudible music.[35]

---

[34] Gottfried von Strassburg, *Tristan*, ed. Friedrich Ranke, 11th ed. (Dublin and Zurich: Weidmann, 1967), lines 8122ff. Translation by A. T. Hatto (Harmonsworth: Penguin, 1982), with some liberties taken here: *Muotgedoene* = mind song, spiritual ditty, spirit-tune; Hatto translates "rapturous music."

[35] The well-shaped presence as an embodiment of musical harmonies was a trope of ethical instruction (see Jaeger, *Envy of Angels*, 165–72). Baudri of Bourgueil takes the musical instrument as a metaphor of the harmoniously governed life. The well-modulated life is one lived in a single mode, and this is the way that God "harmonizes our

Gottfried's image implies an aesthetic of the physical presence, shared by music and body. The body becomes music, and music becomes a body. Isolde's double song continues the logic of the agonal relationships between body and text, but representation and presence achieve balance.

The passage from Hildebert that was our point of departure shares the basic premises of those just discussed: it posits a contest between presence and representation, and it shows the text superior to the body. Hildebert confronts charismatic presence (the gods) with charismatic texts (their statues)—and gives precedence to representation. The gods long to be like their statues because their statues are greater, more impressive, more beautiful. Symbolic presence is superior to real presence.

This reading of Hildebert's lines locates them in the body-text relationship: the charisma of representation, having appropriated personal charisma, takes precedence over it. In this stage the charismatic text emancipates itself from its ties to a single individual and embodies abstract virtue. The biography is no longer the dominant form, but rather the fictional narrative is. The charismatic text still presupposes the human body and charismatic presence as its grounding (no statues without gods), but neither immediate presence nor the memorializing motive are involved.

The fundamental mode of literature in this phase is the fictionalizing of virtue and the enfabulation of charisma. It is projected into the realm of the "marvelous," the "merveilleux." The courtly romance in its origins is a product largely of clerical authors who shared the education of Hildebert of Lavardin, a humanist, cathedral-school education. This is the point of contact between Latin and vernacular culture. At the very moment when an old, humanist program is collapsing and being forced out of the schools of Paris, a new narrative form, created by humanists displaced from the schools and seeking employment at worldly courts, develops into a "novel of education," a "Bildungsroman"—the courtly romance. And this narrative form makes courtly virtue accessible through *aventure*.

The courtly romance presupposes charisma and virtue, but not a living human being who embodies these qualities, in contrast to the biography, letter, or portrait. The charismatic text renders the charismatic

---

manners and our bodies, so that the mystical symphony of our life will be pleasing." *Baldricus Burgulianus Carmina* 218, ed. Karlheinz Hilbert (Heidelberg: Winter, 1979), 287–88.

presence secondary and lives from it at the same time. It is independent from models, but not from that which they represent. This train of thought suggests the relevance for the twelfth and thirteenth centuries of a formula of Hans Ulrich Gumbrecht, that literature begins "in the leave-taking from the body."[36]

It would be possible to develop an aesthetic of the courtly romance from the body-text dichotomy. It is an aesthetic of hyper-mimesis.[37] A hyper-mimetic literature is beyond and above nature. It wants to do for the reader or viewer what the Roman statues do for the gods: astonish them, put them to shame by showing them a world which is theirs, but higher, purer, more perfect. It wants to draw them into that higher world and inspire them to imitate it.

The charismatic text operates on an aesthetic that injects life into the work of art. The representation re-establishes in illusion the properties of presence; it simulates voice, impersonates physicality, enacts presence, counterfeits authority, performs charm, insinuates sexuality. The world evoked through the abstract and wholly unsensual letters of the text is sensual in the highest degree possible for the conceptual, ideal, but its sensuality is hollow-holo-graphic, like the shade of Helen of Troy in *Faust Part 2*.

The charismatic text is functioning when it makes the viewer or reader want to be like it. S/he wants to live in the work of art and according to its laws.[38] The romances had this effect on Don Quixote,

---

[36] Hans-Ulrich Gumbrecht, "Beginn der 'Literatur' / Abschied vom Körper?" *Der Ursprung von Literatur: Medien, Rollen, Kommunikationssituationen zwischen 1450 und 1650*, ed. G. Smolke-Koerdt et al. (Munich: Fink, 1988), 15–50.

[37] That is one reason for the serious problems in Erich Auerbach's essay on courtly romance in *Mimesis: The Representation of Reality in Western Literature*, trans. Willard Trask (New York: Doubleday, 1957). Analyzing romance's representation of reality, he was forced to posit a purposelessness of the knighthood in social and political life which generated the unreality of romance. Recent research has shown that the knighthood was just gaining a role as a self-conscious social group in the late twelfth century, not losing it.

[38] Rilke's poem, "Archaïscher Torso Apollos," observes the charismatic work of art exercising this force. As the poet looks at a headless torso in the Louvre, some magnetism suffusing the statue takes command of him. It is watching him more powerfully than he is watching it, and the poet loses the contest of gazing: "denn da ist keine Stelle, / die dich nicht sieht. Du mußt dein Leben ändern" (Rainer Maria Rilke, *Gesammelte Gedichte* [Frankfurt am Main: Insel, 1962], 313). The marble torso, headless though it is, has eyes and vision and light in its every contour, because the missing head has sublimated itself and diffused vision through the remaining parts: "There is no point that does not see you." The cryptic final line, "You must change your life," is understandable within the logic of the charismatic text: the museum visi-

IX

in whom we have an approximate counterpart of Hildebert's gods vis-à-vis their statues. The living human being senses his inferiority to the fiction, and wants to be like the counterfeit: "cupiunt fictis vultibus esse pares." Don Quixote has no resistance to this wish. His identity submerges in the more powerful identity of the narratives.

Mimesis is humble by comparison with charismatic representation. The basic impulse of imitation is to create a world that is the reader's equal and compel him by similarity to love it as himself. What is not possible in the affection of like for like that mimesis aims at is transformation. There is only stagnation—remaining the same, and loving it—and Narcissus is the defining myth of mimesis for that reason. The basic impulse of hyper-mimetic art is to create a world that is greater and grander than the reader/viewer's, a world of supernaturally beautiful bodies and faces, sublime emotions, motives and deeds, grand and magnificent fates—in order to draw the humbled viewer up into its realms, dazzle, educate and transform him/her through the vision of the higher being s/he could become, as Don Quixote was "educated."

The image of the dazzled gods in Hildebert's Rome poem is located at this point in the historical unfolding of charismatic aesthetics: representation emerges from its subservient position and comes to dominate charismatic presence, which is replaced by the charismatic text. Texts appropriate the representing force that had resided in bodies; the aura of the gods fades; the aura of the work of art intensifies.

This development has a final stage. "Classical" and "charismatic" art are bought at a price to the culture which produces them. Having bargained for charisma, texts overstep their contract. Their humble threadbare presence turns tyrannical, shows itself a Uriah Heep. What characterizes this late phase of the body-text dynamic is: texts suffocate bodies. To keep to the terms of the textual contract by which representation can promise immortality, texts become body-snatchers. They take over force, authority, and sensuality. They are counterfeits, but fakes too want dominance, and they can get it by taking it. Textualization is a threat to embodied charisma.

The cultures which rejected the textual contract knew perfectly what the costs were, and were unwilling to pay them. The native Americans

---

tor is in the force field of the statue; it has imposed its will and authority on the weaker living presence. The missing head symbolizes lost or hidden presence sublimated and working through the charismatic work of art. The headless, eyeless body gazes more powerfully just because it has performed that act of sublimating vision into the body.

who refused to have their pictures taken because they imagined the camera would entrap their souls understood the dangers of representation. If they read Virgil, Shakespeare and Tolstoy, they might well say, if it goes on like this, you won't have any more warriors and heroes—or rather, the only ones will be artists.

A phase in the dynamics of body and text in which texts usurp life is a historical experience and not just a critical/theoretical construct. The connection between the loss of a culture's vitality and growing textualization is observable for instance at the turn of the nineteenth to the twentieth century. The artists of European decadence were well aware that brilliance of art coincides with a culture's loss of vitality. Nietzsche invented the term "Alexandrine man" to describe the person or culture that surrenders life to the book.[39]

The twelfth and thirteenth centuries were presented with the same bill for their artistic flourishing. We can witness the culture's capitulation to representation by comparing two texts, one from the late eleventh, the other from the late twelfth century, that address the relative value of living presence and symbolic presence.

The first is from a remarkable but little-read work by Sigebert of Gembloux, *The Passion of the Theban Legion*. Written around 1075 by a schoolmaster with imperial leanings after his retirement from teaching at Metz to the monastery of Gembloux,[40] the work is a blend of heroic epic and martyr legend. It takes its peculiar character partly from a series of highly polished and interesting orations that precede, comment on, and follow the martyrdom of a legion of Christian warriors,

---

[39] Awareness of this dynamic abounds in the modern period: Faust in the beginning of Goethe's play desperately seeking release from the intellect and from suffocation through texts, buying, at the cost of his soul, the return to life in its vitality and immediacy; "Burckhardtianism," fashioned around the vision of Renaissance Italy in *The Civilization of the Renaissance*; the contest of Dionysian vitalism and Apollonian formalism in Nietzsche's *The Birth of Tragedy*; the opposition of woman (dynamic, vital) to man (intellectual) in Shaw's *Man and Superman*; a vision of the "wasteland" of an old, paralyzed, sick culture superseded by a new vitality shared by T. S. Eliot and German Expressionists, and appropriated by National Socialist vitalism opposing a "degenerate" intellectual culture.

[40] Still the best general appraisal of Sigebert is Max Manitius, *Geschichte der lateinischen Literatur des Mittelalters*, Handbuch der Altertumswissenschaft 9.2 (Munich: Beck, 1923, rpt. 1973), 3: 332-50: "Einer der vielseitigsten und bedeutendsten Schriftsteller des 11. und beginnenden 12. Jahrhunderts" (332).

who refuse an order from the Roman emperor Maximian. One of the speeches is delivered by the warrior saint and officer of the legion, Maurice. He begins by urging his comrades to passive resistance and martyrdom, quoting sayings and stories of Christ. But then he interrupts the Biblical examples with the cry, "Non opus exemplis: exemplum vos magis estis" ("There is no need for examples [from books]: you yourselves are the example").[41] He develops the opposition of written history to living, embodied history and ends,

> "Legimus hactenus hec, audivimus hactenus istec,
> sanctorum tanti recitantur in orbi triumphi,
> Hic video coram fieri que facta legebam. . . .
> En mihi quos imiter, sunt presto quos bene mirer?"

"We have read this, we have heard that. So many triumphs of the saints are reported throughout the world. But here I see with my very eyes those deeds I have read about. . . . Are not those whom I should imitate and those at whom I should marvel right here in front of me!"[42]

A very different attitude to the living as opposed to the textual presence registers in the beginning of Hartmann von Aue's *Iwein*, written in the last decade of the twelfth century. He describes a springtime festival at King Arthur's court with its intense joy, then turns to a lament about the lack of joy in the present. But he takes the *stories* of the ancient heroes as compensation for the dreariness of the contemporary world:

> ichn wolde dô niht sîn gewesen,
> daz ich nû niht enwaere,
> dâ uns noch mit ir *maere*
> sô rehte wol wesen sol:
> dâ tâten in diu *werc* vil wol.

I would not want to have lived then if I had to give up the present and [the Arthurian] *stories* that give us such pleasure. In those days it was *deeds* that gave satisfaction.[43]

---

[41] Sigebert of Gembloux, *Sigeberts von Gembloux Passio sanctae Luciae virginis und Passio sanctorum Thebeorum* 2.448, ed. Ernst Dümmler, Akademie der Wissenschaften, Berlin. Phil.-Hist. Klasse. Abhandlungen 1 (Berlin, 1893), 83.

[42] Ibid. 2.505–13, 85.

[43] Hartmann von Aue, *Iwein*, 7th edition, ed. G. Benecke, K. Lachmann, L. Wolff (Berlin: De Gruyter, 1968), lines 48–58, emphasis added.

Hartmann's verses are the full antithesis of Sigebert's. St. Maurice lives the heroic moment and renounces the recorded and reported words of Christ himself, the Christian hero of the past, in favor of the heroic deeds of living men; Hartmann is willing to trade in the heroic age of deeds and intensely lived pleasures for the dreary contemporary world with its alluring stories of the past. The narrated is preferable to the experienced past. The contemporary world may be unheroic, but it has what the heroic past never had: stories about their great men. It is a gesture that, for this reader at least, has the aura of resignation from life of the writers of European decadence. For Sigebert (or St. Maurice), Truth is in the immediate presence of an exemplary human being; the living presence, equipped with the weapons of virtue, outdoes even sacred history. For Hartmann, the stories have become the bearers of exemplary force, pleasure and entertainment. Virtue is enfabulated.

The culture and intellectual life of the thirteenth century experienced the collapse of immediacy and vitality, and sensed that one of its symptoms was its text-boundness. An anecdote of Jacques de Vitry must stand here in place of a fuller treatment of the topic.

A master of a Paris school, so the story runs, was visited one night by an apparition. It is the ghost of a former student, recently dead. The ghost wears a winding-sheet, "heavy as a stone tower." This shroud is a large piece of parchment, covered at every point with tiny letters and characters. The teacher asks what the writings mean, and the student answers that they spell out the sophisms and vain questionings on which he had wasted his time as a student. The ghost is sweating profusely from his burden, and the teacher experiences its sufferings when a drop of sweat falls onto the back of his hand. Acid-like it eats a hole in his hand that remains as a permanent reminder of the visit. The next morning the professor resigns his chair and enters a Cistercian monastery.[44]

The anecdote captures a cultural malaise in the air in the mid-thirteenth century, and depicts suffocation through texts as its cause. This ghostly man of letters, human presence fully textualized, can serve as a paradigm image of an age that has surrendered its vitality to representation and the book.

---

[44] Jacques de Vitry, *The Exempla or Illustrative Stories from the Sermones vulgares of Jacques de Vitry*, ed. Thomas F. Crane (1890; rpt. New York: Franklin, 1971), 12.

X

The Courtier Bishop in *Vitae* from the Tenth to the Twelfth Century

The *vitae* of bishops who came to office via service in the royal chapel of the Ottonian-Salian kings regularly contain a description of the court service of the young cleric, of his appearance, personality, and character. From these descriptions, which are at the same time vivid revelations of court life and manners, there emerges a picture of the aristocratic cleric as royal servant and future bishop in the imperial church.

The circumstances that brought the figure of the "courtier bishop"[1] to prominence in the Ottonian empire are well known, but they are so closely tied to the subject of this paper that it will be useful to summarize them briefly.[2] The close connection between court service and the bishop's office originated in the influence that rulers exerted on the appointment of bishops. Service to the ruler had been an avenue to the episcopate since late antiquity, and this continued in Carolingian times. But the frequency of this route, as well as its political importance, changed radically under Otto the Great and his successors. Otto built the episcopal office into an important political instrument, a buffer against the opposition of the feudal nobility. Loyal bishops could become powerful secular lords while holding ecclesiasti-

---

This is an expanded version of a lecture given in March 1980 to the Mittelalterkreis of the University of Münster and in May 1980 to the Deutsches Seminar of the University of Freiburg. I am very grateful to Professors Friedrich Ohly, Karl Hauck, and Peter von Moos, who generously placed at my disposal the facilities of the Institut für Mittelalterforschung in Münster, and to the Fulbright commission, which made possible a year's research leave in Germany.

[1] I take the term from Peter Damian, who referred contemptuously to bishops who had risen through court service as *episcopi curiales: Contra clericos aulicos*, PL 145:472C: "[episcopi] qui Ecclesiae militando promoti sunt, vocantur ex more pontifices; ita qui famulando principibus fiunt, dicantur a curia curiales." In clerical parlance *curialis* began as a pejorative, but by the twelfth century it could be a term of high praise. See the list of cardinal bishops in the *Gesta Alberonis* 23: "Guido Cremensis, vir . . . valde curialis," in *Lebensbeschreibungen einiger Bischöfe des 10.–12. Jahrhunderts*, ed. Hatto Kallfelz, Ausgewählte Quellen zur deutschen Geschichte des Mittelalters, Freiherr vom Stein Gedächtnisausgabe (AQDG) 22 (Darmstadt, 1973), p. 596, and *Gesta episcoporum Autissiodorensium* 19: Bishop Guido de Mellotto, "vir tocius curialitatis" (MGH SS 26:584).

[2] See Albert Hauck, *Kirchengeschichte Deutschlands*, 3rd ed. (Leipzig, 1906), 3:28 ff.; Edgar N. Johnson, *The Secular Activities of the German Episcopate, A.D. 919–1024*, University of Nebraska Studies 30 (Lincoln, Neb., 1932), p. 67 ff.; Josef Fleckenstein, *Die Hofkapelle der deutschen Könige*, MGH Schriften 16/1, 2 (Stuttgart, 1959–66), 2:50 ff., 111 ff.; and the extensive survey by Oskar Köhler, "Die Ottonische Reichskirche: Ein Forschungsbericht," in *Adel und Kirche: Gerd Tellenbach zum 65. Geburtstag*, ed. Josef Fleckenstein (Freiburg, 1968), pp. 141–204, esp. p. 173 ff.

cal office. The court chapel played a major role in this transformation of the imperial power structure.[3] Otto and his successors were able to seat members of their chapel — often their relatives or close friends — in vacant bishoprics. The chapel provided a pool of clerical advisors close to the emperor and loyal to him. Their advancement depended entirely on his favor. Though the emperor technically had only an advisory role in choosing bishops — a right reserved by canon law to "clergy and populace" — the Ottos were effective in advancing their own candidates. Of the twenty-four bishops from the tenth to the twelfth centuries whose *vitae* I consider here, seventeen came to their office via service in the royal chapel. The Ottos managed to prevent the seating of candidates they opposed and were willing — Otto III at least — to exercise this power even in cases where the diocese held the privilege of free elections.

As a result the chapel became the training ground for higher office, successful and loyal service the prerequisite for ecclesiastical preferment.[4] Future prelates were groomed at the court, under the scrutiny of the ruler, for another kind of service to the ruler as bishops. The royal chapel attracted talented, educated men of the high nobility. This development produced an educated aristocracy or at least greatly swelled the numbers and importance of this group, both at the court and in the empire. The fertile possibilities inherent in the creation of an elite community at the court were further enhanced by the extraordinary legal status of the chapel. The chaplains were not members of the church hierarchy. As "spiritual vassals" of the king, to whom, like other vassals, they owed *servitium,* the chaplains lived according to special rights and privileges and were not subject to any epis-

---

[3] Of the rich literature on the chapel I will cite only the works to which I refer directly: Siegfried Görlitz, *Beiträge zur Geschichte der königlichen Hofkapelle im Zeitalter der Ottonen und Salier bis zum Beginn des Investiturstreites,* Historisch-Diplomatische Forschungen 1 (Weimar, 1936); Hans-Walter Klewitz, "Cancellaria: Ein Beitrag zur Geschichte des geistlichen Hofdienstes," *Deutsches Archiv für Erforschung des Mittelalters* 1 (1937), 44–79 (repr. in his *Ausgewählte Aufsätze zur Kirchen- und Geistesgeschichte des Mittelalters* [Aalen, 1971], pp. 13–48). The standard work is Fleckenstein, *Die Hofkapelle.* Following Fleckenstein, Siegfried Haider on the episcopal chapel: *Das bischöfliche Kapellanat,* 1: *Von den Anfängen bis in das 13. Jahrhundert,* Mitteilungen des Instituts für Österreichische Geschichtsforschung, suppl. vol. 25 (Vienna and Cologne, 1977). Cf. the review article by Stefan Weinfurter, "Zum bischöflichen Kapellanat und seiner Bedeutung für Köln: Bemerkungen zu einer Neuerscheinung über die Bischofskapelle," *Archiv für Kulturgeschichte* 60 (1978), 203–12. On the chapel of Frederick II, Hans Martin Schaller, "Die staufische Hofkapelle im Königreich Sizilien," *Deutsches Archiv* 11 (1954/55), 462–505; idem, "Kanzlei und Hofkapelle Kaiser Friedrichs II.," *Annali dell' Istituto storico italo-germanico in Trento — Jahrbuch des italienisch-deutschen Instituts in Trient* 2 (1976), 75–116.

[4] Klewitz calls the royal chapel "eine Schule der Reichsbischöfe" in his article, "Königtum, Hofkapelle und Domkapitel im 10. und 11. Jahrhundert," *Archiv für Urkundenforschung* 16 (1939), and *Ausgewählte Aufsätze,* p. 14. Cf. Fleckenstein, *Die Hofkapelle,* 2:289. The election of Wazo to the bishopric of Liège in 1041 was opposed by "flatterers of the king" who objected, "Ex capellanis pocius episcopum constituendum, Wazonem numquam in curte regia desudasse, ut talem promereretur honorem . . .": *Anselmi gesta episcoporum Leodiensium* 50, MGH SS 7:219.

copal authority. Ordinarily they numbered poets, scholars, and artisans in their ranks, and they largely determined the cultural life of the court.[5] Even when placed in a bishopric, the courtier bishop often spent more time at the king's court than at the cathedral attending to the religious life of his diocese.[6]

These circumstances favored the development of an ethic of public service appropriate to the office, reflecting the hybrid nature of its holder, who was both courtier and prelate. The set of values formed in the chapel, based as much on Ciceronian as on Christian notions of state service and the conduct of public life, might appropriately be called "courtly humanism."[7] Some of its central conceptions were to surface in the ethic of *courtoisie* of vernacular romance; they also shape a prototype of the Renaissance courtier.

Despite the social, political, and cultural importance of the courtier bishop, modern scholars have neglected this figure.[8] Two factors seem to have shielded him from the scrutiny particularly of the historian of ideas and manners. The first is the assumption that clerics had to be pious churchmen in order to become bishops. Friedrich Heer points to this factor as a hindrance in understanding the political role of the imperial bishop, who was first and foremost an administrator, statesman, and diplomat. If a cleric, having assumed the office of bishop, also turned out to be pious and saintly,

---

[5] See Fleckenstein, *Die Hofkapelle*, 1:30, 40–42; and Schaller, "Staufische Hofkapelle," p. 462: "Dieser Verband, exemt gegenüber der kirchlichen Hierarchie, immun gegenüber der staatlichen Verwaltung, frei von Steuern und Abgaben, war eine nach besonderem Recht lebende Gemeinschaft, die anscheinend durch eine Art Vasallitätsverhältnis zwischen den Kapellänen und dem Herrscher gekennzeichnet war." On the cultural role of the chapel, ibid. p. 462, and Siegfried Haider, "Zum Verhältnis von Kapellanat und Geschichtsschreibung im Mittelalter," in *Geschichtsschreibung und geistiges Leben im Mittelalter: Festschrift für Heinz Löwe zum 65. Geburtstag*, ed. K. Hauck and H. Mordek (Vienna and Cologne, 1978), pp. 102–38.

[6] Johnson, *Secular Activities*, and Fleckenstein, *Die Hofkapelle*, 2:18 f. In a study of the court service of Spanish bishops in the mid-twelfth century, Bernard Reilly can coin the term "absentee prelate": "The Court Bishops of Alfonso VII of Leon-Castilla, 1147–1157," *Mediaeval Studies* 36 (1974), 67–78.

[7] I have taken this term, *humanisme courtois*, from Jean Frappier, *Le roman breton: Les origines de la légende arthurienne: Chrétien de Troyes* (Paris, 1951), p. 101 ff. He applies it to the poet-clerics who created the courtly romance. Cf. also C. Stephen Jaeger, *Medieval Humanism in Gottfried von Strassburg's Tristan und Isolde* (Heidelberg, 1977), pp. 16 ff., 80 ff. It is a useful and accurate term to describe the culture and ethical values of court clergy generally.

[8] Karl Bosl, "Geistliche Fürsten," in *Lexikon für Theologie und Kirche*, 2nd ed. (Freiburg, 1960), 4:622: "Eine abschliessende Würdigung des g.F. in Deutschland ist mangels Vorarbeiten noch nicht möglich." Friedrich Heer could write in 1952: "Es ist erstaunlich und nur durch die Einseitigkeit der Forschung begreiflich, dass die für Kultur und Lebensstil des 'alten Reiches' wichtigste und repräsentativste soziologische Schicht bis heute noch keine rechte Würdigung gefunden hat, obwohl sie in monumentaler Grösse bis ins 12. Jahrhundert das Antlitz des Sacrum Imperium mit- . . . formt" (*Die Tragödie des heiligen Reiches* [Stuttgart, 1952], p. 9). A valuable study of a major figure from the episcopal milieu in twelfth-century France is Peter von Moos's *Hildebert von Lavardin: Humanitas an der Schwelle des höfischen Zeitalters*, Pariser historische Studien 3 (Stuttgart, 1965).

so much the better. But piety was not a requisite quality for the position in the same way that statesmanship and administrative skill were. In late antiquity the old Roman senatorial nobility could regard a bishop's office as practically hereditary (the case of Sidonius Apollinaris), and the notion that a bishopric could be all but a prerogative of the aristocracy and the ruler's favorites lasted well beyond the Middle Ages. Stendhal in his *Charterhouse of Parma* could still have a court intriguer map out a career for a talented young nobleman which had a tradition of more than a thousand years behind it: "Note . . . that I do not intend to make him an exemplary priest, like so many you see. No, he is a great noble first and foremost; he can remain perfectly ignorant if it seems good to him, and will none the less become a bishop and archbishop, if the prince continues to regard me as a man who is useful to him."[9] The only idea in this passage that owes more to Stendhal's cynicism than to the realities of a certain ecclesiastical career is that the future bishop could afford to be ignorant.

The second factor is the notion that the ideals of the office, if not the social and political realities of it, were orthodox Christian ones. The orthodox ideal of the episcopate (see below, p. 319 and nn. 95–97) had next to nothing to do with the conception of the court chaplain and future bishop in the Ottonian-Salian imperial church. Here the ideals and qualities appropriate to an aspiring bishop are hardly distinguishable from the qualities appropriate to the character and obligations of a chaplain serving the king.

The purpose of this paper is to analyze these qualities, define the type of the courtier bishop, and indicate the influence of this "courtly humanism."

Of the variety of sources pertinent to the culture of the royal courts in this period,[10] the biographies of courtier bishops are the most informative.[11] As a genre, the episcopal *vitae* must be clearly distinguished from hagiographic legends and saints' lives. The latter are popular works collecting legends from oral tradition, assembling reports about the saint's life and activity, and

---

[9] *The Charterhouse of Parma*, trans. Margaret Shaw (Harmondsworth, 1978), p. 129 (ch. 6).

[10] Still the standard work on court life and the development of courtly literature is Reto Bezzola, *Les origines et la formation de la littérature courtoise en occident (500–1200)*, 3 parts in 5 vols. (Paris, 1958–63). But Bezzola had his eye much more firmly on literary productivity than on the history of manners and ideas. The result is that in selecting texts he paid no attention to the *vitae* of bishops.

[11] Studies of the depiction of personality in medieval history and biography regularly draw on them: e.g., Robert Teuffel, *Individuelle Persönlichkeitsschilderung in den deutschen Geschichtswerken des 10. und 11. Jahrhunderts*, Beiträge zur Kultur des Mittelalters und der Renaissance (BKMR) 12 (Hildesheim, 1914; repr. 1974). An excellent work which leans heavily on the *vitae* is Paul Kirn, *Das Bild des Menschen in der Geschichtsschreibung von Polybios bis Ranke* (Göttingen, 1955). The only good study specifically concerned with the representation of bishops in the *vitae* is Oskar Köhler, *Das Bild des geistlichen Fürsten in den Viten des 10., 11. und 12. Jahrhunderts*, Abhandlungen zur mittleren und neueren Geschichte 77 (Berlin, 1935).

The Courtier Bishop

combining these with available commonplace legends and tales of miracles.[12] The bishop's *vita,* on the other hand, stands in the tradition of ancient rhetoric and historiography and of the biography of late antiquity. Although this form idealizes its subject to some extent, the ideal models are quite different from those of the saint's life and legend,[13] even in cases where the bishop became a saint. The educated aristocracy, whose highest representative was the courtier bishop, kept classical-humanistic, Ciceronian ideals alive, found a social context for them in public service to the empire, and amalgamated them with Christian ideals. It is this amalgam of classical and Christian ideals of the active public life which is reflected in the descriptions of a court cleric and future bishop in the *vitae.*

Another consideration important for my purposes is a development within the genre of episcopal biography. In Merovingian and Carolingian *vitae* the beginning chapters, describing the period prior to the cleric's promotion to church office, tend towards a stereotypical idealizing of the future bishop according to monastic-ascetic models. In the *vitae* from the Ottonian-Salian period this is no longer the case. With the exception of the earliest biographies, for instance those of Brun of Cologne (†965; *Vita* ca. 968) and Ulrich of Augsburg (†973; *Vita* between 982 and 993), the description of the character and activities of the future bishop becomes almost wholly secularized. The young cleric may well be praised for his *pietas* and *sanctitas,* but these virtues play next to no role in the life of the future bishop before his rise to office. This posed a problem for the biographers of courtier bishops who became saints. The biographers of Otto of Bamberg and Thomas Becket, for instance, had to show the development from worldly court servant and administrator to saint and, in Becket's case, martyr. The biographies of these two, and of many others who pursued similar careers, fall into two parts and represent two distinctly different types: the courtier-cleric prior to his becoming bishop; the man of the church thereafter.[14]

---

[12] See Hippolyte Delehaye, *The Legends of the Saints,* trans. D. Attwater (New York, 1962), p. 3 ff. and passim.

[13] Cf. Friedrich Lotter, "Methodisches zur Gewinnung historischer Erkenntnisse aus hagiographischen Quellen," *Historische Zeitschrift* 229 (1979), 310: "Neben dieser eher den Bedürfnissen des einfachen Volkes angepassten Form [i.e., the monastic-ascetic saint's life] entstand im gleichen Raum und zur gleichen Zeit eine den Ansprüchen der Bildungsschicht eher angemessene Gattung, die noch weitgehend der Tradition der spätantiken Biographie und Rhetorik verpflichtet war und von der in sich geschlossenen fortschreitenden Prosadarstellung beherrscht wurde. Auch sie idealisiert den Helden, indem sie entweder als Gedenkschrift seine historischen Taten und Leistungen herausstreicht oder als reine Laudatio in Wesen und Taten die Tugenden sichtbar macht...."

[14] This can easily be observed by comparing the portrait of the courtier bishop prior to his assuming office with the descriptions of the same man in the funeral orations or eulogies which frequently end the *vita.* On the division of the personality depiction into two types, see Friedrich Lotter, *Die Vita Brunonis des Ruotger: Ihre historiographische und ideengeschichtliche Stellung,* Bonner historische Forschungen 9 (Bonn, 1958), p. 28 ff.

The *vitae* with which we are dealing, then, are a secularized form of Christian biography. One could characterize their style generally as realistic, the perspective of the biographer as relatively objective. The classical statement of a commitment to "realistic" depiction is by Abbot Norbert of Iburg in his life of Benno II, bishop of Osnabrück (†1088).[15] He rejects the method of those biographers who make saints out of their subjects, inventing tales of their miracles; instead he claims to describe the man as he actually was, not omitting his vices or exaggerating his virtues.[16] Repeatedly the authors of bishops' lives shrink from the reproach of flattering their subjects, and though this may well be a topos of medieval historiography,[17] it appears to have been a topos with a real power to guide the observation of a biographer. Adam of Bremen's famous description of the life of Adalbert of Bremen is anything but a pious saint's legend and idealized life of a man of the church. It is the tragedy of a courtier who neglected his first duty to the church in order to pursue the vainglory of worldly fame and power at the court of King Henry IV. But if Adam attains something like "objectivity" in his portrayal of Adalbert, it is in part because he shrinks from flattering a man whom flattery had driven to ruin.[18]

[15] The *Vita* is one of the most secularized. In spite of all individual features, Benno fits quite neatly the image of the courtier bishop. He served at the courts of Henry III, Bishop Azelinus of Hildesheim, Henry IV, and Archbishop Anno of Cologne. On his court service, see Heinrich Spier, "Benno II. von Osnabrück am Goslarer Königshof," *Harzzeitschrift* 7 (1955), 57–67. For a general characterization of Benno in contrast to the orthodox model of a bishop, see R. W. Southern, *Western Society and the Church in the Middle Ages*, The Pelican History of the Church 2 (Harmondsworth, 1970), pp. 181–83.

[16] "Nec enim imitanda hic videtur quorundam magis temeraria quam religiosa assentatio, qui in eorum, quos describunt, tantummodo laude versantur et non tam, quid egerint, attendere videntur, quam quid egisse debuerint. . . . Itaque non eum verbis sanctificare contendimus . . . sed eius vitam sine fuco . . . depromimus": *Vita Bennonis* 8, ed. Bresslau, repr. in *Lebensbeschreibungen* (n. 1, above), p. 388. In general, when several editions are available, I cite the most recent and refer the reader to the discussion of others in W. Wattenbach and R. Holtzmann, *Deutschlands Geschichtsquellen im Mittelalter: Die Zeit der Sachsen und Salier (DGQ)*, rev. F.-J. Schmale, 3 vols. (Darmstadt, 1971–78). On Benno II, *DGQ*, 2:578 ff. Another statement of a commitment to an "objective" representation of the subject occurs in Herbord of Michelberg's prologue to his *Dialogue on the Life of Otto of Bamberg* (edition cited below, n. 31), p. 7: "Since we [i.e., the participants in the dialogue] loved him especially, we must be especially careful, *ne ob eius dileccionem rem non vere auxisse videamur.*" Anselm of Havelberg seems to indicate in the verse prologue to his *Vita* of Adalbert II of Mainz that an official interdict on flattering a bishop existed: ed. P. Jaffé, *Bibliotheca rerum Germanicarum*, 6 vols. (Berlin, 1864–73), 3:569, ll. 33–39. In any case, what was possible in the saint's legend — stylization of the man's youth according to models of sainthood; montage of conventional, interchangeable episodes; and tales of miracles — was clearly not possible in the life of a bishop.

[17] Gertrud Simon, "Untersuchungen zur Topik der Widmungsbriefe mittelalterlicher Geschichtsschreiber biz zum Ende des 12. Jahrhunderts," part 2, *Archiv für Diplomatik* 5–6 (1959–60), 100.

[18] Adam von Bremen, *Hamburgische Kirchengeschichte* 3.65, ed. B. Schmeidler, 3rd ed., MGH SSrG (Hannover and Leipzig, 1917), p. 212. Cf. *DGQ*, 2:566. A particularly good treatment of this biography is by Georg Misch, *Geschichte der Autobiographie*, 3/1 (Frankfurt am Main, 1959), p. 168 ff. See also Kirn (above, n. 11).

X
The Courtier Bishop

I have drawn generally on the lives of German bishops, but my study is not concerned with distinguishing conditions in Germany from those found elsewhere in Europe. The focus is the court service of clerics. This circumstance was not restricted to Germany, and the ideals of court clergy in France and England seem to have varied little from those which Anno of Cologne, Otto of Bamberg, and others cultivated as chaplains of the German royal court. Therefore I have drawn freely on any biographical material from the period which opens to view the values of clerics at secular courts.

In spite of the sense of individual destiny and character that the bishops' biographers generally evince in describing their subjects, a model of the future bishop emerges from the opening chapters of the *vitae*. In this section I want to formulate the model, explore some of the notions which comprise it, and account for its coherence.

The following scheme summarizes the typical pattern for describing the person and career of a court cleric prior to his assumption of office. He is of high nobility. It was rare for a non-noble to become bishop, and those who did (Gerbert of Aurillac, Anno of Cologne, and Benno II of Osnabrück, for example) are praised for their nobility of mind, spirit, and manners. The cleric's inborn potential or promise *(indoles)* as well as his personal gifts are apparent from his earliest days: physical beauty, quickness of mind, ease of speech, graceful manners. His parents send him to school, *litteris imbuendus*. He excels in his studies and swiftly leaves all his fellow students behind. At school he shows himself to be diligent, learned, wise, and eloquent, friendly to all men and beloved of all. He is taken into the service of a bishop, becomes head of the school, then provost. The bishop makes him his confidant and personal advisor. Various lords, secular and ecclesiastical, compete with each other for his services. The king hears of this gifted young man and makes his acquaintance, perhaps while the young cleric is on a diplomatic mission at the king's court. Before he enters the king's service, there is often a description of the young man's appearance, character, and virtues. These occasionally function to explain his acceptance into the royal chapel. He is handsome, tall, and well proportioned. His character and manners *(mores)* are praised, then his virtues: he is discreet and wise *(discretus et prudens)* farsighted, diligent, and skilled *(providus, strenuus, sollertus)*, but at the same time humble, meek and gentle, patient and pious *(humilis, mansuetus, patiens, pius)*. Other personal qualities frequently mentioned are *gravitas, moderamen, affabilitas, amabilitas*. The king makes him his chaplain, perhaps over the objections of the bishop, to whom he has become indispensable. At the king's court he wins the favor of all by his good manners, affability, and gentleness. He wins the special affection and favor of the king, who takes him into his confidence and seeks his advice on all matters. A bishop dies, whereupon the king casts about for a successor and hits upon our man, perhaps with the help of miraculous urging. After initial refusals ("canonical reticence") he is raised to the bishop's seat.

X

298   The Courtier Bishop

This is obviously not a prescribed or obligatory catalogue of virtues, but rather a list of some of the most important qualities and most common experiences of the courtier bishops described in the *vitae*. The scheme applies rather neatly to the youths of some of the greatest bishops from the tenth to the twelfth century: Bernward of Hildesheim, Meinwerk of Paderborn, Anno of Cologne, Benno II of Osnabrück, and Otto of Bamberg, to mention only a few. One of the most difficult problems in commenting on this scheme is to determine the source of its consistency and unity. Hagiographic-legendary elements play next to no part. There are three constituent elements which it is important to distinguish: literary-biographic tradition, be it Christian or classical; the actual qualities observed in the subject by his friends and contemporaries or by his biographer; and finally the qualities requisite for the court chaplain and future bishop.

As to the first, literary tradition, the selection and arrangement of topics in the above scheme were governed by a rhetorical model. Quintilian for one had formulated it in enumerating the topics of "praise of persons." He lists: parents, birth, nobility; portents and miracles before and during birth; physical strength and beauty; *indoles* or natural talent; education; virtues; and finally deeds.[19] This sequence governs the choice and disposition of topics in bishops' lives as early as the Merovingian period.

The task of separating personal qualities of a man from qualities appropriate to the office he holds is especially difficult.[20] (The difficulty will be evident to anyone who has tried to evaluate academic letters of recommendation.) To distinguish between qualities appropriate to the office of chaplain of the royal court, literary tradition, and personal qualities, I have drawn broadly on nonbiographic sources, historical and literary.

1. Episcopal Beauty

An impressive appearance was all but a requirement for a bishop. It is a commonplace in the *vitae*,[21] and other sources indicate that it was important

---

[19] *De institutione oratoria* 3.7.10–18. Cf. H. Lausberg, *Handbuch der literarischen Rhetorik: Eine Grundlegung der Literaturwissenschaft* (Munich, 1960), 1:204 (par. 376) and 1:132 ff. (par. 245). On the development of personal description from antiquity to the Middle Ages, see Franz Bittner, *Studien zum Herrscherlob in der mittellateinischen Dichtung*, Diss. Würzburg 1961 (Volkach, 1962), p. 9 ff.; Hilde Vogt, *Die literarische Personenschilderung des frühen Mittelalters*, BKMR 53 (Hildesheim, 1934; repr. 1972), p. 6 ff.; Erich Kleinschmidt, *Herrscherdarstellung: Zur Disposition mittelalterlichen Aussageverhaltens untersucht an Texten über Rudolf I. von Habsburg*, Bibliotheca Germanica 17 (Bern and Munich, 1974), p. 11 ff.

[20] Martin Heinzelmann discusses some of the methodological problems in his study of bishops' epitaphs, fourth to seventh century: *Bischofsherrschaft in Gallien: Zur Kontinuität römischer Führungsschichten vom 4. bis zum 7. Jahrhundert: Soziale, prosopographische und bildungsgeschichtliche Aspekte*, Beihefte der Francia 5 (Zurich and Munich, 1974), p. 88. Frequency of occurrence of an epithet is ambiguous. It could indicate either wide literary influence or the actual association of a quality with an office. To conclude the latter requires synchronic confirmation from other sources.

[21] The following examples represent some of the epithets describing episcopal, or pre-

The Courtier Bishop

among the qualities constituting episcopal *idoneitas*. The biographer of Ulrich of Augsburg points to Ulrich's impressive appearance as a factor in the two major steps in his rise to the position of bishop of Augsburg: he was accepted into the service of Bishop Adalbero of Augsburg "propter nobilitatem parentum et bonam eius indolem et formositatem"; the king (Henry I) accepted the nomination of Ulrich as bishop, "intuens herilitatem staturae illius, et comperiens doctrinae suae scientiam. . . ."[22] Certainly physical beauty will be attributed to monks and rulers, but it was by no means a qualification for either of those estates. It was in a sense a qualification for a bishop. Ugliness or puniness could be raised as an objection to a candidate. The election of Bardo, formerly abbot of Hersfeld, to the archbishopric of Mainz in 1031 was opposed by "evil and envious men" who, says his biographer, scorned his monkish background and "disgusting appearance."[23] Hiltdolf of Cologne (†1078), who must be among the most wretched and inglorious bishops of the earlier Middle Ages, stood up badly in comparison with his mighty predecessor Anno *(statura procerus, vultu venerandus)*. When Henry IV proposed Hiltdolf as archbishop, people and clergy rejected him as "homo statura pusillus, vultu despicabilis, genere obscurus," possessing virtues neither of body nor of mind appropriate for a bishop.[24] His slightness of *statura* became a legend. He is said to have cut off the end of Anno's crozier in order to accommodate it to his own size, and Anno then appeared in a dream and drove him from the bed he had occupied.[25] Physical beauty and imposing stature were desirable qualities in a

---

episcopal, beauty. Adalbero II of Metz (†1005): "corpore plus cunctis sui temporis venustus, statura decorus, forma elegans, oculis amantissimus" (MGH SS 4:661). Gunter of Bamberg (†1065): "vir tam corporis elegantia quam animi sapientia conspicuus" (MGH SS 12:230); Lampert of Hersfeld reports that Gunter so far surpassed other mortals in "formae elegantia ac tocius corporis integritate" that in Jerusalem great crowds gathered around him wherever he went in order to marvel at his beauty (Lampert von Hersfeld, *Annalen*, ed. O. Holder-Egger, AQDG 13 [Berlin, n.d.], p. 104 [1065]). Anno of Cologne (†1075): "Erat autem preter virtutes animi et morum gloriam corporis quoque bonis ornatissimus, statura procerus, vultu decorus" (Lampert, *Annales*, p. 328 [1075]). Frederick I of Cologne (†1131): "vir pulcherrimus" (MGH SS 20:427). Norbert of Xanten, archbishop of Magdeburg (†1134): "forma et habilitate corporis beneficio naturae gaudens" (*Lebensbeschreibungen*, p. 452, and MGH SS 12:671). Rainald of Dassel (†1167): "personae spectabilitas gratiosa" (MGH SS 24:345). On this aspect of medieval bishops see Köhler, *Das Bild* (above, n. 11), p. 73.

[22] *Vita Oudalrici* 1, in *Lebensbeschreibungen*, pp. 56–58. *DGQ*, 1:257 f.

[23] ". . . monachum et hominem aspectu deformem Maguntinensi praesidere dedignantes deridebant . . ." (*Vita Bardonis*, in *Bibliotheca rerum Germanicarum*, ed. Jaffé, 3:524). Cf. Köhler's commentary in *Das Bild*, p. 73. A *miles stolidus* murmured against Wolfgang of Regensburg that he was "a ragged and despicable fellow" (*Vita Wolfkangi* 21, MGH SS 4:535).

[24] *Annales* (above, n. 21), p. 342 (1076).

[25] *Translatio Annonis* 3, MGH SS 11:516. Cf. F. W. Oediger, *Die Regesten der Erzbischöfe von Köln im Mittelalter*, Publikationen der Gesellschaft für Rheinische Geschichtskunde 21 (Bonn, 1954–61), #1130.

man of the world,[26] qualities expected specifically of court servants and royal advisors and appearing as such in the earliest documents describing those offices. A court officer, Hincmar of Rheims wrote in his *De ordine palatii*, should be *nobilis corde et corpore*.[27]

2. Education

The education of a courtier bishop is a rich topic. The *vitae* are a mine of information on the history of education in the Middle Ages and on the development of the cathedral schools. A good education, a sharp and practiced mind, knowledge and eloquence are qualities praised in every *vita*.[28] It is important to point here to the role that cathedral schools came to assume in the imperial political-ecclesiastical system. Josef Fleckenstein, in his study of the court chapel, has shown that the cathedral school began to loom large in the education of royal chaplains under Otto I. Before the second half of the tenth century, court chaplains received their education in monastic schools. In the middle of Otto's reign, this changed. Increasingly the men of stature in the chapel, those who advised the king and anticipated receiving bishoprics, were educated at a cathedral school. Chaplains with a monastic education became fewer and took over the comparatively tedious chancellery tasks. The central figure in this development is Brun of Cologne, the brother of Otto, chancellor of the royal court and later archbishop of Cologne. Under Brun the cathedral school of Cologne came to take on the function of educating young men, cleric and lay, for service to the king at court and in the imperial church.[29] This development is important, since it indicates that an institutional basis existed for the cultivation of the qualities and talents which crystallized into the type of the courtier bishop. If the cathedral schools provided a preparation for court service and the office of imperial bishop, then certainly ideas must have been formed and propagated there of the qualities appropriate for those positions. Since we find a clear picture of those qualities in the *vitae*, it stands to reason that we are formulating an ideal maintained and inculcated at the cathedral schools.

---

[26] The parents of Adalbert of Prague decided on a worldly career for him "prae nimia pulchritudine" (*Vita Adalberti* 2, MGH SS 4:582).

[27] Hinkmar von Reims, *De ordine palatii* 4, ed. and trans. Th. Gross and R. Schieffer, MGH Fontes iuris Germ. antiq. 3 (Hannover, 1980), p. 66. This late Carolingian tract is one of the earliest to detail qualities appropriate to a court minister. The paucity of parallels to later listings of such qualities would seem to confirm the idea that the type of the courtier bishop has its roots in the tenth/eleventh century.

[28] On the education of bishops and chaplains, see Haider, *Das bischöfliche Kapellanat* (above, n. 3), pp. 274 ff., 335 ff.

[29] See Josef Fleckenstein, "Königshof und Bischofschule unter Otto dem Grossen," *Archiv für Kulturgeschichte* 38 (1956), 38–62; idem, *Die Hofkapelle*, 2:50 ff.

3. Mores

Praise of a man's *mores* is an obligatory topic in medieval biography. *Mores* are learned or learnable qualities, acquired at school along with *litterae*.[30] "Proper behavior" is a more accurate translation than "character" or "morals," though the term includes both an internal disposition to the good and the outward bearing that brings it to expression. Such formulations as *probitas morum, nobilitas morum,* and *boni mores* are completely commonplace, in no way specific to the milieu under consideration. But a formulation which has a specific and important meaning for a courtier bishop is *elegancia, venustas,* or *gratia morum*. These terms indicate a shift in the meaning of *mores* from the ethical to the aesthetic sphere. When behavior or manners become aestheticized, then we approach the artificial atmosphere of court life and court etiquette, and the courtier ideal of "the self as a work of art" will not be far behind. Indeed we find these terms in the *vitae* in the context of behavior appropriate to the court.

Otto of Bamberg possessed these qualities in abundance. At least each of his three biographers ascribes them to him.[31] The Monk of Prüfening says that all the prelates of Poland "marveled at the elegance of his *mores*."[32] Ebo says that the abbess of Niedermünster placed all the affairs of the monastery in his hands, "having observed the elegance of his person and his *mores*."[33] According to Herbord, he won the favor of the "great and powerful" of Poland not only through his talents and virtues, but also with the help of his physical elegance ("suffragante sibi eciam corporis elegancia").[34] Beauty of *mores* occurs very early as a quality of the court cleric (Notker of Liège, chaplain of Otto III, was, according to the brief sketch of his personality by

---

[30] Cf. Philippe Delhaye, "L'enseignement de la philosophie morale au XIIe siècle," *Mediaeval Studies* 11 (1949), 77–95. Bernward of Hildesheim was sent to school "literis imbuendus, moribus etiam instituendus" (*Vita Bernwardi* 1, in *Lebensbeschreibungen*, p. 275; cf. *DGQ,* 1:58 ff., 3:23 [Nachtrag]). Wazo of Liège exercised the discipline "tam morum quam litterarum" (MGH SS 7:210).

[31] New editions of these important *vitae* have appeared in recent years: (1) The Monk of Prüfening (ca. 1140/46): *S. Ottonis ep. Babenbergensis vita Prieflingensis,* ed. Jan Wikarjak and Kazimierz Liman, Monumenta Poloniae Historica, ser. nov. (MPH) 7/1 (Warsaw, 1966). (2) Ebo of Michelsberg (ca. 1151/59): *Ebonis vita S. Ottonis ep. Babenbergensis,* ed. Wikarjak and Liman, MPH 7/2 (Warsaw, 1969). (3) Herbord of Michelsberg (1159): *Herbordi dialogus de vita S. Ottonis ep. Babenbergensis,* ed. Wikarjak and Liman, MPH 7/3 (Warsaw, 1974). On these now standard editions, see the review articles by Jürgen Petersohn, "Bemerkungen zu einer neuen Ausgabe der Viten Ottos von Bamberg, 1: Prüfeninger Vita und Ebo," *Deutsches Archiv* 27 (1971), 175–94; and "Bemerkungen . . . , 2: Herbords Dialog," *Deutsches Archiv* 33 (1977), 546–59. On earlier editions, *DGQ,* 2:483 ff.

[32] Prüfening 1.3, p. 7: ". . . his artibus cunctorum sibi sapientium concivit affectum . . . ut ipsi illius terre pontifices . . . morum elegantiam mirarentur."

[33] Ebo 1.3, p. 12.

[34] Herbord 3.32, p. 198.

Anselm of Liège, "very distinguished for the elegance of his manners"),[35] and persists beyond our period.

It is possible to determine with some certainty both the function of this ideal in the milieu of the courtier bishop and the exact meaning of the term. As to the first, elegance, beauty, or grace of behavior is consistently said to attract the admiration and wonderment of lords secular and ecclesiastical and to qualify the cleric who possesses it for court service. Bernward of Hildesheim was sought after by several lords who admired his *morum gratia*.[36] Meinwerk of Paderborn was judged worthy of service at the king's court because of the elegance of his *mores:* "Meinwercus autem, regia stirpe genitus, regio obsequio morum elegantia idoneus adiudicatur evocatusque ad palatium regius capellanus efficitur."[37] We could hardly ask for a more lucid illustration of the connection between elegance of manners and court service. The earliest occurrences of the term in the context of entry to the royal chapel are in Germany, but it occurs in France as well, for instance in the *vitae* written by Marbod of Rennes (†1123). In his *Vita Licinii* (written before 1096) he relates that in his youth Licinius (bishop of Angers, †ca. 610) left school to seek service at the court of King Clotarius, who willingly received him "because of his close family ties, his dignified and excellent appearance, and his elegant manners."[38] These passages bring us very close to a sharp focus on the factors that determined entry to the court. High on the list, perhaps first, is beauty or elegance of manners. It was the one quality sought above others; it endeared the cleric to the ruler[39] and bespoke promise of a rise to high office.[40] A final text that lays out very clearly the importance of beautiful manners in the career of a courtier is from Saxo Grammaticus's *Gesta Danorum*. The passage in question probably dates from the last decade of the twelfth century. Writing on the fringes of Europe. Saxo — chaplain of the archbishop of Lund, educated in France or Germany

---

[35] *Gesta episcoporum Leodiensium* 25, MGH SS 7:203: "admodum omni morum elegantia insignitus."

[36] *Vita Bernwardi* 3, *Lebensbeschreibungen,* p. 278: ". . . fit . . . inter episcopum et comitem de tantae indolis iuvene religiosa concertatio, ut uterque pro morum gratia illum sibi adoptare intenderet."

[37] *Das Leben des Bischofs Meinwerk von Paderborn* 5, ed. F. Tenckhoff, MGH SSrG (Hannover, 1921), p. 7. Cf. *DGQ,* 1:70–72.

[38] PL 171:1496A: "Quem rex Clotarius, cum propter sanguinis propinquitatem, tum propter egregiae formae dignitatem ac morum elegantiam quae in adolescente eminebant, libens suscepit . . . inter amicos habere coepit, dignum plane cognitum, cum quo de magnis rebus, et regni administratione tractaret." Cf. Marbod, *Vita S. Gualteri,* PL 171:1567: as a young man at school, ". . . ingenii singularis vivacitas et elegans suavitas morum latere non potuit."

[39] *Vita S. Udalrici Cellensis,* MGH SS 12:254: "Quid vero de gloriosae reginae dicam devotione, quae famulum Christi speciali dilexit affectione. Illius etenim delectabilium morum conventa suavitate, suis eum obsequiis voluit adhaerere . . ." (*Vita posterior* 5).

[40] *Vita Altmanni episcopi Pataviensis,* 40 MGH SS 12:241 (on Hartmann, abbot of Göttweih): ". . . morum exuberans elegantia [erat]. Unde principibus totius regni erat acceptissimus, et ipsi regi Heinrico V familiarissimus, qui et eum in archiepiscopatu Iuvavensi sublimare disposuit. . . ."

or both — was familiar with the language of the European courts. Here he describes the early tribulations of Iarmericus (the Ostrogoth Ermanaric, in Saxo's version son of the Danish king Sywardus). A hostage with Ismarus, king of the Slavs, Iarmericus was released from prison to become a farm laborer. He distinguished himself for administrative ability, became master of the king's slaves, and eventually was taken into the close circle of the king's retainers:

> Ubi cum se iuxta aulicorum ritum egregia morum amoenitate gessisset, brevi in amicorum numerum translatus primum familiaritatis locum obtinuit ac veluti quibusdam meritorum gradibus fretus ab infima sorte ad spectatum honoris fastigium concessit.... Grata omnibus Iarmerici indoles erat....[41]

Here the central role of "charm of manners" in a courtier's career is quite apparent. The passage raises the question whether the quality applied equally to laymen and clerics at court, and the question would be well worth pursuing in another context. Suffice it to say for the moment that Saxo's use of a variant of "elegance of manners" reveals that by ca. 1200 it had become a quality commonly cultivated by courtiers *(iuxta aulicorum ritum)*, and it could account for a dazzling rise to high position.

Since this quality was highly important in the career of a *curialis*, it will be worthwhile to investigate the history of the terms which express it. They are not common in antiquity, but they occur in contexts which make their meaning in classical Latin evident. In his letter-tract *Ad Marciam de consolatione,* Seneca traces various stages of Marcia's grief: at first she actively imposed it upon herself, now (at the time of writing) she is passively permitting it to continue, but soon, he urges her, she must put an end to it of her own will: "Quanto magis hoc morum tuorum elegantiae convenit, finem luctus potius facere, quam expectare" (8.3). Tacitus praises Pomponius in the *Annals* for his *morum elegantia*, "dum adversam fortunam aequus tolerat" (5.8). Evidently *elegantia morum* belongs to the vocabulary of Stoicism (though its infrequent occurrence and the fact that it never occurs in Cicero suggest that it was not a central conception). It indicates a calm and graceful mastering of adversity, restraint of passion. It did not entirely lose this meaning in the Middle Ages. Thomasin von Zirclaere is evidently using the German equivalent when he writes, "swer in zorn hat schoene site, / dem volget guotiu zuht mite."[42] Here also the mastering of powerful and "negative" emotions constitutes "beautiful manners." However, neither in the episcopal *vitae* nor in any other Latin texts from the tenth to the twelfth century have I found a single occurrence of the classical meaning. *Elegantia morum*, in its medieval usage, appears to have referred almost exclusively to "courtly"

---

[41] *Saxonis gesta Danorum* 8.10.1, ed. J. Olrik and H. Raeder (Copenhagen, 1931–57), 1:230–31.
[42] *Der Wälsche Gast des Thomasin von Zirclaria*, ed. Heinrich Rückert, Bibliothek der gesammten deutschen Nationalliteratur 30 (Quedlinburg and Leipzig, 1852), ll. 679–80.

manners and not to moral fortitude.[43] And this is true whether the context is ecclesiastical or secular.

An incident in Herbord's *Dialogue on the Life of Otto of Bamberg* gives us a very clear idea of the meaning of elegant *mores* in the milieu of the courtier bishop. The incident occurs on Otto's first proselytizing mission to Pomerania. The narrator, Siegfried, praises Otto's fastidious preparations for baptism. Otto separates the men from the women and has an elaborate system of curtains hung around the baptismal fonts, so as to preserve decorum. In the winter the water is warmed, and spices and scented oils are added. The participants in the dialogue interrupt here to exclaim about the refinement and decorousness of these arrangements *(disciplinata et honesta baptizandi forma)*:

> "It is small wonder that you are amazed," [the narrator replies.] "We who were present were also amazed not only at this, but at many other indications of his manners and his virtues *(morum atque virtutum insignia)*. For in each and every one of his acts he showed a special gift of singular fastidiousness and, if I may say so, of an elegant and urbane sense of orderliness. Never, under any circumstances — in eating or drinking, in word, gesture, or dress — would he tolerate anything indecorous, inappropriate, or unbecoming, but rather in every act of the outer man he manifested the harmony that reigned within him. . . ."[44]

This passage places us in the midst of a highly articulated Latin vocabulary of courtesy. *Elegans et urbana disciplina*[45] is the summation of Otto's *insignia morum*. That is, he displayed a scrupulous, refined sense of modesty and decorum, not only in the baptismal arrangements but also in the entirely courtly context of table manners, speech, gesture and dress *(in cibo aut potu, sermone, gestu vel habitu)*.

---

[43] Guido de Basochis († 1203), a cleric of St. Stephens of Châlons, writes to Archbishop Henry of Rheims, praising him for preeminence in "imperiosa generis dignitate . . . et lucidiori morum . . . venustate." These two "crowns," high birth and *morum venustas*, are above all other things necessary "ad elegantiorem persone dignioris ornatum" (*Liber epistularum Guidonis de Basochis*, ed. H. Adolfsson, Acta Universitatis Stockholmiensis, Studia Latina Stockholmiensia 18 [Stockholm, 1969], p. 1, Ep. 1, l. 9 ff.). Clearly the refined courtly elegance of the aristocratic clergy, and not Stoic restraint, was the main area of reference of the phrase. John of Salisbury uses *venustas morum* fully in the context of refinements of banqueting: *Ioannis Saresberiensis episcopi Carnotensis policratici sive de nugis curialium et vestigiis philosophorum libri VIII* 8.10, ed. Clemens Webb (Oxford, 1909), 2:284, l. 20. Von Moos refers to Hildebert's frequent use of *venustas morum*. Hildebert (above, n. 8), p. 94.

[44] Herbord 2.16, p. 90: "Nec mirum te ista mirari. Etenim, qui ea vidimus, mirabamur et ipsi tam hec quam alia complura morum eius atque virtutum insignia. Ipse namque in omni accione sua, quod et paganis dignum laude videbatur, quandam singularis mundicie atque — ut ita dixerim — elegantis et urbane discipline prerogativam habebat, ita ut nichil unquam indecens aut ineptum inhonestumve quid in cibo aut potu, sermone, gestu vel habitu admitteret. Sed in omni officio exterioris hominis, quenam esset composicio interioris, ostendebat. . . ."

[45] These are qualities which St. Augustine had rejected as vanities of his youth: "elegans et urbanus esse gestiebam abundanti vanitate" (*Confessiones* 3.1.1.).

X

The Courtier Bishop

The classical version of the Tristan romance by Gottfried von Strassburg, dated ca. 1210,[46] is a witness to the courtly meaning of *elegantia* and *venustas morum* in a secular context. The formula *schoene site* expresses a central concept of courtesy in this most courtly of romances. Young Tristan is kidnapped by Norwegian merchants, who admire his *schoene site* (2240 ff.) and hope to turn a good profit by selling this child prodigy. Freed by the kidnappers in Cornwall, Tristan meets two pilgrims and chats with them. He speaks flowingly and answers their questions with such mastery of word and gesture *(rede und gelaze,* 2740) that the two begin to marvel at his talents. They observe his bearing and his manners *(sine gebaerde und sine site),* his handsome figure. They cannot take their eyes off his splendid clothing. Finally they exclaim: "Who is this child, whose manners are so beautiful!" *(des site so rehte schoene sint,* 2754). There are many other occurrences, but the context and meaning is clear. *Schoene site* is evidently the German translation for *elegancia* or *venustas morum*.[47] Gottfried did not take the term from the Provençal or Old French vocabulary of *courtoisie,* which seems to have nothing comparable.[48] The term itself and the phenomenon to which it gives expression appear to be basically the same in *Tristan* and the *vitae*. In both, beauty of manners makes a man sought after and admired at court. In *Tristan* as in Herbord's *Dialogue* the quality shows itself in externals, in word, gesture, and dress *(sermo, gestus, habitus; rede, gebaerde, kleit).*

We can be fairly sure, then, that *elegantia morum* was connected with courtly cultivation of form and decorum, with refinement of speech and manners, splendor of dress, and politeness at table — that is, with *courtoisie* and *hövescheit*. Modern scholarship has not always distinguished the two constituent elements of *courtoisie:* refined, modest, polite manners and "courtly love."[49] The evidence of the *vitae* suggests that the first of these

---

[46] Citations are from Gottfried von Strassburg, *Tristan und Isold,* ed. Friedrich Ranke (Dublin and Zurich, 1967).

[47] The most common gloss for Lat. *elegantia* is MHG *schoenheit*. For *elegans* there are *schön* and *hövesch,* among others. Lorenz Diefenbach, *Glossarium Latino-Germanicum mediae et infimae aetatis* (Frankfurt am Main, 1857), p. 197. Diefenbach's glosses are from the late Middle Ages, but they are still helpful for usage in the twelfth–thirteenth century, even if not decisive in determining equivalents.

[48] Neither in the standard lexica (Godefroy and Tobler-Lommatzch) nor in the rich secondary literature on the Provençal and Old French vocabulary of courtesy can I find any terms to correspond to *disciplina/zuht, elegantia morum/shoene site* in the context of courtly refinement of behavior. This would suggest that the MHG terms for some central conceptions of courtesy, if not the phenomena to which they refer, derive from clerical culture at German courts, not from French courts and French literature. Unfortunately, there is no literature on the German and Latin vocabulary of courtesy to correspond to the various studies of Provençal and Old French. Cf. the bibliography in Glynnis M. Cropp, *Le vocabulaire courtois des troubadours de l'époque classique,* Publications romanes et françaises 135 (Geneva, 1975).

[49] See Jean Frappier's insistence on the distinction in "Vues sur les conceptions courtoises dans les littératures d'oc et d'oïl au XIIe siècle," *Cahiers de civilisation médiévale* 2 (1959), 135 ff. On the other hand, on the important connection between love and courtesy, see Joan M. Ferrante, "*Cortes Amor* in Medieval Texts," *Speculum* 55 (1980), 686–95.

developed as a social and ethical ideal at European courts some time before it became joined to the second and found its literary embodiment in the knight of courtly romance. At any rate "elegance of manners" was undoubtedly a clerical idea in origin. This is indicated both by its occurrences in the *vitae* and the Stoic and/or Ciceronian provenance of much of its vocabulary *(elegantia morum, honestas, decorum)*. In itself the idea that courtesy arose as an ideal of court clerics is not new.[50] But the opinions on the subject have largely to do with clerics as the authors of romance. The evidence of the *vitae* suggests that the ethical code which surfaced in courtly literature was practiced at the royal chapel some fifty to a hundred years prior to the cult of courtesy among the lay nobility of France.

Dating the evidence for *elegantia morum* is a problem. Current wisdom on the study of medieval biography and hagiography has it that the values expressed in a *vita* must be taken as representing those of the author, not those of the subject; the greater the period of time separating the two, the more strictly this rule applies.[51] Notker of Liège *(morum elegantia insignitus)* was chaplain under Otto III. Anselm's description of him is dated ca. 1056. Bernward of Hildesheim *(morum gratia)* was the favorite of the Empress Theophanu and the tutor and chaplain of Otto III. This is an interesting constellation, since Theophanu, niece of a Byzantine emperor, is known to have imported customs of the Byzantine court into Germany.[52] Her son Otto III, an admirer of urbanity,[53] adopted customs and offices of the refined and polished Byzantine court and at the same time attracted some of the most gifted clerics in Europe to serve in his court chapel.[54] Certainly the circumstances for cultivating an ideal of elegant and graceful manners were present at this court. But unfortunately, Bernward's *vita*, long dated ca. 1022 and ascribed to his teacher Thangmar, has recently been shown to contain later additions, and the description of his youth and court service would appear to be among them.[55] These passages, hence the epithet *gratia morum*,

---

[50] Cf. Frappier, "Vues," p. 146. And one need only mention the names of Edmond Faral, Hennig Brinkmann, Alfred Jeanroy, and Reto Bezzola. Peter von Moos, in his study of Hildebert (above, n. 8), has shown the clearest indications of the connections between the clerical milieu and courtesy. Hennig Brinkmann even attempted to trace the forms of expression of Provençal love lyric to the clerical-episcopal milieu in France. See his *Entstehungsgeschichte des Minnesangs* (Halle, 1926), p. 18 ff.

[51] Lotter, "Historische Erkenntnisse" (above, n. 13), pp. 320 ff., 342.

[52] See Percy Ernst Schramm, *Kaiser, Rom und Renovatio: Studien zur Geschichte des römischen Erneuerungsgedankens vom Ende des karolingischen Reiches bis zum Investiturstreit*, 2nd ed. (Darmstadt, 1957), 1:109 ff., and Bezzola, *Origines*, 1:256 ff.

[53] See his letter inviting Gerbert d'Aurillac to his court to oppose its "Saxon boorishness": *Die Briefsammlung Gerberts von Reims*, ed. Fritz Weigle, MGH Briefe der deutschen Kaiserzeit 2 (Berlin, 1966), p. 222 (Ep. 186). Cf. Bezzola, *Origines*, 1:258.

[54] P. E. Schramm, *Kaiser, Könige und Päpste: Gesammelte Aufsätze zur Geschichte des Mittelalters* (Stuttgart, 1969), 3:277-97.

[55] R. Drögereit, "Die Vita Bernwardi und Thangmar," *Unsere Diözese (Hildesheim) in Vergangenheit und Gegenwart* 28 (1959), 2-46.

The Courtier Bishop

are tentatively dated mid-twelfth century. Meinwerk *(regio obsequio morum elegantia idoneus)* was chaplain under Otto III and Henry II. His *vita*, however, dates also from the mid-twelfth century. Otto of Bamberg is described as elegant, either in manners or appearance, in all three of his *vitae*. This could indicate reliable testimony from his lifetime, but not necessarily. We are still in the middle of the twelfth century. The single reference in Anselm of Liège, reliably dated mid-eleventh century, is too little evidence to place the origins of an ideal of elegant manners among the Ottonian emperors, probable as this may be on the surface of the matter. We can conclude, however, that elegance of manners in the context of court etiquette was an ideal of German courtier bishops by the middle of the twelfth century at the latest — that is, some two decades before courtly ideals appeared in German romance — and that this ideal most likely is much older.[56]

4. Virtues

The list of virtues which characterized future bishops in royal service is long and varied. The biographers were keen observers and had generally a view of the strengths and weaknesses of their subjects unclouded by the urge to sanctify them. Still, it is possible to filter out some characteristics, relying on frequency and confirmation from nonbiographical sources, which clearly constituted requisite or desirable qualities in royal, clerical administrators. The virtues fall into three categories: (1) Religiosity: *pietas* or *sanctitas*. These occur in catalogues of virtues, but the biographers very rarely tell incidents which illustrate them. (2) Virtues connected with the exercise of administrative duties: *discretione providus, auctoritate gravis, acumen ingenii, strenuitas, diligentia, moderamen, facundia, eloquentia, sollertia, astutia*. (3) Personal qualities: *gravitas, compassio, moderamen, mansuetudo, humilitas, probitas, patientia, amabilitas, affabilitas*. In general, the qualities of the courtier bishop produce an odd blend of virtues from the active and contemplative life: authority and humility, zealousness and compassion, gravity and affability. It is an ideal of understated human greatness which has its counterpart in qualities which Cicero had assigned to the ideal Roman statesman: those are right who urge that "the higher we are set above other men, the more we should bear

---

[56] This is not to pin the entire phenomenon of courtesy on a single phrase. There is much evidence for the practice of courtly ideas at German courts as early as the mid-eleventh century, perhaps the best of it contained in the Latin romance epic *Ruodlieb*. A striking bit of evidence which to my knowledge has never been considered in discussions of the beginnings of courtesy is in the *Fundatio ecclesiae Hildesheimensis*, MGH SS 30/2:945. Writing around 1080, the author reports the spread of *ambiciosa curialitas* into Hildesheim under Bishop Azelinus (1044–54, formerly a chaplain of Henry III). This *curialitas* expressed itself in a relaxing of monastic discipline, a love of "courtly sophistication" *(curialis facetia)* among the clergy, refined taste in food, sumptuous taste in clothing, a more elegant and refined way of living, and a soft, effeminate way of dressing (on the text, see *DGQ*, 2:576). The modifier *ambiciosa* indicates the social context of this *curialitas*: it is a mode of behavior adopted by those vying for preferment at court.

308   The Courtier Bishop

ourselves as their inferiors."⁵⁷ This formulates an essential feature of the courtier bishop, and occurs in the *vitae* in a number of variations. The mighty Heribert of Cologne "protested his inferiority, whereas he was superior to all men."⁵⁸

Virtues, like human beings, adapt to the circumstances into which they are placed. Affability in the context of pastoral care and the bishop's love for his congregation is one thing; as a virtue which governs the relations of a court cleric to a king, it is something quite different. What constitutes the originality in the type of the court cleric is neither the addition of new virtues to the canon nor the particular combination of traditional ones, but rather the transformation of virtues traditional to the episcopal office when these are placed in the context of court service.⁵⁹ Though many of the virtues listed above deserve commentary, I will concentrate on two which illustrate especially clearly the transformation produced by the circumstances of court life: *mansuetudo* and *affabilitas*.

Mansuetudo. "Gentleness" is a ruler's virtue in the classical laudation.⁶⁰ It is a virtue ancillary to *clementia*. In Christianity it is biblical, Pauline, patristic, indeed so widespread that an attempt to assign it to a particular social group would be pointless. Nevertheless, it was certainly associated with the office of bishop in late antiquity and the early church,⁶¹ and this continued through Merovingian and Carolingian *vitae*.

Mansuetudo is gentleness of spirit, a placid, benevolent passivity shown to friends and enemies alike.⁶² Associated virtues are *humilitas, patientia, modestia*. The *vir mansuetus* suffers abuse without murmuring; he knows no anger or resentment. Lampert of Hersfeld can praise Bishop Gunter of Bamberg

---

⁵⁷ Cf. Cicero, *De officiis* 1.26: "quanto superiores simus, tanto nos geramus summissius."

⁵⁸ MGH SS 4:742: "superior cunctis inferiorem se aliis protestans." Cf. the praise of Brun of Cologne: "in maximo nobilitatis fastu humilis et mansuetus era" (*Vita Brunonis* 11, in *Lebensbeschreibungen*, p. 194. *DGQ*, 1:8–10, 84–91). And that of Conrad of Constanz: "quanto magnus sit, eo magis sectetur humilitatem" (MGH SS 4:431); and Udalrich of Zell: "tantum in se est humiliatus, quantum super alios exaltatus" (MGH SS 12:255). The latter refers to Ecclesiasticus 3.20: "Quanto maior es, humilia te in omnibus."

⁵⁹ For an analysis of the forces which shape the values within the *familia* of a "charismatic ruler," see Norbert Elias, *Die höfische Gesellschaft: Untersuchungen zur Soziologie des Königtums und der höfischen Aristokratie*, 4th ed., Soziologische Texte 54 (Darmstadt and Neuwied, 1979), pp. 188–90.

⁶⁰ Bittner, *Herrscherlob* (above, n. 19), pp. 24–25; Ernst Jerg, *Vir venerabilis: Untersuchungen zur Titulatur der Bischöfe in den ausserkirchlichen Texten der Spätantike als Beitrag zur Deutung ihrer öffentlichen Stellung*, Wiener Beiträge zur Theologie 26 (Vienna, 1970), p. 214.

⁶¹ Gregory the Great, *Regula pastoralis* 2.10, PL 77:44B ff.; Heinzelmann, *Bischofsherrschaft* (above, n. 20), pp. 36, 38, 152 ff.; and K. L. Noethlichs, "Materialien zum Bischofsbild aus den spätantiken Rechtsquellen," *Jahrbuch für Antike und Christentum* 16 (1973), 33 ff.

⁶² See von Moos's discussion of *mansuetudo* as an element in Hildebert's ideal of *humanitas*: *Hildebert*, pp. 148–49, 172.

The Courtier Bishop

for meekly tolerating insults from his own servants.[63] It is accordingly anything but a heroic virtue and frequently forms a contrasting pair with the warlike spirit of the ruler or knight. Otto of Freising gives a detailed description of Rainald of Dassel and Count Palatine Otto of Wittelsbach as imperial legates of Barbarossa in Italy. After a long list of qualities which both have in common, he distinguishes them by opposing Otto's *gladii severitas* to the *mansuetudo* appropriate to Rainald as a cleric.[64]

This virtue has two aspects particularly relevant to its role in court life: gentleness as a strategy of self-assertion in court intrigue, and as a strategy in the courtier's art of self-display.

An incident from Walter Daniel's *Life* of Ailred of Rievaulx[65] gives us a vivid example of the first. The famous Cistercian was in service at the court of King David of Scotland from his fourteenth to his twenty-fourth year (1124–33). He became steward of the royal court and personal advisor to the king and was placed in charge of the business affairs, internal and external, of the court. The king planned to procure a bishopric for him, but in 1133 Ailred entered the Cistercian monastery of Rievaulx, where he later became abbot. His biographer describes him with formulae common in the lives of courtier bishops, though he injects monastic elements which never occur in the German *vitae* (for example, Ailred falls into a mystical ecstasy while serving at the king's table). The king loved him ("Rex vehementer amabat eum," ch. 2) and placed many officials under his command. He became "as it were a second lord, an alternate prince" (loc. cit.). Ailred pleased all men in all things. He knew no rancor or resentment against any man, and though in a position to do harm to many, he did good to all. Such an abundance of affability and benevolence *(benignitas)* met in him that no abuse, no slander could provoke him to anger or revenge. He was loved by all, except that he had a particularly unpleasant enemy, a certain "thick-skinned and stiff-necked knight, blunt-hearted and utterly untamable" *(miles durus et rigidus valde stolidique cordis et penitus indomabilis)*. This knight hated and envied Ailred because he was loved by the king and by all the court. He began to work secretly against him, telling "envious words and idle tales of detraction," but was ignored. Finally his anger broke out in public, and he reviled

---

[63] *Annales*, p. 104 (1065). It sounds like the behavior of a Christian saint. But the immediate inspiration is probably classical. Cicero had held up Ulysses as a paragon of affability for tolerating insults from his servants to achieve his ultimate end (*De officiis* 1.31.113). John of Salisbury devotes a chapter of the *Policraticus* (3.14) to the virtue of *patientia*, showing Greek and Roman statesmen and generals bearing abuse patiently. He gives no examples from the Bible or Christian hagiography.

[64] *Gesta Frederici* 3.22: ". . . prope moribus equales, preter quod uni ex officio et ordine clericali necessaria inerat mansuetudo et misericordia, alteri . . . gladii severitas dignitatem addiderat" (F.-J. Schmale and A. Schmidt, ed. and trans., *Die Taten Friedrichs oder richtiger Cronica*, AQDG 17 [Berlin, 1965], p. 440).

[65] Ca. 1170. Cited here from *The Life of Ailred of Rievaulx by Walter Daniel*, ed. and trans. F. M. Powicke (New York and Oxford, 1951).

Ailred openly before the entire court, uttering imprecations which the biographer shrinks from relating. To his charge that Ailred was unworthy to enjoy such intimacy and esteem from the king, Ailred responded, composedly and patiently, *mansuetissima elocucione:* ". . . you say well, excellent knight, and everything you say is true; for, I am sure, you hate lying and love me. Who indeed is worthy to fight for King David, or to serve him as he should be served? I know only too well, and hold myself in deep displeasure, that I am a sinner, and have failed much in my service. . . ." Ailred's superior bearing and gentle eloquence won even more affection and trust from the king, who began to place important business into his hands. But Ailred also won over the knight, who pondered long over his own humiliation and Ailred's victory. In the end they became firm friends (ch. 3).

The incident is highly embroidered, it goes without saying.[66] But its idealizing aims at depicting Ailred as the successful court cleric, not as the future abbot. Here the Christian virtues of *mansuetudo, patientia,* and *humilitas,* born by *eloquentia,* are transformed into weapons of the active life, instruments for asserting a superior form of humanity over the rough-cut warrior boorishness of the knight. The irony of the pointed comments ("you hate lying and love me") shows that the stance of humble self-denial is a calculated one. In the intrigue-filled atmosphere of the court, the cleric, who could not reach for his sword in the face of insult,[67] had the superior weapons of intellectual suppleness and long-suffering. In this scene we can observe the contest between knight and cleric as a sociological reality. The confrontation must have been common in court life, and the same opposition produced the love debates in Middle Latin and Old French poetry in which noble ladies compare knight and cleric as lovers. In both fields of confrontation — court life and love — the cleric was normally the victor, not only because clerics depicted the contest, but because the nature of court life itself favored the stifling of conflict, not the open airing of it.[68] In this field of battle, composure, submissiveness, irony, and a fine and gentle bearing were much more effective weapons of self-assertion than headlong assaults. Ailred's *mansuetudo* is a close relative of the "humility" of the splendid and powerful Cardinal Wolsey, lauded by David Lloyd: "To be humble to

---

[66] The stance of suffering contumely to turn it back on the offender may well be adapted from Cicero's *De amicitia* (21.77), which of course Ailred, and presumably his biographer, knew well. But that a knight is assigned the role of boorish slanderer is significant both in the sociology of court life in the twelfth century and in the context of the cleric's biography. The *miles stolidus* is a frequent antagonist of the court cleric (see above, n. 23).

[67] The interdict on a cleric's bearing weapons had a profound effect on his life at court. The cleric-lover in a dialogue of Andreas's *De amore* is reproached by the lady he is wooing with lack of fighting spirit, a quality she prizes in knights. He responds that, were he not restrained by law and custom, he would like nothing better than "actus bellicos exercere et cordis audaciam demonstrare." *Andreae Capellani regii Francorum de amore libri tres,* ed. E. Trojel, 2nd ed. (Munich, 1972), p. 192.

[68] See Elias, *Die höfische Gesellschaft* (above, n. 59), p. 186.

X

The Courtier Bishop

superiors is duty; to equals is courtesie; to inferiors, is nobleness; and to all, safety; it being a virtue that for all her lowliness commandeth those souls it stoops to."[69] These qualities were also appropriate to court life because, to put it at its lowest, they offered a natural camouflage to the intriguer.

In the scene just discussed from the *Life of Ailred* we see also the social circumstances which would have commended an ideal of elegant, gentle courtesy to a warrior class. The tamed *miles indomabilis* is an embodiment of the knighthood's willingness to appropriate for itself a clerical ideal of gentleness, or at least to recognize its superiority. The results of this willingness are evident in the hero of the courtly romance. The ability to conquer the urgings of pride and warrior hotheadedness becomes an essential element of *courtoisie*.[70]

Mansuetudo also produced a strategy of courtier self-display. In the hothouse atmosphere of court life the court cleric faced the real dilemma of having to display the talents and skills which would win him the favor of the ruler without arousing envy among his competitors.[71] The solution to this dilemma was to set up a counterpoint between the brilliance of his talents and the humbleness with which they were put forward. This solution produced an important courtier virtue. We can observe it at three stages in its development. (1) The Christian virtue: Baudri of Bourgeuil describes an incident in the life of St. Hugh (archbishop of Rouen, †730) at the court of Charlemagne (the anachronism is due to Baudri's uncritical rendering of his source). One day a debate took place at court on theological questions. Hugh sat silently and listened as others put forward their opinions. Soon the issue was clouded and the debate was at an impasse. Then the others turned to Hugh and demanded his response. When he finally spoke, he did so with such wisdom that all hung on his words; they marveled at his knowledge and declared that the Holy Spirit spoke through him. The incident was reported to the emperor, and Hugh's bearing so pleased him that he began to love him more dearly and to heap honors on him.[72] What pleased all and won the favor of the emperor was not only that Hugh possessed great wisdom, but

---

[69] *State Worthies: or, the Statesmen and Favourites of England from the Reformation to the Revolution: Their Prudence and Policies, Successes and Miscarriages, Advancements and Falls* (London, 1766), 1:32.

[70] Guillaume de Lorris says of the lady named *Cortoisie* in the *Roman de la Rose*, "onc ne fu hom par li desdiz, / ne ne porta autrui rancune": ed. F. Lecoy, Classiques français du moyen âge 92 (Paris, 1965), 1:39, ll. 1236–37. I cannot help thinking that the author of the *Ruodlieb* was parodying this courtier virtue in his characterization of the two white dancing bears that the *rex minor* gives as a gift to the *rex major*. They eat from dishes like men, they dance with the ladies, they twitter gently instead of roaring, and they do not get angry no matter how they are wronged ("Non irascantur, quodcunque mali paterentur," 5, l. 98): *The Ruodlieb: Linguistic Introduction, Latin Text and Glossary*, ed. Gordon B. Ford, Jr. (Leiden, 1966). They have overcome their animal nature, are civilized, and behave themselves as courtiers are supposed to.

[71] Cf. Castiglione, *Il libro del cortegiano* 2.7, ed. Bruno Maier, 2nd ed. (Turin, 1964), p. 198.

[72] *Vita S. Hugonis*, PL 166:1167A–B. The work dates from before 1120, probably ca. 1117.

that he concealed his understanding, great as it was, until forced to speak. (2) Tristan, the reticent prodigy: calculated underplaying of talents: The stage at which the Christian virtue becomes wholly secularized is seen in the arrival at court of the young prodigy Tristan in Gottfried's version of the romance. After Tristan has struck awe into the Cornish hunting party by a dazzling display of hunting skills, he states that he has now done the best he was capable of; had it been in his power he would have served them better (3045 ff.). Of course none of the Englishmen could have done as well. When the awestruck hunters ask him who he is, he claims to be the son of a merchant, though in fact he is the son of the lord of Parmenie (3096 ff.).[73] At King Mark's court, Tristan listens to the performance of a musician, the best they had at the court. He comments on the performance in a way that indicates he knows a thing or two about music. When asked by the musician whether he himself can play, Tristan replies that he once could, but now has grown so rusty that he dare not (he is only fourteen years old at the time!). When he finally takes up the instrument, he plays so skillfully that the entire court is in raptures. The king asks him whether he knows other instruments; Tristan answers, no. The king insists. Tristan replies that he knows all sorts of instruments, but not as many as he would like to know. And besides, he has not been at it for long, only seven years or so. The instrument which he plays best, the *sambjut*, has never even been heard of in backwoods Cornwall. The court breaks into new and fervent acclaims of Tristan's almost superhuman endowments (3656 ff.). Asked whether he knows any foreign language besides French, Latin, and English, he replies that he knows some "tolerably well" *(billiche wol)*. Then he is addressed in the various languages known at court — Norwegian, Irish, German, Scottish, and Danish — and handles himself like a native in each. The courtiers can only gasp in rapt admiration (3690 ff.).[74] There are other examples, but the pattern is clear: in each there is a calculated underplaying of his skills, accomplishments, and social standing — all the things from which he ought to derive status and preferment at court. The result is that the awed admiration of the onlookers is increased by the secondary admiration for his nonchalance. The pattern is essentially the same as in the scene from Baudri's *Life of St. Hugh,* with the great difference that the effect was calculated in the case of Tristan's performance. What was a virtue has become a stratagem. By concealing great talents or trivializing them, he magnifies them and multiplies the harvest of honor he collects from a wondering court. (3) *Sprezzatura* in the Renaissance

---

[73] See the comments of Siegfried Grosse, " 'Vremediu maere': Tristans Herkunftsberichte," *Wirkendes Wort* 20 (1970), 289–302; and Jaeger, *Medieval Humanism* (above, n. 7), p. 69 f.

[74] Though all these incidents were in Gottfried's (lost) source, Thomas of Brittany, Tristan's posed modesty appears to be Gottfried's addition, at least if Thomas's translator into Old Norse, Brother Robert, renders his source accurately. See *The Saga of Tristram and Ísönd,* tr. Paul Schach (Lincoln, Neb., 1973), p. 26 ff.

The Courtier Bishop

courtier: Count Ludovico da Canossa, the proponent of the perfect courtier in Castiglione's *Il libro del cortegiano,* stipulates that the courtier must at all costs avoid affectation in the display of attainments. He can do this by practicing in all things a certain disdainful attitude towards his own accomplishments *(una certa sprezzatura),* "which conceals all artistry and makes whatever one says or does seem uncontrived and effortless. . . . Grace springs especially from this, since everyone knows how difficult it is to accomplish some unusual feat perfectly, and so ease in such things excites the greatest wonder. . . . So we can truthfully say that true art is what does not seem to be art, and the most important thing is to conceal it" (1.26). That is, the courtier treats his own best accomplishments as if they amounted to nothing, as though he had acquired the skills involved with no effort whatsoever.[75] *Sprezzatura* aims at arousing in the observer the impression that if the courtier can perform something so difficult with such ease, he could with effort accomplish a great deal more.[76] The stance is perfectly apparent in young Tristan's apologies for his awesome skills and his protestations of discontent with his own accomplishments. The scenes from the *Life of St. Hugh* and Gottfried's *Tristan* suggest that Castiglione was giving a new name to a courtier's virtue which had long since been discovered and cultivated at European courts.[77]

Affabilitas-amabilitas-benignitas. There is a broad complex of virtues in the *vitae* connected with the amiability of the courtier bishop. Some of the formulae are *affabilis, amabilis, omnibus carus, gratus, gratiosus, omnibus gratus.* We frequently encounter some variant of St. Paul's *omnibus omnia factus sum* (1 Cor. 9.22), though when applied to a court cleric it is rarely the virtue of the proselytizer: *ut omnes salvos facerem.* Judging from its frequency, affability (which I take as the characteristic virtue of this group) was obligatory in a courtier bishop; it or some variant characterizes virtually every bishop whose *vita* is considered here.[78] Affability is not biblical. It occurs occasionally in

---

[75] On *sprezzatura,* see Erich Loos, *Baldassare Castigliones "Libro del Cortegiano": Studien zur Tugendauffassung des Cinquecento,* Analecta Romanica 2 (Frankfurt am Main, 1955), p. 116; and Joseph Mazzeo, "Castiglione's *Courtier:* The Self as a Work of Art," in idem, *Renaissance and Revolution: The Remaking of European Thought* (New York, 1965), p. 145 f.

[76] *Il libro del cortegiano* 1.28, p. 128; 2.7, p. 198.

[77] He calls *sprezzatura* "una nova parola" (1.26, p. 128). Studies on the source of *sprezzatura* are summarized in Loos, *Studien,* pp. 116–17.

[78] Brun of Cologne (†965): "Arridebant ei omnia" *(Lebensbeschreibungen,* p. 182); Franco of Worms (†999): "cunctis affabilis erat, cunctis benignus extitit" (MGH SS 4:833); Adalbero II of Metz: "Omnibus omnia factus . . . universis non modo clericis et laicis. . . . Hunc omnis sexus et aetas, hunc omnis ordo et conditio . . . miro affectu mentis venerabantur ac diligebant" (MGH SS 4:661); Bernward of Hildesheim: ". . . Deo gratae et hominibus acceptae indolis gratia domno episcopo . . . omnique congregationi dignus et familiaris efficiebatur, propinquorumque dilectioni probatissimus habebatur" *(Lebensbeschreibungen,* p. 276); Meinwerk of Paderborn: "omnibus carus et amabilis, aspectu et colloquio affabilis" (ed. Tenckhoff, p. 6); Anno of Cologne: "cunctorum oculis gratiosus, omnium animis amabilis" (MGH SS 11:467); Otto of

antiquity. Cicero discusses it as a quality which a statesman can cultivate in order to win the favor of the people.[79] In late antiquity it is quite common as an epithet for a bishop, and it establishes itself firmly in Merovingian *vitae*.[80] It is connected with the quality of the bishop which Heinzelmann calls "paternalism."[81] A bishop was father and mother to his flock, and was to help and serve all men: *miseris et pauperibus affabilis* is a frequent formula of praise.

But again, at the courts of the Ottonian-Salian kings the virtue took on quite a different complexion. Here affability and amiability found a broad social context and a distinct social function, but both context and function were not only foreign to the Christian significance of the virtues; they were directly contrary to it. In court life affability was connected with a central concern in the life of the courtier: winning and maintaining the favor of the lord and his court. It was a token of success in court life to make oneself beloved of all. This applies to laymen and clerics alike.[82] It is the overarching concern of Castiglione's *Il libro del cortegiano*,[83] and it is simply a fact that the ruler's favor is the prime mover of court life. Affability and amiability are prominent means of winning it. The biographer of Burchard of Worms tells that Burchard's brother and predecessor as bishop of Worms, Franco (†999), so enjoyed the trust and intimate friendship of the emperor (Otto III) that while still a youth he participated in the king's important councils and was privy to his secrets: "Cunctis affabilis erat, cunctis benignus extitit, . . . ab imperatore multum honoratus et carus prae aliis habitus, illius consilio . . . rem publicam in pace regebat."[84] It would be entirely in the spirit of the passage to translate the first phrases causally: *Because* he was affable and benevolent to all, and *because* he was loved and preferred by the emperor,

---

Bamberg: "omnibus gratus" (Herbord, ed. Wikarjak, p. 198), "se multa opportunitate ac modestia duci aptavit et toti curie gratum fecit" (ibid.), and "Tanta . . . industria et bonitate se . . . gessit, ut ab omnibus curialibus amaretur" (ibid., p. 202); Rainald of Dassel: "illaris, affabilis" (MGH SS 18:640), and "iocondus et affabilis omnibus" (MGH SS 16:464).

[79] See the discussion in *De officiis* 2.14.48. Sallust describes the young Jugurtha as "omnibus carus" (*Bellum Jugurthinum* 6.1). It is a ruler's virtue in the Carolingian *Fürstenspiegel*. See Smaragdus, *Via regia*, PL 102:946A: "[Prudentia] . . . te cunctis amabilem reddat"; and Sedulius Scotus, *Liber de rectoribus Christianis* 2, PL 103:296A: "Ergo per affabilitatem et beneficia procuret ut diligatur. . . ." On this virtue in the saint's legend, see L. Zoepf, *Das Heiligenleben im 10. Jahrhundert*, BKMR 1 (Hildesheim, 1908; repr. 1973), p. 41.

[80] Cf. Heinzelmann, *Bischofsherrschaft* (above, n. 20), p. 163; Jerg, *Vir venerabilis* (above, n. 60), pp. 88, 96, 186 (*deo amabilis*).

[81] "Väterliche Herrschaft" (*Bischofsherrschaft*, p. 152 ff.).

[82] After Ruodlieb impresses the king by his talents in fishing, he "wins the affections of all" the members of the court ("affectans sese cunctis," *Ruodlieb* 2.50).

[83] Cf. Castiglione's statement of purpose in his introduction, *Il libro del cortegiano* 1.1, p. 79; He will describe ". . . la forma di cortegiania più conveniente a gentilomo che viva in corte de' prìncipi, per la quale egli possa e sappia perfettamente loro servire in ogni cosa ragionevole, *acquistandone da essi grazia e dagli altri laude* . . ." (italics added).

[84] *Vita Burchardi* 3, MGH SS 4:833.

X

The Courtier Bishop   315

the kingdom could be governed in peace with his advice. This biographer and many others saw a direct connection between affable manners, the affection of king and court, and high position and influence. The biographers had a keen eye for the sequence of events by which an amiable prodigy rose to preferment: a cleric, called to the court, wins the affection of all by his affability, dazzles all by his talents, is taken into the inner circle of the king's advisors, becomes his most intimate friend and advisor, and finally governs all the business of the court, ruling at the emperor's side, or even in his stead.[85]

Here we must recall the historical circumstances of the court chapel after Otto I. The Ottos increasingly drew bishops from the ranks of their chaplains and chancellors, building the episcopate into an important instrument of imperial politics by filling vacancies whenever possible with men strictly loyal to the emperor. Under these circumstances it lay in the nature of the position of court chaplain and future bishop that his relation to the emperor or king was an extraordinarily close and personal one. The love and trust of the emperor amounted to prerequisites for preferment at court and advancement to a bishop's seat.[86] In the *vitae* after Otto I we no longer encounter the miraculous selection of a bishop common in Carolingian lives. Gone are the days when the emperor appointed a lowly and obscure servant to a vacant seat because he saw a marvelous light breaking from the man's body as he slept.[87] While the Ottonian-Salian biographers no longer felt obligated to testify to the sanctity of a courtier bishop as young man, virtually every one attested to his affability and trustworthiness. Otto III seems particularly to have cultivated close relations with his chaplains.[88]

---

[85] Bernward of Hildesheim: "Benignissime suscipitur [by the empress Theophanu] atque in brevi summae familiaritatis locum apud illam obtinuit" (*Lebensbeschreibungen*, p. 278), and "Praecipua itaque familiaritate magistrum suum [i.e., Bernward] amplectebatur [i.e., Otto III]" (ibid.); Meinwerk of Paderborn: "cum irreprehensibiliter conversaretur, et regalis celsitudo et procerum multitudo eum reverebatur" (ed. Tenckhoff, p. 8), and "Meinwercus . . . regi . . . notissimus, de karo fit karissimus, factusque est ei in negotiis publicis et privatis comes irremotissimus" (ibid., p. 15); Wazo of Liège († 1048): "Imperatori in brevi fit gratissimus" (MGH SS 7:216); Anno of Cologne: "in palacium assumptus, brevi apud eum [Henry III] pre omnibus clericis, qui in foribus palacii excubabant, primum gratiae et familiaritatis gradum obtinuit" (Lampert, *Annales*, p. 328 [1075]); Arnold of Mainz († 1160): "ab extremo ungue usque ad supremum calculum per dignitatum gradus ascendens . . . ut splendore indutus principum, imperialis aule illustrissimus cancellarius, quasi alter imperator in latere imperatoris imperii prestaret officio . . ." (*Bibliotheca rerum Germanicarum*, ed. Jaffé, 3:608).

[86] Hauck, *Kirchengeschichte*, 3:31. On the same circumstance at a bishop's court, Weinfurter (above, n. 1), p. 205: "Von Anfang an . . . zeigt sich, dass die Beziehung zwischen Kapellan und Bischof in einem engen persönlichen Treueverhältnis beruhte. . . . Hierin lag die grosse Aufstiegschance der bischöflichen Kapelläne . . . begründet."

[87] Kunibert of Cologne († 648; *Vita* second half of ninth century). The miraculous selection of a bishop is perfectly common in chronicles from the tenth–twelfth century. Thietmar of Merseburg has a miracle to relate for practically every episcopal election. Perhaps some genre consideration excluded the miraculous selection from the *vitae*?

[88] Fleckenstein, *Die Hofkapelle*, 2:110 f.

Peter Damian tells of the cleric Tammo, the brother of Bernward of Hildesheim, that he was so beloved of the emperor and on such close terms with him that they wore the same clothes and at table ate from the same bowl, joining their hands together when they met in the dish.[89] The relationship of the chaplain to the king is regularly described with the vocabulary of friendship, love, and blood relationship.[90]

The predominant values of the courtier bishop have so far been described schematically, but the same ensemble of qualities and ideals may be observed in a single representative figure, Otto of Bamberg.[91] Otto's life is richly documented, and his court service, first with Judith, wife of Duke Wladislaw of Poland and sister of Henry IV, then with Henry IV himself, lasted fourteen years, from 1088 to 1102.

Otto was born in Swabia of noble but poor parents. He was "an elegant lad" (Ebo 1.3). It was apparent from his earliest days that he was a "magni meriti vir" (Monk of Prüfening 1.1). His elder brother, a knight, inherited his father's possessions, and Otto was sent to school. Having studied the poets and philosophers, and lacking the wherewithal to continue his studies, he left Germany for Poland, where he knew there was a "dearth of literate men" (Herbord 3.32). In Poland he soon had learned the customs and the language so well that he passed for a native (Monk of Prüfening 1.2). The three major biographers give widely differing versions of his early activities in Poland. Herbord says that he took over a school for boys, was soon rich and honored, "omnibus gratus"; he began to serve "rich and powerful men" who favored him for the elegance of his appearance. He was well suited for diplomatic missions for the "greats of the land" (3.32). According to Ebo, he went to Poland to become the chaplain of Judith. He served her most faithfully and made a great name for himself, so that the noble and powerful men of the region positively competed to have their sons accepted into his tutelage. He became wealthy in gold and silver. Judith frequently sent him, laden with magnificent gifts, on missions to her brother Henry, and the authority and circumspectness with which he carried out his legations ex-

---

[89] Schramm, *Kaiser, Rom und Renovatio* (above, n. 52), 1:111.

[90] Otto III "very much loved" Burchard of Worms ("valde illum dilexit," MGH SS 4:833); Meinwerk of Paderborn showed Henry II the "flames of his intimate love" ("flammas dilectionis intime," ed. Tenckhoff, p. 17); Henry IV embraced Otto of Bamberg "as if he were his only son" (Ebo 1.3, p. 12). See the discussion of these formulations in Wolfgang Hug, "Elemente der Biographie im Hochmittelalter: Untersuchungen zu Darstellungsform und Geschichtsbild der Viten vom Ausgang der Ottonen bis in die Anfänge der Stauferzeit" (Diss. Munich, 1957), pp. 108–9.

[91] On Otto's *vitae* see above, n. 31. Also the articles by Jürgen Petersohn, "Probleme der Otto-Viten und ihrer Interpretation: Bemerkungen im Anschluss an eine Neuerscheinung," *Deutsches Archiv* 27 (1971), 314–72, and "Otto von Bamberg und seine Biographen: Grundformen und Entwicklung des Ottobildes im hohen und späten Mittelalter," *Zeitschrift für bayerische Landesgeschichte* 43 (1980), 3–27 (with rich bibliography).

X

The Courtier Bishop

cited the admiration and wonder of the emperor (1.1). According to the Monk of Prüfening, he taught young boys, won the love and affection of all wise men, and became so widely known that all the prelates of the land loved him sincerely, not only for his splendid eloquence, tenacious memory, sharp mind, and learning, but also for the elegance of his manners. He served these lords and won high favor with them. He also won the favor of Duke Wladislaw and served him on diplomatic missions (1.3).

Herbord says that Otto came to the attention of Duke Wladislaw while on such a mission. He found great favor with the duke and with his entire court. The service of such a cleric, so the duke thought, must do honor to his house (3.33). At this point Herbord relates a romanticized version of Wladislaw's courtship of Judith, with Otto serving as his suitor.[92] Otto won the bride and became her chaplain. But he had come to the attention of the emperor while in Germany, and eventually he entered the service of Henry, who had to explain to his disappointed sister that "such a cleric" was necessary for service at the imperial court (Herbord 3.33; cf. Ebo 1.3). Otto so conquered Henry by the nobility of his bearing (*nobilitate morum*) and his sincere loyalty that the king embraced him as if he were his only son, making him his private secretary and chancellor and placing all that was precious and valuable in the palace in his charge. He also placed him in charge of the building of the cathedral of Speyer (Ebo 1.3–5). He was loved and honored by all members of the court, was dear to the greatest and the least, and governed all things in the king's court like a second Joseph (Herbord 3.35).

At this point both Ebo and Herbord tell the anecdote of Otto and the repairing of the king's psalter. One day Henry took Otto aside to a more private place ("secrecius eum compellans"), says Ebo (1.6), and asked him whether he knew the psalter well and could sing it to him. Yes, replied Otto, to the king's delight. He bade him sit by his side when no one else was about, and together they sang the psalter. Herbord says that whenever the king read and prayed in private, Otto was there to discuss and meditate on the texts with him. Seeing him pleased by this, he continued presenting hymns, psalms, prayers, and readings from Scripture throughout the year. Otto was always at hand to bring the king his psalter, because "in his skill and shrewdness he thought he should neglect nothing which could win him the favor of his lord" ("Nichil enim Ottonis sollercia negligendum putabat, quo sibi gratiam domini conciliare valeret . . . ," 3.34). Otto noticed that the book was torn and soiled from use and set about repairing it. The king one day asked for it, and Otto was at hand with the restored book. "Not this one,"

---

[92] This and other episodes show how romance motifs could accrete around the figure of the courtier bishop. Benno II of Osnabrück so distinguished himself in Henry III's campaign in Hungary that popular vernacular songs were composed about him ("populares fabulae et cantilenae vulgares," *Lebensbeschreibungen*, p. 382). One source reports that Thomas Becket's mother was the daughter of the emir of Palestine whom his father met on a crusade while held prisoner of the emir (*Quadrilogus* 1.2).

said the king. "I want my psalter." "This is it," said Otto. " 'This is well done,' replied the king, loving him in his heart more than his words indicated" (3.34). The king is less restrained in Ebo's version. He was "struck dumb" (*obstupefactus*) by the splendor of the restoration, and when he found out that it was Otto's work, he embraced him lovingly and called out: "Just as you . . . have restored my psalter, replacing its old cover with a new one, so also I shall raise you to new heights of honor, replacing your pauper's clothing." From that time on he sought an opportunity of promoting Otto to bishop (1.6).

Here the ideal of the courtier bishop is recorded so clearly and so consistently that the presentation is occasionally startling. An idealized picture of Otto as royal adviser and courtier emerges from all three versions. In each of the *vitae* Otto's early career stands under the sign of *captatio benevolentiae*, the winning of favor. The biographers do not focus on stages in a rise to sainthood, but rather on stages in a worldly career. Otto arouses love and amazement in his lords for his elegant ways, his appearance, his skill as diplomat and administrator, his attentive and loyal service. He is courted by prelates and lords at every stage of his career.[93] Ebo and Herbord also focus sharply on the degree of intimacy which Otto enjoyed with the king. Henry speaks with Otto in private ("remotis aliis") and makes Otto his partner in private prayer. Herbord can motivate the episode of the book repair by stating that Otto, skilled and shrewd as he was ("Ottonis sollercia"), felt he should leave no stone unturned in winning the favor of his lord, and this consists in bringing him his book, repairing it, and taking part in his private meditations. But while the book is a psalter and the sessions are devoted to prayer, neither Herbord nor Ebo praises Otto's *pietas et sanctitas*. It is his skill in winning the king's favor that impressed them, and so the trivial service of repairing the book can become the central event in his rise to preferment. Ebo even explains his promotion to bishop as the king's response to the book repair. It is obviously an apocryphal explanation, suggested to Ebo by the rhetorical *translatio* of newly bound book to Otto's "renewal" and elevation. But it is significant that Ebo, a Michelsberg monk and priest who apparently advocated the Hirsau reform,[94] can envision the rise to the bishop's office in this way. To such an extent had the model of the courtier bishop become entrenched and legitimate that it could be put forward uncritically by a

---

[93] The *vir expetibilis*, for whose services powerful lords compete, is an admired figure. Bernward of Hildesheim: "fitque inter episcopum et comitem de tantae indolis iuvene religiosa concertatio, ut uterque pro morum gratia illum sibi adoptare intenderet" (*Lebensbeschreibungen*, p. 278); Benno II of Osnabrück: "optimatibus terrae illius in brevi est cognitus et honestissima contentione decertatus, cuius potissimum dominio subesse deberet" (*Lebensbeschreibungen*, p. 380), and "Hac itaque caeterisque, quas in eo diximus sitas, virtute conspicuus exteris quoque potentibus et dominis fama vulgante coepit esse expetibilis" (ibid., p. 390).

[94] See Petersohn, "Otto und seine Biographen" (above, n. 91), p. 15. Herbord apparently belonged to a more liberal faction.

X

The Courtier Bishop

monk favoring the church reform. Clearly neither Ebo nor Herbord regarded it as their task to make Otto into a pious man and future saint in the description of his court service. They described a gifted and highly successful courtier, even allowing glimpses of the worst side of that figure to slip into the depiction.

An orthodox model of the Christian bishop as a young man existed in the Middle Ages, of course. Its chief sources were 1 Timothy 3.2-7 and Gregory the Great's *Regula pastoralis*. The latter established the definitive orthodox model of episcopal *idoneitas*,[95] but its influence on the image of the courtier bishop in the *vitae* was negligible.[96] Orthodox writings on the office of bishop, far from advocating our type, argue against it.[97] The Ottonian royal chapel in its relation to the imperial church was the social matrix which produced a new ideal type: the mighty, skillful royal advisor who is the darling of the king and court and the humble servant of all men.

The ideals which crystallized around this figure were not restricted to the royal chapel. They evolved into a Christian-humanist ethic of worldly service.[98] This ethic was broadly influential,[99] cultivated by clerics at secular

---

[95] On the importance of the *Regula pastoralis*, see R. W. Southern, *Western Society and the Church in the Middle Ages* (above, n. 15), pp. 172-73; and Heinz Hürten, "Gregor der Grosse und der mittelalterliche Episkopat," *Zeitschrift für Kirchengeschichte* 73 (1962), 16-41. Hürten shows that the transformation of the bishop into "Reichsfürst" under the Ottos was directly contrary to Gregory's model (p. 17 ff.).

[96] Köhler made Gregory's call for a balance between the bishop's worldly and spiritual duties a guiding idea of his study, *Das Bild des geistlichen Fürsten* (above, n. 11). But even this limited reliance on Gregory is disputed by Hürten (above, n. 95), pp. 19 f. and 40 f. See also Hürten's article, "Die Verbindung von geistlicher und weltlicher Gewalt als Problem in der Amtsführung des mittelalterlichen deutschen Bischofs," *Zeitschrift für Kirchengeschichte* 82 (1971), 18 (criticism of Köhler's and Heer's treatment of the influence of Gregory).

[97] There is a dramatic juxtaposition of the two types in Peter Damian, *Epistolarum libri octo* 2, Ep. 1, PL 144:253 ff. For two twelfth-century formulations, see John of Salisbury, *Policraticus* 7.20, and Peter of Blois, Ep. 15, PL 207:51 ff. See also R. Egenter, "Bischofsstand und bischöfliches Ethos nach dem heiligen Thomas von Aquin," in *Episcopus: Studien über das Bischofsamt. M. Kardinal von Faulhaber zum 80. Geburtstag* (Regensburg, 1949), pp. 164-84; and Martin Grabmann, "Die Lehre des Erzbischofs und Augustinertheologen Jakob von Viterbo (†1307/8) vom Episkopat und Primat und ihre Beziehung zum Heiligen Thomas von Aquin," in *Episcopus*, pp. 185-206.

[98] This ethic did not find its great formulator in the Middle Ages, but rather in the Renaissance. Still, I believe that Colin Morris in his excellent study, *The Discovery of the Individual, 1050-1200* (New York, 1973), p. 46, slightly underestimated its prevalence: "All these administrators in the service of the Church, and many of those who worked for secular governments, were clergy, and they were faced by the personal problem that there was no plan of ethical behavior to guide and justify their way of life." See also Morris's article, "Zur Verwaltungsethik: Die Intelligenz des 12. Jahrhunderts im politischen Leben," *Saeculum* 24 (1973), 241-50.

[99] Görlitz argues that service in the royal chapel was "das höchste erstrebenswerte Ziel jedes jungen Geistlichen" (*Königliche Hofkapelle* [above, n. 3], p. 26). Even though this might be somewhat overstated, it certainly holds true that the standards of the royal chapel must have been widely influential.

courts generally.[100] It is easy to account for its influence. The royal chapel was cosmopolitan; its members were among the most gifted and talented men in Europe. They provided a model which spread to lesser courts and shaped the values of clerical administrators generally. The cathedral schools, pedagogic instruments of Ottonian policy and educators of courtier bishops, assisted in the propagation of those values.

Having elucidated individual attributes of the courtier bishop and the tradition behind them, I now want to look at some representations of character in texts which clearly draw on our type but which originated outside of the context of the episcopal office in the imperial church.

The Curialis *Mythologized: Matthew of Vendôme's Portrait of Ulysses*

In his *Ars versificatoria,* Matthew of Vendôme, a master of grammar and student of Bernardus Silvestris, included a series of portraits to serve as models for the description of particular types. The first is a pope, the second a ruler (Caesar), the third Ulysses.[101] The social order of the figures is evident, except in the case of Ulysses.[102] But our preceding discussion makes it possible to classify him. Matthew describes him as "adorned with eloquence, gladdened by good sense, invested with grace of manners *(morum gratia),* blessed by fame." He is of incisive eloquence, foresighted, great in cunning. He is unsurpassed in genius, a servant of the Good *(servitor honesti).* Some twenty-five lines are devoted to the theme "the wisdom of his words proceeds from the wisdom of his mind." Then the list of virtues continues. What he has received from nature he outstrips through acquired virtue, and this faithful master is "the intimate vassal of the outer man" ("intimus est hominis exterioris homo," ll. 31–32). He weighs difficult cases in the balance, determining whether deeds are good or evil. Age cannot impoverish his virtues, but rather it increases his wisdom. No arrogance defiles the flower of his mind.

The characterization is of an aged servant and counselor living in the "world" (he has attained fame, l. 2; honor, 51–52). The meaning of "intimate vassal of the outer man" is not immediately clear. But a ruler has vassals, Ulysses is in the retinue of Agamemnon, and the "intimacy" no doubt places him in the *familia* of this ruler. The phrase probably means, then, "servant of

---

[100] Two formulations of the type outside the genre of bishop's *vita* are Phillip of Harvengt's letter to a former friend and schoolmate, now bishop (Ep. 13), PL 203:97–119, and Henry of Huntingdon, *Epistola ad Walterum de mundi contemptu, sive de episcopis et viris illustribus sui temporis,* PL 195:979 ff. See especially the description of Simon, deacon of Huntington, son of the king's chancellor and a man "regaliter enutritus": while still a youth, ". . . in summam regis amicitiam et curiales dignitates mox provectus est. Erat autem celer ingenio, clarus eloquio, forma venustus, gratia coruscus, aetate junior, prudentia senilis . . ." (983B).

[101] Edmond Faral, *Les arts poétiques du XIIe et du XIIIe siècle* (Paris, 1924), p. 120 ff.; Ulysses, pp. 123–25.

[102] Cf. Hennig Brinkmann, *Zu Wesen und Form mittelalterlicher Dichtung* (Halle, 1928), p. 60, n. 1: "Ulixes fällt etwas heraus."

The Courtier Bishop

a ruler." He combines wisdom with eloquence, the Ciceronian ideal of education commonly encountered also in the *vitae*. His manners are gracious, surpassing ordinary mortals ("Moribus excedit hominem," 33). The martial virtues are hardly represented at all. Even *fortis* in lines 53 and 57 and *conflictu Caesar* in line 61 most likely refer to strength of character, fortitude in the trials of public life. In any case, moral and intellectual virtues far outstrip any others in the passage. There is also a suggestion that Ulysses is of a gentle and modest disposition, is a *vir mansuetus*, since he knows no arrogance (51).

Had Matthew entitled this portrait according to social rank, as he did that of the pope, he would undoubtedly have used the word *curialis*. Ulysses here and elsewhere appears as one of two characters whom the court cleric appropriated to serve as his mythical counterparts,[103] the other being Joseph in Egypt.

The Royal Counselor in Fürstenspiegel

If we are indeed dealing with the type of the *curialis*, then this type must turn up in the *Fürstenspiegel* of the high and later Middle Ages,[104] which ordinarily include a section listing qualities of the king's advisors. But these works, particularly in their treatment of royal counselors, were strongly influenced by the polemics against the court clergy that arose as a response to the autonomy of this class and gained fuel from the investiture controversy.[105] Peter Damian's *Contra clericos aulicos,* John of Salisbury's *Policraticus,* and Peter of Blois's Epistle 14 to the clerics of Henry II's court established a tradition of anticurial polemics which lasted into the Renaissance and beyond and which in the high and later Middle Ages smothered any literature idealizing the court cleric. But even in these works we find indications that our type survived, though viewed from a negative perspective. His *affabilitas* and *amabilitas* are seen as flattery and obsequiousness; his *mansuetudo* as lack of character; his talent, impressive bearing, and willing service as ambition.[106]

---

[103] See the poetic disputations between Ulysses and Ajax from the twelfth century published by P. G. Schmidt, " 'Causa Aiacis et Ulixes I-II': Zwei Ovidianische Streitgedichte des Mittelalters," *Mittellateinisches Jahrbuch* 1 (1964), 100–132. Ulysses clearly takes over the role of cleric, Ajax that of knight.

[104] See Wilhelm Berges, *Die Fürstenspiegel des hohen und späten Mittelalters,* MGH Schriften 2 (Leipzig, 1938), and Lester K. Born, "The Perfect Prince: A Study in Thirteenth- and Fourteenth-Century Ideals," *Speculum* 3 (1928), 470–504.

[105] This large body of writings has been of some interest lately. See Claus Uhlig, *Hofkritik im England des Mittelalters und der Renaissance: Studien zu einem Gemeinplatz der europäischen Moralistik,* Quellen und Forschungen zur Sprach- und Kulturgeschichte der germanischen Völker, Neue Folge 56 (Berlin and New York, 1973); Peter Dronke, "Peter of Blois and Poetry at the Court of Henry II," *Mediaeval Studies* 38 (1976), 185–235; Rolf Köhn, " 'Militia curialis': Die Kritik am geistlichen Hofdienst bei Peter von Blois und in der lateinischen Literatur des 9.–12. Jahrhunderts," in *Miscellanea Mediaevalia,* 12: *Soziale Ordnungen im Selbstverständnis des Mittelalters,* ed. Albert Zimmermann (Berlin and New York, 1979), pp. 227–57.

[106] Cf. Innocent III, *De contemptu mundi* 2.26, PL 217:727: "Ambitiosus . . . honestatem

322   The Courtier Bishop

By the early Renaissance this perspective was no longer totally dominant. In an English version of the *Secretum secretorum* from 1445, a *Fürstenspiegel* in the form of Aristotle's teachings for Alexander the Great, we find a "trew counseiler or servaunt" of the king characterized by "perfeccion of lymmes," "godnes of lernyng and wille to understonde," a good memory, and a clear and level head in difficult situations. He must be "courtly, faire spekyng, of swete tonge . . . sped in eloquence"; learned; "of good maners and complexion, softe, meke and tretable"; composed and moderate in his manners, "yevying himself curiously to men benyngly tretying."[107] Many tracts on the counselor, legate, and ambassador from the Renaissance could be cited here,[108] but this catalogue gives us a concise and remarkably comprehensive list of the chief characteristics of our type. The Latin vocabulary for most of these is readily at hand: *lineamentorum gratia, eloquentia, moderamen;* "softe, meke and tretable" are the counterpart of *mansuetus, mitis et tractabilis;* "men benyngly tretying" is *benignitas* and *affabilitas.*

The Ideal Courtier in Gottfried's Tristan

The hero of the German Tristan romance represents the literary realization of the courtier ideal in the high Middle Ages. Gottfried's hero[109] possesses the essential features of our type, and these are integrated fully into the values of *courtoisie* and chivalry. Of course, the hero of romance is an amalgam of clerical and chivalric values,[110] but in *Tristan* the clerical, courtier virtues provide the basis for the hero's character and far outweigh chivalric prowess in their importance. The basic showplace of human talents

---

mentitur, affabilitatem exhibet, benignitatem ostendit, sub- et obsequitur, cunctos honorat, universis inclinat, frequentat curias, visitat optimates, assurgit et amplexatur, applaudit et adulatur. . . ." And the ambitious man does all this ". . . ut judicetur idoneus, ut reputetur acceptus, ut laudetur ab hominibus, et a singulis approbetur." Also Guibert de Tournai (†1288) on the chameleon as symbol of the flatterer: the chameleon is ". . . animal naturaliter mansuetum, licet quando infirmatur se esse simulet mansuetum. Eos designat qui in domibus regum sunt et . . . voluntatibus omnium se conformant. . . ." *Le traité Eruditio regum et principum de Guibert de Tournai,* ed. A. de Poorter, Les philosophes belges 9 (Louvain, 1914), p. 54 (Ep. 2, ch. 10). Also ibid., p. 61 (Ep. 2, ch. 15); "Hii [i.e., clerici saeculares in curiis] sunt qui callide omnium venantur in praesentia gratiam."

[107] *Secretum Secretorum: Nine English Versions,* ed. M. A. Manzalaoui, EETS 276 (Oxford, 1977), 1:79.

[108] For an extensive list of such tracts, see Ruth Kelso, *The Doctrine of the English Gentleman in the Sixteenth Century,* University of Illinois Studies in Language and Literature 14 (Urbana, 1929), pp. 169–277. Especially close to the type of the courtier bishop is the scheme of the counselor in *Of Councils and Counselors,* trans. (from the Spanish of Federico Furió Ceriol, *El consejo i consejeros del principe,* 1559) V. B. Heltzel (Liverpool, 1954), p. 17 ff.

[109] It is of course Thomas of Brittany who created the character of Tristan the courtier, but Gottfried clearly understood the figure from first hand, and added much to Thomas's conception.

[110] See Frappier, "Vues" (above, n. 49), p. 149: "Les deux figures [i.e., cleric and knight] . . .

The Courtier Bishop

in this romance is the court, not, as in the romance generally, the battlefield and forest, the tournament and war. In the early scenes at the court of King Mark of Cornwall, there is not a single tournament. The talents in the foreground are intellectual, social, and artistic: knowledge of languages, skill in music, book learning, knowledge of hunting customs and the French terms for them. Tristan's charm, affability, and beauty of body and manners win him the love and favor of the court and the king. He puts forward his talents with *sprezzatura*, defusing envy and producing twofold amazement in the court. These are accomplishments of *cortegiania*, not of chivalry. He is called "a beloved courtier" ("ein lieber hoveman," l. 3487). Down to the details of wording, Gottfried has adapted the iconography of the court cleric which we have observed in the *vitae*. Tristan repeatedly displays *elegantia morum — schoene site*. He makes himself "all things to all men": "er kunde und wolte in allen leben" (3496); he is *omnibus carus* and *omnibus gratus*: "swaz er getet, swaz er gesprach, / daz duhte un waz ouch alse guot, / daz im diu werlt holden muot / und inneclichez herze truoc" (3746–49); he makes himself beloved of the court (cf. *se toti curie gratum fecit*): "sus was der ellende do / da ze hove ein trut gesinde" (3742–43); but he is especially dear to the king (cf. *regi, imperatori praecipue carus*): "der sach in gerne und was sin vro" (3396), and "er truoc im harte holden muot" (3404).

In regard both to the personal qualities of Tristan and to his experiences, we are in the secularized and chivalric atmosphere of the youth of a courtier bishop. This is especially clear if we compare the court service of young Tristan with that of Otto of Bamberg. Both men travel in their youth to foreign lands and learn the languages and customs so well that they can pass as natives,[111] though Tristan far surpasses Otto in his knowledge of countries and languages. Both impress all they meet through their eloquence, beauty, elegance of bearing, and manners. Both are court servants of a lady of high nobility: Otto the chaplain of Judith, Tristan the tutor of Princess Isolde. Both propose a bride to their lord, mastermind the wooing expedition, win the bride, and bring her back to their lord. Both are *viri expetibiles*, courted by the lords they serve. Both are invited to the private chamber of the lord to sing to him: Otto psalms and hymns, Tristan presumably Breton and Latin *lais*.[112] Both are constantly at the king's side, "ready at hand" to

---

tendent à se fondre en un type nouveau, le gentilhomme cultivé et galant, héros du roman courtois."

[111] On Otto, p. 316 above. Cf. *Tristan*, ll. 2131 ff., 3690 ff.

[112] Ebo 1.6, p. 15: ". . . imperator Heinricus fide et prudencia pii Ottonis agnita, secrecius eum compellans, an psalterium cordetenus psallere posset, inquisivit. Quo respondente: Etiam, gavisus imperator eum sibi assidere precepit, et remotis aliis psalmodie cum eo vacabat. . . ." *Tristan*, l. 3648 ff.: "Marke sprach: 'Tristan, ga her / . . . / dine leiche ich gerne hoeren sol / underwilen wider naht, / so du niht geslafen maht. / diz tuostu wol mir unde dir.' / 'ja herre, wol'. . . ."

serve him.¹¹³ Finally, both are placed in the role of "only son" of the king, and they take over the business of the court.¹¹⁴

I am not suggesting that these parallels are accounted for by literary influence, but rather that the early careers of Tristan and Otto arose from a common sociological ground: the ideals, ambitions, and representative experiences of court servants. We can draw two conclusions: that the representation of the hero in Gottfried's Tristan romance drew on the iconography of the court cleric as we find it in the *vitae*, and that in this romance the values and the ideal type of the court cleric were lifted out of the clerical context altogether and joined to chivalric ideals, the latter subordinated to the former.

The biographies of clerics with court service at some stage in their careers are, it should be evident, important documents bearing on court life and manners in the Middle Ages. These texts provide a means of studying the clerical element in court society. Traditionally the chivalric element has commanded the attention of social and literary historians. The reason for this is evident: knighthood stands in the foreground of courtly literature. But clerics had no small hand in writing that literature. The romance was the creation of clerical authors — Geoffrey of Monmouth, Wace, Layamon, Benoît de Ste.-Maure, and probably Chrétien de Troyes were clerics — who undoubtedly had an important role to play in the forging of what are now one-sidedly called "chivalric" ideals. Historians have long pointed to the importance of this group in the cultural life of the court.¹¹⁵ In recent years sociological interpretations of courtly literature, like those of Erich Köhler and Gert Kaiser, have considerably sharpened our eyes to the way in which the values of the poet and his class shaped his work. Obviously clerical values need to be examined much more closely in their relation to courtly romance and lyric than has been the case.

Some of my findings suggest that the role of the German royal courts in the formation of an etiquette of courtesy may have been underestimated in the past. The royal-imperial courts in the early Middle Ages provided the

---

¹¹³ Herbord 3.34, p. 201: ". . . aliisque capellanis alias intentis hic semper presto erat . . . mane vespere et omni tempore cum psalterio suo ad manum imperatoris presto se exhibuit." *Tristan*, l. 3399 ff.: "wan er was zallen ziten / höfschliche an siner siten / und truog in sinen dienest an / als ofte, als er sin state gewan. / swa Marke was oder swar er gie, / da was Tristan der ander ie. . . ."

¹¹⁴ Ebo 1.3, pp. 12–13: ". . . ita sibi prudentissimum imperatorem . . . devinxit, ut eum quasi unicum amplectens filium, secretalem intimum et custodem capitis sui poneret cunctis diebus . . . queque preciosa vel cariora in palatio habuit, eius fidei commisit." *Tristan*, l. 4299 ff.: "Tristan, ga her und küsse mich! / und zware, soltu leben und ich, / ich wil din erbevater sin." And l. 4460 ff.: "dar zuo wil ich dir stiure geben: / min lant, min liut und swaz ich han, / trut neve, daz si dir uf getan."

¹¹⁵ Cf. Karl Hauck, "Mittellateinische Literatur," in *Deutsche Philologie im Aufriss*, ed. Wolfgang Stammler, 2nd ed. (Berlin, 1960), col. 2570 ff.

The Courtier Bishop

social and political context in which a clerical ethic of state service based on classical and Christian models could flourish. The court chapel, a product of the Carolingian court which came to glory under the Ottonian emperors, was the social and political matrix for this ethic. It imposed gracious, elegant, modest, unassuming, and affable manners on court clergy, and if these manners turn up in romances written by clerics in part for the education of the lay nobility, it is entirely possible that we are dealing with the diffusion of ideals of the imperial court chapel. This explanation at least can account for the fact that the earliest known occurrence of the Latin *curialitas* and the first known detailed description of the phenomenon come in a complaint against the influence which a German courtier bishop exercised on the church of Hildesheim between 1044 and 1054 (see above, n. 56). The subject clearly deserves further investigation.

Finally, it is likely that the Renaissance courtier traces his social foundations to the milieu under discussion here. The ideal courtier which Baldessare Castiglione described in his *Libro del cortegiano* (1528) takes over many features we have observed in courtier bishops. Indeed we had to call on Castiglione to help illuminate one aspect of *mansuetudo* as a court virtue. The medieval origins of the Renaissance courtier are imperfectly understood and seem to have escaped serious study. The current formula has it that Castiglione drew on classical antiquity and "medieval chivalry" as his two main sources.[116] The role of court clergy in the development of the courtier has hardly received mention,[117] even though the most important historical constant in this development is demonstrably the ecclesiastical career which leads a *curialis* from court service to the office of bishop. Castiglione himself, a courtier during his mature life, then papal legate to Charles V, was offered the position of bishop of Avila shortly before his death in 1529.

---

[116] See, for instance, Loos, *Studien* (above, n. 75), pp. 171–73; Mazzeo, "The Self as a Work of Art," p. 133: "the courtier ideal . . . is in part a continuation and adaptation of the best elements of the chivalric tradition"; Ernest Barker, "The Education of the English Gentleman in the 16th Century," in *Traditions of Civility: Eight Essays* (Cambridge, Eng., 1948), p. 124; and Kelso, *The Doctrine of the English Gentleman* (above, n. 108), p. 70. The only serious studies of the origins of the courtier focus on Castiglione's literary sources, restricted to classical ones (see Loos, *Studien*, pp. 171–73).

[117] Wilhelm Berges mentioned casually the connection between twelfth-century *curialis* and Renaissance courtier: "Die Figur des glatten Hofmannes, des 'cortegiano,' die im 12. Jahrhundert auftaucht und von Johann von Salisbury und seinen Nachfolgern gehässig verfolgt wird, spielt in der Politik der kommenden Jahrhunderte eine Rolle ohnegleichen" (*Fürstenspiegel* [above, n. 104], p. 65), but no one has taken up the suggestion.

XI

BEAUTY OF MANNERS AND DISCIPLINE (*SCHOENE SITE, ZUHT*): AN IMPERIAL TRADITION OF COURTLINESS IN THE GERMAN ROMANCE

The ideas that have longest given shape to our conception of the past are the ones that should be looked at most critically. The architecture of ideas, unlike that of buildings, does not require careful engineering to stand. Often cultural predispositions, prejudices, or simply the authority of the man or men who constructed them, suffice to hold great edifices of thought in place. One of the most fruitful tasks of American *Germanistik* is to serve as a kind of inspector of buildings and of the rooms in them, to survey foundations, add support where it is lacking or bring down constructions that stand without them. The scrupulous architect and inspector to whom this Festschrift is dedicated teaches, by example and precept, a healthy respect for firm foundations. If some of the positive critical spirit that characterizes his work and thought has made its way into the present study, then an open word of thanks to him as a teacher will be unnecessary.

A prominent historian said recently that the sources of medieval history ought to be reevaluated every forty years or so; new methods, new materials, new perspectives allow a new generation to see them in a wholly different light from the preceding one. This is certainly true of the traditional conception of medieval courtliness and its history. Peter Ganz has shown recently that the long tradition of scholarship on medieval German literature has not produced a satisfactory definition of one of the central concepts in courtly romance and lyric: *höveschheit*.[1] The same is true of the

---

1. "Der Begriff des 'Höfischen' bei den Germanisten", *Wolfram-Studien IV*, ed. W. Schröder, (Berlin, 1977), 16-32. The earlier study by

history of this concept. The great work of Bezzola is still a mine of information on medieval courts and court life.² But he had his eye fixed firmly on literary productivity of the courts. The most important sources for the social and ethical values of medieval German courts are the *Vitae* of bishops who came to their office via service in the royal/imperial courts.³ These works open to view an entirely new perspective on court life and courtliness as a social and historical reality in medieval Germany. The present study draws on these sources to illuminate the history of two important MHG concepts of courtesy, *zuht* and *schoene site*, their development from Latin, their social context.

1.) Schoene site – elegantia morum

Gottfried von Strassburg's exposition of the *lere, moraliteit*, runs as follows:⁴

under aller dirre lere
gab er ir eine unmüezekeit,
die heizen wir moraliteit.
diu kunst diu leret schoene site:
da solten alle vrouwen mite
in ir jugent unmüezic wesen.
moraliteit das süeze lesen
deist saelic unde reine.
ir lere hat gemeine
mit der werlde und mit gote.
si leret uns in ir gebote
got unde der werlde gevallen:
sist edelen herzen allen
zeiner ammen gegeben,

Werner Schrader, *Studien über das Wort höfisch in der mittelhochdeutschen Dichtung*, (Würzburg, 1935), is only useful as a collection of material. See also the forthcoming article by Hubert Heinen "The Concepts *hof, hövesch* and the Like in Hartmann's *Iwein*".

2. Reto Bezzola, *Les Origines et la formation de la littérature courtoise en occident (500-1200)*, (Paris, 1958-63), 3 parts in 5 vols.

3. See my article "The Courtier Bishop in *Vitae* from the tenth to the twelfth Century", *Speculum*, 58 (1983), 291-325.

4. References are to Gottfried von Strassburg, *Tristan und Isold*, ed. Friedrich Ranke, 11th ed., (Dublin/Zurich, 1967), here lines 8002ff.

> daz si ir lipnar unde ir leben
> suochen in ir lere;
> wan sin hant guot noch ere,
> ezn lere si moraliteit.

Certainly the concept *moraliteit* could be the key to entering and penetrating the ideas of the passage; it has been recognized as such,[5] even though there is no satisfactory study of the intellectual history of the concept *moraliteit, moralitas*. But I want to call attention here to the line, "diu kunst diu leret schoene site". If Gottfried-research has so much as nodded towards the term "schoene site", the reference has escaped me. Perhaps it has been read not as a concept but as a descriptive term; beauty of manners or beautiful manners is simply an individual and original circumscription of the results of instruction in *moraliteit*, as if we were to say of a courtly person, "his manners are certainly beautiful". But no, it is a fixed concept, one whose content and history are as approachable as that of *moraliteit*, perhaps more so. Gottfried uses the formulation fairly regularly. The Norwegian sailors who kidnap young Tristan are amazed at his abilities in language, in chess, in music, at his impressive appearance, his beauty, his clothes and flowing speech, and the sum of their admiration:

> nun geduhte si nie jungelinc
> so saelecliche sin getan
> noch also schoene site han. (2240ff.)

They consider this a marketable quality, and resolve to profit from it (2300ff.). Likewise when Tristan, stranded in Cornwall, meets two pilgrims, they are astonished by his courtly qualities, summed up by the same term:

> "a herre got der guote,
> wer oder wannen ist diz kint,
> des site so rehte schoene sint"? (2752ff.)

The quality is prominent also during his debut at the court of Cornwall. there is a portrait of the young prodigy as he is introduced to King Mark, a scene thickly laced with the forms of high courtly fashion, and the portrait ends:

---

5. See the comments of Ganz in Gottfried von Strassburg, *Tristan*, ed. Bechstein, rev. Peter Ganz, (Deutsche Klassiker des Mittelalters, N.F., Vol. IV; Wiesbaden, 1978), I, p. 352 (note to line 8008).

an gebaerde unde an schoenen siten
was ime so rehte wol geschehen,
daz man in gerne mohte sehen. (3348ff.)

It is worth noting that the term keeps close company in each of the above passages with *hövesch, hövescheit, hovebaere*. And it should be evident from the scant description just given, that *schoene site* is the epitome of courtly bearing. It includes fine dress, gentle, courteous, eloquent speech, graceful gestures, suaveness and affability in greeting, skill in court games and pastimes. It strikes those who observe it with awe and amazement, endears its bearer to king and court, and makes him desirable as a courtier.

The term seems to have entered German literature via Gottfried's *Tristan*, though both Veldeke and Hartmann use the term *schoene zühte*. After Gottfried it is commonplace in ethical works and romance. Thomasin von Zirclaere is fond of linking the two, *zuht und schoene site*. Oddly enough, there is no direct verbal counterpart either in Provencal or in Old French. Neither in the standard lexica, nor in the rich scholarship on the Romance vocabulary of courtesy is a term corresponding to *schoene site* to be found.[6] There is no form *beles manieres* or *meurs elegantes*. We find *bones mors* and *bonnes meurs*,[7] and these are clearly loan translations of the Latin *boni mores*. There is also *de meurs bien*

---

6. See Hans Krings, *Die Geschichte des Wortschatzes der Höflichkeit im Französischen*, (Bonn, 1961); Glynn Burgess, *Contribution a l'étude du vocabulaire précourtois*, (Publications romanes et françaises, vol. 110; Geneva, 1970); Glynnis Cropp, *Le Vocabulaire courtois des troubadours de l'époque classique*, (Publications romanes et françaises, vol. 135; Geneva, 1975). Burgess devotes a chapter to the entire Old French vocabulary of beauty in the area of courtly fashion and ideal, op. cit., pp. 115-133. But there is no phrase that corresponds directly to the MHG *schoene site*. This is not to say that the concept comprehended by this term did not exist in France. The term *cointe* seems to carry a comparable meaning. Cf. Burgess, p. 114 (with ref. to Frances Norwood): "...*cointe* évoquait cette beauté recherchée qui résultait de l'éducation...". The point is, while the courtly aesthetic of manners was international, the Latin terms expressing it were adapted in MHG but not in Provencal and Old French.

7. Alfred Tobler & Erhard Lommatzsch, *Altfranzösisches Wörterbuch*, (Wiesbaden, 1925 ff.), VI, p. 289, line 52.

ordinez (Tobler-Lommatzsch, VI, 291, 29), clearly modeled on Latin *mores bene compositi*. But these are part of the general European ethical vocabulary; they lack specific connection to the court and to *courtoisie*. They suggest merely behavior which is good, while *schoene site* are beautiful. The shift from the ethical to the esthetic cannot be explained by the notion that Gottfried took the concept from the Old French. This does not necessarily mean that Gottfried did not learn the concept from the forms of social life practiced at French courts. He may have invented the term to give expressions to ideals of the French chivalric class. On the other hand if there is a model closer to home in which a term for "beautiful manners" conveys a courtly ideal of behavior, then we would have to exclude the possibility of French influence. And there is.

Schoene site is undoubtedly based on the Latin *elegantia morum*, a common term in court literature with many variants: *venustas*,[8] *suavitas, gratia, speciositas, pulchritudo* or *amoenitas morum*. The history of the term will make Gottfried's dependence on the Latin evident.

At its most general the identifying of the ethical with the esthetic, of the Good with the Beautiful, is a constant of aristocratic societies.[9] As a philosophical position it owes its formulation in the west to early Stoicism.[10] But the verbal ancestors of Gottfried's phrase are to be found among Roman writers of the empire. Seneca, in his letter-tract, *Ad Marciam de consolatione*, traces various stages of Marcia's grief: at first she actively imposed it on herself, now (at the time of writing) she is passively permitting it to continue. But soon, he urges her, she must put an end to it by an act of the will: "Quanto magis hoc morum tuorum elegantiae convenit, finem luctus potius facere quam expectare" (8, 3).

---

8. Peter von Moos refers to the frequent use of *venustas morum* by Hildebert: *Hildebert von Lavardin, 1056-1133: Humanitas an der Schwelle des höfischen Zeitalters*, (Pariser historische Studien, vol. III; Stuttgart, 1965), p. 94.

9. Werner Jaeger, *Paideia: The Ideals of Greek Culture*, 2nd ed., trans. G. Highet, (New York, 1965), vol. I, p. 12f.

10. Robert Philippson, "Das Sittlichschöne bei Panaitios", *Philologus*, 85, N.F. XXXIX (1930), 357-413.

XI

Quintilian praises Seneca's writing, in which there is "multa... morum gratia legenda" (*De inst. orat.*, X, i, 129). Tacitus praises Pomponius in the *Annals* for his *morum elegantia*, "dum adversam fortunam aequus tolerat" (V, 8). Evidently the phrase belongs to the vocabulary of Stoicism, though its infrequent occurrence and the fact that it never occurs in Cicero indicate that it was not a central concept. The meaning in classical Latin is clear from the above texts: *elegantia morum* is a calm and graceful mastering of adversity, restraint of passion. It had not entirely lost this meaning in the Middle Ages. Thomasin is using the German equivalent when he writes, "swer in zorn hat schoene site,/ dem volget guotiu zuht mite".[11] Here also the mastering of powerful and "negative" emotions constitutes "beautiful manners", but to my knowledge the Latin terms do not occur in the Middle Ages in the sense of Stoic restraint. Here the context of beautiful manners is different. It is an ideal of decorous, courtly behavior, and its social context is the ruler's court, specifically the imperial/royal courts of Germany. We will first look at the social context, then turn to the courtly sense of the term.

Repeatedly *elegantia morum* and its variants occur in the context of the entry of a gifted cleric into service in the royal chapel.[12] This quality constitutes the epitome of *idoneitas*, suitability, for royal service. Meinwerk of Paderborn, chaplain under Otto III and Henry II, later Bishop of Paderborn, was judged worthy of service to the king because of the elegance of his manners: "Meinwercus autem, regia stirpe genitus, regio obsequio morum elegantia idoneus adiudicatur evocatusque ad palatium regius capellanus efficitur".[13] We could hardly ask for a more lucid illustration of the connection between this quality and court service, Elegance, beauty, or grace of manners regularly appear as qualites which attract the admiration and wonderment of lords secular and

---

11. *Der Wälsche Gast des Thomasin von Zirclaria*, ed. Heinrich Rückert, (Deutsche Nationalliteratur, vol. XXX: Quedlinburg & Leipzig, 1852), lines 679f.

12. Argued with more examples in my "Courtier Bishop", *supra*, note 3.

13. *Das Leben des Bischofs Meinwerk von Paderborn*, ed. F. Tenckhoff, (MHG, Script. rer. germ. in us. schol.; Hannover, 1921), p. 7 (ch. 5).

ecclesiastical and which qualify the cleric who possesses them for court service.[14] The elegant-mannered *vir expetibilis* is sought after and courted by lords hoping to win him for their service.[15] *Elegantia morum* can also commend its possessor for advancement to a bishopric. The author of the *Vita* of Altmann of Passau describes the cleric Hartmann, later Abbot of Göttweig, as

> ...summo religionis studio deditus, prudentia tam saeculari quam spirituali eximie praeditus, copiosa disertus eloquentia, morum exuberans elegantia. Unde principibus totius regni erat acceptissimus, et ipsi regi Heinrico V familiarissimus, qui et eum in archiepiscopatu Iuvavensi sublimare disposuit...[16]

His abundant elegance of manners placed him high in the favor of all princes of the land, and disposed Henry V to elevate him to the Archbishopric of Salzburg. Again, the text reveals the social context of this quality with dazzling clarity. It shows us *elegantia morum* as a key ethical and social concept functioning within a particular historical setting: the "imperial church system" of the Ottonian/Salian kings. The church structure is integrated into the imperial administrative system; the king/emperor establishes a buffer zone against the traditional opposition of the feudal nobility by filling vacant bishoprics wherever possible with his court chaplains, men loyal to him, trained for imperial service at court under the guidance of the king.[17] It is in the context of service at

---

14. Cf. Marbod of Rennes' *Vita Licinii* (ca. 1095), Licinius received into the service of King Clotarius "propter egregiae formae dignitatem ac morum elegantiam quae in adolescente eminebant" (PL 171, 1496A).

15. The bishop of Utrecht competes with a count palatine for the services of Bernward of Hildesheim, who is attractive to them because of his "grace of manners": "fitque inter episcopum et comitem de tantae indolis iuvene religiosa concertatio, ut uterque pro morum gratia illum sibi adoptare intenderet". *Vita S. Bernwardi Ep. Hildesheimensis*, ch. 2, *Lebensbeschreibungen einiger Bischöfe des 10.-12. Jahrhunderts*, trans. Hatto Kallfelz, (Darmstadt, 1973), p. 278.

16. *Vita Altmanni*, ch. 40, MHG, SS 12, p. 241.

17. The circumstances are well known. See the survey by Oskar Köhler, "Die Ottonische Reichskirche: Ein Forschungsbericht". In: *Adel und Kirche: Gerd Tellenbach zum 65. Geburtstag*, ed. J. Fleckenstein, (Freiburg, 1968), 141-204, esp. pp. 173ff.

the imperial courts of Germany that the phrase first occurs.[18] But by the twelfth century we will find its variants in the context of court service throughout Europe. An especially instructive instance is in the *Gesta Danorum* of the learned Danish cleric, Saxo Grammaticus, a contemporary of Gottfried. Saxo speaks the language of the European courts, and his work is an important source for the Latin vocabulary of courtesy. In a passage written probably in the last decade of the twelfth century, he describes the early tribulations of Iarmericus (the Ostrogoth Ermanaric, in Saxo's version son of the Danish king Sywardus). A hostage with the king of the Slavs, he is released from prison to become a farm laborer. Here he distinguishes himself for administrative ability and becomes master of the king's slaves. From here he is taken into the close circle of the king's retainers:

> Ubi cum se *iuxta aulicorum ritum* egregia morum amoenitate gessisset, brevi in amicorum numerum translatus primum familiaritatis locum obtinuit ac veluti quibusdam meritorum gradibus fretus ab infima sorte ad spectatum honoris fastigium concessit... Grata omnibus Iarmerici indoles erat...[19]

By the end of the twelfth century, "charm of manners", *amoenitas morum*, clearly a variant of *elegantia* and *venustas morum*, forms a regular part of the *ritus aulicorum*, the "ways of courtiers". It accounts for a gifted courtier's swift rise to intimacy and familiarity with the king. The resonance with the *schoene site* displayed by Tristan on his rise to favor at the court of King Mark is clearly audible.

We can learn a great deal from Latin sources about the content of this concept. Each of the three *Vitae* of Otto of Bamberg (died 1139) describes him as elegant either in manners or appearance. The anonymous biographer, a monk of Prüfening writing around 1140/46, says that as a young man in Poland, Otto had amazed all the prelates of the land by the "elegance of his manners".[20] Ebo of

---

18. Anselm of Liège, writing ca. 1056, describes Notker of Liège, chaplain of Otto I, as "admodum omni morum elegantia insignitus". *Gesta ep. Leodiensium*, ch. 25, MHG, SS 7, p. 203.

19. *Saxonis Gesta Danorum*, VIII, x, 1, ed. J. Olrik and H. Raeder, (Copenhagen, 1931), I, pp. 230-31.

20. *S. Ottonis ep. Babenbergensis vita Prieflingensis*, ed. J. Wikarjak &

Michelsberg (ca. 1151/59) writes that Otto was placed in charge of the monastery of Niedermünster when the abbess observed "the elegance of his person and his *mores*".[21] But a passage that interests us particularly occurs in Herbord of Michelsberg's *Dialogue on the Life of Otto of Bamberg* (1159). The narrator, who relates Otto's conversion of Pomerania, tells of his fastidious and considerate preparations for baptising the heathens. Otto separates the men from the women and has an elaborate system of curtains hung around the baptismal fonts so as to preserve decorum when the pagans step naked into them. In the winter the water is warmed, and spices and scented oils are added. The participants in the dialogue interrupt here to exclaim about the refinement and decorousness of these arrangements ("disciplinata et honesta baptizandi forma").[22] The narrator replies that this was only one of the many indications of his manners and virtues ("morum atque virtutum insignia"). He showed in his every act a particular fastidiousness (*munditia*) and an "elegant and urbane breeding" ("elegans et urbana disciplina"). He would tolerate nothing indecorous or unseemly, either in eating or drinking, in speech, gesture or dress, but rather "in each act of the outer man he showed the harmony that reigned within him".[23] This remarkable text places

---

K. Liman, (Monumenta Poloniae historica, ser. nov., VII/1; Warsaw, 1966), p. 7 (I, 3): "...his artibus cunctorum sibi sapientium concivit affectum... ut ipsi illius terre pontifices...morum elegantiam mirarentur".

21. *Ebonis vita S. Ottonis ep. Babenbergensis*, ed. Wikarjak & Liman, (MPH, ser. nov., VII/2; Warsaw, 1961), p. 12 (I, 3): "Que cernens persone et morum eius elegantiam,...rerum suarum tociusque domus dispensatorem constituit".

22. *Herbordi dialogus de vita S. Ottonis ep. Babenbergensis*, ed. Wikarjak & Liman, (MPH, ser. nov., VII/3; Warsaw, 1974), p. 90 (II, 16).

23. "Nec mirum te ista mirari. Etenim, qui ea vidimus, mirabamur et ipsi tam hec quam alia complura morum eius atque virtutum insignia. Ipse namque in omni accione sua...quandam a Spiritu sancto...cuiusdam singularis mundicie atque, ut ita dixerim, elegantis et urbane discipline prerogativam habebat, ita ut nichil unquam indecens aut ineptum inhonestumve quid in cibo aut potu, sermone, gestu vel habitu admitteret. Sed in omni officio exterioris hominis, quenam esset composicio interioris, ostendebat, bonitate, disciplina et prudencie cautela conspicuus" (loc. cit.).

us in the midst of a highly articulated Latin vocabulary of courtesy. The arrangements show Otto's refined and scrupulous sense of propriety, his well-bred considerateness. The elegant and urbane breeding is the outer sign of inner virtue; the decorousness of the outer man (his *mores*) reflects an inner harmony (*virtutes*). We can also see that Otto's sense of modesty and decorum is not confined to the Christian context of conversion and baptism, but rather the passage suggests that the proper context of this sensibility is the entirely worldly one of table manners, speech, gesture and dress ("in cibo aut potu, sermone, gestu vel habitu"), the "acts of the outer man". But these were the very things that were included in the ideal *schoene site* in *Tristan: rede, gebaerde, kleit*.

Nonetheless *elegantia morum* is a virtue, or set of virtues that are entirely acceptable to orthodox Christian sentiments; it in no way implies the vain frivolities of worldly ways. The aristocratic cleric Ulrich of Zell (died 1093), who abandoned the service of Henry III and Agnes of Poitou to take up the monastic life, is praised by his biographer for shunning the levity of the court and setting a pattern of moral behavior for the king and queen. But it was his "suavitas delectabilium morum" that won him the love of the king and the position of private chaplain to the queen (MHG, SS 12, p. 254). Hartmann of Göttweig, we recall, was praised as both "summo religionis studio deditus" and "morum exuberans elegantia", beloved of the king and princes of the land because of these qualities. In short there is no contradiction between the love and service of God and the *elegantia morum* which makes a man sought after at court. But this is what Gottfried had told us of the *moraliteit* which teaches *schoenē site*:

    ir lere hat gemeine
    mit der werlde und mit gote.
    si leret uns in ir gebote
    got unde der werlde gevallen. (8010ff.)

"Beautiful behavior" had been a legitimate formula and ethical guideline for Christians living in the world since St. Ambrose formulated a Christian ethic of state service in his adaptation of Cicero, *De officiis ministrorum*. He defined *pulchritudo vivendi* as "rendering to each sex and to each person the things appropriate to him", and called this "the highest rule of conduct, the lustre appropriate to each action...".[24] In the Middle Ages *elegantia* and *venustas morum* become central components in a "natural ethic" which crystallized in the milieu of the educated clergy at the ruler's court. This ethic is more closely related to ethical ideas of antiquity than to Pauline-Augustinian Christianity, but is nonetheless legitimate and thoroughly acceptable in medieval Christianity. The imperial church had created a need for skilled administrators at court; the cathedral schools educated them, not only in letters but also in the ways appropriate to the court, in *mores*, and here was the institutional basis for the propagation of an ethic of state service.

"Beauty of manners" as a held ideal of medieval courtiers is in its origins a clerical ideal. I mean by that, an ideal of the worldly clergy employed at episcopal or secular courts. This class of men should not be confused with monks or even for the most part devout Christians. Rainald von Dassel and Thomas Becket as royal chancellor are two of its highest and most typical representatives. Occasionally it happened that these men proved themselves pious Christians loyal to the church once they had taken over the office of bishop, as did Becket. But piety and orthodoxy had much less influence in the guidance of their lives at court than did ideals like beauty of manners, affability, moderation, urbanity, sophistication (*facetia*), gentleness and magnanimity. It was among this class that ideals of courtliness first were cultivated, and from which they spread outwards to other classes of aristocratic society. It was the German royal/imperial courts that first provided the social matrix in which an ideal of elegant behaviour could flourish.[25]

But these social and ethical ideals did spread outward from the greater courts to the lesser, from the court clergy to local dioceses, from clerical courtiers to the laity. This diffusion of ideals from the royal courts represents the most powerful civilizing force in Europe since ancient Rome. From the end of the eleventh century on, the knighthood begins to adapt courtliness. The ruler and his clerical advisors enjoined on the growing throngs of knights the

---

24. *De off. min.*, I, xix, 84; PL 16, 49A.
25. See the discussion, *infra*, of the "courtliness" imported into Hildesheim in the mid-eleventh century by the courtier bishop Azelinus.

kind of ideals of restraint practiced by the higher members of the court. This education of the knighthood was in part a necessity for a growing population of warriors,[26] but it had to do as well with the susceptibility of the European nobles to ideals. The same susceptibility showed itself in their willingness to go on Crusades. Gottfried von Strassburg gave a very clear picture of this willing acceptance of courtly ideals in his portrait of young Rivalin, his youthful violence and volatility, his subsequent training in court manners at the court of King Mark.

But the best non-literary (or half-literary) text that represent this "Verhöflichung der Krieger" (Elias' term) is in Saxo's *Gesta Danorum*. The passage depicts the education of knights at the court of Canute the Great, and is important for us because it places this entire civilizing process under the aegis of "beauty of manners". It is a "half-literary" text because Saxo's source was an historical document, the *Lex castrensis sive curiae*, a Latin redaction of the Law imposed by Canute on members of his court.[27] But Saxo has turned this piece of military law into the courtly education of a boorish warrior class, and this had broad resonance in the courts of Europe.

After a series of victories in war, there is a period of peace, and the result is an influx of warriors into Canute's court, many of whom are "more weighty of muscle than grave of manner" (*Gesta Dan.*, X, xviii, 1). They had distinguished themselves on the field, but had no sense of the "honorable conduct of life", and they brought violence and squabbling into the court itself. They were governed "by a jumble of chaotic impulses": some were hotheaded, others envious, others wrathful and vengeful. Their ways are so unbridled that they threaten to disturb not only domestic peace, but the conduct of state affairs as well. Now the king calls on his wise counselor, Opo of Seeland, to impose military disci-

---

26. See the analysis of forces which produce a "Verhöflichung der Krieger" in Norbert Elias, *Über den Prozess der Zivilisation: Soziogenetische und psychogenetische Untersuchungen*, 2nd ed., (Suhrkamp TB Wissenschaft, vol. CLIX; Frankfurt, 1979), vol. II, pp. 351-368.

27. For a discussion of the texts, see Thomas Riis, *Les institutions politiques centrales du Danemark, 1100-1332*, (Odense University Studies in History and Social Sciences, vol. 46; Odense, 1977). pp. 31-47.

pline and teach the maturity appropriate to knights through a "most exacting program of education" ("exactissimis institutis"). His program is summed up in the sentence, "In order to ally courteous affability with boldness, he imbued the most courageous knights with the most lovely manner of conduct" ("...ut audaciae comitatem adiceret, fortissimo militi speciosissimum moris habitum ingeneravit..."). The details of this education, basically a system of rewards and punishments, do not interest us, but Saxo tells us that they aim generally at enforcing the "duties of social life" ("societatis officia"). If we are to take this passage as a paradigm for *speciositas morum* then this concept would seem to consist in the imposition of government on impulses earlier unbridled and contentious; "beauty of conduct" is subjection of the "chaotic impulses" to the "duties of social life", respect, considerateness, sensitivity to the rights of others. I believe that it also gives us a marvelously clear look into the origins of the civilizing process in the Middle Ages. It is obviously a rather primitive stage, and the "beauty of conduct" learned by Canute's knights is far indeed from that mastery of manners practiced by Tristan. But we have touched two boundaries of the word-field "beauty of manners": at the one end it is harmonious self-government based on principles of respect for the social order and the rights of other men[28]; at the other the conduct of life becomes a work of art aimed at charming and winning the affection of the beholder.

2) zuht – disciplina

The MHG word *zuht*, like *schoene site*, conveys one of the central social and ethical ideals of medieval German court society. It appears as such first in the *Rolandslied*, and it is common — even more — ubiquitous, in MHG courtly romance and lyric. *Zuht* is the result of fine courtly breeding and education in proper behavior. It suggests self-restraint and moderation. The singular

---

28. See Gerald of Wales (Giraldus Cambrensis), *De principis instructione liber*, ed. George Warner, (Rolls Series, Vol. XXI/8; London, 1891), p. 9 (I, i): "Cum autem morum venustas cuilibet ad se regendum apprime in vita sit utilis et accommoda, nulli tamen adeo ut illi qui multitudinem regit est necessaria".

and plural forms are more or less interchangeable, and the word is open to the aestheticising we observed also in *site, mores: schoene zühte* occurs, as I mentioned earlier, in both Veldeke and Hartmann. *Zuht* also has in common with *schoene site* that there is no direct verbal equivalent either in the Provencal or the Old French vocabulary of courtesy. Chrétien uses the adjective *bien apris* to describe a courtly hero, and the formulation has much in common with MHG *zuht*, though the range of meanings is narrower in Old French. Also the phrase is rare in Chrétien, whereas *zuht* occurs over 100 times in Hartmann's narrative works, and about 160 times in *Parzival*. *Bien apris* was not a central conception of *courtoisie* in France; *zuht* certainly was in Germany. We can put aside the idea that it might be a loan translation from Old French.

Like *schoene site, zuht* is undoubtedly a loan translation from Latin, in this case *disciplina*. In the sense of social sophistication and fine breeding the word has no tradition in classical Latin. Here its main fields of reference were school learning and military order. In the Middle Ages it functioned in both of these areas. Another major context was monastic rule and the ordered religious life in general, more specifically, chastisement, flagellation. But from the mid-eleventh century onward *disciplina* comes to take on the meaning of courtly restraint. Again the originating context is the imperial courts, and this also *disciplina-zuht* has in common with *elegantia morum-schoene site*. The first occurrences are in the *Ruodlieb*, a work with clear ties to the court of Henry III.[29] At the end of a scene which is a mirror of court ceremonial — table manners, etiquette of greeting and leave taking — the legates of the *rex major* to the conquered *rex minor* are provided with a guide to lead them out of the kingdom. He is praised for his good services:

"Disciplinate noster ductor vel honeste
Servivit nobis in simplicitateque cordis
Huius dum regni confinia vidimus ampli".[30]

The stress is on the guide's lack of guile. He guides them in good faith, and the suggestion of restraint refers to the implied stifling of

29. See Karl Hauck, "Heinrich III. und der Ruodlieb", *PBB*, 70 (1948), 372-419.
30. *The Ruodlieb: Linguistic Introduction, Latin Text and Glossary*, ed. Gordon B. Ford, Jr., (Leiden, 1966), IV, 170-172.

any impulse to misguide and rob men at his mercy. In general, scenes depicting the court of the two kings in *Ruodlieb* stress the restraint and affection which govern human interactions: the atmosphere is free of anger, resentment, deceit, boorish self-assertion; there is gaiety and amiability among members of the court, low and high. The restraint and good will implied in *disciplinate* are entirely at home in this atmosphere.

But admittedly in the *Ruodlieb* the connection of the word to court etiquette is a fairly loose one. By the first half of the twelfth century, *disciplina* has become a virtue at home in the courts. The author of the *Vita* of Paulina of Zell (written 1135-50) praises bishop Wernher of Merseburg (died 1093) for his "courtly disciplines" in a revealing context. There is a convening of the royal court (of Henry IV) at Goslar. In attendance are "princes of the realm", among whom Wernher so distinguished himself for his "curiales disciplinae" and brilliance of mind that "among courtiers and men preeminent for worldly glory he appeared glorious indeed, banishing all trace of rustic simplicity".[31] The passage is useful for juxtaposing courtliness with rusticity, as well as for placing *disciplina, disciplinae* precisely in the context of the king's court. It is worthwhile observing that "curiales disciplinae" would translate into MHG as *hövesche zühte*, a phrase too comon in romance and lyric to require the citing of examples. Also, we see that in the Latin as in MHG the singular and plural forms are interchangeable.

We should now recall the passage in Herbord's *Dialogue on the Life of Otto of Bamberg* in which Otto's baptismal arrangements were praised. *Disciplina* is the overarching virtue. There is reference to the "disciplinata et honesta baptizandi forma" (p. 90). Otto's refinement and humane delicacy derive from a gift of "elegans et urbana disciplina". He is praised as "conspicuous for goodness, fine breeding and far-sighted wisdom" ("bonitate,

---

31. "...inter quos et aderat ipse Werenherus curialibus disciplinis et splendida quadam claritudine mentem adeo informans, ut inter aulicos et viros mundana gloria prefulgidos nichil rusticanae simplicitatis admitteret omnibusque gloriosus appareret" (MGH, SS 30, p. 920). The *Vita* of this same bishop praises his sister-in-law, a prominent figure at the court of Henry IV, for her *morum disciplina* (MHG, SS 12, p. 245).

disciplina et prudencie cautela" — loc. cit.). The phrase "elegans et urbana disciplina" is of particular interest. Again, we can render it in MHG and find ourselves dealing with prominent courtly ideals: "schoene und hövesche zuht". It also allows us to separate the virtues of Otto from those traditionally linked to the Christian proselytizer and saint: "elegans et urbanus" were qualities that St. Augustine had rejected as the vanities of his youth.[32] But the phrase is perfectly commonplace in Cicero, and this shows us in whose company Otto's biographers placed him: they see Otto, who in his younger days was an important and highly favored courtier under Henry IV, as the heir — in his personal qualities — more of the Roman statesman than of the Christian bishop and saint.

Disciplina had a glorious future in the vernacular. By the late twelfth century it becomes a key ethical concept in the MHG vocabulary of courtliness. Much later, Middle English takes over the Latin word and makes it into a central concept of courtesy. The fifteenth century tract on the education of boys, *Stans puer ad mensam*, urges, "My dere child, first thiself enable / With all thin herte to vertuous disciplyne...".[33] And Edmund Spenser still writes in the prefatory letter to his *Faerie Queen* that the intent of the work is "to fashion a gentleman or noble person in virtuous and gentle discipline".

******

The traditional notions of the origin and spread of the phenomenon known in Provencal as *cortezia*, in Old French as *cortoisie*, in MHG as *hövescheit*, have it that it began in Provence, spread to northern France and from there was imported to Germany. But this idea is oriented altogether to the history of courtly vernacular literature. Courtliness, as a phenomenon separable from "courtly love", was a reality of social life in medieval Europe from at least the mid-eleventh century on, and as such its history should be viewed quite apart from that of courtly literature. This identification of courtly literature with courtliness has obscured the

---

32. *Confessiones*, III, i, i: "elegans et urbanus esse gestiebam abundanti vanitate".

33. *The Babees book, The Bokes of Nurture etc.*, ed. Frederick Furnivall, (Early English Text Society, old series, vol. 32; London, 1868), p. 26.

existence of an imperial tradition of court manners which was completely independent from customs of the French chivalric class, indeed probably contributed significantly to courtly ethical ideals in France. This brief excursion into the history of the words *schoene site – zuht* opens a window onto the imperial tradition. It shows us the existence of a Latin vocabulary of courtesy, of which *elegantia morum* and *disciplina* are only two examples. Other important ideals within this tradition were gaiety (*hilaritas*), affability (*affabilitas*), wit or sophistication (*facetia*), gentleness (*mansuetudo*), moderation (*moderamen*), and finally the words which gave expression cellectively to these ideals: *urbanitas* and *curialitas*. It is completely in accord with this notion of an imperial tradition that the earliest known occurrence of the Middle Latin word *curialitas* in the sense of courtly sophistication is in a chronicle of the church at Hildesheim, in which the writer laments the influence of the courtier bishop Azelinus on the manners of the local clergy. Azelinus (in office 1044-1054), formerly a chaplain of Henry III and placed in the see by the king, is accused of replacing the pious simplicity and rusticity of the diocese with *ambiciosa curialitas*, "which — being more gentle and effeminate in dress, more elegant and refined in manner of living, more scrupulous in every aspect of culture, seeking to inspire love rather than fear — led to the softening of monastic rigor".[34] The passage deserves a detailed commentary, but for the present purpose it must suffice to observe that this earliest occurrence of *curialitas* in the sense of courtly refinement is fully in the context of the spread of court manners outward from the imperial court, borne by a courtier appointed by the king to a bishopric. His influence results in the education of a rustic clergy to refined social life. The text was written in 1080, referring to events in the mid-eleventh century. The first use of *corteiz, cortezia* in Provencal is in the poems of William IX of Aquitaine, not before 1100. The first use of Old French *cortois* is in the *Song of Roland*, notoriously hard to date, probably 1125-50, but certainly not earlier than 1086.

The few studies of the MHG vocabulary of courtesy procede from the unshakeable assumption of a complete dependence of the

---

34. *Fundatio ecclesiae Hildesheimensis*, MGH. SS 30:2, p. 945.

MHG chivalric terminology on the Old French.[35] Hence we are well informed on the provenance of the terms for stirrups, tents, lances and other chivalric bric-a-brac. But the roots of the MHG courtly ethical vocabulary remain largely in the dark in spite of the rich discussion on the "chivalric system of virtues". There is quite simply a blind spot in our perception of the history of courtesy, one created not least of all by a whole complex of presuppositions, not to say prejudices, concerning the cultural relations of France and Germany. But the existence of an imperial tradition of court manners explains the fact that MHG authors could adapt the ethical language of courtly romance and lyric in part from an *indigenous Latin vocabulary* of courtesy. That this was a tradition of the German royal courts explains why French poets did not necessarily rely on it in forging their own vocabulary of courtesy.

To end, I would like to suggest a model of the beginnings and spread of medieval courtesy that can come to terms with our findings. A "courtly ethic" developed at the imperial courts. In its earliest form it was an ethic of state service based on classical models. It was propagated at the cathedral schools throughout Germany and France, and spread from the eleventh century on through the ranks of *curiales*. Its mastery became a qualification for court service. These values, still largely in the province of the educated aristocratic clergy, spread to other levels of society through various channels. One was the influence of courtier bishops on local dioceses (e.g. Azelinus at Hildesheim). Another was that of rulers who wished to keep peace among crowds of knights at court, and hence called upon their clerical advisors to impose "courtly behavior" on the knightly class (Canute the Great and Opo of Seeland). This development occurred first in Provence and France, and it was all the more successful for combining ideals of courtesy with the cult of courtly love which sprang up at the same time. Here the knighthood willingly accepted and sought

---

35. Cf. Felic Piquet, *De vocabulis quae in duodecimo saeculo et in tertii decimi principio a Gallis Germani assumpserint*, (Paris, 1898); Hugo Palander, "Der französische Einfluss auf die deutsche Sprache im 12. Jahrhundert", *Mémoires de la Société Neophilologique de Helsinki*, 3 (1902), 75-204, and 8 (1929), 1-310; Emil Öhmann, *Die MHD Lehnprägung nach altfranzösischem Vorbild*, (Helsinki, 1951).

instruction in courtliness, and a rich vernacular literature developed, in part as an instrument of this education. At this point "courtly" values are transformed into "chivalric" ideals; they pass from the province of the court clergy to that of the chivalric class. The German lay nobility — whom we must distinguish sharply from the kings and the educated aristocracy — lagged well behind their French counterparts. But when they saw the French nobles behaving themselves like modest, elegant, urbane gentlemen, particularly when they encountered the ideal of the courtly knight of romance, then they wanted nothing more than to be like them, suave in speech and manner, well-groomed, courtly in love-making. But in taking up courtliness the German lay nobles were adopting patterns of behavior which had been in their own back yard — or rather front yard — for generations, practiced at the royal court by the king and his courtiers. As long as courtiers and bishops — after all, the traditional allies of the emperor and political rivals of the feudal nobility — behaved in softer, more civilized ways, these patterns of conduct were merely *pfafflich*. But if the French lay aristocracy began to behave in the same way, that was a different matter. Now the German nobility required enlightenment, instruction, guidance in courtly ways, and they found it in the form of clerical tutors and the courtly romance. In this way the romance was imported from France and with it a whole chivalric vocabulary. But the teachers of courtesy in Germany could also draw on the pre-formed ethical vocabulary of the imperial tradition. Hence *disciplina* became *zuht; elegantia morum* became *schoene site*. And so the imperial tradition made its way in significant trickles into German romance and lyric, while the main flood of chivalric and courtly vocabulary entered via France.

XII

The Text as a Symbol of Decadence

In a volume dedicated to the authority of the text, it might not be inappropriate to reflect on the resistance that texts had to overcome in order to establish their authority. One hindrance to textual authority was the opposition of vitality to textualizing, of life to the book. The history of written traditions in the West contains an important strain of resistance to writing, in which books and texts stand for loss of intellectual vitality.

In the spell of Thomas Mann's *Buddenbrooks*, Rilke wrote a poem called "Der Sänger singt vor einem Fürstenkind," included in his *Buch der Bilder* from 1906.[1] It is full of the jeweled and perfumed imagery, the posed and mannered tiredness that played well in neoromantic circles, and it added the Nietzschean, Thomas-Mannian motif of early generations using up a limited supply of vitality, leaving their heirs sapped of life-force but rich in intellect, aesthetic sense, and artistic mission. Rilke has his pale, sickly prince parade down an ancestral hall where his forebears, bold warriors and beautiful women, vital, robust, sensuous, and dangerous, stare down at him from portraits, and find that his effeteness justifies their reluctance to bring him forth. He holds in his hand a "little book" that is bound in the bridal garments of his ancestors, an image of vitality transmuted into the intellectual: when a bride wore the dress it signaled love, sexuality, fecundity, coupling, and coming life; as bookbinding it signals a kind of parasitism of the intellect. It appropriates the symbolism of life to decorate the sterile, secondhand pleasures of the mind.

This is the book as a symbol of decadence from a writer who recognized himself and his generation as representatives of Decadence with a capital D. The Book has many valences in Western traditions. Curtius could write a long chapter on the subject in his *European Literature and the Latin Middle Ages*.[2] In Judeo-Christian prophetic traditions it symbolized, among other things, the predestined, recorded course of history, the scenario of the apocalypse. The Middle Ages made it into a symbol of a transparent nature and a "readable" universe. The book occurred persistently in images of Melancholy, reading being one of its causes; the angel of Dürer's *Melencolia I* holds a large book in her lap.[3] That is just a brief glance at a few of its many meanings in the premodern world.

From *The Construction of Textual Authority in German Literature of the Medieval and Early Modern Periods* edited by James F. Poag and Claire Baldwin. The University of North Carolina Studies in Germanic Literatures, No. 123. Copyright © 2001 by the University of North Carolina Press. Used by permission of the publisher.

In modern Germany the book has a strong tradition as a symbol of lost vitality. Nietzsche invented the term "Alexandrine man" (in *The Birth of Tragedy*) to designate the representative of a culture whose highest accomplishments are the arts of writing and bookmaking and their museal counterpart, the library. Alexandrine man finds life worth living because its minor puzzles open themselves so conveniently to his shrewd solutions, and he represents for Nietzsche the trivializing of life in its tragic aspect. The godfather or great-grandfather of this thought is Faust in his study at the beginning of Goethe's play, where we find the scholar stifled by dusty books and studies and by a scholastic mentality that "curls up human beings into scraps of paper." He desperately seeks release from the bondage to intellect and the suffocation through texts.

The text as a symbol of decline is, of course, not in a specifically German tradition. It is far broader. Plato's seventh letter is a classic attack on the writing and making of books, texts, tracts, as threats to a tradition of intellectual inquiry that relies on dialogue, on the development of thought in immediate exchange, and, that means, on the living presence of teacher and learners.[4] In the *Phaedrus* he satirizes the pseudo-wisdom of letters: they *appear* to have some form of intelligence and understanding, but they cannot be questioned; they always signify one and the same thing; letters cannot speak, cannot choose their audience, and cannot answer its objections, refute its arguments, or capitulate to its proofs. Letters are ultimately powerless because lifeless, and their appearance of energy and force is illusion and deception.[5] Writing is also dangerous and contrary to the purpose of inquiry, because it erodes the main human faculty of cognition, the memory, and replaces wisdom with desiccated symbols of knowledge.

Cicero sketched an intellectual history of early Rome in the *Tusculan Disputations,* locating its true genius in its archaic period, which had a culture of banqueting, poetry performance, and hermetic transmission of knowledge from mouth to ear, from connoisseur to initiate.[6] He blamed the decline of this culture on published writings, which simplified learning and made it available to the masses. Prior to this decline Roman philosophers had practiced the most bountiful of all arts, the discipline of the good life, and they had preferred to do this in their behavior rather than in writings, a neat juxtaposition of vital, embodied philosophy and dead letters. It speaks a language Rilke and Thomas Mann would have warmed to: "vita magis quam litteris" (life rather than letters).

Saint Paul would have warmed to it too. A strong Christian anti-intellectual tradition rejected written knowledge in favor of the embodied spirit of the living God. Paul declared the Christians of Corinth the "true epistle of Christ, written not with ink but with the spirit of the living God; not in tables of stone, but in fleshy tables of the heart." The flesh, and not letters on parchment, is the medium of the New Testament, "for the letter kills but the spirit gives life" (2 Corinthians 3:6).

In 1022 two learned clerics in Orleans were tried, along with a group of their followers, for heretical teachings. Careful records were kept on their arrest and their trial. The interrogations make clear that these men rejected learning and study as corrupting the true faith. Asked whether they accepted various orthodox beliefs, they replied that they left such questions to those "who believe the fabrications which men have written on the skins of animals. We believe in the law written within us by the Holy Spirit, and hold everything else, except what we have learned from God . . . , empty, unnecessary, and remote from divinity."[7]

This is an important juxtaposition of two media: the written text and the body imprinted or infused with spiritual lessons. The former is as contemptible to them as the animal skin it is written on. True knowledge beats in the heart and circulates in the blood, their testimony implies; true teachings ring in the living voice and beam from the body and face of the teacher.

That dim view of texts was not their heresy. On the contrary, solid spokesmen of orthodoxy could share such mistrust of book learning. There is the phenomenon that Dennis Green calls "Theology of the spoken word," which prefers the oral to the written transmission of Christ's teachings.[8] Bernard of Clairvaux praised his brother Gerard for his ignorance of written letters: "non cognovit litteraturam" (he knew no letters/Latin/literature),[9] a monastic formula of praise rejecting worldly learning in favor of inspired knowledge, which turns up only slightly varied in the well-known and much studied passage of Wolfram's *Parzival*.[10] For conservative orthodoxy, or even for a conservative lay noble, ignorance of letters and writing can be high praise, insofar as the inward illumination of the Holy Spirit or some indwelling genius replaces it. In the Latin tradition it lives in the context of the thought that Christ has chosen simpletons to confound the vain wisdom of the world (1 Corinthians 3:18–20; also 1 Corinthians 1:18–25).

There is also the widespread conservative opposition to worldly learning in the twelfth century: Bernard of Clairvaux juxtaposes wisdom-charged living presence with dead letters in a letter to a learned English cleric, Henry Murdac, urging him to convert to the Cistercian order. Henry claims, so Bernard argues, to seek Christ in his studies. If so, then he will find him in imitating him more than in reading: "Quid quaeris verbum in Verbo, quod jam caro factum praesto est oculis? . . . O si semel paululum quid de adipe frumenti, unde satiatur Jerusalem, degustares! Quam libenter suas crustas rodendas litteratoribus Judaeis relinqueres! . . . Experto crede: aliquid amplius invenies in silvis, quam in libris. Ligna et lapides docebunt te, quod a magistris audire non possis."[11] The living presence of Christ speaks a higher language; so does nature, which fills its forests with a language perceptible to those living in claustral paradise, their ears and minds cleansed of the raucous crowing of worldly professors. When charismatics like Bernard compare the living presence with the written word, the latter inevitably appears threadbare and contemptible, and that can include Scripture.

A remarkable work from the late eleventh century gives dramatic highlight to living presence over written word: Sigebert of Gembloux's *Passion of the Theban Legion,* written around 1075. Sigebert, a schoolmaster in Metz and spokesman of the imperial cause in the investiture controversy, wrote this odd work in retirement. It is a blend of heroic epic and martyr legend with direct ties to the Latin epic *Waltharius.* A Roman legion from Thebes in Egypt refuses a direct order from the emperor Maximian to slaughter a Germanic tribe. They (the Theban legionaires) are converted Christians, and the emperor takes revenge on them for refusing his order by insisting that they renounce their faith or face martyrdom. They choose the latter, and die in a terrible slaughter at the hands of the emperor's army. The warrior saint Maurice addresses the legion in a grand oration before the battle; he urges them to passive resistance and martyrdom, first by citing sayings and stories of Christ. But then he interrupts his own sermon and cries: "Non opus exemplis? exemplum vos magis estis." He goes on to contrast written history to living, embodied history and ends:

> Legimus hactenus hec, audivimus hactenus istec,
> Sanctorum tanti recitantur in orbe triumphi,
> Hic video coram fieri que facta legebam.
> . . . .
> En mihi quos imiter, sunt presto quos bene mirer.[12]

Again, we have a juxtaposition of mediated, textual presence with living presence, to the advantage of the latter. The Theban martyrs in Sigebert's version are heroes of the present moment and the living deed, not the recorded word. And their heroism has greater exemplary force than the recorded teaching of the Christian hero par excellence, Christ.

That is the structure within which the text serves as a symbol of decline: the lived as opposed to the recorded heroic moment. We can take as a definition of decadence with a small "d": decline from a once firm norm of vitality, virtue, greatness; a move from embodied to recorded heroism, wisdom, vitality.

The Text as a Symbol of Decadence

There is a phase in the transition from orality to literacy where the living voice and the physical presence are preferable to writing, textualizing, indeed any form of representation. This has been noted often in studies of transition in media from the earlier to the High Middle Ages.[13] The conservative posture ("the new medium means things are going to hell") is also evident in the early twentieth century in the rejection of technology and modernism in favor of older modes of production, recording, transmitting, and receiving art. And it is still now evident in the mistrust of many colleagues in academia toward the computer, which is seen as destroying the good old discipline of handwritten essays and books.

But to call the new mode a sign of "decadence" or "decline" requires a specific historical situation. I think we can locate this situation in a much discussed passage from the beginning of Hartmann's *Iwein*. Hartmann, like Sigebert, juxtaposes lived heroism with heroic stories. But his attitude is very different. He interrupts his description of the great joy of the springtime festival at Arthur's court to complain about the joylessness of the present age: such intensity of feeling has passed out of the world, he laments, and now we must compensate ourselves with the stories from those vital times. But then he makes a remarkable commitment to the joyless but story-filled present:

ichn wolde dô niht sîn gewesen,
daz ich nû niht enwaere,
dâ uns noch mit ir *maere*
sô rehte wol wesen sol:
dâ tâten in diu *werc* vil wol.

(*Iwein*, 48–58)[14]

The passage has loomed large in the discussion of the emergence of "Fiktionalitätsbewusstsein" in the twelfth century.[15] But I want to stress the author's placement of himself in a *historical* trajectory. Hartmann presents the Arthurian past as a heroic age of deeds and the present as a weak and dark age of words and stories. It is the historicizing of a well-known opposition of men of deeds with men of words. The topos that distinguished Achilles from Ulysses becomes an age of deeds opposed to an age of words. Hartmann, remarkably, is willing to trade in the age of heroic *deeds* and intensely lived pleasures for the dreary contemporary world with its vivid *stories* of the past.

In Hartmann's mind there is a sharp opposition between deeds and words, deeds and intentions, that becomes a theme of *Iwein*. Deeds count, not words or intentions; deeds give dignity and worth. The timorous, self-pitying Kalogrenant picks himself up from the ground after losing his battle with Ascalon and soothes his ego by the thought that his intentions were good, but his deeds just could not quite match them; Iwein himself, however, can blame no one else for losing his lady's favor when his acts do not match his words, and he can only regain it by heroic deeds.[16] Certainly, Hartmann is fond of putting himself ironically in an unheroic position, as does his narrator in *Gregorius,* who claims he cannot understand real suffering in love because he has never experienced it.[17] And the passage at the beginning of *Iwein* may be an ironic posture in this sense. But it resonates clearly with an attitude in the air that beats the age of words with the stick of the heroic age.

Wolfram is following the same logic of words versus deeds when he refuses to concede that his epic is a book at all. If any woman loves him for his poetry, she must be a fool. His deeds are what count and what establish his worth (*Parzival,* 115.11–18). His commitment to deeds over words perhaps scoffs at Hartmann's effete posture on the same question. It seems probable that Wolfram had the beginnings of *Der Arme Heinrich* and *Iwein* in mind when he declared that *Parzival* was not a book. I think it just as likely that Hartmann's preference was for an age of written stories to an age of action, whereas Wolfram had his eye on his proud rejection of book learning in favor of chivalric action.

Whatever Hartmann's real attitude to past and present, he and Wolfram both see the agonistic relationship between deeds and their records, between vitality and texts. Worth noting is that these two observers of the primacy of heroism over texts are nearly alone as knights writing in the classical period of Middle High German narrative, the only other member of their class being Wirnt von Gravenberc. The major representatives of courtly narrative poetry in France, Germany, and England were clerics, and of course these learned authors were inevitably advocates, at least willing beneficiaries, of a transition in media that so clearly favored their talents. Chrétien considers himself the savior of the Arthurian romance, rescuing it from the feckless butchers of tales who regularly ruin them in oral recitation before kings and counts,[18] and Gottfried, the learned cleric par excellence, sees love stories and poems as precisely the medium to rescue love from its present decline and restore a past when love had dignity.[19]

A transition in media inevitably stirs conflict and polarizes opposed attitudes. Alongside the clerical affirmation of texts and a culture of writing there was a conservative attitude closer to Christian anti-intellectualism that opposed writing to heroism or to direct, physical-oral revelation. Whether or not he actually preferred the less to the more vital age, Hartmann had a sense of living in an age of decline, as we defined it earlier; texts, books, stories were compensation for the passing of vitality from the world.

The Text as a Symbol of Decadence   81

But it would be good to corroborate this sense from other sources than courtly romance, because otherwise we might suspect that this is not a held conviction at all, but just the posture of golden age thinking and the topos of praise of times past, *laudatio temporis acti*. What we need to pin down the argument is a sense of decline in which writing, poetry, texts, representation are complicitous.

Here is an example from the context of chivalry and knighthood, but from a very different genre. Peter of Blois, a prolific letter writer, wrote to a certain Archdeacon John.[20] It is an attack on John's two nephews, who are knights, and through them, on knighthood in the present day generally. Peter accuses them of many vices: they slander and malign clerics; their speech is foul and their behavior undisciplined; their highest esteem is reserved for those whose speech is filthiest, whose curses are most scurrilous, and whose respect for the church is lowest. They claim the license to rob and slander. Hardly girded with the sword of knighthood, they turn to plundering the church, persecuting mercilessly those who are poor and suffering. They let their exorbitant lusts and desires run riot. Slothful and drunken, corrupted by leisure, they neglect their duty to fight. They betray an ideal of knighthood established in Roman antiquity by heroes like Aeneas, Scipio Africanus, Pompey, and Caesar. These modern knights go to battle as if to a banquet, their pack animals laden with wine and cheese. Instead of weapons, they carry sausages and roasting forks. Now comes the reproach that interests us; they have their shields gilded and encrusted with jewels, which are so precious that they want to protect them from sword blows at all costs: "Bella tamen et conflictus equestres depingi faciunt in sellis et clypeis, ut se quadam imaginaria visione delectent in pugnis, quas actualiter ingredi, aut videre non audent."[21]

Whatever the power to indict and convict knighthood in reality, it is clear that Peter of Blois's criticism shares the structure of Hartmann's juxtaposing of past and present. Knights of the past were stringent in their ideals, bold, brave, and honest; those of the present take pleasure not in combat itself but in its representation in gilded and jewel-encrusted fantasy images, as Hartmann prefers the stories of King Arthur to the real world of chivalry they depict. Both prefer to read or view the heroic life than to live it.

The twelfth century is an age of new things; it is also an age of proliferation. The categories, a period of transition and radical transformation, seem to me to "rescue the phenomena" better than the often quoted and belabored "renaissance of the twelfth century." Johan Huizinga pointed out some years ago Westerners' gullibility for all that can be called a Renaissance.[22] And it is perennially in effect rescuing Haskins's great study that stamped that term on the twelfth century.

No one could deny the accomplishments of that age. Modern scholars credit it with the creation of courtly literature, of courtly love, the discovery of individualism, a renewal of studies and the Latin classics, of Latin poetry, of historical writing, science, and philosophy—a new humanism, in short—and new schools that developed into the institution of the university, brilliant teachers and philosophers, a new style of architecture and sculpture, and a revival of Roman jurisprudence. That is a résumé of the table of contents of Haskins's book, and then some. And because we are still living in customs and working in institutions founded then—courtesy and universities, for instance—we are strongly tempted to glorify those beginnings, as we tend to glorify origins generally.

Curiously, next to no one in the twelfth century glorified the age or those accomplishments. It is very difficult to find optimistic voices, and impossible to find voices, apart from those of monastic reformers, who think of their own age as a period of renewal.[23] One could go through that entire list of accomplishments just rehearsed and cite a host of powerfully critical voices. Enthusiasm about any of those trends and innovations is very limited indeed. For this essay I limit myself to two items that might well have aroused enthusiasm in an age that both renewed and thought of itself as renewing: the conception of history, the conception of love.

Otto of Freising was for Charles Homer Haskins a perfect example of a philosophizing historian,[24] in the mainstream of his time, educated in Paris, in touch with recent trends in philosophy and theology, Cistercian, bishop and uncle of Frederick Barbarossa, he seems to touch all bases—or most of them—of the twelfth-century Renaissance.[25] His *Chronicle or History of the Two Cities* adapts a work of immense polemical energy and exuberant Christian optimism, Augustine's *City of God*, and it uses the apparently optimistic structure of *translatio imperii* and *translatio studii* as one frame of development in universal history. And yet Otto's *Chronicle* is a work of profound and cynical pessimism. The purpose of histories in general, the author writes in his prologue, is to tell the "tragedies of mortal woes."[26] A wise God wanted it that way so as to scare humans away from transitory things. The men of the present age do not need histories so much, however, because they are living amid vivid examples of the miseries of existence in the city of Babylon, the Roman Empire. The empire in its wanderings has not grown better: it has declined. It has sunk to the last position instead of the noblest and foremost. It has become senile and decrepit, marred with innumerable stains and defects, as it passed from Babylon to Greece to Rome, to Germany. The fate of the chief world power reflects the world's misery and foretells the imminent fall of the whole structure.

Otto wrote the *Chronicle* during the turbulence prior to the election of his nephew as emperor in 1152. His view of the present age brightened in his later work, the *Gesta Friderici*, which he began in 1157 and left as a fragment of two books at his death in 1158.[27] His conception of a worldly history doomed to steady decline through a series of tragic events gives way to a new age of exemplary deeds of the emperor. But, in other respects, the skepticism remains. The comprehensive and predetermined development of history is interrupted by Friedrich's rule, but not suspended.

His skepticism shows in an area important for our topic, studies and learning, that locus of energy and accomplishment which in modern eyes above all distinguished the twelfth from earlier centuries. In his *Chronicle*, he sees the learning of his day as a participant in the general decline that characterizes his age. Although it is true that all learning originated in the East and moved West, that development occurs, he says, because knowledge is destined to end here.[28] Otto agrees with what we also can observe: that studies and learning indeed proliferate in the present age, but he sees this trend as fulfilling the prophecy of Daniel, who had received God's word that the period of decline before the last judgment would be marked by a proliferation of studies: "Pertransibunt plurimi et multiplex erit scientia" (Daniel 12:4),[29] and their running is inane busy-ness, the increase of useless publications. Otto sees the proliferation of studies in his own time in this light: the old age of the world favors the increase of knowledge; his own age is placed strategically to see the fulfillment of earlier prophecies, that the world is already failing and drawing the last breath of extreme old age. This is not the vaulting self-confidence of an age of renewal but rather the resignation of an embittered old man. There is hardly even the limited satisfaction at being a dwarf who can see further than the giants whose shoulders he is sitting on. His age is a weary traveler come exhausted to the end of its road, and all the intellectual energy of his age is but a look back to the dreadful tragedies of the road just traveled.

Many medievalists believe that the twelfth century invented romantic love.[30] It is hard to take issue with that conviction. But it is nowhere in evidence in the twelfth and early thirteenth centuries. Poets of courtly love represent love as in a state of decline. Not one of them, to my knowledge, shares C. S. Lewis's conviction that what they depicted was "an entirely new way of feeling," or Peter Dinzelbacher's that they were among the discoverers of love in the West. Chrétien begins his *Yvain* by complaining about the decline of love:

> mes or i a molt po des suens,
> qu'a bien pres l'ont ja tuit lessiee,
> s'an est Amors molt abessiee,
> car cil qui soloient amer
> se feisoient courtois clamer
> et preu et large et enorable;
> or est Amors tornee a fable.[31]

And Gottfried von Strassburg laments:

> Ez ist vil wâr, daz man dâ saget:
> "Minne ist getriben unde gejaget
> in den endelesten ort.
> wirn haben an ir niwan daz wort.
> uns ist niwan der name beliben."
>
> (*Tristan*, 12279–86)[32]

Of course, these statements also may be variants of the topos, *laudatio temporis acti*. But it does seem early in the history of romance to be sounding that particular motif, and given that the originator of Arthurian romance himself tended to irony and satire of love, it may be a statement of a real sense of loss.

Chrétien and Gottfried thought of themselves as trying to breathe new life into a dying ideal. Gottfried blames the decline of love on the lack of "steadfast friendship" in love in the present day (*der staete vriundes muot*). In a poem from the *Carmina Burana*, the god of love himself would make a similar complaint:

> vigor priscus abiit, evanuit iam virtus.
> Me vis deseruit, periere Cupidinis arcus![33]

It might be objected that the apparent pessimism is precisely the ground out of which the new grows, and that the real answer to the quest for good love positively presented is precisely the romances of *Yvain* and *Tristan*, the lyric poetry of a new love—whatever their authors may say about contemporary conditions. However, that pessimism is widely shared, not only among court poets. I could find no one who wrote about love of any kind or who observed love from noncourtly social sites in the twelfth century, who thought that the practice of love represented a bright new discovery and a happy broadening of the spectrum of human amatory experience. The sense of the decline of good love is widely shared and registers often in nonliterary sources. Cicero had said that true friendships are rare, but the twelfth century took the comment seriously and personally and created or at least stoked a nostalgia for a kind of friendship that had passed from the earth:

> Non amor est hodie quo se Pylades et Orestes,
> Quo se amaverunt Laelius et Scipio.
> Fidens vel fidus rarus in alterutrum.[34]

One of the speakers in Aelred of Rievaulx's dialogue on friendship, *De spiritali amicitia*, puts a peculiar spin on this motif by turning it into an indictment of the Christian era: "Cum tanta sit in amicitia vera perfectio, non est mirum quod tam rari fuerunt hi quos veros amicos antiquitas commendavit. Vix enim, ut ait Tullius, tria vel quatuor amicorum paria in tot retro saeculis fama concelebrat. Quod si nostris, id est christianis temporibus, tanta est raritas amicorum, frustra, ut mihi videtur, in huius virtutis acquisitione desudo, quam me adepturum, eius mirabili sublimitate territus, iam pene despero."[35] Aelred himself jumps in at once to defend Christian friendship, and so the voice of an unworthy present intimated by a glorious past is not unopposed here. Heloise in her letters to Abelard as abbess of the Paraclete strongly affirmed the passion of her youth, but at the same time she lamented the loss of love and "natural vigor" in men at present because the world is old. She called for a new rule of the religious life, one that would take into account male frigidity over against the rule of Saint Benedict, which was written in a time when men were still capable of loving: "Senuisse iam mundum conspicimus hominesque ipsos cum ceteris quae mundi sunt pristinum naturae vigorem amisisse, et . . . ipsam caritatem non tam multorum quam fere omnium refriguisse."[36] She is, of course, generalizing from her own castrated husband and measuring the difference that separates the passion of their early days from the frigid consolations of philosophy, theology, and the religious life. Bernard of Clairvaux recalls the days when the patriarchs burned with desire for the presence of Christ in the flesh, and he weeps for the lukewarmness and frigid unconcern of these times.[37]

Whatever such statements may say about the experience of love in the period, it does indicate that the new paradigm of love was perceived by contemporaries as a response to a decline of good love and friendship.

Unquestionably, these are topoi of golden age thinking; but that does not discredit them as revelations of the self-definition of the age. The same age had other topoi of Christian optimism at its disposal in abundance—as, for instance, Augustine's City of God, which saw a rise to dignity in Christian history. The point is: the age sounded the decline motif regularly, and the voice of optimism is barely heard.

Whatever value we may place on the impressive creations and accomplishments of the twelfth century, we cannot get around the pervasive pessimism and sense of crisis that dominates contemporary judgments of the age: crisis in language, in poetry, in learning, in the schools, in the law, in an earlier ethical discipline. The age thought of itself by and large as an age of decline. I think Giles Constable's phrase "Reformation of the Twelfth Century" fits and accommodates the sense of renewal and reform present in the period far better than "Renaissance."[38]

The text as a symbol of decline fits into this broader context. It is beyond dispute that the age produced a delightful and new form of literature. The late nineteenth and early twentieth centuries also produced an extremely vivid and rich literature—and the very movement that produced that literature judged and called itself "decadent." The evaluation of a sudden proliferation and innovation will be judged variously by various viewers and readers. But we should be careful in forming our own judgment not to ignore that of contemporaries.

I end with an anecdote that shares the deep gloom evoked earlier, but that at least presents the sapping effects of learning and texts with a touch of humor. A legend grew up around the conversion of Serlo of Wilton, a twelfth-century English master in Paris. He wrote poems on grammatical and bawdy subjects in his youth, but then gave up his worldly career to convert to monasticism, and he eventually became abbot of the Cistercian abbey of L'Aumône in 1171. The legend was retold by Jacques de Vitry in the mid-thirteenth century in the following form:[39] One evening the master was visited in his room by the ghost of a former student, recently dead. He is wearing a winding sheet, "heavy as a stone tower." The shroud is a large piece of parchment covered at every point with tiny letters and characters. The teacher asks what the letters mean, and the student answers that they spell out the sophisms and vain questions on which he had wasted his time as a student. The ghost is sweating profusely from his burden, and the teacher experiences its sufferings when a drop of sweat falls on the back of his hand. Acid-like it eats a hole in his hand that remains as a permanent reminder of the apparition. The next morning the professor resigns his chair and enters a monastery.

The student is weighed down not by the moral debts incurred in life, like his colleague in suffering, Jacob Marley, but by parchment and writing, by thought, its visible representation and its mediators. The killing influence of the text and the letter continues even in the afterlife. But at least the apparition can save one professor from textual suffocation.

Notes

1. Rilke, *Das Buch der Bilder,* book 2, part 1.
2. E. R. Curtius, *European Literature and the Latin Middle Ages,* trans. Willard Trask (Princeton: Princeton University Press, 1953; rpt., 1990), 302–47 ("The Book as Symbol").
3. See Erwin Panofsky, Fritz Saxl, and Raymond Klibansky, *Saturn and Melancholy: Studies in the History of Natural Philosophy, Religion and Art* (London: Nelson, 1964). C. S. Jaeger, "Grimmelshausen's Simplicius and the Figure of the Learned Madman in the 17th Century," *Simpliciana* 3 (1981): 39–64.
4. See Eric Havelock, *Preface to Plato* (Cambridge, Mass.: Harvard University Press, 1963).
5. Plato, *Phaedrus,* 275e–276a.
6. Cicero, *Tusculan Disputations,* 4.2, 3–7.
7. The basic documents and bibliography on the events are given in Edward Peters, *Heresy and Authority in Medieval Europe: Documents in Translation* (Philadelphia: University of Pennsylvania Press, 1980), 66–71; quotation from 71.
8. Dennis Howard Green, *Medieval Listening and Reading: The Primary Reception of German Literature, 800–1300* (Cambridge: Cambridge University Press, 1994).
9. *Sancti Bernardi opera,* ed. J. Leclercq, C. H. Talbot, and H. M. Rochais (Rome: Editiones Cistercienses, 1957), 1:175, Sermo super Cant. Cant., 26.V.7.
10. *Parzival,* 115.27: "ine kan decheinen buochstap."
11. Bernard of Clairvaux, Epist. 106, in *Sancti Bernardi opera,* ed. J. Leclercq, C. H. Talbot, and H. M. Rochais (Rome: Editiones Cistercienses, 1957), 7:266–67: "Why seek the Word in words, when it stands before your very eyes in the flesh? . . . Once you've tasted from the fruit of the wheat . . . you would soon leave the husks for those teachers of mere letters to chew on. . . . In the forests you will find more wisdom than in books; the trees and stones will teach you things no professors know."
12. *Sigeberts von Gembloux Passio sanctae Luciae virginis und Passio sanctorum Thebeorum,* 2.448, ed. Ernst Dümmler, Akademie der Wissenschaften Berlin. Phil.-Hist. Kl. 1 (Berlin, 1893), 2.448, 83, and 2.505–13, 85: "Who needs examples from books? You yourselves are the example. . . . We have read this, we have heard that. So many triumphs of the saints are reported throughout the world. But here I see with my very eyes those deeds I have read about. . . . Are not those whom I should imitate and those at whom I should marvel right here in front of me!"
13. There are good examples in Michael Clanchy's book *From Memory to Written Record: England, 1066–1307,* 2d ed. (Oxford: Blackwell, 1993), and in Haiko Wandhoff's *Der epische Blick: Eine mediengeschichtliche Studie zur höfischen Literatur* (Berlin: Schmidt, 1996).

14. "I would not want to have lived then if I had to give up the present where their *stories* (of King Arthur) give us such pleasure. In those days it was *deeds* which gave satisfaction" (emphasis added). Hartmann von Aue, *Iwein*, 7th ed., ed. G. Benecke, K. Lachmann, and L. Wolff (Berlin: de Gruyter, 1968).

15. See Walter Haug, *Literaturtheorie im deutschen Mittelalter von den Anfängen zum Ende des 13. Jahrhunderts* (Darmstadt: Wissenschaftliche Buchgesellschaft, 1985), 124.

16. *Iwein*, 756–72.

17. Hartmann von Aue, *Gregorius*, 13th ed., ed. Hermann Paul, rev. Burghart Wachinger, Altdeutsche Textbibliothek, 2 (Tübingen: Niemeyer, 1984), 789–804.

18. See the prologue to *Erec et Enite*. Chrétien de Troyes, *Erec and Enide*, ed. and trans. Carleton W. Carroll (New York: Garland, 1987), 19–22.

19. See the prologue to *Tristan*, esp. *Tristan*, 155–236. Especially worth reflecting on is the claim "wir lesen ir leben" (*Tristan*, 35). Its unquestioned presupposition of the textualizing, or the textualizability, of life, the reprocessing of vitality into the written word, must have appeared as typically clerical and therefore contemptible to Wolfram.

20. Peter of Blois, Epist. 94, PL 207, 293–97. See my "Courtliness and Social Change," in *Cultures of Power: Lordship, Status and Process in Twelfth-Century Europe*, ed. Thomas N. Bisson (Philadelphia: University of Pennsylvania Press, 1995), 291–94.

21. PL 207, 296A: "They have scenes of combat painted on their saddles and shields, so that they may take pleasure in a kind of fantasy vision of battles, which in reality they would not have the courage even to watch, let alone to take part in."

22. Johan Huizinga, "The Problem of the Renaissance," in his *Men and Ideas: History, The Middle Ages, The Renaissance: Essays*, trans. James S. Holmes and Hans van Marle (New York: Meridian, 1959), 243–87.

23. Gerhart Ladner, who studied the language of renewal, noted with emphasis the reluctance of contemporaries to apply it to their age as a whole: "It is very remarkable that philosophers of nature and natural scientists of the twelfth century, such as Adelard of Bath and Herman of Carinthia—while they considered nature as an innovating force under God in generation and conservation—do not seem to have designated their own time as an age of either rebirth or reform." "Terms and Ideas of Renewal," in *Renaissance and Renewal in the Twelfth Century*, ed. Robert Benson and Giles Constable (Cambridge, Mass.: Harvard University Press, 1982), 7.

24. C. H. Haskins, *The Renaissance of the Twelfth Century* (1927; rpt., New York: Meridian, 1955), 224–75 (on historical writing), 241–44 (on Otto of Freising).

25. On Otto's career, his view of history, and its context, see Hans-Werner Goetz, *Das Geschichtsbild Ottos von Freising: Ein Beitrag zur historischen Vorstellungswelt und zur Geschichte des 12. Jahrhunderts* (Cologne and Vienna: Böhlau, 1984).

26. *The Two Cities: A Chronicle of Universal History to the Year 1146 A.D. by Bishop Otto of Freising*, trans. Charles C. Mierow, Records of Civilization,

Sources and Studies (New York: Columbia University Press, 1928), 94–95 (prologue to book 1); original text in Otto Bischof von Freising, *Chronik oder die Geschichte der zwei Staaten,* ed. Walther Lammers, trans. Adolf Schmidt, Ausgewählte Quellen zur deutschen Geschichte des Mittelalters, 16 (Darmstadt: Wissenschaftliche Buchgesellschaft, 1974), 10–14.

27. See Goetz, *Das Geschichtsbild,* 275, on this change of attitude.

28. *Chronicle,* prologue, ed. Lammers, 12–14; trans. Mierow, 94–95.

29. "Many shall run to and fro and knowledge shall be increased." There is a problem in understanding the line in the Bible. See the commentary in *The Interpreter's Bible* (New York: Abingdon Press, 1956), 6:544–45. But decisive for our context is Otto's understanding of the line. And he clearly understood "pertransire" as scurrying and the "multiplicity" of knowledge as a phenomenon of final decline: "Hanc in senio mundi ex his, quas dixi, causis sapientiam fore multiplicandam propheta previdit, qui ait, *Pertransibunt plurimi*" (The Prophet foresaw this growth of wisdom in the old age of the world for the reasons I have cited [namely corruption and senility], and so he said "Many shall hurry to and fro"). *Chronicle,* book 5, prologue, ed. Lammers, 372; trans. Mierow, 322.

30. C. S. Lewis, *The Allegory of Love: A Study in Medieval Tradition* (London: Oxford University Press, 1936; rpt., 1972), 4, 11; Peter Dinzelbacher, "Über die Entdeckung der Liebe im Hochmittelalter," *Saeculum* 32 (1981): 185–208.

31. "Nowadays it has few adherents, since almost all have abandoned love, leaving it much debased. For those who used to love had a reputation for courtliness, integrity, generosity and honour; but now love is made a laughing-stock." Chrétien de Troyes, *Yvain ou Le Chevalier au Lion,* ed. Jan Nelson, Carleton W. Carroll, and Douglas Kelly (New York: Appleton-Century-Crofts, 1968), 18–24. English quoted from Chrétien de Troyes, *Arthurian Romances,* trans. D. D. R. Owen (London: Dent and Tuttle, 1993), 281. Also the troubadour Giraut de Borneil complains that all pleasure has passed from the world, and "worth" (*pretz*) is banished. He has given up his attempt to rescue these values. Minstrels no longer praise noble ladies; therefore their "worth" (*pretz*) is in ruins. Their lovers now prefer to practice deceit than to praise them. Giraut de Borneil, *Sämtliche Lieder des Trobadors Giraut de Bornelh,* ed. Adolf Kolsen (Halle: Niemeyer, 1907), 412–20, no. 65 ("Per solatz revelhar").

32. "They are right who say that Love is hounded to the ends of the earth. All that we have is the bare word, only the name remains to us." Gottfried, *Tristan,* ed. F. Ranke, ed. and trans. Rüdiger Krohn (Stuttgart: Reclam, 1985). English by A. T. Hatto, *Tristan with the "Tristran" of Thomas* (Harmondsworth: Penguin, 1985), 203.

33. *Carmina Burana: Die Lieder der Benediktbeurer Handschrift,* ed. A. Hilka, O. Schumann, and B. Bischoff, trans. Carl Fischer (Munich: Deutscher Taschenbuch Verlag, 1979), no. 105, 6.3–4. "The ancient vigor has passed away [from love]; its virtue has vanished; my strength has failed me and Cupid's bow shoots no more!"

34. Hugo Sotovagina, in *Anglo-Latin Satirical Poets,* ed. Th. Wright, Rolls Series, 59 (London: Longman, 1872), 2:219: "That love which Pylades felt for

Orestes and Laelius for Scipio does not exist today. Confidence and loyalty in either partner is rare."

35. Aelred of Rievaulx, *Spiritual Friendship*, 25, trans. Mary Eugenia Laker (Kalamazoo, Mich.: Cistercian Publications, 1977), 56; *De spiritali amicitia,* ed. A. Hoste, Corpus Christianorum Continuatio Mediaevalis, 1 (Turnholt: Brepols, 1971), 293: "There never were many friends . . . but in this age of Christianity, friends are so few, it seems to me that I am exerting myself uselessly in striving after the virtue which I, terrified by its admirable sublimity, now almost despair of ever acquiring."

36. Heloise, "Letter 5 to Abelard," in *The Letters of Abelard and Heloise,* trans. Betty Radice (Harmondsworth: Penguin, 1974), 167; "The Letter of Heloise on Religious Life and Abelard's First Reply," ed. J. T. Muckle, *Mediaeval Studies* 17 (1955): 246: "We see that the world has now grown old, and that with all other living creatures men too have lost their former natural vigour; and . . . amongst many or indeed almost all men love itself has grown cold." She changes the biblical reference (Matthew 24:12): "because iniquity shall abound, the love of many shall wax cold" so that a senile world and not "iniquity" is responsible for frigidity—gendered masculine in Heloise's text. On the motif in literature, see James M. Dean, *The World Grown Old in Later Medieval Literature* (Cambridge, Mass.: Medieval Academy of America, 1997). On the cooling of charity with reference to Heloise's statement, 62–66; as a literary motif ("The Decline of Love"), 99–102.

37. *Serm. in Cant.,* 2.1.1. Cf. Richard of Saint Victor, *De gradibus charitatis,* ch. 4, PL 196, 1204C–D. And Peter of Blois, *De amicitia Christiana,* prologue, PL 207, 871A.

38. Giles Constable, *The Reformation of the Twelfth Century* (Cambridge: Cambridge University Press, 1996).

39. Jacques de Vitry, *The Exempla or Illustrative Stories from the Sermones vulgares of Jacques de Vitry,* ed. Thomas F. Crane (1890; rpt., New York: Franklin, 1971), 12. On the genesis of the legend of Serlo of Wilton, see Stephen C. Ferruolo, *The Origins of the University: The Schools of Paris and Their Critics, 1100–1215* (Stanford, Calif.: Stanford University Press, 1985), 202–3.

INDEX

Abbo of Fleury I, 580
Achilles XII, 79
Acts of the Apostles IV, 43
Adalbero of Augsburg X, 299
Adalbero II of Metz X, 299, 313
Adalbert of Bremen I, 573; II, 167; X, 296
Adalbert of Prague VIII, 549, 566; X, 300
Adalbold of Utrecht I, 590
Adam of Bremen I, 573; II, 167; X, 296
Adam of Perseigne, *Letters* III, 59
Adela of Blois II, 146, 167
Adelard of Bath XII, 88
Adèle of Champagne VIII, 560
Adelman of Liège I, 574, 587, 603, 604
Ademar of Chabannes I, 602
Aegidius of Paris V, 6
Aelred of Rievaulx, VIII, 549, 567, 568; X, 309, 310
  De spiritali amicitia XII, 85, 90
Aeneas VII, 293
Agamemnon X, 320
Alan of Lille I, 569, 584, 585, 599–601, 614, 615; II, 145; IV, 49; V, 11
  Anticlaudianus I, 584, 585, 599–601, 608, 615; II, 145
Alberic of Reims IV, 32, 54
Albrecht von Halberstadt VI, 47
Albrecht von Scharfenberg V, 11; VI, 47
Alcuin I, 593, 595; III, 60, 66; VIII, 549, 557, 566
Alexander the Great X, 322
Altmann of Passau XI, 33
Amadeus of Lausanne, Bishop II, 168
Ambrose, Saint, Bishop of Milan I, 585, 587, 596; III, 66; IV, 53; V, 3; XI, 36
  De officiis ministrorum III, 66; XI, 36
Amphion II, 146
Andreas Capellanus, *De amore* VII, 304; VIII, 569; X, 310
Angelran of St. Riquier I, 586
Anno of Cologne X, 296, 297, 298, 299, 313, 315

Anselm of Bec VIII, 550, 557, 558, 567
Anselm of Besate I, 591; II, 142, 143, 162
  Rhetorimachia I, 591; II, 142
Anselm of Havelberg *Vita of Adalbert of Mainz* X, 296
Anselm of Laon I, 571, 589, 602, 605, 606, 607; IV, 44, 49
Anselm of Liège II, 158, 166; X, 302, 306, 307; XI, 34
Archpoet II, 142
Arion II, 146
Aristotle III, 322; VIII, 555, 568
  Nicomachean Ethics III, 63
Arn of Salzburg VIII, 557, 566
Arnold of Mainz X, 315
Arnulf (Onulf) of Speyer I, 581, 582, 583, 590
  Colores rhetorici I, 581, 590
Arthur, King VII, 301, 307; VIII, 564; XII, 81
Astralabius I, 606
Augustine, Saint III, 52, 58; IV, 43, 52, 53; V, 3; VIII, 551, 568; XI, 42
  City of God XII, 82, 86
Azecho of Worms, Bishop I, 591
Azelinus of Hildesheim, Bishop I, 579; X, 296, 307; XI, 43, 44

Bacon, Roger III, 56, 57
  Opus Majus III, 57
Balderich of Trier I, 588, 593
Bardo X, 299
Baudri of Bourgueil II, 141, 146, 153; IX, 131; X, 311, 312
  Life of St. Hugh X, 312
Benedict of Chiusa I, 602
Benno II of Osnabrück, Bishop I, 579; X, 296, 297, 298, 318
Benoît de Sainte-Maure VI, 45, 47, 57; X, 324
  Roman de Troie VI, 57
Berangar of Poitiers IV, 32, 47, 51
Berengar of Tours I, 574, 589, 590, 593,

603, 604; VI, 53
Bern of Reichenau I, 597; II, 164, 165
Bernard of Chartres I, 570, 608, 610; V, 11
Bernard of Clairvaux I, 588, 599, 600;
    II, 167; III, 56; IV, 31–34, 38, 39,
    42–49, 51, 52, 54; V, 4, 12, 13,
    14; IX, 123–126, 129, 130; XII,
    77, 78, 85, 87
    De consideratione III, 56
Bernard of Utrecht II, 141
Bernardus Silverstris I, 569, 585, 615; II,
    168X, 320
    Cosmographia I, 585, 615
Bernward of Hildesheim I, 577; X, 298,
    301, 302, 306, 313, 315, 318; XI,
    33
Boccaccio, Giovanni *Decameron* VIII, 570
Boethius I, 583, 591; II, 148; III, 58
    Consolatio philosophiae I, 583
Boswell, James VI, 58
Brun of Cologne I, 570, 572, 574, 575,
    609, 611; II, 150, 162; X, 295,
    300, 308, 313
Bruni, Leonardo III, 51
Bruno of Merseburg *Brunos Buch vom
    Sachsenkrieg* VII, 297
Burchard II of Worms I, 579; VIII, 549; X,
    314, 316

Caesar VII, 293
Calliope II, 146, 147
Cambridge songs II, 142
Canossa, Ludovico da X, 312
Canute the Great XI, 38, 39, 44
Carmina Burana VI, 48; XII, 84, 89
Cassiodorus II, 148
Castiglione, Baldesar *Il libro del
    cortegiano* I, 588, 615; VIII,
    569X, 311, 313, 314, 325
Distichs of Cato I, 585
Cerberus II, 151
Charlemagne III, 66; VI, 52; VIII, 549, 557
Charles I VIII, 567, 568
Charles V X, 325
Charon II, 151
Chrétien de Troyes III, 75; VI, 45, 46, 47,
    57; VII, 307; X, 293, 324; XI, 40;
    XII, 80, 84, 88, 89
    Cligés VI, 46, 57
    Erec VI, 46, 54, 57; XII, 88
    Yvain III, 75; VI, 46, 57; VII, 307; XII,
    84, 89
Cicero I, 578, 583, 585, 589, 592, 593,
    594, 596, 598; II, 141, 160; III,
    58, 60, 65, 66, 68; IV, 54; VII,
    299; VIII, 555, 556, 557, 568; X,
    308, 309, 310, 314; XI, 32, 36,
    42; XII, 76, 85, 87
    De amicitia VIII, 555, 556; X, 310
    De officiis I, 585, 594; III. 60, 65;
    X, 308, 309, 314
    De oratore I, 594
    Tusculan Disputations I, 583, 592,
    593, 594, 598; III, 60, 61, 66;
    XII, 76, 87
Conan of Brittany VIII, 559, 560
Conrad of Constanz X, 308
Conrad of Hirsau I, 597
Constance of Britanny VIII, 559, 560,
    561, 570
Constance of Castille VIII, 560

Daniel (Old Testament prophet) IV, 40,
    42, 44, 52
Daniel, Walter VIII, 567; X, 309
    Life of Ailred of Rievaulx X, 309, 311
David, King of Israel II, 160, 165, 168;
    VII, 298; VIII, 548
David and Jonathan II, 157, 158; VIII,
    548
David of Scotland (King) VIII, 549; X,
    309, 310
De mensa philosophie II, 142
De nuptis Mercurii et Philologie (11th
    century poem) II, 144, 145, 150,
    151, 153, 168
Dietrich of Bern VII, 300
Dis, King of underworld II, 146, 147, 153,
    160, 161
Don Quixote VII, 307, 308; IX, 133–134
Drogo of Paris III, 72
Dürer, Albrecht *Melencolia I* XII, 75

Eacus II, 151
Ebalus of Reims I, 580
Ebo of Michelsberg X, 301, 316, 317,
    318, 319; XI, 34
Eberhard I of Salzburg II, 166
Ecbasis captivi II, 149
Edward III VIII, 563, 564, 570
Eigil of Fulda, *Vita sancti Sturmi* III, 66
Eleanor of Aquitaine VI, 56, 57
Eliot, T. S. IX, 135
Elyot, Thomas VIII, 567
Eraclius of Liège I, 593
Erluin of Gembloux II, 162
Eugenius V, 13
Eumenides II, 151

INDEX

Eurydice II, 145, 146, 147
Eusebius II, 148

Fanshame, Richard VIII, 567
Fitzstephen, William I, 611, 612; III, 78
    Vita Thomae III, 78
Franco of Worms X, 313, 314
Frederick I of Cologne, Archbishop
    X, 299
Fredrick I Barbarossa II, 166; V, 11; X,
    309; XII, 82
Fredrick II X, 292
Froumund of Tegernsee II, 143
Fulbert of Chartres I, 570, 573, 580, 586,
    587, 590, 603, 604, 608; II, 163
Fulcoius of Beauvais II, 167
Fulk of Deuil IV, 52; V, 10
Furies II, 146, 147

Gautier II, 144, 153
Gawain VII, 308
Geoffrey of Auxerre IV, 32, 33, 47, 48
Geoffrey of Chartres IV, 31, 44, 51
Geoffrey of Clairvaux IX, 129–130
Geoffrey of Monmouth VI, 47, 56; X, 324
Geoffrey the Fair of Anjou VI, 48
Gerald of Aurillac II, 163; VIII, 554
Gerald of Wales I, 596, 614; XI, 39
    De principis instructione I, 614; XI,
    39
Gerbert of Aurillac I, 570, 572, 573, 575,
    582, 589; II, 161, 165; X, 297,
    306
Gerold of Avranches VI, 52
Gervase of Canterbury VIII, 548, 566
Gilbert Foliot V, 6
Gilbert, Sir Humphrey I, 615
Gilbert of Poitiers IV, 45
Gilduin of St. Victor, Abbot III, 74
Giraut de Borneil XII, 89
Godefroy of Rhiems II, 144, 145
Godfrey of St Victor III, 59, 73, 74, 77
    Fons philosophie III, 77
Goethe, J.W. IX, 135; XII, 76
    Faust XII, 76
Goswin of Mainz (Gozechinus) I, 573, 587,
    588; III, 72
Gottfried von Strassburg I, 612–14; VI,
    47; IX, 130; X, 305, 312, 313,
    322, 323, 324; XI, 28, 29, 30, 31,
    34, 36, 38; XII, 80, 84, 89
    Tristan I, 612–614; IX, 130; X, 305,
    312, 313, 322, 323, 324; XI, 29,
    30, 34, 39; XII, 84, 89

Gregory the Great V, 3, 5, 8; X, 308, 319
    Regula pastoralis X, 308, 319
Gregory VII, Pope VII, 297
Guibert de Tournai X, 322
Guibert of Nogent II, 143; VII, 295, 299
Guido de Basochis X, 304
Guido di Castello IV, 42
Guillaume of Lorris X, 311
Guitmund of Aversa I, 589
Gunther of Bamberg, Bishop I, 577, 595;
    VI, 52, 53; X, 299, 308
Gunzo of Novara I, 602

Hamlet I, 596
Hartmann of Göttweig, Abbot XI, 33, 36
Hartmann von Aue VI, 45, 47, 48; VII,
    307; IX, 136, 137; XI, 28, 30, 40;
    XII, 79, 80, 88
    Der arme Heinrich XII, 80
    Gregorius XII, 80, 88
    Iwein IX, 136; XI, 28; XII, 79, 80, 88
Heinrich vonVeldeke VI, 45, 47, 57; XI,
    30, 40
    Eneit VI, 47
Heloise I, 606; IV, 44, 46, 48, 50, 51; V,
    6, 7, 8; XII, 85, 90
Henry I, King II, 166; X, 299
Henry II, King I, 596, 610; III, 68; VI,
    53, 56, 57; VII, 293; VIII, 547,
    548, 549, 560; X, 307, 316
Henry III, King I, 591; II, 164, 165, 166;
    X, 307, 315; XI, 36, 40, 43
Henry IV, King VII, 297; X, 296, 299,
    316, 317; XI, 41, 42
Henry V, King XI, 33
Henry Murdac XII, 77
Henry of Huntington X, 320
Henry of Reims X, 304
Henry of Sens, Archbishop IV, 31
Henry the Liberal of Champagne VI, 53
Henry the Lion VI, 48
Herbert of Bosham IX, 130
Herbord of Michelsberg X, 296, 304,
    305, 316, 317, 319, 324; XI, 35,
    41
    *Dialogue on the Life of Otto von
    Bamberg* III, 67; X, 296, 304,
    305; XI, 35, 41
Herbort of Fritzlar *Liet von Troye* VI, 47
Heribert of Cologne X, 308
Heribert of Eichstätt II, 155
Herman of Carinthia XII, 88
Hermann, Landgraf von Thüringen VI, 57
Hermann of Reims I, 586; III, 72

Herod IV, 35, 36
Hezilo of Hildesheim, Bishop II, 159
Hildebert of Lavardin I, 580, 593; II, 141, 149, 155, 167; III, 72, 73, 77; IV, 52; IX, 117–120, 124, 126, 129, 132, 134; X, 293, 304, 308; XI, 31
   Par tibi Roma nihil IX, 117
Hildegar I, 586, 587
Hiltdolf of Cologne X, 299
Hincmar of Reims I, 609; III, 60; X, 300
   De ordine palatii X, 300
Holbein, Hans (the younger) IX, 128
Horace II, 148, 149
Hotspur VIII, 567
Hrabanus Maurus III, 54, 60
   De institutione clericorum III, 54
   De universo III, 60
Hugh of Avranches VI, 52
Hugh of Die II, 167
Hugh of Flavigny VII, 300
Hugh of Rouen, Archbishop X, 311
Hugh of St Victor I, 584, 587, 597, 605, 614; III, 53, 54, 56, 57, 61, 62, 63, 64, 67, 68, 69, 70, 73, 77, 79; IX, 122–123
   De arca Noe morali III, 57
   De institutione novitiorum III, 53, 54, 56, 57, 59, 60, 61, 64, 67, 68, 69, 70, 74, 77, 79
   De modo dicendi et meditandi III, 57
   *De scripturis et scriptoribus s*acris III, 56
   Didascalion III, 54, 57, 79
   Epitome Dindimi in philosophiam III, 57
   Expositio in Hierarchiam Coelestem S. Dionysii III, 57
Hugo of Besançon I, 597
Hugo Sotovagina XII, 89
Hugues of Champfleury VIII, 559
Huzmann of Speyer III, 72
Hyacinth (Pope Celestine III) IV, 42, 53
Hydra II, 151

Innocent I, Pope IV, 35, 38
Innocent II, Pope IV, 46
Isaiah IV, 41
Isidore of Seville II, 164; III, 60
Isolde IX, 131, 132; X, 323
Ivo of Chartres IV, 50

Jacques de Vitry XII, 86, 90
James of Viterbo (Jakob von Viterbo) X, 319

Jean de Marmoutier VI, 48
Jean Gerson V, 9
Jephtha's daughter IV, 43, 51
Jerome, Saint IV, 43; V, 3; VI, 52, 54
Jesus I, 592; II, 161, 168; IV, 31, 35–44, 51, 53; V, 6, 8, 12; IX, 121; XII, 78
Joan, Countess of Kent and Salisbury VIII, 563, 570
Job V, 8
Johannes de Hauvilla V, 11
Jonathan VIII, 548
John, Evangelist IV, 35, 40
John of Ford IV, 49
John of Salisbury I, 569, 582, 583, 607, 608, 610, 613, 615, 616; II, 168; III, 52, 72; V, 11; VI, 51, 52; X, 304; X, 309, 319, 321, 325
   Entheticus VI, 51
   Metalogicon I, 582, 607, 608, 615; III, 52
   Policraticus I, 615; II, 168; VI, 51, 52; X, 309, 319, 321
Johnson, Samuel V, 14; VI, 57; VII, 307, 308
Joseph (Patriarch) X, 321
Judith X, 323
Julius Caesar VII, 300

Kaiserchronik VI, 46, 54
Kalogrenant XII, 79
Kei VII, 308
Kent VIII, 549
Klâge VI, 56
König Rother VI, 47
Konrad, Pfaffe VI, 47
   Rolandslied VI, 47
Kunibert of Cologne X, 315

de Lafayette, Mme. *La princesse de Clèves* VIII, 557
Lampert of Hersfeld X, 308
   Annalen X, 299
Lamprecht *Alexander* VI, 46
Lancelot VIII, 563
Lanfranc I, 590
Lawrence of Westminster III, 73
Layamon VI, 56
Lear, King VIII, 549
Leo IX, King I, 597
Liber ordinis Sancti Victoris III, 53, 63, 64, 69, 74, 76
Lloyd, David X, 310
Lotulf of Novara IV, 32

Louis VII, King VIII, 559, 560, 561, 570
Louis the German I, 609; III, 60
Lucan IV, 54
Lucidarius VI, 49, 50, 53
Luke, Evangelist IV, 35, 36

Mainz, Cathedral School VII, 296
Malcolm IV of Scotland VIII, 560
Manasses of Reims, Archbishop II, 159, 160, 163, 164, 167; VII, 297, 298, 299, 303
Manegold of Lautenbach I, 570, 571, 585, 587; III, 71
    Liber ad Gebehardum I, 587
Manegold of Paderborn I, 580
Mann, Thomas XII, 75, 76
Marbod of Rennes II, 141, 145, 150, 153; X, 302; XI, 33
    Vita Licinii X, 302; XI, 33
Marcellinus, Pope V, 8
Margaret of Clèves VI, 57
Marie de Champagne VI, 57
Marie de France VI, 47, 54
    Lais VI, 54
Mark, King of England IV, 35; X, 323, 324; XI, 29, 34
Martianus Capella I, 602, 607; II, 143, 145, 146, 155
Martin of Braga II, 155
Mary Magdalene IV, 44, 54
Matthew, Evangelist IV, 35, 36
Matthew of Vendôme X, 320
Matthew Paris I, 612
Maurice (monk of Bec) VIII, 557, 558; IX, 136
McPherson, James V, 14
Meinhard of Bamberg I, 570, 577, 578, 580, 581, 586, 590, 592, 595, 597, 598, 599, 600; III, 67, 72; VI, 52, 53
    De fide I, 578
Meinwerk of Paderborn I, 596; VIII, 549; X, 298, 302, 307, 313, 315, 316; XI, 32
Mondonus Belvaleti VIII, 570
Muses II, 145
Mythographus Vaticanus II, 145

Nibelungenlied VI, 56; VII, 300
Nicolas of Clairvaux V, 11–14
Nietzsche, Friedrich VIII, 553; IX, 135; XII, 76
Norbert of Iburg X, 296
Norbert of Xanten X, 299

Notker of Liège X, 301, 306; XI, 34

Odo of Cluny II, 163; VIII, 554
Odo of St Victor III, 75, 77
Ohtricus of Magdeburg I, 572, 574
Ophelia I, 596
Opo of Seeland XI, 44
Order of the Garter VIII, 562, 564, 565, 570
Orderic Vitalis IV, 49; VI, 52
    Historia ecclesiastica VI, 52
Orleans Heretics XII, 77
Ossian V, 14
Otloh of S. Emmeram I, 571, 580, 602; II, 155
Otto of Bamberg I, 599; III, 67; X, 295, 297, 298, 301, 303, 307, 314, 316, 317, 318, 323; XI, 34, 36, 42
Otto of Freising IV, 44, 48, 51; X, 309; XII, 82, 83, 88
    Chronicle or History of the Two Cities XII, 82, 83, 88, 89
    Gesta Friderici IV, 48; XII, 83
Otto I (The Great) I, 572, 574, 602, 609; II, 155, 162; X, 291, 300, 315, 324; XI, 34
Otto II I, 572
Otto III I, 596; VIII, 549; X, 292, 301, 306, 314, 315, 316; XI, 32
Ovid II, 148; VIII, 564

Paraclete IV, 35, 44, 46, 52, 54
Paschasius Radbertus II, 149
Paul, Saint IV, 43; V, 8; XII, 76
Paulina of Zell XI, 41
Percy, Lady VIII, 567
Pernolf of Wuerzburg II, 143, 155
Peter Abelard I, 570, 582, 589, 600, 602, 603, 605, 606, 607, 616; III, 56, 72; V, 1, 2, 5, 8, 10; XII, 85, 90
    Apologia contra Bernardum IV, 52
    Apologia universis IV, 34, 40, 42, 52
    Carmen ad Astralabium IV, 52, 54
    Dialogus inter Philosophum, Iudaeum et Christianum I, 582; III, 56
    Fidei confessio ad Heloisam IV, 52
    Historia calamitatum IV, 31, 34, 39, 44, 45, 46; V, 1
    Planctus de filia Iephtae IV, 54
    Planctus Israel super Samson IV, 54
    Problemata Heloissae IV, 31, 45, 54
    Sic et non I, 606
Peter Comestor IV, 49
Peter Damian I, 571; II, 141, 163, 167,

168; VIII, 566; X, 316, 319, 321
Contra clericos aulicos X, 321
Peter of Blois II, 155, 167; VI, 53; VII, 291, 292, 293, 294, 295, 296, 297, 301, 302, 306, 307, 308; VIII, 568; X, 319, 321; XII, 81, 88, 90
 De amicitia Christiana XII, 90
Petrus Alfonsi II, 155
Petrus Riga IV, 49, 52; V, 6
Pilate IV, 35, 36, 49, 50
Pilgrim, Bishop of Passau VI, 56
Philip Augustus I, 600; VIII, 547, 548, 557, 560, 561, 565
Philip of Flanders VI, 53
Philip of Harvengt III, 54; VI, 53; X, 320
Philip I, King of France VI, 53
Phyllis and Flora VI, 48
Plato I, 570, 571, 584; VIII, 555; XII, 76, 87
 Symposium VIII, 555
 Phaedrus VIII, 555; XII, 76, 87
 Seventh Letter XII, 76
 Timaeus I, 570, 571, 584, 585, 610
Pluto II, 147, 157, 159
Poeta Saxo I, 596
Polydore Vergil VIII, 564, 570, 571
 Historia Anglica VIII, 564
Pompey VII, 293
Popo of Würzburg, Bishop I, 572; II, 155

Quid suum virtutis II, 144, 149, 167
Quintilian I, 578, 594; II, 148; III, 58, 60; X, 298; XI, 32
 Institutes of Oratory I, 594; X, 298

Rainald of Dassel X, 299, 309, 314; XI, 37
Raoul de Cambrai VII, 300
Regensburg rhetorical Letters I, 584, 591, 592, 593; III, 61
Regula canonicorum III, 52
Renaut de Beaujeu (Bâgé) VI, 48
Rhadamanthus II, 151
Richard of Saint-Vanne VII, 300
Richard of St. Victor I, 594; III, 69, 78; XII, 90
 De gradibus charitatis XII, 90
Richard the Bishop I, 607; III, 72
Richard the Lion Heart VIII, 547, 548, 557, 561, 565
Rilke, Rainer Maria IX, 133; XII, 75, 76, 87
Robert de Boron VI, 48

Robert of Melun I, 594; III, 78; IV, 34, 48; V, 6
Robert of Torigny III, 69
Robert the Pious II, 163
Roger of Howden VIII, 547, 548, 557, 565, 566
Roland VII, 300
Roman d'Eneas VI, 47
Roman de Thèbes VI, 47
Roscellinus IV, 47, 51
Rudolf I von Habsburg X, 298
Rudolf Agricola III, 51
Rodulfus Glaber II, 166
Ruodlieb II, 165X, 307, 311; XI, 40, 41
Ruotger I, 575, 609; II, 162
Rupert of Deutz IV, 49, 50

Saint-Denis VIII, 560
Sallust X, 314
Samson IV, 43
Samson of Reims, Archbishop IV, 49, 51
Saul II, 160; VII, 298; VIII, 548
Saxo Grammaticus VII, 300, 302, 303; X, 302, 303; XI, 34, 38
 Gesta Danorum X, 302; XI, 34, 38
School of Chartres I, 570; II, 168
Scipio Africanus VII, 293
Scotus Eriugena I, 593
Sedulius Scotus II, 149; X, 314
 Liber de rectoribus Christianis X, 314
Seneca I, 585; III, 60; V, 3, 7; VI, 52; X, 303; XI, 31, 32
 Ad Marciam de consolatione X, 303; XI, 31
Serlo of Wilton XII, 86, 90
Shakespeare, William I, 596; VIII, 549, 567
Sidonius Apollinaris X, 294
Sigebert of Gembloux II, 150, 160, 161, 162; III, 58; IX, 135, 137; XII, 78, 79, 87
 Gesta abbatum Gemblacensium III, 58
 Passion of the Theban Legion XII, 78, 87
Simon, Deacon of Huntington X, 320
Sir Gawain and the Green Knight VIII, 563, 564, 570
Sisyphus II, 159
Smaragdus of St. Mihiel, *Via regia* X, 314
Socrates IX, 121
Song of Roland XI, 43
Spenser, Edmund, *Faerie Queen* XI, 42

Stefan of Novara I, 572, 602, 607, 610; II, 155
Stendhal (Henri Beyle) *Charterhouse of Parma* X, 294
Stephen, Saint IV, 43, 53
Stephen of Paris, Archbishop IV, 31
St Gildas of Rhuys IV, 35, 48
St Remi of Reims VII, 297
Strozzi, Niccolò III, 51
Susanna IV, 31, 40–44, 52, 53; V, 8, 9, 10, 12

Tacitus X, 303; XI, 32
  Annals XI, 32
Tammo X, 316
Tantilo II, 159
Thangmar X, 306
Theobald of Canterbury, Archbishop I, 611
Theodulf of Orleans II, 148
Theophanu, Empress X, 306
Theresa of Avila VII, 308
Thietmar of Merseburg X, 315
Thierry of Chartres I, 570; IV, 52
Thierry, (Theoderich), Abbot of St.-Hubert, Andage, Belgium II, 163, 164; VII, 298
Thierry of St. Trond II, 149
Thomas Becket I, 611, 612; III, 78; VI, 51, 52; IX, 130; X, 295; XI, 37
Thomas More IV, 43, 53
Thomas à Kempis V, 9
Thomas Aquinas V, 5; X, 319
Thomas Wolsey, Cardinal X, 310
Thomas of Brittany X, 312, 322
Thomasin of Zirclaere I, 597, 614; VI, 53; VII, 287; X, 303; XI, 30, 32
  Der welsche Gast I, 614
Trajan VII, 293, 300

Udalrici codex I, 579
Udo of Tournai I, 573
Ugo of Parma II, 141
Ulrich of Augsburg X, 295, 299
Ulrich of Bamberg II, 143, 154, 155, 168
Ulrich of Cluny III, 58
  Consuetudines antiquiores Cluniacenses III, 58, 59
Ulrich of Lichtenstein VII, 308
Ulrich of Zatzikoven VI, 47
Ulrich of Zell X, 308; XI, 36
Ulysses X, 309, 320, 321; XII, 79

Venantius Fortunatus II, 148
Vincent of Beauvais I, 614; III, 60
  De eruditione filiorum nobilium I, 614; III, 60
  Speculum morale (Pseudo-Vincent of Beauvais) III, 59
Virgil II, 148
Vita Meinwerci VIII, 566
Vita Theoderici Abb. Andaginensis VII, 298

Wace VI, 45–47, 50, 56, 57; X, 324
  Roman de Brut VI, 46
  Roman de Rou VI, 50, 57
Walahfrid Strabo II, 161
Walo of St. Arnulf (Metz), Abbot II, 159, 160, 164; VII, 297, 298, 299, 302, 303
Waltharius XII, 78
Wazo of Liège I, 577; II, 158, 166; III, 78; X, 292, 301, 315
Werner of Basel I, 604
Wernher of Merseburg XI, 41
Wibald of Stablo I, 580, 588, 590, 593, 594, 604; IX, 124
William IX of Aquitaine XI, 43
William of Champeaux I, 571, 580, 593, 606, 607, 610, 611; III, 71, 72, 77; IV, 44
William of Conches I, 584, 585, 590, 607, 610, 611; III, 67, 68, 72, 73
  Dragmaticon I, 610
  Moralium dogma philosophorum I, 585, 610; III, 67, 68
  Philosophia mundi I, 585, 610
William of Hirsau, Abbot VII, 294
William of Malmesbury I, 595
William of Orange VI, 52
William of St. Thierry I, 610; IV, 31, 39, 51
Willigis of Mainz I, 588
Wipo, *Tetralogus* II, 166, 167
Wirnt von Gravenberc XII, 80
Wladislaw X, 317
Wolfgang of Regensburg I, 577, 602; II, 155
Wolfhelm Brauweiler I, 571
Wolfram von Eschenbach V, 11; VI, 47; VII, 295, 301, 302, 303, 305, 306; VIII, 570; XII, 80
  Parzival VI, 47; VII, 295, 301, 305, 306, 308; XII, 80